Pierson Millennium

Richard E. Pierson, U.S.A.
and
Jennifer Pierson, N.Z.

HERITAGE BOOKS
2007

HERITAGE BOOKS
AN IMPRINT OF HERITAGE BOOKS, INC.

Books, CDs, and more—Worldwide

For our listing of thousands of titles see our website
at
www.HeritageBooks.com

Published 2007 by
HERITAGE BOOKS, INC.
Publishing Division
65 East Main Street
Westminster, Maryland 21157-5026

International Standard Book Number: 978-0-7884-0742-0

FOREWORD

Pierson Millennium covers the approximate period 850 AD to 1850 AD, a thousand years, though some data earlier than 850 and later than 1850 is presented. All Pearson, Peirson, Pierson spellings apply to the surname's place-name origin about 1100 AD in Yorkshire, England, at the vill of Pericne alias Persene settled by descendants of Danish Vikings.

The book includes the investigation and successful results of ten Pierson legends: (1) the legend that the Pierson line descended from Vikings; (2) the legend that the Pierson name originated in the East Riding of Yorkshire, England; (3) the legend that Thomas Pierson of Beverley, East Riding, Yorkshire, England, who inherited the estate of Moscraft (about 1615) which passed to his descendants, was of the American Pierson line; (4) the legend that three Pierson brothers came to New England together; (5) the legend that the immigrant Thomas Pierson Sr. of Branford, Conn., was a brother of Rev. Abraham Pierson; (6) the legend that the immigrant Henry Peirson arrived on a Mayflower ship; (7), the legend that the immigrant Rev. Abraham Pierson was born 1613 in Yorkshire, England; (8) the legend that the immigrant Stephen Pierson of Derby, Conn., came from Suffolk county, England, as the apprenticed son of a widowed mother; (9) the legend that the immigrant John Pearson of Lynn and Reading was born 1615 at Yorkshire, England; and (10) the legend that the Pierson family owned an island in New York harbor. The position always taken in the beginning is that some element of truth is present in the legend until proven otherwise. Then, as many facts are added as possible to test the legend. Conclusions are then drawn about the validity of each legend.

The English ancestors of six Pearson/Peirson/Pierson American immigrants of the 1600s were investigated with results & family inter-relationships provided: (1) Rev. Abraham Pierson of Southampton, L. I., in 1640, later of Branford, Conn., and Newark, N. J.; (2) Bartholomew Pierson of Watertown, Mass. in 1639; (3) Henry Peirson of Southampton, L. I., in 1643; (4) John Pearson of Lynn, Mass. in 1637; (5) Stephen Pierson of Derby, Conn., in 1667; and (6) Thomas Pierson Sr. who m. Maria Harrison at Branford, Conn., in 1662. With regret, it is reported that Deacon John Pearson of Rowley, Mass., in 1643, and Samuel Peirson of Philadelphia, Penn., in 1699, were also investigated, but their English ancestors were not discovered. However, see Appendix B for unfinished research on these two.

Thirty four coats of arms are provided for Pearson/Peirson/Pierson arms of England, Scotland, and the Netherlands with all known genealogical associations. No Pearson/Peirson/Pierson arms were found for Wales nor Ireland.

The Pearson, Peirson, Pierson descendants of the American immigrants of the 1600s from England are provided primarily from Lizzie B. Pierson, *Pierson Genealogical Records*, published 1878, to provide a basis upon which American Pearson-Peirson-Pierson family researchers can tie into the English research provided in this book. Two additional reasons for republishing the descendants is to provide an every-name index for them (Lizzie Pierson only indexed heads of families) and to use the data as a structure to footnote additional information against. The Pierson descendants include, with corrections, those published in 1887 by George Rogers Howell, in 1895 by Frederick Lockwood Pierson, in 1911 by Cuyler Reynolds, in 1917 by Silas Spencer Peirson, and in 1945 by Arthur Newton Pierson. The individual numbering scheme comes from Lizzie Pierson's book and is a consecutive numbering system where the older generations are assigned the smaller numbers and persons of non-Pierson surname are not numbered. Some numbers have letters with them indicating an added different person (this eliminates renumbering Lizzie Pierson's system which leads to errors).

Among the sources referenced in this book are two books which can only partially be bettered by primary records:

Lizzie B. Pierson, *Pierson Genealogical Records*, Joel Munsell, Printer, Albany, NY, 1878: Lizzie Pierson wrote more than 1,000 letters to Pierson families and personally interviewed many family members to create Pierson family genealogies in her book. Additionally, she wrote many letters to England in an attempt at finding the origins of Rev. Abraham Pierson hoping thus to learn if Abraham, Thomas and Henry were "the three brothers, who together left their native land, and sought a home on the rocky shores of New England." Thus, her work represents primarily family records including bible records and as such will not all be found to have a better primary record elsewhere. It is noted of her work that many female children are missing from her genealogies and that often the generations did not provide birth or death dates. Lizzie Pierson is of the Thomas Pierson Sr. line of Branford, Connecticut in 1662. Lizzie Pierson went to northern China as a missionary to join her brother, Rev. Isaac Pierson, there about the time of the publication of her book in 1878. As a religious person, she attempted to prove that all the Pierson families of New England were related to Rev. Abraham Pierson of Southampton in 1640 - which she was unable to prove. Because of this conviction, she made comments in her book that Rev. Abraham, Thomas, and Henry Pierson were probably brothers. Others later took this comment, arbitrarily said they were brothers, and in at least one case provided a fictitious family for them based on fragments of English records and changed dates. In spite of others twisting Lizzie Pierson's information, she has been truthful and has always advised when she was presenting a theory. Lizzie Pierson's work will always be an irreplaceable Pierson family record, and is therefore referred to in this book extensively.

George Rogers Howell, *The Early History of Southampton, L. I., New York, with Genealogies*, 2nd Edition, Weed, Parsons and Company, Albany, NY, 1887: The Rev. George Rogers Howell was born in Southampton in 1833. Although a clergyman, he devoted the greater part of his life to literary pursuits including his "*The Early History of Southampton ...,*" 1st edition 1866, 2nd edition 1887. George Howell earned his Master of Arts degree from Yale University. He was Archivist of the State of New York and Secretary of the Albany Institute for many years. He "lived" in Southampton historical research almost all his life and his 2nd edition book reflects his expertise. He provided genealogies for all Southampton families from Southampton records, wills, probate records, burial records, and other official state records. He accepted some genealogy information from families, but only if the records had good basis. The biggest benefit of using George Howell's book as a reference is his ability to tie Southampton families together. Many marriages are provided between families based on comments in wills which would otherwise not be found. The information provided by George Howell's life work would be extremely difficult to replace. George Howell is a distant cousin of Susannah Howell who married Col. Henry Peirson ca. 1681.

While careful attention has been paid to eliminating errors, there is bound to be some that slipped by the authors in a document of this size. Please accept our apologies in advance for any inconvenience this may cause. Many of the errors residing in George Rogers Howell's and Lizzie B. Pierson's data have been corrected in carrying forward their data to this book, but again some may have slipped by the authors. In adding new data to the structure of the old experts, a few "may", "possible," or "perhaps" pieces have been added since the authors didn't want to leave out certain valuable new data. The proof of those suggested connections is left to the reader. However, the suggested connections came about by an extensive every-word computer search of the entire book to review all of the possibilities before the choice was made of where a new piece of data might belong. Thus, the chance of error in a suggested connection point has been reduced but not eliminated since it is known that all Piersons are not present in this book. Additional verification of these connections has been made to determine that the given names of the new data are in use by the families to which connected.

It has been the policy in developing this book, to not carry non-Pierson lines beyond the children of a Pierson daughter. However, several exceptions have been made when the data is considered new to the research community, especially in England.

The authors have attempted to create a new standard for genealogy books in this writing by including all sources used and placing those sources on the page where the data was mentioned without chasing the "ibid." except where the bulk of the chapter is based on a single source, then that reference is given at the beginning of the chapter. This eliminates the need for a re-work of the research by the reader to find the specific sources, and allows easy verification for problem areas. This is a monumental step upward from early genealogy books that provided just a bibliography at the end of a dozen major sources that were not all-inclusive of the data presented. Where a theory is being presented due to lack of data, the authors have explained the rationale used in the presented text. While perhaps not all such rationales will hold up over the years, the explanations will allow the facts to be ascertained at a later date.

CONTENTS

Chapter 1
Surname Origin

Surname Originated in Yorkshire, England

In 1878, Lizzie Pierson stated[1] that the tradition of the Pierson family is that the surname was established in an honorable and independent condition from a very early period in the East Riding of the county of York, England. A footnote in Lizzie Pierson's book[2] by George Rogers Howell states: "There can be no doubt as to the origin of the name. The baptismal name Pierre (as it is in the French language), as it passed into England after the conquest often took the form of Piers, thus becoming half anglicized. And when surnames began to be used, John the son of Will became John Wilson and his neighbor, John the son of Piers, became John Pierson. - G.R.H." Howell ignores the fact that early spellings of Pierson were more likely to be Pearson or Peresone. The conquest to which George Howell refers took place in 1066 led by William, Duke of Normandy, in France.

In England, before about 1100 AD, most people had only one name. But as the population grew, surnames evolved to distinguish among individuals based upon occupation, place lived or place from which originated, the father's name (patronymic), or a personal characteristic or physical feature. The patronymic surname development discussed by Howell above assumes that Pierre and Piers were in use during surname development in England between 1066 and about 1100, being brought from Normandy during and after the conquest. This assumption could not be verified. On the contrary, the names found in the 1086 tax register, 20 years after the conquest, seemed to be English or Scandinavian such as Dunstan, Godelind, Harold, Hugh, Northmann, Otbert, Weleret, William, Alfgrimr, Authulfr, Bjornulfr, Ecgbeorht, Gamalbarn, Selakollr, Sunnifa, Svartr, Uhtred, and Ulfketill. This statement is based on a search for Pierre or Piers of any spelling as names of the landowners in York, Somerset, and Middlesex counties in the *Domesday book*[3], published by King William I in 1086. No Pierre, Piers, or anything close to it were recorded as names of that era.

However, in other documents of the 1300s, two Piers were found. One was Sir Piers as recorded in 1308 at the first Dunstable knight's tournament. Dunstable is located in the southern part of Bedford County, just north of London. Sir Piers carried the banneret of Henry Percy of Topcliffe, a castle in the North Riding of Yorkshire. Henry Percy is probably a descendant of Baron William Percy who founded the castle at Topcliffe in the period after the 1066 conquest. The only other name of Piers found was from William Langdon's poem, "Piers Plowman," about 1376. This was a political and religious poem describing a vision concerning Piers the plowman. In the poem, Piers has diverse roles as man, plowman, king, overlord, the Pope, St. Peter, Adam, and Christ. In summary, two

---

[1]Lizzie B. Pierson, *Pierson Genealogical Records*, Joel Munsell, Printer, Albany, New York, 1878, p.8.

[2]Lizzie B. Pierson, *Pierson Genealogical Records*, Joel Munsell, Printer, Albany, New York, 1878, p.8, footnote by George Rogers Howell.

[3]*Domesday Book, A Survey of the Counties of England*, compiled by direction of King William I, Winchester, England, 1086.

Piers were located: one was probably a Percy and the other one was a symbol of the perfect man. It appears that use of the name Piers in England began after the development of surnames there and was not a factor in surname development for Pierson.

With these results, one must consider the other ways of surname development: occupation, personal characteristics, physical features, and location. Pierson is not an occupation, a personal characteristic, or a physical feature. That leaves location, a place called Pierson (or some near spelling), as the possible source of the surname.

The Vill of Persene alias Pericne

One of the reasons for looking in Yorkshire, England, when reviewing the *Domesday Book* of 1086 for Piers was the family tradition mentioned in Lizzie Pierson's book that the Pierson name had originated there "from a very early period." While Pierre and Piers names were not found in Yorkshire, a vill[4] named Persene[5], alias Pericne (indicates a pronunciation of

---

[4] In 1086, the basic social and economic unit was the vill. The vill was not necessarily a single settlement but could be a complex of settlements spread over a wide area, belonging wholly to one manor or shared between several. The people within the vill were involved directly with the cultivation of the soil.

Pierson or Pearson), in the *Domesday Book*, was found there and it was located near the center of East Riding, three and a half miles north of Beverley (see map above). This location, along with about 22 Pierson family lines of various spellings in the 1500s in Yorkshire (see Chapter 3 for details), compels one to consider that the name Pierson (also Pereson, Person, Pearson, Peirson, Peerson, Pearsonne, Persone ... all spellings) in England and perhaps Scotland, where it is commonly spelled Pearson, originated from the vill of Pericne alias Persene. Pearsons (includes all spellings) were living in most of the counties of England in the 1500s. Records prior to that time are sparse.

Exactly, where was Persene in 1086 and who owned it? It was one of the properties of the Bishop of Durham[6] in 1086 (see map). Persene had 6 bovates (about 90 acres) taxable with 1 plough (about 120 acres) possible. Persene was part of the land that was Lund Manor in 1066, which was then held by Morcar, Earl of Northumbria, and son of Aelfgar, Earl of Mercia. But Lund is called waste (not in use) in the 1086 tax reckoning, though 12 carucates (about 1440 acres) were taxable to the Bishop of Durham. William of Percy held Persene from the Bishop of Durham in 1086. William Percy, in addition to being a sub-tenant of Bishop William of Durham was also one of the few Yorkshire sub-tenants of Hugh, Earl of Chester. Persene was later (*Domesday Gazetteer*[7] 1977) referred to as a lost vill

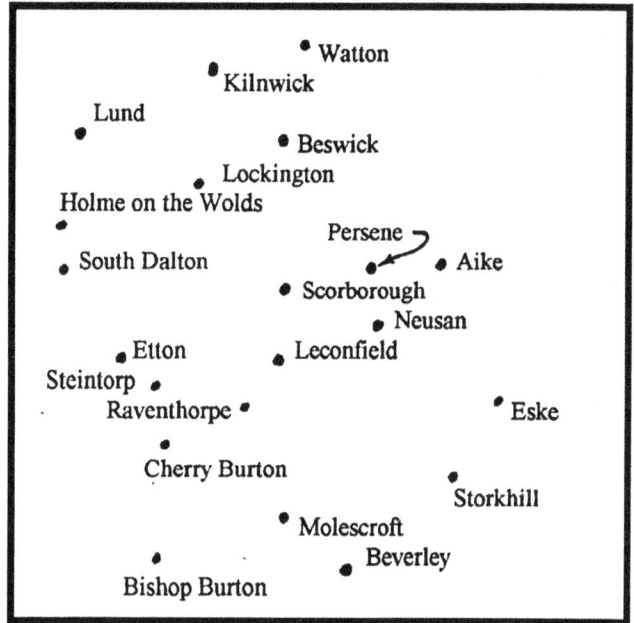

Lost Villages of Yorkshire, Vill of Persene 1086

subsequently part of Scorborough township. The Domesday Gazetteer provided a map which locations are reproduced here. In 1086, Scorborough was part of the Sneculfcros Hundred (area of about 12,000 acres)[8] of Yorkshire and taxable to the Bishop of Durham at 1 carucate (about 120 acres). Under Welton Manor[9], it is said that William of Percy holds Scorborough from the Bishop of Durham, where he has a mill, and 3 villagers with 1/2 plough (about 60 acres plowed). In 1955, Scorborough village, according to "The Lost Villages of Yorkshire," *Yorkshire Archaeological Journal*[10], was "very shrunken and seems to

[5]*Domesday Book, A Survey of the Counties of England*, compiled by direction of King William I, Winchester, England, 1086.

[6]John Morris, General Editor, *Domesday Book, Yorkshire*, Volume 30, Phillimore & Co. Ltd., Chichester, England, 1986, Part 1, p. 304c.

[7]H. C. Darby & G. R. Versey, *Domesday Gazetteer*, Cambridge, England, 1977, p.478, with map pp. 56-57.

[8]John Morris, General Editor, *Domesday Book, Yorkshire*, Volume 30, Phillimore & Co. Ltd., Chichester, England, 1986, Part 2, p. 381d.

[9]John Morris, General Editor, *Domesday Book, Yorkshire*, Volume 30, Phillimore & Co. Ltd., Chichester, England, 1986, Part 1, p. 304c.

[10]M. W. Beresford, "The Lost Villages of Yorkshire," *Yorkshire Archaeological Journal* xxxviii, 1955, p.67.

have lain in the park." An 1875 map[11] shows it as "Scorbrough Hall" along with a dot which seems to show an old building location at Persene.

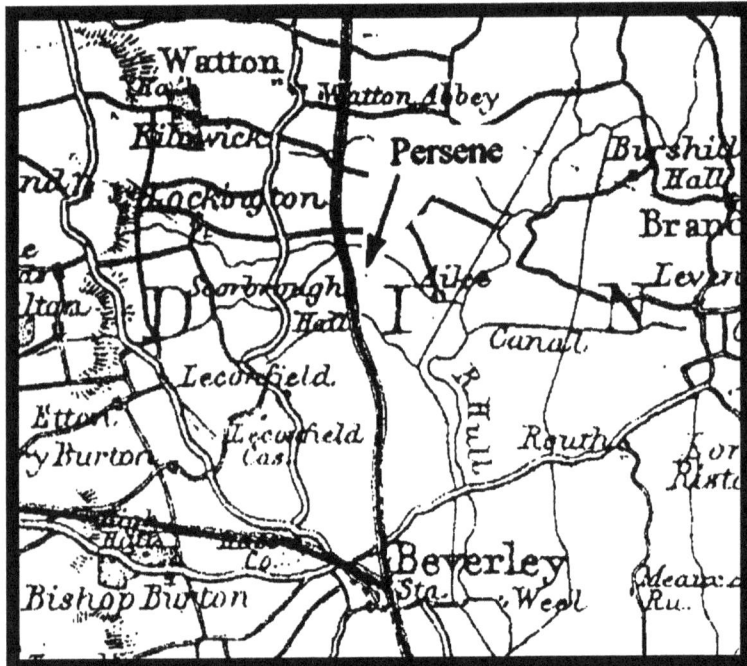

1875 Map, Vill of Persene Location

William of Percy is a key person to the use of the vill of Persene. Who was he? William of Percy's[12] surname is probably derived from the town of Percy in the arrondissement of Saint-Lo in the department of La Manche, France, although it should be noted that there are three other places called Percy in the department of Calvados, France. William of Percy's parentage is unknown, but he seems to have had early connections with Hugh, Earl of Chester. Earl Hugh was the son of Richard of Goz and nephew of King William. The tradition in the Whitby Cartulary is that Earl Hugh and William Percy came to England together in 1067. William Percy was connected with Yorkshire as early as 1070 and he was present on the Scottish campaign of 1072. He founded a castle at Topcliffe (20 miles northwest of York), though the principal family seat was at Spofforth (15 miles west of York). He refounded Whitby Abbey where his brother Serlo became prior and his nephew the first abbot. His wife was Emma, daughter of Hugh de Port, who was an important landholder in Hampshire and the Midlands. He joined the First Crusade with Robert Curthose and died in Palestine in 1099. His eldest son Alan succeeded him. The Percy estate shows considerable extension in the early 1100s.

Based upon the 1086 Domesday Book (tax record) which also recorded 1066 ownership at the time of the conquest, the vills of Molescroft (alias Moscraft, see Chapter 3), Scorborough, and Persene did not exist in 1066. The vill of Pericne was named sometime between about 1070 when William of Percy became principle tenant and the 1086 tax record. One assumes that William of Percy named Pericne (Persene) vill to describe which part of the unoccupied manor of Lund was under his lordship. Persene (pronounced Pierson) most likely means 'belonging to Percy.' In an example from the *Bible* at Matthew, chapter 27, verse 56, Mary Magdalene means Mary, inhabitant of (or belonging to) Magdala.

---

[11]Black's Map of Yorkshire, published by A. & C. Black, Edinburgh, about 1875, reproduced from an original engraving by Jonathan Books, Albany, N.Y. 12220.

[12]John Morris, General Editor, *Domesday Book, Yorkshire*, Volume 30, Phillimore & Co. Ltd., Chichester, England, 1986, Part 2, Appendix.

Descended from Vikings

In 1991, "The Pierson Family Tradition[13], based on American immigrants, was sent to John and Jenny Pierson in New Zealand, which stated in part: "The tradition of the family is that the surname was established in an honorable and independent condition from a very early period in the East Riding of Yorkshire, England. From 793 to 1042, with continuous invasions and major migrations (876-918) by Vikings from the area now known as Denmark, the principal influence on the people of Yorkshire was Danish Vikings." The New Zealand Piersons responded[14]: "The discussion on Danish Vikings created quite a stir. Would you believe I had made a note of a conversation John and I had recently which was to be included in my next letter to you. The note said tell Dick of the long-standing tradition in our New Zealand Pierson families (Charles William Joshua Pierson Jr., Herrick Roosevelt Philetous Pierson, and Albert Ernest Frederic Pierson) of early Viking ancestry, or Scandinavian descent. Charles, Phi, and Fred were born in 1903, 1906, and 1911 and were all third generation descendants of William Pierson of Cairo, New York. When we read your Pierson traditions, I'm sure you can imagine our surprise. John exclaimed 'I always said there was Viking blood.' He's quite right! When we were first married, I often teased John about his 'Viking looks.' With his red hair and bushy red beard, long narrow face and fair skin, he could have been mistaken for a Viking. He used to tell me, 'It isn't such a joke, there is Viking blood in the Pierson family!' " New babies of Richard Pierson's United States line are usually born with red hair which turns blond during the first year of childhood. Richard Pierson, one of the authors, descends from Henry Peirson (1615-1680) of Southampton, Long Island, New York colony, as do the New Zealand Piersons. Whether the red hair comes from the Vikings 30 generations before is unknown, but some Vikings were known to have red hair.

In 1086, the East Riding of Yorkshire, England, contained about 1200 families. It had been 200 years since the Danish Vikings had conquered Northumbria and created the area known as the Danelaw. After about six generations, these people, once about 80 percent pure Vikings were now a mixture called English who were proud of their Viking heritage and were still deep in Viking tradition though Viking slavery in Yorkshire was a thing of the past. When Duke William conquered England in 1066, most of the Vikings living in Yorkshire were smallholders working land that they owned (originally called an Army living off the land). The area of East Riding was not fully conquered until about 1069 with the "Harrying of the North" where King William commanded that "their houses and corn, with all their implements and chattels, be burnt without distinction, and great herds of cattle and beasts of burden (oxen) be butchered wherever they were found." This resulted in a cruel famine where many thousands of this fine Viking race died in Yorkshire. It is believed that the vill of Persene was established just after this "Harrying" when William Percy arrived in Yorkshire about 1070.

According to the Domesday Book[15], William of Percy had 14 dwellings of the following men (who owned the dwellings in 1066 before the invasion): Bjornulfr; Gamalbarn; Svartr;

---

[13]Lt. Col. Richard E. Pierson, "The Pierson Family Tradition," unpublished, Citrus Heights, California, 1991.

[14]Letter, Jennifer Pierson of New Zealand to Richard Pierson of California, U.S.A., dated 6 December 1991.

[15]John Morris, General Editor, *Domesday Book, Yorkshire*, Volume 30, Phillimore & Co. Ltd., Chichester, England, 1986, Part 1, p. 298a.

Ecgbeorht; Selakollr; Alfgrimr; Northmann; Dunstan; Authulfr; Weleret; Ulfketill; Godelind; Sunnifa; Otbert; and he has the church of St. Mary at York in Yorkshire. He also has, from Earl Hugh, two dwellings of two reeves of Earl Harold, but the burgesses say that one of these had not been the Earl's, but they say the other had been forfeited to him. William also claims to hold the Church of St. Cuthbert at Durham in Durham county from Earl Hugh and seven very small dwellings containing 50 feet in width (probably part of St. Cuthbert's). Furthermore, concerning one dwelling of a certain Uhtred, the burgesses say that William of Percy had carried it off for himself into the castle after he returned from Scotland (in 1072). But William himself denies that he had had the land of this Uhtred, but he says that through the orders of Hugh the Sheriff he had borne off Uhtred's house into the castle in the first year after the destruction of the castles. It is noted that all the previous owners had Viking names. William Percy's principle Yorkshire properties[16] were at Bolton Percy, Spofforth, and Topcliffe:

"In Bolton (Percy), Ligulfr, Thorketill and Earnwine had 8 carucates (960 acres) of land taxable (in 1066 before the invasion), where 4 ploughs are possible (480 acres are plowable). Now Rozelin has (it) from William (of Percy). He (William) has there 2 ploughs (240 acres under lordship); and 6 villagers with 2 ploughs (240 acres under plow). Meadow, 20 acres. There, a priest and a church. Woodland, 1/2 league long and 1/2 wide (about one and a half miles long and the same wide). The whole (of Bolton Percy), 1 league long and 1/2 wide (about three miles long and one and a half miles wide). Value before 1066, 40 shillings; now 30 shillings."

"In Spofforth, Gamalbarn had 3 carucates (360 acres) of land (before 1066). 2 ploughs possible there (240 acres plowable in 1066). Now William (of Percy) has there 4 ploughs (480 acres); and 9 villagers and 10 smallholders with 4 ploughs (plows). 1 mill, 2 shillings; meadow, 4 acres; woodland pasture, 1 league long and 1 wide (about 3 miles long and as wide). The whole, 16 furlongs long and 12 wide (about 2 miles long and a mile and a half wide apparently excluding the woodland pasture). Value before 1066, 20 shillings; now 60 shillings."

"In Topcliffe, Crakehill, Dalton, Asenby and Skipton (on Swale), Bjornulfr had 26 carucates (3120 acres) of land taxable, where 15 ploughs are possible (1800 acres plowable). Now William (of Percy) has there 3 ploughs (360 acres); and 35 villagers and 14 smallholders with 13 ploughs (plows). There, a church and 2 priests, who have 1 plough. 1 mill, 5 shillings; woodland pasture, 4 furlongs long and 4 wide. The whole manor, 3 leagues long and 2 wide (about 9 miles long by 6 miles wide). Value before 1066, 4 pounds; now 100 shillings."

William Percy had 60 other properties in Yorkshire, which are not mentioned here, each smaller than the size of the three properties above. William's principle residence was at Spofforth and his largest work force at Topcliffe where he built a castle. Virtually all of the properties had owners before 1066 with Scandinavian names indicating that all of the villagers were Viking descendants.

---

16 John Morris, General Editor, *Domesday Book, Yorkshire*, Volume 30, Phillimore & Co. Ltd., Chichester, England, 1986, Part 1, p. 298a.

Near Persene, in 1086, were the following staff and conditions by others outside William Percy's control (see the earlier map in the vicinity of Persene): Kilnwick had only a small woodland pasture in use; Lund was not in use; Lockington had 9 villagers, 1 mill, and 360 acres under plow; Etton had 2 smallholders, 18 villagers, and 840 acres under plow; Cherry Burton had 12 villagers, and 360 acres under plow; Bishop Burton and other outliars of Beverley including Skidby had 20 villagers and 1200 acres under plow; Beverley housed the Canons at St. John's, and had 3 soldiers of the Bishop of York, 15 smallholders, 18 villagers, and 840 acres under plow plus 40 square miles of woodland pasture; Molescroft had 2 villagers.

Under William Percy's lordship in 1086 near Persene were: Leconfield which had 8 villagers, 300 acres under plow, a 4,000 eels per year fishery, and a woodland pasture of 6 miles by 6 miles; Scorborough[17] had 3 villagers, 1 mill, and 60 acres under plow; and at Persene, 90 acres were under plow. Of these three vills, only Leconfield existed in 1066 and it was then called the Manor of Gytha, and was owned by Osbern, Wulfgeat, and another Osbern. The staff there were believed to be primarily of Viking blood. It is believed that Scorborough and later Persene were staffed from Leconfield, but if from other Percy holdings were also from Viking descent. There apparently were no living quarters at Persene in 1086, but it was likely a vill supporting residences by the early 1100s. According to the archaeologist reports, Persene eventually became part of Scorborough Township, was lost in Scorborough as a separate entity, and then Scorborough was lost as a vill, probably prior to 1500. In 1875, the vill of Scorborough location was known as Scorbrough Hall on maps, and in 1955 that area was referred to as a park. The 1875 map shows an old structure foundation location at the site of the vill of Persene. The estimate for the period in which people resided at Persene is 50 to 400 years beginning about 1100. Very few written records were kept in that era by the church because few could read or write, and no records were kept outside the church which was the center of learning. Most early records have deteriorated (the Domesday Book is an exception) as they were not done on parchment paper which began in the late 1500s. Thus current records consist primarily of archaeological analysis and those records put to pen after parchment paper came into use, from legends handed down generation to generation verbally.

The Peresone Migration Process

It was about 1100 in Europe, when surnames began to be used to further identify individuals within the increasing population. Therefore, when William Percy's son Alan, who succeeded William, staffed Persene at about this time, the villagers might be known as Gamall the Blacksmith or Ormr of Spofforth, and so on, depending on their given name and where they were from or possibly their occupation. When Gamall had children, his sons born in, say 1102 and 1104, at Persene might be known as Gamalbarn (born of Gamall) of Persene and William of Persene. By 1123, Gamall would possibly be seeking an education for one of his sons. Having named one of his sons after William of Percy, Gamall may have urged William of Percy's son Alan to educate his son William at one of the churches where reading and writing was taught. This request may have been well received by Alan Percy because of the loyalty that Gamall had shown in making flawless swords as

---

[17] The vill of Scorborough should not be confused with Scarborough on the sea in North Riding which is a different town.

part of his duties as blacksmith and armorer for Percy in the past (this is a fictitious example). Percy called him Gamall the Smith and he called his son William of Persene (Peresonne). William of Percy owned several church resources, which now were in control of Alan, to train individuals to read and write and to learn about church duties such as recorder, vicar, or possibly rector, thus preparing them for jobs of higher responsibility and higher remuneration for services. Those church resources included Bolton Percy, Whitby Abbey, St. Mary's at York, and St. Cuthbert's at Durham. While St. John's at Beverley was the closest church training center, it was not likely that William of Persene rated the request of a favor from the Archbishop of York who owned it. Nor did Percy wish to let William of Pericne move into the control of the Archbishop and lose his future value as a trained employee capable of such jobs as recorder, vicar, rector, subdean, dean, or sheriff. Of course, the higher jobs had to be earned through loyalty and trustworthiness since they involved great responsibility and power. In this fictitious case, let us say that William of Persene qualifies for a job after training for five years and receives a job as recorder at St. Mary's in York. Thus a Peresonne has migrated to York from the vill of Persene. Under the feudal system brought to England in 1066 by King William I, villains (villagers) were required to remain in the village they were born in by law, but the land owners and tenants did not have to abide by that rule. Thus villagers who sought to leave their village must do so through the desires of their overlord. This law was enforced until the Peasant's Revolt of 1381.

The Persene migration process continued until there were Peresonnes in several locations in Yorkshire and Durham. Their descendants gradually moved to other parts of England, gaining more trust and higher positions. Between 1240 and 1856, thirty-four coats of arms were registered to Peresons (of various spellings) in England, Scotland, and the Netherlands (see Chapter 5). In 1298, Wautier Pieressone was the Count of Berwick. In 1440, William Pereson was rector of Thoresby in Yorkshire. In 1452, Thomas Peirson (Pereson) was the Sheriff of Yorkshire, having earlier been the rector of Bolton Percy and the Subdean of York. In 1477, Nicholas Pierson was the Sheriff of Yorkshire. In the period 1561-1600, John, Henry, Nicolas, Andrew, David, Arche, George, James, and John Peirson were having children in Dunfermline, Fife County, Scotland. In 1637, John Pearson left Howden, Yorkshire, for Lynn, Massachusetts, in America. In 1639, the Rev. Abraham Pierson, Henry Peirson, and Bartholomew Pierson departed London together and sailed to New England in America. About 1645, the widow Anne (Clough) Peirson of Suffolk county, England, sent her son Stephen Peirson to Branford, Connecticut, in America for a carpenter apprenticeship. He stayed and moved to Derby, Connecticut, as an adult. About 1661, Thomas Peirson Sr. left Yorkshire and moved to Branford, Connecticut, in America to be with his uncle, the Rev. Abraham Pierson. About 1860, Charles Anson Crocker Herrick Philetous Pierson moved to the gold fields on the South Island of New Zealand from Cairo, New York, in America. Thus the Peresonne migration continues and is discussed in detail in later chapters.

Chapter 2
Our Viking Ancestors

The name *Viking* probably comes from the Norse word *vik*, meaning bay or creek. Adopted by the Scandinavians in the 9th century, *Viking* meant "sea voyage."[1]

Prior to 600 A.D., the Vikings were a purely Scandinavian people. Their minstrels sang the same songs of old warrior heroes common to all. They all spoke the same language, Old Norse, shared the same way of life on isolated farms, and worshipped the same pagan gods.

The Scandinavians had a written language called runes. The first runic alphabet is thought to have originated about the time of the birth of Christ. It consisted of 24 letters or phonetic symbols, organized in three families of eight, and with minor variations in the shape of some of the letters, was common to all the rune-using Germanic people.[2]

The Viking era, or Viking Age proper, is considered by historians to be 780 to 1070, during which time Scandinavian nations attempted to expand their area of control in the world to include the British isles.

Sweden emerged as a separate country around the 7th century out of the union of two peoples, the Gotar and the Svear governed by a single king descended from the kings of Uppsala.

Norway began its attempts at unification in the 6th century and succeeded by the end of the 9th century under King Harald Finehair's reign.

Denmark was sufficiently unified under King Godfred and powerful enough in the year 800 that they attacked Charlemagne.

By 800, Scandinavia (Norway, Sweden, and Denmark) had about two million inhabitants. But in the 9th century its population began to increase significantly due to a warmer climate period improving food production and reducing the mortality rate. Additionally, the traditions of the Vikings included polygamy. This practice of more than one wife, including concubines from the slave class, produced a large number of children.

The Vikings were a class society represented by three classes - the unfree, the free, and their rulers. The Thralls were the unfree. They did the dirty work, such as carrying loads, lugging firewood, dunging fields, feeding pigs, and cutting peat. Some of the unfree women bore children for their masters. The free men did tasks such as making a loom, taming oxen, building houses, barns and wagons, and making & handling the plow. The free women did tasks such as bearing children, spinning, weaving, providing meals and clothes for her family, managing the household, carrying house keys, and holding purse-strings. The rulers lived in splendor. The master, when young, learned to use bow and arrow, shield and spear, to hunt with horse and ride with hound, and practiced

---

[1] Yves Cohat, *The Vikings, Lords of the Seas*, Discoveries, Harry N. Abrams, Inc., Publishers, New York, New York, 1992, p.11.
[2] Gwyn Jones, *The History of the Vikings*, 2nd Edition, Oxford University Press, Oxford & New York, 1984, p.419.

swordsmanship and swimming. He also was taught the art of writing with runes, and urged to take possession of his hereditary estates. Eventually, he went on Vikings (sea voyages) that resulted in captured treasure, animals, and white slaves. He came to own many dwellings, and in true lord's fashion dealt out some of the looted treasure to his friends and followers. His mistress learned to act like a lady, dress well, eat well, and bear noble children.

In June 793, the sacking of the monastery at Lindisfarne, on the northeast coast of England, signaled the beginning of the Viking rampage. A few drakkars (dragon ships) appeared on the sea's horizon and quickly approached the shore. A small band of Norwegian Viking warriors poured onto the beach and launched an attack on the Lindisfarne monastery. The Vikings hacked their way through the English defenders with sword, ax, spear, and dagger, leaving a bloody massacre behind. The houses and religious buildings were pillaged, treasures seized, and the buildings set afire. The Vikings departed with everything of value in their drakkars including the church treasures, coinage, sheep, oxen, women, and able-bodied men. The captured English were sold into slavery.

In the summer of 794, the Norwegian Vikings attacked Jarrow on the coast of Northumbria, 50 miles south of Lindisfarne. These raids depended upon the element of surprise and a high speed of execution.

By 800, the Norwegian Vikings had attacked eleven monasteries in Scotland, England, and Wales, but only the monastery at Monkwearmouth had succeeded in repulsing such a Viking raid.

These summertime daylight raids heralded the beginning of nearly three centuries of ever more violent and more frequent Viking seagoing expeditions against the island of Britain (England, Scotland and Wales), Ireland, and western Gaul (coastal areas of France and Belgium).

The Danish Vikings were besieged on every side - to the north by the Norwegians, to the east by the Swedes, to the south by the powerful Slavs, to the west by the Carolingian empire. Instead of engaging in piratical raids like the Norwegians, the Danes preferred to launch themselves on Europe with professional armies composed of trained men and elite troops led by great warlords.

At the end of the 8th century, the Danish King Godfred established a line of fortifications called the Danevirke. From these fortifications, he launched numerous attacks on the eastern Carolingian empire, England, and the Frisian islands (belonging to the Netherlands) in the North Sea. Charlemagne, and later his son, Louis the Pious, succeeded in repulsing the Danes for about 35 years.

While the Norwegians and Danes were pillaging western Europe, the Swedish Vikings were taking furs and slaves from the great Russian plain and trading for silks southerly on rivers to the East. The Swedes differed from the Norwegians and Danes in that the primary purpose of the Swedes was trade, whereas the Norwegians and Danes intended to expand their territory. In spite of this, the Swedes founded a New Russian State in the last half of the 9th century covering 600 miles from Novgorod to Kiev primarily to control the trade routes.

Since it was the Danish Vikings that took the region of Yorkshire in England and integrated with the existing English race, becoming the dominant racial influence there by 1066, we shall study these Vikings as the primary race from whom the men of the vill of Pericne (Persene) in the East Riding of Yorkshire, England, descended.

By 834, the Danish Vikings had established a large professional army selected from the finest soldiers recruited from all Scandinavia. They launched attacks and successfully sacked first Dorestad, then Hamburg, followed by Rouen, Chartres, and Tours in France using a fleet of several hundred ships carrying between 10,000 and 15,000 Viking warriors. They eventually attacked Paris in 885 using 700 Viking ships to carry 30,000 Viking warriors up the river Seine.

Beginning in 835 and for almost every year through 900, the Danish Vikings made a series of furious assaults on England. The Danes established fortified bases along the river Thames. From these they mounted violent attacks inland. Over a thirty year period they ravaged the south and center of England.

These attacks were not by small bands of untrained men. The Viking warrior was protected by a breastplate padded with leather. Wealthy warriors might substitute a coat or shirt of mail. His head was protected by a conical metal helmet often with a nose guard made of leather or iron. The warrior's normal weapon was a bow made from yew, reinforced with leather. In hand to hand fighting, the Viking warrior used a shield of linden wood, reinforced with iron panels. He could handle a dagger, javelin, ax, or sword with great skill. Select foot soldiers, chosen for their height and strength, wielded very heavy long-handled battle-axes for defending against opposing cavalry. These special battle-ax groups would form a solid front and when the horse and riders reached them, they were capable of felling a horse or cleaving through a shield with a single blow. The Viking cavalry were mostly Magyars recruited from Hungary. These skilled horsemen would shoot their arrows from a full gallop in a special formation that allowed all horsemen a field of fire on the enemy without other members of their cavalry being in the way. The Viking cavalry were also skilled in the use of sword, lance, and dagger. The long sword was a favorite weapon in close combat and the typical Viking sword had a richly ornamented pommel and a heavy razor-sharp double-edged blade about 30 inches long. This sword was wielded with one hand.

Viking warriors were transported to battle in dragon ships, called drakkars. These ships were marvelously designed to be powered by sail, rowing, or both at the same time. They could reverse direction without turning around simply by rowing in the other direction because the keel

Viking Drakkar

and stern design were similar. These 80-foot-long dragon ships were capable of navigating the high seas or up rivers with their shallow draft. Their center-located single sail mast rose 60 to 66 feet above the bridge and supported a sail, usually of double thickness raw wool, of 330 square feet or more.[3] The ships had 28 to 32 oars and usually carried about 45 warriors each with all their weapons, shields, and personal belongings.

One name probably stands out as the instigator of the historical situation which resulted in the settlement of Vikings in Yorkshire. That name is Bjorn Ironside, son of Lothrocus king of Dacia (Denmark), known in legend as Ragnar Lodbrok[4]. During the years 856 to 862, Ragnar plundered France, Spain, North Africa, Italy, and the island of Oissel (Oscellus). The wealth he pirated exceeded all previous Vikings. In about 862, Ragnar came to England with two ships' crews (about 90 men), likely moving inland along the Humber River. Here he encountered King Ella of Northumbria, who had Ragnar thrown into a pit and stung to death by snakes. Before he died, he was heard to say, "The piglings would be grunting if they knew the plight of the boar!"

In 865, an army of Danish Vikings attacked East Anglia and Mercia[5] in England (the piglings were grunting) causing great damage there. The following year the Vikings captured York in Northumbria. Northumbria[6] had just driven out their king Osberht and

accepted Ella, a king not of the royal line. Too late, the two kings joined forces, marched on York, which was now in Danish hands, and suffered there an overwhelming defeat in 867. Both kings were killed and the Old English kingdom of Deira (Northumbria) passed into Danish keeping. The Viking leaders of the Danish Army were Ivar (Yngvarr) called the Boneless, Ubbi, and Halfdan. Legend tells us that they came from Scandinavia and Ireland to avenge the death of their father, Ragnar. Legend also tells us that these sons of Ragnar "carved the blood eagle" on King Ella's back. This inhuman rite consisted of cutting away the victim's ribs from his spine, then pulling out his lungs and spreading them like wings on his back.

After attacking Mercia, Ivar and Ubbi with their armies moved south in 869 into East Anglia, defeated the English, and captured and executed King Edmund. In 870 Halfdan, accompanied by a second king and many "jarls", led the Danes

[3]Yves Cohat, *The Vikings, Lords of the Seas*, Discoveries, Harry N. Abrams, Inc., Publishers, New York, New York, 1992, p.72.
[4]"Ragnarr Lodbrok in the British Isles," Proceedings of the Seventh Viking Congress, Dublin, 1973.
[5]Michael Wood, *Domesday, A Search for the Roots of England*, BBC Books, London, England, 1986, p.91.
[6]Gwyn Jones, *The History of the Vikings*, 2nd Edition, Oxford University Press, Oxford & New York, 1984, pp.218-9.

against Wessex, and seized and fortified the key town of Reading. Mercia had collapsed by 874, and now the Danish Army, which had held together since 865 (ten years), broke into two. The roughly 2500 men were at Repton on the Trent river in 875 when the Army divided with part going to Deira (Northumbria) under Halfdan while Guthrum and two other kings departed for Cambridge in East Anglia. From Deira, Halfdan made war on the Picts and Strathclyde Welsh to secure his northern frontier.

The actual occupation of English territory by the Danish Vikings was about to begin. In 876, Halfdan "shared out the lands of Northumbria, and the Danes engaged themselves in plowing and making a living[7]." With this permanent base established, Halfdan set off against the Norwegians of Dublin and died in 877. The area partitioned was approximately that of modern Yorkshire. The freeborn Danish soldiers settled as farmers[8] dependent on the army bases established at the main towns. Each army based on the Danelaw towns could muster several hundred men or more. This military origin was long reflected in the social organization of the Danelaw towns. In the tenth century, a hundred years after they settled the area, they still called themselves "armies."

During the period, 876 to 918, Danish settlement in the five boroughs of the Danelaw (York, Nottingham, Lincoln, Derby, and Leicester) took place in two steps, and did not involve displacement of the English. First, there was the Danish army established upon the soil in 876, and second, after 877, an influx of Danish immigrants came via the Humber and Trent rivers, often with their womenfolk, to take plots of land and plow. The government was formed by army councils, "holds," into boroughs (fortified towns larger than villages) run by oligarchies led by important landowners, "earls" (a Viking word).[9] The main period of Danish migration was over by 918.

By 886, the Danish Vikings had fully conquered Northumbria, installed themselves at York and at Nottingham, laid siege to Mercia, and taken London and Cambridge. Alfred, the English king of Wessex, who was skilled in strategic warfare, put up strong resistance. Later in 886, Alfred recovered London from the Danes and liberated a large part of southern England. But in 899, he died and the arrival of fresh Danish Viking troops reversed much of his success.

The Danelaw in Northern England

By 900, the majority of England from the north of Yorkshire to the Thames river had come under Danish Viking rule. This territory was called the Danelaw because it was subject to Viking law. It was defended by six fortified towns: Derby, Leicester, Lincoln, Nottingham, Stamford, and York. The official language became Norse.

The Norwegian Viking, Rognvald, was a marauder in Scotland and the Isle of Man. In 919, Rognvald captured York and made himself king of Northumbria. For Rognvald, this was the resolution of a struggle between Danes and Norwegians that went back 50 years. In 920, Rognvald, the sons of Eadulf, and all those who dwelt in Northumbria (English, Danish, and Norwegians) accepted King Edward as father and overlord. By the acceptance

---

[7] Gwyn Jones, *The History of the Vikings*, 2nd Edition, Oxford University Press, Oxford & New York, 1984, pp.221.

[8] Michael Wood, *Domesday, A Search for the Roots of England*, BBC Books, London, England, 1986, p.134.

[9] Michael Wood, *Domesday, A Search for the Roots of England*, BBC Books, London, England, 1986, p.130.

of the overlordship, Rognvald was confirmed in his recently won kingdom and spared an attack by King Edward at a time when the Danish and Christian part of his realm wished to rise against him. In 921, Rognvald died and was succeeded by his kinsman Sigtrygg. Sigtrygg Gale had earlier recovered Dublin, and had slain the high-king Njall. Sigtrygg was also king of the Liffey Norsemen. In 925, Athelstan of Wessex took Northumbria from the Norwegian Vikings, but this didn't last long. In 927, King Edward chased off the Norwegian Vikings and retook York. In succeeding years, the Danes allied themselves with the English to fight the Norwegian Vikings. By 928, the overlordship of the West Saxons over Britain was achieved: a powerful and well-organized kingship south of the Humber river, client-ruled north of the Humber (Northumbria), and a system of tribute imposed on the kings of the Celtic lands[10]. The Danish courts were merged into the West Saxon system-of-hundred courts. The Danes could administer their own law, with their own lawmen, but no man could now be without a lord according to Athelstan's Grately code.

In the Danelaw, the land dependent on each borough (fortified town) was not yet known as a shire (county), as it would be in the 1086 Domesday Book. Its administrative divisions were wapentakes, as compared with hundreds in the south. Wapentake meant the symbolic brandishing of weapons by which decisions at a public meeting were confirmed. The larger territories within the Danelaw were too unwieldy to have a single council and were divided into what the Danes called ridings or "third parts", especially in the territory called Yorkshire[11].

The West Saxon kings from Alfred to Edgar progressively expanded the power and landed wealth of the monarchy and were successful in building several powerful families in the old kingdoms, with a class of thegns below them, and in imposing extremely heavy taxes. By about 930, when King Athelstan issued his law code at Grately, landowners were required to provide two mounted men for every plow when the king went to war. Presumably this tax was commuted into money or kind in time of peace.

The men who did the fighting were not the peasantry but the landowner class, the thegnhood. They provided the well-armed and well-trained army. Their investment in their skills and equipment was great. A thegn's fighting equipment, which he was required by law to bring to battle, included many expensive items such as helmets, chain mail, swords, and horses. The horse was an important possession, a noble animal in every sense, whereas oxen were the beasts of the field. Because of the investment in training, equipment, and stud farms, Athelstan's laws prohibited the sale of horses abroad[12]. Great expense was lavished on the best weapons, with fantastic ingenuity and skill going into the creation of the great pattern-welded sword blades. Earl Aelfgar of Essex, for example, who died in the 940s, left in his will a mass of weapons including a single sword "worth 120 mancuses of gold" with another four pounds of silver plated on the sheath (about a $2,000 set in today's U.S. money).

---

[10]Michael Wood, *Domesday, A Search for the Roots of England*, BBC Books, London, England, 1986, p.105.

[11]Michael Wood, *Domesday, A Search for the Roots of England*, BBC Books, London, England, 1986, p.132.

[12]Michael Wood, *Domesday, A Search for the Roots of England*, BBC Books, London, England, 1986, p.105.

In 937, on the unidentified battle ground of Brunanburh, the army of Wessex and Mercia under Athelstan and his brother Edmund fought it out with the Norsemen of Ireland under Olaf, the Scots under Constantine, and the Strathclyde Welsh under Eugenius. The army of Wessex and Mercia won the battle. Never until now on the island of Britain was there greater slaughter of an army with the sword's edge. When Athelstan died in 939, Olaf of Dublin with his Irish Norsemen was back in York, and in 940 was raiding triumphantly through the Midlands. He took over officially by treaty in 940 and died in 941. Sigtrygg's son Olaf, nicknamed Kvaran, took over and he lost to Edmund in 942 the five boroughs won earlier by Olaf of Dublin. What followed was almost an annual exchange of kings at York between the Norwegians and English until 954 when Eric Bloodaxe, the last Viking king, was expelled. The kingdom at York would be free of Norwegian and Danish assault for almost 30 years.

Minor raids against the area began anew in the 980s. By this time, the Viking villagers of Yorkshire had been there for about three generations (about a hundred years) and they thought of Yorkshire as their homeland. Having sided with the English against the Norwegians, the Yorkshire Vikings now gave their allegiance to the English kings. Beginning in 991, the Danish Vikings invaded England again. In 1002, the English king Ethelred gave the order that all Danes on English soil were to be killed, the target being the new Danes of the last ten years. The massacre that followed provoked King Sven Forkbeard of Denmark to make terrible reprisals on the English and by 1014, England once again fell under control of the Danish Vikings. King Forkbeard's successor, Knut the Great (King Canute), eliminated the last pockets of English resistance driving out the house of Wessex. In 1016, Canute, king of Denmark and Norway, also made himself king of England. When King Canute of Denmark died in 1035, his sons took over and frittered away his control of England. By 1042, an English king, Edward, was elected to the English throne.

By the 11th century, Scandinavian influence ran deep in the fabric of life in Yorkshire. Organization, language, land tenure, and names of people and places were influenced[13]. In the area of England under Danelaw in the tenth century (roughly from Bedfordshire north to the Scottish border), about 500 place names are denoted as Scandinavian (also called Viking and Danish) and are identified by compounded names with 'by', there are nearly 200 of these such as Thoresby; or by words containing the word 'thorp,' meaning farmstead, such as Lowthorpe; and lastly by pure Scandinavian words such as Eakring (oak ring or circle of oak trees).[14]

The Blood-feud of Northumbria (1016 - 1073)

Northumbria can be described as the land in England between the Humber and Tweed rivers with its northern government and church at Durham and its southern government and church at York. By the 11th century, it was clear to the Anglo-Scandinavian nobility of Northumbria that it would be impossible to maintain it as a separate kingdom. Thus their goal was to maintain it as an earldom with as little interference from the king as possible. Therefore, 11th century politics can be summarized as the attempts of various factions to

[13]Michael Wood, *Domesday, A Search for the Roots of England*, BBC Books, London, England, 1986, p.132.

[14]Michael Wood, *Domesday, A Search for the Roots of England*, BBC Books, London, England, 1986, p.134.

take and hold the effectively vice-regal position of earl. In the late 10th century, the English kings had re-established the descendants of the old Northumbrian ruling house as earls of Northumbria, with the additional safeguard of at times splitting the earldom into northern and southern sections divided by the river Tees. Under the Scandinavian king Knutr, however, the ascendancy of the Bamburgh line was challenged primarily by southern Northumbrian Danish interests. This is the background for the famous blood-feud, described below, which lasted from 1016 to 1073.

Around 1000, the house of Bamburgh was represented by Earl Waltheof. His son and successor Uhtred supported Aethelred against Knutr, but met with opposition from the Danish faction in York, represented by a thane called Thorbrandr and his followers. Despite Uhtred's eventual submission to Knutr, he was killed by Thorbrandr with Knutr's connivance. This led to some twenty years of confusion. The Bamburgh line continued to hold power north of the Tees river where Uhtred's brother and his two sons, Aldred and Eadwulf succeeded him in turn as Earl. Aldred avenged his father's murder by killing Thorbrandr, but was himself killed by Thorbrandr's son Karli. Meanwhile Knutr's nominees for the earldom, first Eric, then Siward - a man of obscure Scandinavian origin - were attempting to take control of the earldom from southern Northumbria. Siward finally established control over the whole of Northumbria in 1041 by the expedient of killing Eadwulf and attempting to unite the two factions by marrying Aldred's daughter. The result was that two main lines of claimants to the earldom traced their origins back to Waltheof, the distinction being between the older line and the newer line represented by Siward and his descendants. Because of the murder of Aldred, Siward's line also became direct participants in the blood-feud against the descendants of Thorbrandr.

Siward ruled successfully until his death in 1055, apparently untroubled by either Northumbrian factions or Edward the Confessor. But his only surviving son was too young to succeed him. Whereupon King Edward and his council, under the dominant influence of the House of Godwine, instead of appointing any of the representatives of the ancient line, gave the earldom to Tosti Godwinson. Tosti was unwelcome as an outsider and maintained his rule only with the support of extensive armed forces. Unlike Siward, he was not successful in the all-important question of relations with Scotland, and it can be assumed that there was internal opposition to his rule. Tosti responded to this in the traditional manner of murdering his opponents. In 1064, he killed Gamall (son of Ormr) and Ulfr (son of Dolgfinnr) in particularly underhand circumstances. The following year, Tosti had Gospatric, the senior representative of the Northumbrian line, killed at the royal court. In response, the Northumbrian nobility, led by Gamalbarn, Dunstan (son of Aegelnothes) and Gluniairnn (son of Eardwulf), in alliance with Mercia, successfully deposed Tosti. Morcar, the younger brother of Edwin, Earl of Mercia, was appointed in his place - presumably the price of Mercian support. Morcar gave the northern part of the Northumbrian earldom to Asulfr (also known to historians as Oswulf), son of the former Earl Eadwulf, which was probably also part of the agreement.

These were the earls in charge of Northumbria when King Edward, the Confessor, died in 1066. The claims to the throne by the House of Godwine were not well received in Northumbria and Tosti was shown outright hostility on his initial incursions. Harold, Earl of Wessex, only obtained Northumbrian support for the throne with difficulty, through his physical presence and his marriage with Edith, sister of Earls Edwin and Morcar. Earls Edwin and Morcar opposed Harold Hardrada's invasion, but sections of the Yorkshire nobility were prepared to support this Norwegian king after his victory at Fulford, until he in his turn, and Tosti with him, were defeated and killed by King Harold's forces at Stamford Bridge (about six miles east of York).

By 1066, William was Duke of Normandy in France and his Danish ancestors had mixed with the Frankish race for five generations. Starting with only 5,000 Danes and mixing with the larger number of Franks, they were mostly Frankish. These people were called Normans and they had lost their affiliation with the Danish Vikings of 155 years ago. Duke William was the second cousin of King Edward, the Confessor, of England, and William had exacted an oath from Harold, Earl of Wessex, to support his future claim to the English throne. King Edward had been elected to the English throne in 1042 after the death of the Danish King Knutr, marking the end of Danish rule in England. William was born in 1027, an illegitimate son of Robert, Duke of Normandy. His mother was a tanner's daughter. He succeeded his father as Duke of Normandy when he was only seven years old. At 24, William had made himself the mightiest feudal lord in all France by various conquests. William's wife, Matilda, a Flemish princess, was descended from the old Anglo-Saxon line of kings. When King Edward died childless in 1066, William, Duke of Normandy, claimed the English crown. However, the English assembly called Witan (wise men) chose Harold as king. The pope supported William, so William gathered together "a host of horsemen, slingers, and archers" and set sail for England. This was not a small unplanned affair. William transported across the English Channel more than five thousand men, horses, equipment, and supplies. Harold met him with foot soldiers armed with battle axes. The two armies battled near Hastings in Sussex county on October 14, 1066. King Harold was killed on the battlefield. The victorious Duke William at age 39 went to London where he was crowned as King William I in Westminster Abbey on Christmas Day.[15]

As a result of William taking the throne by force, England received a new royal dynasty, a new nobility, a new church, a new art and architecture, and a new language of government (Norman French). The leaders and rank and file of the army which had won at Hastings were the first to benefit. After casualties, they numbered about five thousand men, and all of them expected to qualify for the spoils, namely land in England. *Domesday Book* (a very complete tax census of 1086) reveals a massive shift in ownership in England in the 20 years between 1066 and 1086. This 1086 tax census had also recorded land ownership at the 1066 invasion time of King William I. In 1086, among the 180 or so tenants-in-chief who possessed large estates (those bringing in over a hundred pounds per year income) only two (1%) were English; of the 1400 or so lesser tenants-in-chief about 100 (7%) were English; of the further 6,000 sub-tenants there was a much larger English element, many of them leasing land which they had owned freely before 1066.[16]

After Duke William's victory at Hastings in 1066, sections of the northern nobility submitted to him at Barking, including Earls Edwin and Morcar of Northumbria (who now had little influence there) and Siward and Aldred (representatives of the Bamburgh line). These two were probably grandsons of Earl Uhtred and so brothers or half-brothers of Earl

[15]F. E. Compton Co., *Compton's Encyclopedia*, William Benton, Publisher, Chicago, Illinois, 1970, Vol.24, p.163.

[16]Michael Wood, *Domesday, A Search for the Roots of England*, BBC Books, London, England, 1986, p.159.

Gospatric. Waltheof, Earl Siward's son, Earl of Northampton and Huntingdon, also submitted to William at Barking. It is likely that the earls of Northumbria had submitted to William because of military weakness rather than acceptance of the Norman king since the most serious challenge to William's rule came from Northumbria in the following years. Significantly, there was no record of Asulfr, Earl in northern Northumbria, coming to terms with King William.

Outright opposition in Northumbria was partly the result of King William's own ineptitude. He not only failed to make an effective alliance with the ancient line but also sent Kofsi to Northumbria as Earl early in 1067. Kofsi had been associated with Tosti's unpopular rule and had maintained himself by piracy along the Northumbrian coast after 1065, before he too submitted to the King at Barking. Most likely he had been instructed to overthrow Asulfr's de facto rule. This he attempted to do with the result that Asulfr killed Kofsi in March 1067. Asulfr retained power until the following autumn when he was himself killed by a robber. King William then decided to accept a representative of the Northumbrian house and accordingly sold the earldom to Gospatric (son of Madalred), the senior member of the line. Presumably the King felt he was giving office to someone acceptable to the northerners but who, unlike Asulfr, had not openly opposed him.

The main objective of the Northumbrian nobility was to minimize English interference in order to preserve their own power. There was already opposition to the royal taxation policy and Gospatric was more committed to his Northumbrian peers than to the English King. By 1068, Edgar Aetheling, who was emerging as a credible alternative candidate to the throne, had fled to Scotland accompanied by the powerful thane Merlesveinn. Also Edwin and Morcar escaped from their honorable captivity to organize a rising in the Midlands. The Northumbrian nobility decided to support this. Unfortunately for them, King William moved rapidly, putting down the rising in the Midlands and marching on York where he built a castle. Gospatric was able to flee to Scotland, but the people of York had little option but to submit. Those that submitted included Arnketill, the most powerful of the Northumbrian nobles, who gave his son to King William as a hostage, and Bishop Alwine of Durham.

So far, Norman power had penetrated only minimally into Northumbria, but any attempt to extend it could expect to meet with resistance. In January 1069, King William, once more ignoring the native nobility, sent Robert de Commines north as Earl. Despite having been warned by Bishop Alwine, Robert de Commines persisted in entering Durham where he was ambushed and killed. This was the signal for another burst of resistance to Norman rule. Robert (son of Richard), one of the custodians of York castle, was caught away from that secure base and was killed, after which the main body of Northumbrian nobles - Gospatric, Merlesveinn, Arnketill, the sons of Karli, along with Edgar Aetheling, prepared to attack York. The castellan, William Malet, sent a desperate message to King William, who once more had to march rapidly north. He relieved the castle, built a second one, and entrusted the governance of the North to one of his chief barons, William Fitz Osbern, who remained there for a short time.

The 1069 rising had been more serious than that of the previous year, for it was bound up with the invasion plans of Sveinn, King of Denmark. Although King William had put down the early stages of resistance, he was aware of the dangers from Scandinavia and ordered his Lieutenants in Yorkshire to prepare themselves against this contingency. The Danish fleet arrived in September 1069, at which point the rising was renewed. The Northumbrians were once again led by Gospatric, Merlesveinn, Arnketill, and the four sons of Karli, joined by Earl Waltheof, Sigvarthbarn, Alwine (son of Northmann) and an unidentified Elnocinus, with Edgar Aetheling also in attendance. Despite William Malet's assurance that York could hold out for a year, the Danes and Northumbrians advanced on York, took the castles, killed most of the garrison, and captured the castellans, William Malet with his family, and Gilbert of Ghent.

This was the greatest threat to Norman rule during King William's reign. Risings occurred all over England. But by Christmas, King William came north again, made an agreement with the Danes whereby they would return to their ships in the Humber river, and then marched on York. King William had probably bought the Danes off in silver as the French had done with Viking raiders during the previous 150 years. From York, William devoted the Christmas festival to starting the infamous 'Harrying of the North.' The object of the policy seems to have been to make the North a wasteland, incapable of mounting any serious threat to the southern part of the country. Those warned in advance retreated before the onslaught - if they could, which effectively meant the ruling class. The peasantry, whose interests were not considered by any of the warring parties, Normans, Northumbrians, or Danes, were left to take the brunt of the devastation. The Bishop of Durham and the nobility fled to Lindisfarne taking with them their greatest treasure, the body of St. Cuthbert. This was possibly not so much to gain the saint's protection, for Cuthbert proved ineffective on this occasion, but more in case anyone stole him to profit from his miracles elsewhere. King William advanced as far north as the Tees river, where both Waltheof and Gospatric submitted to him, returned through Yorkshire, devastating as he went, and continued his destructive journey southwest into Cheshire. Later, on his death bed, William describes his 'Harrying of the North': "I fell on the English of the northern shires like a ravening lion. I commanded their houses and corn, with all their implements and chattels, to be burnt without distinction, and great herds of cattle and beasts of burden to be butchered wherever they are found. In this way I took revenge on multitudes of both sexes by subjecting them to the calamity of a cruel famine, and so became barbarous murderer of many thousands, both young and old, of that fine race of people."

Others have listed the villages that were ravaged during the 'Harrying of the North' in December 1069 and the vill of Pericne was not among them, though many villages nearby were destroyed. Pericne, Scorborough, and Molescroft are believed to have been established about 1070 and Pericne not occupied until about 1100. Therefore, these three vills were probably established after the "Harrying of the North."

With this area finally under the control of King William in 1070, one could expect the new land owners, including Earl Hugh (to be Earl of Chester), William of Percy and the Bishop of Durham, to arrive from France and take charge of the lands now to be under their lordship. The population of Yorkshire was now of about 80 percent Danish Viking heritage with Viking village skills including farmers, cattlemen, tanners, smiths, merchants, carpenters, weavers, and armorers. These Viking freemen now become villagers (villeins) under their new landowners.

By 1070, the main Northumbrian resistance had been broken. There was little material basis in either supplies or manpower for renewed opposition. The ruling class were not too badly effected, Edgar Aetheling returned to Scotland accompanied by Merlesveinn, Sigvarthbarn, Alwine (son of Northmann), and others. Bishop Alwine subsequently joined them in their exile. For most of them active resistance was at an end except for the bishop and Sigvarthbarn who later joined Hereward in Ely where they were captured and afterward imprisoned. Bishop Alwine died the same year, 1071, at Abingdon, but Sigvarthbarn remained imprisoned in Normandy for 16 years until released by Robert Curthose on King William's death in 1087.

Northumbria did not remain entirely quiet, but the involvement of the native Northumbrian ruling class in risings against Norman rule was effectively at an end. For reasons of convenience, King William restored Gospatric to his earldom in 1070, in which capacity he actively opposed Malcolm of Scotland, who had seized this opportunity to wreak further damage by extensive raiding into Northumbria. Despite this, Gospatric was replaced as Earl after King William's successful Scottish campaign of 1072 which was concluded by his agreement with King Malcolm and included a requirement that all English exiles be expelled from Scotland. William of Percy (holder of the vill of Pericne), one of Earl Hugh's (Earl of Chester) few sub-tenants in Yorkshire, was present on the Scottish campaign of 1072 with King William. After Gospatric was replaced as Earl, he went first to Flanders and afterwards to Scotland, where King Malcolm made him Earl of Dunbar and gave him lands in Lothian.

Waltheof, son of the Earl Siward that had died in 1055, was made the new Earl of Northumbria by King William. The sons of Karli, who had been involved in the 1069 rising, had possibly made their peace with King William, as they seem to have been living in Yorkshire. In pursuance of the ancient blood-feud, Waltheof had four sons of Karli killed treacherously at Settringham (near York) in 1073. This finally avenged the murder of his grandfather by their grandfather and ended the vendetta - possibly because Waltheof himself did not long survive his enemies. In 1075, he joined the revolt of the Norman earls, but abandoned the rebellion in its early stages and sought a reconciliation with the King. It did him no good however, as he was executed at Winchester in 1076. Waltheof was the last non-Norman of the ruling class to be Earl of Northumbria. After Waltheof's death, Bishop Walcher of Durham became the Earl of Northumbria. Walcher, an outsider of Norman alliance, attempted to combine the duties of bishop and earl resulting in him being killed during internal faction fights. The next Earl was Aubrey of Coucy, a Norman. But he was dismissed as incompetent. He was succeeded by Robert of Mowbray, another Norman. Robert used his position as a base from which to attack the royal government during the reign of King William Rufus (1087 - 1100).

Chapter 3
Near the Vill of Pericne
Yorkshire, England

If all Pearson, Peirson, and Pierson families originated at the vill of Pericne alias Persene in East Riding, Yorkshire, England, you would expect to get closer to that location as you study earlier generations, if you could go back far enough in the family of interest. And you do get closer to the vill of Pericne with most of the American immigrant lines.

This chapter analyzes English records of all Pierson spellings to locate ancestors of the American immigrants to New England in the mid-1600s. The historical background and history of record keeping in England is provided. As you will see, records availability will limit the research on direct line ancestors to about 1500 A.D. with only little pieces of data being available earlier than that.

Pierson lines are not divided by different spellings of the surname in this early period. One Peeresone might have his name spelled Peresone, Peresonne, Peirson, Pierson, Pearson, and Person during his life time depending on the whim of the writer of the records. Every Peeresone knows how to pronounce his surname, but no recorder appears to ask him how to spell it (most Piersons could write). Thus, the surname spelling is recorded as found in this chapter, but disregarded as to whether it implies any particular family. Often one can see when the recorder changed by the change in the spelling of the surname of the same family, but it implies nothing else.

Genealogical Record Keeping in England

Prior to the Norman invasion in 1066, no records of birth, death, parents, and marriage were kept for the general population. Some minuscule records are found for kings and the nobility. With the coming of the Normans, the system of record-keeping began. The Domesday Book of 1086, ordered by King William I, was the earliest record, but it was set down for property assessment for taxes and contains no genealogical information.

Between 1066 and 1538 when Henry VIII received some compliance from his orders that all Parishes should maintain records of baptisms, marriages, and burials, only a very few records of any sort were in existence, partly of course, because so few members of the population could read or write. Even in the families of the nobility and landed gentry, where a certain amount of recording was carried out, there is little which survives further back than 1500 A.D. Where records earlier survive, they are principally hearsay evidence which has survived being told by father to son up to the time when eventually committed to paper.

In spite of Henry VIII's order, many Parishes were very dilatory in complying with the instruction and for this reason only a few Parish records go back as far as 1538. However, by 1600, most parishes had some form of record-keeping in operation, though not always accurate and complete.

In 1837, an Act of Parliament decreed that records of births, marriages and deaths in both England and Wales should be registered at Somerset House.

Historical Events Affecting Data Available[1]

1534 - Henry VIII assumes title of head of the Church of England.

1536 - First order issued for the keeping of Parish Registers.

1538 - Second order issued for the keeping of Parish Registers. Approximately 600 English and Welsh parishes comply.

1547 - Third order issued for the keeping of Parish Registers. Approximately 1,250 English and Welsh Parishes comply.

1553-1558 - Mary I makes every effort to force people to return to Roman Catholicism. This has considerable affect on registers of this date.

1559 - Elizabeth I issues order for keeping Parish Registers.

1571 - Introduction of Presbyterianism into England.

1589 - Records of over 5,000 English Parishes exist back to this date or earlier. Many others have lost early records.

1592 - Congregational (Independent) Church formed in London. Earliest records however commenced 1644.

1597 - Elizabeth I orders that Parish Registers be kept on parchment, all earlier records at least back to 1558 to be recopied. The same order requires copies of Christening, Marriage and Burial entries to be sent yearly to the office of the Bishop of the diocese. These are known as Bishop's Transcripts.

1601 - Poor Law Acts of 1597-1601 order the appointment of two overseers of the poor in each Parish. These records are of genealogical value.

1603 - Orders to keep Parish Registers reiterated.

1620 - Emigration of Congregationalists to America in Mayflower.

1642 - The commencement of civil war in England. This had considerable effect on the keeping of Registers until 1660. Many early records lost or destroyed.

1644 - Earliest Presbyterian and Independent (Congregational) Registers.

1647 - Earliest date for Baptist Registers.

1649 - Records of about 6,600 English Parishes exist back to this date or earlier. Commencement of Commonwealth period, many Parish incumbents left their duties unattended.

1653 - Begin civil commission to grant probates - these records absorbed into the Prerogative Court of Canterbury in London.

---

[1]Colonel A. G. Puttock, *A Dictionary of Heraldry and Related Subjects*, Genealogical Publishing Co., Inc., Baltimore, Md., 1970, pp. 135-6.

1654 - Marriages restricted to Justices of the Peace. Commonwealth requires Parish Registers to record births, marriages and deaths, but many fail to comply.

1660 - Parish ministers, if still living, returned to their Parishes but many registers prior to this date were lost or destroyed. Provincial ecclesiastical probate courts reopened. All Parishes again record christenings, marriages and burials in the normal manner.

Prior to 1858 in England, the proving of wills was in the hands of the Church. If a man had property in two or more diocese his will would have to be proved in either the Prerogative Court of Canterbury or the Prerogative Court of York. If property was held in the area of both courts, the proof would be found at Canterbury. There was no bar to a will being proved in a higher court which was frequently adopted because of the reluctance of having family affairs dealt with locally.

The Church as Educational Centers

After King William took control of England in 1066, the archdiocese of York was reduced to having control only over the York and Durham dioceses. Within this archdiocese there were four ministers, of which three were in Yorkshire at York, Ripon, and Beverley. Ripon had been established in the mid-seventh century by Bishop Wilfred, and was originally a monastic house (a monastery where monks and nuns live alone with religious vows). Beverley was founded by St. John of Beverley (Archbishop of York 705-718), and was originally monastic. All three foundations, including York, functioned as houses of secular canons (clergymen belonging to the staff of a cathedral or collegiate church and not bound by monastic vows) by the 11th century and served as local centers of the archdiocese. St. Peter's, York, although a house of secular canons, operated under a rule which was monastic in tone. The diocese at Durham was established in 995 and the foundation of secular canons was called the Clerks of St. Cuthbert, under the dean. About 1080, the old canons, who were married and lived in buildings surrounding Durham Cathedral, were driven out by Bishop William of St. Calais (the new Bishop of Durham) who established a fully monastic house following the Benedictine rule (devoted to scholarship and liturgical worship). New churches were established by the Normans: Selby in Yorkshire was founded about 1070; Whitby was refounded under the patronage of the Percy family; and St. Mary's, York, which had its origins in the pre-Conquest monastery of St. Olaf, was refounded by Count Alan of Brittany. Foreign monks and bishops, brought in by the Normans, made the monasteries centers of learning. Anyone who wanted to study went into the church as a matter of course. The king's secretaries, judges, and most of his civil servants were churchmen, because only churchmen had the necessary education.

William of Percy, who had control of the vill of Pericne, also had control of the churches of St. Mary's at York, St. Cuthbert's at Durham, and Bolton Percy in 1086 according to the Domesday book. The Percy family had also refounded Whitby in Yorkshire. Thus, an individual of the vill of Pericne seeking and gaining the right to education through decisions of William of Percy would likely be educated at Bolton Percy, York, Durham, Whitby, or possibly the other churches at Ripon and Beverley, the latter of which is a few miles from the vill of Pericne in Yorkshire.

During the 13th century, new learning was brought into England by friars and other scholars from the Continent. Oxford University, Oxfordshire, won renown all over Europe.

Historical Conditions and Laws for Villeins

In 1066, when Duke William conquered England, he established the feudal system there. Most existing owners including the Danes of Yorkshire were stripped of their land and forced into serfdom as villeins (villagers). Under the feudal system, no villein could leave the village he was born in. Of course, exceptions were made by their lords for well-deserving villeins to go to a collegiate church for training in jobs requiring education, such as reading and writing skills. Lords with higher amounts of property, such as earls and their sub-tenants, also might move some of their villeins from one vill to another to fill needed voids on occasion. This Statute of Laborers was enforced until the Peasant's Revolt of 1381.

In 1086, King William I had a survey made of all the property in England. His agents visited every manor, found out who owned it, how many people lived there, and reported what the lord ought to pay the king in taxes and feudal service. The findings were recorded in the famous Domesday Book. It was called Domesday (day of doom) because no one could escape its tax judgment.

Henry I, born in England 1068, was the youngest son of William I. At his accession to the English throne, Henry I issued the famous Charter of Liberties, which became the basis of the Magna Carta, the foundation of the liberties of the Anglo-Saxon world. He married Matilda, daughter of King Malcolm III of Scotland.

Henry II spent most of his long reign, 1154 to 1189, in his French possessions; yet he became one of England's great rulers. Henry II sent out trained judges on circuit to different towns in England to sit in judgment in the county courts. The judges kept records of their cases, and when one judge had decided a case, other judges trying the same kind of case were likely to adopt the decision that has been recorded. In the course of years, legal principles came to be based on these decisions. Because this case law applied to all Englishmen equally, it came to be called the *common law*. The circuit justices also made more extensive use of juries and started the grand jury system in criminal law.

Angered by King John's tyrannical rule, the English barons drew up a list of things that even a king might not do. On June 15, 1215, they forced John to set his seal to this Great Charter (in Latin, Magna Carta) of English liberties. The rights it listed were feudal rights of justice and property that had been recognized by previous kings; but now, for the first time, these rights were insisted upon against the king's will. Thus, an important principle was established - the king himself must govern according to law.

Henry III, John's eldest son, was crowned at the age of nine and ruled 56 years, 1216 to 1272. Under his rule, the earliest English heraldic record, the "Roll of Arms," was written between 1240 and 1245. It included the names and Arms of the Barons and Knights of his reign.

Henry III's son, Edward I, who ruled England 1272 to 1307, wisely accepted the limitations on the king's authority. His parliament of 1295 is called the Model Parliament because it included representatives of both shires and towns as well as the Great Council. Many of the laws passed in Edward's reign exist in modified form today. Edward I conquered

Wales and joined it to England but failed in his effort to subdue Scotland. In 1298[2], Wautier Pieressone was the Count of Berwick in Northumberland. He was mentioned in the Ragman's Roll of 1298 as pledging allegiance to Edward I when he invaded Scotland.

In 1307, Edward I died on his way north to put down an uprising led by the great Scottish hero Robert Bruce. His incompetent son, Edward II, then took up the task and was decisively defeated at Bannockburn.

In 1327, Parliament used its new power to depose Edward II and place his son, Edward III, on the throne. Knighthood was still in flower while Edward III was king, 1327 to 1377. The king himself excelled in "beautiful feats of arms." He soon had a chance to prove his skill. During his reign began the long struggle with France called the Hundred Years' War (1337-1453).

In 1346, Edward III's army won a brilliant victory at Crecy, in France, with a new English weapon, the longbow. The next year (1347), Edward took Calais, a French seaport.

The Hundred Years War was brought to a temporary halt when the Black Death (bubonic plague, a germ carried by a flea that lives on rats) swept over Western Europe 1348 through 1349. When the great plague had spent its fury, more than a fourth of England's population had perished. Whole villages were wiped out, and great areas of farmland went to weeds.

In 1356, Edward III's son, the Black Prince, won the famous battle of Poitiers against the French.

Richard II was 10 years old when he became king in 1377. During his reign in 1381, the serfs initiated the Peasant's Revolt and demanded high money wages. If their lord refused, they moved to another manor. The government tried to halt the rise in wages and bind the laborers to their manors once more, but it could not enforce its Statute of Laborers. The landlords sought labor at any price, and the laborers formed combinations (what would now be called unions) to resist the law. The serfdom of the villeins began to die and this gave place to a new class of farmers - free yeomen.

The Battle of Agincourt[3], fought 25 October 1415 near the village of Agincourt in northern France, was the third great battle won by the English against the French during the Hundred Years' War (1337-1453). The young king, Henry V, had recently succeeded to the throne of England. On the advice of his father, Henry IV, he resolved to revive England's claim to the French throne. Henry's forces landed in Normandy and captured the port of Harfleur. Enroute to the port of Calais, then held by England, their way was blocked by a great French army. The French knights, four times as numerous as the English foot soldiers, foolishly dismounted. They advanced in their heavy armor through the deep mud of newly plowed fields. Three times the French knights came on in a narrow defile between two woods. Three times they were forced back by clouds of arrows let fly by skilled English archers. More than 5,000 Frenchmen were killed, including many princes and nobles. The English lost only 113 men. This decisive battle proved the superiority of the long bow over the crossbow and hastened the end of the heavily armored knight.

---

[2]Ragman's Roll of 1298.
[3]Compton's Encyclopedia, F. E. Compton Co., Chicago, Illinois, Vol. 1, p. 100.

Shortly after the battle, Henry V knighted a number of his followers and confirmed the armorial bearings of all of those who had borne them "at Agincourt."

Henry VI, son of Henry V, was the king of England 1422-1461. During the reign of Henry VI and under the Church of England, William Pereson was rector of Thoresby in North Riding, Yorkshire, England in 1440[4]. In 1452[5], Thomas Peirson, perhaps the son or brother of William Pereson, was a sheriff of Yorkshire. In harmony with the Committee, he held court, maintained order, collected taxes, and raised armies for King Henry VI. This Thomas Pereson was also subdean of York (a collegiate church), was Rector of Bolton Percy (8 miles SW of York in West Riding), and founded St. Friedeswides Chantry in York Cathedral.

In 1455, two years after the Hundred Years' War ended, the House of York and the House of Lancaster plunged into a long and bloody struggle for the crown called the War of the Roses (1455-1485). The emblem of the Yorkists was a white rose and that of the Lancastrians a red rose - thus War of the Roses. The families of York and Lancaster were descended from King Edward III. Henry VI of the house of Lancaster was captured and murdered in 1461. Edward the IV, of the House of York, spent most of his reign fighting to keep his crown. In 1477[6], Nicholas Pierson, perhaps the son of Thomas Peirson who was sheriff in York earlier, was sheriff of Yorkshire. When he died in 1490 a Latin inscription to his memory was erected in the church of St. Martin/St. Gregory at York.

The last Yorkist king, Richard III, gained the throne in 1483 when Edward's sons were declared not to be the rightful heirs. Thomas Pearson of Spratton, Northamptonshire, was confirmed a coat of arms during the reign of King Richard III (1483-1485): "Ermine, on two bars gules (red) three bezants (gold coins) two and one[7]." Spratton is located 7 miles north of Northampton and is 15 miles northwest of Olney, Buckinghamshire.

The end of the War of Roses and peace came with Richard's death in the battle of Bosworth Field in 1485. The battles and executions of the War of the Roses had thinned the ranks of the nobles, and their fortified castles were no longer impregnable because of the invention of gunpowder. Country squires, the landed gentry, grew wealthy. England was now the chief cloth exporting country in the world.

In 1497, Henry VII encouraged John Cabot to pilot his ship across the Atlantic Ocean to Newfoundland, five years after Columbus discovered the New World.

Henry VIII ruled 1509-1547 and is famous as the king who had six wives in succession. When he put aside his first wife, Catherine of Aragon, the pope of the Church of England excommunicated him. Henry, enraged, had Parliament cut the ties that bound the English church to the papacy (1534) and forced the English clergy to acknowledge the king rather than the pope as the only supreme head of the Church of England. Yet Henry all his life

---

[4]Lizzie B. Pierson, *Pierson Genealogical Records*, Joel Munsell, Printer, Albany, New York, 1878, pages 70-73.

[5]Lizzie B. Pierson, *Pierson Genealogical Records*, Joel Munsell, Printer, Albany, New York, 1878, pages 70-73.

[6]Lizzie B. Pierson, *Pierson Genealogical Records*, Joel Munsell, Printer, Albany, New York, 1878, pages 70-73.

[7]Sir Bernard Burke, Ulster King of Arms, *The General Armory of England, Scotland, Ireland and Wales, comprising a Registry of Armorial Bearings from the Earliest to the Present Time*, Harrison and Sons, Printers in Ordinary to Her Majesty, London, England, First published 1842, Second Edition (with Supplement) 1884, Facsimile Edition by photolitho 1961, Second Impression 1962.

claimed to be a devout Roman Catholic. His attack on the papacy was prompted in part by greed. By dissolving the monasteries, he was able to seize their immense wealth in lands and buildings and the costly ornaments of the shrines. He used some of his new riches to fortify the coasts and build England's first real Navy. At his death, the royal fleet numbered 71 vessels, some of which were fitted with cannon.

Henry VIII's only son, Edward VI, was ten years old when he came to the throne in 1547. Edward died six years later at age 16 in1553. The Lord Protectors who ruled in his stead favored the Protestant cause. They forbade the Catholics to hold Mass and required Thomas Cranmer's English Prayer Book to be read instead of the Latin Mass.

Mary, daughter of Henry VIII and Catherine of Aragon, ruled England 1553-1558 as Mary I, known as Bloody Mary because of the religious persecutions of her time. Mary had been brought up in the Catholic faith and the right to say the Latin Mass was returned to the Catholics.

Elizabeth I, Mary's half sister, ruled England 1558-1603. England prospered during this long reign, English glassworks supplied small clear glass panes, the British defeated the Spanish Armada in 1588, and an Act for the Relief of the Poor was passed in 1601.

The Tudor dynasty came to an end when Elizabeth I died in 1603. The crown of England then passed to the Stuart line of Scotland. The new king was called James VI in Scotland and James I in England. James boldly announced that he would rule as an absolute monarch, responsible to God alone. This view of monarchy was called the divine right of kings. It was generally accepted on the continent of Europe, but it ran counter to the nature of the English people. Parliament resisted James at every point. James allowed the Navy to decay and suppressed privateering. Yet it was in his reign that colonial expansion began and the British Empire was born.

Under King Charles I[8], who ruled 1625 to 1649, active colonization continued in America. Charles was glad to have the troublesome Puritans leave England, including John Pearson who departed in 1637 from the Howden, Yorkshire, area, and Henry Peirson, the Rev. Abraham Pierson and Bartholomew Pierson who departed England in May 1639 for New England in America.

The Source of Given Names in England

According to old English law, only one given name was allowed (no middle name)[9]: "The old English law was very definite as to the naming of children and, according to Coke, 'a man cannot have two names of baptism.' It is requisite, the law goes on, 'that the purchaser be named by the name of his baptism and his surname, and that special heed be taken to the name of baptism.' Royal personages have always been allowed to have more than one given name, but as late as 1600, it is said, there were only four persons in all England who had two given names. In 1620 the Mayflower sailed for America and there was not a man or woman on it who had a middle name. Even a century and a half ago (1840s), double names were very uncommon. The English used to dodge the law at times by ingeniously compounding names. Thus an old parish register in England may occasionally show

---

[8]F. E. Compton Co., *Compton's Encyclopedia*, William Benton, Publisher, 1970, Vol. 7, p. 238.
[9]From the Ottawa County Genealogy Society, Miami, Oklahoma.

combinations such as Fannasabilia, which is Fanny and Sybil joined together, and Annamaria, made up of Anna and Maria." This law so carried over to the United States that the first five presidents of the United States had no middle name. In England, of the period we are researching (1500-1700), there will be found many John, Thomas, Robert, and William Piersons making absolute identification by name alone impossible. But analysis that views place, dates, and groups of family names in use for children can leave one feeling fairly sure of which families go together in many cases. Given name groups are carried down consistently in English Pearson families except when the father dies when his son is young.

The given names of William, Henry, Stephen, Richard, John, and Edward are popular in the Pearson, Peirson, and Pierson line. Such names were made famous, or infamous as the case may be, by the English kings of the middle ages. They were:

Kings of England	Ruled
William I, the Conqueror, from Normandy, France	1066-1087
William II, William Rufus, the Red King	1087-1100
Henry I, also ruled Normandy, France	1100-1135
Stephen, a gallant knight	1135-1154
Henry II, grandson of Henry I	1154-1189
Richard I, the Lion-Hearted, son of Henry II	1189-1199
John, brother of Richard I	1199-1216
Henry III, eldest son of John	1216-1272
Edward I, son of Henry III	1272-1307
Edward II, son of Edward I	1307-1327
Edward III, son of Edward II,	1327-1377
had son Edward the Black Prince	
Richard II, son of Edward the Black Prince	1377-1399
Henry IV, cousin of Richard II	1399-1413
Henry V, son of Henry IV	1413-1422
Henry VI, son of Henry V	1422-1461
Edward IV,	1461-1470 & 1471-1483
Richard III, the middle ages ended 1485	1483-1485

Other male names used in the Pearson, Peirson, and Pierson line were:

Abraham in Hebrew means literally "father of many," and the original form Abram means "father is exalted." In the *Bible*, Abraham is the first patriarch and ancestor of the Hebrews.

Bartholomew, in Middle English Bartelmeus, meaning literally "son of Talmai." Bartholomew was one of the twelve apostles in the *Bible*. He is also called Saint Bartholomew and his day is August 24.

Cuthbert was a saint who lived about 635 to about 687 A.D. He was an English monk and bishop and his day is March 20. Several churches are named St. Cuthbert after him in the counties of Durham, York, and Bedford in England.

Hillary, in Latin Hilarius, meaning cheerful, a male and female name.

Hugh, in Old French Hue, in Old German Hugo, probably from hugu meaning heart, mind.

James was a Christian apostle, also called Saint James and his day is July 25. James I was king of England 1603-1625.

John was a king of England 1199-1216. But he is probably better known as a Christian apostle of the *Bible* who is credited with writing the fourth Gospel, the three Epistles of John, and the Book of Revelation. He was called the Evangelist, the Divine, and Saint John.

Leonard means "strong as a lion." In 1288, there was a manor of St. Leonard near Hastings in East Sussex, England, which was named from the dedication of a church. Of late, a St. Leonard's Chapel was dedicated in Lincolnshire, England.

Nicholas was a saint who lived about 800 to 867 A.D. Many churches are named St. Nicholas after him in England. Many kings and popes of Europe were named Nicholas. In 1254, a manor of St. Nicholas at Wade, Kent County, England, was named from the dedication of a church.

Philip means "fond of horses." He was one of the twelve apostles in the *Bible*. He is also called Saint Philip and his day is May 1st. Several kings of European countries were named Philip.

Robert, in Old French and Old High German Hruodperht, meaning fame + bright. Robert was the duke of Normandy 1028-1035. He was the father of King William I who conquered England in 1066.

Roger, in Old English Hrothgar, meaning fame + spear.

Thomas was one of the twelve apostles in the *Bible* who doubted at first the resurrection of Jesus. He is also called Saint Thomas and his day is December 21.

Most early parish records in England were written in Latin by the church record keepers. Many of those record keepers tried to Latinize the given names and sometimes the surname also. Thus the names, with inconsistent spelling, were written: Anna (Anne), Alicia (Alice), Cuthbertus (Cuthbert), Dionisia (Diane), Dorothea (Dorothy), Edmundus (Edmund), Edvardus (there is no W in Latin, they used a V to represent a U pronunciation) or Edrus or Edv. (Edward), Elizabetha or Eliz. (Elizabeth), Ellena (Eleanor or Helen), Georgius (George), Gracia or Gratia (Grace), Hellena (Helen), Henricus or Harry or Harrie (Henry), Hyllarius (Hillary), Hugonis (Hugh), Humfridi (Humphrey), Isabella (Isabel), Jacobus (Jacob or James), Jana (Jane), Johanna (Joanne), Johannes or Johannis or Johes. (John), Katherina (Catherine), Lawrentius or Lawrentij (Lawrence), Lucea (Lucille or Lucy), Margeria (Margery), Margreta or Margareta (Margaret), Maria (Mary), Nickolei or Nichus. or Nich. (Nicholas), Richardus or Ricus. (Richard), Robertus or Robtus. (Robert), Thomae or Tho. (Thomas), Tomasine (not Latin, a female name for Thomas), Vrsula (a V represents a U pronunciation) (Ursula), and Guillmus or Guilieli (there is no W in Latin, the G is silent) or Willelmus or Willus. (William). On the occasions when the Pearson (also Pierson and Peirson) surname was Latinized, it was spelled "Person." See examples below with

(Nickolei Person) and without (Thomas Pereson) Latin names on tombstone or monument inscriptions.

Pierson Records (all spellings) Prior to 1500 in England

In 1298[10], Wautier Pieressone was the Count of Berwick, a county in southeastern Scotland. Earlier, Berwick was part of the Saxon kingdom of Northumbria. It had become part of Scotland in the 11th century. England had sacked Berwick in 1296 and taken control of it. Wautier Pieressone was mentioned in the Ragman's Roll of 1298 as pledging allegiance to Edward I of England when he invaded Scotland. Wautier Pieressone had descendants in the area of Ellingham, Northumberland county, England, from 1330 to 1451 (see Angus Baxter, "The Pearson Family," Heritage Quest Magazine, American Genealogical Lending Library, Issue #58, July/Aug 1995, p. 39).

In 1440[11], William Pereson, was rector of Thoresby in North Riding, Yorkshire, England. A rector in the Church of England is a clergyman who holds the rights and tithes of his parish, distinguished from a vicar who receives a salary only and the tithes go elsewhere. The record is of an educated man expected to be a descendant of a man who earlier left the vill of Pericne since education at a church was the primary way of villeins being able to leave their village between 1070 (when William of Percy named the vill of Pericne) and 1381 (the Peasant's Revolt).

In 1452[12], Thomas Peirson was the sheriff of Yorkshire. Sheriff is derived from shire reeve meaning the chief officer, under the king, of the shire (county). He held court, maintained order, collected taxes, and raised armies for King Henry VI. Thomas Pereson, subdean of York during these years, was Rector of Bolton Percy (8 miles SW of York in West Riding), Yorkshire, and founded St. Friedeswides Chantry (a chapel endowed for the chanting of masses commonly for the founder) in York Cathedral. He was probably an Oxford man. He was buried in York Minster (a church attached to a monastery), in the nave (the middle part of the church extending from the railing of the choir to the main entrance) about opposite the two pillars from the west door; and has this Latin inscription on the stone; "Hic jacet Thomas Pereson hujus ecclesia cathedralis subdecanus, qui obiit XXVIII die mensis Octobris A.D. 1490, cujus animae propitietur Deus, Amen. (Here lies Thomas Pereson who was ecclesiastical cathedral subdean, who died the 28th day of the month of October 1490 A.D., whose rational soul favorably inclined God, Amen.)" If Thomas Pereson was about 30 years old when Sheriff in 1452, then he was born about 1422. Based on the education required for these positions, Thomas may be a son of William Pereson who was Rector of Thoresby (38 miles NW of York in North Riding), Yorkshire, in 1440. As subdean of York Cathedral, Thomas may well have been educated at Oxford University, but no proof of that education has been found. Since Thomas was an officer of King Henry VI and may have had a father William, one might expect his children to be named William, Thomas, and Henry, among others. Thomas Pereson died 28 October 1490 (about age 68).

1475. Saye Pierson (b. ca. 1475) of Barking, Essex County, had son Thomas Pierson (b. ca. 1499) of Barking, Essex, who married a daughter of John Brooke of Ilford, and had children

---

[10]Ragman's Roll of 1298.
[11]Lizzie B. Pierson, *Pierson Genealogical Records*, Joel Munsell, Printer, Albany, New York, 1878, pages 70-73.
[12]Lizzie B. Pierson, *Pierson Genealogical Records*, Joel Munsell, Printer, Albany, New York, 1878, pages 70-73.

Thomas, Johan (Joane), and John. See the coats of arms and descendants in a later chapter under (3) Pierson/Gwynne of London, (4) Pierson of Essex county, and (5) Pierson of Stafford county.

In 1477[13], Nicholas Pierson was sheriff of Yorkshire. The following Latin inscription to his memory was erected in the church of St. Martin/St. Gregory at York; "Orate pro anima Nickolei Person quondam civis et vicecomitis istius civitatis, et pro animabus Alicia et Ciceley uxorum ejusdem qui obiit vicesimo die Aprilis Anno Dom. MCCCCLXXXX (Advocate of the soul Nickolas Pierson former citizen and sheriff of this city, and appreciative of his loving Alicia and Ciceley, lawful wives, who died the 20th day of April 1490 A.D.)." This Nicholas would have been born about 1447 and is possibly the son of Thomas Pereson above, who was sheriff of York a generation earlier in 1452, because of a job inheritance opportunity. However, Nicholas died six months before Thomas Pereson. During Nicholas' duties as sheriff, he represented King Edward IV of the House of York. Thus one might expect his children to be named Nicholas, Thomas, and Edward, among others.

1483[14]. Coat of Arms for "PEARSON (Tankerton, and Maize Hill, Greenwich, co. Kent; descended from Thomas Pearson, of Spratton, co. Northampton, living temp. Richard III [reigned 1483-5]). Escutcheon - Erm. on two bars gu. three bezants. Crest - A boar's head couped sa. in his mouth an acorn or., leaved vert. Motto - Perduret probitas (Through hardness, honesty, and virtue)." Greenwich is now in Greater London. The Thomas Pearson of Spratton, Northamptonshire, has the same coat of arms probably confirmed during the reign of King Richard III (1483-1485) or earlier: "PEARSON (co. Northampton). Erm. on two bars gu. three bezants two and one." Spratton is located 7 miles N of Northampton and is 15 miles NW of Olney, Buckinghamshire.

In "1496[15] A.D., Bartholomew Pearson, of Duffield, took sanctuary in Beverley Minster, for the murder of John Eliot." Duffield means an open field frequented by doves. There is a Duffield in Derbyshire and a North and South Duffield in Yorkshire. Since Beverley Minster is in the East Riding of Yorkshire at Beverley near Kingston Upon Hull, perhaps one of the Duffields in Yorkshire was intended in this quote. N. Duffield and S. Duffield are located 22 miles west of Beverley near Bubwith which is 5 miles northwest of Howden. Whether Bartholomew Pearson is guilty of the murder charge, if he is what cause he had, and the outcome of the charge is unknown.

Pierson Families of the 1500s in Yorkshire

Pearsonne ancestors are believed to have originated at the vill of Pericne, three & a half miles north of Beverley, in East Riding of Yorkshire. Therefore, it is possible that a large group of Piersons are still in Yorkshire in the 1500s. We will look at the Pierson family

---

[13]Lizzie B. Pierson, *Pierson Genealogical Records*, Joel Munsell, Printer, Albany, New York, 1878, pages 70-73.

[14]Sir Bernard Burke, Ulster King of Arms, *The General Armory of England, Scotland, Ireland and Wales, comprising a Registry of Armorial Bearings from the Earliest to the Present Time*, Harrison and Sons, Printers in Ordinary to Her Majesty, London, England, First published 1842, Second Edition (with Supplement) 1884, Facsimile Edition by photolitho 1961, Second Impression 1962.

[15]Lizzie B. Pierson, *Pierson Genealogical Records*, Joel Munsell, Printer, Albany, New York, 1878, page 70.

Yorkshire distribution between 1500 and 1600. I queried the LDS IGI database[16] for Yorkshire Pearson (all spellings) marriages prior to 1600. I obtained about 300 Pearson marriages whose dates fell between 1539 and 1599 of which 152 were male Pearson marriages. Because I was interested in the Pearson surname families, I summarized the Yorkshire male marriages by location as follows (the towns with the largest number of male Pearson marriages first):

Miles from Beverley	Town	No. Male Marr.	Earliest Marr. Date	Male Pierson Names Married (repeated names are not written twice)
52 SW	Sheffield	25	1564	Francis, Henry, Hugh, John, Laur., Nicholas, Robert, Thomas, William
19 SW	Howden	17	1546	Christopher, George, Henry, John, Richard, Robert, Thomas, William
29 NW	York	11	1553	Bryan, Francis, George, John, Laur., Leonard, Peter, Robert, Thomas
44 W	Leeds	10	1573	Christ., Francis, Richard, William
33 W	Monk Frystone	7	1539	Hugh, John, Roger, William
47 SW	Rotherham	6	1556	Alexander, Henry, John, Thomas
39 NW	Alne	5	1560	Edward, Lancelot, Robert, William
42 W	Rothwell	5	1547	John, Robert
45 N	Danby in Cleveland	4	1587	John, Thomas
50 SW	Ecclesfield	4	1558	John, Robert, Thomas
41 NW	Aldborough	4	1554	James, William
12 NE	Atwick	4	1573	John, Marmaduke, William
46 NW	Thirsk	3	1557	George, Thomas
25 N	Filey	3	1577	Henry, Nicholas, William
9 SW	South Cave	2	1558	John, Thomas
56 NW	Kirkleatham	2	1564	Nicholas, Robert
54 W	Bradford	2	1599	George
14 NW	Huggate	2	1585	Robert
7 NE	Brandesburton	2	1559	Hillary, Robert
12 W	Holme Upon Spalding Moor	1	1574	Thomas

---

[16]Church of Jesus Christ of Latter-Day Saints International Genealogical Index on CD ROM accessible through the FamilySearch computer program at Family History Centers.

| 4 S | Cottingham | 1 | 1581 | John |
| 6 S | Kirk Ella | 1 | 1579 | William |

There are another 27 Yorkshire towns with one Pearson family (one male marriage) in each town which are mostly outliars of the larger groups mentioned. This provides a picture of the situation with about 150 Pearson families in Yorkshire representing about three generations. Thus about 22 lines of Pearsons (all spellings) must have existed in 1550 in Yorkshire. Pearson families are doubling each generation at this time and place based upon an average 2 wives having combined 8 children, 4 of which survive to adulthood, 2 of which are males that marry and have children. Most first wives died near a child birth, a few living to be widows. The vill of Pericne no longer exists in 1500 and has been referred to as one of the lost villages of Yorkshire in a 1977 publication, the *Domesday Gazetteer*.

William Peirson (Father of Henry) of Olney, Buckinghamshire

In searching for the parents of the American immigrant Henry Peirson (1615-1680) of Southampton, Long Island, New York colony, the following information was found:

25 Jul 1609, Bishop's Transcripts for Olney, Buckinghamshire, England: "William Person[17] and Wyborro Grigges were marr[ied] the xxvth day of July Anno Dom 1609." This is the marriage record for William Peirson and Wyborro Griggs.

10 Dec 1615, Bishop's Transcripts for Olney, Buckinghamshire, England: "Harry Pearson[18] sonne of Will[iam] Pearson was baptized the same Day [xth] of Decem[ber] [1615]" This is the christening of Henry Peirson (1615-1680) of Southampton, Long Island, New York colony. The dictionary gives Harry as a diminutive of Henry in middle English.

28 July 1616, burial record for "William Pearson" at Lavendon (two miles north of Olney), Buckinghamshire, England. This is thought to be Henry's father as Henry's father, William, is believed to have died between Henry's birth of 1615 and his mother's (Wyborro [Griggs] Peirson) 2nd marriage in 1618 to John Cooper.

18 Oct 1618, Bishop's Transcripts for Olney, Buckinghamshire, England, provide: "John Cowper[19] and Wyborough Pearson was maryed the xviiith of October [1618]." This is John Cooper and the widow Wyborro (Griggs) Peirson.

April 1635. New England[20]: "Passinger Wch passed from Ye Port of London, Primo Aprill 1635, in the *Hopewell* of Lond m' Wm Bundocke V's New Engld. Jon Cooper 41 yers of Oney (Olney) in Buckinghamsher, Wibroe 42 yrs wife of Jon Cooper, Mary Cooper 13, Jon Cooper 10, Tho. Cooper 7, Martha Cooper 5, (all) Children of Jon Cooper Aforsaid, Phillip Phillipp 15 Yers Servt to Jon Cooper," (plus others). The *Hopewell* sailed early in April from

---

[17] Bishop's Transcripts for Olney, Buckinghamshire, England, located at Buckinghamshire County Record Office, Aylesbury, England.
[18] Bishop's Transcripts for Olney, Buckinghamshire, England, located at Buckinghamshire County Record Office, Aylesbury, England.
[19] Bishop's Transcripts for Olney, Buckinghamshire, England, located at Buckinghamshire County Record Office, Aylesbury, England.
[20] John Camden Hotten, *List of Emigrants to America 1600-1700*, Genealogical Publishing Company, Baltimore, MD, 1974, p. 44.

London and arrived at Boston, Massachusetts, in June[21]. Wyborro (Griggs) (Peirson) Cooper is Henry Peirson's (1615-1680) mother and John Cooper is Henry's step-father.

10 April - 10 May 1639[22]. "John Woode, Abraham Pomfrett, Christopher Vivion, Samuell Andrewes and Thomas Barnard shippers[23] of goods in the *Mayflower*, Master William Caine, bound from London to New England with passengers and planters." No passenger record was available for this ship. However, this record coincides with the date Henry Peirson left old England (May 1639 as shown in the 1663 English court record below) and two Pierson family legends about the American Pierson immigrant arriving in America aboard the Mayflower and three Pierson brothers (or kinsmen) coming to America together (probably Henry, Rev. Abraham, and Bartholomew Pierson as they all arrived in New England in 1639).

A deed[24] dated 12 May 1662 and signed by "Henry Peirson" and John Cooper (Jr.) was written at Southampton, Long Island, and is now at the Staffordshire County Record Office, Stafford, England. The signatures match those of Henry Peirson and John Cooper Jr. in the Southampton town records. In the deed, Henry Peirson and John Cooper Jr. convey to Ignatius Fuller of Sherrington, county Bucks., (apparently the son of Edward Fuller of Olney, mentioned in the latter's will) two pieces of property in Olney, England. The grantors describe themselves in the deed as:

> "Henry Peirson formerly of Olney in the Countie of Buckingham in old England sonne of William Peirson late of the same towne deceased and now of Southampton upon Long Iland in New England gent: And John Cooper of the same towne of Southampton upon Long Iland aforesaid Brother of the said Henry Peirson by the Mothers side gent."

In addition to showing that Henry is the son of William, this deed also shows that Henry Peirson and John Cooper Jr. have the same mother. She was Wyborro Griggs, who married 1st William Peirson 25 Jul 1609, Olney, Buckinghamshire, England, and 2nd John Cooper Sr. 28 Oct 1618, also at Olney. This record also shows a continuing relationship between Henry Peirson and the Fuller family (it is believed that Henry married Mary Fuller, daughter of Edward Fuller of Olney and sister of Ignatius Fuller of Sherrington (three miles south of Olney) mentioned here, though a marriage record for Henry Peirson has not yet been located.

7 May 1663[25]. English Court record: "Item 35, C.5/421/171 and C.6/22/113, 7 May 1663. Bill of Complaint of Henry Pearson of Southampton in Long Island in America versus John Kirby of Olney, Bucks. Before **Henry Pearson went out of England in May 1639**, he lent Job Brymley of Olney, Buckinghamshire, yeoman, 120 pounds, at the rate of 5%. For

[21]Charles Edward Banks, *Planters of the Commonwealth 1620-1640*, Boston, Massachusetts, 1930, p. 158.

[22]Peter Wilson Coldham, *The Complete Book of Emigrants 1607-1660*, Genealogical Publishing Co., Inc., Baltimore, Maryland, 1987, p. 205.

[23]Public Record Office at Chancery Lane, London WC2A 1LR, 'England, record E190/433/6, read and summarized by Peter Wilson Coldham 1987.

[24]Deed, 12 May 1662, Ref. D742/B/15/1, Staffordshire County Record Office, Stafford, England. A copy was provided to Thomas W. Cooper, II, by Elizabeth Knight, an Olney historian.

[25]Noel Currer-Briggs, *Colonial Settlers and English Adventurers*, Genealogical Publishing Co., Inc., Baltimore, MD, 1971, pp. 71-2.

security, Job Brymley mortgaged 3 acres of land to the plaintiff in Olney with the proviso that Job Brymley should pay Pearson the interest of the 120 pounds by half-yearly installments for 5 years and the principal sum of 120 pounds at the end of the 5 years, otherwise the land would be forfeited. However Job Brymley neglected to pay Pearson the interest and principal at the end of 5 years and died in debt to the plaintiff. He left the three acres at his death to his daughter Jane, who afterwards married Daniel Howes of Olney, yeoman. Henry Pearson having occasion to go to the parts beyond the seas did by his letter of attorney, appoint Edward Fuller of Olney, gent, William Geynes of the same town, and Thomas Constable of the same town, mercers, all now deceased, his attorneys, amongst other things to receive the interest money during the 5 years, and the principal at the end of it. He left with them the deed of mortgage the better to enable them to maintain his title to the lands. By virtue of this they entered, received the profits, and shortly after died. Daniel Howes, in right of his wife Jane, entered the land and sold it to John Kirby of Olney, haberdasher of hats, charged with the payment of the 120 pounds. Notwithstanding John Kirby bought the three acres charged with the payment as aforesaid, and notwithstanding he was abated the sum in his purchase price, yet he refuses to pay the principal sum of 120 pounds as he ought to do. John Kirby being a soldier in the Parliament army against the King by some indirect means has gotten into his hands the mortgage deed so that the plaintiff is unable under the Common Law to make his title to the lands and so cannot recover possession of them." This record shows that Henry Peirson left England for America in May 1639. It also shows a relationship of Henry Peirson to Edward Fuller of Olney, thought to be Henry's wife Mary's father.

The Search for William Peirson's Ancestors

In summary, what we know of William Peirson is that he married "Wyborro Grigges" 25 Jul 1609 at Olney, Buckinghamshire; he had son "Harry Pearson" who was christened 10 Dec 1615 at Olney; and that he probably was the "Wm. Pierson" buried 28 Jul 1616 at Lavendon (two miles north of Olney), Buckinghamshire. Unfortunately, Olney and Lavendon records did not reveal William's christening record there:

Name	Parents/Spouse	Chris./Marr. Date	Place (Bucks.)
William Person	Wyborro Grigges	m. 25 Jul 1609	Olney
Harry Pearson	William	c. 10 Dec 1615	Olney
John Cowper	Wyborough Pearson	m. 18 Oct 1618	Olney
William Pearson	not given	bur. 28 Jul 1616	Lavendon
Thomas Pearson	John	c. 26 Apr 1582	Lavendon
Cuthbert Pearson	Margarett Heames	m. 21 Oct 1602	Lavendon
Susan Pearson	Cuthbert	c. 1 Nov 1603	Lavendon
Joyce Pearson	Cuthbert	c. 21 Aug 1608	Lavendon
Mary Pearson	Cuthbert	c. 16 Jan 1613	Lavendon

| Sara Pearson | Cuthbert | c. 21 May 1616 | Lavendon |
| William Pearson | Cuthbert | c. 21 Feb 1618 | Lavendon |

No relationship could be found between the families of John and Cuthbert Pearson in the table and William Peirson of Olney. Cuthbert heads the only Pearson family known to be at Lavendon in 1616 when William Peirson is buried there. However, William's widow, Wyborro (Griggs) Peirson, responsible for William's burial, is believed to have a brother, George Griggs, who married Alice Sibthorpe 11 May 1618 at Lavendon. Expanding the search circle beyond the Olney/Lavendon area reveals a large number of William Pearsons, especially in Bedfordshire, but with no method of determining which one, if any, is our William Peirson. Additional clues were sought to find the ancestors of William Peirson of Olney, Buckinghamshire.

A clue in the search for William Peirson's English ancestors is a comment in Lizzie Pierson's 1878 book, *Pierson Genealogical Records*, under English Notes:

"Pierson of Yorkshire[26]. Of this branch, came the American Piersons:

70 Thomas Pierson (born about 1591 based on his grandson's christening in 1637), recorder of Beverley in Yorkshire. He inherited the estate of Moscraft, which escheated to the crown, 1700 or 1800, by death of last Pierson. He had chd. 71 Nickolas and 72 Hugh.

71 Nickolas (M.D.) (born about 1614 based on his son's christening in 1637), was supposed to have been a doctor before taking orders and becoming vicar of St. Mary's, Beverley. Removed from Beverley, during the civil wars (1642 to 1660), and appears to have been a Puritan. He h. chd. 73 Samuel, bapt. at St. Mary's, Beverley, 1637, and 74 Nick. (Jr.) bapt. at St. Mary's, 1638, M.D. or V.M.D. At the time of the restoration (1660) was incumbent of a parish in the Isle of Perbeck, in Dorset, d. 1693. Had w. Mary Hayward, and chd. 75 Nick. (III) b. 1691 (who mar. Constance Budden), and a dau. b. 1666, who was mar. and left Eng.,1689, and d. in France.

72 Hugh, of Moscraft, near Beverley, was buried in the Minster, 1669."

Lizzie Pierson's comment "Of this branch came the American Piersons" is part of a large group of information whose source is given by Lizzie as obtained from English state papers, wills, subsidies, and church records, and from family records of all Pierson families in America who responded to her letters in 1877. Nothing in the information itself shows an American connection. The year information in parenthesis above is estimated by this author to more easily determine the search years for ancestors of "70 Thomas Pierson." It is estimated that this Thomas Pierson was born about 1591, 46 years before his first grandson, 73 Samuel, was baptized in 1637. With the three generations after 70 Thomas Pierson containing a Nickolas, one would expect Nicholas to appear in his ancestors list.

The chart on the next page includes Lizzie's information above, plus two earlier generations, a christening within Lizzie Pierson's information, and a wife's name within Lizzie's information:

[26]Lizzie B. Pierson, *Pierson Genealogical Records*, Joel Munsell, Printer, Albany, New York, 1878, page 72.

"Of this branch came the American Piersons."

Robert Pearson
b. ca. 1539, butcher, bur. 18 Nov 1581 Howden, Yorkshire
m. 16 Sep 1560 Hellen (Ellinor bur. 19 Sep 1581) at Howden, Yorkshire
|
Nicholaus Pearson
c. 22 Oct 1565 Howden, Yorkshire
|
Thomas Pierson
(c. 7 Dec 1591 Howden, Yorkshire)
(m. ca. 1614)
Recorder of Beverley (East Riding, Yorkshire)
Inherited the Estate of Moscraft (2 miles north of Beverley)
which escheated to the crown 1700-1800 by death of last Pierson

Rev. Nickolas Pierson	Hugh Pierson
(b. ca. 1615)	(b. ca. 1617)
M.D., Vicar of St. Mary's, Beverley	of Moscraft near Beverley
Puritan, left Beverley civil wars (1644-1660)	buried Beverley Minster 1669
(m. ca. 1636 Mary [see adm. bond Apr 1645])	
had chd:	

Samuel Pierson	Rev. Nickolas Pierson Jr.
c. 1637 St. Mary's Beverley	c. 1638 St. Mary's Beverley
	1660 Isle of Perbeck, Dorset
	died 1693
	m. Mary Hayward (ca. 1665)

daughter Pierson	Nickolas Pierson III
b. 1666	b. 1691
m. & left Eng. 1689	m. Constance Budden
died in France	

Thomas Pierson's christening 7 Dec 1591, father Nicholas Pearson[27], was found 19 miles west of Beverley at Howden, Yorkshire. From parish records of Howden, Thomas had siblings: John bur. 9 May 1589; another John c. 8 Oct 1590; Henrie c. 30 Sep 1593, bur. 3 Jan 1593/4; and Robert c. 6 Jan 1597/8, bur. 10 Jan 1597/8. No marriage was found for Thomas Pierson, though a diligent search was made. For Thomas Pierson's son, Nicholas (b. ca. 1615), record of his estate administration and wife's given name were located:

"Administrative bond granted April 1645 to Mary Pearson, relict of Nicholas Pearson of Kingston Upon Hull."[28]

No marriage was found for Thomas' father, Nicholas Pearson, who was christened 22 Oct 1565 at Howden, Yorkshire, father Robert[29]. From parish records of Howden, Nicholas had siblings: Janeta c. 7 Dec 1561; Francis (M) c. 7 Feb 1562/3; Elizabeth c. & bur. 13 Aug 1564; Katherina c. 16 May 1568, bur. 6 Nov 1568; Joan bur. 17 May 1569; Alicia c. 23 Jan 1572/3, bur. 11 May 1574; Catherine c. 6 Dec 1576; and Frances (F) bur. 1 Dec 1583.

Nicholas' father, Robert Pearson, was born about 1539 (parents unknown), was a butcher, and was buried 18 Nov 1581 at Howden, Yorkshire[30]. Robert Pearson married 16 Sep 1560 Hellen (surname unknown) at Howden, Yorkshire (called Ellinor when buried 19 Sep 1581 at Howden) [31]. Further defining her name, a land sale (feet of fines) in 1567 shows that "Robert Pereson and Elienora his wife" sold two tracts of land with the buildings thereon in Howden to John Gregory[32].

While Robert Pearson's parents are unknown, location and others present indicate that he may have been the eldest son of John Pearson who was buried 21 Oct 1570 at Howden, Yorkshire, called "Old John Pearson" in the Howden parish burial record. While no marriages were listed in parish registers for Old John Pearson, it is believed that he married 1st about 1538 Catherine _____, who was buried at Howden 7 Oct 1546, and 2nd about 1548 Elizabeth _____, who was buried at Howden 6 Jan 1564/5. This belief is based on placing all Piersons in Howden records in a family position based on birth date, location within Howden parish, and children's names. Ten siblings have been assigned to Robert Pearson (includes children from both wives of Old John Pearson) and six siblings have been assigned to Old John Pearson. See Appendix A for Howden parish records and Pearson families formed by analysis.

---

[27] *The Registers of the Parish of Howden, Co. York*, Vols. I (published 1904, marriages 1542-1644 and baptisms 1542-1659), & II (published 1905, burials 1543-1659), edited by G. E. Weddall, privately printed for the Yorkshire Parish Register Society, Beck & Inchbold Ltd., Printers, Oriel Press, Leeds, Yorkshire, England.

[28] The Yorkshire Archaeological and Topographical Association, Record Series, Vol. IV, Wills in the York Registry from 1636 to 1652, Robert White, Printer, Worksop, 1888, p. 113.

[29] *The Registers of the Parish of Howden, Co. York*, Vols. I (published 1904, marriages 1542-1644 and baptisms 1542-1659), & II (published 1905, burials 1543-1659), edited by G. E. Weddall, privately printed for the Yorkshire Parish Register Society, Beck & Inchbold Ltd., Printers, Oriel Press, Leeds, Yorkshire, England.

[30] *The Registers of the Parish of Howden, Co. York*, Vols. I (published 1904, marriages 1542-1644 and baptisms 1542-1659), & II (published 1905, burials 1543-1659), edited by G. E. Weddall, privately printed for the Yorkshire Parish Register Society, Beck & Inchbold Ltd., Printers, Oriel Press, Leeds, Yorkshire, England.

[31] *The Registers of the Parish of Howden, Co. York*, Vols. I (published 1904, marriages 1542-1644 and baptisms 1542-1659), & II (published 1905, burials 1543-1659), edited by G. E. Weddall, privately printed for the Yorkshire Parish Register Society, Beck & Inchbold Ltd., Printers, Oriel Press, Leeds, Yorkshire, England.

[32] *The Yorkshire Archaeological and Topographical Association Record Series*, Vol. 2, "Feet of Fines of the Tudor Period," Part I, Robert White, Printer, Worksop, Co. Nottingham, England, 1887, p. 336.

Attempting to corroborate the inheritance of the estate of Moscraft by Thomas Pierson, land records (Yorkshire Feet of Fines) were searched for Moscraft, alias Molescroft. You will recall that Molescroft shows on the maps of the area of the vill of Pericne in an earlier chapter in 1086 when it belonged to the Archbishop of York under control of St. John's at Beverley in the East Riding of Yorkshire. In the dozen or so land transactions found for Molescroft, no Piersons were found in these records. But private and royal ownership existed at Molescroft for various different property pieces there in the 1500s and 1600s.

Armed with the idea that our William Peirson might be born in Yorkshire near Howden, a computer search was accomplished in Yorkshire IGI records[33] for the christening of William Peirson. The conditions selected were (1) christened during the 15 years before 1588 (21 years before his 1609 marriage) and (2) within 20 miles of Beverley in East Riding. The reason for using a 15-year search period is that William died in 1616, seven years after his marriage making the possibility that he was significantly older than 21 years at marriage in 1609. One record qualified. It was at Howden, located 19 miles SW of Beverley - a record which makes William age 32 at marriage in 1609 and age 39 at death in 1616:

Guillmus (William) Pearson c. 19 Sep 1577, Howden, Yorkshire, father Thomae (Thomas). The IGI record was confirmed by Howden parish records, which showed that William did not die or have children at Howden, and expanded his ancestors to additional generations below [34]:

William's father, **Thomas Pearson, was c. 18 Nov 1549 at Howden, Yorkshire, father John.** Thomas was a butcher, and was bur. 15 Feb 1583/4 at Howden. Thomas married 23 Nov 1572 Elizabeth Fawne at Howden. They had children, christened and/or buried at Howden: Elizabetha c. 18 Apr 1574, bur. 19 Aug 1574; Johanna c. 13 Jul 1575, bur. Joane 13 Mar 1577/8; Guillmus (William) c. 19 Sep 1577; Elena c. 24 Feb 1579/80, bur. Eleanor 3 Nov 1582; and Dorothea c. 10 Feb 1582/3.

Thomas' father, John Pearson, was born about 1517, and is the one called **"Old John Pearson" who was buried at Howden 21 Oct 1570.** It is believed that he married 1st about 1538 Catherine _____ who was buried 7 Oct 1546 at Howden, Knedlington, or Booth (all in Howden parish), and married 2nd about 1548 Elizabeth _____ who was buried 6 Jan 1564/5 at Howden. The only firm record of children is Thomas who was c. 18 Nov 1549 (William Peirson's line). However, based on the analysis shown in Appendix A on Howden Parish records, John Pearson is believed to have had:

Children by his 1st wife, Catherine:

1. Robert Pearson, born about 1539, butcher, bur. 18 Nov 1581 at Howden, and had grandchild Thomas who inherited the estate of Moscraft alias Molescroft near Beverley;

33 Part of the 67 million English records in the Church of Jesus Christ of Latter-Day Saints International Genealogical Index.
34 *The Registers of the Parish of Howden, Co. York*, Vols. I (published 1904, marriages 1542-1644 and baptisms 1542-1659), & II (published 1905, burials 1543-1659), edited by G. E. Weddall, privately printed for the Yorkshire Parish Register Society, Beck & Inchbold Ltd., Printers, Oriel Press, Leeds, Yorkshire, England.

2. William Peerson, born about 1541, of Asselby (4 miles west of Howden within Howden parish), bur. 16 Mar 1587/8, m. 23 Jan 1562/3 Julian Collin, had grandchild Rev. Abraham Pierson who went to America in 1639 (see a full analysis of this family in Chapter 4), also had grandchild John Pearson who went to America in 1637 (see a full analysis in Chapter 4);

3. John Pearson, born about 1543, buried 18 Mar 1546/7 (no parent given) at Howden, Knedlington, or Booth;

4. Agnes Pearson, born about 1545, buried 10 Jul 1546 (no parent given) at Howden, Knedlington, or Booth.

Children by his 2nd wife, Elizabeth:

5. Thomas Pearson, c.18 Nov 1549 Howden, butcher, bur. 15 Feb 1583/4 Howden, m. 23 Nov 1572 Elizabeth Fawne at Howden, had grandchild Henry Peirson who went to America in 1639;

6. Henrie Pearson, born about 1551, m. 27 Apr 1574 Margaret Williamson at Howden;

7. Jennet Pearson, born about 1553, m. 8 May 1571 William Dun Jr. at Howden;

8. Marion Pearson, born about 1559, m. at Howden 15 Sep 1577 Thomas Middleton of Hambleton (12 miles west of Howden);

9. John Peerson, born about 1561, of Skelton and Howden, bur. 1 Oct 1592 Howden, m. 15 Nov 1584 Elizabeth Stamp of Kilpin at Howden;

10. Edward Pearson, born about 1563, of Howden, bur. 22 Aug 1619, m. 1st about 1584 Isabell _____ (bur. 9 Dec 1592), m. 2nd about 1593 Anne _____;

11. Joan Peerson, born about Jan 1564/5, m. 5 Aug 1583 Richard Leaven of Goole at Howden.

A. Old John Pearson, born about 1517, probably having all of the 11 children listed above, is the oldest generation of record in Howden Parish. We are at the beginning of written records for ordinary citizens at this location. However, these same Howden records show others within Howden parish who are likely Old John Pearson's siblings or cousins:

B. Thomas Pearson, born about 1520, bur. 27 Mar 1569 of Saltmarshe, probably had seven children, see Appendix A;

C. William Pearson, born about 1523, of Howden, who had children Robert c. 24 Jul 1545 (no parent given) (who probably had grandchild Bartholomew Pierson who went to America in 1639), Margaret bur. 10 Mar 1549/50, George c. 3 Apr 1550 (bur. 16 Nov 1551), and Cuthbert c. 17 Apr 1552 (perhaps the father of Cuthbert Pearson of Lavendon, Buckinghamshire, mentioned earlier in this chapter, who had son William & 4 daus.);

D. George Pearson, born about 1525, bur. 8 Feb 1569/70 at Howden, m. 27 Jul 1546 Agnes _____ (bur. 28 May 1571 Howden), had children, all at Howden, John bur. 12 Dec 1550, George c. 25 Nov 1550, Alicia c. 17 Feb 1551/2 (who m. 10 Aug 1572 Thomas Richardson of Howden), Richard b. ca. 1556 (m. 5 Jul 1579 Alice Hartfirth), and Dorothie bur. 19 Dec 1559;

E. Richard Pearson, born about 1533, m. about 1554, had child Anna c. 26 Feb 1555/6;

F. Robert Pearson, born about 1540, bur. 13 Sep 1589 Swinefleet (located 4 miles south of Howden on the south side of the River Ouse within Howden Parish);

G. Alicia Pearson c. 16 Jul 1546 at Howden, no parents given.

The parents of the probable 7 siblings of Old John Pearson are not identified in Howden Parish records. Between Old John Pearson and his siblings and Nicholas Pierson, who was sheriff of York in 1477, lie two unknown generations. It is unknown if a direct line exists between them, though a Nicholas given name does carry down in the A. 1. Robert Pearson (b. ca. 1539) and A. 2. William Peerson (b. ca. 1541) lines above. See Appendix A for Howden parish records of all Pearsons present and family groups determined by analysis. Descendants of many of those mentioned above are listed there in the analysis.

Historically, Howden was the capital of a district called Howdenshire, which was a Wapentake in the East Riding of Yorkshire under the Danelaw in 900 AD. According to Pratt's History of Howden[35], it is probable that its early inhabitants were of Danish extraction due to its close and constant connection with Denmark. That is consistent with the Viking history in Chapter 2.

A collegiate church existed at Howden beginning sometime after the 1066 Conquest, but it was dissolved in the first year of the reign of King Edward VI (1547) and its facilities became vested in the crown where they remained until 1582 when Queen Elizabeth granted them by letters patent under the great seal of England to Edward Frost, John Walker, and others, their heirs and assigns forever. [36]

Howden Manor extends along the River Ouse for 30 miles from Cawood to Welton. It includes portions of the following parishes and townships: Asselby, Barmby-on-the-Marsh, Belby, Cliffe-cum-Lund, Eastrington, Ellerker-cum-Brantingham, Howden, Kilpin, Knedlington, Riccall, Saltmarshe, Skelton, Walkington, and Welton-cum-Melton. [37]

"Howden is a market town of considerable antiquity and of local importance. As early as the year 1200, King John granted a license to Philip de Poictou, Bishop of Durham, to hold an annual fair at Howden, on the second and following day of October. The fair is held in a field near the town, but the general business extends over a full fortnight, and is carried on in every town and village around, as well as in the town of Howden." [38]

As an example of the local path to becoming a minister: Asselby in Howden parish was the birth place of the Rev. J. Noble, who was born in 1611, and educated at Christ's College, Cambridge. He became vicar of St. Giles at Pontefract[39], 17 miles southwest of his birth place.

---

[35]*History of the Church, Parish, and Manor of Howden*, W. F. Pratt, publisher, Bride-Gate, 1851, p. 9.

[36]*History of the Church, Parish, and Manor of Howden*, W. F. Pratt, publisher, Bride-Gate, 1851, p. 27.

[37]*History of the Church, Parish, and Manor of Howden*, W. F. Pratt, publisher, Bride-Gate, 1851, pp. 14 & 15.

[38]*History of the Church, Parish, and Manor of Howden*, W. F. Pratt, publisher, Bride-Gate, 1851, pp. 9 & 57.

[39]*History of the Church, Parish, and Manor of Howden*, W. F. Pratt, publisher, Bride-Gate, 1851, p. 62.

Life in Howden, Yorkshire, is illustrated from 1579 through 1656 from Parish record extracts below[40]:

From April 1579 through July 1579, a large number of people were buried in the Howden Parish apparently due to some disease. At the peak of the deaths, 52 died in June 1579 compared to the normal monthly rate of 10 the year before. William Peirson of Olney was at Howden and less than two years old at the time, but escaped this 4-month epidemic with his life.

20 Aug 1602. "Elizabeth a wich died at Knedlington." There were no notes on how she died or who she was related to. Today, it would be unfathomable for a church clerk to write something like this into parish records.

23 May 1620, An Pearson of Howden was excommunicated. (Listed with burials: It is not clear if she was buried on this date and previously excommunicated or if she was just excommunicated on this date - deprived of rites of the church.) This could be An Pearson c. 31 Jul 1598 (age 22), dau. of Edward, or Anne Pearson the 2nd wife of this Edward, or An Pearson the wife of C. 1. (1) John Pearson as mentioned in Appendix A. Edward is believed to be the son of Old John Pearson of Howden. Thus the daughter An Pearson is probably a 1st cousin of William Pearson of Olney. Anne, the 2nd wife of Edward Pearson, is mentioned as his wife in a 1615 Howden land transaction.

1642, the English civil war began in earnest and Howden parish records from then to 1660 were meager or nonexistent. A few Pearson descendants from the Howden area managed to emigrate to America before the fighting and turmoil of the civil war broke out: John Pearson left in 1637; Henry Peirson, Rev. Abraham Pierson, and Bartholomew Pierson departed in May 1639. See the details in later chapters. But their marriages were not recorded at Howden, Yorkshire, and have not been found elsewhere in England at this writing. Perhaps the Puritan discrimination had begun making parish records of the Church of England meager or nonexistent for Puritans.

14-21 September 1654. "This year diverse of ye Londoners deserted ye faire (usually kept from ye 14 Sept to ye 21) (and) sold their goods at Beverley ye reason unknown to mee."

13 January 1654/5. "The thirteenth of ye monthe of January being Saturday at Whitgift the ferry-boat unfortunately sunke where John Pyecocke and Marmaduke Maskell of Adlingfleet with six other persons were drowned three escaped." Whitgift is located five miles southeast of Howden on the south shore of the Ouse river and within Howden Parish.

31 January 1654/5. "God's blessed Providence producing Plenty wheate some say for Twentypence a Bushell. But some for Twelvepence a Bushell sold at Howden in this month of January ... To God be only Praise."

10 March 1654/5. "It was spoken for truth (in my hearing) that upon Saturday the tenth of this month there was bought in Howden Markett Twenty Nine Egges for three pence

---

40 *The Registers of the Parish of Howden, Co. York*, Vols. I (published 1904, marriages 1542-1644 and baptisms 1542-1659), & II (published 1905, burials 1543-1659), edited by G. E. Weddall, privately printed for the Yorkshire Parish Register Society, Beck & Inchbold Ltd., Printers, Oriel Press, Leeds, Yorkshire, England.

(though seeminge here impertinent) yet for these and other Plenty by the Almighty Providence bestowed upon us a Thankfulness ought to be Remembered."

8 April 1655. "In remembrance of old Thomas Heward aboves (buried ye 8th) ye sume of forty shillings was distributed to ye poore of Howden and here inserted to animate others to ye like charytable Worke."

21 April 1655. "Whether it were by the Salors neglect or want of water it the ship called ye Constant wher Richard Chapman of Howden goeth Master being fraugh with three hundred qters. of Corn and other Nescessaries touchinge her voyage set forward from Howden-dike at Skelton upon Saturday the One and Twentyth of this Month it hapned the said Vessell came foule upon some Stake or Pyle Wherby she received a Breach (then sinking) and thus caused great losse in the ship the corn and other provisions beside the hinderance of the present voyage."

5 May 1655. "Pity yt sad accident upon Saturday the fifth of this month happened at Fockerthrop in ye house of Francis Blancherd, husbandman, being himselfe his wife and two sons at Howden Market one at home - some nieghbor servant came to fetch fire (ye wind southward) it seemed some sparke scattered in ye dunghill, kindled in ye straw, ascended the barne and dwelling-house - being remote from help, it consumed there his substance - (oh hevie returne) the Lord in mercie divert the judgments our sins so much deserve."

31 August 1655. "This year in ye month of August fell a great Raine wherr in some places the waters exceeded their Boundes, swept away much Hay, some Corne and other Hay corrupted by the unseasonable Season (ye like scarce memorable). It enlarged the price of Corne yet in mercie ye Lord comunicates above our Deserts his Blessings towards us."

September 1655. "This year the Londoners (though ye last year some absent) completed the faire kept it wholy at Howden accordinge to its former freedoms."

29 September 1655. "This Years Brought forth great Plenty of Orcharde fruits insomuch that upon the Nine & Twentyth Day of this Month (it's said) Apples was sold at Selby faire for one penny the Pecke." Selby is located 9 miles west northwest of Howden in Yorkshire.

1 October 1655. "This year ye workmen upon Munday ye first of ye Month at Howden began to sinke one Drawinge Well in a place called ye Corne Market Hill, Mr. Henery Gunson, Constable ye first day."

31 December 1655. "In ye Month ye River Ouze was (in some places) so frozen yt at Langrick & also Betweene Airsmouth & Booth people went over on ye Ice yet not much Snow." The mid-1600s were known as the mini-ice-age in Europe. Scientists who study the sunspot cycles know this period as the "Maunder minimum" - a period when few sunspots were seen on the sun's surface, coinciding with unusually cold weather on earth.

December 1655. "The marriages at Howden solemnized (are) upon ye days of publique meetings (of) the Justices of Peace (first Tuesday each month or as accasion require) hearinge and determininge matters and controversies amongst neighbors so depending with sundry other publique affairs."

January 1655/6. "Joshua Lamley of Howden, shoemaker & deputy bailife, was apprehended at Howden for doing murder (neere North Cave ye day before on ye body of William Pearson of Kirk Ella, shoemaker). Thence he was sent to jail at York, there received and loosed within four or five days after upon whar bail (if bailable) I know not but home he came which thing seemed very strange to men of good understanding. And within four days did fly for it from Howden." The murdered man, William Pearson of Kirk Ella (located 17 miles east of Howden near Kingston Upon Hull), is likely the one who married 8 Feb 1643/4 Elizabeth Browne at Kirk Ella and had children William b. ca. 1644, Phillip c. 26 Dec 1645, Mergretta c. 16 Aug 1646, Jane c. 25 Nov 1649, and Elizabetha c. 7 Dec 1651. That Pearson line has lived in Kirk Ella at least since 1571 [Susanna c. 18 Oct 1571 Kirk Ella, father Willelmi (William); and Willelmus (William) Pearson m. 24 May 1579 Elizabeth Lilfurth at Kirk Ella], but they are not known to be connected to the Howden Pearsons within the existing period of records.

June 1656. "For the yeare last past. The cause and reason why no Comunion was administered to the parisherners of Howden is best known to Mr. John Thomson our Minister." This is part of the religious turmoil caused by the rule of the Puritans. Oliver Cromwell had returned from the battle fields in 1653, had dismissed Parliament, and nominated the Barebone's Parliament. The Commonwealth had taken on the name of Protectorate, with Cromwell as Lord Protector. His rule was more despotic than the King's. Many ministers did not know what they could do legally and feared for their jobs and their lives. The Rump Parliament under Oliver Cromwell's leadership had beheaded King Charles on January 30, 1649, and no one doubted the power of Cromwell. The majority of ministers in the Church of England simply vacated their duties at the church, including communion, christenings, and the keeping of records of births, marriages, and deaths, until 1660 when the Puritan rule was over. It is presumed that marriages continued to be carried out by the Justices of the Peace, though records were meager or non-existent.

In 1850, Howden Township including Howden-dike was still small containing only 2,332 inhabitants and 2,800 acres of farm land.

More Family Connections to Howden, Yorkshire

Within Howden parish records of Yorkshire , England, it is noted that Jane Cowper (Cooper) m. 15 Nov 1621 Philip Pearson of Yokefleet. It was sought to determine if she was related to John Cooper who married William Peirson's widow, Wyborro (Griggs) Peirson, in 1618 at Olney, Buckinghamshire. John Cooper, Wyborro's second husband, was age 41 on the passenger record of the Hopewell in 1635 when he went to America with Wyborro. That makes John Cooper's birth year 1594 that we seek.

But parish records at Howden, Yorkshire, did not reveal the christening of Jane Cooper that married Philip Pearson nor of John Cooper that married Wyborro (Griggs) Pierson. However, search in the nearby towns of Snaith (8 miles SW of Howden) and Pontefract (11 miles W of Snaith) revealed:

Snaith parish records[41]:

---

41 William Brigg, *The Parish Registers of Snaith, Co. York*, Printed for The Yorkshire Parish Register Society, Vol. 57, Part I, Baptisms 1558-1657, Marriages 1537-1657, 1917, p. 63.

10 Apr 1604 "baptised Jane Cowper da. of Richard of Goldall" (Gowdall within Snaith parish).

Pontefract parish records[42]:

28 July 1594 "Robart Cowper and An Barweeke were married."

22 Dec 1594 "baptised John son of Robart Cowper."

6 Jan 1598 "baptised Robart son of Robart Cowper."

11 Dec 1600 "baptised Mary dau. of Robert Cowper."

20 Aug 1602 "buried Thomas son of Robt Cowper of Tanshelf."

24 Dec 1605 "Robt Cowper was buried." (husband of Anne Barwick?)

While a relationship may exist between Howden and Pontefract Coopers, it was not found. Regardless, the christenings of Jane Cooper who married at Howden, Yorkshire, and John Cooper who married at Olney, Buckinghamshire, were found in Yorkshire at Snaith and Pontefract, respectively. In the Cooper records at Pontefract parish, no other records other than those stated above were found that connect to this family. The marriage of John Cooper's parents, Robert Cooper and Anne Barwick, was found along with John Cooper's christening. The Robert Cooper that was buried in 1605 is believed to be John Cooper's father, since no additional children were christened after the burial date and no parent of the buried Robert is given (rules out the son Robert).

Given-name check against John Cooper's parents in Pontefract:

The children of John Cooper and Wibroe (Griggs) Peirson were named Anne, Mary, John, Thomas, and Martha. John after his father, Martha after her mother, Martha Wyborro, Anne from John's mother, Anne Barwick, and Mary and Thomas from siblings of John Cooper at Pontefract. The Pontefract Cooper family looks like a reliable match for the parents of John Cooper. While no son is named Robert for John Cooper's children, this is typical when a son's (John's) father dies when the son is young (age 10 in this case). This lack of carrying down the father's name in children's names also occurred for Henry Peirson (1615-1680) of Southampton with relation to his father William who died when Henry was age 1.

Finding as many connections to Howden as possible for Pierson and other allied families is part of a larger proof by preponderance of evidence that William Peirson of Olney, Buckinghamshire, England, is the one christened at Howden, Yorkshire, England, 19 Sep 1577. See the next chapter for additional Pierson immigrant connections to Howden, Yorkshire, England.

[42]Thomas B. Willis, *The Parish Records of Pontefract 1585-1641*, Printed for The Yorkshire Parish Register Society, Vol. 122, Doncaster, Yorkshire, England, 1958, pp. 26, 33, 38, 160, 170, 253.

Chapter 4
American Immigrant Inter-Relations
in England

The investigations begin with the legend of the three Pierson brothers and end with several other American Pierson immigrants whose origins have been mysteries, for example:

1878, Lizzie Benedict Pierson, " An attempt has been made in England to find from records an account of the emigration to America of Rev. Abraham Pierson & his contemporaries ..."

1895, Frederick Lockwood Pierson, "All attempts to trace Stephen Pierson in Suffolk County (England) or beyond have failed."

But since those books were published in the 19th century, over 100 years have passed. The Church of Jesus Christ of Latter-Day Saints (LDS) has been gathering records in their International Genealogical Index (IGI) for many years now, which are currently on CD ROM disks and accessed through their computer program "FamilySearch" available at local Family History Centers for individual use of members and non-members of the Church of Jesus Christ of Latter-Day Saints. The most recent updates are their 1994 IGI Addendum disks which added about 20 percent more records than previously contained therein. The number of English records now in the IGI and computer accessible is 67,507,124. A large percentage of these 67 million entries are from Parish records of England relating christenings and marriages. The computer program FamilySearch can search these records by name, county, and date range. Thus, a new data pool with quick access is now available for searching for hard-to-find ancestors in England. This capability is used extensively in the following searches for Pierson immigrants. After a probable answer is found, it is then necessary to search by other methods for corroborating information including actually looking at the parish records, wills, military records, etc. to prove a case. But the task of where to look is made easy with the computer and those vast records of the church.

The Three Brothers to New England Legend

Lizzie B. Pierson, in her book *Pierson Genealogical Records*, 1878, presents a Pierson legend[1]: "An attempt has been made in England to find from records an account of the emigration to America of Rev. Abraham Pierson and his contemporaries, hoping thus to learn if **Abraham, Thomas and Henry,** were *'the three brothers, who together left their native land, and sought a home on the rocky shores of New England.'* "

All Pierson legends have carried some element of truth and this legend is not an exception. Above, Lizzie Pierson suggests that the three brothers include Henry. If this is so, then we are looking for three Pierson brothers who came to New England in May 1639. To test this theory, we will look at the Piersons that first appear in New England records in 1639 or shortly thereafter.

---

[1]Lizzie B. Pierson, *Pierson Genealogical Records*, Joel Munsell, Printer, Albany, NY, 1878, Introduction p. v.

"**Rev. Abraham Pierson**[2] came first to **Boston** in **1639**, was on Long Island a short time, but his life and labors were particularly in Branford, Connecticut, and in Newark, New Jersey." Later in Lizzie Pierson's book[3], she states "In 1613, Abraham Pierson was born in Yorkshire, England; graduated at Trinity college, Cambridge, 1632; in pursuit of religious freedom came to America, 1639. He was in Boston and Lynn, Massachusetts, 1640; went to Southampton, Long Island, where he remained till 1647; then removed to Branford, Connecticut, from which place he again removed, in 1666, to Newark, New Jersey, where he died, August 9, 1678. His wife was Abigail, daughter of Rev. John Wheelwright of Lincolnshire, England, who removed to New Hampshire." Further details are provided by George Howell[4]: "Rev. Abraham Pierson arrived in America in 1639." "On the 11th of October, 1640, Mr. (Abraham) Pierson was appointed[5] at Boston (Massachusetts), to be the minister of the colony then settled and residing at Southampton (Long Island). In November 1640, Rev. Hugh Peters attended the ordination of Mr. Abraham Pierson at Lynn (Massachusetts), and the organization at the same time and place of a church composed of individuals who had emigrated from Lynn and settled at Southampton."

Abraham Pierson arriving in New England the same year as Henry Peirson suggests that they could be two of "the three brothers." From records of Henry Peirson, we know that his parents, William Peirson and Wibroe Griggs, married 25 Jul 1609 at Olney, Buckinghamshire, England; Henry was baptized 10 Dec 1615 at Olney, and a "William Pearson" was buried 28 Jul 1616 near Olney at Lavendon. No other Pierson baptisms appeared in the Bishop's Transcripts for Olney. It is concluded that Rev. Abraham Pierson is not likely to be a sibling of Henry but could still be a kinsman.

Watertown, Massachusetts[6]: "1639. Bartolemew Person (**Bartholomew Pierson**), An homestall of six acres bounded the north with the highway, the south with Edmund White, the east with the common, and the west with John Perse." Bartholomew and Ursula Pierson had chd. Bartholomew (1st)[7] b. 7 Sep 1640, bur. 27 Oct 1640; Bartholomew (2nd)[8] b. 26 Feb 1641/42; Martha[9] b. 17 Sep 1643; Jonathan[10] b. 12 Aug 1648; and Joseph[11] b. 8 Nov 1650. At Woburn in 1652, John Burge[12] sold his house and lands to Bartholomew Pierson of Watertown. At Woburn, Bartholomew and Ursula Pierson had dau. Mary b. 10 Apr 1652.

Only three 1639 records of first appearing Pierson "planters" in New England have been found. Therefore, Bartholomew is probably the third "brother" in the three brothers legend with Henry and Rev. Abraham Pierson.

---

[2]Lizzie B. Pierson, *Pierson Genealogical Records*, Joel Munsell, Printer, Albany, New York, 1878, Introduction p. vi.

[3]Lizzie B. Pierson, *Pierson Genealogical Records*, Joel Munsell, Printer, Albany, New York, 1878, p. 10.

[4]George Rogers Howell, *The Early History of Southampton, L.I., New York*, 2nd Edition, Weed, Parsons and Company, Albany, NY, 1887, pp. 15-16.

[5]George Rogers Howell, *The Early History of Southampton, L.I., New York*, 2nd Edition, Weed Parsons and Company, Albany, NY, 1887, pp. 21-22.

[6]Watertown, Massachusetts Land Records. First Inventory, p. 63.

[7]Watertown, Massachusetts, *First Book of Births, Marriages and Deaths*, p. 8.

[8]Watertown, Massachusetts, *First Book of Births, Marriages, and Deaths*, p. 9.

[9]Watertown, Massachusetts, *First Book of Births, Marriages, and Deaths*, p. 11.

[10]Watertown (Massachusetts), *First Book of Births, Marriages, and Deaths*, p. 14.

[11]Watertown (Massachusetts), *First Book of Births, Marriages, and Deaths*, p. 15.

[12]*The New England Historical and Genealogical Register*, Volume XL, p. 260.

Middleton, Massachusetts[13]: "**John Pierson**, of Middleton, 1640, d. 1677; and left one son, who died young."

This 1640 record of John Pierson is one year after Henry came in 1639.

Watertown, Massachusetts[14]: "**Hugh Pierson**, of Watertown, Massachusetts, 1640, had child Ruth. He died in 1675, very poor, as he had lived."

This 1640 record of Hugh Pierson is one year after Henry came in 1639.

"**Thomas Pierson Sen.**[15] is first recorded in America at Branford, Connecticut. The Town Records of Branford say Thos. Pierson mar. Maria Harrison, both of Branford, Nov. 27, 1662. At Branford, he was closely associated with Rev. Abraham Pierson and in all probability they were brothers (Lizzie Pierson comment) who had together or at the same time left old England. Records of Thomas are meager. He was a weaver. Thomas was one of the signers of Heads of Families at Branford Oct. 30, 1666, that agreed to move to Newark, New Jersey. Accordingly that fall, with Rev. Abraham Pierson at their head, they went to Newark." He (Thomas) had chd. Samuel b. 1663; Hannah; Eliza; Abigail; Mary; and Thomas b. 1678.

Thomas is one generation too young to be a brother of the Rev. Abraham Pierson. Lizzie Pierson's comment that Thomas left old England at the same time as Abraham is unsubstantiated as Abraham arrived 1639 and the earliest record for Thomas is his 1662 marriage at Branford. However, Thomas could be a kinsman of the Rev. Abraham Pierson. The conclusion is that this Thomas is not one of the three brothers in the legend.

For the *three brothers to New England legend*, only three Piersons have been found in New England records which fit the general legend criteria of arriving at the same time. These three Piersons are Abraham, Bartholomew, and Henry. But records of England have yet to show that Henry had any brothers. However, I could believe that the legend of the three Pierson brothers referred to three Piersons who were not siblings but were brothers in the sense of "any male relative, kinsmen[16]" (one of the alternate meanings of brother). If this latter definition of brothers is the one meant to be used in the legend, then Abraham, Bartholomew, and Henry are the three Pierson brothers of the legend and all three came to America together on the same ship in May 1639.

Having traced the Henry Peirson line to Howden, Yorkshire, England, in the previous chapter, the other two "brothers" of the legend will now be traced to see if they descend from that area.

The Rev. Abraham Pierson of Yorkshire and Branford, Connecticut

"Thus far[17], I only find of Rev. Abraham Pierson, in England, that 'he was born in Yorkshire, 1613, and that he matriculated at Cambridge, 1632.' " This statement was made by Lizzie Pierson in her 1878 book.

---

[13]Lizzie B. Pierson, *Pierson Genealogical Records*, Joel Munsell, Printer, Albany, NY, 1878, p. 66.

[14]Lizzie B. Pierson, *Pierson Genealogical Records*, Joel Munsell, Printer, Albany, NY, 1878, p. 66.

[15]Lizzie B. Pierson, *Pierson Genealogical Records*, Joel Munsell, Printer, Albany, NY, 1878, p. 34.

[16]*Webster's New World Dictionary*, 2nd College Edition, William Collins Publishers, Inc., 1980, p. 181, def. 5.

[17]Lizzie B. Pierson, *Pierson Genealogical Records*, Joel Munsell, Printer, Albany, NY, 1878, p. 73.

The Rev. Abraham Pierson of whom she speaks was born in Yorkshire, England, about 1613, attended Trinity College in Cambridgeshire in 1632, and was ordained in England (some say at Newark-on-Trent, Nottinghamshire). He came to New England (Boston) in 1639 and became the first minister at Southampton, Long Island, New York colony in 1640. In 1647, through a disagreement with the power of the church in government affairs, Abraham left Southampton with some of his followers to form his own town and church in Connecticut (Branford). He had been at Southampton for eight years with Henry Peirson (note surname spelling) and during this time Abraham spelled his name Pierson. It is said in legend that Abraham named Branford after the town he came from in Yorkshire. However, there is no Branford in Yorkshire, but there is a Bradford. The English counties of Herefordshire and Worcestershire do have a "Bransford" which means "ford by a hill." In 1086, it was spelled Bradnesford there. In Abraham Pierson's will he refers to Branford, Connecticut, as "Brandford." It is evident from Abraham's education and by his spelling of Brandford for his town in Connecticut that he sees Branford and Bradford as the same name. Thus, we can believe that he was referring to having come from Bradford, Yorkshire, for the following analysis of his ancestors. In 1666, the Rev. Abraham Pierson moved his church and followers to Newark, New Jersey, which some say he named after the place he was ordained in England.

The Rev. Abraham Pierson Jr., Abraham's son, was the first President of Yale College at New Haven, Connecticut, 1701-1707, acting as its rector. A statue of Abraham Pierson Jr. is displayed at Yale University at New Haven, Connecticut.

Because of the superb reputation of these two Abrahams, many Pierson families have sought connection to that fine line. It was stated by Lizzie Pierson in her 1878 book[18] that she thought that the Rev. Abraham Pierson was a brother of Henry Pierson of Southampton, Long Island, and Thomas Pierson of Branford, Connecticut, of her line. Her reasoning was that they might possibly be the three Pierson brothers of family legend that came to America together. But she could find no proof of those suspicions.

According to Arthur Newton Pierson in his 1945 book[19], "Peletreau and Brown's *American Families of Historic Lineage* (no date, estimated publication 1906) traces the Pierson family back to St. Mary's, Shadwell Parish, Stepney, England." He provided the Pierson family: Abraham (b. 1590) mar. Christine Johnson July 31, 1612 (date has apparently been modified - see below) and had two chd. Rev. Abraham and Henry. He also gave two earlier generations of Richards for Abraham (b. 1590). Frankly, the children of the families provided by Pelletreau and Brown are fictitiously connected! Unfortunately, others besides Arthur Newton Pierson were taken in by the unsupported data.

Prior to 1990, Elmer Meyer published the Abraham Pierson and Christine Johnson family of England in *Pierson Kinship Historical Newsletter No. 1*, p. 1, with chd. Rev. Abraham, Henry, and Thomas. With Elmer Meyer's newsletter as a reference, in 1990, it was published[20] in *Seek and Ye Shall Find, Pearson, Volume III*.

---

[18]Lizzie B. Pierson, *Pierson Genealogical Records*, Joel Munsell, Printer, Albany, NY, 1878.

[19]Arthur Newton Pierson, *Genealogy, Our Pierson Family, Marsh Family, Clark Family, Baker Family*, 1945.

[20]Bettina Pearson Higdon Burns, *Seek and Ye Shall Find: Pearson, Volume III*, The Gregath Company, Cullman, Alabama, 1990, p. 839-841 (her reference was Pierson Kinship Historical Newsletter #1, p. 1, by Elmer Meyer).

But the following record of that family group is all that exists:

"31 July 1615[21]. Marriage of Pearson, Abraham (Pierson), of Shadwell, parish of Stepney, co. Middlesex (now Greater London), sailor, and Christian Johnson, of said parish, widow of Barnard Johnson, late of same, tailor - at All Hallows Barking, London."

No records of children's births could be found to go with this marriage. Therefore, it is recommended that all association between this data and Abraham, Henry, and Thomas Pierson be dropped. It has already been proven that Henry Peirson was born 1615 at Olney, Buckinghamshire, England, father William (see Chapter 8 for details).

The ancestors of the Rev. Abraham Pierson will now be addressed using the legend that he is from Bradford, Yorkshire.

The LDS International Genealogy Index (IGI) for England was searched for Abraham Pierson, born about 1613 in Yorkshire. Three church christening records are worthy of review:

Name	Chris. Date	Parents	Location in England
Abraham Pearson	24 Jul 1599	William	Bradford, Yorkshire
Abraham Person	14 Aug 1608	not given	Guiseley, Yorkshire
Abraham Peerson	**22 Sep 1611**	**Thomas**	**Guiseley, Yorkshire**

The 1599 christening is the location we seek in England, but the year is probably too early for the Abraham we seek of about 1613. The 1608 christening is not too far off 1613 and Guiseley is located only 6 miles north of Bradford, Yorkshire. Not bad, but Guiseley parish records indicated that he was buried 30 Sep 1608 at age 1 1/2 months. The 1611 christening, father Thomas, is at Guiseley near Bradford in Yorkshire and is even closer to the 1613 date. This makes the best selection for our Abraham Pierson as christened 22 Sep 1611, father Thomas, at Guiseley, Yorkshire, just 6 miles from the desired Bradford.

According to parish records of Bradford[22] and Guiseley[23], "Thomas Pearson" married 14 Aug 1593 "Grace Marshall" at Guiseley Church and had children:

1. "Child of Thomas Pearson of Bradford" bur. 21 Jan 1597/8 Bradford (christening records are not available before 1599 at Bradford);

2. "Robert, son of Thomas Pearson of Bradford, baptism" 24 Jun 1599 Bradford, perhaps this is the Robert Pearson that, along with Richard Stanhope and William Kitchin, purchased land and a "moiety of a messuage (half of the premises) at

[21]*London Marriage Licenses & Allegations*, 1521-1869, Col. 1035, microfiche in State Library at Sydney, Australia, ref. 10/N929.3421/2. Photocopied by Jenny Pierson of Wellington, New Zealand.

[22]LDS Library 35 mm microfilm No. 1648142, Item 1 (Baptisms 1599-1715), Item 2 (Marriages 1596-1700), Item 4 (Burials 1596-1700)· Church of England, *Parish Church of Bradford (Yorkshire), Parish Register Transcripts, 1596-1734*, Item 1 pp. 2 & 11, Item 4 p. 5.

[23]William Easterbrook Preston and Joseph Hambly Rowe, *A Transcript of the Early Registers of the Parish of Guiseley in the County of York, 1584 to 1720, Together with a Transcript of the Early Registers of the Chapelry of Horsforth, 1620 to 1720, with Notes on Guiseley Families*, Percy Lund, Humphries & Co. Ltd., Bradford, Yorkshire, 1913, pp. 14 (Thomas marriage), 75, 80, 81, 83, 85, 86, 90, 94, 95, 97, 101, 103 (Thomas burial), 110 (Grace 2nd marriage), 120.

Horsforth[24] in Michaelmas Term (the quarter of the year containing September 29), 1624" (Horsforth is a Chapelry of Guiseley Parish);

3. "William, son of Thomas Pearson of Bradford, bap." 12 Jul 1601 Bradford, bur. at Bradford 20 Nov 1601 "child of Thomas Pearson of Bradford" (this burial belongs to either this William or his brother Robert);

4. "Samuell Person, baptysing" 27 Feb 1602/3 Guiseley, "sonne of Tomas Person";

5. "Mercye Person bap." 5 May 1605 Guiseley (no parent given), buried "(blank) Person" 18 Aug 1605 Guiseley (this is likely Mercye at 3 1/2 months old because a second child was named Mercye in this family);

6. "Rebeckca Pearson bap." 12 Oct 1606 Guiseley (no parent given), bur. at Guiseley 14 Dec 1625 "Rebeckah Personn of Carelton" (died age 19 & living at Carlton with mother and stepfather in 1625 [see details below] - Carlton is located 13 miles SE of Guiseley, or 5 miles south of Leeds);

7. "Abraham Person bap." 14 Aug 1608 Guiseley (no parent given), bur. at Guiseley 30 Sep 1608 "Abraham Person" (age 1 1/2 months);

8. "Grace Person bap." 29 Oct 1609 Guiseley (no parent given), this is probably the Grace Pearson who married 8 May 1633 Thomas Swain at the Cathedral, Bradford, Yorkshire;

9. **"Abraham Peersone bap." 22 Sep 1611 Guiseley, "sone of Thomas Peerson";**

10. "Mercye (2nd) Person bap." 7 Nov 1613 Guiseley (no parent given), "Tomas Pearson('s) child" bur. at Guiseley 16 Nov 1613 (this is likely Mercye at 9 days old);

11. "Isack Pearson bap." 10 Sep 1615 Guiseley (no parent given), "Isack Person" bur. Guiseley 9 Mar 1616/7 (age 6 months).

Since there appeared to be no other Pearson/Peerson/Person family at Guiseley, the other Pearson/Person children christened at Guiseley with no parent given were assigned to this Thomas (their christening dates fit well together). The first three children were buried or christened at Bradford, a connection deduced from no other Thomas eligible as a father at Bradford and from the marriage, burial and christening date spacings of Thomas and his other children at Guiseley. Thomas Pearson appeared to be a member of the Bradford Parish Church after marrying at Guiseley in 1593, but about 1602 he and his family became members of the Guiseley Parish Church, six miles to the north. Whether, Thomas physically moved his residence at this point is unclear. There was another Thomas Pearson at Bradford, but he was born about 1591 and married Dorothy Hawksworth 2 Sep 1616 and could not be the father of the earlier children buried or christened at Bradford in 1597/8, 1599 and 1601. The birth record of Thomas Pearson of Guiseley, father of Rev. Abraham Pierson, was not found near Bradford in Yorkshire (pre-dates existing records, but see later analysis). "Tomas Persone" was buried 18 Apr 1617 at Guiseley Church, Yorkshire. The eldest surviving son appears to be Robert, who would inherit the majority of his estate.

---

[24]The Yorkshire Archaeological Society, *Record Series Vol. 58, Yorkshire Fines for the Stuart Period Vol. 1*, Edited by William Brigg, printed for the Society, 1915, p. 242.

Thomas' widow, "Grace Person", married 2nd 26 Jan 1621/2 "Edward Roodes" at Guiseley Church, Guiseley, Yorkshire. "Grace Roods, wife of Edward Roods of Carelton," was buried at Guiseley Church 8 Aug 1629 after her 19-year-old daughter "Rebeckah Personn of Carelton" was buried there 14 Dec 1625. Edward Roodes must have remarried as Guiseley Parish records show that "Grace Roodes, daughter of Edward Roodes of Carelton," was baptized at Guiseley 26 Aug 1632. "Edward Rhodes of Carelton" was buried at Guiseley Church 18 Mar 1672/3.

Before 1641 (birth year of his first known child), the Rev. Abraham Pierson (c. 22 Sep 1611) married Abigail, daughter of Rev. John Wheelwright of Lincolnshire, England[25]. The following table is a given-name check of the Rev. Abraham and Abigail Pierson's children against his presumed father and siblings above:

Father, Wife, or Siblings of Abraham	Children of Abraham and Abigail
Abraham, husband	Abraham, son b. 1641 Lynn, Mass.
Thomas, father	Thomas, son b. 1641/2 Southampton
John Wheelwright, father-in-law	John, son b. 1643 Southampton, NY
Abigail, wife	Abigail, dau. b. 1644 Southampton
Grace, mother & sister b. 1609	Grace, dau b. 1650 Branford, Conn.
(wife Abigail's sister?)	Susanna, dau b. 1652 Branford, Conn.
Rebeckca, sister b. 1606	Rebecca, dau b. 1654 Branford, Conn.
(From the Bible?)	Theophilus, son b. 1659 Branford, Conn
Isack, brother b. 1615	Isaac, son
(wife Abigail's sister?)	Mary, dau.

That's a good match, and represents an exceptionally good family relationship. It indicates a pattern of using sibling's names for children's names and Abraham and Abigail taking turns naming the children, after their fathers and own names were used up.

Based on that pattern, there was one John Wheelwright family in Lincolnshire, England, at Mumby, that matched the possible names for Abigail Wheelwright's probable sisters, Susan and Mary. Mumby is located 21 miles northeast of Boston, Lincolnshire near Alford. The marriage for this family is recorded in parish records[26] as "Anderby Marriages. John Whelewright & Elizabeth Smyth 20 Oct 1603." Anderby is located one mile NE of Mumby. Mumby parish records[27] show the following christenings and burials:

---

[25]Lizzie B. Pierson, *Pierson Genealogical Records*, Joel Munsell, Printer, Albany, NY, 1878, p. 10.

[26]Thomas M. Blagg and Reginald C. Dudding, *Lincolnshire Parish Registers Marriages*, "Anderby Marriages," W. P. W. Phillimore, general editor, London, 1913, Vol. 10, p. 22.

[27]LDS Library 35 mm microfilm No. 0505772 (Vol. 4), Church of England, Parish Churches of Mumby, Bilsby, and Laceby, *Parish Register Extracts, 1573-1724*, Mumby baptisms pp. 370-1, Mumby burials p. 373, Bilsby baptisms and marriages p. 386, Bilsby burials and vicars p. 387, Laceby baptisms p. 391.

Wheelwright	Chris. or Bur.	Parents	Lincolnshire
Susan	c. 25 Feb 1603/4	John	Mumby
Mary	c. 11 Dec 1605	John	Mumby
Elsabeth (sic)	c. 3 Apr 1608	John	Mumby
John	c. 10 Jan 1609/10	John	Mumby
John	bur. 26 Feb 1609/10		Mumby
Isabel	c. 9 Feb 1610/11	John	Mumby
Isabel	bur. 21 Apr 1611		Mumby

According to Mumby parish records[28], "Alice, wife of John Whelewright," was buried 11 Jan 1602/3 at Mumby. This is either another John Whelewright (Robert, son of John Whelewright, bap. 18 Feb 1586/7 at Mumby) or John Wheelwright's first wife and son, and Elizabeth Smyth, mother of Susan and Mary and three other children above, is his second wife. It is probable that Elizabeth (Smyth) Wheelwright died after daughter Isabel was born as a third marriage is recorded at Bilsby[29] for "John Wheelwright & Marie Storre 8 Nov 1621." Bilsby is located 3 miles NW of Mumby. Marie Storre is believed to be a relative, perhaps a daughter, of Rev. Thomas Storre, vicar of Bilsby parish, which vicar Thomas died 26 Mar 1623. Rev. John Wheelwright succeeded Rev. Thomas Storre at Bilsby as its vicar[30] from 25 Mar 1625 to 25 Mar 1633. Rev. John Wheelwright then moved to Laceby (near Great Grimsby in Lincolnshire), 24 miles NNW of Bilsby. John and Marie Wheelwright had children at Mumby or Bilsby, and Laceby[31] as follows:

Wheelwright	Chris. or Bur.	Parents	Lincolnshire
Abigail	**b. ca. 1622 (no record)**	**John**	**Mumby or Bilsby**
William	bur. 19 May 1627	John	Bilsby
Katherine	c. 4 Nov 1630	John	Bilsby
Mary	c. 19 May 1632	John	Bilsby
Marie	bur. 28 Jul 1632	John	Bilsby
Elizabeth	c. 9 Jun 1633	John & Mary	Laceby

[28]LDS Library 35 mm microfilm No. 0505772 (Vol. 4), Church of England, Parish Churches of Mumby, Bilsby, and Laceby, *Parish Register Extracts, 1573-1724*, Mumby baptisms pp. 370-1, Mumby burials p. 373, Bilsby baptisms and marriages p. 386, Bilsby burials and vicars p. 387, Laceby baptisms p. 391.
[29]LDS Library 35 mm microfilm No. 0505772 (Vol. 4), Church of England, Parish Churches of Mumby, Bilsby, and Laceby, *Parish Register Extracts, 1573-1724*, Mumby baptisms pp. 370-1, Mumby burials p. 373, Bilsby baptisms and marriages p. 386, Bilsby burials and vicars p. 387, Laceby baptisms p. 391.
[30]LDS Library 35 mm microfilm No. 0505772 (Vol. 4), Church of England, Parish Churches of Mumby, Bilsby, and Laceby, *Parish Register Extracts, 1573-1724*, Mumby baptisms pp. 370-1, Mumby burials p. 373, Bilsby baptisms and marriages p. 386, Bilsby burials and vicars p. 387, Laceby baptisms p. 391.
[31]LDS Library 35 mm microfilm No. 0505772 (Vol. 4), Church of England, Parish Churches of Mumby, Bilsby, and Laceby, *Parish Register Extracts, 1573-1724*, Mumby baptisms pp. 370-1, Mumby burials p. 373, Bilsby baptisms and marriages p. 386, Bilsby burials and vicars p. 387, Laceby baptisms p. 391.

In this family, Rev. Abraham Pierson's wife, Abigail Wheelwright, has been placed as a child of John and Marie (Storre) Wheelwright based on believing she is a half-sister of Susan and Mary, though no record has been found for Abigail's christening. The records at Bilsby were meager during these years with voids in the christenings. Thus the records were not kept or were destroyed or lost. Regardless, this is believed to be Abigail Wheelwright's family because of the presence of Susan and Mary and John Wheelwright being a minister (Lizzie Pierson stated in her 1878 book[32] that the Rev. Abraham Pierson's "wife was Abigail, dau. of Rev. John Wheelwright of Lincolnshire, England, who [Abigail] removed to New Hampshire.")

A birth record for the Rev. Abraham Pierson's father, Thomas, was not found in the records of towns near Bradford, Yorkshire. However, if Abraham is related to Henry Peirson of the three brothers legend, then we should look for Thomas' birth at Howden, Yorkshire, from which place the Henry Peirson line appears to descend. If Thomas Pearson's birth year is estimated as 21 years before his 14 Aug 1593 marriage to Grace Marshall, the estimated year is 1572. When searching Howden, Yorkshire records for a Thomas born about that time, having no burial record, and having no children there (seeming to depart), one record fits the requirement: **Thomas Pearson c. 17 Jul 1574 at Howden, father William Peerson** of Asselby (who married 23 Jan 1562/3 Julian_ Collin at Howden). That means that Thomas married at age 19 at Guiseley. Which marriage age is reasonable considering that his father, William, died when Thomas was age 14. Thomas' first two named sons, born at Bradford, Robert and William, match Thomas' father William and probable uncle Robert (who was grandfather of Thomas Pierson of Beverley that inherited an estate at Moscraft). Henry Peirson's grandfather Thomas is probably another uncle of Thomas Pearson of Bradford and Guiseley. William Peerson's children (baptised at Asselby in Howden parish) are: Dorothea c. 24 Oct 1563, Alice bur. 14 Aug 1565, Margareta c. 30 Dec 1565, Thomas c. & bur. 27 Dec 1570, Nicholas c. 2 Feb 1572/3 & bur. 19 Feb 1572/3, **Thomas c. 17 Jul 1574**, Christopher b. ca. 1576, and John b. ca. 1580 (see Appendix A for details). William's wife, Julian, probably died about 1580/1. This William is believed to be the William of Kilpin (Howden parish) bur. 16 Mar 1587/8 who (William of Kilpin) married (2nd) 19 Oct 1581 Alison Bushbie (bur. 3 Mar 1586/7 Howden). All of William Peerson's children were by his first wife Julian Collin.

If this Pierson family analysis is correct, then the ancestors of two of the "Pierson brothers of legend" now go back to Howden parish in Yorkshire. See Chapter 7 for descendants of Rev. Abraham Pierson, American immigrant.

Bartholomew Pierson of Yorkshire and Watertown, Massachusetts

Having related Henry Peirson and Rev. Abraham Pierson to a probable Howden, Yorkshire, England connection, Bartholomew, the third of the three Pierson brothers of legend, is investigated below.

According to Lizzie Pierson, in her 1878 book[33], "Bartholomew Pierson was admitted freeman in Watertown, Mass., 1648. He came to Watertown in 1639; removed to Woburn,

[32]Lizzie B. Pierson, *Pierson Genealogical Records*, Joel Munsell, Printer, Albany, NY, 1878, p. 10.
[33]Lizzie B. Pierson, *Pierson Genealogical Records*, Joel Munsell, Printer, Albany, NY, 1878, p. 66.

Mass., 1652; died 1687; left wife Ursula, who d. 1694, and had chd. Bartholomew, b. 1641-2, d. 1661; Martha; Jonathan, b. 1648; Joseph, b. 1650. The Colonial Records say, 'Porsune was selectman of Woburn, 1665-6.' Probably this same Bartholomew."

According to town records of Watertown, Massachusetts[34], Bartholomew Pierson purchased land there in "1639. Bartolemew Person, An homestall of six acres bounded the north with the highway, the south with Edmund White, the east with the common, and the west with John Perse." Bartholomew and Ursula Pierson had chd. Bartholomew (1st)[35] b. 7 Sep 1640, bur. 27 Oct 1640; Bartholomew (2nd)[36] b. 26 Feb 1641/42; Martha[37] b. 17 Sep 1643; Jonathan[38] b. 12 Aug 1648; and Joseph[39] b. 8 Nov 1650.

At Woburn, Middlesex county, Massachusetts, in 1652, John Burge[40] sold his house and lands to "Bartholmew Pierson of Watertown." At Woburn, Bartholomew and Ursula Pierson had daughter Mary[41] b. 10 Apr 1652 who d. 21 Dec 1721. Mary Pierson m. 28 Oct 1672 John Richardson at Cambridge, Middlesex county, Massachusetts, and they had Richardson chd. Mary 1674, Jacob 1675, and William 1678.

At Yorkshire, England in "1496[42] A.D., Bartholomew Pearson, of Duffield, took sanctuary in Beverley Minster, for the murder of John Eliot." There is a Duffield in Derbyshire and a North and South Duffield in Yorkshire. Since Beverley Minster is in the East Riding of Yorkshire at Beverley near Kingston on Hull, perhaps one of the Duffields in Yorkshire was intended in this quote. N. and S. Duffield are located near each other at 22 miles west of Beverley near Bubwith which is 5 miles northwest of Howden.

The above reference of Bartholomew Pearson taking sanctuary at Beverley is not intended to connect the Bartholomew Pierson of Watertown, Massachusetts or his ancestors to this incident. It is provided to determine where the name, Bartholomew Pearson, is being used in England. The five miles from Howden, Yorkshire, has led to the discovery that a family with the Bartholomew surname exists in the Howden parish.

John Pearson of Barmby (within Howden parish) was born about 1581 (bur. 6 Apr 1627 of Barmby) and married about 1602 to An (no marriage record found). They had children at Barmby: Elizabeth c. 2 Jul 1603 who m. 5 Feb 1624/5 Thomas Richman of Osgodby; William c. 25 Oct 1605, bur. 3 May 1665 of Barmby; An c. 25 Oct 1605 (twin to William?); Grace c. 3 Sep 1608; Thomas c. 28 Oct 1610; Savage c. 6 Feb 1612/3, bur. 4 Feb 1666/7 Balkholme (within Howden parish), m. 17 Jan 1655/6 Anne Lyon and had chd. John bur. 17 Dec 1658 Laxton; Dorothie c. 2 Mar 1615/6; Robert c. 27 Nov 1619, tailor, bur. 29 Nov 1687, wife Ann bur. 12 Apr 1681 and had chd. Marie, Joseph c. 8 Jul 1649, Robert, & Ann; Dorcas bur. 17 Oct 1624 (no parent given). They may have had an additional child,

---

[34]Watertown, Massachusetts Land Records. First Inventory, p. 63.

[35]Watertown, Massachusetts, *First Book of Births, Marriages and Deaths*, p. 8.

[36]Watertown, Massachusetts, *First Book of Births, Marriages, and Deaths*, p. 9.

[37]Watertown, Massachusetts, *First Book of Births, Marriages, and Deaths*, p. 11.

[38]Watertown (Massachusetts), *First Book of Births, Marriages, and Deaths*, p. 14.

[39]Watertown (Massachusetts), *First Book of Births, Marriages, and Deaths*, p. 15.

[40]*The New England Historical and Genealogical Register*, Volume XL, p. 260.

[41]LDS computer Ancestral File, 1994, from Richardson family records.

[42]Lizzie B. Pierson, *Pierson Genealogical Records*, Joel Munsell, Printer, Albany, New York, 1878, page 70.

Bartholomew Pearson, born about 1618, whom we seek. John's son Thomas, c. 28 Oct 1610 of Barmby, bur. 26 May 1672 Asselby (within the Howden parish), m. 20 May 1638 Marie Underwood (bur. 21 Jan 1670/1) and they had chd. John c. 22 Jan 1638/9, bur. 26 Dec 1639; **Bartholomew** c. 27 Apr 1641, bur. 1 May 1641; and Joseph bur. 29 Dec 1653.

Because of John Pearson's grandson Bartholomew, John's wife An, is believed to be the Anne Bartlemewe c. 4 Sep 1580 at Warborough, Oxfordshire, father Thomas. Her father, Thomas Bartlemewe, was born in 1557 at Barmby in Howden parish, Yorkshire, father Richard Bartlemewe. Richard Bartlemew m. 22 Apr 1553 Alice (surname unknown, bur. 25 Nov 1557) of Barmby and they had chd. at Barmby, Yorkshire: Margareta c. 5 Feb 1553/4, bur. 10 Feb 1553/4; Frances c. 7 Jul 1555, bur. 25 Sep 1555; and Thomas c. 1 Aug 1557. Thomas Bartlemewe married 1st about 1579, wife unknown, and had chd. Anne c. 4 Sep 1580 at Warborough, Oxfordshire. Thomas m. 2nd 11 Nov 1582 Elizabeth James at Warborough and they had chd. at Warborough: Jane c. 9 Jun 1583; Ales c. 19 Apr 1586; and Richard c. 26 Nov 1589. From the Index of Wills[43], Oxfordshire, "Bartelmew als Martine, Thomas, husbandman, 6 Dec 1619, Shellingford near Dorchester, Dorchester Peculiar Court, Will and Inventory." Perhaps the Bartholomew Pearson we seek was born to Anne Bartlomew, wife of John Pearson of Barmby, in 1618 when she went to Oxfordshire to see her ailing father, Thomas. Thus, the birth of Bartholomew could have occurred on a path in England between Howden, Yorkshire, and Warborough, Oxfordshire, and a record of birth or christening may or may not have been registered with a parish. Warborough is located 9 miles SSE of Oxford in Oxfordshire.

Though the christening of Bartholomew Pierson of Watertown, Mass., was not found, he is believed to be from the Howden parish, Yorkshire. Bartholomew Pierson married Ursula about 1638 and they settled in Watertown, Massachusetts, in 1639. This marriage was searched for in England and not found.

No proof of Bartholomew Pierson's relation to the families of the other two brothers of legend was found. However, he is still believed to be one of the three brothers of legend and the only possible connection might be as a 3rd cousin to Henry Peirson and Rev. Abraham Pierson who are probably 2nd cousins to each other. Since we are at the earliest records in England now, it is not likely that the relationship between the three "brothers" of legend will ever be proven.

Suffice it to say that the three brothers legend means: **Abraham, Bartholomew, and Henry Pierson came to New England together, departing London in May 1639, aboard the Mayflower of London.** This is not the pilgrim ship. It probably landed at Boston, Massachusetts, near the end of July 1639. See Chapter 6 on the Pierson Mayflower legend.

Other Pierson Immigrant Inter-Relationships

John Pearson of Yorkshire and Lynn, Massachusetts

According to Lizzie Pierson in her 1878 book[44],"1 John Pearson was born in 1615 in Yorkshire, England. He married Maudlin and they arrived at Lynn (then Saugus),

---

[43]Index of *Wills, Oxfordshire and Buckinghamshire*, England, LDS microfilm No. 0095109.
[44]Lizzie B. Pierson, *Pierson Genealogical Records*, Joel Munsell, Printer, Albany, New York, 1878, page 57.

Massachusetts, in 1637. They had children 2 Mary, 3 Bertha, and 4 Sarah at Lynn; and 5 John (b. 1650/53) and 6 James at Reading, Massachusetts, where they had moved in 1639. John Pearson is said to have been one of seven men who founded the church and town of Reading in that year. John Pearson died at Reading, Massachusetts in 1679." According to Howell[45], 2 "Mary Pierson married at Lynn, Mass., 3 Dec 1663 Thomas Burnett."

If 1 John Pearson's wife, Maudlin, had three children at Lynn between 1637 and 1639, she must have arrived pregnant and left late in 1639 for Reading. The only name basis for a father of John is his first son's name John, though the son could be named after himself. His son James was probably named after James I, king of England 1603-1625 while John was growing up.

While Lizzie Pierson gives "born in 1615 in Yorkshire" as a firm date for John Pearson's birth in her 1878 book, the year is probably an approximation based on John being at least 21 years old at marriage and having his first child in 1637. That formula gives born in 1615 or earlier.

The location of John Pearson at Lynn, Massachusetts, from 1637 to 1639 coincides with the presence of John Cooper and his wife Wyborro, Henry Peirson's step-father and mother, who arrived in Lynn (Saugus) in 1635 aboard the ship Hopewell, and departed in 1640 to settle at Southampton, Long Island. Henry Peirson of Southampton, Long Island, also arrived at Lynn (Saugus) in 1639 from old England (reference a letter from England to Governor Winthrop of the Massachusetts Bay colony in 1640 mentioning a letter from "Henry Person" earlier in Saugus (Lynn); also Henry Peirson's declaration in English court papers that he left England in May 1639). Thus, with all these Peirsons in Lynn at the same time, they must be related in England. It was typical to have someone to sponsor a new individual into a settlement like Lynn, and these seem to be the clues to whom John Pearson knew at Lynn.

Therefore, the criteria for the search in England for John Pearson is: (1) from Yorkshire, England; (2) born in 1615 or earlier; (3) probably related to Henry Peirson of Southampton, Long Island (Henry's father, William, is believed to have been born at Howden in Yorkshire in 1577); and (4) probably has a father named John. Armed with this criteria, the LDS IGI in Yorkshire, England, was searched for John Pearson christenings between 1605 and 1615. One record met all four criteria:

"John Pearson c. 8 Dec 1608 at Howden, Yorkshire, England, father John."

Who is John's father, John Pearson, and what is the relationship to the Henry Peirson line of Southampton, Long Island? There are three John Pearson's having children at about the same time in Howden Parish when our John Pearson of Lynn is born. However, they were easily separated upon close scrutiny of the Howden Parish records[46]. One John Pearson of Barmby within Howden parish m. An (Bartholomew?) and had children from 1603 through

[45]George Rogers Howell, *The Early History of Southampton, L.I., New York*, 2nd Edition, Weed, Parsons and Company, Albany, NY, 1887, p. 206.

[46]*The Registers of the Parish of Howden, Co. York*, Vols. I (published 1904, marriages 1542-1644 and baptisms 1542-1659), & II (published 1905, burials 1543-1659), edited by G. E. Weddall, privately printed for the Yorkshire Parish Register Society, Beck & Inchbold Ltd., Printers, Oriel Press, Leeds, Yorkshire, England.

1619 (including Bartholomew Pearson?) in Barmby. Another John Pearson of Howden and Skelton m. 1584 Elizabeth Stamp and they had children from 1585 through 1592. See Appendix A for details of these two families. The John Pearson (father of John c. 8 Dec 1608 at Howden) was born about 1580 and bur. 7 Feb 1635/6 at Howden, Yorkshire. John (b. ca. 1580) m. 1st 19 Feb 1603/4 Jane (surname unknown, died about 1617), and 2nd ca. 1618 Mary (bur. 16 Oct 1656, of Asselby within Howden parish). John had children by his 1st wife Jane, all at Howden: Elizabeth c. 3 May 1604, bur. 19 Nov 1604; Elizabeth c. 9 Oct 1605, bur. 17 Sep 1607; William c. 5 Nov 1607, bur. 16 Nov 1607; **John c. 8 Dec 1608**; Frances c. 9 Feb 1610/11, bur. 14 Sep 1612; Thomas c. 16 Jan 1612/3; William c. 17 Dec 1614 (died before 1636?); and An c. 11 Feb 1616/7 (sister Hannah of Edward?). John had children by his 2nd wife Mary, all at Howden: Mary c. 27 Mar 1619, bur. (Marie) 22 Nov 1621; Edward c. 11 Nov 1620; Jane c. 15 Dec 1622, bur. 1 Sep 1624; and Elizabeth c. 8 Jan 1624/5.

John Pearson (b. ca. 1580) died in nearby Beverley, Yorkshire, and left a will: "Wills at York. 1636. John Pearson, of Beverley, Mary, widow, children Elizabeth, Thomas, John, and Edward mentioned." As can be seen from the christenings, John c. 8 Dec 1608 is the eldest surviving son in 1636. He now, at age 28, had the money to get married and journey to Lynn, Massachusetts, in America in 1637.

The John Pearson of Beverley (b. about 1580), who had a will in 1636, is believed to be the son of William Peerson who m. 23 Jan 1562/3 Julian Collin at Howden, based upon the rationale of which Pierson family is having children at the time (and considering the children's names). William Peerson (m. 23 Jan 1562/3) is the grandfather of the Rev. Abraham Pierson (1611-1678) and is also believed to be the brother of Thomas Pearson (see Appendix A), the grandfather of Henry Peirson (1615-1680) of Lynn, Massachusetts, and Southampton, Long Island. John (b. about 1580) Pearson's son, Edward Pearson (c. 11 Nov 1620 at Howden), was probably the " Edward Pearson who was at Beverley in 1650[47] with children Mary and Elizabeth, and sister Hannah."

In summary, John Pearson of Lynn (1608-1679) is likely the first cousin of Rev. Abraham Pierson (1611-1678) of Branford, Conn., and Newark, N.J., and he is likely the second cousin of Henry Peirson (1615-1680) of Lynn, Mass., and Southampton, Long Island. John Pierson of Lynn, Massachusetts, was christened 8 Dec 1608 at Howden, Yorkshire, England, parents John and Jane Pearson who married 19 Feb 1603/4. John's father died in 1636 and John came to Lynn, Massachusetts, the following year in 1637. He had wife Maudlin and children at Lynn and Reading, Massachusetts, and died at Reading in 1679 at age 71. For descendants of John Pearson, American immigrant, see Chapter 15.

Thomas Pierson Sr. of Yorkshire and Branford, Connecticut

"Thomas Pierson Sen.[48] is first recorded in America at Branford, Connecticut. The Town Records of Branford say Thos. Pierson mar. Maria Harrison, both of Branford, Nov. 27, 1662. At Branford, (Connecticut) he was closely associated with the Rev. Abraham Pierson (witnessed his will). He was a weaver. Thomas was one of the signers of Heads of Families at Branford Oct. 30, 1666, that agreed to move to Newark, New Jersey.

---

[47]Lizzie B. Pierson, *Pierson Genealogical Records*, Joel Munsell, Printer, Albany, New York, 1878, page 71.

[48]Lizzie B. Pierson, *Pierson Genealogical Records*, Joel Munsell, Printer, Albany, NY, 1878, p. 34.

Accordingly that fall, with Rev. Abraham Pierson at their head, they went to Newark." Thomas had chd. Samuel b. 1663; Hannah; Elizabeth; Abigail; Mary; and Thomas b. 1678.

Excerpts from the will[49] of Thomas Pierson: "Jan. 12, 1697-8. The will of Thomas Pierson Sr. of Newark, New Jersey. Children -- Samuel, Thomas (youngest son), Hannah, Abigail, Mary, Elizabeth. Real and personal estate. Son(-in-law), Samuel Lyon, executor. Witnesses -- Zophar Beech, Jonathan Tichnar, Benjamin Lyon. Proved March 3, 1700/1. May 1, 1701 letters issued to Samuel Lyon, of Newark. E. J. D., Lib. G, pp. 278-279."

Thomas is one generation too young to be a brother of the Rev. Abraham Pierson as suggested by Lizzie Pierson in her book. Lizzie Pierson's comment that Thomas left old England at the same time as Abraham is unsubstantiated as Abraham arrived 1639 and the earliest record for Thomas is his 1662 marriage at Branford, Connecticut. However, Thomas could be a kinsman of the Rev. Abraham Pierson.

Based upon the birth name and date of Thomas Pierson's first child Samuel in 1663, Thomas Pierson's father could be "Samuell c. 27 Feb 1603/4 Guiseley, Yorkshire, England, father Thomas." This Samuell c. 1603/4 is the brother of the Rev. Abraham Pierson (see the earlier analysis under the Rev. Abraham Pierson). If Samuell is Thomas Pierson's father, Thomas would be born in England near Bradford, Yorkshire between 1626 (22 years after his father's birth) and 1641 (21 years before his marriage to Maria Harrison).

Records of Rotherham, Yorkshire, England, show that a Samuel Pierson married 19 Jan 1629/30 Elizabeth Armitage[50]. Rotherham is 29 miles southeast of Bradford, Yorkshire, and Samuell was born at Guiseley, 6 miles north of Bradford. From Dewsbury parish records[51], Samuel and Elizabeth Peirson settled at Dewsbury, Yorkshire, (8 miles southeast of Bradford) where they had children:

1. "A yonge daughter of Mr. Sam. Peirson not baptised was buried" 2 Feb 1630/31;

2. "Samuell son of Mr. Samuell Peirson clerke baptised" 11 Apr 1632;

3. **"Thomas son of Mr. Samuell Pearson baptized" 6 Aug 1634;**

4. "Abraham son of Mr. Samuell Pearson baptised" 1 Dec 1636;

5. "Isaac sonne of Samuell Pierson preacher baptized" 2 Oct 1639;

6. "Elizabeth daughter of Mr. Samuell Pierson baptized" 20 Apr 1642;

7. "James son of Mr. Samuell Pierson baptized" 29 Jun 1648.

The children born at Dewsbury are certain to belong to the Rev. Abraham Pierson's brother Samuell because of the match of the children's names to Samuell (b. 1604), the Rev. Abraham (b. 1611), their brother Isaac, and their father Thomas. The birth date criteria for

[49]Edited by A. Van Doren Honeyman, *Documents Relating to the Colonial History of the State of New Jersey*, Volume II -- 1730-1750, The Unionist-Gazette Association, Printers, Somerville, N.J., p. 563.

[50]LDS International Genealogical Index, 1994.

[51]Samuel Joseph Chadwick, *The Registers of Dewsbury, Yorkshire, Vol. 1, 1538-1653*, Joseph Ward & Co., Dewsbury, Record Series of the Yorkshire Archaeological Society, no publication date given (near 1900), pp. 123, 125, 130, 136, 141, 147, 160.

the Thomas we seek is met with this 1634 christening record for Thomas, son of Samuell, at Dewsbury.

The marriage of Samuel Pierson to Elizabeth Armitage 19 Jan 1629/30 at Rotherham is confirmed as the one we seek by her child named Elizabeth and her death record at Dewsbury[52]:

"Elizabeth wife of Samuell Pierson Vicar of Dewsburie buried the 27th day September 1651."

Elizabeth Armitage's christening was not found at Rotherham where the marriage took place. In searching for her christening in Yorkshire, the most likely result was "Elizabeth Armitage c. 31 Jul 1603 at Calverley, Yorkshire, father Thomas Armitage." Calverley is located 3 miles south of Guiseley where Samuel Pierson was christened. It is likely that Samuel Pierson and Elizabeth Armitage grew up together. It is not known why they went to Rotherham to get married.

We are witnessing an occupation promotion for Samuell Peirson in the baptisms and burial above where he is a clerk in 1632, a preacher in 1639 (achieved in 1633), and vicar in 1651 (achieved in 1642). Dewsbury parish records reflect that the Rev. Samuell Pierson had the following activities:

> 26 Jan 1632/3, baptised Alice Rodlye at home in the night of Saturday.
> 11 Apr 1632, listed as clerke at his son Samuel's baptism.
> 28 May 1635, baptised Timothye Brooke at Ossett Chappell.
> 10 Jun 1635, married a couple at Woodchurche.
> 25 Nov 1635, married a couple at Mourley Chappell.
> 2 Oct 1639, listed as preacher at his son Isaac's baptism.

Lizzie Pierson said of Samuel Pierson in her 1878 book[53], "In 1642, the Rev. Samuel Pearson was presented to the vicarage of Dewsbury in Yorkshire, vacated by Rev. H. Adams." His career was further elaborated on in the transcribed registers of Dewsbury[54]:

A couple "maryed by * Samuell Pearson, clarke, preacher at Dewsburye of God's worde." *(footnote) "The Rev. Samuel Pearson became Vicar of Dewsbury in July 1642 and was buried 6th October 1656. He brought an action against the Vicars of Huddersfield, Almondbury, Kirkheaton, and Bradford, to recover the pensions payable by them to him as Vicar of Dewsbury; and the depositions in this action, taken in Michaelmas Term (the quarter of the year containing September 29), 1653, are printed in the 26th and 27th Articles on Dewsbury Parish Church, which appeared some years ago in the *Dewsbury Reporter*. Mr. Pearson is said to have been ejected from his living by the Puritans (during Cromwell's reign), but if so , he must have been allowed to return, for he obtained an order dated 4th November, 1651, from the Committee for Plundered Ministers, for £30 a year, to be paid for increase of his maintenance, out of the impropriate titles of Hartshead, and this allowance

---

[52]Samuel Joseph Chadwick, *The Registers of Dewsbury, Yorkshire, Vol. 1, 1538-1653*, Joseph Ward & Co., Dewsbury, Record Series of the Yorkshire Archaeological Society, no publication date given (near 1900), p. 165.

[53]Lizzie B. Pierson, *Pierson Genealogical Records*, Joel Munsell, Printer, Albany, New York, 1878, p. 70.

[54]Samuel Joseph Chadwick, *The Registers of Dewsbury, Yorkshire, Vol. 1, 1538-1653*, Joseph Ward & Co., Dewsbury, Record Series of the Yorkshire Archaeological Society, no publication date given (near 1900), p. 115 & footnote.

continued to be made until sometime in the year 1655, when we find Mr. Pearson petitioning the Commissioners for Managing Estates Under Sequestration, that the allowance may be continued to him and the arrears paid (Royalist Composition Papers, 1st Series, Vol. 50, p. 317). The above-mentioned tithes would be part of the property of the Rectory of Dewsbury, which in 1348, was appropriated to St. Stephen's College, Westminster."

In summary, it is probable that Thomas Pierson Sr. of Branford, Connecticut, was christened 6 Aug 1634 at Dewsbury, Yorkshire, England, father Rev. Samuell Pierson (c. 27 Feb 1603/4 Guiseley, Yorkshire), grandfather Thomas Pearson (c. 17 Jul 1574 Howden, Yorkshire). By this analysis, the Rev. Abraham Pierson is Thomas Pierson Sr.'s uncle. Thomas Pierson probably emigrated from England to New England sometime between his 21st birthday (1655) and his marriage at Branford, Connecticut, 27 Nov 1662 to Maria Harrison of Branford. The most likely emigration year would be 1661 after training as a weaver was complete and after Puritan rule in England ended in 1660. See the section under Rev. Abraham Pierson above for ancestors of Thomas Pierson's father, Samuell, of Guiseley and Dewsbury in Yorkshire, England. See Chapter 13 for descendants of Thomas Pierson Sr.

Stephen Pierson of Suffolk County, England, and Derby, Connecticut

In 1895, Frederick Lockwood Pierson provided the following several paragraphs: "Stephen Pierson[55], the Immigrant Ancestor, born in Suffolk County, England, in 1645, was apprenticed there by his mother (probably a widow) to Thomas Mulliner of Branford, Conn., to learn the carpenter trade, and landed at New Haven in 1654. Mulliner first appeared in New Haven in 1640. June 30, 1657, Stephen Pierson testified in court in New Haven in a case of slander brought by Meeker against Mulliner for saying that Meeker's pigs were bewitched. In Oct., 1658, Stephen Pierson appeared in the Probate Court at New Haven in a complaint made against Thomas Mulliner for not fulfilling an agreement to teach him the carpenter trade. On March 15, 1667, Stephen Pierson was one of eight recorded residences of Derby, then called Paugassett, and in all probability was there in 1666. His first wife, and mother of all his children, was Mary Tomlinson, daughter of Henry Tomlinson and his wife Alice _____ of Stratford, Connecticut."

"Henry Tomlinson came from Watertown, Mass., in 1644; to Milford, Conn., in 1652; and thence to Stratford, Conn., in 1665, where he died in 1681. His widow, Alice, married John Birdsey Sr. under a contract of Oct. 8, 1688."

"Henry Tomlinson[56] was son of George Tomlinson and Maria Hyde of Yorkshire, England, who married in Jan. 1600. They moved from Yorkshire to Derby, Derbyshire. Henry was a weaver by trade."

Since this statement by Frederick Lockwood Pierson in 1895, parish records provide that: Henry Tomlinson c. 22 Nov 1606 St. Peters, Derby, Derbyshire, England, father George

---

[55]Frederick Lockwood Pierson, *The Descendants of Stephen Pierson of Suffolk County, England and New Haven and Derby, Conn., 1645-1739*, Walsh & Griffen, Printers, Amenia, N.Y., 1895, p.3.
[56]Frederick Lockwood Pierson, *The Descendants of Stephen Pierson of Suffolk County, England and New Haven and Derby, Conn., 1645-1739*, Walsh & Griffen, Printers, Amenia, N.Y., 1895, p.32, notes & errata.

Tomlinson, mother Maria Hyde. George Tomlinson m. 19 Jan 1600 Maria Hyde, St. Peters, Derby, Derbyshire, England. Georgius (George) Tomlinson c. 16 Aug 1567, Howden, Yorkshire, England, father Johannis (John) Tomlinson (mother Barbara). The location of George Tomlinson's christening at Howden is interesting in that the ancestors of Henry Peirson of Southampton, Long Island, New York Colony (1640), the Rev. Abraham Pierson of the same place and time, John Pierson of Lynn, Massachusetts (1637), Thomas Pierson of Branford, Connecticut (1662) and probably Bartholomew Pierson of Watertown, Massachusetts (1639) all descend from Howden, Yorkshire, England.

"Stephen Pierson's wife, Mary Tomlinson, died in Derby Sept. 25, 1715. Stephen died in Derby (now Oxford) May 14, 1739, aged 94, leaving a second wife, Esther.

"Children of the Immigrant, Stephen Pierson and Mary Tomlinson, all born in Derby, Connecticut: Sarah m. 21 Jan 1679(/80?) John Twitchell; Stephen Jr. (eldest son), m. 12 Oct 1697 Mehetabel Canfield; Mary m. 19 Sep 1700 Josiah Baldwin; Joseph, who drew lots in Derby March 12, 1702, probably another son of Stephen; John, probably a bachelor, d. about 1704; Abraham (called Sergeant) b. 1681, m. Sarah _____; Bathsheba m. Adam Blackman of Stratford, Connecticut; Daniel (b. ca. 1687), who drew lots in Oxford in 1713, was probably their son, but could find no proof of that." See chapter 14 for further descendants of Stephen Pierson.

The statements in Frederick Pierson's book indicate that Stephen Pierson immigrated to Branford, Connecticut, in 1654 at the age of nine to take on an apprenticeship. In searching Suffolk County, England for Stephen's christening record, the best fit from the LDS IGI records was:

"Stephen Peirson c. 13 Feb 1642/3 Ubbeston, Suffolk, England, father Edward Peirson, mother Anne." This information was confirmed in Ubbeston parish records[57].

If this is the correct choice, Stephen would be 11 years old when immigrating in 1654 and 96 years old at death. It makes his apprentice age reasonable. To check this christening record, we will list all Peirson families of Ubbeston to see if Stephen's father dies or stops having children because his mother is probably a widow in 1654. Ubbeston is located 22 miles NNE of Ipswich.

The earliest Peirson family recorded at Ubbeston[58] in Suffolk county is "Richard Peirson and wife Anna who had chd. Mary c. 28 Apr 1586, John c. 24 Dec 1587, Sara c. 27 Dec 1590, Sara (2nd) c. 16 Apr 1593, and Judith c. 28 Mar 1597."

The next oldest family recorded at Ubbeston[59] and believed to be of direct lineage to Stephen is "**Edward Peirson** who had chd. **Edward c. 10 Jul 1600**, Elizabethe c. 18 Mar 1605/6 (no parents given), Steven c. 15 Nov 1608, Edmund c. 27 Nov 1611, Sara c. 30 Apr 1614, and Anne c. 23 Nov 1620. "Elizabethe" was attached to this family because no other

---

[57]LDS microfilm No. 0919634, Church of England, Parish Church of Ubbeston (Suffolk Co.), original Parish Registers, 1555-1837.

[58]LDS microfilm No. 0919634, Church of England, Parish Church of Ubbeston (Suffolk Co.), original Parish Registers, 1555-1837.

[59]LDS microfilm No. 0919634, Church of England, Parish Church of Ubbeston (Suffolk Co.), original Parish Registers, 1555-1837.

Peirson was having children in Ubbeston in 1605 and a hole in the child spacing was available there. These two Edwards are believed to be Stephen's father and grandfather because they are at the same town in which Stephen was christened and the name "Steven" is carried in this line and no other there. From Ubbeston Parish records, Edward Peirson Sr. was buried at Ubbeston 2 Apr 1628.

Stephen's parents in Ubbeston, Suffolk County, are believed to be "**Edward Peirson (c. 10 Jul 1600)** and Anne who had chd. Leonard c. 19 Apr 1640, **Stephen c. 13 Feb 1642/3**, and Thomas c. 13 Jan 1644/5. This data fits the story about his mother (Anne as seen here) sending Stephen to Branford, Connecticut, for an apprenticeship. He would be traveling at the age of 11 years in 1654. If his mother Anne was a widow in 1654, no more children would be born after about 1653 (and in this case no children occur after 1645).

Per Haveningham Parish records[60], "Edward Peirson & Anne Clough were married 22 Dec 1631." Haveningham is located one mile east of Ubbeston, in Suffolk County. Therefore, this is believed to be the correct marriage and wife's maiden name. That would make Edward about age 31 at marriage, if he is the one christened in 1600. Since there is nine years between the marriage date and the first child's christening found, Suffolk County was searched for another location they may have lived at during those years but no other christenings were found.

An Edward Pearson was known to be a member of King Charles' army in 1638-9:

"Muster Rolls for Military Service 32 Counties in England[61], 5 Jan 1638-9, Suffolk County (ages 16-60), Hundred of Loe, Marlesford, **Edward Pearson**." Marlesford is located 10 miles south of Ubbeston. With the christening of the last child Thomas on 13 Jan 1644/5, Edward Peirson could have died in battle in 1644 or 1645. In 1644, Cromwell's Puritans defeated Charles' Cavaliers at Marston Moor (six miles west of York in Yorkshire). In 1645, Cromwell gained a decisive victory over Charles' army at Naseby, Northamptonshire (not far from Suffolk County). Based on this information, it would be fair to say that Stephen's father, Edward, probably died about 1645.

In summary, Stephen Pierson of Branford and Derby, Connecticut, was christened 13 Feb 1642/3 at Ubbeston, Suffolk County, England. His parents were Edward Peirson and Anne Clough. The widow Anne (Clough) Peirson sent Stephen to Branford, Connecticut, for his apprenticeship. Edward Peirson was christened 10 Jul 1600 at Ubbeston, Suffolk County, England, father Edward, and died about 1645 probably a casualty of the English civil war. Stephen Pierson died at Derby, Connecticut, on 14 May 1739 at age 96. For descendants of Stephen Pierson, American immigrant, see Chapter 14.

---

[60]LDS microfilm No. 0919613, Church of England, Parish Church of Haveningham, "Parish Registers, 1539-1886."
[61]Able Men of Suffolk (England) 1638, Calkins Press, Boston, Mass., 1931, p. 38.

Chapter 5
Pierson Coats of Arms (all spellings)

(England, Scotland, Ireland, Wales, and Netherlands)

In the period from King William I through King Richard III (1066-1485), knights increased the amount of armor that they wore until it completely covered their heads and bodies. There grew up the custom of emblazoning devices on shields and surcoats so that the soldiers could find their commanders and rally around them in the press of battle. The surcoat, a garment worn over the body armor, was the original 'coat of arms.' Heraldry gets its name from the heralds who were the official representatives of kings and lords. They were the masters of ceremony at tournaments. They were also the court chroniclers, and it was their duty to keep track of family relationships and of the intricate etiquette governing coats of arms.

A complete coat of arms is known in heraldry as the achievement. It always includes the shield or escutcheon, which is the most important element, the crest, and the motto. The achievement may also be embellished with a helmet; a torse or wreath out of which the crest rises above the helmet; and the mantling or lambrequin which is a scarflike decoration hanging from the helmet. The lambrequin's two sides are of different colors, so it is doubled over in places to show both surfaces. The blazon is the verbal description of a shield. The dexter is the side of the shield at the right of the person wearing it and the sinister at the left of the person wearing it. The color of the field is always named first (in Norman French as all blazons were written by heralds); then the principal charge or charges with their location and color; then the secondary charges. The charge is a figure or symbol on the shield. A great variety of charges are used, including geometrical figures, weapons, animals, and plants. A common charge is the lion in various positions: rampant (erect on one hind leg); passant (walking); couchant (lying with the head raised); or dormant (asleep).

Sir Bernard Burke, Ulster King of Arms, published his book[1] of Coats of Arms in 1842, and second edition in 1884. It represents a complete United Kingdom registry of coats of arms from 1200 to 1884 and is based upon the heraldic writings of Dugdale, Camden, Guillim, Edmondson, Berry, Nicolas, county histories, and the herald's visitations to counties from 1500 to 1699. It contains 29 Pierson, Peirson, or Pearson coats of arms.

The heraldic writings are based on the following documents:

The earliest English heraldic record is the "Roll of Arms" written between 1240 and 1245. It included the names and Arms of the Barons and Knights of the reign of Henry III (1216-1272).

---

[1]Sir Bernard Burke, Ulster King of Arms, *The General Armory of England, Scotland, Ireland and Wales, comprising a Registry of Armorial Bearings from the Earliest to the Present Time*, Harrison and Sons, Printers in Ordinary to Her Majesty, London, England, First published 1842, Second Edition (with Supplement) 1884, Facsimile Edition by photolitho 1961, Second Impression 1962.

In February 1301, a poem "The Siege of Caerlaverock" was written describing the Banners of the Peers and Knights of the English army under King Edward I who were present at the siege of Caerlaverock Castle in Scotland in 1300/01.

Between 1308 and 1314, "The Roll of Arms of the time of Edward II" was written. This list was divided into counties and included the names and arms of about 1,160 persons. It is kept in the Cottonian Library, British Museum.

Between 1337 and 1350, "The Fourth Roll in the time of Edward III" was compiled embracing the arms of all the Peers and Knights in England in the order: (1) The King, the Earls and Barons, (2) The Knights under their respective counties, and (3) The Great Personages who lived in earlier times.

Ensigns (Coats of Arms) were, in the beginning, taken up at any gentleman's pleasure, yet they were later made the rewards of merit or the gracious favors of princes. In the reign of Henry V (1413-1422), a proclamation was issued prohibiting the use of heraldic ensigns to all who could not show an original and valid right, except those "who had borne arms at Agincourt." The Battle of Agincourt[2], fought 25 October 1415 near the village of Agincourt in northern France, was the third great battle won by the English against the French during the Hundred Years' War (1337-1453). Shortly after the battle, Henry V knighted a number of his followers and confirmed the armorial bearings of all of those who had borne them "at Agincourt." In spite of the proclamation by Henry V, abuses of the use of Ensigns occurred causing Herald's Visitations, documents of high authority and value, beginning in the early 1500s and lasting approximately every generation for 200 years. All persons who could deduce descent from an ancestor whose armorial ensigns had been acknowledged, in any one of the Visitations, were entitled to carry those Arms by right of inheritance. Otherwise, bearers must be grantees or descendants of grantees. In England and Wales, Arms were granted under the authority of the Earl Marshal by the Garter King of Arms and one of the Provincial King of Arms, according to his jurisdiction. In Scotland, Arms were granted by the Lyon King of Arms, and in Ireland, the Ulster King of Arms.

Below are listed 34 Pierson, Peirson, and Pearson Coats of Arms including 29 from Burke's *General Armory*, one from the Herald's visitation of London 1568, two corroborating that family from Lizzie Pierson's 1878 *Pierson Genealogical Records* English Notes, one from Burke's *Encyclopedia of Heraldry*, and one from Rietstap's *Armorial General*. These knights are all believed to be descendants of the Viking villagers of Pericne dating from about 1100 AD in the East Riding of Yorkshire, England.

---

[2]Compton's Encyclopedia, F. E. Compton Co., Chicago, Illinois, Vol. 1, p. 100.

The heralds of England recorded all coats of arms in Norman French. The listings from Burke and Rietstap combine English and Norman French. The more common French and heraldic terms are defined as:

gules (gu.)	Red.	or	Gold.
azure (az.)	Blue.	vert	Green.
argent (ar.)	Silver.	sable (sa.)	Black.
proper (ppr.)	Natural colors.	ermine (erm.)	White fur with black spots.
of the first	Of the 1st color mentioned. erminois		Gold fur with black spots.

of the second	Of the 2d color mentioned.
fess	Centered horizontal bar.
per fess	Centered horizontal line.
pale	Centered vertical bar.
per pale	A vertical line separating left and right shield.
chevron (chev.)	Inverted V, usually separating upper & lower shield.
per chevron	Inverted V line separating upper & lower shield.
chevronel	Narrow inverted V, usually borne in two or more.
canton	A square area filling one third of chief (upper third of the shield) on the dexter side unless stated as sinister.
dexter	The right side of the wearer.
sinister	The left side of the wearer.
embattled (emb.)	Crenallated, the apertures of an embattled wall showing.
indented	A notched line.

The Entitlement to Bear Arms

No one is entitled to bear arms unless they have been granted by the College of Arms in England, Lyon office Edinburgh in Scotland, the Chief Herald of Ireland or by the Heraldic authority of the country from which the armiger originated, or they can trace lineal male descent, which must be conclusively proved, from a properly registered armiger[3].

In Scotland, the right to bear arms does not extend to younger sons until the arms have been matriculated with such marks of cadency as the Lord Lyon may determine. The bearings thus differenced again descend to the heir male whose younger brothers must again matriculate to receive further differences.

Armigerous persons may display their arms in one or more of the following places: a Heraldic banner; wall plaques and paintings for use in the house; on the side of a vehicle; on decorative scroll work either on gates or on furniture; table silver and table mats; cigarette boxes; cigarette cases; lighters; cuff links; rings; stationery, seals and bookplates.

---

[3] Colonel A. G. Puttock, *A Dictionary of Heraldry and Related Subjects*, Genealogical Publishing Co., Inc., Baltimore, Maryland, 1970.

England

The Three Suns Group

A **sun** is generally borne in splendour which is represented by a charge with a human face (eyes, nose and mouth) drawn within the circle of the sun which is encircled by rays. The "sun in splendour" was one of the two badges used by King Richard II who reigned 1377-1399. A badge is a mark of distinction somewhat similar to a crest but not placed on a wreath nor worn on the helmet. In early days it was generally embroidered upon the sleeves of servants and followers.

(1) "PIERSON (co. Devon). Per fess embattled gu. and az. **three suns** in splendour or. Crest - Out of a mural coronet chequy or and az. a parrot's head ppr."

The "Crest" is a leather or metal object worn atop the helmet for recognition. A "mural coronet" or "mural crown" is a circlet with four block-like embattlements, three of which appear in representation with lines showing the individual mason blocks (called masoned and embattled). 'Chequy or and az.' is French for checkered gold and blue. The mural coronet frequently appears in civic Heraldry.

(2) "PIERSON (co. Bedford). Per fess embattled gu. and az. **three suns** or." This blazon is identical to the one for "(1) Pierson of Devon county", "(3) Pierson portion of Pierson/Gwynne impalement of London", and "(5) Pierson of Stafford" except that no crest is given. Therefore, these Piersons are related to the Pierson of Bedford county who registered this coat of arms.

(3) PIERSON/GWYNNE (London), 1568. The herald's *Visitation of London 1568*[4] provides the Pierson ensign above impaled with what is believed to be the ensign of Gwynne of Windsor and also provides some pedigree information on the Piersons of this ensign:

"**PIERSON** 33b[5] (collated with College of Arms MSS G.10. f.44 and F.1. 314b and Harleian Society volume 31):

ARMS: DEXTER: Per fesse embattled gules and azure, **three suns** in splendour or.

CREST: On a torse or and gules a bird close vert, beaked and legged gules. [The bird is drawn like a chough (a European bird of the crow family with red legs and beak and glossy black feathers) in Queen's College MS 72, College of Arms MS G.10 and F.1, although Harleian Society vol. 31 describes it as a parrot.]

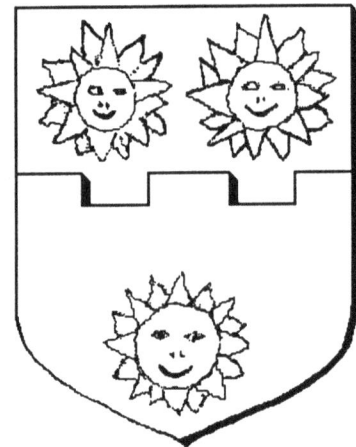

---

[4] *The 1568 Visitation of London* from MS 72 in the Library of the Queen's College, Oxford, England.

[5] Sophia W. Rawlins, edited from the transcripts prepared and annotated by the late H. Stanford London, Norfolk Herald Extraordinary, *Visitation of London 1568 with Additional Pedigrees 1569-90, the Arms of the City Companies and a London Subsidy Roll 1589*, The Harleian Society, Vols. 109 & 110 for the years 1957 & 1958, printed by John Whitehead and Son Limited, London, Great Britain, 1963, p. 34.

SINISTER: Pierson impaling an unfinished trick with a fesse, and a demi-beast in base. [The impaled coat in College of Arms MS F.1 seems to be *Azure, on a fess gules between three beasts* (hinds?) *statant argent 3 chevrons* (?) *or*. What the charges on the fesse are meant for is quite uncertain; they look like rather narrow inverted letters V (three chevronels). Presumably the coat is for Gwynne of Windsor.]

The 17 of June (1568). **Thomas Pierson** of Barkinge in Essex maryed the doughter of John Brooke of Ilford and by her hathe yssue: Thomas Pierson his eldist Sonne; Johan maryed to John Frithe of Essex.

Thomas Pierson of London gent. Citesen and Skryvenor of the same Citie maryed Johan the doughter of Mathew Gwynne of Wyndesor and by her hathe yssue: John his eldist Sonne is of the age of xxi yeres; Mary maryed unto John Chilester of London goldsmythe; Elizabethe and Philip are unmaryed. [In College of Arms MS G.10. 'citesen' to 'Citie' is omitted, and also John's age.]"

(4) PIERSON (co. Essex). Lizzie Pierson in *Pierson Genealogical Records* further identifies the family above[6]:

"Pierson of Essex: Saye Pierson, of Barking, Essex, h. chd. John or Thomas of Barking, who mar. dau. of John Broke, of Ilford. Their chd. were Joane (w. of J. Frith), and Thomas, of London, who mar. Joane Gwynne, of Windsor. The last Thomas had chd. Edw., John, Mary (mar. J. Chichester, of London), Eliz., and Philip.

Arms, Party per chevron indented gu. and b. (blue) **three suns** or. Crest, a parrot vert beaked and legged gu."

"1582, Thomas Pearson, bought manor of Little, Ilford, Essex." This belongs to the Thomas that married Joane Gwynne of Windsor.

The blazon listed above under Pierson of Essex does not match the other descriptions, and it seems to be a differencing rather than a marshalling of the Pierson and Gwynne ensigns. The indented chevron is the type of differencing attributed to a 4th son. So perhaps this is the ensign of Philip, son of Thomas. No registration of this indented chevron ensign being granted was found in official heraldic records.

(5) PIERSON (co. Stafford). Lizzie Pierson in *Pierson Genealogical Records* further identifies the families above[7]:

"Peirsons of Stafford: 1 Thomas Pearson, of Barking, Essex, h. w. (dau. of John Brooke of Ilford) and chd. 2 John, 3 Thomas, and Joanna. 2 John, h. chd. Eliz., Cath., and Anne. 3 Thomas, h. chd. Eliz. (w. of William Brookbank), Mary (w. of John Chillister) of London, 4 Edward of London, and 5 John of London. 4 Edward, h. w. Marg't Richardson, and chd. 9 Edward, living in Stafford 1614 (w. was Joan Mead)

---

[6]Lizzie B. Pierson, *Pierson Genealogical Records*, Joel Munsell, Printer, Albany, New York, 1878, pages 70-73.
[7]Lizzie B. Pierson, *Pierson Genealogical Records*, Joel Munsell, Printer, Albany, New York, 1878, pages 70-73.

who had chd. 10 Edw. and Jane. 5 John, h. w. Eliz. Brett, and chd. 6 Thomas and 7 John. 6 Thomas (w. was dau. of Barnes of Essex), h. chd. 8 Thomas and Mary.

The coat of arms, party per fess emb. g. (gules, red) and b. (blue) **three suns** or. Crest, a parrot vert beaked and legged gu."

The blazon of the Peirsons of Stafford matches the arms of (1) PIERSON (co. Devon), (2) PIERSON (co. Bedford), and (3) the PIERSON portion of the PIERSON/GWYNNE impaling. This ensign represents Edward Pierson, who had father Edward and wife Joan Mead.

Because there is several mentions above of Barking in Essex for this family, an explanation of its location is needed. Currently, Barking in Essex is part of Greater London. Thus, this location is sometimes improperly confused with Bocking in Essex or Barking in Suffolk. Combining the family data, the six Pierson (Peirson, Pearson) generations that belong to the above coats of arms are:

I. Saye Pierson (b. ca. 1475) of Barking (now Greater London), Essex, had son:

A. Thomas Pierson (b. ca. 1500) of Barking, Essex, married a daughter of John Brooke of Ilford, and had children:

1. Thomas (b. ca. 1525), his eldest son, of London, gent., citizen, and scribe; married Johan (Joane) daughter of Mathew Gwynne of Windsor (Berkshire); Pierson coat of arms (three sons in splendour) recorded as impaled with Gwynne of Windsor (three chevronels) on 17 Jun 1568; bought Manor of Little in 1582 at Ilford (now Greater London), Essex , and had children:

(1) John of London, eldest son, age 21 in 1568 (b. 1547), married Elizabeth Brett (who was a widow in 1606), and had children:

i. Thomas, married (27 Nov 1606) a daughter of Barnes of Essex (Mary Barnes of Barking, now Greater London), had children Thomas and Mary.

ii. John.

(2) Mary of London, married John Chillester of London, goldsmith.

(3) Elizabethe, unmarried 1568, married William Brookbank.

(4) Philip, unmarried 1568.

(5) Edward of London, married Margaret Richardson, and had Edward (living in Stafford 1614) who married Joan Mead and had children Edward and Jane.

2. Johan (Joane), married John Frithe (Frith) of Essex.

3. John, had children Elizabeth, Catherine, and Anne.

(6)"PEARSON, or PIERSON (London). Per fesse embattled az. and gu. **three suns** or." This blazon uses a blue fess instead of the red fess in other blazons above. Notice the two surname spellings provided by the herald. This is the period when the surnames previously spelled as Peresone, Pearsonne, and Pearson are being changed to be spelled

Pierson, Peirson, and Person by some families. This resulted in Pearson, Pierson, and Peirson as the most common modern spellings which derive from the same families. The objective in changing the spelling was to gain correct pronunciation of the surname. Thus different regions tend to use the spelling that works best there. For example, Pearson in Scotland.

(7)"PEARSON, or PIERSON. Per fesse embattled az. and gu. **three suns** or. Crest - Three savages' heads conjoined in one neck, one looking to the dexter, one to the sinister, and one upwards."

The blue fess is again used in this blazon. Perhaps the crest represents Pierson families migrating in three different directions.

(8)"PIERSON (Dean of Salisbury, Wiltshire). Per fess az. and gu. **three suns** or. Crest - A demi lion ppr. holding in the dexter paw a sun or."

This escutcheon is similar to (6) and (7) Pierson, but has been differenced by omitting the embattlement on the fess. A crest is not part of the escutcheon passed down father to son. Since the escutcheon retains the three gold suns, fess, and the two colors, it is believed to belong to a descendant of (6) or (7) Pierson. Salisbury is located in Wiltshire 30 miles northwest of the Isle of Wight. 'Dean' is the title of the presiding official of a cathedral or collegiate church.

(9)"PIERSON. Sa. **three suns** in pale or., betw. two palets erminois."

Here, the three gold suns are in a vertical row in the black pale with a vertical row of erminois on each side. Erminois is a fur in heraldry and is represented by a gold field with black spots. Because the blazon is similar to (10) Pearson, its owners may be related to that family.

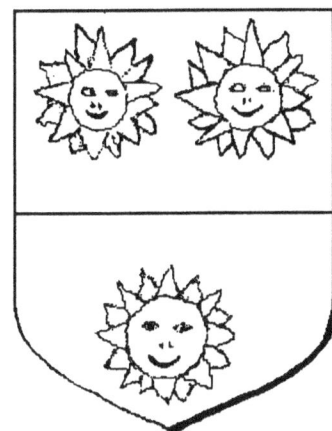

(10)"PEARSON (Tyers Hill, co. York). Az. betw. two pallets wavy erm. **three suns** or. Crest - A sun ppr. issuing out of a cloud."

Erm. is the abbreviation for ermine, a fur in heraldry, and is represented by a white field with black spots. The three gold suns would be placed vertically on a blue field centered between the two ermine pallets with wavy borders. This crest is similar to part of the badge ("the sun's rays descending from clouds proper") of King Edward III who reigned 1327-1377.

"Tyers Hill" has not been located in Yorkshire, England, but a similar named place, "Tyresall," is stated in two Pearson records in the LDS IGI . Perhaps these are the Pearsons of this coat of arms (see below). The year of the herald's visitation is unknown, but a Yorkshire visitation is noted in (11) Pearson of 1665.

"John Pearson born 5 Jul 1640 Tyresall, father Chrystopher;" and

"Chrystopher Pearson born 1642 Tyresall, father Chrystopher."

(11)"PEARSON (Lowthorpe, co. York, 1665). Per fesse embattled gu. and az. **three suns** in splendour or, a canton ar."

This is the same blazon as (1) and (2) Pierson except that it has been differenced by adding a silver canton. A canton is placed in the upper corner (right side of the wearer, left side as you view it), represented by a square consuming about a third of the chief. The chief is the upper third of the shield. In this case, no charge has been placed in the canton. Lowthorpe is in the East Riding of Yorkshire, 14 miles north of Beverley, and about 9 miles north of the vill of Pericne.

This coat of arms appears to belong to John Pearson and his three sons William, John, and Matthew Pearson of Lowthorpe in 1665 (see the family below):

"Pearson of Yorkshire[8].   Mathew Pearson from I. of Cley, came to reside at Cleveland, Yorkshire, and h. chd. 1 John, of Cleveland, who mar. Jane Philip. 1 John, h. chd. 2 Thomas of Harpsham, York, d. 1640 (who mar. Marg't Philips); 3 William, of Cleveland; and 4 Matthew, of Kilham. 2 Thomas, h. chd. 5 William of Besingby, and **6 John of Lowthorpe, b. 1589 (who mar. Eliz. dau. of John Pearson of Mowthorpe). 6 John h. chd. 57 William, 58 John and 59 Matthew.**"

Cleveland is believed to be the region around the Cleveland Hills in North Riding of Yorkshire which in 1974 became a new county named Cleveland which encompasses part of North Riding (Yorkshire) and part of Durham county on both sides of the Tees River. "Besingby" is the Bessingby located 10 miles northeast of Great Driffield near Bridlington in Yorkshire. "Mowthorpe" is the Mowtharp located 4 miles west of Scarborough on the sea. "Lowthorpe" is the Lowthorpe located 4 miles northeast of Great Driffield, and "Kilham" is located 3 miles north of Lowthorpe.

(12)"PEARSON (granted, 1714, to Hugh Pearson, son of Matthew Pearson, son of Daniel Pearson, descended from a family of Pearson, of Wisbeach, Isle of Ely, Cambridge). Per fess embattled az. and gu. **three suns** in splendour or. Crest - On a mural crown or, a paroquet vert, beaked and legged gu."

This is the same blazon as (6) Pierson of London and (7) Pierson of unknown location. The identification below of the Pearson families related to Hugh Pearson will provide the Pierson families associated with all three of these coats of arms.

The following may be ancestors of Hugh Pearson:

"Pierson of Cambridge[9]. Nick. Peerson, was descendant of Personnes of Yorkshire, and had chd. Thomas, of Wisbeach, Cambridge, who mar. Eliz. Gayton. This Thomas had chd. Thomas, 1619, who h. w. Mary Best, and chd. Eliz., Anna, Thomas, Robert and Andrew."

---

[8]Lizzie B. Pierson, *Pierson Genealogical Records*, Joel Munsell, Printer, Albany, New York, 1878, page 72.
[9]Lizzie B. Pierson, *Pierson Genealogical Records*, Joel Munsell, Printer, Albany, New York, 1878, pages 70-73.

The Two Chevronels Group

A chevron is an ordinary said to have been derived from a pair of rafters and occupying approximately one fifth of the field. It has a diminutive called a **chevronel** which is generally about half the width of a chevron.

(13)"PIERSON (cos. Gloucester and Hertford, and Westminster; granted 1577; borne by Pierson, of Hitchin, co. Hertford). Ar. **two chev.** sa. on a canton of the last an eagle displ. of the first. Crest - Out of a ducal coronet or, an ostrich's head betw. two ostrich feathers ar."

Westminster is now part of greater London. An "eagle displayed or" was part of the badge of King Henry IV who reigned 1399-1413. The eagle displayed in the canton here is silver, whereas the eagle displayed in the badge of King Henry IV was gold.

The crest coronet is usually emblazoned as "a ducal coronet" but it has no relationship to ducal rank and no resemblance to the coronet worn by the Duke. It was originally used as an alternative to the wreath. The wreath was a six-fold band placed on top of a helm and said to represent the "lady's favour" with which the old knights went into battle. The crest coronet is seldom granted today but is frequently found in earlier arms. It is represented by a silver gilt circlet chased as if gemmed, but with no actual jewels, surmounted by four strawberry leaves, of which one and two halves are visible to the viewer and between each pair of leaves stands a small silver gilt protuberance fully surrounded by nine small circlets.

Ostrich feathers were used in the badges of King Stephen (reigned 1135-1154, "ostrich feathers in plume") and King Edward III (reigned 1327-1377, "an ostrich feather and also a falcon").

Since we know where and when this coat of arms was placed, the following information on the family is provided from christening and marriage records at Hitchin in Hertfordshire.

Four Peerson families were known to be present at Hitchin in Hertfordshire:

> Symon Peerson who had son Richard c. 1562 at St. Mary.

> John Peerson who had son John c. 1562 at St. Mary.

> Timothie Peirsone married 1579 Elizabeth Papworth.

> William Pearson married 1614 Joan Wilkinsen at St. Mary.

In 1577, when the coat of arms was registered with the herald, the three families that could be present are Symon, John, and Timothie. But only one family seemed to be actively living there in 1577. John is the Hertfordshire representative:

John Peerson (b. about 1538) had children at Hitchin: John c. 1562 (died young?), Roger c. 1568 (died young?), Agnes c. 1570 (m. 1607 Robert Richardson), John 2nd c. 1573, Roger 2nd c. 1576.

John Peerson 2nd (c. 1573) m. 1st 1620 Elizabeth Rugmer at Hitchin, and m. 2nd 1622 Elizabeth Packe at Hitchin. They had children at Hitchin: Susan c. 1624, William c. 1626, Marye c. 1628, and Elizabeth c. 1630.

Roger Peereson 2nd (c. 1576) m.1606 Anne Jordan at Hitchin, and had children at Hitchin: John c. 1607 (m. 1630 Mary Knott), Sara c. 1608, Edward c. 1609, William c. 1612 (m. 1635 Elizabeth Drap), Henrie c. 1615 (m. 1638 Elizabeth Chambers), Marie c. 1617, and Thomas c. 1620.

(14)"PEARSON, or PIERSON (Westminster). Ar. **two chev.** sa. on a canton of the second an eagle displ. or."

An "eagle displayed Or" is part of the badge of King Henry IV who reigned 1399-1413. Therefore, the canton suggests service under King Henry IV.

Perhaps this is the individual referred to in the (13) Pierson blazon above in Westminster. The escutcheon has been differenced only in changing the eagle to gold from silver.

(15)"PIERSON (confirmed to Thomas Pierson, 21 Oct. 1577). Ar. **two chev.** sa. betw. three oak leaves erect ppr."

This escutcheon repeats the two black chevronels of (10) and (11) Pierson and adds three green oak leaves. He is said to be of Westminster (Greater London) and only had female heirs to this coat of arms. See the comments under (16) Pierson and (18) Pierson below. Because the coat of arms is "confirmed", he inherited it from his father of whom we have no name.

(16)"PIERSON (granted by Segar, Garter, to Richard, son of Thomas Pierson, of Olney, co. Bucks). Ar. **two chevronels** az. betw. three leaves vert. Crest - A hind's head couped ar. charged with two chevronels az."

The Order of the Garter was instituted by King Edward III of England in 1348, but the recipients were limited in number, and then it was only awarded to the greater members of the Nobility.

Richard Pierson's ensign is the same as (15) Thomas Pierson's ensign (confirmed 21 Oct 1577) except that the chevronels are blue instead of black. A hind is a doe (deer). Here, "of Olney, co. Bucks" seems to refer to Richard and not Thomas. Yet below, under (18) Pierson's "borne of Henry," the herald's records show Richard as a "citizen of London." Perhaps Richard moved from Olney to London by 1633-35 when the herald's visitation occurred. Other records below under (18) Pierson show (15) Thomas Pierson to be from Westminster (greater London area) and having coheirs (no male heirs, just two or more female heirs). Thus (15) Thomas is not the Thomas who is the father of Richard.

The only record found for a Richard Pierson near Olney is: "Richard Pierson c. 1 Jan 1620 Moulsoe (6 miles S of Olney), Buckinghamshire, no parents given." However, this cannot be the Richard of the coat of arms above since with a wife and four children in 1634, the Richard we seek would have been at least 26 years old in 1634 (born before 1608). The

Richard Pierson of the coat of arms married Elizabeth, daughter of Edmond Chrich of London & of Thomasin, his wife (daughter of Simon Henden). Richard Pierson and Elizabeth Chrich had children: Henry Peirson, eldest son; Edward; Richard; and Margaret (only daughter). The coat of arms was inherited by Henry Peirson who in 1634 was living at Benenden, Kent County. Henry's children ("born of Henry" apparently after 1634) were registered with their own coat of arms in 1634 which was the same as Richard's and Henry's except that it had the two chevronels in black to match Thomas Pierson's 1577 confirmed arms, who must therefore be deceased in 1634. This matching arms indicates some family relation that is not evident here.

(17)"PIERSON (London). Ar. **two chev.** az. betw. three leaves erect vert. Crest - A doe or hind's head couped ar. charged with two chev. az."

This Pierson's escutcheon and crest are identical to Richard Pierson's above. Therefore, it is probably an entry, after the original grant to Richard Pierson, based on the 1633-35 London visitation of the herald (see framed information next to shield of Henry Peirson).

(18)"PIERSON (Visit. London 1634, borne by Henry Pierson, then residing at Benenden, co. Kent). Same arms (as Thomas Pierson, 21 Oct 1577). (Ar. **two chev.** sa. betw. three oak leaves erect ppr.) Crest - An ounce sejant az. armed and langued gu."

In 1869, the Harleian Society was formed in England whose goal was to publish previously unpublished heraldic documents, which they published for many years at the rate of one or two volumes per year. In 1883, they published *The Visitation of London, Anno Domini 1633, 1634, and 1635*, Volume II, made by Sir Henry St. George, Knight and Richmond Herald, and Deputy and Marshal to Sir Richard St. George, Knight and Clarencieux King of Arms.

Vide the last booke of certificates in the office of Armes for the funerall of Pierson per Mʳ Lennard

It contains one Pierson coat of arms complete with facsimile of the shield and a description of the family:

"Pierson.

Cordwayner Ward.

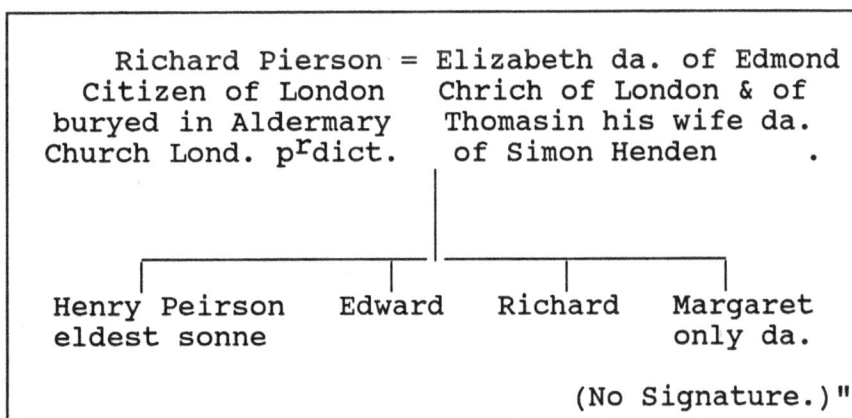

```
Richard Pierson = Elizabeth da. of Edmond
Citizen of London   Chrich of London & of
buryed in Aldermary Thomasin his wife da.
Church Lond. pʳdict. of Simon Henden      .
                     |
        ┌────────────┼──────────┬──────────┐
Henry Peirson    Edward     Richard     Margaret
eldest sonne                            only da.

                              (No Signature.)"
```

Henry's father and mother are given here and it is certain to be the Richard Pierson, granted by Segar, above since the escutcheon is the same. The escutcheon and crest depicted here is that of Henry Peirson (surname spelling difference noted) because of the azure (blue) chevronels shown. Above, Henry's son is entitled to the sable (black) chevronels of Thomas Pierson, while Richard has azure chevronels with a different crest.

Now that we have four generations of coats of arms for Thomas Pierson, Richard Pierson, Henry Peirson, and the son of Henry Peirson, some additional information can be added to identify this family further:

In 1880, the Harleian Society published *The Visitation of London, Anno Domini 1633, 1634, and 1635*, Volume I, made by Sir Henry St. George, Knight and Richmond Herald, and Deputy and Marshal to Sir Richard St. George, Knight and Clarencieux King of Arms. On p. 375, "Symon Henden had children: Edward, Serjeant at law; John, who married Susan dau. of Robert Brickenden, widow of Champion Brickenden; and Thomazine, wife of Edm. Chrich of London, remar. to Ed ... A ... of Betherden (Bethersden) in Kent Esq." Additionally, it states Symon's son "John Henden of Biddenden" remarried to "Elizabeth dau. of Edmund Chritch, widow of **Richard Pereson**." This establishes a relation to Piersons and locations that include Benenden (Kent county) and London. The "Ed ... A ..." may be Edward Ackreth as identified in a confused note in Lizzie Pierson's English Notes[10] which states: "Pierson of London, Richard Pierson, citizen of London, bur. in Aldermary church, h. w. Eliz. (dau. of Edw. Ackreth, of London and of Thomasine, his wife), and chd. Edw., Rich., Henry and Margaret." This is clearly the family in the London visitation above for Henry, but with Elizabeth Critch's father listed as her mother's 2nd husband.

In 1909, the Harleian Society published *The Visitation of the County of Buckingham, made in 1634*, by John Philipot, Esq., Somerset Herald, and William Ryley, Bluemantle Pursuivant, Marshals and Deputies to Sir Richard St. George, Knight and Clarencieux King of Arms and Sir John Borough, Knight, Garter, who visited as Norroy by mutual agreement. On pp. 13-14, the Bowyer family of Denham, Buckinghamshire, is given in support of arms. In part, it states "Francis Bowyer of London, m. Elizabeth dau. and heir of William Tillesworth of London; had chd. 1. Sir William Bowyer of Denham, Bucks Knight, m. Mary dau. and coheir of **Thomas Peirson** of Westminster, she remarried to James Ley E. Marlboro; 2. Robert Bowyer of London 2d son; 3. John Bowyer 3d son; 4. Francis Bowyer of Hertford 4th son." An additional three Bowyer generations therein given for descendants of Sir William and Mary (Peirson) Bowyer are omitted here. The Thomas Peirson mentioned here is believed to be the Thomas Pierson that had a coat of arms confirmed above on 21 Oct. 1577. The "coheir of Thomas Peirson" for Mary Peirson means that there are no living male heirs of Thomas Peirson and that there are currently more than one female heir.

The Three Charges and Chevron Group

(19)"PEARSON (co. Chester). Ar. a **chev.** erm. betw. three laurel leaves ppr."

(20)"PEARSON (registered, 1698, to Lieut.-Col. John Pearson). Quarterly, 1st and 4th, per fess embattled az. and or. in chief two suns in splendour of the last, and in base a sun in splendour gu.; 2nd and 3rd, gu. a **chev.** erm. betw. three oak leaves or. Crest - A demi griffin segeant az. beaked or. and charged on the shoulder with a sun of the arms."

10Lizzie B. Pierson, *Pierson Genealogical Records*, Joel Munsell, Printer, Albany, NY, 1878, p. 73.

(21)"PEARSON (York, 1715). Ar. a **chev.** betw. three roses gu."

The Weavers Group

(22)"PEIRSON. Az. **three shuttles** or., **quills** ar. Crest - A deer's head issuing, or."

Shuttles and quills are used in weaving and this coat of arms represents a professional weaver named Peirson. Usually, companies adopted these escutcheons but families with a history of weavers also established their own escutcheon as in the case of Peirson. The shuttle is a half-decked, canoe-shaped device which holds in a cavity a bobbin of thread called a quill. It is used to weave in and out across a perpendicular course of threads in making cloth material. Lizzie B. Pierson, in her book[11], says of Thomas Pierson Sr. who married Maria Harrison of Branford, Connecticut, in 1662: "At Branford, he was closely associated with Rev. Abraham Pierson (witnessed the Reverend's will). He (Thomas) was a weaver."

The Five Fusils Group

A **fusil** is a charge resembling the lozenge but longer and narrower. The lozenge is a figure resembling the diamond on a playing card.

(23)"PEARSON (co. Lancaster). Az. **five fusils** in fesse or. within a double tressure flory counterflory ar."

(24)"PEARSON (Storrs Hall, co. Lancaster). Az. **five fusils** in fesse or. within a double tressure flory counterflory ar."

The Three Bezants Group

A **bezant** is a gold roundlet. It represents the old coin of Byzantium. It was introduced into English Heraldry by the crusaders.

(25)"PEARSON (co. Northampton). Erm. on two bars gu. **three bezants** two and one." This coat of arms belongs to Thomas Pearson of Spratton, Northamptonshire [see comment in (26) Pearson below].

(26)"PEARSON (Tankerton, and Maize Hill, Greenwich, co. Kent; descended from Thomas Pearson, of Spratton, co. Northampton, living temp. Richard III [1483-5]). Erm. on two bars gu. **three bezants.** Crest - A boar's head couped sa. in his mouth an acorn or., leaved vert. Motto - Per duret probitas (Through hardness and honesty)." Greenwich is now in Greater London.

The Three Horses Group

(27)"PEARSON (Upper Gloucester Place, London). Ar. billetty az. on a pile of the last **three horses'** heads erased of the field. Crest - A horse's head erased sa. billetty and gorged with a mural crown or."

[11]Lizzie B. Pierson, *Pierson Genealogical Records*, Joel Munsell, Printer, Albany, NY, 1878, p. 34.

The Two Lions Group

A **lion** rampant is an erect lion with his left hind paw on the ground.

(28)"PEARSON   (New Sleaford, co. Lincoln, and Tunbridge Hall, near Godstone, co. Surrey).   Or on a pale az. betw. **two lions** ramp. respecting each other gu. a sun in splendour of the field.   Crest - A cock's head erased az. combed and wattled gu. betw. two palm branches vert, holding in the beak a heart's ease or pansy ppr. and charged on the neck with a sun in splendour or."

Scotland

It is believed that the Pearson/Peirson/Pierson surnames of Scotland are descendants of the vill of Pericne alias Persene in Yorkshire, England. The following is the earliest records found of Pearson/Peirson/Pierson as it relates to Scotland.

In 1286, the death of Scotland's Alexander III left as heiress to the throne of Scotland his young granddaughter Margaret, the "Maid of Norway." With the treaty of Birgham, 1290, the guardian government agreed that Margaret should marry the heir of Edward I of England. Scotland remained a separate kingdom under this agreement. But Margaret died in 1290 shortly after the agreement was concluded.   There followed 13 claimants to the throne of which Robert Bruce and John Balliol, descendants of a younger brother of Malcolm IV and William, emerged as the leading competitors.   In 1292, Edward I of England, acting as arbitrator, named John Balliol as king.   But when Edward sought to exert his overlordship by taking law cases on appeal from Scotland and by summoning Balliol to do military service for England in France, the Scots resisted.   Thus in 1295, Scotland concluded an alliance with France. But Edward was determined to have his way by force and sent his army north to force Scottish compliance. At the Scottish border in 1296, the English sacked Berwick.   Balliol of Scotland was forced into submission by the superior forces of Edward. National Scottish resistance began to grow against English rule. William Wallace, a knight's son, led the resistance and defeated the British at Stirling Bridge in 1297.   But in 1298, Edward I of England, counterattacked and defeated William Wallace at Falkirk. Wallace lived to be executed in London in 1305.

It is likely that Wautier Pieressone was appointed the Count of Berwick under King Edward I in 1296 shortly after Berwick was sacked by Edward's army, since Wautier Pieressone was listed as the Count of Berwick in the Ragman's Roll of 1298 as pledging allegiance to Edward I when he invaded Scotland. It is likely that Wautier Pieressone was the first Pierson/Peirson/Pearson knight and may have participated in the sacking of Berwick in 1296. Based on the Ragman's Roll, Wautier Pieressone and his forces were likely part of Edward's army at the battle of Falkirk where King Edward defeated William Wallace and his Scottish forces.

The earliest records found for Pearson/Peirson/Pierson christenings in Scotland are for the period 1561 to 1600. At that time, Peirsons were settled in the counties of Perth and Fife, with most of them at Dunfermline, Fife, Scotland. Those with male children are mentioned below:

In Perth, Perth county, Scotland, male children were born: John Persone had son Daniel c. 5 Oct 1572; Robert Peirsone had son Johne c. 10 Oct 1574.

In Dunfermline, Fife county, Scotland:

John Peirson and Margaret Watson had chd. David c. 8 Feb 1561/2, John c. 9 Jul 1564, Harry c. 21 Apr 1566, Bessie c. 18 Apr 1568, and David (2d) c. 17 Sep 1570.

Henry Peirson and Bessie Reid had chd. John c. 3 May 1562, Andrew c. 20 Jun 1565, and Margaret c. 6 Mar 1568/9.

Nicolas Peirson and Katherine Hendirson had son Robert c. 25 Apr 1563.

Andrew Peirson and Christian Loudian had chd. Janet c. 9 May 1568, and John c. 2 May 1571.

David Peirson and Christian Stirk had chd. Peter c. 21 Jan 1572, and Katherine c. 20 Feb 1574.

Henry (Harry) Peirson and Marjory Dewar had chd. Patrick c. 1 Jan 1575, Christian (f) c. 24 Nov 1577, Nans (f) c. 30 Nov 1580, Margaret c. 26 Feb 1583, Marjory c. 26 Feb 1584, Nans (2d) (f) c. 14 Jun 1587, and Marjorie (2d) c. 29 Jul 1590.

Henry Peirsone and Katherine Edisone had chd. Robert c. 17 Mar 1576, Beatrix c. 26 Nov 1581, Thomas c. 21 Mar 1584, Janet c. 9 Apr 1587, and Margaret c. 7 Dec 1589.

Arche Peirson and Effie Aitkin had chd. William c. 15 Apr 1576, Kaetie c. 20 Apr 1578, William (2d) c. 3 Jul 1580, Nans (f) c. 2 Sep 1582, Janet c. 15 Mar 1583/4, Archie c. 21 Nov 1585, James c. 21 Jan 1587, and Alison c. 21 Dec 1589.

Arche Peirson and Isobel Dik had son Adam c. 4 Jul 1591.

George Peirson and Effie Phillen had chd. Gelis (f) c. 14 Oct 1582, Janet c. 4 Oct 1584, David c. 14 Jun 1587, Nans (f) c. 25 Sep 1588, and David (2d) c. 18 Apr 1591.

James Peirson and Grizel Tomson had chd. Isobel c. 27 Mar 1583, and John c. 19 Jan 1588.

David Persone and Margaret Cuningham had chd. John c. 24 Oct 1585, Robert c. 28 Jan 1587, and David c. 19 May 1599.

John Persone (Peirson) and Grizel Mestertoun (Mastirtoun) had chd. John c. 14 Mar 1590, and Harry c. 26 Apr 1600.

It is unknown if these Scottish Peirson families are related to any of the following Scottish coats of arms.

The Two Swords Group

The usual form of the sword is a long straight blade with a cross handle. Any variations of this form will be given in the blazon. A cinquefoil is a bearing derived originally from a plant of the clover type; however, in modern Heraldry, from its general shape, is frequently looked upon as representing the narcissus flower.

(29)"PEIRSON - Scotland. Ar. **two swords** chevronways, az. sustaining on their points a heart gu. In base, a rose of the last, stalked and leaved vert. Crest - A lion's paw, holding a heart gu."

This Peirson of Scotland escutcheon is from Burke's *Encyclopedia of Heraldry* dated prior to 1878, and is not included in Sir Bernard Burke's *General Armory* of 1884.

(30)"PEARSON, or PIERSON (Balmadies, co. Forfar). Ar. **two swords** chevronways az. piercing a man's heart in chief ppr. in base a cinquefoil of the second. Crest - A dove holding an olive branch in her beak ppr. Motto - Dum spiro spero (While I live, I have hope)."

Forfar is currently the county seat of Angus county, Scotland. This escutcheon is also listed in the Lion Register.

(31)"PEARSON (Westhall, co. Forfar, 1672). Ar. **two swords** chevronways az. hilted and pommelled or, piercing a heart gu. betw. two crescents in chief and a cinquefoil in base of the second."

(32)"PEARSON (Bielside, co. Haddington, 1856). Ar. on a fess gu. a saltire of the first, over all **two swords** chevronways ppr. hilted and pommelled or, piercing a heart in chief of the second, in base a cinquefoil az. Crest - A dove holding an olive branch in her beak ppr. Motto - Dum spiro spero (While I live, I have hope)."

The Two Daggers Group

The **dagger** is a charge that is a shortened form of the sword, but it is given a much more pointed blade than the sword.

(33)"PEARSON (Kippenross, co. Stirling). Ar. **two daggers** in bend and bend sinister, conjoined in point az. piercing a man's heart in base ppr. in the honour point a cinquefoil sa. Crest - A tower ppr. Motto - Rather die than be disloyal."

This escutcheon is also listed in the Lion Register.

Ireland and Wales

Although Burke's *General Armory* includes Ireland and Wales, there were no coats of arms for Piersons of any spelling listed from those two countries for the period 1200 to 1884.

Netherlands

Rietstap's *Armorial General*, published in France in 1884, lists one coat of arms for Pierson:

The Chevron and Five Charges Group

(34)"PIERSON - Amsterdam. De gu. au chev, d'azur, ch. de cinq roses d'arg. et acc. de trois lions d'or; en chef un ecusson d'arg., br. sur la cime du chev. et ch. d'une epee de sa. Brl. de gu., d'or et d'azur. C: l'epee, entre un vol d'or, les plumes ext. de gu. L. d'or, de gu. et d'azur." Translated: "Red, a blue **chevron** charged with five silver roses and accompanied by three gold lions; in the chief a silver shield, superposed on the apex of the chevron and charged with a black sword, adorned in red, gold and blue. Crest: The sword of the arms between a set of golden wings, the feather tips of which are red."

This Amsterdam is in the Netherlands (Holland) and has a chance of being related to English Piersons. Lions and roses also appear in some English escutcheons. Lizzie B. Pierson[12] in her English notes quoting the vicar of Newark-upon-Trent states "About 1666,

many of the Piersons were Puritans, and settled in Cambridge, England. They suffered much because of their Puritan views of religion, and some are thought to have sought refuge from persecution in Holland (Netherlands)."

"In 1615[13], was proved the will of John Peerson, of the manors Bramridge and Eastley, in the Isle of Wight. He had children Thomas, John, and Anne. He speaks of John Peerson of the Lowe Countries. He speaks of land at Brooke, in the Isle of Wight. To his son Thomas he leaves land at Hallowell, Huntingdonshire. Speaks of his brother William Bowman."

This Peerson family is obviously well-to-do and the reference to the "Lowe Countries" is to the European mainland, i.e. the Netherlands (or Holland). Perhaps this coat of arms belongs to a John Pierson of Amsterdam, Netherlands, who emigrated there before 1615.

[12]Lizzie B. Pierson, *Pierson Genealogical Records*, Joel Munsell, Printer, Albany, NY, 1878, p. 73.
[13]Lizzie B. Pierson, *Pierson Genealogical Records*, Joel Munsell, Printer, Albany, NY, 1878, p. 70.

Chapter 6
The Pierson Mayflower Legend

A contemporary writer, Capt. Edward Johnson[1], relating to the settlement of Massachusetts, wrote: "For fifteen years space to the year 1643, ... the number of ships that transported passengers ... is 298. Men, women, and children passing over this wide ocean is 21,200 or thereabouts." Of the estimated 21,200 passengers to the Massachusetts territory between 1628 and 1643, Banks[2] lists 2,646 probable passengers between the period 1620 and 1640. While 298 ships are estimated by Johnson, Banks finds written reference to 177 ships in a slightly different period but only has passenger or ship's names for about 100 of these.

Charles Banks[3] states that the names of many of these early emigrants to America, though not in English Custom House records, are to be found recorded in "diaries, letters, court proceedings, and in modern books that relate to traditions of our colonial families."

Cuyler Reynolds, in his 1911 genealogy book, provided information on the Pierson families in the Hudson-Mohawk valleys of New York[4]:

> "There is a well-believed tradition that the first Pierson came over in the *Mayflower* as ship's carpenter, not as a passenger."

Cuyler Reynolds referenced descendants of Henry Pierson of Long Island via Eli Pierson of Fulton County that were present in 1911 in the Hudson and Mohawk valleys of New York. At first, it was thought that the Mayflower tradition was fabricated in 1911 by Cuyler Reynolds and not factual. But in 1991, Jenny Pierson, wife of John Charles Pierson of New Zealand (John is a 10th generation descendant of Henry Peirson of Long Island), stated in her letter to Richard Pierson[5]:

"According to Uncle Fred's and John's families, the original Pierson came over to America in the *Mayflower*, being one of the Pilgrims."

Uncle Fred refers to John Charles Pierson's uncle. John Charles Pierson is the fourth New Zealand generation descending from Charles Anson Crocker Herrick Philetous Pierson who came to New Zealand about 1860 from Cairo, Greene County, New York. Prior to the 1991 communication between the New Zealand and California Piersons, Jenny Pierson said she "was rather inclined to dismiss them (the Mayflower and Viking family legends), but now feels (after hearing of the Viking location origin of the Pierson surname), garbled as the information is, there may be more than a grain of truth in it."

Since the New Zealand Pierson Mayflower legend was passed down from Piersons who left America in the 1860s, the 1911 Pierson Mayflower version presented by Cuyler Reynolds

---

[1] Capt. Edward Johnson, *Wonder-Working Providence, 1628-1651*, Chapter XIV.

[2] Charles Edward Banks, *Planters of the Commonwealth 1620-1640*, Boston, Massachusetts, 1930, p. 13.

[3] Charles Edward Banks, *Planters of the Commonwealth 1620-1640*, Boston, Massachusetts, 1930, p. viii.

[4] Cuyler Reynolds, *Hudson-Mohawk Genealogical and Family Memoirs*, Lewis Historical Publishing Co., New York, NY, 1911, Vol. II, p. 775.

[5] Jennifer Pierson of New Zealand, Letter to Richard Pierson of California, U.S.A., 18 September 1991, p. 2.

may also have more than a grain of truth in it. The New Zealand Mayflower legend indicates that the legend existed in the New York Pierson family line in the 1860s.

Those passing down each Mayflower legend seemed to assume that their version of the legend referred to the 1620 Mayflower that landed at Plymouth in America. Yet, reference was found to seven Mayflower sailings from England to America between 1620 and 1641. Therefore, it is possible that the first Pierson immigrant came to America on a ship named Mayflower and that it sailed between 1620 and 1641 and landed in New England. The following investigations are an attempt to discover from where, upon which ship, which date, and to what port the American immigrant Henry Peirson sailed to America.

The 1620 Mayflower to Plymouth

On September 16, 1620, the *Mayflower* set sail from Plymouth, England, under the command of Captain Christopher Jones. The voyage across the wintry Atlantic Ocean took 65 days. Crowded on board were the men, women, and children who founded Plymouth, the first permanent colony in America settled by English families. These people, now called the Pilgrims or Pilgrim Fathers, were the first colonists to come to America to gain religious liberty[6]. The *Mayflower* arrived in Provincetown Harbor, Massachusetts Bay, on November 11, 1620. A month later on December 11, 1620, they selected Plymouth as the site of their new colony. The number of passengers depends upon whether one counts William Butten, who died at sea; Oceanus Hopkins, born at sea; and Peregriene White, born on the ship after it reached Plymouth harbor. Governor Bradford's *Of Plimoth Plantation* contains a list of about 100 passengers. No Piersons of any spelling appear on the list of passengers. Of the crew members he states:

> "John Alden was hired for a cooper, at South-Hampton (England), where the ship victuled; and being a hopeful young man, was much desired, but was left to his own liking to go or stay when he came here; but he stayed and married here."

> "John Allerton and Thomas Enlish were both hired, the latter to go (be) mr (master) of a shalop (open boat) here, and the other was reputed as one of the company, but was to go back (being a seaman) for the help of others behind. But they both died here, before the ship returned."

> "There were also two other seaman hired to stay a year here in the country, William Trevore, and one Ely. But when their time was out, they both returned."

The conclusion drawn from this passenger and crew list is that an immigrant Pierson did not come on the 1620 *Mayflower* to Plymouth. This is confirmed by a review of the early records of Plymouth which do not show any Piersons present.

---

[6]F.E. Compton Co., *Compton's Encyclopedia*, William Benton, Publisher, Chicago/Toronto/Rome/Sydney/Tokyo, 1970, Vol. 14, p.182.

The 1629 Mayflower to Salem & Plymouth

Banks, in his *Planters of the Commonwealth*, mentions about a 100 ship's names which came to New England 1620 to 1640. Among these are three *Mayflower* sailings (1620, 1629, and 1630). Of the 1629 *Mayflower* sailing, Banks states[7]:

"*Mayflower*, William Peirce, Master, left Gravesend (in Kent county, England) in March with thirty-five passengers, mostly from Leyden, Holland, destined for Plymouth."

Only 23 of the 35 passengers are named in Banks' book, but because the destination was Plymouth and Salem and no Pierson records appear in those towns, this is not considered to be the *Mayflower* sailing of Pierson tradition. However, this is clear evidence that a ship named *Mayflower* was transporting passengers to the Massachusetts area in 1629. This is probably the same *Mayflower* ship that became part of the Winthrop fleet in 1630 which fleet delivered 700 passengers to the Massachusetts Bay Colony.

The 1630 Mayflower to Charlestown

Charles Edward Banks, in his book[8], *The Winthrop Fleet of 1630*, provides information about the preparation in 1629 and the voyage in 1630 of a fleet of eleven ships of which only seven (including the *Mayflower*) carried passengers. A reconstructed passenger list of the fleet was compiled by Banks from survivors of the Massachusetts Bay Colony expedition who appeared in local Massachusetts records after the fleet's arrival in 1630. Therefore, those that died enroute or shortly after arrival, or returned, are not included in the list. Except for a few dignitaries, it is not known upon which of the seven ships the passengers traveled. But the names of all eleven ships are known and which ones carried passengers. "Winthrop, in a letter to his wife written just before sailing, told her that there were seven hundred passengers aboard (the fleet).[9]" The eleven vessels secured for carrying the Great Immigration were:

Arbella	Talbot	Hopewell	Trial
Ambrose	Mayflower	Whale	Charles
Jewel	William & Francis		Success

"It can be inferred from available records that only the four leaders of the fleet ... (*Arbella, Talbot, Ambrose,* and *Jewel*) ... carried passengers, as well as the *Mayflower, Whale,* and *Success*. The others were used to transport freight and live stock."

In another book[10] by Banks, he states: "The first five ships sailed April 8 from Yarmouth, Isle of Wight, and arrived Salem June 13 and following days. The other half of the fleet (including the *Mayflower*) sailed in May (1630) and arrived in July at various dates (*Mayflower* July 1, 1630 at Charlestown)."

---

[7] Charles Edward Banks, *Planters of the Commonwealth 1620-1640*, Boston, Massachusetts, 1930, pp. 64-5.
[8] Charles Edward Banks, *The Winthrop Fleet of 1630*, Originally published Boston, 1930, Reprinted Genealogical Publishing Co., Inc., Baltimore, MD, 1989.
[9] Charles Edward Banks, *The Winthrop Fleet of 1630*, Originally published Boston, 1930, Reprinted Genealogical Publishing Co., Inc., Baltimore, MD, 1989, p. 46.
[10] Charles Edward Banks, *Planters of the Commonwealth 1620-1640*, Boston, Massachusetts, 1930, p. 65.

In Banks' book[11], he provides a reconstructed passenger list of 571 persons of whom he shows origins for 416 of those passengers.

There are no Piersons of any spelling in this reconstructed list because none appeared in local New England records shortly after arrival of the Winthrop fleet at the towns settled by this Massachusetts Bay colony. Therefore, the 1630 Mayflower sailing is not believed to be the voyage of the Pierson legend.

The 1633 and 1634 Mayflower to Virginia

September 1634[12]. "Petition[13] of Edward Kingswell that, having undertaken a plantation in Carolina, he contracted with Samuel Vassall to take a company there. When Vassall failed in his obligations, the petitioner on the persuasion of Peter Andrews, commander of the *Mayflower*, landed the passengers in Virginia in October 1633. They remained there in distress until May 1634 without means of getting to Carolina. The petitioner has obtained a warrant against Andrews and asks for a hearing to take place against him and Vassall."

November 1634[14]. "Depositions[15] re the voyage of the *Mayflower*, Mr. Peter Andrewes, in 1633 and 1634 from London to Virginia carrying passengers including Mrs. Wingate and her maidservant Margaret Dalton. Peter Andrewes of Limehouse, Middlesex, mariner aged 39, deposes that in 1632 Samuel Vassall fitted out the *George* of London, Mr. Henry Taverner, for a voyage of discovery to Carolina alias Florida to seek a place suitable for a new plantation."

February 1635[16]. "Petition[17] of Samuel Vassall. He was imprisoned in the Fleet on 4 February because of his differences with Edward Kingswell and asks to be set at liberty. A report is enclosed on the losses sustained by Kingswell in the transportation of 40 persons to Carolina. Kingswell insisted on using the *Mayflower* though Vassall told him there was not enough water on the Carolina coast and it was at Kingswell's wish that the company went to Virginia to winter. A ship was sent in the spring to transport the company to Florida. Kingswell's partner, Mr. Wingate, with his wife and family came from Virginia in March 1634 and Kingswell came in June 1634. Vassall's ship arrived in Virginia in July 1634 and would have transported Kingswell had he not already left."

---

[11]Charles Edward Banks, *The Winthrop Fleet of 1630*, Originally published Boston, 1930, Reprinted Genealogical Publishing Co., Inc., Baltimore, MD, 1989, Appendix A, pp. 57-99.

[12]Peter Wilson Coldham, *The Complete Book of Emigrants 1607-1660*, Genealogical Publishing Co., Inc., Baltimore, Maryland, 1987, pp. 118-119.

[13]W. Noel Sainsbury, editor, *Calendars of State Papers, American and Colonial Series, 1574-1660*, Longman & Green, 1860, with Addenda 1, 1574-1674, H.M.S.O., 1893, and Addenda 2, 1653-1687, Hon. J. W. Fortescue, editor, H.M.S.O., 1899.

[14]Peter Wilson Coldham, *The Complete Book of Emigrants 1607-1660*, Genealogical Publishing Co., Inc., Baltimore, Maryland, 1987, p. 119.

[15]Peter Wilson Coldham, *English Adventurers and Emigrants*, Vol. I, Genealogical Publishing Co., Inc., Baltimore, Maryland, 1984.

[16]Peter Wilson Coldham, *The Complete Book of Emigrants 1607-1660*, Genealogical Publishing Co., Inc., Baltimore, Maryland, 1987, p. 124.

[17]W. Noel Sainsbury, editor, *Calendars of State Papers, American and Colonial Series, 1574-1660*, Longman & Green, 1860, with Addenda 1, 1574-1674, H.M.S.O., 1893, and Addenda 2, 1653-1687, Hon. J. W. Fortescue, editor, H.M.S.O., 1899.

11 May 1635[18]. "A further report[19] upon the petition of Edward Kingswell. Henry Taverner, Master of the *Thomas*, was hired by Samuel Vassall to take 28 passengers if any should have died on the *Mayflower* and the ship arrived in Virginia in July 1634 by which time Kingswell had left there."

Since these 1633 and 1634 Mayflower sailings transported passengers from England to Virginia and Virginia to Carolina (alias Florida), it is not expected that the Henry Peirson passage that we seek occurred here, even though a definitive passenger list does not exist to verify this assumption. This *Mayflower* is believed to be the same ship that sailed from England to New England in 1629 and 1630 since wooden ships of that era lasted 10 to 20 years if they did not sooner have a destructive accident.

The 1639 Mayflower to New England

10 April - 10 May 1639[20]. "John Woode, Abraham Pomfrett, Christopher Vivion, Samuell Andrewes and Thomas Barnard shippers[21] of goods in the *Mayflower*, Master William Caine, bound from London to New England with passengers and planters."

This *Mayflower* departed London, Master William Caine, in about May 1639 and arrived in New England, probably Boston, in about July 1639 (7 to 10 week trip) carrying passengers, some of whom (planters) would settle in New England. No passenger list has been found for this voyage.

Thomas Cooper, in his article[22] in *The American Genealogist*, with reference to a 1663 lawsuit involving property in Olney, Buckinghamshire, England, had quoted Henry Pierson as stating that he had emigrated from Olney to New England "in or about the month of May 1639[23]" This *Mayflower* departure matches the month Henry Peirson left England. Therefore, it is believed this sailing is the source of the Pierson Mayflower legend.

In Thomas Cooper's article, the Isaac Lovell letter[24] to John Winthrop of 11 May 1640, states that "the party who gave his father (goodman Fuller) notice of (John Fuller's intended marriage) his name is Henry Person (sic) sonne in law (then included step-son) to goodman Cooper dwelling at Sawgust (Saugus, later Lynn)." Lovell of England had, on behalf of his wife's uncle Fuller of Olney in Buckinghamshire, asked Governor John Winthrop of New England to counsel Fuller's son, John Fuller of the Boston area. This means that Henry

[18]Peter Wilson Coldham, *The Complete Book of Emigrants 1607-1660*, Genealogical Publishing Co., Inc., Baltimore, Maryland, 1987, p. 144.

[19]W. Noel Sainsbury, editor, *Calendars of State Papers, American and Colonial Series, 1574-1660*, Longman & Green, 1860, with Addenda 1, 1574-1674, H.M.S.O., 1893, and Addenda 2, 1653-1687, Hon. J. W. Fortescue, editor, H.M.S.O., 1899.

[20]Peter Wilson Coldham, *The Complete Book of Emigrants 1607-1660*, Genealogical Publishing Co., Inc., Baltimore, Maryland, 1987, p. 205.

[21]Public Record Office at Chancery Lane, London WC2A 1LR, 'England, record E190/433/6, read and summarized by Peter Wilson Coldham 1987.

[22]Thomas W. Cooper, II, "The Cooper-Pierson-Griggs Connection, Long Island, Massachusetts, and Buckinghamshire, England" *The American Genealogist*, October 1989, Vol. 64, No. 4, pp. 193-200.

[23]Pearson vs. Kirby, Public Record Office, England, C5/421/171.

[24]*Winthrop Papers 4*, Boston, Massachusetts, 1944, pp. 239-40.

Peirson is in Lynn (Saugus), located 10 miles north of Boston in Massachusetts colony, with his step-father John Cooper prior to Isaac Lovell's 11 May 1640 letter.

In summary, in agreement with the Pierson Mayflower legend, it appears that Henry Peirson left London on the *Mayflower* in May 1639, sailed to Boston arriving about July 1639, and joined his mother Wibroe (Griggs) (Peirson) Cooper and step-father John Cooper in Lynn. See the three brothers legend in Chapter 4.

This 1639 *Mayflower* is probably the same "Mayflower of London" that sailed from England to America in 1629, 1630, 1633, 1634, and 1641. That is a 12-year span and possible for a single wooden ship. She did not always sail with the same Master and she was capable of carrying 140 passengers (note the 1641 sailing below) though ships of this era were built as freighters. That puts her in the 120 to 150 ton class.

The *Mayflower of London* was apparently lost at sea on a voyage to Virginia in 1641 as no further record of her is found after the "accident:"

> 20 October 1641[25]. "Pass[26] for the *Mayflower* of London, Mr. John Cole, to proceed to Virginia with passengers."

> 18 October 1642[27]. "Depositions[28] re accident to the *Mayflower*, Mr. John Cole, bound from London to Virginia with 140 passengers in 1641."

---

[25]Peter Wilson Coldham, *The Complete Book of Emigrants 1607-1660*, Genealogical Publishing Co., Inc., Baltimore, Maryland, 1987, p. 220.
[26]Acts of the Privy Council of England (1613-1631), H.M.S.O., 1921-1964.
[27]Peter Wilson Coldham, *The Complete Book of Emigrants 1607-1660*, Genealogical Publishing Co., Inc., Baltimore, Maryland, 1987, p. 223.
[28]Peter Wilson Coldham, *English Adventurers and Emigrants*, Vol. I, Genealogical Publishing Co., Inc., Baltimore, Maryland, 1984.

Chapter 7
Descendants of Rev. Abraham Pierson
American Immigrant

The following descendants of the Rev. Abraham Pierson (1611-1678) are copied from Lizzie B. Pierson, *Pierson Genealogical Records*, Joel Munsell, Printer, Albany, N.Y., 1878, pp. 10-22. Lizzie Pierson's footnotes, errata, and related appendices are incorporated within the text which is modified by footnoted additional research by the authors of *Pierson Millennium*. An every-name index is provided at the back of *Pierson Millennium* whereas only heads of families are indexed in *Pierson Genealogical Records*. The + symbol after an identifying number indicates more information is provided in a later paragraph beginning with the same number in this chapter.

1 Abraham Pierson was born in Yorkshire, England (christened 22 Sep 1611, Guiseley, Yorkshire, England[1], see chapter 4). He graduated at Trinity College, Cambridge, England, 1632; and came to America in 1639. He was in Boston and Lynn, Mass. 1640; went to Southampton, Long Island, where he remained till 1647; then moved to Branford, Ct.; from which place he again moved, in 1666, to Newark, New Jersey, where he died, Aug. 9, 1678. The tradition in America is that "he was ordained in Newark, Eng." But search has been made in Newark (on the Trent), and no records can be found there concerning him. He married Abigail (dau. of Rev. Jno. Wheelwright of Lincolnshire, Eng.), who moved to New Hampshire. See the Wheelwright family in Chapter 4.

He was ordained in Boston, as a Congregational minister. At Lynn 1640, "finding themselves straightened, about 40 families, with Pierson as their minister," departed from Lynn, and attempted to make a settlement on the west end of Long Island. But the Dutch had made sure of that end, so they repaired to the east end, and laid the foundations of Southampton. The first church of that town was started as a Congregational church, but it afterwards became Presbyterian (Howell's Hist. of Southampton 1st edition). He was most rigid in his desire to have the "civil as well as the ecclesiastical power all vested in the church, and to allow none but church members to act in the choice of officers of gov't, or to be eligible as such." This led to a division of the colony; and in 1647, Abraham Pierson with a small part of his congregation, attempted another settlement, across the sound, on the Connecticut shore, where they organized and formed the town of Branford. There, for 20 years, he "enjoyed the confidence and esteem not only of the ministers, but the more prominent civilians connected with the New Haven colony." He early interested himself in behalf of the Indians, made himself familiar with their language, and prepared a catechism for them, that they might know of God. In 1665, he united with John Davenport in opposing the union of the two colonies, Connecticut and New Haven, with great inflexibility. He was rigid to excess in church communion, and disapproved of the

---

[1]William Easterbrook Preston and Joseph Hambly Rowe, *A Transcript of the Early Registers of the Parish of Guiseley in the County of York, 1584 to 1720, Together with a Transcript of the Early Registers of the Chapelry of Horsforth, 1620 to 1720, with Notes on Guiseley Families*, Percy Lund, Humphries & Co. Ltd., Bradford, Yorkshire, 1913, pp. 14 (Thomas marriage), 75, 80, 81, 83, 85, 86, 90, 94, 95, 97, 101, 103 (Thomas burial), 110 (Grace 2nd marriage), 120.

liberality of the clergy in the Connecticut colony. In this respect; he differed with them upon the ordinance of infant baptism, as no person in the New Haven colony could be made a freeman unless he was in full communion with the church. He fully agreed with Davenport and others in the colony, that no other government than that of the church should be maintained in the colony. In 1666, because of this belief, he with most of his congregation, left Branford, and repaired to N. J. In New Jersey, on the Passaic, they purchased land of the Indians, and laid the foundations of the now flourishing city of Newark. During 1666 and 1667 some sixty-five men came from Branford and two neighboring towns to Newark. Each man was entitled to a homestead lot of six acres. They brought their church organization with them from Branford, and became the First Church of Newark, which afterwards became a Presbyterian church. At Newark, for 12 years, Abraham led his flock of devoted followers.

Abraham wrote his will[2] 10 Aug 1671 which was proved 12 Mar 1678 at Newark, New Jersey: "Will of Abraham Pierson of Newark. Wife, Abigail. Daughters -- Devenporte, Mary and two others not named. Sons -- Abraham, Thomas, Theophilus, Isaac. Executors -- Jasper Crane, Robert Treat, Lieut. Swaine, brother Tomkins, brother Lawrence, brother Serjant Ward. Witness Thomas Pierson." On March 12, 1678-9, his Inventory was made by John Ward, Michel Tomkins and Thomas Pierson (£854.17.7). On March 18, 1678-9, the administration was granted to Abigail Pierson, the widow (E. J. D., Lib. 3, pp. 153-155).

He had children 2+ Abraham, b. 1641; 3+ Thomas Jr., b. 1641-2; 4 John, b. 1643 at Southampton, d. before 1671; 5 Abigail, b. 1644, mar. 1663 at Branford, John Davenport Jr. (son of Jno. Davenport, 1st minister of New Haven); 6 Grace, b. 1650 at Branford, mar. Sam. Kitchell (afterwards of Newark); 7 Susanna, b. Dec. 1652 at Branford, mar. Jonathan Ball (of Stamford); 8 Rebecca, b. 1654 at Branford, d. Nov. 1732, mar. Jos. Johnson (of Newark); 9+ Theophilus, b. 1659 at Branford, d. 1713 in Newark; 10 Isaac; and 11 Mary.

2 Abraham Pierson (Rev. and rector) was born 1641 at Lynn, Mass., and died May 5, 1707 at old Killingworth, Conn. He was with his father at Southampton, moved to Branford; where there mar. Abigail Clark (dau. of Geo. Clark of Milford); grad. at Harvard coll. 1668, and moved with his father to the new settlement of Newark. At that time the people of Woodbridge (a neighboring settlement in N. J.) sought the young Abraham as their pastor. But as his father was advanced in years, and in need of an assistant, the town at once secured young Abraham and settled him as a colleague with Rev. Abraham, July 28, 1669. At the death of his father 1678, he became sole pastor, which office he filled till 1692; then he returned to Conn. In 1694 he became pastor of the ch. at Killingworth, which position he retained even after he was chosen president. In 1701, when the wise fathers established Yale college, 2 Abraham was made her president or "rector," thus, for the last six yrs. of his life did he perform the duties of both pastor and rector. Pres. Abraham Pierson instituted at Yale college, a "System of Natural Philosophy," which the students of Yale continued to use, many years. Pres. Abraham received from his father 1 Rev. Abraham, his Library, which was composed of 440 volumes, very valuable for those early colonial days. The most of these he bequeathed to the Library of Yale college. While his father, 1 Abraham, was a strict Independent, he was a Moderate Presbyterian. Two fine monuments have been

2 Edited by A. Van Doren Honeyman, *Documents Relating to the Colonial History of the State of New Jersey*, Volume II -- 1730-1750, The Unionist-Gazette Association, Printers, Somerville, N.J., p. 563.

erected to his memory, one in old Killingworth, the other on the grounds of Yale college, New Haven.

He had chd. 12+ Abraham, b. 1680; 13 Sarah; 14 Susanna; 15 Mary; 16 Hannah; 17 Ruth; 18 James; 19 Abigail; 20+ John, b. 1689 at Newark, d. Aug. 3, 1770, at Hanover, N.J.

12 Abraham Pierson was born in 1680 at Newark, N.J., and died 8 Jan 1752 at Long Hill in Killingworth, Clinton, Conn. He mar. 1710 Mrs. Mary Hart. He was an old colonial magistrate, in Conn., of great learning and usefulness, and a pillar in the church and state. He had chd. 24 Jedediah, b. Sept. 17,1711; 25 Mary, b. Feb. 10, 1713; 26 John, b. May 13, 1717; 27 Phineas, b. Dec. 29, 1718; 28+ Samuel, b. Apr. 15, 1721; 29+ Dodo, b. 1724; 30 Nathan, b. Mar. 24, 1726; 31 Sarah, b. Aug. 8, 1728; and 32 Sarah, b. July 9, 1732. These were all probably born at Killingworth, Conn.

28 Samuel Pierson was born Apr. 15, 1721, and died in 1801, probably at Killingworth, Conn. This family bore an important part in the town and church interests of old Killingworth. Samuel had chd. 50 Submit; 51 Lydia; 52 Sarah; 53+ Samuel, b. July 29, 1750, d. 1801; 54 Martha; 55 Rachel; 56 Sarah.

53 Samuel Pierson was born July 29, 1750, at Killingworth, Conn., and died 1801 (the same year in which his father died). He mar. 1773 Rebecca Parmele. They had chd. 79+ John Russell, b. Nov. 30, 1773, d. 1844; 80 Lydia; 81+ Simon; 82+ Josiah, b. Mar. 19, 1781; 83+ John; 84 Elizabeth; 85+ Philo; 86 Thankful; 87 Sally; 88+ Linus.

79 John Russell Pierson was born Nov. 30, 1773 in Killingworth, Conn., and died in 1844. In 1815, he emigrated from Conn., to Genesee Co., New York, and there joined his five brothers who had preceded him by a few years. He had chd. 124 Luther G., b. 1800, d. Nov. 26, 1862; 125 Edwin, b. 1805, d. Mar. 12, 1867; 126+ Samuel Willis, b. 1813; 127 John B.; 128 Adolphus; 129 Mary, d. 1829; 130 Phileta.

126 Samuel Willis Pierson (Rev.) was born 1813 in Killingworth (now Clinton), Conn. While young, he was brought to Genesee Co., N.Y. In 1833, he mar. Aurilla Tullar. He is a minister of the gospel. He resides (1878) in Painsville, Ohio. He had chd. 187+ Samuel Fletcher, b. 1835; 188 Mary E., b. 1838 (w. of S. C. Hotchkiss, and has 3 chd.); 189 Martha M., b. 1839 (w. of S. E. Fink, and has 4 chd.).

187 Samuel Fletcher Pierson was born 1835, mar. 1st, Mary F. Bower and 2d Deborah I. McWade. Now (1878) is in Cleveland, Ohio.

81 Simon Pierson was born in Killingworth, Conn. In 1806-7, he and his four younger brothers emigrated to Genesee Co., N.Y., which was then a "howling wilderness, Where nothing dwelt but beasts of prey, Or men as fierce and wild as they." He had chd. 131 Philo; 132 David M.; 133 Clarkson.

82 Josiah Pierson (Rev.) was born Mar. 19, 1781 in Killingworth (Clinton), Conn., and died Mar. 6, 1846, in Bergen, N.Y. In 1806, he emigrated in company with his brothers to Bergen, Genesee Co., N.Y., where the remainder of his life was spent. He was a minister of the gospel; and had chd. 134+ Hamilton W.; 135 Ebenezer; 136 Josiah; 137 Parmelia (w. of Henry Dibble, Bergen, N.Y.); 138 Carlos.

134 Hamilton Wilcox Pierson (D. D.) was born at Bergen, N. Y.; educated at Union College, and at Union Theo. sem.; was elected president of Columbia coll., Ky., 1858: is the author of

Jefferson at Monticello, and the *Private Life of Thos. Jefferson,* and other works. He remained at his post, in Ky., till forced to leave, in the time of the rebellion (Civil War). Now (1878) in western N.Y.

83 John Pierson, was born in Killingworth (Clinton), Conn.; and emigrated to Genesee Co., N. Y. in 1806-7. He had chd. 139 Harlow W.; and one daughter.

85 Philo Pierson, was born in Killingworth (Clinton), Conn., and emigrated, with his brothers, to Genesee Co., N. Y., in 1806-7. He had chd. 140 William; 141 Daniel; and several daughters.

88 Linus Pierson, was born in Killingworth (Clinton), Conn., and moved, with his brothers, to Genesee Co., N. Y., in 1806-7. He had chd. 142 Edward; and two daughters.

29 Dodo Pierson (Dea.) was b. 1724, at Killingworth (Clinton), Conn.; and died at the same place, January 19, 1796. Tradition says that a maiden aunt objected to having such a name as Dodo put upon the child; but her objections were overruled, and he was so named; and the name of "Dea. Dodo Pierson," now stands out bright and honored in the annals of old Killingworth. During the Revolutionary War, he was a Private in the Connecticut militia.[3] "It appears from a letter from Jeh'd Ward, that Dodo went down to Rye, Westchester Co., N. Y., when the army was encamped there, either as a volunteer in the service, or perhaps to make a visit to his son; at any rate, there being some call for more force, the old man took his musket and went on duty, as a sentinel. This led Mr. Ward to write to Dodo's son Abraham as follows: 'I believe, that through the blessing of God, we shall have better times before long. I have seen your honored father standing sentry, which made me feel otherwise at first. But when I came to consider the grand cause he was in, I found myself rejoiced to think, that men of his rank and age, were willing to turn out.' " Dodo mar.[4] Mary Seward, and they had chd. 57+ Abraham, b. 1756.

57 Dea. Abraham Pierson was born April 11, 1756[5], in Killingworth, Conn., and died there, May 11, 1823. He was treasurer of the school and Ecclesiastical societies, town clerk, selectman, justice of the peace for 32 years and for 24 yrs. represented his town in the gen'l assembly of the state of Conn. But as the "good Deacon Abraham" he was best known. He took an active part in the revolutionary war, and was an officer (Ensign in Connecticut)[6] in the army. "Col. Abraham Pierson was paymaster in Washington's army, the pay roll being still preserved in the family; and in the times that tried men's souls, when our fortunes and finances were at a low ebb, he paid the needy soldiers from his own private purse."[7] He

---

[3]*DAR Patriot Index,* Centennial Edition, National Society of the Daughters of the American Revolution, 1994, part 3, p. 2257.
[4]*DAR Patriot Index,* Centennial Edition, National Society of the Daughters of the American Revolution, 1994, part 3, p. 2257.
[5]*DAR Patriot Index,* Centennial Edition, National Society of the Daughters of the American Revolution, 1994, part 3, p. 2256.
[6]*DAR Patriot Index,* Centennial Edition, National Society of the Daughters of the American Revolution, 1994, part 3, p. 2256.
[7]Lizzie B. Pierson, *Pierson Genealogical Records,* Joel Munsell, Printer, Albany, N.Y., 1878, footnote on p. 22.

mar.[8] Lydia Redfield and had two chd. 89+ William Seward, b. Nov. 1788, d. July 16, 1860; 90 Lydia, b. June 19, 1785 (w. of Rev. Hosea Beckley).

89 William Seward Pierson (M.D.) was born in Killingworth (Clinton), Conn., Nov. 1788 and died July 16, 1860. He was graduated at Yale coll. 1808 and studied medicine; received his M.D. at Dartmouth. He resided, the most of his life, at Windsor, Conn. where he was much beloved and prized as a physician, and as a citizen. His name Wm. Seward was after one of the former and honored inhabitants of old Killingworth. He mar. Nancy Sargeant (dau. of Capt. J. Sargeant, of Hartford, Conn.), 1814. (She died Sept. 17, 1863). They had chd. 143+ William Seward, b. 1815; 144 Nancy S. (w. of R. P. Spalding, of Cleveland, O.), b. 1817; 145 Lydia b. 1819 (w. of C. H. Dexter, of Windsor Locks); 146 Olivia b. 1820 (in Windsor, Ct.); 147 Abraham, b. 1822, d. 1841; 148 Jacob S., b. 1824, d. 1827; 149 Luther P., b. 1826, d. 1827; 150 Julia Ann, b. 1827 (w. of Rev. S. H. Allen, of Windsor Locks); and a babe.

143 William Seward Pierson was born at Windsor, Conn., in 1815; was graduated at Yale coll. in 1836; for many years counselor at law in New York city; and resided several years in Sandusky, Ohio (where he was mayor of the city). He served nearly three yrs. in the war of the rebellion; and had command of a depot for confinement of rebel officers, and prisoners of war, of whom 7,000 were placed in his charge. He now (1878) resides in Windsor, Conn., and is an officer or director in different banks, Ins. Co., R.R. and canal, and manufacturing cos.: is held in high repute in Windsor. He mar. Mary E. Beers (dau. of Dr. T. Beers, of New Haven, 1840).

20 John Pierson (Rev.), was in born in Newark, N.J., in 1689, and died in Hanover, N.J., Aug. 3, 1770, at the home of his son-in-law J. Greene. His early days were spent in Newark, under the instruction of his father. He moved with his father to Conn., and graduated at Yale, 1711. In 1714, he went to Woodbridge, N. J., to preach, where he was ordained over the Presb. ch. April 29, 1717, "with a salary of £80 a year and the use of the parsonage." He continued in charge there till 1752. He was one of the first board of trustees of the College of New Jersey. He mar. Ruth (dau. of Rev. Timothy Woodbridge, of Hartford, Ct.) She died Jan. 7, 1732, aged 38, and was buried in Woodbridge. He moved from Woodbridge to Mendham, N. J., in 1753, where he remained for 10 yrs. and preached the gospel. He married again J. Smith, and moved to her farm, on Long Island. After her death he returned to N. J., and spent his declining days at Hanover, with his dau. Eliz. (w. of J. Greene), where he died, after a ministry of 56 years. He had chd. 33 Abraham; 34+ John, b. 1723, d. 1772; 35 Wyllis; 36 Abigail (w. of ____ Graves, and h. ch. Ruth); 37 Anna; 38 Elizabeth, b. 1726 (w. of Rev. Jacob Greene, and mother of Dr. Ashbel Greene, the 8th pres. of Princeton coll.); 39 Margaret; 40 Hannah.

34 John Pierson (M.D.) was born 1723 at Woodbridge, N. J., and died 1772, at the same place. He was buried by the side of his mother. The inscription on his tombstone "In memory of Doct. John Pierson, who deceased Feb. 21, 1772, ag. 49 yrs. A sensible man and skillful physician." The widow "Mary Pierson" was listed on the tax list[9] at Woodbridge Twp., Middlesex Co., N.J., on Aug. 1784. She died Aug. 14, 1792. He had chd. 58 Abigail,

---

[8]*DAR Patriot Index*, Centennial Edition, National Society of the Daughters of the American Revolution, 1994, part 3, p. 2256.
[9]MicroQuix, *Colonial America - Pre-1790 Census Indexes, Tax Lists*, No. CD136, Automated Archives, Inc., 1992.

d. 1773, ag.17 yrs.; 59 Theodosia, b. 1750, d. 1761; 60 Theodosia, b. Feb. 24, 1767, d. June 1793 (w. of Nath. Marshall).

3 Thomas Pierson, Jr., was born 1641-2 at Southampton, Suffolk Co., N.Y., and died in Newark, N. J., before the year 1684. In childhood he moved with his father to Branford, Conn., where he mar. Mary Brown. When his father and others of that colony moved to Newark, N.J., he also moved to the same place, where he had a house-lot of 6 acres set off to him. He had chd. 21+ Abraham, b. 1676, d. 1756-8; and possibly 21a Samuel.

21 Abraham Pierson was born 1676 in Newark, N.J., and died there in 1756 or 8. He lived on an allotment of land belonging to Thomas Pierson Jr. He mar. Hannah _____ (b. 1676 and d. 1727), and had chd. 41+ Benjamin, b. 1701, d. 1783; 42+ Abraham, b. 1707, d. 1777; 43+ Isaac, b. 1718, d. 1803; 44 Mary (w. of ____ Plum); 45+ John.

41 Benjamin Pierson was born 1701 at Newark, N.J., and died in 1783. He moved from Newark to a tract of land called Piersonville, three miles east of Morristown on the road from Whippany to East Hanover (now Madison), a portion of which land is now (1878) occupied by the Roman Catholic convent and school. He owned a large and beautiful tract of land there, which he afterwards divided among his children, the most of whom settled thereon. "He was of size under the average, grave, and much respected for his religious character and solid worth." Benjamin recorded[10] his cattle ear marks in 1753 at Morris Twp., Morris Co., N.J. He posted for strays[11] in Hanover, N.J., on 3 Dec 1755, 14 & 24 Nov 1768, 29 Nov 1771, and 16 Nov 1775. In Oct. 1768, Benjamin Pierson was listed[12] with tax ratables at Morris Twp., Morris Co., N.J., consisting of land 12£ 10s, 223 acres, 14 horses & cattle, 19 sheep, 1/2 sawmill, and no single men. Benjamin mar. Patience Coe, who d. in 1785; and they had chd. 61+ Elijah, b. 1728-30, d. 1795; 62+ John, b. 1731; 63 Sarah, b. 1733 (w. of ____ Cook, and mother of Benj. Cook of Bottle Hill); 64+ Benjamin, b. 1736; 65+ Moses, b. 1738, d. 1768; 66 Isaac[13], perhaps had chd. 105 Darius & 106 Penira; 67+ Aaron, b. 1746; 68 Keziah (w. of Dea. Munson); 69 Abraham; 70+ Daniel, b. 1750, d. 1831. See the 1771 census[14] in Chapter 17 for Piersonville, Morris Twp., Morris Co., N.J.

61 Elijah Pierson was born 1728 or 30 in Newark, N.J., or Piersonville, N.J., and died in 1795. He was buried at Morristown, N.J. He settled on a farm near Greene Village, N. J., and in Oct. 1768 was rated[15] in Morris Twp, Morris Co., N.J., with land 12£ 10s, 330 acres, 11 horses & cattle, and 17 sheep. He had chd. 91+ George; 92 Moses (who never married); 93+ Benjamin, b. Nov. 25, 1757; 94 Sarah (w. of ____ Crane); 95 Jane (w. of ____ Durham); 96 Phebe (w. of ____ Furnam).

---

[10]Harriet Stryker-Rodda, *Some Early Records of Morris County, New Jersey 1740-1799*, published under the patronage of Morris County Archives Publications Committee, Polyanthos, Inc., New Orleans, La., 1975, p. 4.

[11]Harriet Stryker-Rodda, *Some Early Records of Morris County, New Jersey 1740-1799*, published under the patronage of Morris County Archives Publications Committee, Polyanthos, Inc., New Orleans, La., 1975, p. 43.

[12]Harriet Stryker-Rodda, *Some Early Records of Morris County, New Jersey 1740-1799*, published under the patronage of Morris County Archives Publications Committee, Polyanthos, Inc., New Orleans, La., 1975, p. 63.

[13]A correction to Lizzie Pierson's book: For the Isaac Pierson that was b. 1737 & d. 1790, see 73 Isaac Pierson, son of 42 Abraham Pierson.

[14]MicroQuix, *Colonial America - Pre-1790 Census Indexes, Tax Lists*, No. CD136, Automated Archives, Inc., 1992.

[15]Harriet Stryker-Rodda, *Some Early Records of Morris County, New Jersey 1740-1799*, published under the patronage of Morris County Archives Publications Committee, Polyanthos, Inc., New Orleans, La., 1975, p. 73.

91 George Pierson was born at Greene Village, N. J., and had chd. 151 Sallie; 152 Phebe; 153 Betsey; 154 John; 155 Andrew; 156 Furnam.

93 Benjamin Pierson was born[16] Nov. 25, 1757, and died[17] Feb. 10, 1832. He settled on a part of the original Piersonville farm near Morristown, N. J. He served in the Revolutionary War as a Private in Capt. Daniel Pierson's Company, Morris Co., N.J. militia (S-719). He mar. Dec. 22, 1779, Abigail Condit. On 24 Apr 1782, he advertised[18] in the New Jersey Journal newspaper, "Benjamin Pierson 3d advertises for rent the farm, formerly the property of Ebenezer Condict, deceased, 170 acres, within 3 miles of Morristown on the road to Baskenridge (Basking Ridge), with a large cider house and mill and an apple orchard. To be sold, livestock, farming utensils and produce." Benjamin is buried[19] in the First Presbyterian Church yard, Morristown, N.J. After Benjamin's death, his widow Abigail (Condit) Pierson joined[20], Nov. 25, 1835, the Presbyterian Church of Madison, N.J., by letter from the Presbyterian Church of Morristown, N.J. Benjamin and Abigail had chd. 157+ Ebenezer Condit; 158+ Silas; 159+ Elijah; 160+ Mahlon; 161+ Julia Ann; 162 Jane (mar. Edwin Ford of Morristown).

157 Ebenezer Condit Pierson mar[21]. Apr. 5, 1803, Betsey Corey. Ebenezer and Betsey were both confirmed[22] May 15, 1808, at the Presbyterian Church at Madison, N.J. They moved[23] in 1814 to Morristown, N.J. They had chd. 190a Mary[24], bap. Jun. 26, 1808; 191 Betsey[25] (Eliza.), bap. Jun. 26, 1808[26]; 190[27] Sylvester Condit[28], bap. Sep. 3, 1809 at age 6 mo.

---

[16]Barbara Hoskins, *Men from Morris County New Jersey Who Served in the American Revolution*, The Friends of the Joint Free Public Library of Morristown and Morris Township, Morristown, N.J., 1979, p. 144.

[17]Barbara Hoskins, *Men from Morris County New Jersey Who Served in the American Revolution*, The Friends of the Joint Free Public Library of Morristown and Morris Township, Morristown, N.J., 1979, p. 144.

[18]Thomas B. Wilson, *Notices From New Jersey Newspapers 1781-1790*, Hunterdon House, Lambertville, N.J., 1988, p. 137.

[19]Barbara Hoskins, *Men from Morris County New Jersey Who Served in the American Revolution*, The Friends of the Joint Free Public Library of Morristown and Morris Township, Morristown, N.J., 1979, p. 144.

[20]Viola E. Shaw and Barbara S. Parker, *Madison, New Jersey Presbyterian Church Vital Records 1747-1900*, The Presbyterian Church of Madison, Madison, N.J., 1982, p. 249.

[21]Viola E. Shaw and Barbara S. Parker, *Madison, New Jersey Presbyterian Church Vital Records 1747-1900*, The Presbyterian Church of Madison, Madison, N.J., 1982, p. 249.

[22]Viola E. Shaw and Barbara S. Parker, *Madison, New Jersey Presbyterian Church Vital Records 1747-1900*, The Presbyterian Church of Madison, Madison, N.J., 1982, p. 249.

[23]Viola E. Shaw and Barbara S. Parker, *Madison, New Jersey Presbyterian Church Vital Records 1747-1900*, The Presbyterian Church of Madison, Madison, N.J., 1982, p. 249.

[24]Viola E. Shaw and Barbara S. Parker, *Madison, New Jersey Presbyterian Church Vital Records 1747-1900*, The Presbyterian Church of Madison, Madison, N.J., 1982, p. 250.

[25]Viola E. Shaw and Barbara S. Parker, *Madison, New Jersey Presbyterian Church Vital Records 1747-1900*, The Presbyterian Church of Madison, Madison, N.J., 1982, p. 250.

[26]Betsey was baptized on the same date as her sister Mary.

[27]Identification number out of order so that birth order can be maintained while using Lizzie Pierson's identification numbers.

[28]Viola E. Shaw and Barbara S. Parker, *Madison, New Jersey Presbyterian Church Vital Records 1747-1900*, The Presbyterian Church of Madison, Madison, N.J., 1982, p. 250.

158 Silas Pierson witnessed[29] a session record in 1824 at the Presbyterian Church of Madison, N.J. He had chd. 192 Delia.

159 Elijah Pierson, had chd. 193 Elizabeth.

160 Mahlon Pierson was confirmed[30] May 26, 1836, at the Presbyterian Church at Madison, N.J. The roll there says he was suspended with no date. He mar[31]. Julia Lindsley (d. May 15, 1856, at Somerville, N.J.), dau. of widow Phebe Lindsley. Reference is made to Morristown N.J. church records for more information.

161 Julia Ann Pierson was a member[32] of the Presbyterian Church at Madison, N.J., from May 29, 1834, to Nov. 1846. She came from before and returned to afterwards the Presbyterian Church of Morristown, N.J.

62 John Pierson was born near Morristown (Piersonville), N.J., in 1731, and had chd. 97 Catherine (w. of ____ Cook, and mother of Dr. Silas Cook); 98 Mary (w. of I. Spaulding); 99 Ruth (w. of I. Spining).

64 Capt. Benjamin Pierson was born near Morristown (Piersonville, near the present Convent Station), N.J., Mar. 30, 1736 [33], settled near the old homestead, and died[34] Jan. 1, 1792. In 1765, "Benjamin Peirson Jr.," recorded[35] cattle ear marks at Morris Twp, Morris Co., N.J. In May 1776, a poll list[36] for delegates from Morris County to New Jersey's First Constitutional Convention included "Benjm Pearson Junr" with place of abode Mendham, Morris Co., N.J. In 1776, men were enlisting[37] in Lt. Benjamin Pierson's Company, Eastern Regiment, Morris County, N.J., Militia. That year, three Continental Regiments came from Fort Ticonderoga to Morristown and Lt. Benjamin Pierson's Company was assigned to guard the Continental stores and prisoners. Benjamin served in the Revolutionary War as both a Lieutenant and a Captain of the Morris Co., N.J., militia, Eastern Battalion (S-405). He mar[38]. Nov. 3, 1756, Phebe Raynor (d. 1799). He was on a tax list[39] July 1783 at

---

[29] Viola E. Shaw and Barbara S. Parker, *Madison, New Jersey Presbyterian Church Vital Records 1747-1900*, The Presbyterian Church of Madison, Madison, N.J., 1982, p. 252.

[30] Viola E. Shaw and Barbara S. Parker, *Madison, New Jersey Presbyterian Church Vital Records 1747-1900*, The Presbyterian Church of Madison, Madison, N.J., 1982, p. 251.

[31] Viola E. Shaw and Barbara S. Parker, *Madison, New Jersey Presbyterian Church Vital Records 1747-1900*, The Presbyterian Church of Madison, Madison, N.J., 1982, p. 251.

[32] Viola E. Shaw and Barbara S. Parker, *Madison, New Jersey Presbyterian Church Vital Records 1747-1900*, The Presbyterian Church of Madison, Madison, N.J., 1982, p. 251.

[33] *DAR Patriot Index*, Centennial Edition, National Society of the Daughters of the American Revolution, 1994, part 3, p. 2256.

[34] Barbara Hoskins, *Men from Morris County New Jersey Who Served in the American Revolution*, The Friends of the Joint Free Public Library of Morristown and Morris Township, Morristown, N.J., 1979, p. 144.

[35] Harriet Stryker-Rodda, *Some Early Records of Morris County, New Jersey 1740-1799*, published under the patronage of Morris County Archives Publications Committee, Polyanthos, Inc., New Orleans, La., 1975, p. 6.

[36] Harriet Stryker-Rodda, *Some Early Records of Morris County, New Jersey 1740-1799*, published under the patronage of Morris County Archives Publications Committee, Polyanthos, Inc., New Orleans, La., 1975, p. 88.

[37] Joseph R. Klett, *Genealogies of New Jersey Families*, Genealogical Publishing Company, Inc., Baltimore, Md., 1996, p. 913.

[38] Barbara Hoskins, *Men from Morris County New Jersey Who Served in the American Revolution*, The Friends of the Joint Free Public Library of Morristown and Morris Township, Morristown, N.J., 1979, p. 144.

[39] MicroQuix, *Colonial America - Pre-1790 Census Indexes, Tax Lists*, No. CD136, Automated Archives, Inc., 1992.

Hanover Twp., Morris Co., N.J. Benjamin is buried[40] in the First Presbyterian Church yard, Morristown, N.J. Benjamin and Phebe had chd. 100+ David, b. 1763; 101 Hannah; 102+ Gabriel, b. 1767; 103 Patience.

100 David Pierson[41] was born Aug. 29, 1763 in Morristown, N. J., and died Mar. 22, 1824. In the Revolutionary War, he served as a Private in Morris Co., N.J. militia (S-719). He mar. Dec. 1789 Abigail Thompson (b. January 13, 1769, and d. Apr. 6, 1842). David is buried[42] in the First Presbyterian Church yard, Morristown, N.J. David and Abigail had chd. 163+ Albert O., b. January 10, 1791, d. Oct. 14, 1862; 164+ Benjamin Thompson, b. Sept. 21, 1793, d. June 18, 1862; 165+ Jonathan, b. Oct. 2, 1795, d. Feb. 20, 1869; 166+ Stephen H., b. Sept. 29, 1797, d. July 12, 1863; 167 Mary Ann (David's only dau.), b. Nov. 6, 1802, d. Oct. 13, 1862 (w. of Isaac H. Bruin of Chatham, N. J., eldest son of Benjamin Bruin); 168+ Charles T., b. July 21, 1804, d. January 26, 1859; 169+ Ira C., b. Apr. 26, 1806, d. 1872 (lived in New York city, mar. M. Garthwaite); 170+ Lewis C., b. Aug. 14, 1808, d. 1869 (he lived in Georgia).

163 Albert O. Pierson[43] was born Jan. 10, 1791, and died Oct. 14, 1862. He mar. Abby Garthwaite, and lived in Newark, N. J. They had chd. 194 Maria Smith, b. 1814, d. Jan. 1877, w. of _____ Headley; 195 Julia Britton, b. 1817, w. of C. A. Dennis; 196 Almira Parkhurst, b. 1820, w. of _____ Miller; 196a David Lafayette, b. 1822, d. 1832; 197 William Henry, b. Nov. 15, 1827, and now (1878) resides in New Orleans; 198 Jerry Garthwaite, b. 1830, and now (1878) resides in New Orleans; 198a Mary Virginia, b. 1836; and two others who died young.

164 Benjamin Thompson Pierson[44] was born Sept. 21, 1793, and died June 18, 1862. He resided in Newark, N. J., and prepared the first "Directory of the City of Newark." He mar. Mrs. P. Gale, and had chd. Paulina.

165 Jonathan Pierson[45] was born Oct. 2, 1795, and died Feb. 20, 1869. He resided at Newark, N. J. He mar. M. Carnes, and had chd. 200a Jane W., b. April 5, 1818, d. Dec. 23, 1857; 200 Mary Ann, b. Oct. 29, 1819, d. Oct. 13, 1855 (w. of A. Ward); 200b Nancy B., b. Sept. 14, 1821, d. young; 199 Abby T., b. Jan. 19, 1823, d. July 15, 1859 (w. of M. Field); 200c Sophia J., b. Apr. 17, 1825, d. Nov. 20, 1835; 200d Paulina G., b. Feb. 6, 1828, d. Sept. 18, 1849; 200e Stephen H., b. Aug. 30, 1830, d. Sept. 12, 1851; 200f Ira Burnet, b. Apr. 2, 1833, d. June 4, 1833; 200g Charles H., b. June 28, 1834, d. Nov. 12, 1854; 201 _____ (mar. _____ Osborn) (she may be one of the other daus. mentioned above).

166 Stephen H. Pierson[46] was born Sept. 29, 1797, and died July 12, 1863. He mar. S. A. Wheeler, in 1820, and had chd. 202 Phebe, d. young; 203 Ann W., (w. of Rev. I. P. Lemoy); 204 Joseph W. (was an Episcopal clergyman in Illinois), now (1878) deceased; 205+ James

---

[40]Barbara Hoskins, *Men from Morris County New Jersey Who Served in the American Revolution*, The Friends of the Joint Free Public Library of Morristown and Morris Township, Morristown, N.J., 1979, p. 144.

[41]Lizzie Pierson's Appendix p. 21 of her book, *Pierson Genealogical Records*, 1878, is integrated.

[42]Barbara Hoskins, *Men from Morris County New Jersey Who Served in the American Revolution*, The Friends of the Joint Free Public Library of Morristown and Morris Township, Morristown, N.J., 1979, p. 145.

[43]Lizzie Pierson's *Pierson Genealogical Records*, Appendix p. 21 of her book is integrated in this family's data.

[44]Lizzie Pierson's *Pierson Genealogical Records*, Appendix p. 21 of her book is integrated in this family's data.

[45]Lizzie Pierson's *Pierson Genealogical Records*, Appendix p. 21 of her book is integrated in this family's data.

[46]Lizzie Pierson's *Pierson Genealogical Records*, Appendix p. 21 of her book is integrated in this family's data.

W. F.; 206 Charles Henry (resides in New York city); 207+ Arthur Tappan; 208 Mary Augusta (resides in Rochester, N. Y.).

205 James W. F. Pierson resides (1878) in New York city, N.Y. He had chd. 219 James H.; 220 Carrie E.

207 Arthur Tappan Pierson (Rev.) graduated at Hamilton college, 1857, and Union Theological seminary. In1878, he was the pastor of a Congregational church in Detroit, Mich. He mar. S. F. Benedict, and they had chd. 221 Helen M.; 222 Laura; 223 Louisa; 224 Delavan; 225 Anna; 226 Edith.

168 Charles T. Pierson[47] was born July 21, 1804, and died Jan. 26, 1859 He mar. Hannah Coe, and resided in Newark, N. J. They had chd. 209a Edward (killed in the late civil war); 209b Abby Henrietta (w. of ____ Baldwin); 209 Annie I. (w. of M. Field); 209c Mary Adelaide.

169 Ira C. Pierson[48] was born April 26, 1806, and died 1872. He resided in New York city, N.Y. He mar. Mary P. Garthwaite, and they had chd. 209d John G. (mar. Miss Valentine); 209e Augustus, d. in 1876; 209f Caroline G.

170 Lewis C. Pierson[49] was born Aug. 14, 1808, and died 1869. He resided in Georgia.

102 Gabriel Pierson was born in 1767, and died[50] Sep 1814 at age 47 (newspaper). He lived near Morristown, N. J.,. He mar. [51] Ruth ____ (d. Mar. 2, 1857 in her 91st year, and is bur. Hillside Cemetery, Madison, N.J.). Gabriel and Ruth had chd.[52] 171 Matthias, mar. [53] Feb. 9, 1811, Charlotte Genung (he of Morristown, she of Bottle Hill [newspaper]), (they lived Sussex co., N.J., & had 6 chd.); 172 Eneas, died young; 173 Sally (w. of Paul Day, of Chatham, N. J.); 173a Phebe[54], b. 1794, d. Feb. 12, 1867 at age 72, bur[55]. Hillside Cem., Madison, N.J., never married; 173b+ Mehitabel; 173c Julia, never married.

173b Mehitabel Pierson[56], b. Dec. 1, 1797, d. July 1, 1872, never married, bur. Hillside Cem., Madison, N.J., in plot with Ruth (widow of Gabriel), Ambrose, and Phebe.

---

[47]Lizzie Pierson's *Pierson Genealogical Records*, Appendix p. 22 of her book is integrated in this family's data.

[48]Lizzie Pierson's *Pierson Genealogical Records*, Appendix p. 22 of her book is integrated in this family's data.

[49]Lizzie Pierson's *Pierson Genealogical Records*, Appendix p. 22 of her book is integrated in this family's data.

[50]Viola E. Shaw and Barbara S. Parker, *Madison, New Jersey Presbyterian Church Vital Records 1747-1900*, The Presbyterian Church of Madison, Madison, N.J., 1982, p. 250.

[51]Viola E. Shaw and Barbara S. Parker, *Madison, New Jersey Presbyterian Church Vital Records 1747-1900*, The Presbyterian Church of Madison, Madison, N.J., 1982, p. 250.

[52]The pre-appendix 171 Albert, 172 Thompson, and 173 Stephen on p. 18 of Lizzie Pierson's book have been dropped as incorrect.

[53]Viola E. Shaw and Barbara S. Parker, *Madison, New Jersey Presbyterian Church Vital Records 1747-1900*, The Presbyterian Church of Madison, Madison, N.J., 1982, p. 251 (Matthias Pierson listed as son of Gabriel), they reference Morris County N.J. Marriage Books A & B.

[54]Viola E. Shaw and Barbara S. Parker, *Madison, New Jersey Presbyterian Church Vital Records 1747-1900*, The Presbyterian Church of Madison, Madison, N.J., 1982, p. 252.

[55]Phebe Pierson buried in plot with widow of Gabriel, Ambrose, and Mehetabel.

[56]Viola E. Shaw and Barbara S. Parker, *Madison, New Jersey Presbyterian Church Vital Records 1747-1900*, The Presbyterian Church of Madison, Madison, N.J., 1982, p. 251.

65 Moses Pierson was born 1738, near Morristown, Morris Co., N.J., at Piersonville, and died in 1768 at age 30. "Moss Person" posted[57] strays at Hanover, Morris Co., N.J., on 6 Dec 1760. He had chd. 104 Keziah.

67 Aaron Pierson was born in 1746[58] at Piersonville, near Morristown, Morris Co., N. J., and died[59] Jan. 2, 1803. He lived (on his father's old homestead[60]) in Hanover Township[61]. Aaron served[62] as Private in Morris Co., N.J., Militia (S-719). He mar. [63] Nov. 25, 1766, Mary Howell. He was at Bottle Hill, N.J., on 2 Oct 1782, per the New Jersey Journal newspaper[64] "Aaron Pierson, Bottle Hill, advertises a mare strayed to his plantation." Aaron is listed in tax lists[65] of Hanover Twp, Morris Co., N.J., in July 1783, July 1785, 1787, Aug. 1788, and Aug. 1789. He is listed[66] as a freeholder 17 Jan 1793 at Hanover Twp., Morris Co., N.J. Aaron contributed[67] at the Presbyterian Church of Madison, N.J., in 1794 and 1795. He is buried[68] in the First Presbyterian Church yard, Morristown, N.J. Aaron and Mary had chd. 107+ Ebenezer D.; 108 Charlotte, d. 1846, (mar. Wm. Jones, and had 9 Jones chd., of whom Charlotte Jones mar. A. Canfield and Louisa Jones mar. O. L. Kirkland).

107 Ebenezer D. Pierson, M.D., was born in Morristown, N. J., graduated Princeton coll. 1791, studied medicine and practiced the same in Morristown till 1816, when he moved with his family to Cincinnati, Ohio. He died there in 1829, after a successful practice. He mar. Phebe Day (and possibly Phebe, the dau. of Abr. Canfield), and had chd. 174 Mary Ann , d. 1825, (w. of ____ DeWitt, of Cincinnati); 175 Nancy (w. of ____ Keyt); 176 Sallie, d. 1846; 177+ Aaron Howell, d. 1875; 178 Charlotte, d. 1831 (w. of ____ Robinson); 179 Emily A., d. 1847 (w. of ____ Orr).

177 Aaron Howell Pierson spent his early days in Cincinnati, and moved to Natchitoches, Louisiana, between 1825 and 1830. For many years he was an imminent lawyer in Louisiana, and died in 1875 at Natchitoches. He mar. Mrs. Creighton (formerly M. G.

---

[57]Harriet Stryker-Rodda, *Some Early Records of Morris County, New Jersey 1740-1799*, published under the patronage of Morris County Archives Publications Committee, Polyanthos, Inc., New Orleans, La., 1975, p. 37.

[58]Barbara Hoskins, *Men from Morris County New Jersey Who Served in the American Revolution*, The Friends of the Joint Free Public Library of Morristown and Morris Township, Morristown, N.J., 1979, p. 144.

[59]Barbara Hoskins, *Men from Morris County New Jersey Who Served in the American Revolution*, The Friends of the Joint Free Public Library of Morristown and Morris Township, Morristown, N.J., 1979, p. 144.

[60]Lizzie B. Pierson, *Pierson Genealogical Records*, Joel Munsell, Printer, Albany, N.Y., 1878, Peirson. 19.

[61]Barbara Hoskins, *Men from Morris County New Jersey Who Served in the American Revolution*, The Friends of the Joint Free Public Library of Morristown and Morris Township, Morristown, N.J., 1979, p. 144.

[62]Barbara Hoskins, *Men from Morris County New Jersey Who Served in the American Revolution*, The Friends of the Joint Free Public Library of Morristown and Morris Township, Morristown, N.J., 1979, p. 144.

[63]Barbara Hoskins, *Men from Morris County New Jersey Who Served in the American Revolution*, The Friends of the Joint Free Public Library of Morristown and Morris Township, Morristown, N.J., 1979, p. 144.

[64]Thomas B. Wilson, *Notices From New Jersey Newspapers 1781-1790*, Hunterdon House, Lambertville, N.J., 1988, p. 146.

[65]MicroQuix, *Colonial America - Pre-1790 Census Indexes, Tax Lists*, No. CD136, Automated Archives, Inc., 1992.

[66]Harriet Stryker-Rodda, *Some Early Records of Morris County, New Jersey 1740-1799*, published under the patronage of Morris County Archives Publications Committee, Polyanthos, Inc., New Orleans, La., 1975, p. 150.

[67]Viola E. Shaw and Barbara S. Parker, *Madison, New Jersey Presbyterian Church Vital Records 1747-1900*, The Presbyterian Church of Madison, Madison, N.J., 1982, p. 249.

[68]Barbara Hoskins, *Men from Morris County New Jersey Who Served in the American Revolution*, The Friends of the Joint Free Public Library of Morristown and Morris Township, Morristown, N.J., 1979, p. 144.

Martin of Rhode Island) and had chd. 210 Edward L.; 211 Augusta L.; 212 Percy S.; 213 Aaron Howell (mar. M. A. Pierce, and now (1878) resides in Natchitoches); 214 Emilie A.; 215 Lelia T.; 216 Eva M.; 217 Charles D.; 218 Horace L.

70 Lt. Daniel Pierson was born near Morristown, at Piersonville, N. J., in 1750, and died[69] Dec. 15, 1831 in Dayton, Ohio. During the Revolutionary War, he served as a 2nd Lieutenant in Capt. Imlay's Company, 3rd Regiment, Continental Army, and was present at the battle of Monmouth. He was discharged[70] with his battalion (S-21; 161), pension (S4-272). On 6 Feb 1782, he advertised[71] in the New Jersey Journal newspaper, "Daniel Pierson, Hanover, advertises for sale a farm of 157 1/2 acres three miles from Morristown on the road to Chatham where the Jersey troops are hutted." He then moved to the village of Morristown and built his house on the corner of South and Pine streets. He later moved to Dayton, Ohio with his whole family, except Charles,. He mar[72]. Feb. 19, 1784, Prudence King (d. 1837). Daniel and Prudence had chd. 109 Clarissa, b. 1785 at Morristown, and d. 1863 at Cin. (w. of ____ Davies); 110+ Charles Edwin, b. 1787, d. 1865; 111 John A., b. 1789, d. 1811; 112 William H., b. 1791, .d. 1820; 113 Eliz. Ann, d. 1794; 114+ Henry A., b. 1795.

110 Charles Edwin Pierson (M.D.) was born in Morristown, in 1787. He graduated from Princeton coll. in 1807. "He commenced the practice of medicine in his native town, as a partner with Dr. Ebenezer D. Pierson. This gentleman soon after died, and his large practice fell into the hands of the young Dr. Chas. Edw. Pierson. His health failed in consequence, and he repaired to London, where he resided 6 yrs. He then returned to New York city and practiced medicine. In his later life, he became interested in the public schools of the city, and devoted much time to devising the best systems for carrying on the schools. He was an earnest Christian, and fond of nature and scientific studies." He mar. A. M. Shaw, and died in Bergen, N. J. in 1865. He had chd. 180 Clara Ann, b. 1817, d. 1853 (w. of F. S. Howe); 181 Charles, b. 1819, d. 1820; 182 John Shaw, b. 1822, graduated Princeton 1840 (mar. C. L. Tuthill, who is now (1878) deceased), now (1878) resides in New York city, and is well known in his connection with the Bible Society; 183 Charles E., b. 1825, (unmarried); 184 Amelia R., b. 1827, d. 1828; 185 Wm. H., b. 1830, d. 1831.

114 Henry A. Pierson, born 1795 and died in Dayton, Ohio, in 1874; had chd. 186 Daniel, b. 1832, d. 1865 Dayton, Ohio.

42 Abraham Pierson, was born in Newark, 1707 and died 1777 in Morristown, N. J. He lived on a farm opposite his brother Benjamin, in Morristown; mar. Mary ____ (who died in 1782), and had chd. 71 Abraham; 72+ Darius; 73+ Isaac, b. 1737; and some others.

72 Darius Pierson had chd. 115 Isaac; 116 Joseph.

---

[69]Barbara Hoskins, *Men from Morris County New Jersey Who Served in the American Revolution*, The Friends of the Joint Free Public Library of Morristown and Morris Township, Morristown, N.J., 1979, p. 144.
[70]Barbara Hoskins, *Men from Morris County New Jersey Who Served in the American Revolution*, The Friends of the Joint Free Public Library of Morristown and Morris Township, Morristown, N.J., 1979, p. 144.
[71]Thomas B. Wilson, *Notices From New Jersey Newspapers 1781-1790*, Hunterdon House, Lambertville, N.J., 1988, p. 131.
[72]Barbara Hoskins, *Men from Morris County New Jersey Who Served in the American Revolution*, The Friends of the Joint Free Public Library of Morristown and Morris Township, Morristown, N.J., 1979, p. 144.

73 Isaac Pierson was born 1737 in Morristown, Morris Co., N.J., and continued to reside there till his death in Aug. 1790. In Oct. 1768, Isaac was rated[73] in Morris Twp, Morris Co., N.J., with land 12£ 10s, 140 acres, 12 horses & cattle, and 17 sheep. Isaac mar.[74] Rhoda ____. After Isaac's death in 1790, the widow Rhoda Pierson mar. 2d 10 Oct 1791 Deacon Jonathan Thompson (b. 1734, d. 20 Dec 1817). Deacon Thompson owned 152 acres in Madison, N.J., known as the Pine Tree Farm. Deacon Thompson's 1st wife, Abigail Haines d. 27 Mar 1791 aged 57 years. Isaac and Rhoda had chd. 117 Darius; 118 Jacob, d. 1770; 119 John; 120 Abraham, b. 1749, and d. 1771; 121 Phebe; 122 Taphena; 123+ Eunice.

123 Eunice Pierson may be the Eunice Pierson that was born 12 Feb 1762, mar. Leonard Coleman (b. 14 Apr 1754 Morris Co., N.J., d. 28 Mar 1839 Belmont, Ohio), and had Coleman chd.: Leonard; William John Pierson; Jacob; Elizabeth; Mary; William Pierson; Charlotte; and Sarah.

43 Isaac Pierson, was born in Newark, N. J.; he mar. Sarah Ogden (b. 1718 and d. 1795), and had chd. 74 John; 75 Uzal; 76 Isaac; 77 Hannah.

45 John Pierson was born between 1702 and 1727 in Newark, Essex Co., N.J., and is known to have been an Episcopal clergyman, in lower New Jersey, and to have chd. 78 Abraham; and perhaps another. The following John and family fit the criteria:

"Will[75] of John Pierson of Salem Town and County, N.J., clerk, dated Oct. 9, 1747, and proved Oct. 29, 1747 (Lib. 9, p. 359). Wife, Ann, sole executrix, and to have personal estate with the profits of my real estate until my three sons will be 21. Sons - Coleman, at 21, to have the plantation called the Fork, which I purchased of Edmund Wetherby, also my Negro boy Prime and my silver tankard; Henry, my dwelling in Salem Town, with the lot belonging, he paying £100 to his sister Mary Pierson, when she will be 21, also my Negro girl and my pint silver can; Abraham, when 21, to have my house, land and marsh in the Town bounds of Salem, with 12 acres in Cow's Neck, and my silver ladle. Daughter, Mary, at 21, or marriage, to have my silver salver and Negro girl, Calia. Unto the expected child (be it male or female) [John, see mother Ann's will below], £100. Witnesses - Andrew Gardiner, Rebekah Coleman, Dan. Mestayer."

John's wife, "Ann Pierson of Salem Town and County, N.J., widow, made her will[76] June 4, 1749, which was proved 1750. Daughter, Mary, to have the Great Bible, Negro woman Flora, two silver pepper boxes, nine large silver spoons, one set of teaspoons and £200, when of age or at marriage, the interest thereof to be used for the bringing up and education of said daughter. Sons - Henry to have £100 at interest, for his bringing up and education; John, one silver porringer, two silver salts, two small silver spoons, together

[73] Harriet Stryker-Rodda, *Some Early Records of Morris County, New Jersey 1740-1799*, published under the patronage of Morris County Archives Publications Committee, Polyanthos, Inc., New Orleans, La., 1975, p. 73.
[74] Helen Martha Wright, *History and Records of the Methodist Episcopal Church, Mendham, Morris Co., N J*, published by author, printed by Charles C. Harman, Jersey City, N. J., 1938, p. 40.
[75] A. Van Doren Honeyman, *Documents Relating to the State of New Jersey*, First Series, Vol. 30, "Calendar of New Jersey Wills, Administrations, Etc," Vol. II 1730-1750, The Unionist-Gazette Association, Printers, Somerville, N.J., 1918, p. 379.
[76] A. Van Doren Honeyman, *Documents Relating to the State of New Jersey*, First Series, Vol. 30, "Calendar of New Jersey Wills, Administrations, Etc," Vol. II 1730-1750, The Unionist-Gazette Association, Printers, Somerville, N.J., 1918, p. 379.

with the sum of £200 to be delivered to him when of age (the £200 to be put to interest for the bringing up and education of my son). Residue of my estate to be divided among my three children, Mary, Henry, and John; the land to be delivered at their respective ages aforesaid. Executor - my brother-in-law, Joseph Sharp. Witnesses - Elizabeth Coleman, George Trenchard. Inventory (missing, no date) but listed as £313.18.6 (Lib. 9, p. 83)."

Based on the above two wills, John Pierson (d. 1747) mar. ca. 1732 Ann Coleman(?) (d. 1750), probably in Salem Co., N.J., and they had chd., all born at Salem, Salem Co., N.J.: 78a Coleman, b. ca. 1733, d. between Oct. 9, 1747 & June 4, 1749; 78b Henry, b. ca. 1736; 78 Abraham, b. ca. 1740, d. between Oct. 9, 1747 & June 4, 1749; 78c Mary, b. ca. 1744; and 78d John, b. within the 6(?) months after Oct. 9, 1747.

9 Theophilus Pierson, the 8th chd. of Rev. Abraham Pierson, was born at Branford, Ct., in 1659 and moved in childhood to Newark, N. J., where he mar. and made his residence. He died in 1713. Had chd. 22+ Jonathan, b. 1687, d. 1771; 23+ David, d. 1732.

22 Jonathan Pierson was born in Newark, N. J., in 1687, where he continued to reside, till his death in 1771. He mar. J. Ward (who d. 1731) and had chd. 46 Rebecca (mar. ____ Lyon, and had Lyon chd. Nathaniel, David and Joanna).

23 David Pierson was born in Newark, N.J., where he probably lived, and died there 1732. His will was dated Dec. 1, 1732, was proved Jan. 11, 1732/3, and his inventory taken Mar. 22, 1732/3. His will[77] states "David Peirson" of Newark, Essex Co., N.J., joiner; children Theophilus, Mary, and Susannah, all under age; expected child; Negro boy, Titus, to be sold towards paying my debts; lands joining lands of Ebenezer Headly and Daniel Harrison; executors: wife Hannah, and brother Jonathan; witnesses: John Crane, John Wall, & J. Styles (Lib. B, p. 373). David and Hannah had chd. 47 Theophilus; 48 Mary; 49 Susanna; and one other b. 1732/3 (see will about expected child).

[77] A. Van Doren Honeyman, *Documents Relating to the Colonial History of the State of New Jersey*, First Series - Vol. 30, "Calendar of New Jersey Wills, Administrations, etc.," Vol. II, 1730-1750, The Unionist-Gazette Association, Printers, Somerville, N.J., 1918, p. 374.

Chapter 8
Henry Peirson (1615-1680)
American Immigrant

Henry Peirson was the son of William and Wyborough (Griggs) Peirson of Olney, Buckinghamshire, England. Henry was baptized 10 Dec 1615 at Olney. This is verified as follows[1]:

A deed[2] dated 12 May 1662 and signed by "Henry Peirson" and John Cooper (Jr.) was written at Southampton, Long Island, and is now at the Staffordshire County Record Office, Stafford, England. The signatures match those of Henry Peirson and John Cooper Jr. in the Southampton town records. In the deed, Henry Peirson and John Cooper Jr. convey to Ignatius Fuller of Sherrington, county Bucks., (apparently the son of Edward Fuller of Olney, mentioned in the latter's will) two pieces of property in Olney, England. The grantors describe themselves in the deed as:

> "Henry Peirson formerly of Olney in the Countie of Buckingham in old England sonne of William Peirson late of the same towne deceased and now of Southampton upon Long Iland in New England gent: And John Cooper of the same towne of Southampton upon Long Iland aforesaid Brother of the said Henry Peirson by the Mothers side gent."

In addition to showing that Henry is the son of William, this deed also shows that Henry Peirson and John Cooper Jr. have the same mother. She was Wyborough Griggs, who married 1st William Peirson 25 Jul 1609, Olney, Buckinghamshire, England, and 2nd John Cooper Sr. 18 Oct 1618, also at Olney. The Bishop's Transcripts at Olney provide[3]:

"William Person and Wyborro Grigges were marr[ied] the xxvth day of July Anno Dom 1609"

"harry pearson sonne of will[iam] pearson was baptized the same Day [xth] of Decem[ber] [1615]"

"John Cowper and wyborough Pearson was maryed the xviiith of October [1618]"

"Anne Cowper Daughter of John Cowper baptized the same day [xxixth of Auguste 1619]"

"Mary Cowper Daughter of John was baptized the xiith of Aguste [1621][4]"

"Jhon Cowper sonne of Jhon [baptized] Mar i [1624/5]"

---

[1]Thomas W. Cooper, II, "The Cooper-Pierson-Griggs Connection, Long Island, Massachusetts, and Buckinghamshire, England" *The American Genealogist*, October 1989, Vol. 64, No. 4, pp. 193-200.
[2]Deed, 12 May 1662, Ref. D742/B/15/1, Staffordshire County Record Office, Stafford, England. A copy was provided to Thomas W. Cooper, II, by Elizabeth Knight, an Olney historian.
[3]Bishop's Transcripts for Olney, Buckinghamshire, England, located at Buckinghamshire County Record Office, Aylesbury, England.
[4]Except for the last two entries in the Bishop's Transcripts for Olney, the day of the date is given in small roman numerals.

"Thomas Coop[er] sonn of Jhon [baptized] March 11 [1626/7]"

"Martha Coop[er] the Daugh[ter] of John [baptized] Nov[e]mb[er] 26 [1629]"

The above record for the baptism of "harry pearson" is believed to be that of Henry Peirson because of the derivation of Harry and because it is the correct location and father's name. From the dictionary[5]: "Harry [Middle English - Herry derived from Henry] a masculine name." Therefore, Henry Peirson was baptized 10 Dec 1615 at Olney, Buckinghamshire, England.

From the above deed and Bishop's Transcripts, it is evident that Wyborough Griggs married twice and that something happened to William Peirson before Wyborough remarried. It is probable that the burial record for "William Pearson" in the adjacent parish of Lavendon on 28 July 1616 belongs to Henry Peirson's father since no other William Pearson is present in the vicinity. Furthermore, members of the Griggs family are known to be from Lavendon as can be seen in the passenger records of the Hopewell in 1635 and in the Lavendon parish register.

Henry Peirson's mother, Wyborough (Griggs) (Peirson) Cooper, and step-father, John Cooper, and most of their children traveled to America on the Hopewell in 1635:

"*Hopewell* of London[6], William Bundock, Master. She sailed early in April 1635 from London and arrived at Boston in June 1635."

Passenger	Age	English Origin	Initial Destination
"John Cooper	41	Olney, county Bucks	Lynn,
Wybroe Cooper	42	wife of John Cooper	Massachusetts
Mary Cooper	13		
John Cooper	10		
Thomas Cooper	7		
Martha Cooper	5	Children of John Cooper aforesaid	
Phillip Phillipp		15 years servant to John Cooper"	

Ann Cooper, age 16, and Henry Peirson, age 20, are not listed as passengers on the Hopewell in 1635. Henry Peirson came to America in 1639. John White was at Lynn, Mass., in 1630, married Ann Cooper, and was living in Southampton in 1647. Thus it is believed that Ann Cooper came on the Hopewell in 1635 and was inadvertently left off the passenger list.

In a 1663 lawsuit involving property in Olney, Henry Peirson stated in writing to an English court that he had emigrated from Olney, Buckinghamshire, England to New England "in or about the month of May 1639[7]." Based on Pierson family legend and a ship and date match, Henry came to New England in America from London, England, May 1639 on the ship *Mayflower* of London as discussed in Chapter 6. It is believed that two other

---

[5] *Webster's New World Dictionary*, 2nd College Edition, William Collins Publishers, Inc., 1980, p. 639.

[6] Charles Edward Banks, *The Planters of the Commonwealth 1620 - 1640*, originally published Boston, MA, 1930, reprinted Genealogical Publishing Co., Inc., Baltimore, MD, 1991, p. 158, Library of Congress Cat. No. 67-30794.

[7] Legal Proceedings in English Courts of Cambridgeshire and Huntingdonshire, England, Item 35, C.5/421/171 and C.6/22/113, 7 May 1663, Bill of Complaint of Henry Pearson of Southampton in Long Island in America versus John Kirby of Olney, Bucks.

Pierson kinsmen accompanied him on this *Mayflower* voyage (see the three brothers legend in Chapter 4).

Both Lizzie Benedict Pierson [8] (1878) and George Rogers Howell[9] (1887), in their books, have stated that Henry Pierson married Mary Cooper and it has been repeated by many. However, it is not true. Both Mary Cooper, age 13 when she came to America on the *Hopewell* with her father John Cooper in 1635, and Henry Peirson have the same mother, Wyborough Griggs, as shown in the 1662 deed earlier. Therefore, Mary Cooper is Henry Peirson's half sister.

From the article[10] by Thomas W. Cooper, II, in *The American Genealogist*, the sources of information for assuming Henry Peirson married Mary Cooper are examined and their true meaning shown. He concluded that Henry Peirson married a Mary, but not Mary Cooper.

To determine in what year the marriage took place, we will review the age of the eldest son Joseph:

"At a towne meeting (Southampton, Long Island) March 6, 1657/58[11] it was concluded that Joseph Pierson and Richard Howell (bap. 1629[12], now age 28) are to receive the hundred pounds for the town's use of the Indians."

Here, Joseph is mentioned for the first time in records and he is the eldest son of Henry Peirson (birth information for Joseph has not been located). If we assume that Joseph is at least 18 years of age in 1658 (reasonable for dealing with Indians and disbursing 100 pounds), then Joseph was born about 1640 in Lynn, Massachusetts or Southampton, Long Island. If this is so, then Henry probably married about age 24 in 1639, probably at Olney, Buckinghamshire, England. Therefore, it is probable that Mary ____, Henry's wife, came to America with Henry Peirson in May 1639. Henry's wife Mary is probably the daughter of Edward Fuller of Olney, Buckinghamshire, England, whom Henry had hold a mortgage for him in Olney before departing in 1639 and to whom Henry sent a letter from Lynn, Massachusetts, in 1639 or 1640 about Edward Fuller's son, John.

At Olney, Buckinghamshire, England[13]: "Mary Fuller Daught(er) of Edward was bapt(ized) the xxiiijth of March 1621 (24 Mar 1621/2)." Baptisms were also recorded there for Mary's siblings Abygall, 31 May 1618; John, 20 Feb 1619/20; and Thomas (same date as Mary).

Will[14] of "Edward Fuller of Olney, Bucks, yeoman, 22 Aug 1656, proved 20 Sep 1656. To my eldest son John Fuller my house, cottage or tenement in Olney, with the arable land &c.

---

[8]Lizzie B. Pierson, *Pierson Genealogical Records*, Joel Munsell Printer, Albany, NY, 1878, p. 22.

[9]George Rogers Howell, *The Early History of Southampton, L.I., New York with Genealogies*, 2nd Edition, Weed, Parsons and Company, Albany, NY, 1887, p. 348.

[10]Thomas W. Cooper, II, "The Cooper-Peirson-Griggs Connection, Long Island, Massachusetts, and Buckinghamshire, England" *The American Genealogist*, October 1989, Vol. 64, No. 4, pp. 193-200.

[11]*Town Records of Southampton*, NY, Liber A, No. 1, p. 143-144.

[12]George Rogers Howell, *The Early History of Southampton, L.I., New York with Genealogies*, 2nd Edition, Weed, Parsons and Company, Albany, NY, 1887, p. 301.

[13]Church of England, *Bishop's Transcripts*, Olney, Buckinghamshire, England.

[14]*The New England Historical and Genealogical Register*, Vol. 50, The New England Historic Genealogical Society, Boston, Mass., 1896, p. 533.

belonging, wherein I now dwell, next the cottage or tenement there now or late of Robert Martin on the one side. To my second son Ignacious Fuller my freehold lands, houses &c. in Olney and Sherrington Bucks. To my third son Thomas Fuller two hundred pounds, to be paid to him a year after my decease. To my daughter Abigail ten pounds, to be paid in a year &c. More to my eldest son John five pounds within a year. The residue to son Ignacious whom I make full and whole executor.   Berkley, 334."

It was hoped that the Edward Fuller will would mention a Mary Pierson, but instead he does not mention her at all. It is concluded that Mary Fuller has already received her share of the estate through her dowry, perhaps as payment for the trip to America in 1639. Thus, Mary Fuller may have been the wife of Henry Peirson, but no proof exists. She is probably the Mary Peirson that was Henry's widow in 1680.

After John Cooper[15] arrived at Boston with his family on the Hopewell in 1635, he was made a freeman at Boston 6 Dec 1636, was an elder of the church at Saugus (Lynn, Massachusetts), when it was formed in 1638, and owned 200 acres in Lynn. John Pearson came to Saugus (Lynn) in 1637 (see chapter 4 for the relationship). Henry Peirson joined his mother, Wyborough (Griggs) (Peirson) Cooper, and step-father John Cooper in Lynn in 1639 after arriving on the Mayflower of London (not the pilgrim ship).

Near Boston, Massachusetts, at Lynn in 1640, eight men formed a company with the intention of establishing their own town. These men were Edward Howell, Edmond Farrington, Edmund Needham, Thomas Sayre, Josiah Stanborough, George Welbe, Henry Walton, and Job Sayre. Before the company departed Lynn, twelve more families were added: Daniel How (ship's Captain), John Cooper, Allen Breed, William Harker, Thomas Halsey, Thomas Newell, John Farrington, Richard Odell, Philip Kyrtland, Nathaniel Kirtland, Thomas Farrington, and Thomas Terry. Edward Howell & Company purchased eight square miles on Long Island from James Farrett for 400 pounds, approved June 12, 1640. The rights to settle a town were said, in the agreement from James Farrett, to be commensurate with those rights enjoyed by "other Plantations of the Massachusetts Bay under its governor, John Winthrop, Esquire." After a false start on the western end of Long Island, the ship, with the Company aboard headed south from Boston toward the eastern end of Long Island and entered the interior of Long Island by sailing up the Great Peconic Bay landing at what is now called North Sea about three miles north of where they settled and named it Southampton.

By July 7, 1640, they had determined the town boundaries. On October 11, 1640, the Southampton men selected as their minister, Mr. Abraham Pierson. Abraham's ordination and the forming of the church took place at Lynn, Massachusetts, in November 1640. The Rev. Abraham Pierson is believed to be the 2nd cousin of Henry Peirson (see Chapter 4 on American Immigrant Inter-Relations in England and Appendix A for their ancestors at Howden, Yorkshire, England).

There were native Indians on Long Island and they now had to purchase their land from them even though they had already paid a British owner. The Indian Deed was obtained

15George Rogers Howell, *The Early History of Southampton, L.I., New York with Genealogies*, 2nd Edition, Weed, Parsons and Company, Albany, NY, 1887, pp. 217-8.

December 13, 1640. The largest signature witnessing the deed for the Southampton settlement was their minister, Abraham Pierson:

"At the time of the settlement of Southampton[16], five tribes of Indians were living in its vicinity. The tract of land originally settled was purchased of the Shinnecocks. The western boundary of the town then was on the borders of the Poosapatuck and Patchogue Indian tribes, and the northern on the borders of the Peaconics. To the east were the Montauk, the royal tribe of the island , whose chief, Wyandanch, a man of noble character, exercised supreme authority over the whole 13 tribes that occupied Long Island. The Montauks are said to have been the most numerous and powerful. Tradition has it, that in early times when drawn out in 'Indian file' the warriors of the Shinnecock tribe extended from Shinnecock gate to the town - this being about two miles would give them at least 2,000 adult men. Nowedanah, a brother of Wyandanch, was the chief of the Shinnecocks." In spite of the warlike reputation of all Indians of New England, "there was never any serious disturbance of the peaceful relations initiated at the settlement of the town." There were occasionally rumors of Indian threats, but these seemed to be caused by those on the mainland who would incite an Indian war. "The friendly feeling (of the Indians on Long Island) was owing partly to the fact of the fair and equitable treatment they universally received from the English; and partly from the circumstances of the Indians. The Montauks and Shinnecocks had been harassed by the Narragansett Indians of Rhode Island, and were glad to enter into a treaty with the English for mutual protection." This mutual protection clause was part of the 1640 deed between the Shinnecocks and the Southampton settlers.

During the next few years[17] (1640-1643), Southampton was further increased in population by 43 families: Richard Barrett, William Barker, William Barnes, John Bishop, Robert Bond (1643), John Bostwick, Thomas Burnett, Ellis Cook, John Cory (1643), Samuel Dayton, Fulk Davis, Christopher Foster, John Gosmer, Thomas Goldsmith, James Hampton, John Hand, James Herrick, Thomas Hildreth, John Jagger, John Jennings, John Jessup, Anthony Ludlam, John Lum or Loom, Robert Merwin, Richard Mills, John Moore, William Mulford, Robert Norris, John Oldfields, John Ogden, Henry Pierson, Richard Post, Joseph Raynor, William Rogers, Robert Rose, Richard Smyth, Richard Stratton, Thomas Talmage, Thomas Topping, William Wells (1643), John White, Isaac Willman, and John Woodruff. It is believed that Henry Pierson, his wife Mary, infant son Joseph, and perhaps another child were living with his step-father, John Cooper, and his mother, Wyborough (Griggs) (Peirson) Cooper, at Southampton before he became a land owner in Southampton and thus appeared in Southampton records in May 1643 as owning a one-acre home lot which he obtained at some earlier point in time:

---

[16] George Rogers Howell, *The Early History of Southampton, L.I., New York, with Genealogies*, 2nd Edition, Weed, Parsons and Company, Albany, NY, 1887, p. 164.
[17] George Rogers Howell, *The Early History of Southampton, L.I., New York, with Genealogies*, 2nd Edition, Weed, Parsons and Company, Albany, NY, 1887, pp. 30-31.

May 29, 1643[18]. "It was ordered by the General court (Southampton) that Richard Barret, John Mulford, Arthur Bostock, Thomas Tomson & Robert Bond, shall have each of them two acres of land divided unto them upon the plain, viz. Richard Barret, John Mulford and Thomas Tomson shall have the aforesaid two acres to lye next unto Henry Pierson's one acre lot ..."

In 1644[19] in Southampton town records, reference is made to "John Cooper the elder." This is Henry Peirson's stepfather and *elder* refers to a church position as opposed to seniority. All references to seniority in Southampton records have used *Senior*. The church here at Southampton referred to itself as "Presbiterians" in 1707 when purchasing land for a church site and again in 1712 when assigning land in Bridgehampton "for use of a Presbyterian ministry and no other."

March 7, 1644/45[20]. The settlers observed that a large number of whales annually beached themselves on the beaches near Southampton. This became a new industry for the settlers. The whale oil was used for lamps and the whale bone (thin plastic-like sheetings hanging from the upper whale jaw) was used for corset stays. Because of the value of these whales and to maintain order, the town had to set rules for their taking:

"It is ordered by this present Court (Southampton) that if by the providence of God there shall be henceforth within the bounds of this plantation any whale or whales cast up. For the prevention of disorder it is consented unto that there shall be fowre (four) wards in this towne, eleven persons in each ward, and by lot two of each ward, if any such whales be cast up, shall be employed for the cutting out of the said whales, who for their pains shall have a double share, And every inhabitant with his child or servant that is above sixteen years of age, shall have in the division of the other part an equal proportion, provided that such person when it fall into his ward (be) a sufficient man to be employed about it. And it is further agreed upon that there shall be in each ward eleven persons:"

Ward "1. For the first ward William Barnes, Geo. Wood, Thomas Cooper, Richard Stratton, Job Sayre, Thomas Burnet, John White, William Mulford, Thomas Halsey Junr, Thomas Talmage Senr, and Mr. Johnes."

Ward "2. For ye second ward Richard Jaques, Thomas Talmage Junior, Mr. [Abraham] Pierson, Robert Rose, Mr. Gosmer, Thomas Halsey Senr, Mr. Stanborough, Richard Barret, Richard Post, Thomas Tomson, Robert Talmage."

Ward "3. For the third ward Richard Gosmer, Arthur Bostock, Henry Pierson [age 30], John Hande, Thomas Hyldreth, John Mulford, John Moore, Ellis Cook, Robert Bond, Fulk Daves, & Mr. Howe."

Ward 4. "For the fourth ward John Cooper Senr [age 51], Tristrum Hedges, John Cooper Junr [age 20], John Cory, Mr. Howell, Mr. Odell, John Howell, Richard Smith, & Thomas Sayre." [Notes in brackets by Richard Pierson.]

---

[18] *Town Records of Southampton*, NY, Liber A, No. 1, p. 21.

[19] George Rogers Howell, *The Early History of Southampton, L.I., New York, with Genealogies*, 2nd Edition, Weed, Parsons and Company, Albany, NY, 1887, pp. 98-9.

[20] *Town Records of Southampton*, NY, Liber A, No. 1, p. 24.

Every able bodied man of 16 years age and older is listed above for Southampton on this date in 1644/45.

June 27, 1646[21]. "At the same court, it is ordered that Henry Pierson shall have full power as clarke (clerk) of the band (of soldiers) to see that all the soldiers bring their arms to the meeting every Sabbath day and to gather six pence upon every default and also to examine when hee see good how every soldier is provided with powder and shot." In essence, Henry Pierson is the officer in charge of the town militia and the sword listed in his 1680 inventory was likely used for that position. However, no rank title was recorded for Henry Pierson as was done in later years for militia leaders at Southampton.

October 6, 1646[22]. "Henry Pierson was censured by the Court of Magistrates (of Southampton) for miscarriage in threatening that if any man should strike his dog he would knock him down, and to pay for the said miscarriage ten shillings and to be of good behavior." The laws written by Rev. Abraham Pierson for Southampton in 1640-41 were partially obliterated or missing, therefore, a law on threatening was not found. Regardless, this unusually trivial violation seems to be an improper mixture of church morals and civil law. Cruelty to animals or damage to Henry's property (his dog) was apparently not a consideration of the court.

October, 1646[23]. "Southampton this _th October 1646, Henry Pierson dothe acknowledge himselfe to owe unto the sayd towne the summe of five pounds, and John Cooper doth acknowledge to owe the sayd towne five pounds to be leavied of their goods & chattels lands and tenements upon this condition that the sayd Henry Pierson shall appear at the next quarter Court holden for this towne, and in the meane whyle to be of good behaviour towards the Magistrates and all other persons. (Note added later:) Henry Pierson appeared this day." Because of the October 6, 1646, fine of ten shillings against Henry Pierson, it is probable that Henry's stepfather, John Cooper, joined Henry in redressing the magistrates for this attack on freedom of speech and for allowing the church to impose such laws on one who was simply protecting his property (his dog). Henry Peirson and John Cooper received five-pound fines for their behavior toward the magistrates. This was the beginning of general town resistance to church ideals being enforced by civil court which culminated in Rev. Abraham Pierson's dismissal as Southampton minister. It is noted that Abraham Pierson is still present June 24, 1647, but does not appear in later town records:

"Southampton[24], June 24, 1647. Wee whose names are underwritten doe witnes that all the inhabitants of this towne except Tho. Vale & Tho. Burnet were present and consenting unto the aforesaid agreement (not stated herein), only Mr Smith was out of towne.

Edward Howell	Jo. Gosmer	Abraham Pierson
Job Sayre	Richard Odell	John Moore
Thomas Halsey	Henry Pierson"	

It was evident that the beliefs of Rev. Abraham Pierson did not coincide with enough members of the Southampton community for him to continue as their minister.

---

[21]*Town Records of Southampton*, NY, Liber A, No. 1, p. 80.
[22]*Town Records of Southampton*, NY, Liber A, No. 1, p. 35.
[23]*Town Records of Southampton*, NY, Liber A, No. 1, p. 38.
[24]*Town Records of Southampton*, NY, Liber A, No. 1, p. 43.

Abraham[25] "was most rigid in his desire to have the civil as well as the ecclesiastical power all vested in the church, and to allow none but church members to act in the choice of officers of government, or to be eligible as such." A small part of his congregation agreed with him, and they, with Rev. Abraham Pierson, moved to Branford, Connecticut, in 1647 where he founded a new church and was its minister for 23 years. Rev. Fordham became the new minister for Southampton. After leaving Branford, Rev. Abraham Pierson was the first pastor of what is now the First Presbyterian Church of Newark, New Jersey. He died on August 9, 1678. His son, Rev. Abraham Pierson Jr., was the first President of Yale College (1701-1707), acting as its rector.

In 1649[26], Mrs. Thomas Halsey was murdered by Indians at Southampton, which caused some apprehension of a general resurrection against the English on Long Island. She was the wife of Thomas Halsey, who died 1678, and who was the first Halsey family at Southampton. A messenger was immediately sent by the magistrates to summon Wyandanch, Chief of the Montauk ruling tribe of Long Island Indians, to appear before them. "His counselors, fearing that he would be summarily condemned to death by way of retaliation, advised him not to obey the summons. Before he expressed his own opinion, he submitted the case to Mr. Gardiner, who happened to be lodging in his wigwam that same night. By his advice, he set out immediately for Southampton, Mr. Gardiner agreeing to remain as a hostage to the tribe, for the safety of their beloved chief. With amazing celerity, he not only accomplished the journey of twenty-five miles, but actually apprehended on his way, and delivered to the magistrates, the murderers of the woman; who instead of being his own subjects, proved to be Pequot Indians from the main; some of whom were generally lurking on the Island for the purpose of promoting disturbances between the natives and the new settlers. These men being sent to Hartford (Connecticut), were there tried, convicted, and executed." This murder is the only known loss of an English settler life at Southampton by Indians. Thomas Halsey remarried ten years later 25 July 1660 Ann, widow of Edward Johnes. On 19 September 1666, Thomas Halsey, in clarifying the right of Wyandanch to sell Shinnecock land, stated:

"I the subscriber, namely, Thomas Halsey do witness that at the time of the trouble in this town of Southampton by reason of murther (sic) committed by the Indians; at a great assembly of the Indians for the settling of matters in fine, I saw Mandush (the great Sachem's son of Shinnecock) cut up a turf of ground in Southampton and delivering it to Wyandanch, gave up all his right and interest (in that land) to him. ... And this I am ready to depose when thereunto called. Witness my hand the 19 day of September 1666. (signed) Thomas Halsey."

Descendants of Thomas Halsey have married into the Peirson line more than once, including the marriage of Josiah Peirson (son of Col. Henry Peirson) in 1724 to Martha Halsey (b. 1699, dau. of Jeremiah and Ruth Halsey). U. S. Fleet Admiral William Frederick Halsey Jr. ("Bull Halsey") of World War II fame is Thomas Halsey's 10th generation descendant (Thomas[1], Thomas[2], Jeremiah[3], Jeremiah[4], Matthew[5], Job[6], Capt. Eliphalet[7], Thomas[8], William Frederick[9], Admiral William Frederick Halsey Jr.[10]). In this line, Capt.

[25]Lizzie B. Pierson, *Pierson Genealogical Records*, Joel Munsell, Printer, Albany, NY, 1878, p. 10.

[26]George Rogers Howell, *The Early History of Southampton, L.I., New York, with Genealogies*, 2nd Edition, Weed, Parsons and Company, Albany, NY, 1887, p. 168.

Eliphalet Halsey[27] was the first whaling Captain from Sag Harbor, Long Island, to round "the horn" (southern tip of South America) in 1817 in pursuit of whales. Fishing in the Anarctic Ocean he returned with 1700 barrels of whale oil.

Southampton[28]: "A list of all the townsmen, May 10, 1649.

Mr Edward Howell	Mr Gosmer	Mr Raynor
Mr Odell	Thomas Halsey	John Howell
John Cooper	Thomas Cooper	Thomas Sayre
Job Sayre	Edward Johnes	Josiah Stanborough
Thomas Talmage	Samuel Dayton	Thomas Vayle
Richard Post	Thomas Hildreth	Henry Pierson
John White	Ellis Cooke	Isaac Willman
Richard Barrett	Richard Smith	Thomas Burnet
George Wood	John Jessup	Wm Rogers"

September 10, 1650[29]. "John Howell, Richard Howell, Mr. Rainer, Thomas Vayle, Joseph Rainer, Thomas Burnet, Thomas Cooper, Henry Pierson, Ellis Cook, and John Halby are to have for their paines 3s per day at the seapoose." Seapoose is an Indian word for "little river" and as found in these records usually refers to the inlet connecting Mecox Bay with the ocean. A considerable amount of digging was needed there to keep the waterway open to Mecox Bay. Three shillings per day per person was paid by the town since the passageway benefited the whole town.

May 10, 1652[30]. "It is concluded by the major pt of the towne (Southampton, Long Island) that the calf heard (herd) shall be left for this ensueing year att Sagabonack (Sagaponack, one mile east of Bridgehampton, also called Sag and Sagg) where they were kept the yeare last past."

June 1, 1652[31]. "An action of trespass upon the case entered by Jonas Wood H against Henry Pierson deft, withdrawn by consent." Jonas Wood was the town Marshall later that year as shown by an October 15, 1652, entry that stated "At a towne meeting Jonas Wood H. being chosen last 6th of October to bee constable & Marshall and now called to take his oath did refuse soe to doe." The exact situation is not known here, but the case against Henry Pierson was withdrawn.

November 15, 1652[32]. "Mr Josiah Stanborough exchangeth with Thomas Pope, and passeth over unto him the home lott of two acres (less or more) which hee the said Thomas Pope now dwells on In consideration of the 3 acres given and granted by this towne October the 6the last past unto the said Thomas Pope, which 3 acres lying next unto the said Mr

---

[27]Mrs. Albert W. Topping, Everett C. Foster, and Editor Paul H. Curts, *Bridgehampton's Three Hundred Years*, The Hampton Press, Bridgehampton, NY, 1956, p. 67.

[28]*Town Records of Southampton*, NY, Liber A, No. 1, p. 63

[29]*Town Records of Southampton*, NY, Liber A, No. 1, p. 85.

[30]George Rogers Howell, *The Early History of Southampton, L.I., New York, with Genealogies*, 2nd Edition, Weed, Parsons and Company, Albany, NY, 1887, p. 192.

[31]*Town Records of Southampton*, NY, Liber A, No. 1, p. 101.

[32]*Town Records of Southampton*, NY, Liber A, No. 1, p. 164.

Stanboroughs his home lot, the said Thomas doth exchange with and passeth over in lyke manner affore said unto the said Mr Stanborough.

Witness *Henry Peirson* Cloark"

"Cloark" was written with a double underline and is the title (Clerk). There is no doubt how Henry spelled his surname in 1652, and with a colonial "S" in Peirson.

1653[33]. "The amicable relations between the two races (Indians and English) was seriously threatened in 1653, when the Narragansetts, perhaps allied with emissaries of the Dutch, endeavored to seduce the Indians on the east end of Long Island into a combination with them to exterminate all white settlers. In this they were unsuccessful, although the apprehension of the English (was high), and for some time unusual care was taken to guard against sudden attack." In the field a guard was continuously kept. At night, none knew at what hour the alarm would sound. On the Lord's day, they went to meeting with rifles as men prepared for instant war. Every male, sixteen years of age and older, was a soldier enrolled in the ranks.

March 8, 1653[34]. The four wards for cutting up beached whales are now four squadrons. Instead of a double portion for their efforts, cutters now get a third of what they cut in addition to their town portion. "Henry Pierson" was listed in the 3rd Squadron for cutting whales. Below the list of squadrons it stated, "Memorandum that after ye squadrons had gone round not orderly, the town began according to order, Mr Smiths Squadron (1st) cut next, Mr Johnes (2nd) at Spring 1655, next John White his Squadron (3rd) cut April 26 1655, Richard Barrets squadron (4th) cut May 1655, Mr Smiths squadron (1st) cut May 9 1655, Richard Post (2nd) cut in Aprill '56." The rate shown here is four beached whales per year for 1655, mostly in the spring, and must vary some from year to year.

January 9, 1653/54[35]. "At a general court, it is concluded that if the Indians will suitably fence one half betweene them & us that then ye towne will fence with 3 rails or that which is answerable thereunto, the other halfe, and what soever else may bee thought necessary to bee done about or concerning the said fencing, as treating & concluding with the Indians about it, & disposing of the fence in regard of placeing it, is referred to 4 men namely Jonas Wood at North Sea, John Jessup, Tho. Goldsmith & Henry Pierson." It is likely that these four men speak the Indian's tongue, Henry having been in contact with the Indians for over 13 years now.

February 4, 1656/57[36]. "At a towne meeting it was agreed that the liquor that was taken from Goodman [Thomas] Gouldsmith, he shall have his money returned namely the town's part of it. Also at the meeting there was a contribution to Goodman [Thomas] Gouldsmith

---

[33] George Rogers Howell, *The Early History of Southampton, L.I., New York, with Genealogies*, 2nd Edition, Weed, Parsons and Company, Albany, NY, 1887, p. 164.
[34] *Town Records of Southampton*, NY, Liber A, No. 1, p. 111.
[35] *Town Records of Southampton*, NY, Liber A, No. 1, p. 118.
[36] *Town Records of Southampton*, NY, Liber A, No. 1, p. 116.

because of his loss by fire: Mr [Thomas] Topping one bushel of wheat, Mr [John] Gosmer two bushels, Mr [Alexander] Field three pecks of wheat, Thomas Sayre one bushel, Henry Pierson the value of half a bushel of wheat, William Ludlam half a bushel of wheat, Isaak Willman half a bushel of wheat, Thomas Halsey Junior 2s 6d, Joseph Rainer half a bushel of wheat, ... (rest of page missing)." [Notes in brackets by author Richard Pierson.] By May 11, 1657, several houses had been burned by Indians including the house of Mrs. Howell, widow of Edward Howell and probably that of Thomas Gouldsmith above (Goodman is not his name, it is a common title of the colonial era). See the court proceeding below, on May 11, 1657, about the Indians that fired Mrs. Howell's house.

April 30, 1657[37]. Southampton: "Half a pound of powder a peece delivered unto ye undernamed persons out of ye magazen: Nathaniel Foster, Isaac Halsey, Thomas Halsey Jr, John Howell, John coopr Jr, Edward Howell, Francis Sayre, John Oldfield, John Jagger, John Bishop, Joshua Barnes, Tho. Pope, John Ogden, Jonas Bower, John White, Ellis Cook, Isaac Willman, Tho. Topping, Elnathan Topping, John Hand, John Jessup, Daniel Sayre, Henry Ludlam, Thomas Cooper, John Woodruf Sen, John Woodruf Jr, David Halsey, John Negro, John Topping, Tho. Burnet, Sergeant Post, Obadiah Rogers, Henry Pierson, James Herrick, Edward Howell, Christopher Foster, John Foster, Joseph Foster, Richard Howell, Joseph Rayner, and there was weighed 9 lb 1/4 of powder and put into the barrel, & remains to be disposed." Here, the town of Southampton is preparing to defend themselves against Indian attackers who have been burning houses. Note the number of family heads listed is 40 and that another 9 1/4 pounds of powder has been readied for instant use.

May 11, 1657[38]. Hartford, Connecticut: "A particular Court ... Magistrates Jno Webster Esq Governor, Mr Wells Deputy, Mr Cullick, Mr Clarke, Mr Tailcoat, Mr Ogden, with Mr Allen & Wm Wadsworth. Upon examination of Wigwagub, he confessed that he was hired to burn Mrs. Howell's house, by two Indians one Awabag, who promised him one gun; and Agagoneagu who promised him 7 shillings 6 pence and he said Auwegenum did not know he was to burn the house two days before it was done - and that himself and the three Indians were together when he was hired, but Auwegenum did not hear their discourse, but Auwabag told Auweganum of it afterward. Upon consideration of the motion made from our friends at Southampton for the presence, countenance and assistance of 20 men from us, and considering their sad distressed present state by reason of the insolent and insufferable outrage of some heathen upon that land and near that plantation by firing several dwelling houses to the undoing of several members of this Colony. This Court order that there shall be 20 men pressed forthwith to go over to their assistance as the case may require together with necessary provision & Ammunition which are to be taken out of the several Towns in the Portion following: Hartford, Windzor, Wethersfield, Farmington, Middletown, Sea Brooke, Pequett - These men to have 25 lb of powder & 50 lb of Bullets."

1657 "Henr Pierson," (sic) census of 61 families, only one Pierson family, center of Main St., east side.

After 1657 "Hen. Pierson," (sic) 3rd whaling group.

---

[37] *Book of Town Accounts*, Southampton, NY.
[38] George Rogers Howell, *The Early History of Southampton, L.I., New York, with Genealogies*, 2nd Edition, Weed, Parsons and Company, Albany, NY, 1887, p. 167, and he gives his reference as From records of particular courts at Hartford, Ct., Liber 2, p. 99, as published in Hist. Magazine, by Charles J. Hoadley.

July 5, 1659. Dorchester and Roxbury, Massachusetts.[39]   First Church at Dorchester, church minutes: "This day the Teaching & ruling elders of our Church as messengers of ye Church met at Rocksbery with ye messengers of other Churches, for to hear the Indians make a relation, of the work of God upon their soul: at which time there were six made their relation in the Indian tongue, & repeated by Mr Eliot in English witnessed unto ye truth of his translation, by Mr Pearson of Long Island, & Goodman Fordgier of Martins Vinyard, & Mr Eliots own son, & because ye time would not permit for ye other two Indians to make their relation at that time, therefore ye relation which they had made ye day before unto Mr Pearson in private it was declared by Mr Pearson, & many questions put to ye Indians in point of knowledge to ye great rejoising of ye hearers & so it was left in ye close of ye day to ye counsel of ye messengers of ye churches what was next to be done." This Pearson on Long Island can only be Henry Peirson in 1659. Both Henry and his son Joseph Peirson dealt with Indians on Long Island and spoke the Indian's language at this date. However, Henry would be the one classified as a "teaching and ruling elder" of the church. Roxbury is a few miles from both Boston and Dorchester in Massachusetts.

January 20, 1660/61[40]. Southampton: "Henry Pierson his daughter Sarah was borne the 20 day of January 1660." This is the earliest primary record of a child's birth for Henry Pierson's children. However, Sarah is believed to be the seventh or eighth child of Henry. Of the first six or seven children, five names are later identified as Joseph, John, Henry, Benjamin, and Daniel. Two of these five children's birth years are determined from age and death date on their tombstones: Col. Henry Peirson born 1652 and Benjamin Pierson born 1655. Theodore and two of the daughters are known to have been born after Sarah.

From Legal Proceedings in English Courts in Cambridgeshire and Huntingdonshire, England[41], Item 35, C.5/421/171 and C.6/22/113, 7 May 1663. Bill of Complaint of Henry Pearson of Southampton in Long Island in America versus John Kirby of Olney, Bucks.: "Henry Pearson" states that he loaned Job Brymley of Olney, Buckinghamshire, 120 pounds, and took as security a mortgage on Brymley's 3 acres of land. Before Henry left England "in May 1639 to go to parts beyond the seas," he left the mortgage with Edward Fuller of Olney and two mercers to collect the interest and then the principle at the end of 5 years. However, the English Civil War began three years into the 5-year mortgage and at its end, Edward Fuller and the two mercers were deceased and the mortgage papers missing. Job Brymley had died, his daughter Jane inherited, and the land was sold to John Kirby who refused to pay the mortgage.

On the 20th of May 1663, the Plea[42] of John Kirby to the Bill of Henry Pearson, stated that he refused to acknowledge any of the matters contained in the bill. Kirby stated further that since the plaintiff has not made oath that he has not the deed in his custody, and for many other defects in the bill, John Kirby pleads not to be compelled to answer. However,

---

[39]George H. Ellis, *Records of the First Church at Dorchester in New England 1636-1734*, Boston, Mass., 1891, p. 30-31.
[40]*Town Records of Southampton*, NY, Liber A, No. 2, 2nd Part, p. 26.
[41]Noel Currer-Briggs, *Colonial Settlers and English Adventurers*, Genealogical Publishing Co., Inc., Baltimore, MD, 1971, pp. 71-2, Abstract.
[42]Noel Currer-Briggs, *Colonial Settlers and English Adventurers*, Genealogical Publishing Co., Inc., Baltimore, MD, 1971, pp. 71-2, Abstract.

the court required him to answer, which occurred one and a half years later on 7 November 1664, Item 36, C.6/22/133, The Answer[43] of John Kirby. Kirby stated that he knew nothing of 21 pounds mentioned in the bill of complaint, or money lent by the plaintiff to John Brimlye, or that Brimlye made any mortgage to the plaintiff of 3 acres of land. And he knew nothing of any Power of Attorney which the plaintiff may have reposed in Edward Fuller, or the mercers. He denies ever having seen any mortgage deed. He admits that about 8 or 9 years ago, he bought the 3 acres of land in Olney in question from Daniel Howes and Jane Brymley his wife, and paid 15 pounds for it. He enjoyed peaceful occupation of it for 4 years before the deaths of the mercer William Geynes and Edward Fuller, who, although they lived in the same town, never claimed the land by virtue of any pretended mortgage.

No further court records were found on the Complaint. Thus it is concluded that the court accepted this answer and dropped further action on Henry Pearson's Complaint. But there are three obvious flaws in Kirby's statement: (1) he knows nothing of 21 pounds (but what about the 120 pounds in question?), (2) he knows nothing about money lent by the plaintiff to John Brimlye (but what about Job Brymley who was borrower?), and (3) Edward Fuller never claimed the land by use of a pretended mortgage (but what about by use of the real mortgage?). Essentially, John Kirby has made a non-statement and the court let him get away with it!

Henry Peirson obviously felt his 120-pound investment had been stolen from him, with the help of the English Civil War and an irresponsible post-war court system. His anger would be suppressed by taking refuge in his religion: George Rogers Howell states in his book[44] that in Henry's own handwriting, he wrote in the town records:

> "Jehovah I upon thee call!
> O make thou haste to me,
> And hearken thou unto my voyce,
> When I do crye to thee."

Donald Pierson of Coloma, California, advises that this prose is from the *Bible*, Verse 1 of Psalm 141. The Geneva version of the *Bible*, published 1560 at Geneva, was used extensively by the Puritans of England and New England in the 1600s, and is a close match to Henry's verse in the town records. It provides:

"PSAL. CXLI.

David being grievously persecuted Under Saul, onely fleeth unto God to have succour, Desiring him to bridle his affections, that he maie paciently abide til God take vengeance of his enemies.

A Psalme of David.

1 O Lord, I[a] call upo' thee:
  haste thee unto me:

[43] Noel Currer-Briggs, *Colonial Settlers and English Adventurers*, Genealogical Publishing Co., Inc., Baltimore, MD, 1971, pp. 71-2, Abstract.
[44] George Rogers Howell, *The Early History of Southampton, L.I., New York with Genealogies*, Second Edition, Weed, Parsons and Company, Albany, NY, 1887, p. 348.

heare my voyce,
when I crye unto thee.

a He sheweth ye there is none other refuge in o'r necessities, but onely to flee unto God for comfort of foule."

In 1664, the English captured New Netherland from the Dutch, and Charles II gave the colony to his brother James, the Duke of York and Albany. In so doing, Charles included all of Long Island as part of the new colony which James renamed New York. James also changed the city names of New Amsterdam to New York and Beverwyck on the Hudson river at Fort Orange to Albany. Southampton became part of New York in the court system, but maintained its military support and trade ties with the Connecticut colony at Hartford.

April 10, 1667[45]. "Know all men by these presents that I the within named Humphrey Hughes doe hereby Assigne unto Mr Nicholas Stephens of Boston one third, and unto John Cooper of Southampton on Long Island another third pt of the Interest I have in the within grant, & the product, or any manner of benefit that may any way whatsoever come or bee obtained thereby. Witness my hand this 10th day of Aprill 1667. Humphrey Hughes.
    Witness   Henry Pierson   Mary X Pierson
                                        her mark"

This is the first appearance of Henry Pierson's wife, Mary, in Southampton records and one of the assignees above is John Cooper. John Cooper Sr. had died five years earlier in 1662[46]. Therefore, the above assignment is to John Cooper Jr., Henry Pierson's half brother.

March 23, 1667/68. "Henry Peirson," 3rd whaling Sqdn., no other Peirsons (of any spelling).

In 1673, the Dutch fleet recaptured New York colony and in August the Dutch requested the English settlements on Long Island to surrender to the arms of the Prince of Orange. Southampton and the other villages on eastern Long Island realized that their military situation was deplorable. Regardless, they intended to resist this takeover to the best of their ability. The Dutch had not been in control of New York colony for nine years (since 1664) and they had never controlled the eastern end of Long Island. But now the Dutch presence was the first threat of foreign takeover of Southampton.

In October 1673[47], the Dutch government required the eastern towns of Long Island to take the Oath of Allegiance to the Dutch government. "This oath was refused to be taken by the men of East Hampton, Southampton, Southold, and Huntington, they understanding that it was to be administered to their Magistrates only in behalf of the people. Whereupon, the Dutch sent a vessel to compel the people to take it. The commissioners came from New York in the frigate *Zeehond*, arrived at Southold, and called a meeting of the inhabitants to

---

[45] *Town Records of Southampton*, NY, Liber A, No. 2, 1st Part, p. 75.
[46] George Rogers Howell, *The Early History of Southampton, L.I., New York with Genealogies*, Second Edition, Weed, Parsons and Company, Albany, NY, 1887, p. 218.
[47] George Rogers Howell, *The Early History of Southampton, L.I., New York with Genealogies*, Second Edition, Weed, Parsons and Company, Albany, NY, 1887, p. 62-3.

take the oath of allegiance to the Dutch government. The flag of the Prince of Orange was brought in and displayed. Failing in their attempts to force the oath on the Southold people, they resolved to break up the assembly and depart." The frigate *Zeehond*'s Journal stated: "On leaving the place, some inhabitants of Southampton were present; among the rest was one John Cooper (half brother of Henry Peirson) who told Mr. Steenwyck, to *take care and not appear with that thing at Southampton*, which he more than once repeated: for the Commissioners, agreeable to their commission, had intended to go thither next morning. Whereupon Mr. Steenwyck asked what he meant by that word *thing*, to which said John Cooper replied, *the Prince's Flag*: then Mr. Steenwyck inquired of John Cooper if he said so of himself or on the authority of the inhabitants of Southampton. He answered, *Rest satisfied that I warn you, and take care that you come not with that Flag within range of shot of our village.*" They did not visit Southampton and East Hampton fearing they would "do more harm than good."

February 25, 1673/74[48]. Earlier, in August 1673, the Southampton people had addressed a letter to the New England colonies, setting forth the demand of the Dutch to surrender to the arms of the Prince of Orange, and their deplorable situation militarily. On the receipt of this, John Winthrop, Major of the Connecticut militia, was sent (after October 1673) with such force as could be spared in a vessel to Southold to assist the Long Island people. Captain John Howell with forty soldiers from Southampton and twenty from East Hampton, had come promptly at the summons of Major Winthrop for assistance. Captain John Howell's forty soldiers from Southampton surely included John and Thomas Cooper (sons of John Cooper Sr.) and three of Henry Peirson's sons, Lt. Joseph (about age 36), Col. Henry (then a Lt. at age 22), and Benjamin (age 20). Colonial soldiers of the period were considered to be those 16 years to 50 years of age though every male that could shoot a gun was used in defense of the community. Henry Peirson, then age 58, may not have participated because of age. The combined forces of Major Winthrop, Captain Howell, and Southold militia probably numbered between 150 and 250, and they stood ready at Southold to defend the eastern end of Long Island against the Dutch.

On February 25, 1673/74, Major Winthrop wrote at Southold of an engagement between his forces and the *Snow*, a Dutch ship, with one ketch and two sloops, who summoned the town of Southold to surrender. Major Winthrop replied "*Sir, I am here appointed by the authority of his Majesty's colony of Connecticut, to secure these people, in obedience to his Majesty, and by God's assistance I hope to give a good account thereof, and you may assure yourself that I will receive you in the same condition as a person that disturbs his Majesty's subjects.*" It is not recorded how many shots were fired (if any) or if the Dutch troops were landed from their ships, but the Dutch withdrew their forces and the last that was seen of them the vessels were on their return passage through Plum Gut (a water passageway from the Great Peconic Bay into Long Island Sound). No casualties were reported for this engagement. The Dutch apparently were not expecting significant armed resistance and may have been outnumbered by the Englishmen. In 1674, the Dutch were compelled to surrender New York colony for the second time to the English crown, the first time being in 1664.

---

[48] George Rogers Howell, *The Early History of Southampton, L.I., New York with Genealogies*, Second Edition, Weed, Parsons and Company, Albany, NY, 1887, p. 64 and Howell gives his source as Winthrop Papers, Massachusetts Historical Collection, 3 s. vol. 10, p. 92.

December 26, 1677[49]. "A list of the fence to bee done by the towne at Shinnecock against the land which ye Indians plant. Of 39 lots: No. 38 Henry Pierson, 150 pounds, 5 poles (of fence). Per me Henry Pierson Register."

November 5, 1679[50]. "At a town meeting ... It is ordered that Mr. Justice Topping (Mr. Justice is a title for John Topping), the constable & overseers attended by Henry Pierson shall appoint all the inhabitants of this towne their proper and distinct places in the meeting house on the Lords day to prevent disorder." The seating in the Presbyterian church of this era required that the elderly sit in front next to the church elders and their wives, and the remainder of the congregation be seated behind them with the younger to the rear or balconies of the church meeting house. The men always sat on one side of the church and the women on the other side. A single family might be scattered over the entire seating area. Over the years, an individual gradually moved from the rear of the church meeting house to up front just before dying. In 1675, the Southampton church had 49 heads of families and if all were present with their children, more than 200 people were required to sit in their assigned place. One can understand how confusion and disorder might reign as the congregation grew larger and simultaneously moved forward to fill the seats of the deceased.

1640-1691. Summary of Land Transactions for Henry Peirson, as taken from Southampton town records, Suffolk Co., New York Colony, on the given dates:

Before May 29, 1643	Lot in Southampton.	1 acre
Nov. 19, 1644	Lot bought from John White.	about 1 acre
Oct. 29, 1645	On the Great Plain.	4 acres
Before Apr. 16, 1646	From Mr. Odell of Southampton.	4 acres
Nov. 6, 1648	Swampland in division of Great Plain.	unk. acreage
Nov. 21, 1653	Henry swaps acreage in old town for acreage on Farington's (Old Town) pond.	3 acre swap
Feb. 2, 1653/4	Division of Sagaponack, 150-pound lot to Henry on east side of Sagaponack pond.	6 acres
Feb. 1654/5	Division of Sagaponack field 23-pound lot to Henry in Seaponack division.	About 1 acre
Oct. 7, 1659	Eastward lotment of meadow at the beach or Pines No. 1.	Guess 4 acres
Jan. 22, 1660/1	Acreage in Halsey's Neck in the Great Plain given to Henry by Southampton.	2 acres
Sep. 9, 1662	Henry trades property in Sagaponack for property in Shinnecock Neck.	6 acre swap

---

49 *Town Records of Southampton*, NY, Liber A, No. 2, 2nd Part, p. 89-90.
50 *Town Records of Southampton*, NY, Liber A, No. 2, 1st Part, p. 127.

Undated between 1662 and 1665	Redefines location of his 10 acres in Southampton town as behind his home lot ye rest by John Jessup's close.	10 acres redefined
Dec. 18, 1665	150-pound lotment at Quaquanantuck.	About 4 acres
Jan. 14, 1667/8	The east side of Littleworth Hollow south of the mill path.	35 acres
May 29, 1673	Meadow at Quaquanantuck from Assops Neck to the 4th Neck. 150-Pounds twice, lots 3 & 9.	About 8 acres
Nov. 15, 1676	Division of the ox pasture north of Southampton at Great Hogg Neck and Little Hogg Neck, 150-pound lot 7 South Division, 150-pound lot 14 North Div.	About 8 acres
May 11, 1677	150-pound lot 17 at Mecox, against Kellie's pond, north of the great Hollow that runs down to Calf Pen creek.	About 4 acres
June 1, 1680	Lot 41 at Hog Neck.	About 4 acres
Apr. 2, 1683	Quaquanantuck purchase: division of meadow at Catchaponack, Potunk and Onunk, lots 29 & 32 (totaling 300 pounds) to Henry's estate.	5 acres
Mar. 21, 1691	The 300-pound lotment to Henry Pierson deceased at Quaquanantuck purchase now belongs to Joseph, Henry (Jr), and Theodore Pierson, and Mathew Howell, assignee of Benjamin Pierson.	5 acres to sons of inheritance
	Total lands registered at Southampton for Henry Pierson	about 100 acres

Henry Peirson's public service spanned 35 years. He was appointed or elected to 24 Southampton public positions requiring his excellent writing skills. Each position was held for one year or less, and some simultaneously with others. Additionally, he accomplished many other short term public tasks on a continual basis ranging from writing letters on behalf of the town to surveying land for distribution grants. During the last 13 years of his life beginning in 1668, he was continuously the Clerk of Suffolk County while simultaneously holding office with Southampton during three of those years.

1646	Clerk of the Band of Soldiers, at age 31
1650	Register
1651	Townsman
1652	Town Clerk, Secretary
1653	Townsman

1654	Secretary
1655	Town Clerk, Secretary
1659	Secretary
1660	Secretary, Register
1661	Register
1663	Register, Town Collector, Assessor
1664	Townsman
1665	Clerk, Recorder, Overseer
1668	Public Notary, Keeper of Cattle Records
1668 thru 1680	Clerk of Suffolk County
1673	Recorder
1680	Recorder, at age 64

1 Jul - 7 Nov 1680. Henry Peirson died after 1 July 1680 when he witnessed a Southampton town record[51] and before 8 November 1680 when the inventory of his property was taken at Southampton[52]. Henry was about 65 years old at death and the cause of death is unknown. Since no will existed, it is presumed that illness or an accident was sudden. Henry Peirson's inventory was taken by Capt. John Howell, John Jessupe, Mr. Edward Howell, and Thomas Cooper (Henry's half brother).

The inventory of Henry Peirson, clearly stated that he was deceased by 8 Nov 1680 and that he spelled his name Peirson. In the inventory, the values were given in English pounds, each of which contains 20 shillings, and each shilling contains 12 pence. Henry's 11 pieces of land totaled about 100 acres and were worth about 700 pounds. His residence with house, barn, and land (about 6 acres) located on the southeast corner of Main and Meetinghouse Lane in the center of Southampton, where the First Presbyterian Church now stands, was worth half of his total land assets. At the Close at the old Towne, Henry owned about 4 acres. The Close at Littleworth refers to Littleworth Hollow where Henry owned 35 acres and perhaps grazed his cattle there. The Great and Little Plains are no longer shown on maps. However, the Great Plain was bounded on the north by Captain's Neck Lane, east by the town pond, south by the beach, and west by Taylor's Creek; thus it included First, Cooper's, Halsey's and Captains necks. Of this, Henry owned 6 acres at Halsey's neck which he plowed for crops. The Little Plain was bounded north by Frog pond or Gin Lane, south by the beach, east by old town pond, and west by the town pond. Henry probably owned about 4 acres in the Little Plain. Henry owned about 2 acres at Hog neck not including his meadow there. His five meadows all totaled about 43 acres where he mowed for winter hay.

Henry had 10 horses worth 39 pounds and no oxen whereas his neighbors had 2 to 10 oxen each for plowing and pulling carts. Since riding horses were then worth about 5 pounds each, it is reasonable to say perhaps only four or five of Henry's horses were riding horses, the others being colts or plow horses for Henry's two plows, harrowteeth, one cart, and three animal yokes. Henry had over 185 pounds of cattle. The value of cattle at that time ranged from 2 pounds 10 shillings for two year old steers to 4 pounds 10 shillings for the

[51]*Town Records of Southampton*, NY, Liber A, No. 2, 1st Part, p. 142.

[52]Thomas W. Cooper, *The Records of the Court of Sessions of Suffolk County in the Province of New York, 1670-1688*, Heritage Books, Inc., Bowie, Maryland, 1993, p. 103-4.

best cows. Using an average of this value range, Henry had 53 cattle. Henry had more than 32 pounds of sheep, hogs, and Indian corn with value lumped together. However, it was typical to have about 7 pounds of corn on hand, based on other inventories of the period locally, and have four times as many sheep as hogs (each worth 10 shillings). Therefore, Henry had approximately 56 bushels of Indian corn (maize), 10 hogs, and 40 sheep. The cattle and hogs were raised for milk, butter, and meat, and Henry probably sold some of them as the quantity seems excess to his family needs. Henry probably raised his sheep for wool only as his inventory lists no sheep skins or sheepskin rugs, only wool. He probably sold the wool and used the money to purchase finished cloths and other household items not raised on his farm as indicated by the large cloth inventory.

Henry had over 35 pounds of wheat, hay, and oats. Using the ratios of these in other inventories of Southampton, the 1679 rates of 5 shillings per bushel wheat & 2 shillings 6 pence per bushel oats or corn, and estimating hay at 6 pence per bushel, Henry had approximately 120 bushels wheat, 20 bushels oats, and 150 bushels hay on hand. While Henry had 18 pounds of flax (probably thread) on hand, he had no listing of flax crops (in bushels) as some of his neighbors did. Thus it is believed that Henry's crops were only wheat, oats, and Indian corn (maize). Hay (grass, alfalfa, or clover) was mowed from his meadows, dried, and used to feed his cattle and horses during the winter. These crops were probably stored in the barn as they were listed with the plows and cart in the original inventory. Wheat was used in porridge or taken to the local mill and made into flour and durum. The flour was used to make bread, wheat cakes (pancakes), cakes, and pastries. The coarsely ground durum meal, a byproduct created in the manufacture of fine flour, was used in making puddings, noodles, spaghetti, and macaroni. Oats were used as cereal for porridge or as horse feed. Corn was probably eaten off the cob in season and the dried corn stored for the winter was either boiled into hominy or milled into corn meal for corn bread and other foods. The hogs probably got table scraps after the dogs and cats got the better parts including the meat scraps. Meats were not listed in the inventory but would have existed as ham, bacon, beef and perhaps some venison from hunting. Chickens were not listed in the inventory, but are believed to have existed at Henry's home based upon the 17 pounds of feathers on hand and the five feather beds, though their source could also be geese. Thus, eggs were probably available. Dogs and cats were not listed in the estate inventory, but it is known that Henry had at least one dog based on a court case about someone striking his dog, perhaps a sheep dog for his 40 sheep. Cats were probably present for rodent and snake control. Fruit is not mentioned in this November inventory and is probably not available in large enough quantities to justify drying for the winter. However, jam and jelly preserves were common in that era, and it is known that most farmers in Southampton had fruit trees based on a law passed to prosecute those that steal fruit from other's fruit trees (likely apple, peach, apricot, cherry). It is clear that Henry Peirson worked hard as a yeoman (gentleman farmer) and he and his family ate well.

The furnishings of the house, tell us how many rooms the house had and what was in each room. It is probable that each room's inventory starts with the major furniture. When it lists a bed, for example, there is only one bed in that room, otherwise it would have said 2 beds. Based on that analysis, there appears to be five bedrooms and a great room which contains the kitchen, fireplace, tables, chairs, pillows, dishes, cooking utensils, etc. Henry's house was built in 1648 when Henry moved to his larger home lot in the center of the current Southampton and probably looked similar to the sketch below of Mr. Sayre's house built there the same year with barn in background. The Sayre house was still standing in 1887 when this sketch was made.

A house built in 1648 at Southampton

The kitchen was on the main floor at the high wall side of the house, fireplace in the middle, two or three bedrooms over the kitchen, with the balance of the bedrooms at the back or sides on the kitchen level. The barn was separate and large. Many frame structures of this exact practical design were built in Southampton at this time. The design was called a saltbox (two-story on the front side and one-story on the back).

Since Henry's books and wearing apparel were listed before the house and fences in the original inventory, it is unknown where they were kept, but it indicates their importance. The three guns shown in the inventory of Henry's estate were powder and shot type rifles used in the defense of the community or for hunting. The word pistols has been used in other inventories of this place and time when gun does not mean rifle. The sword probably signifies his status as an officer in colonial armed forces of the community, but only a record of him being "Clerk of the Band of Soldiers" in 1646 (age 31) has been found. It probably meant that he was in charge since no commander was mentioned at the time.

Henry was not listed as owning slaves in the inventory of his estate, but his half brother, John Cooper Jr., was shown as owning "2 Negroes & 2 chd" worth 90 pounds when he died in 1678. This means that Henry had opportunity to own slaves, but chose not to do so. In the greater Southampton area in a 1698 census, there were 83 Negro slaves representing about 8 percent of the total population. Many of these were freed by the owners in the 1700s as recorded in Southampton records.

Many words are used in the inventory of Henry's estate which are not familiar today. A looking glass is a mirror and only one was in Henry's house in a bedroom that was not his, though he kept his guns and sword in that room. Flax is a plant with blue flowers and narrow leaves of which the seeds are used for linseed oil and the fibers are spun into linen thread. A porringer is a small shallow bowl for porridge. A saltser is a saltcellar which is a small dish or container with a perforated top for holding salt. A tankard is a large drinking cup with a handle and often has a hinged lid. A posnett is probably a device which heats posset over the fire place. Posset is a hot drink made of milk curdled with ale, wine, etc. and usually spiced. One can see Henry leaning back in a cushioned chair in front of his fire place on a cool winter evening, sipping the steaming spiced posset from his tankard, and watching the fire flicker in Mary's eyes.

A coverlid is now called coverlet, bed covering, or bedspread. Henry's home contained all of the following cloths mentioned in his inventory. "A pcs Manchester" and "a remt Penistone" refer to cloths made in those towns in England and nowhere else. Manchester was then located in southeastern Lancashire which is adjacent to the southwest border of Yorkshire. Penistone is in southern Yorkshire just across the county border from Manchester. The port of trade for these cities was Liverpool which served the textile industries of northern England. The appearance of these cloths in Henry's house and others of Southampton acknowledges trade between northern England and Connecticut where Southampton traded. Kersy is a coarse lightweight woolen cloth usually ribbed and with a cotton thread warp (lengthwise). Broad cloth is a fine smooth woolen (also cotton or silk) cloth made on a wide loom. Serge is a strong twilled fabric made of wool or silk with a diagonal rib. Cambric (a city in northern France where the fabric was originally made) is a very fine thin linen. Duffel (a town in northern Belgium) is a coarse woolen cloth with a thick nap. Fustian is a coarse cloth of cotton and linen. Holland (first made there) is a linen or cotton cloth used for clothing and window shades. Drugget was then a woolen or part woolen material used for clothing. Diaper was then a cloth or fabric with a pattern of repeated small figures such as diamonds. Ticking is a strong heavy cloth, often striped, used for casing mattresses and pillows.

March 2, 1680/1[53]. "Att a Court of Sessions held at Southampton Begune the 2nd day of March 1680/1 Was Presented to the Court by Mary Peirson Relict & Widow of Henry Peirson of South Hampton deceased an Inventory of her said Husbands estate Aprized by Mr John Howell, Edward Howell, John Jessupe, Thomas Cooper who were Sworne by Mr John Tapping Justice of the Peace which Inventory and Aprizemt was allowed by the Court & Ordered to be Recorded; being as Followeth (dated 8 Nov 1680, see above). Upon the Petition of the said Mary Peirson for Liberty to Administer upon the aforesaid Estate as also to Ascertain her third of the whole estate according to Law. The Court doth Admit her the said Mary Peirson to be sole Administratrix of the whole Estate she performing the same according to Law as also her third pt of said according to her petition."

---

[53] Thomas W. Cooper, *The Records of the Court of Sessions of Suffolk County in the Province of New York, 1670-1688*, Heritage Books, Inc., Bowie, Maryland, 1993, p. 102-4.

March 3, 1680/1[54]. "Henry Peirson Inventory. There is a petition of Mary Peirson, widow of the deceased, dated 3 March 1680/1. She has several small children and asks letters of administration and that the court decide, after her one-third is deducted, how much shall be given to her sons and daughters and that she have the guardianship of the younger children."

Mary Peirson remarried to the Rev. Seth Fletcher[55] in May 1682 who was the son of Robert Fletcher of Concord, Massachusetts. Seth Fletcher had married 1st Mary, daughter of Bryan Pendleton of Portsmouth, New Hampshire. Seth Fletcher became the minister in Southampton in 1676 and remained as minister until about the beginning of 1679. The Reverend was installed as minister at Elizabethtown, New Jersey, in 1680. He died in 1682, after marrying 2nd Mary Peirson, leaving an estate valued at 559 pounds, 5 shillings, 8 pence.

March 21, 1691/2[56]. (Abstract by Wm. Pelletreau[57]) "Whereas there are several pieces of meadow laid to a 300 pound lotment to Henry Pierson deceased, lying at Quaquanantuck purchase, in 4 lots, and 5 acres, which now by agreement belong to Joseph, Henry, and Theodore Pierson, and Mathew Howell assignee to Benjamen Pierson. The said Henry, Joseph and Theodore (Pierson) make over to Mathew Howell all that lot of meadow at Quaquanantuck Neck. Witness John Howell, Joseph Wickham March 21, 1691." This documentation leaves little doubt about the names of four of Henry Peirson's sons.

Children of Henry and Mary (Fuller?) Peirson

Henry and Mary Peirson had children: Lt. Joseph, b. ca. 1640, d. aft. 1698, Southampton; dau. #1 b. ca. 1642, Southampton; dau. #2 b. ca. 1645; John b. ca. 1648; Col. Henry, b. 1652, d. 1701; Benjamin, b. 1655, d. 1731; Daniel b. ca. 1657; Sarah, b. 20 Jan 1660/61; dau. #4, born ca. 1665; Theodore, b. 1669; and dau. #5, b. ca. 1673. Detailed records of the children Lt. Joseph, Col. Henry, Benjamin, and Theodore Peirson are contained in Chapters 9, 10, 11, and 12, respectively, of this book. Records of the other children are described below.

Dau. #1 (ca. 1642-   ) and Dau. #2 (ca. 1645-   )

It is possible that two other children exist between Joseph (b. ca. 1640) and John (b. ca. 1648). It is probable that these children either died young or were female for which records are not known.

John (ca. 1648-   ) and Daniel (ca. 1657-   ) Peirson

From Lizzie B. Pierson's book[58], "Henry Pierson ... had children John (whose descendants are not traced); Daniel (not traced); Joseph; Henry; Benjamin; Theodore; Sarah." But

[54]Kenneth Scott and James A. Owre, *Genealogical Data From Inventories of New York Estates 1666-1825*, New York Genealogical and Biographical Society, New York, 1970, p. 32.
[55]George Rogers Howell, *The Early History of Southampton, L.I., New York with Genealogies*, Second Edition, Weed, Parsons and Company, Albany, NY, 1887, p. 105.
[56]*Town Records of Southampton*, NY, Liber A, No. 2, 1st Part, p. 194.
[57]Henry Hedges, Wm. Pelletreau, Edward Foster, *The Second Book of Records of the Town of Southampton, Long Island, N.Y. with other Ancient Documents of Historic Value*, John H. Hunt, Printer, Sag Harbor, NY, 1877, p. 126-127.
[58]Lizzie B. Pierson, *Pierson Genealogical Records*, Joel Munsell, Printer, Albany, NY, 1878, p. 22.

George Rogers Howell, noted expert on Southampton and author of several books on the subject, says of Lizzie's listing[59]:

"I fear Miss Pierson is mistaken in saying Henry had sons John and Daniel, as in all the lists of inhabitants of Southampton and in their records covering all sorts of transactions, no such names ever appear."

It is true that no such sons appear in Southampton records, as only four sons (Joseph, Henry, Benjamin, and Theodore) inherited land owned by Henry Peirson (see the March 21, 1691, entry above). However, there is room for two more children in the spacing of the known children at birth years about 1648 and 1657. Perhaps John and Daniel fall at these two birth years and died in their youth. Lizzie Pierson did not give her source for the names John and Daniel, but it is known that she wrote to many Pierson families for information in about 1877. It is presumed that the names, John and Daniel, come from family records.

Sarah Peirson (1661-   )

January 20, 1660/61[60]. "Henry Pierson his daughter Sarah was borne the 20 day of January 1660."

June 2, 1680[61]. "Jonathan Raynor gives in the day of marriage with Sarah Pierson by Justice John Topping to be upon the 2d day of June 1680." The Topping family also later married into the Pierson family.

March 4, 1681/82[62]. "Jonathan Rainer gives in the birth day of his son Jonathan March 4, 1681."

1698[63]. A town census: "A list of ye Inhabitants of ye Towne of Southampton (Long Island) ... Anno. 1698:

Jonathan Raynr	Sarah Raynr
Jonathan Raynor, jur.	Debrah Raynr
	Hanah Rayner"

This Sarah Raynor is the daughter of Henry Peirson and wife of Jonathan Raynor. Jonathan Jr., Debrah, and Hanah are probably all children of Jonathan and Sarah (Peirson) Raynor.

Daughter #4 (ca. 1665-   ) and Daughter #5 (ca. 1673-   ) Peirson

"In a prenuptial agreement[64] made between Mary Peirson and Seth Fletcher (Mary's 2nd husband), besides numerous monetary arrangements, this clause was included: *and to take three of her children with her as long as she shall see cause to have them so to be with her.*" The

---

[59]Lizzie B. Pierson, *Pierson Genealogical Records*, Joel Munsell, Printer, Albany, NY, 1878, p. 22, footnote.

[60]*Town Records of Southampton*, NY, Liber A, No. 2, 2nd Part, p. 26.

[61]*Town Records of Southampton*, NY, Liber A, No. 2, 2nd Part, p. 68.

[62]*Town Records of Southampton*, NY, Liber A, No. 2, 2nd Part, p. 122.

[63]George Rogers Howell, *The Early History of Southampton, L.I., New York with Genealogies*, 2nd Edition, Weed, Parsons and Company, Albany, NY, 1887, p. 37. Howell gives his source as Manuscripts in office of Secretary of State, Albany, NY.

[64]Arthur Newton Pierson, *Genealogy, the Pierson Family, the Marsh Family, the Clark Family, the Baker Family*, published by author, 1945, p. 3, a copy is in Library of Congress, Washington, DC.

existence of these children is further verified in Mary Peirson's petition to the Court of Sessions in Southampton on March 3, 1680/1 (see above). This means that Mary, took her three minor children, daughter #4 (b. ca. 1665, about age 17), Theodore (b. 1669, age 13), and daughter #5 (b. ca. 1673, about age 9) to live with her in Elizabeth Town. Theodore returned to Southampton about 1690 (age 21). Since no sons, other than "Joseph, Henry, Benjamen, and Theodore," inherited land (see the 1691 entry above), it is presumed that the other two children were female (names not known). The approximate birth years of these two females is based upon known child birth dates and typical child spacing for this family. Others believed that Benjamin was one of those three children, but Benjamin (b. 1655) was age 27 in 1682 and would not have been dependent on his mother at that time. It is true, however, that Benjamin also went to Elizabethtown, New Jersey, at about the same time as his mother, and there raised a family of his own (see Chapter 11).

The American Immigrant Wall of Honor

In 1992, the large Ellis Island immigration station in New York harbor celebrated its 100th anniversary. As part of the celebration, they decided to erect "The American Immigrant Wall of Honor." They would put immigrant's names and country of origin on plaques along this wall. Furthermore, they would not limit the names to those that used the Ellis Island entry port. They would allow any United States immigrant to be represented there including those that settled the original colonies. To fund this project, they would accept immigrant's names from those who would donate a minimum of $100 per name to cover the expense of the wall and plaque. The administration of this project was arranged by the federal government to be The Statue of Liberty-Ellis Island Foundation, Inc., the same non-profit organization that handled the refurbishing of the Statue of Liberty in New York harbor in 1986 when it was a 100 years old. In 1992, the name "Henry Peirson of England" was submitted by one of the co-authors, Richard Pierson, for the American Immigrant Wall of Honor. The Statue of Liberty-Ellis Island Foundation issued an Official Certificate of Registration. The plaque should now be in place for public viewing on Ellis Island in New York harbor.

Chapter 9
Descendants of Lt. Joseph Pierson
Son of Henry

Lt. Joseph Pierson is the eldest son of Henry and Mary Peirson. The following descendants of Lt. Joseph Pierson (ca. 1640 - aft. 1706/7) are copied from Lizzie B. Pierson, *Pierson Genealogical Records*, Joel Munsell, Printer, Albany, N.Y., 1878, pp. 22-29, as a framework to present new data upon. Lizzie Pierson's footnotes, errata, and related appendices are incorporated within the text which is modified by footnoted additional research by the authors of *Pierson Millennium*. An every-name index is provided at the back of *Pierson Millennium* whereas only heads of families were indexed in *Pierson Genealogical Records*. The + symbol after an identifying number indicates more information is provided in a later paragraph of this chapter beginning with the same number.

1 Henry Pierson had chd. 2 John; 3 Daniel; **4+ Joseph**; 5 Henry, b. 1652, d. 1701; 6 Benjamin, d. 1731; 7 Theodore; 8 Sarah, b. Jan. 20, 1660/61. See chapter 8 for more children and information on 1 Henry Peirson's family.

4 Joseph Pierson (Lieut.), was born (about 1640, see analysis in chapter 8) at Southampton, L. I.; was known as lieut.; and was active in settling the new town. He dealt with Indians for the town March 6, 1657/58[1]; and at age 30, still single, he exchanged 20 acres of land in Southampton on June 19, 1670[2]. He mar. Amy Barnes (probably the dau. of Joshua Barnes of Southampton[3]), Nov. 17, 1675[4] (she died Oct. 3, 1692[5]). After her death[6], Joseph mar. Joana, wid. of Thomas Cooper. In 1681[7], Joseph had cattle earmarks registered at Southampton, the cattle probably being inherited from his father who died the year before with about 53 head of cattle on hand. In 1682[8], Joseph was elected as one of Southampton's overseers including responsibility for preparing the Town Estimate in 1683[9] along with John Foster, John Jagarr, and John Howell Jr. Of the 143 individuals listed in the estimate, three were Piersons: Benj. Peirson £51; Joseph Pierson £127; and Henry Peirson £136. Of Joseph and his two brothers Benj. and Henry, only Joseph spelled his name Pierson at that time. In 1686[10], Joseph was a townsman (Assessor, etc.) for Southampton. He received

---

[1]*Town Records of Southampton*, NY, Liber A, No. 1, pp. 143-144.

[2]*Town Records of Southampton*, NY, Liber A, No. 2, 1st Part, p. 127.

[3]George Rogers Howell, *The Early History of Southampton, L.I., New York with Genealogies*, 2nd Edition, Weed, Parsons and Company, Albany, NY, 1887, p. 202.

[4]*Town Records of Southampton*, NY, Liber A, No. 2, 2nd Part, p. 67.

[5]*Town Records of Southampton*, NY, Liber A, No. 2, 2nd Part, p. 109.

[6]George Rogers Howell, *The Early History of Southampton, L.I., New York with Genealogies*, Second Edition, Weed, Parsons and Company, Albany, NY, 1887, pp. 348-9.

[7]*Town Records of Southampton*, NY, Liber A, No. 2, 2nd Part, p. 96.

[8]*Town Records of Southampton*, NY, Liber A, No. 2, 1st Part, p. 155.

[9]George Rogers Howell, *The Early History of Southampton, L.I., New York with Genealogies*, Second Edition, Weed, Parsons and Company, Albany, NY, 1887, pp. 44-5, and his reference is given as Doc. Hist. of N.Y., Vol. 2, page 536.

[10]*Town Records of Southampton*, NY, Liber A, No. 2, 1st Part, pp. 167-168.

land grants from the town of Southampton in 1686[11] at Accobogue Meadows, and 1687[12] at the meadow at the beach and pines.

In 1687, Joseph owned one of 14 whaling companies of 12 men each in the greater Southampton area who reported whale oil in their possession - two of them were: "Att ye Pines, Joseph Pierson & Co., 240 bbls" and his brother "Att Sagabonick, Lift Henery Peirson & Co., 276 bbls." "For generations before the settlers came[13], the Indians had cut up stranded whales blown ashore in the winter storms, and had gone out in dugout canoes, driving the whales ashore by shooting numbers of arrows into them. Companies were licensed to ship out off the south shore as 'adventurers on ye whayle designe,' the first in 1650." Joseph held Southampton town offices: in 1688 as Commissioner, Townsman, & Trustee; in 1692 as Viewer and Surveyor of Highways; in 1693 as Surveyor; in 1694 as Surveyor of Highways and Fences; and in 1695 as Trustee and the Town Rate. In the 1694 town records, he is called "Ensign" Joseph Pierson for the first time which title continued through the 1698 census prior to his death. An Ensign is an entry level Lieutenant and he was likely in the local colonial militia as was his brother Henry. In the 1696 Town Estimate for Southampton[14], the three Piersons listed were: "Theodore Pierson £38, Joseph Pierson £75, Col. Henry Pierson £130." In the 1698 Southampton town census[15], he was listed as "Ensign Joseph Peirson with children Henry, Joseph Jr., Mary, Ephraim, and Sam'll Peirson." His second wife Joana, widow of Thomas Cooper, is believed to have died before 1698 since she does not appear in the town 1698 census. After 1698, Joseph was mentioned two more times in Southampton records (both times as Lieutenant): 5 Dec 1700[16] "Jeremiah Culver was married to Mary Pierson ye daughter of Left. Joseph Pierson;" and 23 Feb 1706/7[17], "Mary Culver daughter of Left. Joseph Pierson, and wife of Jeremiah Culver departed this life Feb. 23, 1706." On 21 Jun 1739[18], land at the 41 lots of meadow on the beach westward from Hill Bank to Dow Little were laid out for the owners who included in Lot 2 "The heirs of Joseph Pierson." This 1739 record applies to Joseph Pierson Jr. since in 1720 Jr. was no longer applied to official records with Jr's. childrens' births. Thus Lieut. Joseph Pierson died between 23 Feb 1706/7 and 1720.

Joseph and Amy (Barnes) Pierson had chd. 10 Amy, b. Oct. 28, 1676 [19]; 11+ Henry, b. Apr. 17, 1678 [20]; 12+ Mary, b. June 12, 1680 [21], mar. Jeremiah Culver 1700; 13+ Joseph, b. Aug. 6,1684 [22]; 14+ Ephraim, b. Jan. 20, 1686/7 [23]; 15 Samuel, b. Feb. 24, 1689/90 [24].

---

[11]*Town Records of Southampton*, NY, Liber A, No. 2, 1st Part, pp. 178-179.

[12]*Town Records of Southampton*, NY, Liber A, No. 2, 1st Part, p. 188.

[13]Co-Chairmen Mrs. Albert W. Topping, Everett C. Foster, and Editor Paul H. Curts, *Bridgehampton's Three Hundred Years*, Hampton Press, Bridgehampton, NY, 1956, p. 66.

[14]Henry Hedges, Wm. Pelletreau, Edward Foster, *The Second Book of Records of the Town of Southampton, Long Island, N.Y. with other Ancient Documents of Historic Value*, John H. Hunt, Printer, Sag Harbor, NY, 1877, pp. 361-4.

[15]George Rogers Howell, *The Early History of Southampton, L.I., New York with Genealogies*, 2nd Edition, Weed, Parsons and Company, Albany, NY, 1887, p. 36.

[16]*Town Records of Southampton*, NY, Liber A, No. 2, 2nd Part, p. 132.

[17]*Town Records of Southampton*, NY, Liber A, No. 2, 2nd Part, p. 301.

[18]*Town Records of Southampton*, NY, Liber B (Vol. 3), pp. 39-40.

[19]*Town Records of Southampton*, NY, Liber A, No. 2, 2nd Part, p. 75.

[20]*Town Records of Southampton*, NY, Liber A, No. 2, 2nd Part, p. 75.

[21]*Town Records of Southampton*, NY, Liber A, No. 2, 2nd Part, p. 75.

[22]*Town Records of Southampton*, NY, Liber A, No. 2, 2nd Part, p. 75.

11 Henry Pierson, born Apr. 17, 1678 [25], at Southampton, Long Island, New York Colony. He was living with his father in the Southampton 1698 census[26] at age 20. He mar. (Abigail Ludlam June 11, 1702) [27], (dau. of Henry and Rachell Ludlom, see Southampton 1698 census)[28]. Henry's wife, Abigail (Ludlam) Pierson, died March 27, 1722[29], just 12 days after her son Samuel's birth. Henry received land grants from Southampton township: in 1712[30] at the Westward Division Speeunk Neck and Tanners Neck and Apocuck Neck, in 1727[31] at Seder Swamps Westward of the Little River, three in 1738 [32] [33] [34] at Lower Division and North Division Quaquanantuck Purchase, and timber land between the Indian line and East Hampton, and in 1739[35] at Canoe Place Division in Quaga Purchase. In 1713[36], he passed through his possession some land from Samuel Clark of North Sea to Sarah Limon, Samuel Clark, and Joab Clark. In 1726[37], Southampton records show this Henry in possession of his grandfather Henry's original home lot in the center of Southampton. He held civil office in Southampton in 1713 when he was constable[38] and in 1727[39] as Trustee, 1734[40] as Trustee, 1741[41] as Fence Viewer, and 1742[42] as Fence Viewer. In 1742, Henry sold his four pieces of property [43] [44] [45] [46] at Southampton township and moved to Cohansey, Salem Co., New Jersey.

"Henry Peirson's" will[47], dated July 10, 1747, at Cohansey, Salem Co., N.J., appoints son Henry executor who is to have all my lands and buildings, except 100 acres bounding upon

[23]*Town Records of Southampton*, NY, Liber A, No. 2, 2nd Part, p. 123.

[24]*Town Records of Southampton*, NY, Liber A, No. 2, 2nd Part, p. 123.

[25]*Town Records of Southampton*, NY, Liber A, No. 2, 2nd Part, p. 75.

[26]George Rogers Howell, *The Early History of Southampton, L.I., New York with Genealogies*, 2nd Edition, Weed, Parsons and Company, Albany, NY, 1887, p. 36, and Howell gives his source as Manuscripts in the Office of the Secretary of State, Albany, NY.

[27]*Town Records of Southampton*, NY, Liber A, No. 2, 2nd Part, p. 306.

[28]George Rogers Howell, *The Early History of Southampton, L.I., New York with Genealogies*, 2nd Edition, Weed, Parsons and Company, Albany, NY, 1887, p. 39, and Howell gives his source as Manuscripts in the Office of the Secretary of State, Albany, NY.

[29]*Town Records of Southampton*, NY, Liber A, No. 2, 2nd Part, p. 306.

[30]*Town Records of Southampton*, NY, Liber A, No. 2, 1st Part, p. 246.

[31]*Town Records of Southampton*, NY, Liber A, No. 2, 1st Part, pp. 296-9.

[32]*Town Records of Southampton*, NY, Liber B (Vol. 3), pp. 166-73.

[33]*Town Records of Southampton*, NY, Liber B (Vol. 3), pp. 184-88.

[34]*Town Records of Southampton*, NY, Liber B (Vol. 3), p. 157.

[35]*Town Records of Southampton*, NY, Liber B (Vol. 3), pp. 189-94.

[36]*Town Records of Southampton*, NY, Liber B (Vol. 3), p. 84. Abstract.

[37]*Town Records of Southampton*, NY, Liber A, No. 2, 1st Part, p. 291.

[38]*Town Records of Southampton*, NY, Liber A, No. 2, 1st Part, p. 267.

[39]*Town Records of Southampton*, NY, Liber B (Vol. 3), p. 135.

[40]*Town Records of Southampton*, NY, Liber B (Vol. 3), p. 137.

[41]*Town Records of Southampton*, NY, Liber B (Vol. 3), p. 139.

[42]*Town Records of Southampton*, NY, Liber B (Vol. 3), p. 139.

[43]*Town Records of Southampton*, NY, Liber B (Vol. 3), p. 82. Abstract.

[44]*Town Records of Southampton*, NY, Liber B (Vol. 3), p. 92. Abstract.

[45]*Town Records of Southampton*, NY, Liber B (Vol. 3), p. 127. Abstract.

[46]*Town Records of Southampton*, NY, Liber B (Vol. 3), p. 151. Abstract.

[47]A. Van Doren Honeyman, *Documents Relating to the State of New Jersey*, First Series, Vol. 30, "Calendar of New Jersey Wills, Administrations, Etc," Vol. II 1730-1750, The Unionist-Gazette Association, Printers, Somerville, N.J., 1918, p. 374.

Nixon and Shepherd's lines, which shall be for my son Azal; Sons William, John, Eli, and dau. Amy to have equally the money from the sale of residue of moveable estate; witnesses: Benjamin Chard, William Casto, John Ogden (Lib. 5, p. 391). The date the will was proved was not found, however, his inventory was taken Feb. 2, 1747/8 by Jonathan Shepherd & John Ogden. Henry is mentioned in Southampton records[48] on Oct. 22, 1747 when he witnessed the sale of 50 acres of land at Smith's Corner in Sag from Josiah Topping to Abram Pierson, Elnathan White, and Job Pierson. Henry was then age 69 and died a few months later in New Jersey.

Henry and Abigail Pierson had chd., all born at Southampton, Suffolk Co., N.Y.: 23 Henry, b. Feb. 1, 1704/5[49]; 24+ William, b. April 1, 1706[50]; 25+ Azel, b. Sept. 13, 1708[51]; 26+ John, b. Dec. 29, 1710[52]; 27 Eli, b. Dec. 30, 1712[53]; 28 Abigail, b. Feb. 28, 1714/15[54]; 29 Amy, b. Oct. 11, 1716[55], probably the one who mar. Elisha Davis in East Hampton May 7, 1739[56]; 30+ Samuel, b. March 15, 1721/22[57].

24 William Pierson was b. April 1, 1706[58] at Southampton on Long Island, New York Colony. He mar. ca. 1727 Elizabeth Howell[59] (b. Jan. 9, 1709), dau. of Daniel Howell (b. 1680 Southampton, N.Y., d. Apr. 25, 1732) of Ewing, N. J. Since later records of Southampton do not reflect William Pierson's continued presence, perhaps he settled in Ewing, N.J. A 1741 census record[60] reflects "William Pearson," Trenton Twp., Hunterdon Co., N.J.

25 Azel Pierson was born 13 Sep 1708[61] at Southampton Twp, Suffolk Co., N.Y., and moved to Cumberland Co., N. J. Azel Pierson's will[62] was dated 3 Feb 1765 at Stow Creek, Cumberland Co., N.J., and proved 8 Apr 1765. The will names his wife Mary ____, and chd.[63] 903 Ruth; 904+ Azel; 905 George; 906 Marce; 907 Zebulon (bap. 25 Oct 1746 Pittsgrove Pres. Ch., Cumberland Co., N.J.)[64]; 908 Abigail; and 909 Reuben.

---

[48]*Town Records of Southampton*, NY, Liber B (Vol. 3), p. 197. Abstract.

[49]*Town Records of Southampton*, NY, Liber A, No. 2, 2nd Part, p. 306.

[50]*Town Records of Southampton*, NY, Liber A, No. 2, 2nd Part, p. 306.

[51]*Town Records of Southampton*, NY, Liber A, No. 2, 2nd Part, p. 306.

[52]*Town Records of Southampton*, NY, Liber A, No. 2, 2nd Part, p. 306.

[53]*Town Records of Southampton*, NY, Liber A, No. 2, 2nd Part, p. 306.

[54]*Town Records of Southampton*, NY, Liber A, No. 2, 2nd Part, p. 306.

[55]*Town Records of Southampton*, NY, Liber A, No. 2, 2nd Part, p. 306.

[56]George Rogers Howell, *The Early History of Southampton, L.I., New York with Genealogies*, 2nd Edition, Weed, Parsons and Company, Albany, NY, 1887, p. 425.

[57]*Town Records of Southampton*, NY, Liber A, No. 2, 2nd Part, p. 306.

[58]*Town Records of Southampton*, NY, Liber A, No. 2, 2nd Part, p. 306.

[59]George Rogers Howell, *The Early History of Southampton, L.I., New York with Genealogies*, 2nd Edition, Weed, Parsons and Company, Albany, NY, 1887, p. 314.

[60]MicroQuix, Colonial America - Pre-1790 Census Indexes, Tax Lists, No. CD136, Automated Archives, Inc., 1992.

[61]*Town Records of Southampton*, NY, Liber A, No. 2, 2nd Part, p. 306.

[62]H. Stanley Craig, *Genealogical Data from Cumberland County New Jersey Wills*, published by H. Stanley Craig, Merchantville, N.J., no pub. date (received 2 Sep 1942 at Genealogical Society of Utah), p. 99.

[63]The children's identifying numbers in the 900s do not represent the generation era they are from, but rather are an added generation among smaller-numbered generations.

[64]Baptism said "Zebulon Pierson, son of Asahel (Azel) and Mary." Source: H. Stanley Craig, *Salem County Genealogical Data Prior to 1800*, Vol. I, published by H. Stanley Craig, Merchantville, N.J., no pub. date (microfilmed by the LDS church 15 Nov 1977), p. 196.

904[65] Azel Pierson was born[66] 19 Jan 1739 in New Jersey and died[67] 16 Oct 1798 in New Jersey. He mar.[68] 1st 4 Dec 1762 Mary Siden in Salem Co., N.J., and mar.[69] 2d? Philithia Sayre. "Azel Peirson" was on tax lists[70] at Hopewell Twp., Cumberland Co., N.J. in Sep. 1773, 1774, May 1778, and Sep. 1779 (spelled Pierson that year). During the Revolutionary War he was a Captain in the New Jersey militia.[71] In January 1781[72], "Azel Pierson" appeared on the tax list at Fairfield Twp., Cumberland Co., N.J. He had chd. 67+ Azel, b. July 1767; perhaps 67a+ Daniel; perhaps 67b+ David; and perhaps others.

67 Azel Pierson, M. D., was born in Cumberland Co., New Jersey, July, 1767, and died 1813. After having been licensed as a practitioner of medicine, he married Phebe ____ (probably Clark based on first son's middle name) and settled in Cedarville. He always visited patients on horseback, and was considered a good rider. In 1804 (at age 37), he was appointed Clerk of Cumberland County, transferred his residence to Bridgeton, and discharged the duties of his office for eight years. He still practiced medicine, along with his clerkship. In the early part of 1813, while visiting a patient with typhus fever, he contracted the disease, and died. He lies interred in the graveyard of the Old Stone church; a plain marble slab alone marks his resting place. His widow, Phebe, had will[73] at Bridgeton, Cumberland Co., N.J., dated 22 Oct 1842, proved 2 Dec 1844, that mentions living children Daniel C. and Azel, and living grand-children Azel and Phebe, chd. of Daniel, and Matilda Fithian, dau. of Azel. He had chd.139+ Daniel Clark, b. 1792; 140+ Azel, b. 1795 (twin), and 141+ Matilda, b. 1795 (twin); 142 Lucius Sayre, b. July 10, 1798, d. July 21, 1805; 143 George, b. Sept. 11, 1800, d. July 14, 1805; 144 Collin, b. Dec. 15, 1802, d. Aug. 1, 1805; 145 Reuben, b. April 27, 1805, d. Oct. 3, 1805; 146 Phebe Ann, b. July 20, 1809, d. Oct. 17, 1809.

139 Daniel Clark Pierson, M.D., born Oct. 9, 1792, moved with his family from Cumberland Co., New Jersey, to Jacksonville, Illinois, in 1833; again, in 1850, moved to Augusta, Illinois, where he died Jan. 29, 1857. Daniel Clark Pierson married Naomi Nixon in 1816. She still (1878) lives in Augusta, Illinois. They had chd. 293+ Azel, b. 1817; 294 Phebe, b. Mar. 28, 1818, mar. Samuel S. Clark, lived in Bunker Hill, Illinois; 295 Ruth, b. Oct. 26, 1819, d. July 31, 1833; 296+ Jeremiah, b. Aug. 16, 1821; 297+ Daniel, b. July 1, 1823; 298 George, b. Dec.

---

[65]Identifying numbers in the 900s do not represent the generation era they are from, but rather are an added generation among smaller-numbered generations.

[66]*DAR Patriot Index*, Centennial Edition, National Society of the Daughters of the American Revolution, 1994, part 3, p. 2256.

[67]*DAR Patriot Index*, Centennial Edition, National Society of the Daughters of the American Revolution, 1994, part 3, p. 2256.

[68]New Jersey Marriage Licenses, as reported by: H. Stanley Craig, *Salem County Genealogical Data Prior to 1800*, Vol. I, published by H. Stanley Craig, Merchantville, N.J., no pub. date (microfilmed by the LDS church 15 Nov 1977), p. 196.

[69]*DAR Patriot Index*, Centennial Edition, National Society of the Daughters of the American Revolution, 1994, part 3, p. 2256.

[70]MicroQuix, *Colonial America - Pre 1790 Census Indexes, Tax Lists*, No. CD136, Automated Archives, Inc., 1992.

[71]*DAR Patriot Index*, Centennial Edition, National Society of the Daughters of the American Revolution, 1994, part 3, p. 2256.

[72]MicroQuix, *Colonial America - Pre-1790 Census Indexes, Tax Lists*, No. CD136, Automated Archives, Inc., 1992.

[73]H. Stanley Craig, *Genealogical Data from Cumberland County New Jersey Wills*, published by H. Stanley Craig, Merchantville, N.J., no pub. date (received 2 Sep 1942 at Genealogical Society of Utah), p. 99.

14, 1824, d. 1825; 299+ George, b. May 10, 1826; 299a Naomi, d. young; 299b William, b. 1830, d. July 20, 1854, mar. L. Devee at Jacksonville, Illinois; 299c Matilda, d. young; 299d Ruth, b. 1834, mar. C. C. Palmer of Knoxville, Tenn., a widow in 1878; 299e Henry Martyn, d. young; 299f Naomi, mar. E. B. Sanner of Illinois.

293 Azel Pierson, b. Jan. 22, 1817, is a farmer, and lives [1878] in Augusta, Illinois. He has [1878] chd. 462 Lillie (w. of Rev. F. Mitchell, of Missouri); 463 Henry, b. 1861.

296 Jeremiah Pierson, born Aug. 16, 1821, resides [1878] in Jacksonville, Illinois. He mar. Sarah E. Catlin, in 1847, and had chd.: 464 Cornelia J., b. 1847; 465 Emma C., b. 1849; 466 Minnie A.; 467 Willie; 468 Daniel Elmer, b. Jan., 1856; 469 Azel, b. Apr. 3, 1858; 470 Mary Lois; 471 James R. C.; 472 Alfred W. E.; 473 Bessie H.

297 Daniel Pierson, M.D., born July 1, 1823, resides [1878] in Augusta, Illinois, and has chd.: 474 Abby, b. 1847; 475 Lawrence D., b. 1854; 476 Clark Morse, b. 1860; 477 Paoli, b. 1869.

299 George Pierson, born May 10, 1826, graduated at Illinois College, 1848, and at Andover Theological Seminary, 1851; mar. Salome Dexter, 1851; went as a missionary of A. B. C. F. M., to the Choctaw Indians, but his health failed and his wife died, so he left the field in 1852. In 1854, he married again, Nancy A. Shaw, and went as a missionary to Micronesia, in 1854. Remaining there till 1860, his wife's health failed, and he returned to America. He took charge of a Presbyterian church at Brooklyn, California, for nine years; and another Presbyterian church at Adel, Iowa, till April 1871. In 1876, moved to Solomon, Kansas, where he now [1878] resides, and has charge of a Presbyterian church. He had chd. 478 Salome Annette, b. 1856; 479 George F.; 480 Mary A.

140 Azel Pierson was born in Cumberland Co., New Jersey, in 1795. He is a twin with 141 Matilda Pierson. From a Pierson Bible record[74], Azel mar. 3 Oct 1820 Phebe Clark[75] at Bloomfield, Cumberland Co., N.J. He resided in Bridgeton, N.J., where he taught school. He died there shortly before his 4th wedding anniversary on Sep. 18, 1824. He had chd.: 301 Lucius C., in 1878 lived in Camden, N.J.; 301a Matilda, mar. ____ Fithian, in 1878 a widow in Cincinnati, Ohio.

141 Matilda Pierson was born in Cumberland Co., N. J., in 1795. She was a twin with 140 Azel Pierson. She mar. Rev. C. Foot who was a pastor in Longmeadow, Mass., in 1878. Matilda died Dec. 1838.

67a Daniel Pierson had chd.: 910 Maria, mar. Alexander Webb (will 7 May 1849, proved 30 Jul 1849) of Bridgeton, Cumberland Co., N.J.

67b David Pierson mar.[76] 1st 19 Dec 1792 Rebecca Fithian at the Fairfield Presbyterian Church, Cumberland Co., N.J. David wrote his will[77] 26 Dec 1812 at Fairfield,

---

[74]H. Stanley Craig, *Genealogical Data from Cumberland County New Jersey Wills*, published by H. Stanley Craig, Merchantville, N.J., no pub. date (received 2 Sep 1942 at Genealogical Society of Utah), p. 18.

[75]Azel's father, 67 Dr. Azel, also married a Phebe Clark(?) ca. 1791, but this marriage record cannot belong to 67 Azel as he died in 1813. Therefore, this marriage belongs here and 140 Azel's son, Lucius C. is probably Lucius Clark.

[76]H. Stanley Craig, Cumberland County (NJ) Marriages (from NJ Archives), pub. by H. Stanley Craig, Merchantville, N.J., reprinted 1978, p. 235.

[77]H. Stanley Craig, *Genealogical Data from Cumberland County New Jersey Wills*, published by H. Stanley Craig, Merchantville, N.J., no pub. date (received 2 Sep 1942 at Genealogical Society of Utah), p. 99.

Cumberland Co., N.J., which was proved 7 May 1813. The will provides his 2d wife Hannah ____, and chd. 911 David, 912 John, and 913 Eli.

26 John Pierson was born Dec. 29, 1710[78], at Southampton, Suffolk Co., N.Y. No further record of John is found in Southampton.

30 Samuel Pierson was born at Southampton, Suffolk Co., New York Colony, March 15, 1721/22[79]. At age 21, about 1743[80], he owned cattle (registered earmark) at Southampton. Samuel is believed to have lived and died at Southampton, but no record is found of him after the birth of his youngest son 69 Samuel in 1754[81]. Perhaps 30 Samuel died before ca. 1759 when his eldest son Timothy married at about age 17. He had chd. 68+ Timothy, (b. ca. 1742); 69+ Samuel, b. Dec. 28, 1754[82] at Southampton.

68 Timothy Pierson (born Southampton ca. 1742, based on his father's birth 1722 and Timothy's eldest child's birth 1760)[83]. Timothy mar. Mary[84] (Mollie[85]) Culver ca. 1759 (based on the 1st child's birth of 1760). Based upon earmarks and brands registered at Southampton, Timothy owned cattle in 1766[86], 1770[87], and 1772[88]. In May 1775, Timothy signed the Association (Associations 30.166, 175) [89] of those against British tyranny at County Hall (Southampton), Suffolk Co., N.Y. On July 22, 1776, the census[90] of the town of Southampton showed "West of the Watermill" Timothy Peirson family, 4 males, 6 females. On Long Island, during the last years of the British occupation, Timothy witnessed Samuel Cooper's will, June 22, 1782[91]. Timothy was one of the signers Dec. 30, 1784[92] of an agreement with the Rev. Joshua Williams to become the ninth pastor of "the first Parish in

---

[78]*Town Records of Southampton*, NY, Liber A, No. 2, 2nd Part, p. 306.

[79]*Town Records of Southampton*, NY, Liber A, No. 2, 2nd Part, p. 306.

[80]*Town Records of Southampton*, NY, Liber A, No. 2, 2nd Part, p. 307.

[81]Comment by the author Richard Pierson after analysis of which records applied to Samuel or his son Samuel. The 1775 Association signing and 1784 Rev. Williams agreement signing, both at Southampton, apply to his son 69 Samuel Peirson.

[82]Silas S. Peirson, *The Peirson Family in Wayne County, New York, 1638-1916*, Arcadia Advertising Co., Newark, NY, 1917, p. 35.

[83]Note by author Richard Pierson. There is insufficient room for both Timothy's father Samuel and Timothy to marry at age 21 or later. It is believed that Timothy, the eldest son, married ca. 1759 at age 17 because his father 30 Samuel had died earlier. Based on other examples in the Pierson line, a son is more likely to marry under age 21 if his father is deceased.

[84]Silas S. Peirson, *The Peirson Family in Wayne County, New York, 1638-1916*, Arcadia Advertising Co., Newark, NY, 1917, p. 33.

[85]Cuyler Reynolds, *Hudson-Mohawk Genealogical and Family Memoirs*, Lewis Publishing Co., New York, NY, 1911, p. 776.

[86]*Town Records of Southampton*, NY, Liber B (Vol. 3), p. 285, Abstract.

[87]*Town Records of Southampton*, NY, Liber B (Vol. 3), p. 356, Abstract.

[88]*Town Records of Southampton*, NY, Liber B (Vol. 3), p. 374, Abstract.

[89]Frederic Mather, *The Refugees of 1776 from Long Island to Connecticut*, Genealogy Publishing Company, Baltimore, Maryland, 1972, p. 1056.

[90]Henry Hedges, Wm. Pelletreau, Edward Foster, *The Third Book of Records of the Town of Southampton, Long Island, N.Y. with other Ancient Documents of Historic Value*, John H. Hunt, Printer, Sag Harbor, NY, 1878, Appendix, pp. 391-9.

[91]Berthold Fernow, *Calendar of Wills*, on file and recorded in the offices of the Clerk of the Court of Appeals, of the County Clerk at Albany and by the Secretary of State (New York) 1626-1836, compiled 1896, p. 85, No. 371.

[92]George Rogers Howell, *The Early History of Southampton, L.I., New York with Genealogies*, 2nd Edition, Weed, Parsons and Company, Albany, NY, 1887, pp. 111-13.

Southampton." Timothy held the following Southampton offices: 1786[93] Fence Viewer, 1787[94] Trustee, 1788[95] Assessor, 1789[96] Overseer of the Poor, 1791[97] Assessor, 1792[98] Assessor and Fence Viewer, 1795[99] Trustee and Fence Viewer, 1798[100] Fence Viewer. No record of Timothy Pierson was found in Southampton after 1798 and it is presumed that he died shortly after that time. Timothy and Mary had sons[101] [102] and daus. [103] [104] 147a+ Phoebe b. 5 Mar 1760[105], who mar. William Herrick[106] and they resided at Southampton; 147+ James, b. 1762, d. 1821; 148+ Charles who moved to Renshaven, Albany Co., New York; 149+ Eli who moved to Johnstown, Fulton Co., New York; 150 Timothy, who died at ten, killed by a whale; 151+ William; 151a Mary, who married William Halsey; 151b Ruth; 151c+ Deborah, who married Ananias Halsey; and 151d Betsy, who married and resided in Southampton.   William and Ananias Halsey are the sons of Joshua$_5$ Halsey[107], (Nathaniel$_4$, Nathaniel$_3$, Thomas$_2$, Thomas$_1$).

147a Phoebe Pierson was born[108] 5 Mar 1760 at Southampton, Long Island, and d.1846. Phoebe married William Herrick about 1782 and they resided at Southampton[109] on Long Island. "William Herrick[110] b. Apr. 27, 1761[111], and d. Nov. 25, 1825. Phoebe Pierson's husband, William Herrick, was Southampton town clerk from 1791 through 1808 and probably for many years thereafter (town records after mid-1808 not reviewed). In addition to this post, he was elected at Southampton, Long Island, to one-year terms as Commissioner of Schools in 1796, 1798, & 1800, and Trustee in 1806, 1807, & 1808. William and Phoebe had Herrick ch.[112] William Peirson, b. Oct. 3, 1783; Stephen, b. Aug. 18, 1785, of Utica, New York; Mary, b. Aug. 18, 1787; George, b. Feb. 13, 1790; Herman, b. March 17,

[93]*Town Records of Southampton*, NY, Liber B (Vol. 3), p. 431.

[94]*Town Records of Southampton*, NY, Liber B (Vol. 3), p. 434.

[95]*Town Records of Southampton*, NY, Liber B (Vol. 3), p. 442.

[96]*Town Records of Southampton*, NY, Liber B (Vol. 3), p. 448.

[97]*Town Records of Southampton*, NY, Liber B (Vol. 3), p. 457.

[98]*Town Records of Southampton*, NY, Liber B (Vol. 3), p. 459.

[99]*Town Records of Southampton*, NY, Liber B (Vol. 3), p. 470.

[100]*Town Records of Southampton*, NY, Liber B (Vol. 3), pp. 485-6.

[101]Lizzie B. Pierson, *Pierson Genealogical Records*, Joel Munsell Printer, Albany, NY, 1878, p. 25.

[102]Silas S. Peirson, *The Peirson Family in Wayne County, New York, 1638-1916*, Arcadia Advertising Co., Newark, NY, 1917, p. 33.

[103]Cuyler Reynolds, *Hudson-Mohawk genealogical and Family Memoirs*, Lewis Publishing Co., New York, NY, 1911, p. 776.

[104]Silas S. Peirson, *The Peirson Family in Wayne County, New York, 1638-1916*, Arcadia Advertising Co., Newark, NY, 1917, p. 33.

[105]*Town Records of Southampton*, NY, Liber B (Vol. 3), p. 488.

[106]George Rogers Howell, *The Early History of Southampton, L.I., New York with Genealogies*, 2nd Edition, Weed, Parsons and Company, Albany, NY, 1887, p. 295.

[107]George Rogers Howell, *The Early History of Southampton, L.I., New York with Genealogies*, 2nd Edition, Weed, Parsons and Company, Albany, NY, 1887, p. 272.

[108]*Town Records of Southampton*, NY, Liber B (Vol. 3), p. 488.

[109]Silas S. Peirson, *The Peirson Family in Wayne County, New York, 1638-1916*, Arcadia Advertising Co., Newark, NY, 1917, p. 33.

[110]George Rogers Howell, *The Early History of Southampton, L.I., New York with Genealogies*, 2nd Edition, Weed, Parsons and Company, Albany, NY, 1887, p. 295.

[111]*Town Records of Southampton*, NY, Liber B (Vol. 3), p. 488.

[112]*Town Records of Southampton*, NY, Liber B (Vol. 3), p. 488.

1792; Abigail, b. May 3, 1794, d. July 16, 1798; Austin, b. April 12, 1796; Edward, b. Sept. 1, 1798, d. March 15, 1800, small pox; and a 2nd Edward, b. Dec. 6, 1801."

147 James Pierson, born 1762, died 1821 at age 59, mar. Sept. 24, 1788[113] (Howell provides[114] Sept. 22, 1788) Phoebe, daughter of Jeremiah$_5$ Culver (Jeremiah$_4$, Jeremiah$_3$ who m. Mary dau. of Lt. Joseph Pierson, Gersham$_2$, Edward$_1$[115]) of Southampton. James was a merchant captain. He was elected Constable at Southampton April 7, 1801[116]. In 1804[117], James was on a committee at Southampton to purchase, repair, and enlarge the schoolhouse. James and Phoebe had chd. 302+ William, of Cairo, Greene Co., New York; 303+ James; 304 Henry; 305+ Philetous, b. 1801, mar. Elizabeth (b. 1802, dau. of Edward Reeves); 306 Milicent (w. of Wm. Wick); and 306a Franklin.

302 William Pierson[118] was born Sept. 15, 1789 in Suffolk Co., New York, and died Jan. 21, 1872 at Cairo, Greene Co., N. Y. He married at Greene Co., New York, 11 May 1816 Eleanor Carbine (b. Jan. 4, 1795; d. May 15, 1858), daughter of Zebulon Carbine and Mary Crocker and stepdaughter of Peter Van Orden. William Pierson was raised at Southampton on Long Island, was first found in Greene County records of New York, 6 Sep 1814 to 10 Nov 1814, as "Private William Person[119] (sic)" attached to a Company of Militia under command of Capt. John Van Vechten, in the 61st Regiment of N.Y.S.D. Militia, commanded by Lt. Col. Barnabas Covva in the service of the United States. However, Capt. John Van Vechten's Company was detached about 6 Sep 1814 and placed under Lt. Colonel Ezra Post in Brig. General Peter S. Van Orden's Brigade at Cairo.[120] Corporal William Pierson was honorably discharged 8 Dec 1814 at Harlem Heights near New York City, New York, having served more than 3 months during the War of 1812. In 1822, he was listed[121] as "Ensign William Pierson" of the 120th Regiment of Infantry at Greene County, New York. After William Pierson married Eleanor Carbine in Greene County, William and Eleanor lived in Cairo, Greene Co., New York, as verified by the 1820, 1830, 1840, and 1850 U. S. censuses. From 1824 to 1830, William was Cairo Town Clerk. From 1832 to 1838, William Pierson (ages 43 to 49) was a Justice of the Peace[122] for the town of Cairo. In the 1855 New York state census, William Pierson, age 66, was a clerk. He was a Justice of the Peace at

[113]Silas S. Peirson, *The Peirson Family in Wayne County, New York, 1638-1916*, Arcadia Advertising Co., Newark, NY, 1917, p. 33.

[114]George Rogers Howell, *The Early History of Southampton, L.I., New York with Genealogies*, 2nd Edition, Weed, Parsons and Company, Albany, NY, 1887, p. 349.

[115]George Rogers Howell, *The Early History of Southampton, L.I., New York with Genealogies*, 2nd Edition, Weed, Parsons and Company, Albany, NY, 1887, pp. 228-9.

[116]*Town Records of Southampton*, NY, Liber B (Vol. 3), p. 492.

[117]*Town Records of Southampton*, NY, Liber B (Vol. 3), p. 516, Abstract.

[118]Information copied from gravestones and monuments by David Stapleton of Greymouth, New Zealand, in October 1992, when he visited Cairo cemetery, Greene Co., N. Y.

[119]*History of Greene County, New York with Biographical Sketches of its Prominent Men*, J.B. Beers & Co., New York city, New York, 1884, p. 30.

[120]Record Group 15, Records of the Veterans Administration. War of 1812 Pension File; Pierson, William; Sworn statement by William Pierson made before Robert Dorlon, Justice of the Peace, Greene Co., New York, Nov. 19, 1850; National Archives, Washington, DC.

[121]*Annual Report of the New York State Historian, Greene County, 1822*, p. 2355.

[122]*History of Greene County, New York with Biographical Sketches of its Prominent Men*, J.B. Beers & Co., New York city, New York, 1884, pp. 207-208.

Cairo from 1852 to 1856.[123] William's wife, Eleanor, died 15 May 1858 at age 63. William was living by himself in the 1860 census at Cairo at age 71. By 1870, William, age 81, had a live-in domestic servant, a black lady Sally Peterson (age 65), perhaps because he could no longer run the household by himself. William Pierson died 21 Jan 1872 at Cairo at age 82.

All of the children of William and Eleanor Pierson are verified from cemetery records[124] except Mary Frances, James M., and Charles. Mary Frances' name comes from her descendants inserting her name in the LDS IGI from family records of William Van Orden Carbine, and is confirmed by the 1830 and 1840 censuses as being the missing daughter born 1825. The name Mary Frances is carried down in her brother Charles family in New Zealand when he names his first child Olla Mary Frances Pierson (b. 5 Sep 1872 in New Zealand). The names and birth years for James and Charles come from the 1850 census. The full five names for Charles are from his death certificate at Kumara, New Zealand. William and Eleanor had chd., all born at Cairo, Greene Co., New York: 600+[125] William H., b. 17 Jul 1818, d. 1841, lost at sea; 601 Elizabeth Ann, b. 6 Aug 1820, d. 29 Jan 1840; 602 George A. H., b. 13 Jun 1823, d. May 1861; 603 Mary Frances, b. 1825, mar. Joshua Fiero Jr.[126]; 604 Malcomb W. B., b. 29 Jul 1826, d. 29 Oct 1827[127]; 605+ James Malcolm, b. 1829; 606 Phebe Elmira, b. 24 Aug 1832, d. May 1841; 607+ Charles Anson Crocker Herrick Philetous (one person), b. 15 May 1838; and two infants died at birth without name.

600 William H. Pierson was born 17 Jul 1818 at Cairo, Greene Co., New York. He became a young whaling ship captain[128] living at Bridgehampton, Long Island, and sailing from Sag Harbor. Captain William H. Pierson lost his life at sea in 1841 at age 23. There is a monument in the burying ground at Sag Harbor on eastern Long Island to six whaling captains that lost their lives in their trade including this William H. Pierson. On one side of the monument are the six captains names and on the other side it states:

"To commemorate that noble enterprise The Whale Fishery and a tribute of lasting respect to those bold and enterprising ship masters Sons Of Southampton who perilled their lives in a daring profession and perished in actual encounter With the Monsters of the Deep, Entombed in the Ocean they live in our memory."

605 James Malcolm Pierson, Captain, was born in 1829 (age 21 in the 1850 census) at Cairo, Greene Co., New York. He was a Union officer[129] at Greene County, New York, during the U.S. Civil War. James joined the 120th New York Infantry Regiment at Greene County 22 Aug 1862 and was discharged as a Captain on 17 Mar 1863. After the war, James moved

[123]*History of Greene County, New York with Biographical Sketches of its Prominent Men*, J.B. Beers & Co., New York city, New York, 1884, pp. 207-208.
[124]Information copied from gravestones and monuments by David Stapleton of Greymouth, New Zealand, in October 1992, when he visited Cairo cemetery, Greene Co., N. Y.
[125]Individual identification numbers of 600 or larger are added by the author Richard Pierson for clarity.
[126]Attorney-in-fact (Greene Co., N.Y., Deeds 84:294 FHL 480 034), and Indenture (Greene Co., N.Y., Deeds 84:436 FHL 480 035).
[127]Year from birth date and death age on first gravestone, month and day from date of death on second gravestone.
[128]Co-Chairmen Mrs. Albert W. Topping, Everett C. Foster, and Editor Paul H. Curts, *Bridgehampton's Three Hundred Years*, Hampton Press, Bridgehampton, NY, 1956, p. 71.
[129]*History of Greene County, New York with Biographical Sketches of its Prominent Men*, J.B. Beers & Co., New York city, New York, 1884, p. 70.

to Kingston, Ulster Co., New York, where he mar. 26 Oct 1865 Inez Clark Decker.[130] James died 15 Dec 1905, aged 75, at Bayonne, Hudson Co., New Jersey.[131] Inez C. (Decker) Pierson died 16 Dec 1909 and was buried beside her husband James Malcolm Pierson at Bay View Cemetery, Jersey City, New Jersey.[132] James and Inez had chd.: 846 William D., b. 21 Dec 1866; 847 Malcolm I., b. 26 Dec 1868; 848 Eleanor H?, b. 7 Apr 1871; 849 Laura M., b. 15 Oct 1874; 850 J. Milton Fiero, b. 25 Dec 1876; 851 James M. Jr., b. 7 Dec 1878; and 852 E. McCready Tremain, b. 20 Mar 1881.[133]

607 Charles Anson Crocker Herrick Philetous Pierson was born 15 May 1838[134] at Cairo, Greene Co., New York. He went to New Zealand for the gold rush there, about 1860[135]. According to Charles's 1904 death certificate, he married Hannah Church, in Hokitika, N.Z. 33 years before he died (1871) (the next of kin, probably wife Hannah, provided the marriage data for the death certificate). On 13 Apr 1876, an Attorney-in-fact[136] was made at Hokitika, Westland, N.Z., by Charles P. Pierson and his wife A. Mary Pierson of Stafford in Westland, N.Z., to appoint Mary F. Fiero (Mary Frances, sister of Charles Pierson) and Joshua Fiero Jr. her husband of Greene Co., N.Y., USA, their true and lawful attorney for sale of the Pierson homestead on Catskill Turnpike Road at Cairo and for James M. Pierson's house and land on Susequehannah Turnpike in Cairo. On 26 Sep 1876, an indenture[137] was made between Mary F. Fiero & Joshua Fiero Jr. her husband of Catskill, Greene Co., N.Y., Charles P. Pierson & A. Mary Pierson his wife of Stafford, Westland, N.Z. (first part) and Wildy Rickerson of Cairo, Greene Co., N.Y. (second part) for the sale of the Pierson homestead and James' house and land in Cairo for $3,150 U.S. currency. Per Kumara marriage records, Charles Pierson married[138] 16 Aug 1895 Hannah Church (b. 16 Aug 1851, London, England, d. 31 Jul 1923, Hokitika,

Charles Anson Crocker Herrick Philetous Pierson (1838-1904)

---

[130]Record Group 15, Records of the Veteran's Administration, *General Affidavit*, January 26, 1906, National Archives, Washington, DC.

[131]Record Group 15, Records of the Veteran's Administration, *A Transcript from the Record of Deaths*, March 29, 1906, National Archives, Washington, DC.

[132]Record Group 15, Records of the Veteran's Administration, Application for Reimbursement of burial costs for Inez C. Pierson from James M. Pierson Jr., 10 May 1910, National Archives, Washington, DC.

[133]Record Group 15, Records of the Veteran's Administration, Department of the Interior, Bureau of Pensions Circular, January 15, 1898, National Archives, Washington, DC.

[134]His marriage record on 16 Aug 1895, age provided by himself, gives age 57, (makes his birth year 1838). The 15 May comes from family records.

[135]Death certificate states he was in New Zealand 44 years in 1904 (since 1860).

[136]Greene Co., N.Y., Deeds 84:294 FHL 480 034.

[137]Greene Co., N.Y., Deeds 84:436 FHL 480 035.

[138]Marriages in the District of Kumara, page 2556, No. 25, "16 Aug 1895 In the dwelling house of Charles Philetous Pierson, Main Street, Kumara (N.Z.), between Charles Philetous Pierson and Hannah Church, Charles age 57, manufacturer, bachelor, born New York, United States, North America, residence Kumara (N.Z.), parents William

New Zealand, dau. of John [a sailor] and Hellen [Lake] Church) at Kumara, Westland, New Zealand. Charles died[139] 16 Oct 1904 at Kumara, Westland, New Zealand. When Hannah Church died, her death certificate stated she died 31 July 1923 at age 72 and that she married at age 20 to Charles Pierson (calculates as born 1851 and married 1871). For more information on Charles and his family see *New York to New Zealand, a Pierson Family History*, by Jennifer Pierson, to be published.

Charles had chd.[140] 608 Olla Mary Frances, b. 5 Sep 1872, d. 30 Nov 1955, mar. 11 Jan 1899 James Hornsby Stapleton; 609+ Charles William Joshua, b. 1 Jul 1874; 610 George Augustus

Victor, b. 6 Aug 1876, d. 20 Dec 1963, mar. 15 Jun 1904 Jane (Jenny) Holley (sister to Sara); 611 James Malcolm Albert, b. 29 Dec 1878, d. 1 Oct 1917; 612 Arthur Ernest Robert, b. 31 Mar 1882, d. 1966, aged 83, Wanganui Hospital, New Zealand, mar. 9 Apr 1917 Elizabeth Annie Griffin (b. 8 Jul 1893 Apiti, Rangitikei, New Zealand, d. 15 Sep 1996 at age 103 at Palmerston North); 613 Thomas Henry Anson, b. 2 Mar 1884, d. 21 Nov 1918, mar. ca. 19 Sep 1913[141] Alice Emily Harris; 614 Phebie Elizabeth Elenor, b. 20 Feb 1886, d. 7 Apr 1967, mar. 8 Jan 1908 Herbert Spencer (Dinny) Kyle; 615 Rose Alice Azalia, b. 26 Feb 1888, d. 21 Aug 1961, mar. 27 Oct 1913 James Philip Nicholas. They were all born on the South Island of New Zealand in Westland, the first being at Hokitika, the next three at Staffordtown, and the last four at Kumara.

609 Charles William Joshua Pierson, known as Josh, was born 1 Jul 1874 at Staffordtown, Westland, New Zealand, and died 8 Oct 1958 at Hokitika, Westland,

Charles William Joshua Pierson Sr. (1874-1958)

Pierson, merchant, and Eleanor (Vanorden) Pierson, Hannah age 45, spinster, born London (England), residence Kumara (N.Z.), parents John Church, sailor, and Hellen (Lake) Church, officiating minister John Smith."

[139]Death certificate, certification No. 046398 dated 8 Jan 1986, registered at Greymouth, New Zealand: "Charles Anson Crocker Herrick Philetous Pierson, Cordial Manufacturer, male, age 63 years, died 16 October 1904 at Kumara (N.Z.), born Cairo (N.Y.) United States of America, 44 years in N.Z. (arrived 1860), father William Pierson, married at Hokitika (N.Z.) at age 30 to Hannah Church, living issue males ages 30, 28, 26, 23, 21, females ages 32, 18, 16, buried 18 Oct 1904 at Kumara, N.Z., cause of death Arterio Sclerosis."

[140]608 Olla Mary Frances Pierson bible records: "Charles Anson Crocker Herrick Phelitous Pierson, born May 15, 1841, America, Cairo; Hannah Church Pierson, born Aug. 16, 1851, London, England; In Loving Memory of Our Father & Brother, Charles Anson Crocker Herrick Phelitous Pierson died Oct. 16, 1905 at Kumara, aged 63; James Malcom Albert Pierson died Oct. 1, 1917 at Hokitika, aged 39; Thomas Henry Anson Pierson died Nov. 21, 1918, at Greymouth, aged 35; Alice Pierson, wife of Henry Pierson, died Dec. 6, 1918, at Greymouth, aged 24; Hannah Church Pierson died July 31, 1923, age 72; Olla Mary Frances Pierson born Sept. 5, 1872 at Hokitika; Charles William Joshua Pierson born July 1, 1874 at Stafford; George Augustus Victor Pierson born Aug. 6, 1876 at Stafford; James Malcom Albert Pierson born Dec. 29, 1878 at Stafford; Arthur Earnest Robert Pierson born March 31, 1882 at Kumara; Thomas Henry Anson Pierson born March 2, 1884 at Kumara; Phebie Elizabeth Elenor Pierson born Feb. 20, 1886 at Kumara; Rose Alice Azalia Pierson born Sep. 20, 1888 at Kumara."

[141]Intent to marry was 18 Sep 1913 and the marriage usually took place within the next week.

New Zealand. He married 18 Aug 1902 at Kumara, Westland, New Zealand, Sara Holley (b. 17 Dec 1874 England, d. 23 May 1951 Kumara, Westland, New Zealand), dau. of William and Mary (Lewis) Holley. Charles and Sara had chd.: 853+ Charles William Joshua Jr., b. 15 Aug 1903; 854 Herrick Roosevelt Philetous, b. 30 Oct 1906 at Kumara, d. 30 Apr 1981 at Kumara Beach, mar. Ellen (Nellie) Catherine Fahey at Kumara; and 855 Albert Ernest Frederic (Fred), b. 20 Feb 1911 Kumara, d. 16 Feb 1984 Napier, New Zealand, mar. 14 Sep 1937 at Hokitika, Phyllis Joan Maunder.

853 Charles William Joshua Pierson Jr. was born 15 Aug 1903 at Kumara, Westland, New Zealand, and died 21 Sep 1977 at Napier, Hawkes Bay, New Zealand. He married 8 Nov 1933 at Riverton, Southland, New Zealand, Dorothy Winifred McNaughton (b. 31 Jan 1909 Riverton, living at age 87), dau. of John and Elizabeth Jane (James) McNaughton. Charles was a professional and amateur runner (sprinter). His professional running career was from 1 Jan 1923 to 21 Apr 1930. He was then re-instated as an amateur runner on 6 Mar 1931 and his running career finished at the end of the 1933 season (about April). Charles served as a Captain with the Infantry of the Second New Zealand Expeditionary Force during World War II under the command of Major General Sir Bernard C. Freyberg. During the war, Charles was captured by the Germans on 30 Nov 1941 at Sidi Rezegh, Libya, and released from Stalag 7A, Moosberg, a German POW (prisoner of war) camp, on 29 Apr 1945, a period of 3 years and 5 months. Charles and Dorothy had one chd.: 856+ John Charles, b. 3 Nov 1936.

856 John Charles Pierson was born 3 Nov 1936 at Invercargill, Southland, New Zealand. He married 1st 18 Jun 1962 Rosemarie Joan Hitchens (b. 9 Dec 1934 Wellington, NZ, d. 19 Feb 1967 New Plymouth, NZ), mar. 2nd 6 Apr 1968 Janis Mary Page (b. 28 Nov 1946 Wellington, div. 23 Jun 1969), and mar. 3rd 7 Jun 1971 at Blenheim, Marlborough, New Zealand, Jennifer Penney (b. 22 Oct 1948 Picton, Marlborough, NZ), dau. of John James and Thelma Elizabeth (Collins) Penney. John had chd. by his 1st wife Rosemarie who were raised by his 3rd wife Jennifer: 857 Craig Stuart, b. 20 Oct 1962 Napier, New Zealand, mar. 1st 2 Apr 1989 Emma Lewis, mar. 2nd 7 Oct 1995 Kylie Woolley at Surfer's Paradise, Queensland, Australia; and 858 Marilyn Rose, b. 28 Dec 1964. Jennifer Penney brought with her a son from a previous marriage to Graeme Ross Gullery: 859 Shane Johnson Gullery who adopted the Pierson name, b. 19 Nov 1966, d. 18 Nov 1994. Jennifer (Penney) Pierson is a co-author of this book, *Pierson Millennium*.

303 James Pierson[142] of Riverhead, Long Island, N.Y., had w. Achsa and chd. 481 Edward; 482 Alice.

305 Philetous Pierson[143], Captain, was born in 1801 at Southampton, Suffolk Co., New York, and mar. Elizabeth (b. 1802, dau. of Edward Reeves). They had chd. 483+ James Henry, b. 1838; 484 Harriet E., b. 1840, w. of Capt. Jetur R. Rogers; 485 Mary L., b. 1842, d. 1877, w. of David H. Burnett (b. 1847) and had chd. David Pierson Burnett.

---

[142] George Rogers Howell, *The Early History of Southampton, L.I., New York with Genealogies*, 2nd Edition, Weed, Parsons and Company, Albany, NY, 1887, p. 349.
[143] George Rogers Howell, *The Early History of Southampton, L.I., New York with Genealogies*, 2nd Edition, Weed, Parsons and Company, Albany, NY, 1887, pp. 207 & 349.

483 James Henry Peirson was born in 1838. In 1910, at age 72, he was "living in Southampton, Suffolk Co., New York. James H. Peirson is a bachelor, and the last representative of our line bearing the name of Peirson living in Southampton. He is a man of sterling qualities, honored and trusted by his fellow citizens. He has represented his district in the State Legislature and is (1910) president of the Southampton Bank."[144]

151 William Pierson was born between 1760 and 1767, fought in the Revolutionary War, and died between 1790 and 1805. A letter, dated 19 Nov 1850, written by his nephew, William Pierson (b. 1789) of Cairo, Greene Co., New York, to the Commissioner of Pensions, read in part, "When a lad an uncle of mine - and of the same name of mine, died - and as I have been told left to me his pocket book containing about one hundred dollars in Continental money which he had received as I was informed for his Services in the Revolutionary War."[145]

151c Deborah Pierson was born at Southampton, Long Island, N.Y., between 1763 (earliest child spacing available) and 1776 (Southampton census with all daughters present), parents Timothy and Mary (Culver) Pierson[146]. Deborah married Ananias Halsey[147] (Joshua$_5$ 148,Nathaniel$_4$, Nathaniel$_3$, Thomas$_2$, Thomas$_1$). "Ananias Halsey[149] (and Deborah Pierson) had Halsey chd. Uriah bap. Sept. 10, 1787; Eli Pierson; and Mary, w. of Daniel Fordham. Eli Pierson Halsey m. Susan, dau. of Abraham Sayre, and had son Edwin P. Halsey." "Daniel Fordham[150] m. Mary, dau. of Ananias Halsey, and had Fordham chd. Mary; Nancy, wife of Silas Tuthill of Southold, N.Y.; Susan, w. of Huntting J. Post of Palmyra, N.Y.; Elizabeth, w. of George G. White; Eli Pierson, who m. Ann Eliza, dau. of Capt. William Post; Henry Augustus; and William Francis. "

148 Charles Pierson was born at Southampton, Suffolk Co., New York, between 1763 (earliest child spacing) and 1772 (21 years before his marriage). He moved to Renshaven, Albany Co., New York. Charles mar.[151] 1793 Elizabeth Howell. Charles and Elizabeth had chd.[152] 616 Sophia; 617+ James; 618 Harriet; 619 Mary; 620+ Charles; 621 Betsy; 622 Ann; and 623 William.

617 James Pierson married Mary Hineman. They had chd. 624 Henry; and 625 Jane.

[144]Silas S. Peirson, *The Peirson Family in Wayne County, New York, 1638-1916*, Arcadia Advertising Co., Newark, NY, 1917, p. 33.
[145]Record Group 15, Records of the Veterans Administration. War of 1812 Pension File; Pierson, William; Letter, William Pierson to J. L. Edwards, Nov. 19, 1850; National Archives, Washington, DC.
[146]Silas S. Peirson, *The Peirson Family in Wayne County, New York, 1638-1916*, Arcadia Advertising Co., Newark, NY, 1917, p. 33.
[147]Silas S. Peirson, *The Peirson Family in Wayne County, New York, 1638-1916*, Arcadia Advertising Co., Newark, NY, 1917, p. 33.
[148]George Rogers Howell, *The Early History of Southampton, L.I., New York with Genealogies*, 2nd Edition, Weed, Parsons and Company, Albany, NY, 1887, p. 272.
[149]George Rogers Howell, *The Early History of Southampton, L.I., New York with Genealogies*, 2nd Edition, Weed, Parsons and Company, Albany, NY, 1887, p. 272.
[150]George Rogers Howell, *The Early History of Southampton, L.I., New York with Genealogies*, 2nd Edition, Weed, Parsons and Company, Albany, NY, 1887, p. 245.
[151]George Rogers Howell, *The Early History of Southampton, L.I., New York with Genealogies*, 2nd Edition, Weed, Parsons and Company, Albany, NY, 1887, p. 349.
[152]George Rogers Howell, *The Early History of Southampton, L.I., New York with Genealogies*, 2nd Edition, Weed, Parsons and Company, Albany, NY, 1887, p. 349.

620 Charles Pierson married and had chd. 626 Mary; and 627 Charles.

149 Eli Pierson[153] was born at Southampton, Suffolk Co., New York, between 1763 (earliest child spacing) and 1777 (22 years before his son Eli's birth). He moved to Johnstown, Fulton Co., New York, before 1799. He mar. Mary Veghte, and had chd.: 628 James; 629 Mary, married William Richardson; 630 Polly, married Conrad Becker; 631+ Eli; 632 Nellie, mar. Philip Argersinger; 633+ Timothy; 634 Eliza, mar. Lewis Dorn; 635 William, d. young."

631 Eli Pierson[154] was born in Johnstown, Fulton Co., New York, Feb. 20, 1799, and died there Feb. 21, 1880. He had grand jury duty[155] in Montgomery Co., N.Y., in 1829 and 1834 where he was listed as of Johnstown, tanner. He was a farmer and a tanner, continuing actively in the tannery until 1870 when he retired. He mar. Amanda Mason (b. Oct. 20, 1802 Dorset, Vermont, d. June 8, 1883 Johnstown, New York) in the spring of 1822. She was the daughter of Isaac and Elizabeth (Cornell) Mason, and granddaughter of Samson Mason, the revolutionary soldier of Adams, Massachusetts. Eli and Amanda had chd., all born at Johnstown, New York: 636+ Mary Ann, b. Feb. 17, 1823, d. March 29, 1873; 637 Abram Veghte, b. Jan. 28, 1826, d. Aug. 27, 1831; 638 Alice Pamela, b. Mar. 22, 1828, d. Dec. 11, 1885; 639 Margaret Caroline, b. Oct. 16, 1830, d. Dec. 26, 1861; 640 William Henry, b. Jan. 9, 1833, d. Dec. 30, 1899; 641+ Abraham Veghte, b. June 19, 1835, d. Jan. 26, 1892; 642 Emily Amanda, b. Nov. 12, 1838, mar. Daniel Yost of Fonda; 643 John Mason, b. June 2, 1840, d. July 31, 1885; 644 Charles, b. Dec. 10, 1842, d. Nov. 14, 1908; 645 Marcus Fayette, b. May 6, 1845, d. May 4, 1896.

636 Mary Ann Pierson was born Feb. 17, 1823, at Johnstown, N. Y., and died March 29, 1873. She mar. James I. McMartin of Johnstown and had dau. Caroline McMartin[156] b. at Johnstown, New York. Caroline McMartin mar. Richard Evans, whom she survives (1911), and resides at Johnstown, N.Y.

641 Abraham Veghte[157] Pierson was born Aug. 10, 1835 (June 19 was given above by Cuyler Reynolds, perhaps one is a christening date), and died in Johnstown, N.Y., Jan. 26, 1892. He was educated in the public schools, and after completing his studies worked with his father in the tannery until 1870, when his father 631 Eli Pierson retired from the business. In 1871, Abraham joined with his brothers 644 Charles and 643 John M. Pierson in the business of glove-making and carried this on for some time before the business was dissolved. He then associated with James Dunn, who had been engaged in glove manufacturing in Johnstown since 1860. The firm of Dunn & Pierson continued as a successful business until 1888, when Abraham withdrew and retired. Abraham mar. Oct. 26, 1858, Jane Dunn (b. Dec. 30, 1837, dau. of John and Elizabeth (Cuyler) Dunn).

---

[153]Cuyler Reynolds, *Hudson-Mohawk genealogical and Family Memoirs*, Lewis Publishing Co., New York, NY, 1911, pp. 776 & 951.

[154]Cuyler Reynolds, *Hudson-Mohawk genealogical and Family Memoirs*, Lewis Publishing Co., New York, NY, 1911, pp. 776 & 951.

[155]Arthur C. M. Kelly, *Grand Jurors of Montgomery Co., N.Y., 1816-1850*, 1989, pp. 11 & 27.

[156]Cuyler Reynolds, *Hudson-Mohawk genealogical and Family Memoirs*, Lewis Publishing Co., New York, NY, 1911, p. 951.

[157]Cuyler Reynolds, *Hudson-Mohawk genealogical and Family Memoirs*, Lewis Publishing Co., New York, NY, 1911, pp. 776-7.

Abraham and Jane had chd.: 646 Elizabeth, mar. David Ireland; 647+ James D., b. Mar. 16, 1864; 648 Amanda, b. July 31, 1868, mar. Oct. 1893 John R. Russell, and had Russell chd Elizabeth b. May 29, 1895, & Catherine b. Dec. 2, 1898; 649 Charles b. July 21, 1871; and 650 Eli, b. Oct. 28, 1872, partner of firm of Pierson Brothers, glove makers of Johnstown, mar. Sep. 5, 1898, Nora E. Dement (b. Sep. 5, 1871), and had son 651 James A., b. Nov. 7, 1901.

647 James D. Pierson[158] was born March 16, 1864 at Johnstown, New York. He was educated at public school and at Johnstown Academy. On reaching a suitable age he was taken in with his father and taught the business of glove making. He was associated with James Dunn after the retirement of his father 641 Abraham Pierson in 1888. In 1889, James Dunn died, and he continued in the glove business with his brother, 650 Eli Pierson, as a partner, forming Pierson Brothers. They manufactured a medium grade of ladies' and childrens' gloves and mittens. James D. Pierson was a director of the Johnstown Bank in 1911.

633 Timothy[159] Pierson married Eleanor V. Dake and had chd.: 652 John McArthur, d. young; 653 Philetus, d. in infancy; 654 Jennie; 655 Julia B., mar. Stephen Wemple; 656 Kate M.; 657 Benjamin, d. in infancy; 658 Amanda W., mar. ____ Sutliff; 659 Hattie B.; and 660+ Winfield Scott.

660 Winfield Scott[160] Pierson was born in Fulton Co., New York. He was a farmer in Fulton county, New York. Winfield mar. Maggie Cornell and they had chd.: 661 Eleanor, deceased (1911 statement); 662 John Fremont, deceased (1911 statement); 663 Earl Winfield; 664 Paul Revere; 665 Mildred Wicks, deceased (1911 statement); 666 Theodore Roosevelt.

69 Samuel Pierson[161] was born Dec. 28, 1754, at Southampton, Suffolk Co., New York Colony. He was a miller at Southampton on Long Island. Samuel mar. Prudence Ball (b. June 7, 1755, d. Mar. 6, 1793, the day her 6th child was born). Prudence Ball is said to have been of the same family as Martha Washington. In May, 1775, Samuel signed the Association of men against the British tyranny[162] at County Hall, Suffolk County (Associations 30.166, 175) at the same time as his brother Timothy signed. Samuel was listed as a refugee to Connecticut during the occupation of Long Island by the British (1776-1783) during the Revolutionary War. According to Frederic Mather's *The Refugees ...*, a "Samuel Peirson" of Long Island may have served in the 6th Dutchess of New York or with the Connecticut militia. Samuel has no known children born between 1771 (son Silvanus) and 1783 (son John), confirmed by his will, indicating that he was busy at a war effort of some kind where he was separated from his wife. From records of The Daughters of the

[158]Cuyler Reynolds, *Hudson-Mohawk genealogical and Family Memoirs*, Lewis Publishing Co., New York, NY, 1911, pp. 776-7.

[159]Cuyler Reynolds, *Hudson-Mohawk genealogical and Family Memoirs*, Lewis Publishing Co., New York, NY, 1911, p. 776.

[160]Cuyler Reynolds, *Hudson-Mohawk genealogical and Family Memoirs*, Lewis Publishing Co., New York, NY, 1911, p. 776.

[161]Silas S. Peirson, *The Peirson Family in Wayne County, New York, 1638-1916*, Arcadia Advertising Co., Newark, NY, 1917, pp. 35-38.

[162]Frederic Mather, *The Refugees of 1776 from Long Island to Connecticut*, Genealogy Publishing Company, Baltimore, Maryland, 1972, p. 1056.

American Revolution[163]: "Samuel Pierson (son of Samuel & brother of Timothy), PS (Patriotic Service, non-military), b. 28 Dec 1754 NY, d. after 9 Aug 1808 NY, m. 1st Prudence Ball, m. 2nd Jerusa Woodhall." The non-military patriotic service for Samuel is identified as the signing of the Association in 1775. Samuel returned to Southampton after the war where he was one of the signers, along with his brother Timothy, of the agreement with Rev. Joshua Williams on Dec. 30, 1784[164] who became the new minister at Southampton. In 1802, Southampton town records show registration of ear marks and a cattle brand[165] for "Samuel Peirson, of town, hollow crop on right, half penny over it and under left, brand S. P. which was his fathers." This is the last town record at Southampton, Suffolk Co., New York, for Samuel Peirson. It indicates his father was "S. P." (Samuel Peirson) and that he went to Sodus, Ontario Co. (became Wayne Co. in 1823), New York, between this year (1802) and the year of his will at Sodus (1808). According to Silas S. Peirson, Samuel moved to Wayne County (then Ontario Co.), New York, about 1807. In Ontario Co., he married his 2d wife, Jerusha Woodhull. Samuel was buried (after his 9 Aug 1808 will) in the East Palmyra Cemetery, Ontario Co. (became Wayne Co. in 1823), New York. Samuel was nearly 7 feet tall. No stone marks his last resting place.

Samuel Pierson's Will, dated 9 Aug 1808, was never proved, but was found in the family papers after his estate had been settled[166]: "In the name of God, Amen, I, Samuel Peirson of the town of Sodus and County of Ontario (became Wayne Co. in 1823), weak in body but of sound and perfect mind and memory, Blessed be God for the same, do make and publish this my last Will and Testament ... I give ... to my eldest son Silvanus Peirson the one half of my real estate ... and the other half of my real estate to my son Silas Peirson. I give to my well beloved wife Jerusha Peirson one bed and bed clothes with two pair of sheets and one coverlet and one set of curtains. And I also give my wife Jerusha Peirson the privilege of living with my two sons while she remains my widow and likewise her wearing apparel to dispose of as she thinks proper and one of the large iron pots and one third of the pewter and one looking glass and one chest. I also give to my eldest son Silvanus Peirson one bed and beddings and one chest. I bequeath unto my daughters Abigail and Ruth Peirson the remainder of my household furniture excepting one chest which I give to my daughter Abigail Peirson to be divided equally between them and my will and meaning is that my two sons maintain my daughters till otherwise provided for. I also give to my son Silas Peirson my gun. My wearing apparel to be divided equally between my two sons Silvanus Peirson and Silas Peirson. I appoint my wife Jerusha Peirson and my son Silas Peirson executrix and executor of this my last Will and Testament ... In witness whereof I the said Samuel Peirson have hereunto set my hand and seal the ninth day of August in the thirty second year of Independence of the United States of America by the Grace of God free and Independent. In the year of our Lord one thousand eight hundred eight. Samuel Peirson (signature). Witnesses: Gilbert Howell, James Burnett."

---

[163]*DAR Patriot Index*, Centennial Edition Washington 1990, National Society of the Daughters of the American Revolution Centennial Administration, Washington, DC (District of Columbia, U.S.A.), copyright 1994, p. 2258.

[164]George Rogers Howell, *The Early History of Southampton, L.I., New York with Genealogies*, 2nd Edition, Weed, Parsons and Company, Albany, NY, 1887, pp. 111-13.

[165]*Town Records of Southampton*, NY, Liber B (Vol. 3), p. 490, Abstract.

[166]Silas S. Peirson, *The Peirson Family in Wayne County, New York, 1638-1916*, Arcadia Advertising Co., Newark, NY, 1917, pp. 36-38.

Samuel had chd., all by his 1st wife Prudence Ball, all at Southampton, N. Y.: 667+ Silvanus, b. Oct. 16, 1771, d. May 4, 1849; 668 John, b. Nov. 6, 1783, probably d. young in Southampton; 669+ Silas, b. May 12, 1786, d. Jan. 28, 1857; 670 Abigail, b. Oct. 19, 1788, deaf & dumb, a resident of Wayne Co., N. Y., not married in 1916; 671 Ruth, b. Jan. 20, 1791, mar. Mr. Butts; and 672 Prudence, b. March 6, 1793, probably d. young in Southampton.

667 Silvanus Peirson[167], was born Oct. 16, 1771 at Southampton, Suffolk Co., New York, deaf and dumb, and died May 4, 1849. Silvanus moved from Southampton, N. Y., to Wayne county (then Ontario Co., N.Y.) about 1810 and settled one mile north of Hydesville by the road running north from the 69 Samuel Peirson farm. Silvanus married Diadama Howe, also a mute. After Silvanus died in 1849, a pot of gold and silver was found under the kitchen floor. Silvanus and Diadama had chd.: 673 John b. 8 Dec 1814, d. 13 Jul 1899, mar. 8 Jun 1837 Sallie Lewis (b. 11 Jan 1819, d. 3 Feb 1899); 674 Joseph b. 16 Mar 1817, moved to Michigan, mar. and had one son; and 675 Elijah b. 28 Feb 1820, d. 9 Sep 1850, never married.

669 Silas Peirson[168] was born May 12, 1786, at Southampton, New York, and died Jan. 28, 1857. Silas learned the carpenter trade in Southampton and at age 21 in 1807 moved to Ontario County, New York, which embraced Wayne Co. (formed in 1823). Silas was part of the Wayne Co. Militia being an Ensign in 1814, a Lieutenant in 1815, and later a Captain in the Cavalry[169]. He was known as a carpenter, farmer, and townsman in Arcadia, Wayne Co., New York, where he held many town offices between 1820 and 1840. The Will of Silas Peirson was dated 11 Apr 1853. It bequeaths to sons Samuel and Henry one dollar each, to two married daughters Hannah and Phoebe two hundred dollars each, to two daughters Mary and Louisa five hundred dollars each, to his wife Mary her legal dower and life lease of dwelling, and to his two sons William C. and George H. his real estate subject to wife's dower. Capt. Silas Peirson died 28 Jan 1857 where he was a member of the Presbyterian church of East Palmyra, Wayne Co., New York.

Silas mar. Hannah DeLong of Southampton and they had dau. 676 Polly b. 16 Feb 1809 (d. 27 Mar 1825 unmarried at age 17). Hannah apparently died shortly after Polly's birth. Silas Peirson mar. 2nd 12 May 1811 Mary Culver (b. 27 Dec 1791, d. 14 Feb 1858), daughter of George and Ruth Culver. Silas and Mary (Culver) Peirson had children, all born on the old homestead just north of Hydesville, New York: 677+ Samuel b. 14 Jun 1812, d. 11 Feb 1898; 678+ Hannah Ann b. 6 Jun 1814, d. 13 Feb 1892; 679+ Henry Rayner b. 22 Jan 1816, d. 29 May 1900; 680+ Phoebe b. 15 Mar 1819, d. 2 Aug 1896; 681+ William Clark b. 6 Apr 1821, d. 26 Jul 1889; 682 Ruth b. 19 Jan 1824, d. 12 Jun 1825; 683+ Mary b. 12 Jun 1826, d. 16 May 1862; 684+ Louisa b. 8 Jun 1830, d. 13 Sep 1892; 685+ George Harrison b. 22 Apr 1833; and 686 Celia b. 6 Apr 1837, d. 10 Apr 1839.

---

[167]Silas S. Peirson, *The Peirson Family in Wayne County, New York, 1638-1916*, Arcadia Advertising Co., Newark, NY, 1917, p. 39.

[168]Silas S. Peirson, *The Peirson Family in Wayne County, New York, 1638-1916*, Arcadia Advertising Co., Newark, NY, 1917, p. 40.

[169]Clark's *Military History of Wayne County*, p. 149.

677 Samuel Peirson[170] was born 14 Jun 1812, and died 11 Feb 1898. He mar. Sept. 30, 1834, Eliza Nicholoy (b. Apr. 8, 1815, d. Apr. 3, 1889). Samuel was a farmer. They had chd.: 687 Ruth, b. July 5, 1835, mar. Feb. 11, 1858, Elezer Mighles Hyde of Hydesville, N.Y. (div. 12 yrs. later); 688+ Henry J., b. May 25, 1838; 689 Andrew Jackson, b. June 9, 1841; 690 Martha, b. April 7, 1845, d. Feb. 5, 1891; 691 Albert S., b. Jan. 22, 1849; 692 Byron, b. May 5, 1851, d. Mar. 9, 1908; and 693 Edwin, b. Mar. 22, 1855, d. in infancy.

688 Henry J. Peirson[171], b. May 25, 1838, mar. May 23, 1865, Syrena S. Prescott (b. Jan. 25, 1844), had chd. 694 Herbert Prescott b. March 3, 1866.

678 Hannah Ann Peirson[172] was born June 6, 1814, and died Feb. 13, 1892. She mar. Jan. 1, 1833 Gilbert Jessup (b. Mar. 5, 1809, d. Aug. 16, 1882). Hannah and Gilbert had Jessup chd.: Silas Lewis, b. Apr. 8, 1834, d. May 31, 1836; William Franklin, b. Aug. 30, 1839, d. Jan. 1, 1912; and George Robert, b. Oct. 30, 1849.

679 Henry Rayner Peirson[173] was born 22 Jan 1816, and died 29 May 1900. He mar. 22 Apr 1840 Calista Reeves (b. 13 May 1820, d. 27 Oct 1896), dau. of Samuel B. and Sally (Harding) Reeves. Henry was buried at East Palmyra, N.Y. They had chd. 695+ Silas Spencer, b. 18 Jun 1841; 696 Mary Calista Adelaide, b. 25 Oct 1843, mar. Rev. M. V. Willson (d. 20 May 1903), no children; 698 Sarah Louisa, b. 11 Oct 1846, mar. 13 Jun 1869 Seward F. Price (b. 17 Feb 1845), and had Price chd. George Henry, Harrison B., and Seward Peirson; 699 Samuel Adelbert, b. 6 Oct 1849, d. 30 Sep 1878, mar. 26 Nov 1872 Lizzie Olive Crosby (b. 18 Jan 1850) & had chd. 697 Adella O. (b. 26 Aug 1873, d. 10 Nov 1878); & 700 Henry Adelman (twins), b. 6 Oct 1849, d. 6 Oct 1866, unmarried; 701 Herbert, b. 12 Aug 1851, d. 13 Sep 1851;and 702 Orpha May, b. 15 Jul 1858, d. 3 Nov 1858.

695 Silas Spencer Peirson[174] was born June 18, 1841, on his father's farm just north of Hydesville, New York. He was the author of the 1917 book, *The Peirson Family in Wayne County, New York*. In 1866, he formed a partnership with E. P. Soverhill and opened a bank under the name of S. S. Peirson & Co., Bankers in Newark, New York. The bank later became the Newark State Bank. The Newark State Bank bought the controlling interest in the First National Bank and they merged under the name of the First National Bank. Silas mar. May 30, 1864 Sarah Armeda Van Wagenen, dau. of Simon and Eliza (Burnett) Van Wagenen. They had chd.: 716 Silas Rayner, b. Nov. 26, 1865, mar. July, 1890 Cora Colton (d. Sep. 21, 1903); 717 Ernest Van, b. Oct. 9, 1867, mar. July 12, 1892 Mary Stuart; 718 Louis Arnold, b. Sep. 12, 1869, ordained Presbyterian minister 1894, mar. 1898 Mary Louise (Mollie) Brooks (b. Sep. 19, 1872, dau. of Micah Wooster Brooks); 719 Mary Armeda, b. May 22, 1872; 720 Winifred, b. Nov. 29, 1883, mar. June 18, 1912 Merle L. Sheffer.

---

[170]Silas S. Peirson, *The Peirson Family in Wayne County, New York, 1638-1916*, Arcadia Advertising Co., Newark, NY, 1917, p. 40.

[171]Silas S. Peirson, *The Peirson Family in Wayne County, New York, 1638-1916*, Arcadia Advertising Co., Newark, NY, 1917, p. 40.

[172]Silas S. Peirson, *The Peirson Family in Wayne County, New York, 1638-1916*, Arcadia Advertising Co., Newark, NY, 1917, p. 40.

[173]Silas S. Peirson, *The Peirson Family in Wayne County, New York, 1638-1916*, Arcadia Advertising Co., Newark, NY, 1917, pp. 40-109.

[174]Silas S. Peirson, *The Peirson Family in Wayne County, New York, 1638-1916*, Arcadia Advertising Co., Newark, NY, 1917, p. 40.

680 Phoebe Peirson[175] was born 15 Mar 1819, and died 2 Aug 1896. She married Jan. 16, 1840, Benjamin A. Bailey and they had Bailey chd.: Mary Evangelia, b. Mar. 16, 1842, d. Mar. 23, 1869; Harriet; William Benjamin; and Calista Antoinette.

681 William Clark Peirson[176] was born Apr. 6, 1821, and died July 26, 1889. He mar. Caroline Clark (b. Oct. 12, 1837, d. Sep. 24, 1880). He was a farmer and lived on the old homestead just north of Hydesville, New York. They had chd.: 703 William Tracy, b. Oct. 6, 1868, mar. Feb. 5, 1890 Anna Smith (b. Aug. 3, 1867) and they had chd. 706 William T. (d. Jun. 10, 1898); 704 George Conway, b. July 30, 1870, mar. Apr. 24, 1889 Mary Farmer (b. Dec. 3, 1868), they had chd. 707 Lucille (b. Feb. 14, 1891); and 705 Mary A., b. Aug. 2, 1866, teacher of the blind and still single in 1916.

683 Mary Peirson[177] was born June 12, 1826, and died May 16, 1862. She mar. Edwin Rogers (b. Dec. 13, 1820, d. Jan. 17, 1906) as his second wife. They had Rogers chd. Mary, b. Dec. 11, 1859 who mar. Nov. 25, 1885 Fred M. Allerton.

684 Louisa Peirson[178] was born 8 Jun 1830, and died 13 Sep 1892. She mar. Feb. 2, 1858, Artemus W. Hyde (b. Sep. 9, 1816, d. Jan. 5, 1892) as his 2d wife. They had Hyde chd.: Artemus Douglas, b. Mar. 28, 1861, d. Feb. 19, 1890, mar. Sep. 29, 1888, Rosa Hoeltzel of Newark; William Henry, b. July 26, 1863, mar. Bertha Jackson, living Denver, Colorado, in 1916 ; and Meda L., d. May 4, 1900, mar. Peter R. Sleight, had Sleight chd. Margory and George.

685 George Harrison Peirson[179] was born 22 Apr 1833. He mar. Dec. 14, 1858, Mary Wakeman (b. Mar. 31, 1838). They had chd.: 708 Eva M., b. Aug. 15, 1860, mar. Feb. 21, 1884 Frank Howell (b. Jan. 21, 1857); 709 Martha, b. Jul. 1, 1864, d. Oct. 23, 1872; 710 Flora, b. Jul. 1, 1867, mar. Sep. 20, 1893 W. D. Quinby; 711 Frances Irene, b. Jun. 9, 1869, mar. Oct. 22, 1895 Leonard Wheat; 712 Myrta Louise, b. Jun. 16, 1875, mar. Nov. 4, 1903 Ernest J. Reed (b. Jan. 18, 1876); 713 George, b. Nov. 16, 1884, mar. Jul. 27, 1910 Selma Van Cise (b. Mar. 7, 1892); 714 Charles William, b. Jun. 15, 1889, not married 1915; and 715 Antoinette Louise, b. Mar. 31, 1891, mar. Nov. 4, 1916 Raymond G. Heim of Lancaster, New York.

12 Mary Pierson was born 12 Jun 1680 [180] at Southampton, Suffolk Co., New York Colony, and died there 23 Feb 1706/7[181]. She mar. 5 Dec 1700 Jeremiah Culver[182] at Southampton.

---

[175]Silas S. Peirson, *The Peirson Family in Wayne County, New York, 1638-1916*, Arcadia Advertising Co., Newark, NY, 1917, p. 40.

[176]Silas S. Peirson, *The Peirson Family in Wayne County, New York, 1638-1916*, Arcadia Advertising Co., Newark, NY, 1917, p. 40.

[177]Silas S. Peirson, *The Peirson Family in Wayne County, New York, 1638-1916*, Arcadia Advertising Co., Newark, NY, 1917, p. 77.

[178]Silas S. Peirson, *The Peirson Family in Wayne County, New York, 1638-1916*, Arcadia Advertising Co., Newark, NY, 1917, p. 79.

[179]Silas S. Peirson, *The Peirson Family in Wayne County, New York, 1638-1916*, Arcadia Advertising Co., Newark, NY, 1917, p. 81.

[180]*Town Records of Southampton*, NY, Liber A, No. 2, 2nd Part, p. 75.

[181]*Town Records of Southampton*, NY, Liber A, No. 2, 2nd Part, p. 301.

[182]*Town Records of Southampton*, NY, Liber A, No. 2, 2nd Part, p. 132.

Jeremiah was the son of Gersham and Mary Culver of Southampton[183]. They had Culver chd.: Jeremiah, b. 22 Apr 1702; Mary, b. 5 Feb 1703/4; and Jesse, b. 20 Feb 1706/7. Jeremiah Culver mar. 2d 9 Dec 1714 Damaris, dau. of Joseph Foster[184].

13 Joseph Pierson Jr. was born 6 Aug 1684[185] at Southampton, Suffolk Co., New York Colony, and was prominent among the early settlers of that region. He had cattle 1700-1705 per cattle earmark registration to Joseph Pierson Jr. [186] The Southampton records do not indicate whom Joseph married between 1705 (age 21) and 1707 (the year before the first child's birth). In the Southampton records from 1721 to 1807, only one record of this family occurs, June 21, 1739[187]: "Whereas Jonathan Raynor, Josiah Halsey and John Howell were ordered by ye owners of ye lots of meadow on ye beach lying from ye westward part of the hill bank to Dow Little to lay out ye said meadows according to every mans right as it now stands recorded upon ye town book: 41 lots with Lot 2 The heirs of Joseph Pierson." This record applies to Joseph Pierson Jr. since his father died after 1706 and before 1720 when Jr. is no longer applied to official records. Therefore, Joseph Pierson Jr. died before 21 Jun 1739. He had chd. [188], all at Southampton: 31+ Joseph, b. 3 Feb 1707/8; 32 Sarah, b. 13 Feb 1709/10; 33 Phebe, b. 2 Jul 1711; 34 Benjamen, b. 5 Feb 1714/15; 35 Daniel, b. 30 Jun 1716; 36 Hannah, b. 6 Mar 1719/20.

31 Joseph Pierson was born[189] 3 Feb 1707/8 at Southampton, Suffolk Co., N.Y. In 1739, he inherited[190] part of his father's estate at Southampton, Suffolk Co., N.Y. He bought land in 1741 located 2 miles west of Morristown, N.J., and settled there. He mar. ca. 1741, 20 Patience Pierson, of Orange, N.J., dau. of 8 Joseph Pierson (see numbers 8 and 20 in Chapter 13). In 1746, "Joseph Pirson" registered[191] cattle ear marks at Morris Twp., Morris Co., N.J. In Oct. 1768, "Joseph Pierson" was listed[192] as a Ratable in Morris Twp., Morris Co., N.J., and described therein as "land 10£, 200 acres, 13 horses & cattle, and 23 sheep." Joseph and Patience Pierson had chd. 866+ Joseph, b. 1735; 867 Jonathan; 868+ David; 869+ Bethuel.

866 Joseph Pierson was born in 1735[193] near Morristown, N.J., and died in 1815[194] in N.J. In 1768, "Joseph Peirson Junr" registered[195] cattle ear marks at Morris Twp., Morris Co.,

[183]George Rogers Howell, *The Early History of Southampton, L.I., New York with Genealogies*, 2nd Edition, Weed, Parsons and Company, Albany, NY, 1887, pp. 35-6. Howell gives his source as Manuscripts in office of Secretary of State, Albany, NY.

[184]George Rogers Howell, *The Early History of Southampton, L.I., New York with Genealogies*, 2nd Edition, Weed, Parsons and Company, Albany, NY, 1887, p. 228.

[185]*Town Records of Southampton*, NY, Liber A, No. 2, 2nd Part, p. 75.

[186]*Town Records of Southampton*, NY, Liber A, No. 2, 1st Part, p. 225.

[187]*Town Records of Southampton*, NY, Liber B (Vol. 3), pp. 39-40.

[188]*Town Records of Southampton*, NY, Liber A, No. 2, 2nd Part, p. 306.

[189]*Town Records of Southampton*, NY, Liber A, No. 2, 2nd Part, p. 306.

[190]*Town Records of Southampton*, NY, Liber B (Vol. 3), pp. 39-40.

[191]Harriet Stryker-Rodda, *Some Early Records of Morris County, New Jersey 1740-1799*, published under the patronage of Morris County Archives Publications Committee, Polyanathos, Inc., New Orleans, La., 1975, p. 2

[192]Harriet Stryker-Rodda, *Some Early Records of Morris County, New Jersey 1740-1799*, published under the patronage of Morris County Archives Publications Committee, Polyanathos, Inc., New Orleans, La., 1975, p. 73

[193]*DAR Patriot Index*, Centennial Edition, National Society of the Daughters of the American Revolution, 1994, part 3, p. 2258.

N.J. He served[196] in the Revolutionary War as a Private in Capt. Austin Bayley's Company, Morristown, N.J., and in the State Troops (S-720) as Sergeant[197]. Joseph lived in Morris Township and had pension S3693. Joseph had chd. 870 Joseph and 871 Timothy.

868 David Pierson had chd. 872+ Lewis Sr., b. 1800; 873+ Elias; 874+ David; 875 Silas; 876+ John; and 877 Phebe.

872 Lewis Pierson Sr. was born in 1800, and lived in Morristown, N.J. He had chd. 880 Wm. A.; 881 John; 882 Edward E.; and 883 L. Harvey.

873 Elias Pierson had chd. 884 Jesse; and 885 Amzi (of Morristown, N.J.).

874 David Pierson had chd. 886 David A. (of Ohio).

876 John Pierson had chd. 887 David Augustus (of Indiana).

869 Bethuel Pierson mar. Rachel Day, and lived in Morristown, N.J. Bethuel and Rachel had chd. 878 Sarah and 879 Isaac, and perhaps others.

14 Ephraim Pierson, born Jan. 20, 1686/87[198] at Southampton, Suffolk Co., New York Colony. He had chd. 37+ Ephraim, b. before 1733; and perhaps others.

37 Ephraim Pearson was born before 1733, and died before 1787. He mar. in 1754, at Windsor, Ct., Hannah Barrett, a lady of French or Huguenot descent, "possessing more than ordinary good looks and gracefulness." They spelt their name Pearson. They had children 70 Hannah (w. of 1st R. Hendee and 2d ____ June, who died in Leroy, N. Y.); 71 Annie, b. 1757, died on the day appointed for her marriage; 72+ Ephraim Jr., b. June 18, 1758; 73+ Jesse, b. 1761; 74+ Benjamin, b. 1763, d. 1843; 75+ John, b. 1765, d. 1812; 76+ Joseph, b. 1767, d. 1843; 77+ David, b. 1769, d. 1844; 77a "Aulif" (Olive), b. ca. 1770, mar.[199] 23 Jul 1787 Joseph Rathbun, both of Duanesburg, N.Y., he son of Jonathan, and she dau. of Ephraim (deceased).

72 Ephraim Pierson Jr. was born[200] June 18, 1758, in Connecticut, and died[201] in 1804 at Savannah, Georgia. During the Revolutionary War, Ephraim was a Private in the Connecticut militia.[202] He married Phoebe Cleveland[203] in Vermont, and they had 4

[194]*DAR Patriot Index*, Centennial Edition, National Society of the Daughters of the American Revolution, 1994, part 3, p. 2258.
[195]Harriet Stryker-Rodda, *Some Early Records of Morris County, New Jersey 1740-1799*, published under the patronage of Morris County Archives Publications Committee, Polyanathos, Inc., New Orleans, La., 1975, p. 7
[196]Barbara Hoskins, *Men from Morris County New Jersey Who Served in the American Revolution*, The Friends of the Joint Free Public Library of Morristown and Morris Township, Morristown, N.J., 1979, p. 145.
[197]*DAR Patriot Index*, Centennial Edition, National Society of the Daughters of the American Revolution, 1994, part 3, p. 2258.
[198]*Town Records of Southampton*, NY, Liber A, No. 2, 2nd Part, p. 123.
[199]C. M. Kelly, *Marriage Records of Two Early Schoharie, NY, Churches*, 1978, Schoharie Reformed Church, p. 14.
[200]*DAR Patriot Index*, Centennial Edition, National Society of the Daughters of the American Revolution, 1994, part 3, p. 2257.
[201]*DAR Patriot Index*, Centennial Edition, National Society of the Daughters of the American Revolution, 1994, part 3, p. 2257.
[202]*DAR Patriot Index*, Centennial Edition, National Society of the Daughters of the American Revolution, 1994, part 3, p. 2257.
[203]*DAR Patriot Index*, Centennial Edition, National Society of the Daughters of the American Revolution, 1994, part 3, p. 2257.

children. He, in company with some others, took a drove of farm stock, said to be hogs, to Boston, chartered a ship to Havana, and while off the coast of the southern states they were captured and robbed by Spanish pirates. He remained south, ten years, acquired property, came back within 10 miles of his old home, and hearing that his wife had married again, returned and lived the remainder of his life at Charleston, S.C., or Savannah, Ga. Years later, his son went south and found his grave. The names of Ephraim's four children are not known by the authors.

73 Jesse Pierson was born May 6, 1761, in Conn., and died Jan. 10, 1837, in New York. During the Revolutionary War, he was a Private in the Connecticut militia, and later received a pension.[204] He mar. 1784 Lydia[205] Stevens (d. 1849), of Wells, Vt. He moved with his wife and children to Avon, N.Y., in 1805, and there bought a farm of his brother, which he lived on till his death. He was a member of the Avon Baptist church. He had chd. 152+ David, b. 1785, d. 1853; 153 Lydia, b. 1786 (w. of C. Alexander), and d. 1861; 154 Charlotte, b. 1788 (w. of Ethan Allen); 155 Clarissa, b. 1792 (w. of N. Merrill); 156 Hannah, b. 1794 (w. of J. Richardson), d. 1831; 157 Orra, b. 1796 (w. of R. Perry); 158 Amanda, b. 1798 (w. of E. Judd), lived in Mich. 1878; 159 Ephraim, b. 1800 (killed by a horse, aged 13 yrs.); 160+ Hiram, b. 1805, lived in N.Y. in 1878.

152 David Pierson, born Mar. 27, 1785, in Vt.; mar. Huldah Churchill, 1811, and died June 17, 1853, at Avon, N. Y. He had chd. 307 Ruhamah, b. 1811 (w. of S. D. Halsey, in Mich.); 308 Margaret, b. 1813, d. 1865; 309 Adelia, b. 1815 (w. of J. Smith, of Mich.); 310 Ann J., b. 1816 (w. of J. Bainbridge, of Mich.); 311 Charles C., b. 1818 (mar. M. Dutton); 312 Jane L., b. 1819 (w. of D. Lacy); 313 Mary E., b. 1821 (w. 1st of Dr. Drake and 2d J. Johnson); 314 Laura, b. 1823 (w. of B. E. Rust, of Mich.); 315 Ephraim, b. 1825 (mar. S. Merrill); 316 Andromeda, b. 1827 (now [1878] living in Leroy, N. Y.); 317 Delos D., b. 1829 (mar. P. Duglass).

160 Hiram Pearson, born Sept. 21, 1805, at Avon, N.Y., where he still [1878] resides; mar. A. L. Hendee in 1827, and had chd. 318 Annetta, b. 1828 (w. of B. E. Stevens, now [1878] of Leroy, N. Y.); 319 Hannah Amarillis, b. 1831.

74 Benjamin Pearson, born May 29, 1763, in Enfield, Conn.; mar. 1st Anna Abbott, in Vt. (who had one child, and both died); mar. 2d Eliz. Smith, in 1792, at Geneva, N.Y., and died Nov, 1834. He was the pioneer of his family of five brothers to Genesee Co., N.Y., preceding them a few years; and in traveling became acquainted with his (2d) wife when stopping at her father's house, in Geneva, N.Y. He lived and died at East Avon, N.Y.; was a prominent member of the Baptist church there: and had chd. 161 Clarissa, b. 1793 (w. of T. Ward), d. 1848, in Avon; 162 Anna, b. 1795, d. young; 163 John, b. 1797, d. young; 164 Eliz., b. 1799 (w. of Dr. G. Graves); 165 Benjamin, b. 1801 (mar. A. Arthur); 166+ Wm. S., b. 1806, in Hartford, N.Y. (now [1878] Avon, N.Y.) (mar. 1st F. M. Arthur, in 1829, and 2d F. Ladd, in 1834); 167 Temperance, b. 1803 (w. of A. Gilbert), d. 1827; 168+ James Leonard, b. 1808

---

[204] *DAR Patriot Index*, Centennial Edition, National Society of the Daughters of the American Revolution, 1994, part 3, p. 2257.

[205] *DAR Patriot Index*, Centennial Edition, National Society of the Daughters of the American Revolution, 1994, part 3, p. 2257.

(mar. Eliz. King), d. 1860; 169 Barrett, b. 1812, d. 1829 (is bur. beside his parents, in the field near the old homestead, now [1878] owned by Mr. Bristol).

166 William S. Pearson, born April 21, 1806, in Avon, N.Y.; mar. 1st, F. M. Arthur and 2d F. Ladd, in 1834, now [1878] resides in Flint, Mich.; a farmer, and of the Presbyterian church. He had chd. 320 Mary, b. 1831, at Avon; 321 Maria S., b. 1835; 322 Herman L., b. 1837 (mar. A. Jenks, of Mendon, N.Y.); 323 Caroline, b. 1839 (w. of R. J. Garvin, of Leroy, N.Y.); 324 Wm. S., b. 1841, in Mich.; 325 Barrett, b. 1843, in Mich.; 326 James L., b. 1846, in Michigan.

168 James Leonard Pearson, born Oct. 17, 1808, mar. Eliz. T. King, 1832, died at Leroy, N.Y., 1860. Elizabeth was the dau. of Rev. B. King of Rockaway, N.J. James and Elizabeth had chd. 327 James B., b. 1834 (mar. M. B. Stanley, and had chd. 721 Gertrude and 722 Stanley King), and was drowned at Albany, N. Y., Dec. 29, 1869; 328 Susan E., b. 1836 (w. of Dr. H. B. Doolittle, of Albion, N.Y.); 329 Benjamin B., b. 1846, d. young; besides a babe.

75 John Pearson, born May 7, 1765, in Ellington, Tolland Co., Conn.; mar. Rebecca W. Hull, 1789, in Schenectady, N.Y., and died Dec. 23, 1812 in Avon, N.Y. His wife was dau. of Capt. Sam. Waterous, and born in Killingworth, Conn., 1765, and the widow of Henry Hull; she outlived John Pearson, and then mar. Col. Sam Blakeslee, and died in Penn. in 1861, at the age of 96 years. John first lived in Duanesburg, N.Y., then moved to Hartford, N.Y. (now Avon, N.Y.) where in the 'howling wilderness,' he established his home. He built the first frame building, two stories high, which was named 'John's industry and Rebecca's economy.' He also built a store and established an extensive trade. He was a man of positive and decided character, and met with success in all that he undertook. He had chd. 170 Amanda, b. 1789, in Duanesburg (w. of W. T. Hosmer, now [1878] in Meadville, Penn.); 171+ Chandler b. 1791 (mar. J. Clarke), d. 1853; 172 Olivia, b. 1792 (w. 1st of J. Brown and 2d G. Reynale, of Dansville, N. Y.); 173+ Horatio, b. 1794 (mar. S. Turner, 1815), d. 1856; 174 Orrel, b. 1796 (w. of G. Clark, now of Clarkson, N. Y.); 175 Mary Ann, b. 1798 (w. of A. Hosmer, 1818), d. at Hartland, N.Y., 1857; 176+ John, b. 1802; 177 Vashti Maria, b. 1803 (w. of Chas. B. Storrs, of Longmeadow, Mass., and mother of Henry M. Storrs of Brooklyn, N. Y.), d. 1839; 178 Henry, b. 1806 (mar. Grace Plumb, of N. Y.), d. in Texas.

171 Chandler Pearson, b. 1791 Duanesburg, N.Y., mar. Jemima Clark, d. Jan. 1, 1853, had chd. 330 Sophia M., b. 1814 (w. of T. B. Hosmer); 331 Erastus, b. 1815, d. 1840; 332 Hamden, b. 1817, d. 1851; 333 Albert H., b. 1819; 334 Mary Jane, b. 1821 (w. of Judge A. Brown, Ogdensburg, N.Y., 1843), d. in 1865; 335 Henry C., b. 1823; 336 Catherine M., b. 1827 (w. of Dr. Sherman, of Ogdensburg, N.Y.); 337 Van Renslaelaer, b. 1829 (mar. 1st E. Vedder and 2d S. J. Vedder), now [1878] lives at Niagara, N.Y.; 338 Sarah, b. 1831 (w. of A. G. Coffin), now [1878] lives in Brooklyn, N.Y.; 339 Harriet E., b. 1835, d. 1866; 340 Edward E., b. 1839.

173 Horatio Pearson, born Aug. 7, 1794, mar. S. Turner, 1815 (who died in 1850) and died Oct. 8, 1856. He was born at Duanesburg, N.Y., and had chd. 341 Ashley, b. 1816 (mar. H. M. Carrington, 1864, and lives [1878] near Sacramento, Cal.); 342 Matilda, b. 1818, d. 1820; 343 Winfield S., b. 1820, d. 1864 (mar. E. Richardson, in 1858, and had 3 chd.); 344 Mary Ann, b. 1822 (w. of C. S. Lowell, in 1852), now [1878] in California; 345 Evelina, b. 1824 (w. of Dr. J. C. Spencer), d. 1856; 346 Thomas C., b. 1826 (mar. S. Isenbise, 1848); 347 Sarah, b. 1829; 348 John T., b. 1830, d. 1856.

176 John Pearson, born Jan. 23, 1802, Avon, N.Y., mar. 1st C. Tiffany, of Canada, and 2d C. F. Passage, of N. J.; now [1878] resides in Danville, Ill.; a lawyer there; a graduate of Princeton college in 1824, licensed to practice law in 1832; went to Chicago, Ill., then to Danville, Ill.; was elected judge of his district for 4 years, and state senator for 2 years; and had chd. 349 Gustavus C., b. 1827, at Ravenna, Ohio (mar. H. P. Brown, 1864), now [1878] of San Francisco; 350 George T., b. 1829, d. 1861 at Springfield, Ill.; 351 Eliz. M., b. 1831 (w. of W. C. McReynolds, 1853, and had 8 chd.); 352 Adelaide C., b. 1845, d. young; Amanda H., b. 1846, d. 1864; 354 Fanny B., b. 1848; 355 Jennie B., b. 1852, d. young; 356 Harriet M., b. 1854.

76 Joseph Pearson, born Apr. 15, 1767, mar. 1st Sarah Waterous, 1789, and 2d C. W. Jenks, 1810, and 3d P. Wheelock, in 1836; and died in 1843. He came to Avon, N.Y., in 1797, with a wife and 4 children. He took up first the farm afterwards owned by his brother Jesse, and then the one in East Avon, N.Y., upon which he lived and died, at which place he was a prominent member of the Congregational church, and he kept a public house, many years, where he was widely known and highly respected. He had chd. 179 Catherine, b. 1791 at Duanesburg, N.Y (w. of 1st M. Hanna, & 2d D. Kneeland, & 3d E. Bachelder), now [1878] resides upon her father's farm, at Avon, N.Y.; 180 Clarenda, b. 1793 (w. of W. Martin); 181 Mary, b. 1794 (w. of W. Jenks), now [1878] lives in Mendon, N.Y.; 182 Nancy, b. 1797 (w. of T. Hanna), d. 1817; 183 Maria, b. 1799 (w. of A. A. Bennett), now [1878] of Rochester, N.Y.; 184 Welthy, b. 1801 (w. of G. G. Cook), now [1878] of Grand Blanc, Mich.; 185+ George, b. 1804; 186+ Frederick Bushnell, b. 1806; 187+ Bradley M., b. 1809 (mar. C. M. Whitbeck).

185 George Pearson, born 1804 at Avon, N.Y., mar. 1st D. Barrows, and 2d ____ in 1845, died 1857, and had chd. 357 Harriet P., b. 1831; 358 Geo. B., b. 1835 (mar. M. J. Wade); 359 Maria J., b. 1843, d. young.

186 Frederick Bushnell Pearson, born at Avon, N.Y., Nov. 22, 1806, mar. F. J. Gibson, now [1878] an extensive farmer in East Avon, N.Y.; and had chd. 360 Sarah, b. 1829 (w. of Rev. E. B. Walsworth formerly the President of Female college, Oakland, California); 361 Joseph K., b. 1831, d. young; 362 Frances J., b. 1835 (w. of J. H. Brummajim), now [1878] of Mariposa, California; 363 Sabrina E., b. 1847, d. young.

187 Bradley M. Pierson, born at Avon, N.Y., Mar. 15, 1809, mar. C. M. Whitbeck, and had chd. 364 Sarah J. (w. of E. Cash), d. 1868 at Paw Paw, Mich.; 365 Joseph P., mar. M. Pelton, d. 1869 at Decatur, Mich.

77 David Pearson was born 6 Oct 1769 in Litchfield Co., Conn., and died in 1844 at Canada West (Ontario, Canada). He mar. 1st 1793 H. Irish, and 2d Mrs. Dewey. He first moved to Cherry Valley, N.Y., and after two years to Avon, N.Y., where he resided for 26 years, and then emigrated to Canada West (Ontario, Canada). That country was then new and unsettled, and he kept a public house near the present city of Brantford (Ontario, Canada). He had chd. 188 Ira, b. 1793, d. 1850; 189 Benjamin, b. 1796; 190 Olive, b. 1798, d. young; 191 Susannah, b. 1800, d. 1823 (mar. ____ Darling); 192 Sarah, b. 1802; 193+ Jesse, b. 1804, d. 1865; 194+ David, b. 1806; 195 Ann, b. 1808 (w. of N. Fowler), now [1878] lives in Canada West (Ontario, Canada); 196+ John K., b. 1810; 197 Laura, b. 1813; 198 Ephraim, b. 1815; 199 Joseph, b. 1817 (mar. L. Gear); 200 Eliz., b. 1819; 201 Hannah, b. 1822.

193 Jesse Pearson was born Sept. 2, 1804, at Avon, N.Y., and died 1865. He mar. H. Slusser who, as a widow, resided in Michigan in 1878. He had chd. 366 Susannah, b. 1831, mar. J. Brason; 367 Egbert, b. 1833, d. 1864 at City Point, Va., mar. M. Cain, served two years in the Civil War; 368 Mary L., b. 1836, mar. R. E. James; 369 Emeretta, b. 1852 in Mich., mar. F. M. James; 370 Sarah A., d. young.

194 David Pearson was born in 1806 in Avon, N.Y., mar. A. Anderson, and had chd., all born in Illinois: 371 John Henry; 372 Hannah C., mar. C. Bradfield; 373 James F.

196 John K. Pearson was born Sept. 26, 1810, at Avon, N.Y. He mar. Roby ____; and had chd. 374 Joseph W., b. 1835; 375 Lydia, b. 1836; 376 Seth W., b. 1839; 377 Lysander, b. 1841; 378 John A., b. 1844; 379 Lucy; 380 Sarah E.; 381 Jesse K. The members of this family have varied the spelling of their name, using both Pierson and Pearson.

Chapter 10
Descendants of Col. Henry Peirson
Son of Henry

Col. Henry Peirson is the son of Henry and Mary Peirson of Southampton, Suffolk Co., New York Colony. The following descendants of Col. Henry Peirson (1652-1701) are copied from Lizzie B. Pierson, *Pierson Genealogical Records*, Joel Munsell, Printer, Albany, N.Y., 1878, pp. 29-33, as a framework to present new data upon. Lizzie Pierson's footnotes, errata, and related appendices are incorporated within the text which is modified by footnoted additional research by the authors of *Pierson Millennium*. An every-name index is provided at the back of *Pierson Millennium* whereas only heads of families were indexed in *Pierson Genealogical Records*. The + symbol after an identifying number indicates more information is provided in a later paragraph of this chapter beginning with the same number.

1 Henry Pierson had chd. 2 John; 3 Daniel; 4 Joseph; **5+ Henry, b. 1652, d. 1701**; 6 Benjamin, d. 1731; 7 Theodore; 8 Sarah, b. Jan. 20, 1660/61. See chapter 8 for more children and information on 1 Henry Peirson's family.

5 Henry Pierson, Col., was born 1652 at Southampton, Long Island. In 1678[1], he witnessed the will of Joseph Raynor at Southampton as "Henry Peirson Jun." In 1679[2], "Henry Pierson Jr" purchased a tract of land by land exchange at Sagaponack (Bridgehampton area) from George Harris. In 1680, his father Henry died (see chapter 8 for details), and the term "Junior" was henceforth dropped from Col. Henry Pierson's name. He mar. ca. 1681 Susannah (b. July 15, 1658, d. 1716 Sagaponack) , dau. of Major John and Susannah Howell[3], and became one of the settlers of Bridgehampton (at Sagaponack alias Sagg), at which place he died Nov. 4, 1701[4]. In the 1683[5] "Estemate of the Towne of Southampton" (includes Bridgehampton) the Piersons present were "Benjamin Peirson £51, Joseph Pierson £127, and Henry Peirson £136." In 1684-1685[6], "Henry Pierson" had cattle as noted by earmarks recorded at Southampton.

For generations[7] before the English settlers came, the Indians had cut up stranded whales blown ashore in the winter storms, and had gone out in dugout canoes, driving the whales ashore by shooting numbers of arrows into them. Companies were also licensed to ship out

---

[1]Berthold Fernow, *Calendar of Wills*, on file and recorded in the offices of the Clerk of the Court of Appeals, of the County Clerk at Albany and by the Secretary of State (New York) 1626-1836, compiled 1896, p. 326, No. 1431.

[2]*Town Records of Southampton*, NY, Liber A, No. 2, 1st Part, p. 134.

[3]George Rogers Howell, *The Early History of Southampton, L.I., New York with Genealogies*, Second Edition, Weed, Parsons and Company, Albany, NY, 1887, p. 302.

[4]George Rogers Howell, *The Early History of Southampton, L.I., New York with Genealogies*, Second Edition, Weed, Parsons and Company, Albany, NY, 1887, p. 349.

[5]George Rogers Howell, *The Early History of Southampton, L.I., New York with Genealogies*, Second Edition, Weed, Parsons and Company, Albany, NY, 1887, pp. 44-5, and his reference is given as Doc. Hist. of N.Y., Vol. 2, page 536.

[6]*Town Records of Southampton*, NY, Liber A, No. 2, 2nd Part, p. 108.

[7]Co-Chairmen Mrs. Albert W. Topping, Everett C. Foster, and Editor Paul H. Curts, *Bridgehampton's Three Hundred Years*, Hampton Press, Bridgehampton, NY, 1956, p. 66.

off the south shore as "adventurers on ye whayle designe," the first in 1650. By 1685, there were seven whaling companies in the greater Southampton area, among them "Henry Pierson and Co. of Sagaponack." In 1687, there were 14 whaling companies of 12 men each in the Southampton area who reported whale oil in their possession, probably the result of one season's whales, including "Att ye Pines, Joseph Pierson & Co (Henry's eldest brother), 240 bbls; Att Sagabonick, Lift Henery Peirson & Co, 276 bbls." This is the first appearance of military rank, and he is a Lieutenant here, pronounced Leif-ten-ant by the British colonial militia.

Being successful in the whaling business, in 1686[8] "Henry Pierson and Thomas Stephens" paid £50 cash to the town of Southampton for a grant of "60 acres of land a piece in the commons somewhere to the eastward of the mill in some convenient place not prejudicial to the highway and watering."

In 1686, Henry Pierson was one of a six-man committee to advise on Southampton Indian land purchases with Governor Thomas Dongan at Fort James which resulted in the Dongan Patent[9], dated Dec. 6, 1686, in which 12 Southampton men are mentioned including "Henry Pearson." Henry held Southampton town offices in 1687[10] Trustee; and 1688[11] "Leift. Henry Pierson", Trustee. Henry had land grants at Southampton in 1691[12] to his father's estate (split between him and his brothers[13] Joseph, Theodore, and Benjamin); and to him in 1691[14] at Assup neck meadow. Henry was a member of the New York Colonial Assembly from Suffolk Co., 1691 to 1695 and from 1698 to 1701. From 1693 to 1695 inclusive, Col. Henry Pierson was Speaker of the House.[15] As early as 1696, he had the title of "Colonel." The 1696[16] "Estimate of Town of Southampton" provided "Theodore Pierson (Henry's youngest brother), £38; Joseph Pierson (Henry's eldest brother), £75; and Col. Henry Pierson, £130."

On Nov. 3, 1696[17], Major John Howell died, father of Col. Henry Pierson's wife Susannah. With regard to Susannah, the will stated: "I do give and bequeath unto my eldest daughter, Susannah Pierson, one hundred pounds of country pay to her & her heirs, she or they allowing what she hath already received out of it." On March 17, 1696/7[18], Col. Pierson gave a receipt for the balance of Susannah's inheritance in the presence of Abraham and

[8] *Town Records of Southampton*, NY, Liber A, No. 2, 2nd Part, p. 117.
[9] George Rogers Howell, *The Early History of Southampton, L.I., New York with Genealogies*, Second Edition, Weed, Parsons and Company, Albany, NY, 1887, p. 460-4.
[10] *Town Records of Southampton*, NY, Liber A, No. 2, 2nd Part, p. 125.
[11] *Town Records of Southampton*, NY, Liber A, No. 2, 2nd Part, p. 130.
[12] *Town Records of Southampton*, NY, Liber A, No. 2, 1st Part, p. 194.
[13] Henry Hedges, Wm. Pelletreau, Edward Foster, *The Second Book of Records of the Town of Southampton, Long Island, N.Y. with other Ancient Documents of Historic Value*, John H. Hunt, Printer, Sag Harbor, NY, 1877, p. 126-127.
[14] *Town Records of Southampton*, NY, Liber A, No. 2, 2nd Part, p. 149-150. Abstract.
[15] George Rogers Howell, *The Early History of Southampton, L.I., New York with Genealogies*, Second Edition, Weed, Parsons and Company, Albany, NY, 1887, p. 349.
[16] Henry Hedges, Wm. Pelletreau, Edward Foster, *The Second Book of Records of the Town of Southampton, Long Island, N.Y. with other Ancient Documents of Historic Value*, John H. Hunt, Printer, Sag Harbor, NY, 1877, p. 361-4.
[17] William S. Pelletreau, *Early Long Island Wills of Suffolk County, 1691-1703, With Genealogical and Historical Notes*, Francis P. Harper, New York, NY, 1897, pp. 129-137.
[18] William S. Pelletreau, *Early Long Island Wills of Suffolk County, 1691-1703, With Genealogical and Historical Notes*, Francis P. Harper, New York, NY, 1897, pp. 129-137.

Prudence Howell, 3rd son and 2nd daughter, respectively, of Major John Howell, deceased: "Paid to Col. Pierson in severals as may appear upon ye book ye sum of £75, 14 shillings as part of his wife's portion of the John Howell estate."

At Southampton on April 6, 1697[19], Henry Pierson, with James Hildreth and Theophilus Howell, set up a mill on Sagg Stream and received a 12-year permit to use the stream providing that they did "Grinding for the Inhabitants of this Towne when they can with conveniency takeing a moderatt Toale or tenth partt."

In 1698, a census was taken in the greater Southampton area of 118 families, listing every first name. Henry's family was listed under "Mecox, Sagg[20], and Bridgehampton." "Lift. Coll. Henry Peirson, Mrs. Susanah Peirson (wife), John Peirson (age 13), David Peirson (age 10), Theophilus Peirson (age 8), Abraham Peirson (age 5), Josiah Peirson (age 3), Hanah Peirson (about age 16), Sarah Peirson (about age 1), Abigale Toping (relation unknown)" (Information in parenthesis by author Richard Pierson).

With regard to Henry's military career, the Society of Colonial Wars[21] lists: "Pierson, Lieut.-Col. Henry, 1652-1701. Lieut.-Col., Suffolk Co. Militia, 1698, Province of N.Y., and under Earle Bellomont, 1700. Speaker 4th Colonial Assembly." Henry held the rank of Lieut. Colonel in the Suffolk County Militia and was entitled to be referred to in short as "Colonel."

On April 17, 1701[22], Col. Matthew Howell was, along with Col. Henry Pierson, a representative for Suffolk County in the Colonial Legislature. That day, Col. Howell was expelled from that body by the Governor, for presenting a paper considered "disloyal to his Majesty, and disaffected to his government," a paper, however, which we now recognize as the early warnings of the Revolutionary War against British tyranny and unrepresented taxation. Four others were rebuked for signing Col. Howell's paper, including Col. Henry Pierson, and Kiliaen Van Rensselaer of Albany, New York. This occurred seven months before Henry's death at age 49.

On August 28, 1701[23], Colonel Henry Peirson wrote his will, "in perfect strength of memory, though weak in body & not knowing ye day of my appointed change," confirming his eight children: "my eldest son, John Peirson; my son, David Peirson; my son, Theophilus Peirson; my two younger sons, Abraham Peirson & Josiah Peirson; my three daughters Hannah Peirson, Sarah Peirson & Mary Peirson, and wife Susannah Peirson." See chapter 17 for an unabridged copy of the will. Henry was buried in the village burying ground at Sagg, near Bridgehampton, Suffolk Co., New York. It is believed that the

---

[19] *Town Records of Southampton*, NY, Liber A, No. 2, 1st Part, p. 216.

[20] So long as the population of the town was almost entirely confined to the village of Southampton, all goods and stores from abroad were landed at North Sea, as the most convenient port, but when the population of Sagaponack and Mecox became numerous, it was necessary to find a nearer port for these areas to save time and labor in transporting goods. This was the beginning of Sag Harbor, which was called Sagaponack harbor for many years, and in bills of lading as late as 1760, it was called the Harbor at Sagg. Thus Sagaponack, Sagg, and Sag are the same place.

[21] The Society of Colonial Wars, *An Index to Ancestors*, New York, NY, 1922, p. 374.

[22] George Rogers Howell, *The Early History of Southampton, L.I., New York with Genealogies*, Second Edition, Weed, Parsons and Company, Albany, NY, 1887, p. 303.

[23] William S. Pelletreau, *Early Long Island Wills of Suffolk County, 1691-1703, With Genealogical and Historical Notes*, Francis P. Harper, New York, NY, 1897, pp. 239-41.

original grave marker stated "died Nov. 4, 1701 in the 50th year of his age." However, Colonel Peirson's tombstone has been restored by Mrs. Russell Sage (granddaughter of 103 Margaret Pierson who mar. John Jermain), his descendant of the fifth generation, according to Pelletreau's 1897 book[24] and the gravestone is now engraved, "Coll. Henry Peirson deceased November the 15 in the 50 year of his age. 1701." The date on the restored tombstone is 11 days after the court record of his death during the proving of his will. This indicates that the date has been <u>inappropriately</u> changed on the tombstone from the Julian calendar in use in English colonies of that era to the date that would appear on the Gregorian calendar in use beginning 1752. Officially, Henry's will was proved on September 2, 1702[25]: "By ye tenor of these presents know ye that on ye 2d day of Sept. 1702 at ye Manor of St. Georges in ye County of Suffolk before Colonel William Smith, Judge of ye Prerogative Court in ye sd County, was proved & approved ye last Will & Testamt of Henry Peirson, late of S'hampton in ye sd. county, **deceased on ye 4 day of Nov. Anno Dom. 1701,** who by his sd last will did nominate & appoint Susannah, his wife, his Sole Executrix to whom was granted the administration of all & singular ye goods & chattels of ye sd dec'd & C."

In 1712[26], it was confirmed that Mrs. Susannah Pierson retained her right of fifty from her husband in commonage of Southampton, and she was granted one and a half fifties of land[27] by the Town of Southampton in 1712 at the Westward Division Speeunk Neck and Tanners Neck and Apocuck Neck. Susannah died, probably in 1716 at Sagg, and her Inventory[28] was taken 4 April 1716 at Southampton, Suffolk Co., N.Y. colony by Isaac Halsey, Lt. Nathan Howell, and Christopher Foster and exhibited on 13 June 1716 by Theophilus Peirson and Josiah Peirson, executors (sons of Susannah). The amount of the estate was £400/19/8 (pounds/shillings/pence). Among the items listed were 2 Negroes and an Indian boy (£75), books and other things (£16/6/-), and cash, plates and other things (£30/3/6).

Henry and Susannah had chd. 16a+ Hannah[29], b. ca. 1682; 16 John b. Nov. 30, 1685, d. Jan. 15, 1704/05[30]; 17+ David, b. 1688; 18+ Theophilus, b. 1690, d. 1742; 19+ Abraham, b. 1693; 20+ Josiah, b. 1695, d. 1776; 20a+ Sarah[31], b. ca. 1697; and 20b+ Mary[32], b. ca. 1700.

---

[24] William S. Pelletreau, *Early Long Island Wills of Suffolk County, 1691-1703, With Genealogical and Historical Notes*, Francis P. Harper, New York, NY, 1897, p. 282.

[25] William S. Pelletreau, *Early Long Island Wills of Suffolk County, 1691-1703, With Genealogical and Historical Notes*, Francis P. Harper, New York, NY, 1897, pp. 239-41.

[26] *Town Records of Southampton*, NY, Liber A, No. 2, 1st Part, p. 240-241.

[27] *Town Records of Southampton*, NY, Liber A, No. 2, 1st Part, p. 246.

[28] Kenneth Scott and James A. Owre, *Genealogical Data From Inventories of New York Estates 1666-1825*, New York Genealogical and Biographical Society, New York, N.Y., 1970, p. 114.

[29] George Rogers Howell, *The Early History of Southampton, L.I., New York with Genealogies*, Second Edition, Weed, Parsons and Company, Albany, NY, 1887, p. 349.

[30] George Rogers Howell, *The Early History of Southampton, L.I., New York with Genealogies*, Second Edition, Weed, Parsons and Company, Albany, NY, 1887, p. 349.

[31] George Rogers Howell, *The Early History of Southampton, L.I., New York with Genealogies*, Second Edition, Weed, Parsons and Company, Albany, NY, 1887, p. 349.

[32] George Rogers Howell, *The Early History of Southampton, L.I., New York with Genealogies*, Second Edition, Weed, Parsons and Company, Albany, NY, 1887, p. 349.

16a Hannah Peirson was born at Bridgehampton, Suffolk Co., N.Y. colony, about 1682 (based on being the eldest dau. in the 1698 Southampton township census, child spacing, and order of children in census and father's will). Her father died the year he wrote his will 28 Aug 1701[33], leaving her: "I give unto my three daughters Hannah Peirson, Sarah Peirson & Mary Peirson, each of them, one hundred pounds current money of this Province, or what may be equivalent thereto, when they shall come to ye age of twenty years, or at ye day of their marriage, as it shall be demanded." She was not yet age 20 nor was she married on that date in 1701.

17 David Pierson, was born at Bridgehampton, Long Island, in 1688 and spent his life in that vicinity, and died 1767[34]. In 1701, when David was age 13, his father died, leaving to him via will dated Aug. 28, 1701[35], and proved 1702: "I give unto my son, David Peirson, to him, his heirs & assigns forever, all that piece of land lying in Bridgehampton on ye West side of ye street bounded with ye land of Robt Norris, Stephen Hedges & Josiah Hand on ye South; with Sag pond on ye West; with ye land of ye sd Norris on ye North, & with ye street on ye East thereof & also all my meadows at Noyack & also one half quarter of a share at Meantake & one horse, two steers of 3 year old & two cows & ten sheep & twenty five pound in money or what shall be equivalent when he shall come to ye age of twenty one years." David held many one-year public offices in Southampton: 1712 Assessor[36]; 1713 Trustee[37]; 1720 Trustee[38]; 1727 Assessor[39]; 1729 Trustee[40]; 1731 Trustee[41]; 1732 Assessor[42]; 1734 Supervisor[43]; 1735 Supervisor & Trustee[44]; 1736 Supervisor[45]; and 1737 Supervisor[46]. David received land grants from the Town of Southampton at: 1727[47] Cedar Swamps; 1738[48] Lower Div. Quaquanantuck; 1738[49] North Div. Quaquanantuck; 1738[50] South & North Div. Timber Land between the Indian line and East Hampton; 1739[51] Canoe Place Div Quaquanantuck; 1745[52] at Sagg Harbor; 1763[53] Awcaubogue Division in Quogue

[33]William S. Pelletreau, *Early Long Island Wills of Suffolk County, 1691-1703, With Genealogical and Historical Notes*, Francis P. Harper, New York, NY, 1897, pp. 239-41.

[34]George Rogers Howell, *The Early History of Southampton, L.I., New York with Genealogies*, Second Edition, Weed, Parsons and Company, Albany, NY, 1887, p. 349.

[35]William S. Pelletreau, *Early Long Island Wills of Suffolk County, 1691-1703, With Genealogical and Historical Notes*, Francis P. Harper, New York, NY, 1897, pp. 239-41.

[36]*Town Records of Southampton*, NY, Liber A, No. 2, 1st Part, p. 239.

[37]*Town Records of Southampton*, NY, Liber A, No. 2, 1st Part, p. 267.

[38]*Town Records of Southampton*, NY, Liber B (Vol. 3), p. 133 Abstract.

[39]*Town Records of Southampton*, NY, Liber B (Vol. 3), p. 135.

[40]*Town Records of Southampton*, NY, Liber B (Vol. 3), p. 136.

[41]*Town Records of Southampton*, NY, Liber B (Vol. 3), p. 136.

[42]*Town Records of Southampton*, NY, Liber B (Vol. 3), p. 137.

[43]*Town Records of Southampton*, NY, Liber B (Vol. 3), p. 137.

[44]*Town Records of Southampton*, NY, Liber B (Vol. 3), pp. 137-8.

[45]*Town Records of Southampton*, NY, Liber B (Vol. 3), p. 138.

[46]*Town Records of Southampton*, NY, Liber B (Vol. 3), p. 138.

[47]*Town Records of Southampton*, NY, Liber A, No. 2, 1st Part, pp. 296-299.

[48]*Town Records of Southampton*, NY, Liber B (Vol. 3), p. 166-73.

[49]*Town Records of Southampton*, NY, Liber B (Vol. 3), p. 184-88.

[50]*Town Records of Southampton*, NY, Liber B (Vol. 3), p. 157.

[51]*Town Records of Southampton*, NY, Liber B (Vol. 3), p. 189-94.

[52]*Town Records of Southampton*, NY, Liber B (Vol. 3), p. 143-6.

(Quaquanantuck); in 1763[54] Aucaubogue Division in Toppings Purchase; and in 1763[55] Little South Division at Southampton. David died in 1767 at age 79. David mar. 1st Esther Conkling and 2d Elizabeth Conkling in 1712/13[56]. He had chd.: 38+ Lemuel of Sagg, b. 1717; 39+ David; 40 John.

38 Lemuel Pierson of Sagg[57] was born on Long Island in 1717. He mar. Apr. 9, 1741, Martha Stratton[58] of East Hampton, Suffolk Co., N.Y. In the Sagg Burying Ground[59], a tombstone reads "In memory of Mrs Martha the wife of Mr Lemuel Peirson who died Augst the 26th 1753 in the 72th year of her age. My sun is set, My Glass is run, My Candle's out, My work is done." This stone cannot be in very good shape as died in 1755 near the birth of her last child Isaac in the 34th year of her age is more likely (I note the "th" after the age year of 72 doesn't fit). During the Revolutionary War, Long Island was occupied by the British from 1776 to 1783. During the occupation one story told was: the soldiers came to the house of Lemuel Peirson and turned him out. Against their orders, Lemuel was determined to carry off some of his furniture and, although the soldiers stood over him with drawn sword, he persisted and got his way. This is probably 38 Lemuel. To avoid taking the oath of allegiance to the British, many left Long Island during the British occupation. Lemuel Peirson's effects were moved[60] from Sagaponack to Stonington, Connecticut, in Sep 1776 by Capt. David Sayre, and on 16 Sep 1776, with ten of his family, Lemuel was moved from Sagaponack to East Haddam, Connecticut, by Capt. Joshua Griffeth. Lemuel had cattle in 1757 ("Lemuel Piersons")[61] and in 1784 ("Lemuel Peirson the first")[62], based on ear marks registered at Southampton. Lemuel was among the Bridgehampton residents that signed the agreement with Rev. Woolworth on 2 July 1787. Lemuel and Martha had chd.: 78a Phebe[63]; 78+ Lemuel, b. 1744, d. 1821; 78b Jemima[64]; 79+ David, b. 1751, d. 1829; 80+ Isaac, b. 1755; 81 Henry; 82 Zipporah (these chd. may not be listed here in order of birth, Isaac is believed to be the last child born).

[53] *Town Records of Southampton*, NY, Liber B (Vol. 3), p. 298-300.
[54] *Town Records of Southampton*, NY, Liber B (Vol. 3), p. 302-06.
[55] *Town Records of Southampton*, NY, Liber B (Vol. 3), p. 320-24.
[56] George Rogers Howell, *The Early History of Southampton, L.I., New York with Genealogies*, Second Edition, Weed, Parsons and Company, Albany, NY, 1887, p. 349.
[57] Sagaponack, located one mile east of Bridgehampton.
[58] George Rogers Howell, *The Early History of Southampton, L.I., New York with Genealogies*, Second Edition, Weed, Parsons and Company, Albany, NY, 1887, pp. 349-50.
[59] George Rogers Howell, *The Early History of Southampton, L.I., New York with Genealogies*, Second Edition, Weed, Parsons and Company, Albany, NY, 1887, p. 190.
[60] Frederic Mather, *The Refugees of 1776 from Long Island to Connecticut*, Genealogical Publishing Company, Baltimore, MD, 1972, pp. 504-8.
[61] *Town Records of Southampton*, NY, Liber B (Vol. 3), p. 220, Abstract.
[62] *Town Records of Southampton*, NY, Liber B (Vol. 3), p. 423, Abstract.
[63] George Rogers Howell, *The Early History of Southampton, L.I., New York with Genealogies*, Second Edition, Weed, Parsons and Company, Albany, NY, 1887, pp. 349-50.
[64] George Rogers Howell, *The Early History of Southampton, L.I., New York with Genealogies*, Second Edition, Weed, Parsons and Company, Albany, NY, 1887, pp. 349-50.

78 Sgt. Lemuel Pierson Jr. was born 1744 in Southampton (see military record below), Suffolk Co., N.Y., and died Nov. 8, 1821[65]. He mar. 1st Sarah[66] ____, who d. July 3, 1771, at age 25, and 2d Mary[67] ____.

Sgt. Lemuel Pierson Jr. served in Col. Mulford's and Col. Smith's Regiments during the Revolutionary War. He was listed as "Sergeant Major Lemuel Pierson," a staff officer in Col. David Mulford's 2nd Regiment of Suffolk Co. on Feb. 10, 1776. He was in Capt. Ezekiel Mulford's 12th Company, which reported[68] on 26 July 1776: Lemuel Pierson, Sergt., residence Southampton, age 32 (makes his birth 1744), born Southampton, 5 ft. 8 in. tall, dark complexion, dark brown hair, occupation weaver.

During the Revolutionary War, the British occupied Long Island from 1776 to 1783. In one story of the occupation, the British soldiers came to Lemuel Peirson's house on Long Island to secure any plunder that might offer itself. Mrs. Peirson was alone in the house with young children, but bravely met them at the door with a kettle of hot water and threatened to scald the first man who attempted to enter her doors. The British soldiers quietly retreated. From this description (with young children), it could only have been Sgt. Lemuel Peirson Jr's second wife, Mary, who had young children Henry and Franklin at home. To avoid taking the oath of allegiance to the British, many left Long Island during the British occupation. Sgt. Lemuel Peirson Jr's family was moved[69] from Sagaponack to East Haddam, Connecticut, in Nov 1776 by Capt. Joshua Griffeth.

After the war, "Lemuel Peirson Jr." had cattle as confirmed by ear mark registration at Southampton in 1785[70]. "Lemuel Peirson" held Southampton town offices: in 1787[71], 1791[72], and 1792[73].as Overseer of Highways 6th District; and in 1794[74] and 1804[75] as Trustee. Lemuel Jr. had chd. (by which wife is not certain): 203 Henry; 204 Franklin.

79 Capt. David Pierson was born 1751, on Long Island, and died Feb. 15, 1829[76]. He was known as 'Capt.' and was in the service of his country during the Revolution. During the Revolutionary War, the British occupied Long Island from 1776 to 1783. To avoid taking the oath of allegiance to the British, many left Long Island during the British occupation.

[65]George Rogers Howell, *The Early History of Southampton, L.I., New York with Genealogies*, Second Edition, Weed, Parsons and Company, Albany, NY, 1887, p. 350.

[66]George Rogers Howell, *The Early History of Southampton, L.I., New York with Genealogies*, Second Edition, Weed, Parsons and Company, Albany, NY, 1887, p. 350.

[67]George Rogers Howell, *The Early History of Southampton, L.I., New York with Genealogies*, Second Edition, Weed, Parsons and Company, Albany, NY, 1887, p. 350.

[68]Frederic Mather, *The Refugees of 1776 from Long Island to Connecticut*, Genealogical Publishing Company, Baltimore, MD, 1972, p. 1005.

[69]Frederic Mather, *The Refugees of 1776 from Long Island to Connecticut*, Genealogical Publishing Company, Baltimore, MD, 1972, pp. 504-8.

[70]*Town Records of Southampton*, NY, Liber B (Vol. 3), p. 424, Abstract.

[71]*Town Records of Southampton*, NY, Liber B (Vol. 3), p. 434.

[72]*Town Records of Southampton*, NY, Liber B (Vol. 3), p. 457.

[73]*Town Records of Southampton*, NY, Liber B (Vol. 3), p. 459.

[74]*Town Records of Southampton*, NY, Liber B (Vol. 3), p. 466.

[75]*Town Records of Southampton*, NY, Liber B (Vol. 3), p. 511.

[76]George Rogers Howell, *The Early History of Southampton, L.I., New York with Genealogies*, Second Edition, Weed, Parsons and Company, Albany, NY, 1887, p. 350.

The Capt. David Peirson family was brought[77] from Sag Harbor by Capt. Elijah Mason and thence from Bridge Hampton to East Haddam, Connecticut on 2 Sep 1776, with five persons and goods. David served as Captain and company commander in Col. Mulford's Regiment, Col. Smith's Regiment, and in Col. Drake's Provisional Regiment.   Frederic Mather[78] attributes the title of Colonel to Capt. David Peirson after the war, but this is in error.   A 1791[79] Southampton record lists town officers including three Davids: "Col. David Peirson, Capt. David Peirson, and David Peirson Jr." Col. David Peirson was the son of Job and Hannah Peirson. David Peirson Jr. is Capt. David Peirson's uncle, son of Capt. David's grandfather, David. After 1791, town records at Southampton continue to refer to 79 David as "Capt. David Pierson." "Capt. David Peirson" had cattle after the war as confirmed by ear marks registered at Southampton in 1784[80], which was the mark of David's father, Lemuel Peirson the first (recorded previously to him). Capt. David held town offices at Southampton: in 1791[81] as Trustee; in 1792[82] as Fence Viewer & Commissioner of Highways; in 1793[83] as 6th District Overseer of Highways; in 1795[84] as Collector; in 1796[85] as Trustee ("Capt. David Peirson Esq."); in 1797[86] as Collector, Trustee, & Fence Viewer; in 1798[87] as Fence Viewer; and in 1799[88] as Commissioner of Schools ("David Peirson").

Capt. David Pierson of Sag Harbor married[89] 1st Elizabeth, dau. of Dea. Maltby and Mary Gelston of Southampton township on Long Island, New York; and married 2d Hannah, dau. of Capt. James Green (2d Connecticut Light Horse) of East Haddam, Connecticut, and widow of Joseph Hungerford. Deac. Maltby Gelston[90] (son of Hugh Gelston b. 1697 Belfast, Ireland), was b. March 20, 1723, and d. Sept. 22, 1783. Elizabeth Gelston was b. Nov. 3, 1746 on Long Island, d. Jan. 1, 1777 at East Haddam, Conn., and is buried there (Lucy Gelston also on tombstone). Hannah (Green) Pierson d. July 2, 1833, aged 78, and is also buried at East Haddam, Connecticut. Capt. David and Hannah (Green) Pierson had son 205+ Jesse, b. 1780.

---

[77] Frederic Mather, *The Refugees of 1776 from Long Island to Connecticut*, Genealogical Publishing Company, Baltimore, MD, 1972, pp. 504-8.

[78] Frederic Mather, *The Refugees of 1776 from Long Island to Connecticut*, Genealogical Publishing Company, Baltimore, MD, 1972, pp. 505.

[79] *Town Records of Southampton*, NY, Liber B (Vol. 3), p. 457.

[80] *Town Records of Southampton*, NY, Liber B (Vol. 3), p. 423, Abstract.

[81] *Town Records of Southampton*, NY, Liber B (Vol. 3), p. 457.

[82] *Town Records of Southampton*, NY, Liber B (Vol. 3), p. 459.

[83] *Town Records of Southampton*, NY, Liber B (Vol. 3), p. 461.

[84] *Town Records of Southampton*, NY, Liber B (Vol. 3), p. 470.

[85] *Town Records of Southampton*, NY, Liber B (Vol. 3), p. 477-8.

[86] *Town Records of Southampton*, NY, Liber B (Vol. 3), p. 481.

[87] *Town Records of Southampton*, NY, Liber B (Vol. 3), p. 485-6.

[88] *Town Records of Southampton*, NY, Liber B (Vol. 3), p. 489.

[89] Statement by Richard H. Greene in Frederic Mather, *The Refugees of 1776 from Long Island to Connecticut*, Genealogical Publishing Company, Baltimore, MD, 1972, p. 505.

[90] George Rogers Howell, *The Early History of Southampton, L. I., New York, with Genealogies*, Weed, Parsons and Company, Albany, NY, 1887, p. 258.

205 Jesse Pierson, was born in 1780 at East Haddam[91], Conn., and died Jan. 27, 1840[92] in Southampton Twp., Suffolk Co., N.Y. (probably at Sagg alias Sagaponack). He lived at Sagaponack, Suffolk Co., N.Y. at property across the street to the west from the Sagg graveyard, which was previously owned by Jonathan Hedges[93]. Jesse built his house there (1842 according to *Bridgehampton's Three Hundred Years*) before he died in 1840. After the death of his grandson, 845 David Emmett Pierson (by which son is not known to this author, but perhaps by 382 David), the place was sold at auction. The homestead was the Hearthstone Inn in 1956. Jesse had w. Elizabeth (b. 1783)[94] and chd. 382 David, b. 1801, m. Susan Cone[95] 1865, and resides Bridgehampton 1878; 383 George; 384 Robert b. 1812[96]; 385 James b. 1815[97], and Marietta[98] b. 1819.

80 Isaac Pierson was born in 1755 on Long Island, N.Y., and died[99] Aug. 19, 1825 in New Jersey. In the Revolutionary War, he enlisted[100] in April 1775 at Southampton, N.Y., in Capt. John Hulbut's Company, 2nd New York Regiment, and in 1776 he was in Capt. David Pierson's Company, N.Y. Regiment as a Corporal[101] in the Minute Men. His occupation[102] was shoemaker. He mar.[103] 1st Hannah ____, and 2d Mary ____. In 1788, he moved to New Jersey, and settled on a tract of land near Morristown, New Jersey, known as Piersonville. He was commonly called "Long Island Pierson" to distinguish him from the other Pierson families of New Jersey. He lived[104] with his son Maltby G. Pierson at the time he applied for a pension in 1823 (Pension R8246). He had chd., by which wife is unknown: 206+ Elisha, b. 1781; 207 Eleazar, b. 1785; 208+ Maltby G. (perhaps named after

[91]Statement by Richard H. Greene in Frederic Mather, *The Refugees of 1776 from Long Island to Connecticut*, Genealogical Publishing Company, Baltimore, MD, 1972, p. 505.

[92]George Rogers Howell, *The Early History of Southampton, L.I., New York with Genealogies*, Second Edition, Weed, Parsons and Company, Albany, NY, 1887, p. 350.

[93]Co-chairmen Mrs. Albert W. Topping and Everett C. Foster, Editor Paul H. Curts, *Bridgehampton's Three Hundred Years*, The Hampton Press, Bridgehampton, N.Y., 1856, pp. 8-9.

[94]George Rogers Howell, *The Early History of Southampton, L.I., New York with Genealogies*, Second Edition, Weed, Parsons and Company, Albany, NY, 1887, p. 350.

[95]George Rogers Howell, *The Early History of Southampton, L.I., New York with Genealogies*, Second Edition, Weed, Parsons and Company, Albany, NY, 1887, p. 350.

[96]George Rogers Howell, *The Early History of Southampton, L.I., New York with Genealogies*, Second Edition, Weed, Parsons and Company, Albany, NY, 1887, p. 350.

[97]George Rogers Howell, *The Early History of Southampton, L.I., New York with Genealogies*, Second Edition, Weed, Parsons and Company, Albany, NY, 1887, p. 350.

[98]George Rogers Howell, *The Early History of Southampton, L.I., New York with Genealogies*, Second Edition, Weed, Parsons and Company, Albany, NY, 1887, p. 350.

[99]Barbara Hoskins, *Men from Morris County New Jersey Who Served in the American Revolution*, The Friends of the Joint Free Public Library of Morristown and Morris Township, Morristown, N.J., 1979, p. 145.

[100]Barbara Hoskins, *Men from Morris County New Jersey Who Served in the American Revolution*, The Friends of the Joint Free Public Library of Morristown and Morris Township, Morristown, N.J., 1979, p. 145.

[101]*DAR Patriot Index*, Centennial Edition, National Society of the Daughters of the American Revolution, 1994, part 3, p. 2257.

[102]Barbara Hoskins, *Men from Morris County New Jersey Who Served in the American Revolution*, The Friends of the Joint Free Public Library of Morristown and Morris Township, Morristown, N.J., 1979, p. 145.

[103]Barbara Hoskins, *Men from Morris County New Jersey Who Served in the American Revolution*, The Friends of the Joint Free Public Library of Morristown and Morris Township, Morristown, N.J., 1979, p. 145.

[104]Barbara Hoskins, *Men from Morris County New Jersey Who Served in the American Revolution*, The Friends of the Joint Free Public Library of Morristown and Morris Township, Morristown, N.J., 1979, p. 145.

Isaac's brother David's father-in-law Dea. Maltby Gelston), b. 1795; 209+ George; 210+ Henry; 211 Miller; 212+ Isaac.

206 Elisha Pierson, born on Long Island in 1781, moved with his father to New Jersey when he was a child, and resided in Morristown (or Piersonville), and had chd. 386 John; 387 Sidney; 388 Eliza; 389 Harriet; 390 Hannah.

208 Maltby G. Pierson, was born 1795 in New Jersey at Piersonville, mar. S. Voorhees, and lived in Monroe[105], Sussex Co., New Jersey. He had chd. 391 Isaac N. (mar. R. Post); 392+ Aaron Voorhees, b. 1824; 393 Charles J. (mar. M. Cobert); 394 Henry W. (mar. M. Budd); 395 David L. (mar. E. Berry); 396+ Maltby Gilson (a spelling variation of Gelston); 397 Allen H. (never married); 398 Wm. (never mar.); 399 Mary Ann; 400 Hannah N.; 401 Harriet; 402 Ellen C.; 403 Sarah L.; and 402a+ Ellen Elizabeth[106].

392 Aaron Voorhees Pierson[107] was born Mar. 28, 1824, and died Jan. 14, 1914, at Schooley's Mountain, N.J. He was buried in Hillside Cemetery, Madison, N.J. He mar. Sarah J. Burch (b. Sep. 10, 1831, d. Jan. 17, 1901, bur. at Hillside Cemetery, Madison, N.J.). He contributed in 1869 to the Presbyterian Church in Madison, N.J. His wife, Sarah, was dismissed Dec. 19, 1897, from the Madison Presbyterian church to the Methodist Episcopal church at Green Village, N.J. Aaron had a dau. Mrs. Dr. (Pierson) Cooper of Westfield, N.J.

396 Maltby Gilson[108] Pierson[109] was a farmer. He was confirmed May 8, 1857, at the Presbyterian Church of Madison, N.J. He mar. Nov. 24, 1858, Caroline Muchmore (d. Jan. 26, 1871, age 32 at Brooklyn, N.Y.), dau. of William Muchmore. He was dismissed in 1859 from the Madison Presbyterian church to the Tabernacle Church of Brooklyn, N.Y. Maltby and Caroline had a child[110] that d. Aug. 3, 1861, at Brooklyn, N.Y.

402a Ellen Elizabeth Pierson[111] mar. (at the home of her brother [which one is unknown] at 92 New St., Newark, N.J.) Oct. 21, 1857, Mahlon M. Miller, mason of Green Village, N.J.

209 George Pierson was born in New Jersey, and had chd. 404 Oliver; 405 Miller; 406 Eliz.; 407 Temperance. In 1878, they were said to be in California.

210 Henry Pierson was born in New Jersey, and had chd. 408 Charles; 409 Caroline.

212 Isaac Pierson was born in New Jersey, and had chd. 410 Edward; 411 Henry; 412 Cecilia; 413 Eliza; 414 Mary.

39 David Peirson Jr. was born on Long Island, probably Bridgehampton based on his father David's location. David owned cattle as confirmed by ear marks and a brand registered at

[105]Viola E. Shaw & Barbara S. Parker, *Madison, New Jersey Presbyterian Church Vital Records 1747-1900*, The Presbyterian Church of Madison, Madison, N.J., 1982, p. 251.

[106]Viola E. Shaw & Barbara S. Parker, *Madison, New Jersey Presbyterian Church Vital Records 1747-1900*, The Presbyterian Church of Madison, Madison, N.J., 1982, p. 250.

[107]Viola E. Shaw & Barbara S. Parker, *Madison, New Jersey Presbyterian Church Vital Records 1747-1900*, The Presbyterian Church of Madison, Madison, N.J., 1982, p. 249.

[108]A variation on the spelling of the Gelston surname.

[109]Viola E. Shaw & Barbara S. Parker, *Madison, New Jersey Presbyterian Church Vital Records 1747-1900*, The Presbyterian Church of Madison, Madison, N.J., 1982, p. 251.

[110]Burroughs undertaking records.

[111]Viola E. Shaw & Barbara S. Parker, *Madison, New Jersey Presbyterian Church Vital Records 1747-1900*, The Presbyterian Church of Madison, Madison, N.J., 1982, p. 250.

Southampton under "David Peirson Jr" in 1762[112]; in 1768[113] (firebrand D. P.); and in 1772[114]. David Jr. held town office at Southampton Township: in 1788[115] Commissioner of Highways; in 1789[116] Fence Viewer; in 1790[117] Fence Viewer; in 1791[118] Fence Viewer. Based on these records, David Peirson Jr. lived ca. 1740 to ca. 1792 at Southampton. No record of marriage or children was found.

18 Theophilus Pierson was born 1690, at Bridgehampton, Long Island, and died 1742 (Howell[119] says he died Sept. 1744, but he is often wrong on dates). When Theophilus was 11 years old, his father, Col. Henry Peirson, wrote his will August 28, 1701[120], proved in 1702. Theophilus inherited: "I give unto my son, Theophilus Peirson, all yt piece of land yt I bought of Mr Peregrine Stanburgh, called ye Swamp Close & also two fifty pound allotments of land in Hog Neck, one of which was my father's No. 41, ye other I bought of Benjamin Foster No. 26, all which said land I give unto him, ye sd Theophilus Peirson, his heirs & assigns for ever - Also one horse, two steers, two cows, ten sheep & twenty five pounds in money, or what may be equivalent thereto, when he shall come to ye age of twenty one years & also one Eighth part of a share at Meantake." Theophilus had cattle as confirmed by his father's will (two steers & two cows) and by ear mark registration at Southampton in 1713[121] at age 23.

Theophilus held one-year public offices at Southampton: in 1718[122] as Assessor; in 1722[123] as Trustee; in 1728[124] as Assessor; in 1729[125] as Trustee; in 1732[126] as Trustee; in 1735[127] as Supervisor of Intestate Estates; and in 1741[128] as Trustee. In 1712, Theophilus bought[129] a right of fifty in commonage throughout Southampton. The town of Southampton granted him land: in 1712[130] at the Westward Division of Speeunk Neck, Tanners Neck, and Apocuck Neck; in 1727[131] at Seder Swamps westward of ye Little River; in 1738[132] at the

[112]*Town Records of Southampton*, NY, Liber B (Vol. 3), p. 281, Abstract.

[113]*Town Records of Southampton*, NY, Liber B (Vol. 3), p. 341, Abstract.

[114]*Town Records of Southampton*, NY, Liber B (Vol. 3), p. 371, Abstract.

[115]*Town Records of Southampton*, NY, Liber B (Vol. 3), p. 442.

[116]*Town Records of Southampton*, NY, Liber B (Vol. 3), p. 448.

[117]*Town Records of Southampton*, NY, Liber B (Vol. 3), p. 455.

[118]*Town Records of Southampton*, NY, Liber B (Vol. 3), p. 457.

[119]George Rogers Howell, *The Early History of Southampton, L.I., New York with Genealogies*, Second Edition, Weed, Parsons and Company, Albany, NY, 1887, p. 350.

[120]William S. Pelletreau, *Early Long Island Wills of Suffolk County, 1691-1703, With Genealogical and Historical Notes*, Francis P. Harper, New York, NY, 1897, pp. 239-41.

[121]*Town Records of Southampton*, NY, Liber A, No. 2, 1st Part, p. 238.

[122]*Town Records of Southampton*, NY, Liber A, No. 2, 1st Part, p. 281.

[123]*Town Records of Southampton*, NY, Liber B (Vol. 3), p. 134.

[124]*Town Records of Southampton*, NY, Liber B (Vol. 3), p. 135.

[125]*Town Records of Southampton*, NY, Liber B (Vol. 3), p. 136.

[126]*Town Records of Southampton*, NY, Liber B (Vol. 3), p. 137.

[127]*Town Records of Southampton*, NY, Liber B (Vol. 3), pp. 137-8.

[128]*Town Records of Southampton*, NY, Liber B (Vol. 3), p. 139.

[129]*Town Records of Southampton*, NY, Liber A, No. 2, 1st Part, p. 240-241.

[130]*Town Records of Southampton*, NY, Liber A, No. 2, 1st Part, p. 246.

[131]*Town Records of Southampton*, NY, Liber A, No. 2, 1st Part, pp. 296-9.

[132]*Town Records of Southampton*, NY, Liber B (Vol. 3), p. 166-73.

lower Division in Quaquanantuck Purchase; in 1738[133] at the north Division in Quaquanantuck Purchase; in 1738[134] at timber land between the Indian line and East Hampton bounds; in 1739[135] at Canoe Place Division in Quaquanantuck Purchase; and on Nov. 19, 1745[136] at Sagg Harbor ("Theophilus Pierson deceased"). This 1745 record is the last town entry for Theophilus Pierson and it confirms that he died before Nov. 19, 1745.

Theophilus mar. Sarah Topping[137] and had chd. 41+ Henry, b. ca. 1720, d. 1783; 42+ Nathan, b. 1723, d. 1826; 42a Susanna[138], w. of Arthur Howell; 42b Keturah[139]; 43+ Stephen, b. 1729.

41 Henry Pierson was born about 1720 probably at Bridgehampton, Suffolk Co., N.Y., and died in 1783, probably at Mendham Township, Morris Co., N.J. Henry received land grants from the town of Southampton: in 1761[140] at Sagg Harbour's Twelve Acres; in 1763[141] at Aucaubogue Division in Topping's Purchase; and in 1763[142] at the Little South Division of Southampton. Henry probably went to New Jersey about 1770 when his sons Shadrach and James were known to have gone there, as no further records of this Henry appear at Southampton. He had chd. 83a Abigail[143] b. ca. 1746, 83+ Shadrach; 84+ James, b. 1750.

83 Shadrach Pierson was born ca. 1748 (based on sister Abigail b. ca. 1646 and brother James b. 1750) in Southampton Township (based on his father Henry's property location), Suffolk Co., N.Y. colony on Long Island, and died before 1810 in upper New York state. He moved to New Jersey in 1770. Shadrach mar. before 1774, 104 Rebecca Peirson (his 2nd cousin, they both had great grandfather Col. Henry Peirson), dau. of 51 Sylvanus and Rebecca (Lupton) Peirson, of Bridgehampton[144], Suffolk Co., New York colony. About 1776, during the Revolutionary War, "Shadrack Pierson" served[145] as a Private in the Morris Co., N.J., militia (S-720). He lived in Morris Township, Morris Co., N.J., according to that military record. By 1779, he had moved to Mendham Township, still in Morris Co. N.J. On March 8, 1779[146], at the First Presbyterian Congregation Church of Mendham,

[133]*Town Records of Southampton*, NY, Liber B (Vol. 3), p. 184-88.
[134]*Town Records of Southampton*, NY, Liber B (Vol. 3), p. 157.
[135]*Town Records of Southampton*, NY, Liber B (Vol. 3), p. 189-94.
[136]*Town Records of Southampton*, NY, Liber B (Vol. 3), p. 143-6.
[137]George Rogers Howell, *The Early History of Southampton, L.I., New York with Genealogies*, Second Edition, Weed, Parsons and Company, Albany, NY, 1887, p. 350.
[138]George Rogers Howell, *The Early History of Southampton, L.I., New York with Genealogies*, Second Edition, Weed, Parsons and Company, Albany, NY, 1887, p. 350.
[139]George Rogers Howell, *The Early History of Southampton, L.I., New York with Genealogies*, Second Edition, Weed, Parsons and Company, Albany, NY, 1887, p. 350.
[140]*Town Records of Southampton*, NY, Liber B (Vol. 3), p.288-90.
[141]*Town Records of Southampton*, NY, Liber B (Vol. 3), p. 302-06.
[142]*Town Records of Southampton*, NY, Liber B (Vol. 3), p. 320-24.
[143]*Genealogies of Connecticut Families*, Vol. 3, Genealogy Publishing Company, Baltimore, Maryland, 1983, p. 254.
[144]Henry B. Hoff, *Long Island Source Records*, Genealogical Publishing Co., Inc., Baltimore, 1987, family records of Margaret Jermain, dau. of Silvanus Peirson.
[145]Barbara Hoskins, *Men From Morris County New Jersey Who Served in the American Revolution*, Friends of the Joint Free Public Library of Morristown, Morristown, New Jersey, 1979, p. 145.
[146]Helen Martha Wright, *The First Presbyterian Congregation, Mendham, Morris County, New Jersey, History and Records 1738-1938*, pub. by author, Jersey City, New Jersey, 1939, p. 67.

Morris Co., New Jersey, Shadrach was chosen as one of a committee of four to be "Collectors of the minister's sallary for the ensueing year and for what is payt." Shadrach was still at Mendham, Morris Co., New Jersey Apr. 4, 1781[147]: The New Jersey Journal, Chatham, "The horse Granby will cover at Shedrick Peirson's, Mendham."

Shadrach and family moved to New York state in 1785, where he was located in the 1790 U.S. census at Schoharie Town, Albany Co. (became Schoharie Co. in 1795), New York: "Person (sic), Shedrick, one male of age 16+, 4 males under 16, and 3 females." This indicates that he had four sons, two daughters, and a wife at home in 1790. From Schoharie, New York, Reformed Church records[148]: 19 Nov 1792 Henrich Richter, son of Henrich (living Dwiensbusch) [Duanesburg, Schenectady Co., N.Y.], married Phobe Parson (sic), dau. of S(adrah) [indexed Shadrac] (living Blikkersbusch) [Bleecker near Gloversville, Fulton Co., N.Y.]. This is believed to be Shadrach's eldest dau. Phoebe Pierson, born ca. 1774 if age 18 at marriage. Neither Shadrach or Rebecca could be found in the 1800 U.S. census. In the 1810 U.S. census at Montgomery Co., New York: "Rebecca Parson (sic), 1 female age 16-26 (daughter #2), 1 female age 45+ (Rebecca Peirson, about age 58)." This is believed to be Shadrach's wife, Rebecca, without Shadrach and the other children. The 1810 census indicates that Shadrach died before 1810.

Shadrach and Rebecca had chd. 213 Henry; 213a Phoebe[149], b. ca. 1774, mar. 19 Nov 1792 Henrich Richter at Schoharie, N.Y.; 214+ Moses, b. 10 Dec 1776 N.J., d. 6 Jun 1863[150]; 215+ James, b. ca. 1778; 216+ Joseph; 217+ Rufus, b. 19 Dec 1787, d. 6 Jun 1865; 217a Dau. #2 (1790 census).

214 Moses Pierson was born 10 Dec 1776 at Mendham, Morris Co., New Jersey, and came to Schoharie, N.Y., with his father in 1785 at age 9. In 1797 or 1798, Moses, age 21 or 22, went to Charleston, Montgomery Co., N.Y. where he took up 150 acres on the Stone-heap Patent[151]. The road leading directly north from Oak Ridge was an old Indian road. The famous stone-heap was situated on this road. Each Indian that passed by threw another stone on the pile. Stone-heap Patent is a tract of land where the stone-heap is located. In the 1855 census of Montgomery County, N.Y., Moses is listed[152] as "Charleston, Moses Peirson, age 79, born New Jersey." Moses died there on 6 Jun 1863[153]. Moses, wife Mary, two daus. & a granddau. are bur. at the cemetery at Oak Ridge, Montgomery Co., N.Y. He mar. 1st ca. 1802 Mary[154] (Priest?)[155] (b. 1780, d. 25 Mar 1839)[156], and 2nd 1840/50 Rachel

---

[147]Thomas B. Wilson, *Records of New Jersey*, Vol. I, "Notices from New Jersey Newspapers 1781-1790," Hunterdon House, Lambertville, New Jersey, 1988, p. 119.

[148]C. M. Kelly, Marriage Records of Two Early Schoharie, NY, Churches: Reformed Church 1732-1892, St. Paul's Lutheran Church 1743-1899, p. 18.

[149]C. M. Kelly, Marriage Records of Two Early Schoharie, NY, Churches: Reformed Church 1732-1892, St. Paul's Lutheran Church 1743-1899, p. 18.

[150]LDS microfilm 17135, Cemetery Inscriptions, Cemetery at Oak Ridge, Montgomery Co., N.Y.

[151]*History of Montgomery and Fulton Counties, N.Y.*, F. W. Beers & Co., 1878, p. 106.

[152]Dr. David Paul Davenport, *The 1855 Census of Montgomery County, New York*, Kinship, Rhinebeck, N.Y., 1989.

[153]LDS microfilm 17135, Cemetery Inscriptions, Cemetery at Oak Ridge, Montgomery Co., N.Y.

[154]LDS microfilm 17135, Cemetery Inscriptions, Cemetery at Oak Ridge, Montgomery Co., N.Y.

[155]Mary had a dau. Mary P. in 1810 which creates the possibility that Mary's maiden surname starts with a P. The 1850 census at Charleston shows Moses with Susan Priest, age 34, living with the Pierson family. Records for Green Hill Cemetery, Amsterdam, N.Y., show that an Elijah Priest d. 22 Dec 1824, aged 47. If Elijah Priest is Mary's father, then Susan Priest could be Mary's sister who would have been age 8 in 1824 when Elijah died.

____ (b. 1788 N.J.)[157]. Moses had chd. (all by 1st wife Mary): 415a Elisabeth[158], b. 13 Mar 1803; 415b Mary P. [159], b. 13 Jan 1810 Mont. Co., N.Y., d. 29 Sep 1847, bur. Oak Ridge, Mont. Co., mar. Mr. Waters; 415+ Henry; 416a Esther A. [160], b. 1816, d. 21 Nov 1842, bur. Oak Ridge Cem., Mont. Co.; 416+ David; 417+ William Nelson, b. 1821, d. 1878.

415 Henry Pierson was born ca. 1813 (based on sibling spacing), had chd. 486 Elizabeth (mar. twice, and both times physicians); 487 Moses (died in N. J., was a physician, left a widow in Bristol, Pa., and had chd. 915 Bowen, 916 Wm. H. and 917 Ely F.); 488 Wm. B. (now [1878] resides in Brooklyn, N. Y., in which place he is a physician).

416 David Pierson was born ca. 1818 (based on sibling spacing), mar. Sophia ____ (b. 29 Mar 1809, d. 12 Sep 1848)[161] and had chd. 489 Emily S., b. 1828, d. 6 Jul 1846[162].

417 William Nelson Pierson was born 1821 on the Stoneheap Patent[163] near Charleston, Montgomery Co., N.Y. and died 1878[164] being buried at the Charleston Four Corners Church. He had grand jury duty[165] 1848 in Montgomery Co., N.Y., where he was listed as "Nelson Pierson of Charleston, farmer." In the 1855 census of Montgomery Co., N.Y., he was listed[166] as "Charleston, Nelson Peirson, age 33, born Montgomery Co., N.Y.," living on the same property or next door to Moses Peirson, age 79, and George N. Peirson[167] (b. Jefferson Co., N.Y.), age 15. He mar. Elmina ____ (b. 1824, d. 1890) [168] and had chd. 490 Carrie (dau.); 491 Frank H. (b. 1857, d. 1913)[169].

215 James Pierson was born 1775-1784 (ref. 1810 & 1820 censuses) at Mendham, Morris Co., N.J. and died before 1830 probably in Montgomery Co., N.Y. The 1810 U.S. census at Charleston Township, Montgomery Co., N.Y., provides "James Parson" (sic), "1 male age 26-45 (James), 3 males under age 10 (Hiel and two of Isaac, Rufus, & Samuel), 2 females under age 10 (daus. #1 & # 2), and 1 female age 26-45 (James wife, name unknown). The 1820 U.S. census at Charleston Township, Montgomery Co., N.Y., provides "James Parsons" (sic), 2 males under 10 & 1 male 10-16 (3 of the 4 sons, perhaps Isaac, Rufus, & Samuel since Hiel, age 19, may be off doing his apprenticeship as a shoemaker), 1 male 26-45 in Commerce (James), and 1 female 26-45 (James' wife)." The 1830 U.S. census at Glen Township, Montgomery Co., N.Y., provides James' son "Hiel Persons" (sic) living with 3 males of the age of his brothers Isaac, Rufus, and Samuel, along with Hiel's wife and young daughter. The conclusion is that something happened to James and his wife before the 1830 census. James mar. ca. 1799 (unk. fem. of German origin based on son's name Hiel, b. 1775-

[156]LDS microfilm 17135, Cemetery Inscriptions, Cemetery at Oak Ridge, Montgomery Co., N.Y.

[157]1850 U. S. census at Charleston, Montgomery Co., N.Y.

[158]Arthur C. M. Kelly, *Baptism Records of the Schoharie Reformed Church*, Rhinebeck, N.Y., 1977, p. 107/

[159]LDS microfilm 17135, Cemetery Inscriptions, Cemetery at Oak Ridge, Montgomery Co., N.Y.

[160]LDS microfilm 17135, Cemetery Inscriptions, Cemetery at Oak Ridge, Montgomery Co., N.Y.

[161]Charleston Ryders Corner (Baptist) Church Cemetery, Montgomery Co., N.Y.

[162]Charleston Ryders Corner (Baptist) Church Cemetery, Montgomery Co., N.Y.

[163]*History of Montgomery and Fulton Counties, N.Y.*, F. W. Beers & Co., 1878, p. 106.

[164]Charleston Four Corners Church Cemetery, Charleston, Montgomery Co., N.Y.

[165]Arthur C. M. Kelly, *Grand Jurors of Montgomery Co., N.Y., 1816-1850*, 1989, p. 76.

[166]Dr. David Paul Davenport, *The 1855 Census of Montgomery County, New York*, Kinship, Rhinebeck, N.Y., 1989.

[167]This is probably 425 George Pierson, son of 216 Joseph Pierson (who may be deceased in 1855).

[168]Charleston Four Corners Church Cemetery, Charleston, Montgomery Co., N.Y.

[169]Charleston Four Corners Church Cemetery, Charleston, Montgomery Co., N.Y.

1784 [ref. 1810 & 1820 censuses]) and had chd. 418a dau. #1[170]; 418+ Hiel, b. 1801[171], d. aft. 1860; 419a dau. # 2[172]; 419 Isaac, b. ca. 1807; 420 Rufus, b. ca. 1810; 421 Samuel, b. ca. 1813. (The birth year estimates for Isaac, Rufus, & Samuel could be out of order, but one is 1810, one is 1804/09, and one is 1811/18, based on 1810 & 1820 censuses and child spacing required).

418 Hiel Pierson Sr. was born in 1801[173] at Charleston, Montgomery Co., N.Y., and died between 1860 and 1870, probably at Amsterdam, Montgomery Co., N.Y. where he lived in 1860[174]. His occupation was shoemaker[175]. He mar. at Montgomery Co., N.Y., 26 Jan 1826, Polly (Mary) Freeman (b. 1 Dec 1801, Guilderland, Albany Co., N.Y., d. 8 Feb 1899, bur. Green Hill Cemetery, Amsterdam, N.Y.), dau. of Robert and Genny (Man) Freeman. The 1855 census of Montgomery County, N.Y., listed[176] him as "Amsterdam, Kiel (should be Hiel) Pierson, age 54, born Montgomery Co., N.Y.," with Rachel R. Knapp, age 57, living next door. A photograph of Hiel Pierson Sr. taken about 1860 was handed down in the family through Hiel Pierson Jr., his son Edward Pierson, his dau. Marguerite (Pierson) Peak, and to her nephew Allen Pierson & reproduced for his two brothers Richard & Donald Pierson. When Mary died, her obituary[177] read, "Mary Pierson, widow of Hiel Pierson, died February 8 at the age of 97. She will be buried in western Green Hill. Her son-in-law is Charles Wetherby." Hiel Sr. and Mary had chd.[178], all born in Montgomery Co., N.Y.: 723+ Olivia Jane (Olive), b. 1827, d. 1905; 724 James I., b. 1830, d. aft. 1884; 725 Josemis (illegible, looks like in 1850 census), b. 1833, idiot; 726+ Hiel Jr., b. 6 Mar 1835, d. 14 Jun 1902; 727 Sarah, b. 1838; 728+ Eliza, b. 1841, d. 25 Jun 1892, mar. Charles Wetherby; and 729 Anna C., b. 1843 Amsterdam.

Hiel Pierson Sr. (1801-186?)

---

[170] 1810 U.S. census at Charleston Township, Montgomery Co., N.Y.

[171] 1855 New York State census, Amsterdam, Montgomery Co., N.Y., Kiel (Hiel) Pierson, age 54.

[172] 1810 U.S. census at Charleston Township, Montgomery Co., N.Y.

[173] 1855 New York State census, Amsterdam, Montgomery Co., N.Y., Kiel (Hiel) Pierson, age 54.

[174] 1860 U.S. census at Amsterdam, Montgomery Co., N.Y.

[175] 1850 U.S. census at Montgomery Co., N.Y. under the name "Hiram Peirson." (This is Hiel based on the children's names.)

[176] Dr. David Paul Davenport, *The 1855 Census of Montgomery County, New York*, Kinship, Rhinebeck, N.Y., 1989.

[177] From a newspaper clipping kept in the family Bible (since lost) of Karl E. Pierson in 1988, no date, city, or newspaper identified, but probably dated about 10 Feb 1899 at Amsterdam, N.Y.

[178] 1850 census of "Hiram Peirson" and 1860 census of "Hiel Piersons", both at Amsterdam, Montgomery Co., N.Y.

723 Olivia Jane Pierson was born in 1827 in Montgomery Co., N.Y. She mar. ca. 1852 Joseph A. Eldrett (b. 1821 England, carriage maker). When Olive died, her obituary[179] read: "Olive Jane Pierson, who married Joseph A. Eldrett, died at home in Sherman (Chautauqua Co.), New York at 78 years old (1905). She leaves two daughters and two sons: Mrs. George Pelton of Sherman, NY; Mrs. Edgar Merry of Dalton, NY; James A. Eldrett of Rochester, NY, and his son Ralph also of Rochester; and Lorimer Eldrett of Buffalo, NY. Nephews and nieces of Olive Jane Pierson in Amsterdam (NY) at the time of her death were Harlan Eldrett, Miss Jossena Eldrett, Mrs. George Lum, Mrs. Delos B. Lewis, and Miss Belle Gardner." Joseph and Olivia had Eldrett chd.: Anna E., b. 1853, mar. either George Pelton or Edgar Merry (see above obituary); Edward I., b. 1857, d. bef. 1905; James A., b. 1858, in Rochester, N.Y., in 1905, had son Ralph; Jannie, b. 1866, mar. either George Pelton or Edgar Merry (see above obituary); Lorimer, b. aft. 1870, in Buffalo, N.Y. in 1905; and a child of J. Eldrett, b. 6 Aug 1871, d. 10 Sep 1871, bur. Green Hill Cemetery, Amsterdam, N.Y.

726 Hiel Pierson Jr.[180] was born 6 Mar 1835 at Glen[181], Montgomery Co., N.Y., and died 14 Jun 1902 at Webb City, Jasper Co., Missouri. He lived at Amsterdam, Montgomery Co., N.Y., and his trade was wagon maker[182]. Hiel Jr. worked for E. & J. A. Eldrett Carriages and Sleighs. Joseph A. Eldrett was the husband of 723 Olivia Pierson, Hiel Jr.'s sister. He mar. at Amsterdam, N.Y., 19 May 1857 Sarah E. Knapp (b. 15 Apr 1838 Glenville, N.Y., d. 30 Oct 1911 Webb City, Mo.), dau. of Elijah and Rachel Randall (Johnson) Knapp Jr. In 1887, Hiel Jr. (age 52), his wife Sarah (age 49), and two daughters, Minnie (age 25) and Libbie (age 14), moved from Amsterdam, New York, to Webb City, Jasper Co., Missouri, where his son Edward had moved to five years earlier. At Webb City, Hiel Jr. and family lived at 1420 W. Joplin Street. His obituary read[183]: "Hiel Pierson (Jr.) died June 14, 1902, at age 67, 3 months, and 8 days (makes his birth 6 Mar 1835). He will be buried in the Webb City Cemetery. He was a resident of Webb City for 15 years

Hiel Pierson Jr. (1835-1902)

(makes his arrival in 1887 before 30 Sep when his dau. Libbie died there). He was married to Sarah Knapp. He was blind several years before his death. Mr. Pierson was a well to do

---

[179]From a newspaper obituary kept in the family bible (since lost) of Karl E. Pierson in 1988, no date, place, or newspaper given, but probably 1905 in Amsterdam, NY.
[180]Hiel Pierson Jr. family data including his children come from Pierson family records coupled with census data.
[181]1860 U.S. Census at Amsterdam, Montgomery Co., NY, family 509.
[182]1860 U.S. Census at Amsterdam, Montgomery Co., NY, family 509.
[183]From a newspaper article, no publisher or date, kept in the Karl Pierson family bible, probably originating from the Webb City Times about 16 June 1902.

member of this community." The Webb City Cemetery record said he died of paralysis. Hiel Jr. and Sarah had chd., all born at Amsterdam, Montgomery Co., N.Y.: 730 Minnie M., b. 16 Jul 1861, d. 19 Aug 1897 Webb City, Mo., mar. James W. Burr; 731+ Edward Melvin, b. 29 May 1865, d. 10 May 1912; 732 unnamed child, b. & d. ca. 1869; 733 Sarah Elizabeth (Libbie), b. 22 Sep 1872, d. 30 Sep 1887 Webb City, Mo., at age 15.

731 Edward Melvin Pierson[184] was born 29 May 1865 at Amsterdam, Montgomery Co., N.Y., and died 10 May 1912 at Claremore, Rogers Co., Oklahoma. He lived at Webb City, Missouri, where he had moved to in 1882 from Amsterdam, N.Y. He started out in Webb City as a lead and zinc miner and owned his own horse-driven ore-pulverizing equipment. A successful miner, he married at Carthage, Jasper Co., Missouri, 24 Jan 1891 Abigail (Abbie) Joanna Speece (b. 3 Jan 1864, d. 7 Feb 1933), dau. of Bowen Wesley and Nancy Jane (Dull) Speece of Carthage. In 1905, he and his family were living in a single story frame house at 1501 W. Joplin Street in Webb City. By 1910, Edward had gone into the coal and feed business and had moved to a two-story house with basement (14 rooms with 6 bedrooms) at 1492 W. Joplin Street in Webb City. E. M. Pierson Coal & Feed was located on East Daugherty street in Webb City, and in this business he became well to do. In 1912, Edward was suffering from dropsy and went to the hot springs at Claremore, Oklahoma, in hope of a cure. But instead, he died there. He was buried at Webb City, Missouri. In

Edward M. Pierson (1865-1912)

1919, the widow Abbie Pierson moved to Kansas City, Missouri, and son Karl joined her there that summer where he attended High School for a short while. On January 1, 1923, at Kansas City, Missouri, Abbie Pierson married 2nd Frank Pearson of Canada who already had daughter Madeline and two other children from a previous marriage. There were no children of this Frank and Abbie marriage. Frank, Abbie, and Karl moved to Los Angeles, California, in 1923, where Abbie died in 1933. Edward and Abbie had chd., all born at Webb City, Missouri: 734 Winifred May, b. 4 Feb 1892, d. 18 Jun 1914 of pneumonia at age 22, single school teacher; 735 Joy Lorene, b. 27 Jul 1898, d. 1970, mar. 15 Jan 1918 George Floyd McCallister, also mar. Frank Dancer, Don Bence, and George Dougherty, and div. all four, no children; 736 Marguerite, b. 3 Dec 1901, d. 20 Mar 1987, mar. 8 Jan 1923 William Archie Peak, no children; 737+ Karl Edward, b. 29 Mar 1905, d. 1 Jun 1991.

---

[184]Edward Pierson family data including his children come from Pierson family data passed down through Bible recordings, Bible held by Karl E. Pierson in 1988 (now lost).

737 Karl Edward Pierson was born 29 Mar 1905 at Webb City, Jasper Co., Missouri, and died 1 Jun 1991 at Roseville, Placer Co., California. He went to California about 1926 and there mar. 1st 31 Jan 1931 (div. 1943) Irene Josephine Barnett (b. 16 Feb 1908 Trinidad, Las Animas Co., Colorado, d. 4 Apr 1959 Anaheim, Orange Co., California) dau. of Frederick and Ida Mae (Thorp) Barnett of Long Beach, California, mar. 2nd 19 Nov 1944 at Vallejo, Solano Co., California, Frances Josephine Cawley (b. 6 Feb 1915 Pocatello, Bannock Co., Idaho), dau. of Charles William and Caroline Elizabeth (Hauser) Cawley. Karl was an electronic engineer, self taught. He headed research and development for the Jackson Bell Company during the peak of midget radio set production (1,500 per day). By that time, Jackson Bell had become Packard Bell and Karl continued another 3 years as design and production engineer. He then worked 3 years for Patterson Radio Company as chief engineer and developed notable communication receivers, including the cherished PR-15 used commercially and by amateur radio operators around the world. Karl was also an amateur

Karl E. Pierson (1905-1991)

radio operator under the call letters W6BGH. When Patterson died, Karl formed Pierson-Delane Incorporated and was president and chief engineer of it for 7 years.

In December 1941, a few days before the Japanese bombed Pearl Harbor in Hawaii, it was announced that Karl had developed an amplitude modulation noise silencer that brought comment from the father of radio, Dr. Lee DeForest. Dr. DeForest said, "Pierson has accomplished what no other radio engineer working with amplitude modulation has succeeded in doing. He employs special silencers which possess the unique quality of cutting out or reducing in their intensity to an astounding degree all sorts of interference. It undoubtedly will prove an important factor in military radio communication." In 1943, at the peak of World War II, Karl became senior development engineer for Raytheon in Massachusetts, working closely with the Massachusetts Institute of Technology radiation laboratory to develop Navy radar and other secret equipment. Karl worked as a communication engineer for Space Technology Laboratories and others in the pioneer days of the space launch program and is credited with solving many communication problems on such launches as Able Star and others. Karl died June 1, 1991, at age 86 while visiting his son Richard in Citrus Heights, California, and was pronounced dead at nearby Roseville Hospital, Roseville, Placer Co., California.

Karl had chd. (by Irene) 738+ Richard Earl & 739+ Donald Karl (identical twins), b. 11 Nov 1934, and 740 Allen Melvin, b. 20 Dec 1938.

738 Lt. Col. Richard Earl Pierson was born 11 Nov 1934 at Glendale, Los Angeles Co., California. He is a co-author of this book, *Pierson Millennium*. Richard served 21 years in the U.S. Air Force (1952-1973) as a fighter pilot and electrical engineer. He enlisted in the USAF as an Airman (Private) in 1952 rising to the rank of Lt. Colonel via the Aviation Cadet program where he received his Pilot aeronautical rating and commission as 2d Lieutenant on 16 May 1955. He married 21 May 1955 at Carmichael, Sacramento Co., California, Roberta Bell Jones (b. 31 Mar 1935 Roseville, Placer Co., California) dau. of Robert Walter and Esther Mae (Bell) Jones. In 1959, Richard received an Air Force scholarship through the Air Force Institute of Technology civilian institutions program to the University of Colorado where he graduated with a Bachelor of Science degree in Electrical Engineering in 1962. Richard served as pilot in propeller-driven aircraft on three combat assignments during the Vietnam War in 1963, 1967, and 1971, during which time he was awarded the Distinguished Flying Cross twice, the Meritorious Service Medal twice, and the Air Medal fourteen times. He retired from military service in 1973 and began his civilian career in solar engineering and management. He retired from management work with the State of California in 1994. Richard and Roberta had chd. 828 Mark Alan b. 16 Aug 1956 Big Spring, Howard Co., Texas, in 1996 was a Commander in the U.S. Navy with submarine experience; 829 Scott Wayne b. 10 Oct 1957 Big Spring, Howard Co., Texas, mar. 4 Jul 1979 Adriane Joyce Ridder, and had chd. 835 Courtney Lynn 22 Aug 1980, 836 Adam Christopher & 837 Ian Nathanial (fraternal twins) 3 Jul 1982; and 830 Jeffery Karl b. 4 Apr 1959 Waco, McLennan Co., Texas, mar. 1st 13 Aug 1983 (div.) Susan Lynn Robinson, mar. 2nd 2 Feb 1991 Lisa Marie Thompson and had by Lisa chd. 838 Ashley Noel b. 26 Dec 1990 and 839 Karli Marie b. 25 Jan 1993.

739 Donald Karl Pierson, Fire Chief, was born 11 Nov 1934, twin of Richard Earl, at Glendale, Los Angeles Co., California. Donald enlisted in the U.S. Air Force in 1952 and served four years as a B-36 gunner in Strategic Air Command. After leaving the service in 1956, he became a fireman in Los Angeles City where he rose to the rank of Captain in charge of a fire station before retiring there with 25 years service. Later, he became the Fire Chief of the Coloma-Lotus Fire District in El Dorado Co., California, for 5 years. He mar. 1st 29 Apr 1955 at Boulder, Boulder Co., Colorado, Elizabeth Loraine Smith (b. 11 Sep 1935 Cheyenne Co., Colorado, d. ca. 1982). They had chd. :831 Linda Marie b. 24 May 1957 Inglewood, Los Angeles Co., California, d. 25 Jun 1963; 832 Daniel Wayne b. 31 Mar 1959 Inglewood, Los Angeles Co., California, mar. 5 May 1995 at Placerville, CA, Elaine Phillips; and 833 Joni Marlene b. 28 Oct 1961 Northridge, Los Angeles Co., California, mar. 28 Apr 1984 at Los Angeles, CA, Jeffery Scott Hitt and had Hitt chd. Samantha Christine 19 Dec 1987 and Angela Blair 20 Aug 1995. Donald mar. 2nd 18 Sep 1982 at Los Angeles, Carol Joyce Clare Caughlin (b. 2 May 1944), dau. of George Caughlin. She brought with her two daughters (by an earlier marriage to James Michael Dove), Laura Evelyn Dove, b. 14 Nov 1977 Belleville, Illinois, and Sara Ann Dove b. 24 Jul 1979 Belleville, Illinois. Donald later adopted 834 Sara Ann Dove who retained the Dove surname.

728 Eliza Pierson was born in 1841 at Amsterdam, Montgomery Co., N.Y., and died 25 Jun 1892 at Hudson, Wisconsin where she had lived since 1867. She married Charles Wetherby.

When she died, her obituary[185] read "Eliza Pierson Wetherby, wife of Charles Wetherby, and daughter of Mary Pierson, died June 25th in Hudson, Wisconsin where she had lived for 25 years. Her mother (Mary Pierson) is over 90 years of age and survives her."

216 Joseph Pierson had chd. 422 John; 423 Joseph; 424 Rufus; 425 George. 425 George may be the George N. Pierson (b. at Jefferson Co., N.Y., age 15 in 1855) living with his uncle Moses Pierson at Charleston in the 1855 Montgomery Co., N.Y., census. Perhaps 216 Joseph Pierson died before 1855, leaving no wife to care for his youngest son. See 214 Moses Pierson and 417 William Nelson Pierson in this chapter for more information.

217 Rufus Pierson was born 19 Dec 1787 in New York state, and died 6 Jun 1865.[186] He lived in N.Y. state and was buried[187] at Esperence Cem., Esperence, Schoharie Co., N.Y. He mar. ca. 1811 Amy ____ (b. 3 Sep 1793, d. 3 Jul 1869) [188]. "Rufus Persons" (sic) is listed in the 1830 U.S. census at Charleston, Montgomery Co., N.Y. with family. "Rufus Pierson" purchased land in Montgomery Co. in 1824, 1829, and 1846. He served as a grand juror[189] in Montgomery Co., N.Y., in 1835: "Rufus Pierson, Charleston, tanner." The 1850 U.S. census at Sharon, Schoharie Co., N.Y. reports "Rufus Pierson, age 63, merchant, b. NY, Emmy (Amy on tombstone) age 57, David Aug. age 12, Elsma age 10, Eustacia F. age 17, M. Ann age 15." Rufus and Amy had chd. 426+ Henry R., b. 1810/15; 427+ A. Judson, b. 1815/20; 427a Eustacia F., b. 22 Aug 1832, d. 1 Dec 1920, bur. Four Corners Church, Charleston, Montgomery Co., N.Y., mar. Rev. H. J. Gordon (b. 26 Apr 1830, d. 20 Oct 1866); 427b Mary Ann, b. 1835; 428 David Augustus, b. 1838; 428a Elsma, b. 1840.

426 Henry R. Pierson was born 1810/15 per the 1830 U.S. census at Charleston, Montgomery Co., N.Y. "Henry R. Pierson, Esq. of New York" mar. 17 Oct 1849 "Sarah H., eldest dau. of Harvey Davis of Schenectady," N.Y.[190] He resided in Albany, N. Y. in 1878, and had chd. 492 Ida; 493 Henry.

427 A. Judson Pierson, resided in New York city 1878, a business man, and has chd. 494 Sarah; 495 William; 496 Frank.

84 James Pierson[191] was born in Oct. 1750, on Long Island, and died 28 Mar 1777 (during the Revolutionary War). He mar. 11 Mar 1773, 105 Martha Peirson (b. 12 Jul 1754), dau. of 51 Silvanus and Rebecca (Lupton) Peirson of Bridgehampton, Long Island, N.Y. James and Martha settled at Mendham Township, Morris Co., N.J., and had chd. in New Jersey: 218 Silvanus, b. 28 Dec 1773, mar. 21 Jan 1804 Elizabeth Hinkel; and 218a Rebecca, b. 11 Mar 1776, d. 27 Apr 1778.

---

[185]From a newspaper obituary kept in the family Bible (since lost) of Karl E. Pierson in 1988, no date, place, or newspaper given, but probably dated about 27 Jun 1892 at Amsterdam, N.Y.

[186]Gertrude A. Barber, *Schoharie County, NY, Cemetery Records*, 1932, vol. 5, p. 29.

[187]Gertrude A. Barber, *Schoharie County, NY, Cemetery Records*, 1932, vol. 5, p. 29.

[188]Gertrude A. Barber, *Schoharie County, NY, Cemetery Records*, 1932, vol. 5, p. 29.

[189]Arthur C. M. Kelly, *Grand Jurors of Montgomery Co., N.Y., 1816-1850*, 1989, p. 29.

[190]Marriages, Schenectady County Newspapers, Item 163: "Freedom's Sentinel or Schenectady Cabinet, Tuesday, October 23, 1849."

[191]Joseph R. Klett, *Genealogies of New Jersey Families*, From the Genealogical Magazine of New Jersey, Vols. I & II, Genealogical Publishing Co., Inc., Baltimore, 1996, pp. 666-667, "Pierson - Sutton Family Records," original in possession of the New Jersey Genealogical Society.

James' widow, Martha Pierson, mar. 2nd 14 Apr 1778 Joseph Sutton (b. 9 Jul 1747, d. 8 Nov 1822) of Mendham, Morris Co., N.J, son of Zebulon and Mary Sutton. Joseph Sutton had siblings: Patience, b. 31 May 1732; Jonathan, b. 23 Mar 1735; Jeremiah, b. 29 Oct 1738; Uriah, b. 21 Jul 1741; Mary, b. 19 Sep 1744; and Anne, b. 20 Dec 1750. Joseph and Martha (Pierson) Sutton had Sutton chd. in New Jersey: Joseph, b. 9 Jul 1747; Uriah, b. 28 Mar 1779, mar. 25 Jan 1807 Ann Howell; Shadrach, b. 28 Mar 1781, mar. 1st 19 Aug 1804 Fanny Seward (d. 25 Jan 1806), mar. 2nd ca. 1807 Sarah (Sally) Stewart (d. 23 Apr 1822); Rebecca, b. 2 Jun 1783, mar. 11 Aug 1803 Luther Conkling; Jonathan, b. 13 Feb 1787, mar. 5 Nov 1809 Martha Upson; Elizabeth Ann, b. 19 Jun 1789, mar. 19 Jun 1811 William Babbitt; Martha Lupton, b. 27 Sep 1792, mar. 27 Feb 1812 Aaron Carson (d. 20 Feb 1823); James, b. 4 Jul 1796, mar. 10 Feb 1818 Julia Ann Beach; Joseph Pierson, b. 9 Nov 1798, mar. 13 Nov 1821 Piersa Horton.

42 Capt. Nathan Pierson was born 1723 on Long Island. He held a one-year town office as Trustee in 1754[192]. He received a land grant from the town of Southampton in 1763[193] at the Little South Division. Nathan moved about 1765 from Long Island to Richmond, Mass., where he established and operated a large and profitable tannery, till the time of his death in 1826. He mar. Abigail (dau. of Daniel Hedges? [194]), and had chd. 85+ Nathan; 86+ Zechariah, b. 1750, d. 1827; 87 Sarah; 88+ Jeremiah."

85 Nathan Pierson, born before May 1759 (at least age 16 at signing the Association) and before 1750 if the eldest son (so indicated by moving to his father's location at his father's death). He signed the Association against British tyranny in May 1775[195] at County Hall, Suffolk Co., New York. He was living in the Bridgehampton area (East of Watermill) during the July 4, 1776 census of Southampton with 2 males and 2 females including he and his wife. He stayed on Long Island during the 7-year British occupation of the Revolutionary War (1776-1783). In 1779[196], he witnessed the will of his great uncle Abraham Peirson at Southampton where he signed "Nathan Peirson, yeoman." In 1782, the town of Southampton granted him property at the last division in Topping's Purchase[197], and at the last division in Quoug Purchase[198]. In 1790[199], Nathan built a home on property located on the west side of Sagg Street, north of Parsonage Lane. In 1804, Nathan was still in the Southampton township as reported by the Southampton Commissioners of Highways which stated "Nathan Peirson, we sold him 8 poles[200] of ground, also sold him a piece of land in front of his Downs lot, containing 6 poles of ground making a straight line from Thos. Peirson's NW corner to David Peirson's SW corner." Between 1804 and probably 1811 (when his son Nathan Jr. is executor to a will 5 miles to the east of

---

[192] *Town Records of Southampton*, NY, Liber B (Vol. 3), p.241.

[193] *Town Records of Southampton*, NY, Liber B (Vol. 3), p. 320-24.

[194] George Rogers Howell, *The Early History of Southampton, L.I., New York with Genealogies*, Second Edition, Weed, Parsons and Company, Albany, NY, 1887, p. 288.

[195] Frederic Mather, *The Refugees of 1776 from Long Island to Connecticut*, Genealogical Publishing Co., Baltimore, Maryland, 1972, p. 1055.

[196] Berthold Fernow, *Calendar of Wills*, on file and recorded in the offices of the Clerk of the Court of Appeals, of the County Clerk at Albany and by the Secretary of State (New York) 1626-1836, compiled 1896, p. 309, No. 1359.

[197] *Town Records of Southampton*, NY, Liber B (Vol. 3), p. 405-410.

[198] *Town Records of Southampton*, NY, Liber B (Vol. 3), p. 410-15.

[199] Co-chairmen Mrs. Albert W. Topping and Everett C. Foster, Editor Paul H. Curts, *Bridgehampton's Three Hundred Years*, The Hampton Press, Bridgehampton, N.Y., 1856, p. 11.

[200] When used as an area, one pole equals a piece of ground measuring 16.5 ft x 16.5 ft.

Richmond) he moved to Richmond, Mass., where he resided and was post-master, till 1828 at about age 80. He had chd., probably all born on Long Island, 219 Jerusha; 220 David; 221 Sanford; 222+ Nathan; 223 J. Sayre; 224 Franklin; 225 Lucy; 226 Eliz.; 227 Catherine; 228 John R.; 229 Sylvanus.

222 Nathan Pierson Jr., born on Long Island, probably moved to Richmond, Mass., after 1804 with his father. In 1811, 5 miles to the east of Richmond, Mass., at Canaan, Colombia Co., New York, Asa Douglass wrote his will dated September 24, 1811; proved May 16, 1812; Abstract: "Asa Douglass, Canaan, Colombia Co., New York. Wife Sarah, sons Asa, Zebulon, Haratio G., daughters Sarah Wright, Olive Warner, Eliza Fordham, Nancy Pierson, Polly Pierson, heirs of son John. Real and personal property. Executors the wife with sons-in-law Daniel Warner and Nathan Pierson Jun.[201] " Thus Nathan Pierson Jr. married either Nancy or Polly Douglass prior to 24 Sep 1811, living perhaps at Canaan, New York. They had chd. 429 John D.; 430 Robbins; 431 Sarah.

86 Zechariah Pierson was born 1750 in Suffolk Co., N.Y., and died Nov. 15, 1827, at Richmond, Mass. In May 1775, he signed the Association of Americans against British tyranny at Southampton (Suffolk County Hall), N.Y. (see Chapter 16). During the Revolutionary War, "Zechariah Pierson" was among the enlisted men included[202] on 10 Feb 1776 in Capt. David Pierson's 2nd Southampton Company of the Minutemen Regiment. In the 4 July 1776 Southampton census, east of the Watermill, he is listed as "Zechariah Peirson" with one male over 16 (Zechariah), 1 male under 16, 1 female over 16 (Zechariah's wife), and 1 female under 16. After the British took and occupied Long Island during the Revolutionary War, Zechariah was moved from Sagaponack to East Haddam, Connecticut, on 2 Sep 1776, with one person and goods by Capt. Elijah Mason; and also in Sep 1776, five persons and goods to Chester, Connecticut, by the same Captain. During or after the war, Zechariah moved to Richmond, Mass., where his father, Capt. Nathan, had gone about 1765. It is known that Zechariah went to Richmond, Mass. before 2 July 1787 when he is not among the signers of an agreement between the residents of Bridgehampton (Suffolk Co., N.Y.) and Rev. Aaron Woolworth. Zechariah was a justice of the peace at Richmond, Mass. He had chd. 230+ James; 231 Jerusha; 232+ Silas; 233 Ketura; 234 Sarah; 235 Mary; 236 Alvah; 237+ William; 238 Henry; 239+ Myron; 240 Lucinda.

230 James Pierson had chd. 432 Franklin; 433 Sarah; 434 James H.; 435 Nathan.

232 Silas Pierson had chd 436 Zechariah; 437 Charles.

237 William Pierson had chd. 438 Edwin D.; 439 Levi R.; 440 Albert.

239 Myron Pierson had chd. 441 Douglas. Perhaps Myron Pierson is the other Pierson married to one of Asa Douglass' daughters, Nancy or Polly Douglass, mentioned in the Asa Douglass will under 222 Nathan Pierson Jr. above.

[201]Berthold Fernow, Compiler, *Calendar of Wills*, on file and recorded in the offices of the Clerk of the Court of Appeals, of the County Clerk at Albany, N.Y., and of the Secretary of State (N.Y.) 1626-1836, 1896, #555.
[202]Frederic Mather, *The Refugees of 1776 from Long Island to Connecticut*, Genealogical Publishing Company, Baltimore, MD, 1972, pp. 995-996.

88 Jeremiah Pierson was born on Long Island. In 1808[203], he was elected to the Southampton office of Overseer of Highways district 9. He had chd. 241 Silas; 242 Henry; 243 Jeremiah; 244 Jerusha; 245 Mary; 246 Laura; 247 James.

43 Stephen Pierson was born in 1729 (1721?) in Bridgehampton, Suffolk Co., N.Y., and died after 2 July 1787 probably at Bridgehampton. There may be a problem with Stephen's birth year of 1729 as given here by Lizzie Pierson since father and son Ens. Theophilus are born only 14 years apart in this record. The Ens. Theophilus birth appears correct, however, since Theophilus had 5 children under 16 in the Southampton 1776 census. Thus Stephen Pierson's birth may have been earlier, about 1721. Stephen witnessed a land transaction at Southampton on Long Island in 1747[204]. In 1760[205], Stephen sold his share in Lot 4, Canoe Place Division in Southampton Township to Ephraim Hildreth. The town of Southampton granted Stephen land in 1763[206] at Little South Division; and in 1782 at the last division in Topping's Purchase[207] and at the last division in Quoug Purchase[208]. In May 1775, Stephen signed the Association of Americans against British tyranny at Southampton (Suffolk County Hall), N.Y. (see Chapter 16). In the Southampton census of July 4, 1776, east of the Watermill, Stephen is listed with one male (Stephen) and one female (his wife, his children have all left home). After the British took and occupied Long Island, Stephen Peirson was moved from Bridgehampton to Stonington, Connecticut, in Sep 1776 by Capt. Eliphalet Budington. On 2 July 1787, Stephen was among the signers of an agreement between the residents of Bridgehampton and Rev. Aaron Woolworth. Stephen's wife is unknown. He had chd. 89+ Theophilus (Ensign), b. 1743; 90+ Elias, b. 1748.

89 Theophilus Pierson, Ens., was born in 1743. In May 1775, he signed the Association against British tyranny[209] at Southampton (Suffolk County Hall), N.Y. The Census of the Township of Southampton, July 4, 1776[210], East of the Watermill, listed the Theophilus Pierson family with 1 male age 16 to 50 (Theophilus), 3 males under 16 (children), 1 female over 16 (Theophilus' wife), and 2 females under 16 (children). This census was taken in preparation of the Revolutionary War. The battle of Long Island was fought a few months later, and Long Island was occupied by the British from 1776 to 1783. After the battle of Long Island in 1776, the surviving remnants of the 2nd Regiment and Minutemen were reconstructed and commissioned 13 Sep 1776 at a mainland site into the 2nd Battalion of Suffolk County with nine companies. The 3rd Company was commanded by Capt. David Pierson[211], and his staff included 1st Lt. Daniel Hedges[212], 2nd Lt. David Sayre, and Ensign Theophilus Pierson. This reorganization took place, as reported by the orders of

[203] *Town Records of Southampton*, NY, Liber B (Vol. 3), p. 535.

[204] *Town Records of Southampton*, NY, Liber B (Vol. 3), p. 200, Abstract.

[205] *Town Records of Southampton*, NY, Liber B (Vol. 3), p. 273, Abstract.

[206] *Town Records of Southampton*, NY, Liber B (Vol. 3), p. 320-24.

[207] *Town Records of Southampton*, NY, Liber B (Vol. 3), p. 405-410.

[208] *Town Records of Southampton*, NY, Liber B (Vol. 3), p. 410-15.

[209] Frederic Mather, *The Refugees of 1776 from Long Island to Connecticut*, Genealogical Publishing Co., Baltimore, Maryland, 1972, p. 1055.

[210] Henry Hedges, Wm. Pelletreau, Edward Foster, *The Third Book of Records of the Town of Southampton, Long Island, N.Y. with other Ancient Documents of Historic Value*, John H. Hunt, Printer, Sag Harbor, NY, 1878, Appendix, pp. 391-9.

[211] Capt. David$_5$, Lemuel$_4$, David$_3$, Col. Henry$_2$, Henry$_1$

[212] Husband of Susanna Peirson and son-in-law of Josiah Peirson.

General Washington, "in order that such as was needed to protect their homes should return, and others as preferred could enlist under a new organization." To escape British occupation and a demand for an oath of allegiance to England, many Long Island families took refuge on the mainland, arriving first at the American-held state of Connecticut, for the duration of the Revolutionary War, including[213] Ens. Theophilus Peirson, who was moved from Bridgehampton to Stonington, Connecticut, in Sep 1776, with five passengers and goods, by Capt. Amos Pendleton; and in Oct 1776, with five passengers and goods, by Capt. David Sayre. It is probable that Theophilus was at Westfield, Essex Co., N.J., when he wasn't on military maneuvers, based on the tax list[214] there in July 1781 which included a "Theophilus Person" along with two other Long Island Piersons (Abraham and Sylvanus) in addition to descendants of Benjamin Peirson of Long Island (William, Daniel, and David). It is clear, in an agreement between the residents of Bridgehampton and Rev. Aaron Woolworth dated 2 July 1787 which was signed by Theophilus Peirson and 19 other Peirsons, that Theophilus returned to Bridgehampton after the British occupation was over in 1783. In 1788[215] and 1798[216], Theophilus was elected at Southampton as Overseer of Highways 6th district.

Theophilus had chd. born at Bridgehampton, Suffolk Co., N.Y. (or at Westfield, Essex Co., N.J.): 248+ Elias Jr.; 249+ Charles; 250 Jeremiah; 251+ Paul; 252 Harvey; 253 Solon; 253a&b two daus. (ref. 1776 Southampton census); and perhaps other daus. born after the 1776 census.

248 Elias Pierson Jr. was called Junior to distinguish him from his uncle 90 Elias Pierson. Elias Jr. was among the signers of an agreement between the residents of Southampton and the Rev. Joshua Williams dated 30 Dec 1784[217].

249 Charles Pierson was born about 1766 at Bridgehampton, Suffolk Co., N.Y. On 2 July 1787, he was among the signers of an agreement between the residents of Bridgehampton and Rev. Aaron Woolworth. He had chd. 442 Henry.

251 Paul Pierson was born either at Bridgehampton, N.Y., or Stonington, Conn., and had chd. 443 James F.; 444 Chas. F.

90 Elias Pierson, Corp., was born 1748 at Southampton (age 28 in 26 July 1776 military record which said born Southampton). He had cattle in 1768 at Southampton[218], Suffolk Co., N.Y., as verified by his "brand S. P., which was his father's" and earmark registration. The S. P. also verifies his father was Stephen Pierson. "Corp. Elias Peirson" served during the Revolutionary War in Col. Smith's and Col. Mulford's Regiment, in the latter under Capt. Zephaniah Roger's 1st Company (raised for protection to the inhabitants and stock of

[213]Frederic Mather, *The Refugees of 1776 from Long Island to Connecticut*, Genealogical Publishing Company, Baltimore, MD, 1972, pp. 504-8.
[214]MicroQuix, *Colonial America - Pre-1790 Census Indexes, Tax Lists*, No. CD136, Automated Archives, Inc., 1992.
[215]*Town Records of Southampton*, NY, Liber B (Vol. 3), p. 442.
[216]*Town Records of Southampton*, NY, Liber B (Vol. 3), p. 485-6.
[217]George Rogers Howell, *The Early History of Southampton, L. I., New York, with Genealogies*, Albany, New York, 2nd Edition, 1887, pp. 112-113.
[218]*Town Records of Southampton*, NY, Liber B (Vol. 3), p. 341, Abstract.

Long Island). His military record read[219] on 26 July 1776: Elias Peirson, Corp., residence Southampton, age 28, born Southampton, 6 ft. 6 in. tall, dark complexion, dark hair, occupation weaver. To escape the British occupation of Long Island and a demand for an oath of allegiance to England, many Long Island families took refuge on the mainland in the American-held state of Connecticut for the duration of the Revolutionary War, including[220] Corp. Elias Peirson[221], from Sagaponack in Bridgehampton to East Haddam, Connecticut, in Sep 1776, brought to Connecticut by Capt. John Harris. After the war was over in 1783, Elias returned to Southampton. Elias was among the signers of an agreement between the residents of Southampton and the Rev. Joshua Williams dated 30 Dec 1784[222]. Elias had chd. 254 Jeremiah.

19 Abraham Pierson was born at Bridgehampton, L. I., in 1693. In 1701 his father, Col. Henry Peirson, died and left a will dated August 28, 1701[223]. It stated, in relation to Abraham:

"I give unto my two younger sons, Abraham Peirson & Josiah Peirson, to them, their heirs & assigns forever, equally to be divided, all yt piece of land which I bought of ye town of S'hampton & of Christopher Leaming, called ye Wood Close, bounded with a highway on ye South, with ye land of Theophilus Howell & ye parsonage land on ye East, with ye land of Capt. Topping, Benoni Flint and common land on North, with ye land of Robt. Norris & a highway on ye West thereof & also a fifty pound commonage throughout ye bounds of S'hampton & also four acres of land lying in S'hampton, join to ye east end of ye lot of Joseph Peirson & I do give unto each of them, my sd two sons, Abraham & Josiah Peirson, twenty five pounds in money, one horse, two steers, two cows & ten sheep as they shall come to ye age of twenty one years."

On April 25, 1726[224], Abraham Peirson's Lot is mentioned in Southampton township records as being at Sagg (Sagaponack in Bridgehampton). His home was located[225] on the east side of Sagg Street, north of Parsonage Lane. The home was next owned by his son Silas and then Caleb. In 1739[226], Abraham and his brother, Josiah Pierson, sell 1/2 of lot 48 of meadow on west beach to Nathan Herrick. In 1747[227], "Abram Pierson," Elnathan White, and Job Pierson made a significant purchase of 50 acres of land from Josiah Topping at Sag, called Smiths corner, bounded W & S by Sagg pond, E by Elnathan White, N by bridge lane, price 585 pounds. Abraham received land grants from the town of

[219]Frederic Mather, *The Refugees of 1776 from Long Island to Connecticut*, Genealogical Publishing Company, Baltimore, MD, 1972, pp. 1003-1004.

[220]Frederic Mather, *The Refugees of 1776 from Long Island to Connecticut*, Genealogical Publishing Company, Baltimore, MD, 1972, pp. 504-8.

[221]Corp. Elias$_5$, Stephen$_4$, Theophilus$_3$, Col. Henry$_2$, Henry$_1$

[222]George Rogers Howell, *The Early History of Southampton, L. I., New York, with Genealogies*, Albany, New York, 2nd Edition, 1887, pp. 112-113.

[223]William S. Pelletreau, *Early Long Island Wills of Suffolk County, 1691-1703, With Genealogical and Historical Notes*, Francis P. Harper, New York, NY, 1897, pp. 239-41.

[224]*Town Records of Southampton*, NY, Liber A, No. 2, 1st Part, pp. 289-90.

[225]Co-chairmen Mrs. Albert W. Topping and Everett C. Foster, Editor Paul H. Curts, *Bridgehampton's Three Hundred Years*, The Hampton Press, Bridgehampton, N.Y., 1856, p. 11.

[226]*Town Records of Southampton*, NY, Liber B (Vol. 3), p. 94. Abstract.

[227]*Town Records of Southampton*, NY, Liber B (Vol. 3), p. 197. Abstract.

Southampton: in 1727[228] at Seder Swamps; in 1738[229] at the south and north divisions of lots of timber land between the Indian line and East Hampton; in 1745[230] at Sagg Harbor; in 1763[231] at Aucaubogue Division in Toppings Purchase; in 1763[232] at Little South Division; in 1782[233] at last division in Topping's Purchase; and in 1782[234] at last division in Quoug Purchase. Abraham held one-year town offices at Southampton: in 1733[235] as Constable; in 1736[236] as Trustee; in 1738[237] as Supervisor of Intestate estates; in 1742[238] as Trustee; in 1748[239] as Trustee; in 1757[240] as Trustee; in 1759[241] as Trustee; and in 1765[242] as Trustee.

In the 4 July 1776 Southampton census, Abraham is listed as one male over 50 and one female over 16. Since his second wife Prudence Howell died in 1776, it is unknown if the female is his wife or daughter Elizabeth.

Abraham wrote his will at age 82 which was dated October 30, 1779[243], and was proved January 31, 1787, when he was age 89 or 90. Abstracted: Abraham Peirson of Southampton, Suffolk County (New York), farmer. Sons William, Zebulon, Matthew, dau. Elizabeth, wife of Lemuel Peirson. Real and personal estate. Executors sons Zebulon and Matthew. Witnesses Nathan Peirson, yeoman, Silvanus Peirson and Silvanus Topping. Recorded Vol. I Wills and Probates, p. 28. His son Silas is not mentioned in the will, but Silas became the next owner of Abraham's home lot. Therefore, it is likely that Silas inherited the home lot before the date of his father's will in 1779. Perhaps Silas also took care of his father Abraham during those last years as part of the deal.

Abraham mar. 1st[244] Jan. 7, 1720, Elizabeth Conkling of East Hampton, and mar. 2nd[245] Prudence Howell[246] (b. 1702, d. 1776), by whom he had chd. 44+ Matthew, b. 1744; 45+ Zebulon; 46+ Silas, (not mentioned in father's will in 1779); 47+ William; 47a Elizabeth,

228 *Town Records of Southampton*, NY, Liber A, No. 2, 1st Part, pp. 296-9.
229 *Town Records of Southampton*, NY, Liber B (Vol. 3), p. 157.
230 *Town Records of Southampton*, NY, Liber B (Vol. 3), p. 143-6.
231 *Town Records of Southampton*, NY, Liber B (Vol. 3), p. 302-06.
232 *Town Records of Southampton*, NY, Liber B (Vol. 3), p. 320-24.
233 *Town Records of Southampton*, NY, Liber B (Vol. 3), p. 405-410.
234 *Town Records of Southampton*, NY, Liber B (Vol. 3), p. 410-15.
235 *Town Records of Southampton*, NY, Liber B (Vol. 3), p. 137.
236 *Town Records of Southampton*, NY, Liber B (Vol. 3), p. 138.
237 *Town Records of Southampton*, NY, Liber B (Vol. 3), p. 138.
238 *Town Records of Southampton*, NY, Liber B (Vol. 3), p. 139.
239 *Town Records of Southampton*, NY, Liber B (Vol. 3), p.201.
240 *Town Records of Southampton*, NY, Liber B (Vol. 3), p.261.
241 *Town Records of Southampton*, NY, Liber B (Vol. 3), p.268.
242 *Town Records of Southampton*, NY, Liber B (Vol. 3), p. 334.
243 Berthold Fernow, *Calendar of Wills*, on file and recorded in the offices of the Clerk of the Court of Appeals, of the County Clerk at Albany and by the Secretary of State (New York) 1626-1836, compiled 1896, p. 309, No. 1359.
244 George Rogers Howell, *The Early History of Southampton, L.I., New York with Genealogies*, 2nd Edition, Weed, Parsons and Company, Albany, NY, 1887, p. 351.
245 George Rogers Howell, *The Early History of Southampton, L.I., New York with Genealogies*, 2nd Edition, Weed, Parsons and Company, Albany, NY, 1887, p. 351.
246 George Rogers Howell, *The Early History of Southampton, L.I., New York with Genealogies*, 2nd Edition, Weed, Parsons and Company, Albany, NY, 1887, p. 306.

mar. her 2nd cousin[247], Lemuel Peirson 3d, son of Job Peirson (children not necessarily in that order).

44 Matthew Pierson was born in 1744, and had chd. 91 Hiram; 92+ Silas, b. 1789[248].

92 Silas, b. 1789, had wife Elizabeth (b. 1797) and chd. 741 Lawrence b. 1823; 742 Caleb b. 1834; 743 Charles b. 1835; and 744 Caroline b. 1838.[249]

45 Zebulon Pierson was born before 4 July 1726 (over age 50 in the 1776 census) at Sagaponack, Suffolk Co., N.Y. colony, and died after 2 July 1787 when he signed the Bridgehampton (Suffolk Co., N.Y.) minister's agreement. He had cattle in 1755[250] as confirmed by his earmark registered at Southampton. In May 1775, he signed the Association of Americans against British tyranny at Southampton (Suffolk County Hall), N.Y. (see Chapter 16). In the 4 July 1776 Southampton census, east of the Watermill, he was listed with one male over 50 (Zebulon), 2 males 16 to 50, 1 male under 16, one female over 16 (Zebulon's wife), and 3 females (daughters) under 16 years of age. After the British took and occupied Long Island, Zebulon and his effects were moved Sep 1776 from Bridgehampton to Saybrook, Conn., by Capt. Zebulon Stow. On 16 Sep 1776, Zebulon and five in the family and goods were moved to East Haddam, Conn., by Capt. Joshua Griffeth. The town of Southampton granted him land in 1782[251] at the last Division in Topping's Purchase. On 2 July 1787, he was among the signers of an agreement between the residents of Bridgehampton and Rev. Aaron Woolworth. His wife is unknown. He had chd. 93+ John; 94+ Abraham; 95+ D. Williams; and 95a, 95b, & 95c at least three daughters (1776 census).

93 John Pierson, Sgt., was born about 1755 (plus or minus 2 years) in Southampton Township, Suffolk Co., N.Y. In May 1775, he was under age 20 (living with his father Zebulon in the 1776 Southampton census) when he signed the Association of Americans against British tyranny at Southampton (Suffolk County Hall), N.Y. (see Chapter 16). On 10 Feb 1776, he was an enlisted man[252] in Capt. David Pierson's 2nd Southampton Company of the Minutemen Regiment. On 10 Aug 1776, he was listed as a Sergeant[253] in Capt. Zephaniah Roger's 1st Company (raised for protection to the inhabitants and stock of Long Island). On 2 July 1787, John was among the signers of an agreement between the residents of Bridgehampton and Rev. Aaron Woolworth. No record of a wife and children was found in Southampton records.

---

[247]George Rogers Howell, *The Early History of Southampton, L.I., New York with Genealogies*, 2nd Edition, Weed, Parsons and Company, Albany, NY, 1887, p. 352.

[248]George Rogers Howell, *The Early History of Southampton, L.I., New York with Genealogies*, 2nd Edition, Weed, Parsons and Company, Albany, NY, 1887, p. 351.

[249]George Rogers Howell, *The Early History of Southampton, L.I., New York with Genealogies*, 2nd Edition, Weed, Parsons and Company, Albany, NY, 1887, p. 351.

[250]*Town Records of Southampton*, NY, Liber B (Vol. 3), p. 242. Abstract.

[251]*Town Records of Southampton*, NY, Liber B (Vol. 3), p. 405-410.

[252]Frederic Mather, *The Refugees of 1776 from Long Island to Connecticut*, Genealogical Publishing Company, Baltimore, MD, 1972, pp. 995-996.

[253]Frederic Mather, *The Refugees of 1776 from Long Island to Connecticut*, Genealogical Publishing Company, Baltimore, MD, 1972, pp. 1003-1004.

94 Abraham Pierson Jr. fought in the Revolutionary War in Col. Smith's Minutemen Regiment, 2nd Southampton Company under the command of Capt. David Pierson. He was part of the 60 Rank and File of enlisted men listed[254] in a 10 Feb 1776 report of that Regiment. After the British took & occupied Long Island in 1776, Abraham joined the Connecticut militia. He returned to Bridgehampton after the war ended in 1783. He had cattle in 1785[255] as confirmed by his cattle earmark registered at Southampton. In 1805[256], he held a one-year town office at Southampton of Overseer of Highways 7th District. He had chd. 255 Huntting; 256 Ruth; 257+ Isaac; 258 Eliphalet.

257 Isaac Pierson lived in Bridgehampton, and had dau.[257], 860+ Malsey.

860 Malsey Pierson[258] was the 1st wife of Nymphas Wright (a farmer of Bridgehampton, who mar. 2d Sophia Halsey), son of Nymphas and Hannah Wright of Middle Haddam, Conn. Nymphas and Malsey had Wright chd. Hannah E. (mar. Samuel O. Hedges), and Morgan P.

95 D. Williams Pierson was among the signers of an agreement between the residents of Bridgehampton and Rev. Aaron Woolworth dated 2 July 1787. He had chd. 259 Nathan; 260 John; 261 Stephen.

46 Silas Pierson was perhaps the eldest child of his father Abraham. Silas is not mentioned in his father's will written in 1779, but Silas becomes the next owner of his father's home lot. He probably is not mentioned in the will because he has already inherited his share by 1779. The next owner of the home lot after Silas was Caleb Pierson. Perhaps Silas had chd. 914 Caleb.

47 William Pierson was born at Sagaponack, Suffolk Co., N.Y. (see father's location in town records of 1726) before 1728 (based on being at least age 14 when he witnessed his first land transaction in 1742). He witnessed land transactions at Southampton, which his father Abraham also witnessed, in 1742[259] and 1752[260]. He is the first son mentioned in his father's will in 1779[261] which was proved 31 Jan 1787, but he did not inherit his father's home lot. His brother Silas, who was not mentioned in the will inherited the home lot probably before the will was written. On 2 July 1787, William was among the signers of an agreement between the residents of Bridgehampton and Rev. Aaron Woolworth.

---

[254] Frederic Mather, *The Refugees of 1776 from Long Island to Connecticut*, Genealogical Publishing Company, Baltimore, MD, 1972, pp. 995-996.

[255] *Town Records of Southampton*, NY, Liber B (Vol. 3), p. 424. Abstract.

[256] *Town Records of Southampton*, NY, Liber B (Vol. 3), p. 519.

[257] Co-chairmen Mrs. Albert W. Topping and Everett C. Foster, Editor Paul H. Curts, Bridgehampton's Three Hundred Years, The Hampton Press, Bridgehampton, N.Y., 1956, p. 10.

[258] George Rogers Howell, *The Early History of Southampton, L.I., New York with Genealogies*, 2nd Edition, Weed, Parsons and Company, Albany, NY, 1887, p. 409.

[259] *Town Records of Southampton*, NY, Liber B (Vol. 3), p. 182, Abstract.

[260] *Town Records of Southampton*, NY, Liber B (Vol. 3), p. 116. Abstract.

[261] Berthold Fernow, *Calendar of Wills*, on file and recorded in the offices of the Clerk of the Court of Appeals, of the County Clerk at Albany and by the Secretary of State (New York) 1626-1836, compiled 1896, p. 309, No. 1359.

20 Josiah Pierson was born at Bridgehampton (Sagg), Long Island, in 1695, and died 1776, in his 82nd year (age 81), at Sagg[262] (Sagaponack, 1 mile east of Bridgehampton, Suffolk Co., NY). Josiah's father, Colonel Henry Peirson, died in 1701 when Josiah was six years of age leaving him in a will dated 28 Aug 1701[263]:

"I give unto my two younger sons, Abraham Peirson & Josiah Peirson, to them, their heirs & assigns forever, equally to be divided, all yt piece of land which I bought of ye town of S'hampton & of Christopher Leaming, called ye Wood Close, bounded with a highway on ye South, with ye land of Theophilus Howell & ye parsonage land on ye East, with ye land of Capt. Topping, Benoni Flint and common land on North, with ye land of Robt. Norris & a highway on ye West thereof & also a fifty pound commonage throughout ye bounds of S'hampton & also four acres of land lying in S'hampton, join to ye east end of ye lot of Joseph Peirson & I do give unto each of them, my sd two sons, Abraham & Josiah Peirson, twenty five pounds in money, one horse, two steers, two cows & ten sheep as they shall come to ye age of twenty one years."

In 1717[264], Josiah owned cattle at Southampton township as verified by earmark registration. He lived on the north side of the main road from Southampton to East Hampton, called the upper road, at its intersection with the west side of Sagg Street and near the "North Burialground" (Poxebug) on the east side of that street. He was buried in the mentioned cemetery.

From 1727 to 1765 (ages 32 to 70), Josiah Peirson was elected 32 times[265] to one-year civil service duties at Southampton on Long Island, New York colony. He was a Trustee of the town of Southampton for four years (1727, 1752, 1755, and 1758). Josiah also served as an Assessor for ten years (1731, 1738, 1752, 1754, 1755, 1758, 1759, 1760, 1763, and 1765). He was chosen a Land Commissioner for 18 years between 1740 and 1759.

Josiah's land transactions from 1718 to 1782 included[266]: 1718 traded 3 acres with Nathaniel Howell; 1727 granted land at Seder Swamps from town of Southampton; 1729 sells some Southampton land rights to John Morehouse; 1732 bought a half lot from Daniel Sayre; 1735 bought acreage from John Norris at Bridgehampton; 1738 bought 12 acres from John and Nathan Norris; 1738 received 3 land grants from town of Southampton at north & south divisions in Quaquanantuck Purchase and at timber land between Indian line and East Hampton; 1739 bought 1/8 share of Montauk; 1739 he and his brother Abraham sell a half lot in meadow on West Beach to Nathan Herrick; 1739 bought 260 acres in Bridgehampton and in north & south divisions of Southampton from Thomas Stephens; 1745 received a land grant at Sagg Harbor from town of Southampton; 1752 swapped 2 acres in harbor area; 1761 received land grant from Southampton in 12 acres division of Sagg Harbor; 1763 received 3 land grants from Southampton at Aucaubogue in Quogue

[262]Henry B. Hoff, *Long Island Source Records From The New York Genealogical and Biographical Record*, "Genealogy of Pierson - The Family of Margaret Pierson, wife of John Jermain, Genealogical Publishing Co., Baltimore, MD, 1987.

[263]William S. Pelletreau, *Early Long Island Wills of Suffolk County, 1691-1703, With Genealogical and Historical Notes*, Francis P. Harper, New York, NY, 1897, pp. 239-41.

[264]*Town Records of Southampton*, NY, Liber A, No. 2, 1st Part, pp. 277-9.

[265]*Town Records of Southampton*, NY, 1727 to 1765 entries.

[266]*Town Records of Southampton*, NY, 1718 to 1782 entries.

Purchase, Aucaubogue in Topping's Purchase, and Little South Division; 1764 bought two small highways laid through amendment in Little South Division; and in 1782 (6 years after Josiah died) received land grant from Southampton in Last Division in Quogue Purchase to "Josiah Pierson's heirs."

When Josiah died in 1776, his will[267] gave all his property to three sons and a daughter who were then in the Bridgehampton area:

"I give unto my son, Mathew Pierson, my house and all my buildings and the one half of the lot of land on the north side of my home lot and the land lying on the east side of the land of Sylvanus Topping and Peter Hildreth, and one half of my lot of land called Sayre's lot on the west side, and one third part of my wood lot lying in the Lots 1 and 2, and one half of fifty throughout the township of Southampton. I give unto my son, Sylvanus Pierson, my buildings and my lot of land called Norrissee Lot, and one half of my lot called Home Lot on the south side, and one third part of my wood Land adjoining on the Lots No. 1 and 2. I give unto my son, Timothy Pierson, my buildings and the lot of land bounded by David Hand's land on the west and the north and Lemuel Pierson on the east, south by the road, and one half of my lot of land called Sears Lot, and one third part of my wood land lying on the south Division. All the rest of my Estate after paying my debts to be divided equally between Mathew, Sylvanus, Timothy and Susannah Pierson."

Josiah Pierson was married four times, and had 17 children[268]:

Josiah married 1st, 1716 at Suffolk Co., New York colony, Martha Petty, probably the daughter of Edward Petty[269] of Southampton. They had chd., all born at Bridgehampton, Suffolk Co., New York colony, 48a Hannah, born about 1717, died in infancy; twins 48b Josiah and 48c Elnathan, born about 1719, both died in infancy. Perhaps the mother, Martha Petty, died at the birth of the twins as Josiah remarries in 1722.

Josiah married 2nd, 1722 at Suffolk Co., New York colony, Mary Gilbert, daughter of Caleb Gilbert of Southampton. They had son 48+ Silas, b. 23 Jan 1723 at Bridgehampton, Suffolk Co., New York colony, d. 26 Feb 1804 at Hamptonburgh, Orange Co., New York. Perhaps the mother, Mary Gilbert, died at Silas's birth as there is no more children of this marriage and Josiah marries again a year later.

Josiah married 3rd, 1724 at Suffolk Co., New York colony, Martha Halsey (b. 1699 Southampton, d. 1774, bur. Poxebug cemetery at Sagg), daughter of Jeremiah and Ruth Halsey. They had 13 children, all born at Bridgehampton, Suffolk Co., New York colony: 50+ Matthew b. 2 Mar 1725, d. 1798; 51+ Sylvanus (twin of 50 Matthew) b. 2 Mar 1725, d. 23 Aug 1795[270] at Bridgehampton; 52+ Paul b. 1726; 55+ Martha b. 1728; 53+ Timothy b. 1731; 54+ Josiah b. Jan 1731/32; 49 John b. 1733, (d. bef. 1736 when the second John was born?);

[267] Orange County Genealogical Society, New York, *The History of Orange County, New York*, records from the family of Silas Pierson, son of Josiah Pierson.
[268] Orange County Genealogical Society, New York, *The History of Orange County, New York*, records from the family of Silas Pierson, son of Josiah Pierson.
[269] George Rogers Howell, The Early History of Southampton, L. I., New York, with Genealogies, second Edition, Weed, Parsons and Company, Albany, New York, 1887, p.436.
[270] Henry B. Hoff, *Long Island Source Records From The New York Genealogical and Biographical Record*, "Genealogy of Pierson - The Family of Margaret Pierson, wife of John Jermain, Genealogical Publishing Co., Baltimore, MD, 1987.

twins 56+ Joseph b. 1736, d. 1802 New York city, N.Y., mar. Anne Vielee; 59 John (twin of 56 Joseph), b. 1736, d. in infancy; 58+ Susannah b. 1737; 57+ Benjamin b. 1741; 61 Henry b. 1746, d. 1756; and 60+ Jeremiah b. 1752. (Children numbered per Lizzie Pierson's book, and sequenced by birth year from Orange Co. NY Genealogical Society information.)

Josiah, at age 79, married 4th, 1774 at Suffolk Co., New York colony, Esther Edwards. There were no children of this marriage. Josiah died in 1776 and Esther predeceased him.

48 Silas Pierson, Capt., was born 23 Jan 1723 at Bridgehampton, Suffolk Co., New York colony, and died 26 Feb 1804 at Hamptonburgh, Orange Co., N. Y., leaving sons Silas Jr., Josiah, & William and daus. Mary, Sarah, & Rachel. In 1749, Silas moved from Long Island to Hamptonburgh, Orange Co., N. Y. In 1760, Silas Sr. was a Captain[271] in the Militia Regiment commanded by Col. Benjamin Tusten Sr., his neighbor. Silas signed the Association to oppose the British in 1775, and was the Assessor of District No. 3 in Old Cornwall that year. He served as Captain in Col. Jesse Woodhull's Regiment during the Revolution (1775-1783) which took an active part in the defense of the highlands. Capt. Silas Pierson married[272] his cousin, Elizabeth Gilbert, daughter of Josiah Gilbert, his mother's brother. They had chd. 96+ Silas Jr., b. 10 Apr 1748; 96a+ Josiah[273], b. 23 Feb 1761; 97 William; 98 Martha; 99 Sarah; 99a Mary[274]; 99b Rachel[275].

96 Silas Pierson Jr. b. 10 Apr 1748[276] N.Y., d. 24 Feb 1804[277] N.Y. He signed the Association in 1775. He mar. Rachel Bull of Hamptonburgh, Orange Co., N.Y.[278], chd. 918 Jubal, b. 1785, who had 919 Albert (b. 1813) who had 920 Mary Ann (b. 1840, Ithaca, N.Y.).

96a Josiah Pierson was born 23 Feb 1761[279] in N.Y., and died 26 Mar 1826[280] in N.Y. During the Revolutionary War, he served as a Private in the N.Y. militia.[281] He married Frances, daughter of Rev. John Moffat of Little Britain, Orange Co., N.Y., and in 1788

---

[271]Orange County Genealogical Society, New York, *The History of Orange County, New York*, records from the family of Silas Pierson, son of Josiah Pierson.
[272]Orange County Genealogical Society, New York, *The History of Orange County, New York*, records from the family of Silas Pierson, son of Josiah Pierson.
[273]Orange County Genealogical Society, New York, *The History of Orange County, New York*, records from the family of Silas Pierson, son of Josiah Pierson.
[274]Orange County Genealogical Society, New York, *The History of Orange County, New York*, records from the family of Silas Pierson, son of Josiah Pierson.
[275]Orange County Genealogical Society, New York, *The History of Orange County, New York*, records from the family of Silas Pierson, son of Josiah Pierson.
[276]*DAR Patriot Index*, Centennial Edition, National Society of the Daughters of the American Revolution, 1994, part 3, p. 2259.
[277]*DAR Patriot Index*, Centennial Edition, National Society of the Daughters of the American Revolution, 1994, part 3, p. 2259.
[278]Orange County Genealogical Society, New York, *The History of Orange County, New York*, records from the family of Silas Pierson, son of Josiah Pierson.
[279]*DAR Patriot Index*, Centennial Edition, National Society of the Daughters of the American Revolution, 1994, part 3, p. 2258.
[280]*DAR Patriot Index*, Centennial Edition, National Society of the Daughters of the American Revolution, 1994, part 3, p. 2258.
[281]*DAR Patriot Index*, Centennial Edition, National Society of the Daughters of the American Revolution, 1994, part 3, p. 2258.

moved to Mt. Hope near Otisville, Orange Co., N.Y. They had sons: 745 Silas; 746 Gilbert; and 747 Henry[282].

50 Matthew Pierson was born 2 Mar 1725 at Bridgehampton, Suffolk Co., N.Y. colony and died 17 Oct 1798 at Sagg[283] in his 74th year (age 73). He is the twin of 51 Sylvanus. Matthew is believed to be the eldest of the twins because he inherited his father's house on his home lot. In 1776, Matthew's father, Josiah Peirson, died and left property to Matthew:

"I give unto my son, Mathew Pierson, my house and all my buildings and the one half of the lot of land on the north side of my home lot and the land lying on the east side of the land of Sylvanus Topping and Peter Hildreth, and one half of my lot of land called Sayre's lot on the west side, and one third part of my wood lot lying in the Lots 1 and 2, and one half of fifty throughout the township of Southampton. All the rest of my Estate after paying my debts to be divided equally between Mathew, Sylvanus, Timothy and Susannah Pierson."

"Matthew Peirson" signed the Association (against British tyranny), in 1775 at Southampton. The Southampton census of 4 July 1776 represented Matthew's family as 1 male over 50 years of age (Matthew), 1 male over 16 (son Henry), 1 female over 16 (Matthew's wife Phebe Moore). In September 1776, he and his family escaped the British occupation of Long Island during the Revolutionary War by moving to Connecticut. Matthew was taken across Long Island Sound initially by Capt. Isaac Sheffield, and later with one passenger and goods by the same. The last trip was on September 27, 1776, with six passengers (probably men to help move the goods) and goods, he was moved over by Capt. Ephraim Pendleton.[284]   In 1782[285], Matthew was granted land by the town of Southampton at the Last Division in Topping's Purchase, a right he inherited from his father. In 1787, Matthew was back on Long Island as confirmed by him signing the Agreement with Rev. Woolworth at Bridgehampton. This branch of the family continues to spell its name Peirson.

He mar. Phebe[286] (d. 23 Feb 1782 at age 52), dau. of Samuel Moore[287]. They had chd. 100+ Lucretia; 101+ Henry.

100 Lucretia Pierson married prior to 4 Jul 1776[288] Caleb Russell, of Morristown, N.J., formerly of Bridgehampton, N.Y. They had 9 Russell chd. including[289] Robert, Israel, & Eliza.

---

[282]Orange County Genealogical Society, New York, *The History of Orange County, New York*, records from the family of Silas Pierson, son of Josiah Pierson.

[283]Henry B. Hoff, *Long Island Source Records From The New York Genealogical and Biographical Record*, "Genealogy of Pierson - The Family of Margaret Pierson, wife of John Jermain, Genealogical Publishing Co., Baltimore, MD, 1987.

[284]Frederick Gregory Mather, *The Refugees of 1776 from Long Island to Connecticut*, Genealogical Publishing Co., Inc., Baltimore, MD, 1972, pp.506-7.

[285]*Town Records of Southampton*, NY, Liber B (Vol. 3), p. 405-410.

[286]George Rogers Howell, The Early History of Southampton, L. I., New York, with Genealogies, second Edition, Weed, Parsons and Company, Albany, New York, 1887, p.352.

[287]Frederick Gregory Mather, *The Refugees of 1776 from Long Island to Connecticut*, Genealogical Publishing Co., Inc., Baltimore, MD, 1972, pp.506-7. Source listed as Miss Alice E. Peirson and she says Matthew Peirson married either Phebe or Elizabeth, dau. of Samuel Moore.

101 Henry Peirson, Esq., was born about 1757 (plus or minus 2 years) in Southampton township, Suffolk Co., N.Y.   He was under age 20 when he signed the Association of Americans against British tyranny in May 1775 at Southampton (Suffolk County Hall), N.Y. He was living with his father 50 Matthew during the Southampton census of July 4, 1776, east of the Watermill. He mar. Phebe Mulford. He was among the signers of an agreement between the residents of Bridgehampton and Rev. Aaron Woolworth dated 2 July 1787. Henry held office at Southampton: in 1787[290], as a commissioner of highways; in 1789[291] as Overseer of Highways District 6; in 1793[292] as a commissioner of highways and as Justice. It was in his 1793 post as Justice that he was henceforth known a Henry Peirson, Esquire.   Henry Peirson Esq. was elected: in 1794[293] as commissioner of highways; in 1795[294] as trustee and continued to sit as Justice; in 1796[295] as commissioner of highways; in 1797[296] continued to sit as Justice; in 1798[297] as Assessor and Commissioner of Highways, and sitting as Justice; and on 2 Apr 1799[298] still sitting as Justice. Henry moved to Richmond, Mass., in 1799[299]. This family spelled their name Peirson. They had chd. 262 Sophia; 263+ Josiah, bapt. 1784; 264 Eliz. M. (Betsey); 265 Harriette; 266 Joseph.

263 Josiah Peirson was born (bapt. 1784) at Bridgehampton, L. I. He mar. [300] Nabby Rossiter, and had chd.[301] 445 Mary Hedges, m. ____ Lucas; 446+ Henry Mulford; 447 Sarah A. Rossiter, m. ____ Perkins; 448 Melissa Rossiter, m. ____ Geer; 449 Abigail (Abbie) E., m. ____ Nichols; 450 Phebe S., m. ____ Dean; and 450a+ Joseph J.

446 Henry Mulford Peirson, resides (1878) at Pittsfield, Mass., a dealer in hardware there; and had chd. 497 Henry R. (who is in the hardware business with his father, in Pittsfield, Mass.); 498 Hattie E.; 499 Fanny F.; 500 Joseph E.; 501 Wm. R.; 502 Frank E.; 503 Mary L.

450a Joseph J. Peirson lived in Richmond, Mass., at the house to which Squire Henry came in 1799. He had chd. Alice E. (source of family information); Gertrude Clark; and Martha Barnes.

---

[288] Southampton, N.Y. census of 1776.

[289] Henry B. Hoff, *Long Island Source Records From The New York Genealogical and Biographical Record*, "Genealogy of Pierson - The Family of Margaret Pierson, wife of John Jermain, Genealogical Publishing Co., Baltimore, MD, 1987.

[290] *Town Records of Southampton*, NY, Liber B (Vol. 3), p. 434.

[291] *Town Records of Southampton*, NY, Liber B (Vol. 3), p. 448.

[292] *Town Records of Southampton*, NY, Liber B (Vol. 3), p. 461.

[293] *Town Records of Southampton*, NY, Liber B (Vol. 3), p. 466.

[294] *Town Records of Southampton*, NY, Liber B (Vol. 3), p. 470.

[295] *Town Records of Southampton*, NY, Liber B (Vol. 3), p. 477-8.

[296] *Town Records of Southampton*, NY, Liber B (Vol. 3), p. 481.

[297] *Town Records of Southampton*, NY, Liber B (Vol. 3), p. 485-6.

[298] *Town Records of Southampton*, NY, Liber B (Vol. 3), p. 489.

[299] Frederick Gregory Mather, *The Refugees of 1776 from Long Island to Connecticut*, Genealogical Publishing Co., Inc., Baltimore, MD, 1972, pp.506-7.

[300] Frederick Gregory Mather, *The Refugees of 1776 from Long Island to Connecticut*, Genealogical Publishing Co., Inc., Baltimore, MD, 1972, pp.506-7.

[301] Frederick Gregory Mather, *The Refugees of 1776 from Long Island to Connecticut*, Genealogical Publishing Co., Inc., Baltimore, MD, 1972, pp.506-7.

51 Silvanus Pierson (twin of 50 Matthew) was born 2 Mar 1725 at Bridgehampton, Suffolk Co., N.Y. colony, and died 23 Aug 1795[302] at Bridgehampton. Silvanus is believed to be the youngest of the twins because his brother Matthew inherited his father's house on the home lot. In May 1775, Silvanus signed the Association of Americans against British tyranny at Southampton (Suffolk County Hall), N.Y. (see Chapter 16). During the 4 July 1776 Southampton census, Silvanus' family showed one male over 16 (Silvanus), one female over 16 (his wife Rebecca Lupton), and one female under 16 (a daughter). In 1776, Silvanus' father, Josiah Pierson, died and provided in his will:

"I give unto my son, Sylvanus Pierson, my buildings and my lot of land called Norrissee Lot, and one half of my lot called Home Lot on the south side, and one third part of my wood Land adjoining on the Lots No. 1 and 2. All the rest of my Estate after paying my debts to be divided equally between Mathew, Sylvanus, Timothy and Susannah Pierson."

When the British occupied Long Island during the Revolutionary War in 1776, Silvanus Peirson[303], with four of his family and goods, moved temporarily from Sagaponack, Suffolk Co., N.Y., to Stonington, Conn., Sep to Dec 1776, by Capt. Josephus Fitch, Capt. Isaac Sheffield, Capt. John Miner 2d, and Capt. Hubbard Latham. In 1779[304], "Silvanus Peirson" witnessed the will of his uncle, Abraham Peirson, who was probably temporarily located in Westfield, Essex Co., N.J. (tax list[305], July 1781, "Abraham Person"). Since two of Silvanus's married daughters (Martha and Rebecca) were in Mendham, New Jersey, Silvanus may have moved to N.J. temporarily, while waiting for the British to leave Long Island, as suggested by the tax list[306] at Westfield, Essex Co., N.J., in July 1781 which listed "Sylvanus Pierson." In 1786[307], now back at Bridgehampton (Sagaponack), Silvanus was elected to Overseer of Highways District 4. Silvanus mar. Rebecca Lupton (d. 9 Jul 1785, age 59), dau. of David Lupton of Boston, Mass. Silvanus married again[308] after the death of Rebecca Lupton. On 2 July 1787, he was among the signers of an agreement between the residents of Bridgehampton and Rev. Aaron Woolworth. Silvanus and Rebecca had chd. 102+ Sarah (Sally); 103+ Margaret (source of family information[309]), b. 14 Mar 1764; 104+ Rebecca; 105+ Martha (source of family information[310]), b. 12 Jul 1754.

102 Sarah (Sally) Pierson married Joshua Hildreth and had 4 children. They resided at Johnstown, Montgomery Co., N. Y.

---

[302]Henry B. Hoff, *Long Island Source Records From The New York Genealogical and Biographical Record*, "Genealogy of Pierson - The Family of Margaret Pierson, wife of John Jermain, Genealogical Publishing Co., Baltimore, MD, 1987.

[303]Silvanus₄ (twin of Matthew), Josiah₃, Col. Henry₂, Henry₁

[304]Berthold Fernow, *Calendar of Wills*, on file and recorded in the offices of the Clerk of the Court of Appeals, of the County Clerk at Albany and by the Secretary of State (New York) 1626-1836, compiled 1896, p. 309, No. 1359.

[305]MicroQuix, *Colonial America - Pre-1790 Census Indexes, Tax Lists*, No. CD136, Automated Archives, Inc., 1992.

[306]MicroQuix, *Colonial America - Pre-1790 Census Indexes, Tax Lists*, No. CD136, Automated Archives, Inc., 1992.

[307]*Town Records of Southampton*, NY, Liber B (Vol. 3), p. 431.

[308]*Long Island Source Records From The New York Genealogical and Biographical Record*, Selected and Introduced by Henry B. Hoff, Genealogical Publishing Co., Baltimore, MD, 1987.

[309]*Long Island Source Records From The New York Genealogical and Biographical Record*, Selected and Introduced by Henry B. Hoff, Genealogical Publishing Co., Baltimore, MD, 1987.

[310]Joseph R. Klett, *Genealogies of New Jersey Families*, From the Genealogical Magazine of New Jersey, Vols. I & II, Genealogical Publishing Co., Inc., Baltimore, 1996, pp. 666-667, "Pierson - Sutton Family Records," original in possession of the New Jersey Genealogical Society.

103 Margaret Pierson was born at Bridgehampton 14 Mar 1764, and died 30 Mar 1833 at Albany, N. Y. She married[311] John Jermain 27 Aug 1781 and had 9 children.

104 Rebecca Peirson mar. 83 Shadrach Pierson (her 2nd cousin, they both had great grandfather 5 Col. Henry Peirson), and had chd. 213a Phoebe[312], b. ca. 1774, mar. 19 Nov 1792 Henrich Richter at Schoharie, N.Y.; 213 Henry; 214+ Moses, b. 10 Dec 1776 N.J., d. 6 Jun 1863[313]; 215+ James, b. ca. 1778; 216 Joseph; 217+ Rufus, b. 19 Dec 1787, d. 6 Jun 1865; 217a dau. #2 (1790 census). See 83 Shadrach Pierson, earlier in this chapter, for location and descendants.

105 Martha Peirson was born 12 Jul 1754 at Bridgehampton, Long Island, N.Y. She mar. 11 Mar 1773, 84 James Pierson[314] (b. Oct. 1750, d. 28 Mar 1777) (her 2nd cousin, they both had great grandfather 5 Col. Henry Peirson). Martha and James had Pierson chd. in New Jersey: 218 Silvanus, b. 28 Dec 1773, mar. 21 Jan 1804 Elizabeth Hinkel; 218a Rebecca, b. 11 Mar 1776, d. 27 Apr 1778. Martha Pierson mar. 2nd 14 Apr 1778 Joseph Sutton (b. 9 Jul 1747, d. 8 Nov 1822) of Mendham, Morris Co., N.J, son of Zebulon and Mary Sutton. Joseph Sutton had siblings: Patience, b. 31 May 1732; Jonathan, b. 23 Mar 1735; Jeremiah, b. 29 Oct 1738; Uriah, b. 21 Jul 1741; Mary, b. 19 Sep 1744; and Anne, b. 20 Dec 1750. Joseph and Martha (Pierson) Sutton had Sutton chd. in New Jersey: Joseph, b. 9 Jul 1747; Uriah, b. 28 Mar 1779, mar. 25 Jan 1807 Ann Howel; Shadrach, b. 28 Mar 1781, mar. 1st 19 Aug 1804 Fanny Seward (d. 25 Jan 1806), mar. 2nd ca. 1807 Sarah (Sally) Stewart (d. 23 Apr 1822); Rebecca, b. 2 Jun 1783, mar. 11 Aug 1803 Luther Conkling; Jonathan, b. 13 Feb 1787, mar. 5 Nov 1809 Martha Upson; Elizabeth Ann, b. 19 Jun 1789, mar. 19 Jun 1811 William Babbitt; Martha Lupton, b. 27 Sep 1792, mar. 27 Feb 1812 Aaron Carson (d. 20 Feb 1823); James, b. 4 Jul 1796, mar. 10 Feb 1818 Julia Ann Beach; Joseph Pierson, b. 9 Nov 1798, mar. 13 Nov 1821 Piersa Horton.

52 Paul Pierson was born 1726[315] at Bridgehampton, Suffolk Co., N.Y. colony. He married Elizabeth Hand of Southampton, Long Island[316]. In 1763[317], Southampton township records mentioned Paul Pierson's lot, which was located at the corner of Sagg road and Country road. In 1764[318], Paul had cattle at Southampton township as verified by ear mark registration there. They moved to Richmond, Mass. in 1769, and then to Ballston,

[311]*Long Island Source Records From The New York Genealogical and Biographical Record*, Selected and Introduced by Henry B. Hoff, Genealogical Publishing Co., Baltimore, MD, 1987.

[312]C. M. Kelly, Marriage Records of Two Early Schoharie, NY, Churches: Reformed Church 1732-1892, St. Paul's Lutheran Church 1743-1899, p. 18.

[313]LDS microfilm 17135, Cemetery Inscriptions, Cemetery at Oak Ridge, Montgomery Co., N.Y.

[314]Joseph R. Klett, *Genealogies of New Jersey Families*, From the Genealogical Magazine of New Jersey, Vols. I & II, Genealogical Publishing Co., Inc., Baltimore, 1996, pp. 666-667, "Pierson - Sutton Family Records," original in possession of the New Jersey Genealogical Society.

[315]Orange County Genealogical Society, New York, *The History of Orange County, New York*, records from the family of Silas Pierson, son of Josiah Pierson.

[316]Orange County Genealogical Society, New York, *The History of Orange County, New York*, records from the family of Silas Pierson, son of Josiah Pierson.

[317]Henry Hedges, Wm. Pelletreau, Edward Foster, *The Third Book of Records of the Town of Southampton, Long Island, N.Y. with other Ancient Documents of Historic Value*, John H. Hunt, Printer, Sag Harbor, NY, 1878, p. 234.

[318]*Town Records of Southampton*, NY, Liber B (Vol. 3), p. 284, Abstract.

Saratoga Co., N.Y. in 1777.[319] Revolutionary War records[320] state that Paul Pierson was assigned in Connecticut during the Revolution, died 9 Jan 1802, age 76 years, and is buried at Hinman Cemetery, West Milton (close to Ballston), Saratoga Co., N.Y. Paul and Elizabeth had chd. 106 John, of Whitestone[321], N.Y.; 107 Josiah; 108 Benjamin; 109 Alanson; 110 David; 111 Susannah, wife of ____ Watrous[322], Ballston, Saratoga Co., N.Y.; 112+ Mary (Polly); 113 Sarah (Sally); ___ (and perhaps another).

112 Mary (Polly) Pierson married ____ Stow[323] of Ballston, Saratoga Co., N.Y. Mr. Stow was killed by Indians. Polly mar. 2nd ____ Spencer and had Spencer chd. Alanson; Harvey; and a daughter who married in Guilford, Conn.

53 Timothy Pierson was born 1731 and died 1802[324] at age 71. In May 1775, Timothy signed the Association of Americans against British tyranny at Southampton (Suffolk County Hall), N.Y. (see Chapter 16). In the 4 July 1776 Southampton census, Timothy's family was listed with one male and four females (3 daughters). In 1776, Timothy's father, Josiah Peirson, died and left a will:

"I give unto my son, Timothy Pierson, my buildings and the lot of land bounded by David Hand's land on the west and the north and Lemuel Pierson on the east, south by the road, and one half of my lot of land called Sears Lot, and one third part of my wood land lying on the south Division. All the rest of my Estate after paying my debts to be divided equally between Mathew, Sylvanus, Timothy and Susannah Pierson."

On 2 July 1787, Timothy was among the signers of an agreement between the residents of Bridgehampton and Rev. Aaron Woolworth. He married Martha Howell[325] and had daus. 114+ Mary (Molly); 115+ Susannah; 114a perhaps a 3d dau. (see 1776 census); and sons[326] 115a Silvanus; 115b Watson; and 115c Timothy.

114 Mary (Molly) Pierson married Silas Hand of Sagg, Long Island, and had Hand chd. [327] Watson, Pierson, and Sylvanus. Watson Hand had son Watson of Texas.

115 Susannah Pierson was bedridden for 40 years.

[319]Orange County Genealogical Society, New York, *The History of Orange County, New York*, records from the family of Silas Pierson, son of Josiah Pierson.
[320]*Connecticut Men in the Revolution*, p. 746, LDS microfilm 1294816, item 10, p. 106.
[321]*Long Island Source Records From The New York Genealogical and Biographical Record*, Selected and Introduced by Henry B. Hoff, Genealogical Publishing Co., Baltimore, MD, 1987.
[322]*Long Island Source Records From The New York Genealogical and Biographical Record*, Selected and Introduced by Henry B. Hoff, Genealogical Publishing Co., Baltimore, MD, 1987.
[323]*Long Island Source Records From The New York Genealogical and Biographical Record*, Selected and Introduced by Henry B. Hoff, Genealogical Publishing Co., Baltimore, MD, 1987.
[324]*Long Island Source Records From The New York Genealogical and Biographical Record*, Selected and Introduced by Henry B. Hoff, Genealogical Publishing Co., Baltimore, MD, 1987.
[325]Orange County Genealogical Society, New York, *The History of Orange County, New York*, records from the family of Silas Pierson, son of Josiah Pierson.
[326]*Long Island Source Records From The New York Genealogical and Biographical Record*, Selected and Introduced by Henry B. Hoff, Genealogical Publishing Co., Baltimore, MD, 1987.
[327]George Rogers Howell, *The Early History of Southampton, L.I., New York with Genealogies*, 2nd Edition, Weed, Parsons and Company, Albany, NY, 1887, p. 280.

54 Capt. Josiah Pierson was born Jan 1731/32 at Bridgehampton, Suffolk Co., N.Y., and died before 25 Apr 1785[328] leaving his 2nd wife and two daus. by his first wife. He married 1st Mrs. Julianna (Gilbert)[329] De Kay, dau. of Josiah Gilbert, and they lived in Newark, N.J. He married 2nd Sarah Gilbert (no known children), sister of his first wife. In 1776[330], Capt. Josiah Pierson's New Jersey Company is mentioned. During the Revolutionary War, Josiah served as a Captain in charge of a Company of the New Jersey militia[331]. On 27 Nov 1782, a New Jersey newspaper article[332] referred to Isaac Pierson and Josiah Pierson as owning land near Newark, N.J. This same article, 27 Nov 1782, mentioned Capt. Josiah Pierson's house in Newark, N.J. Josiah and Julianna had chd. 748+ Hannah; and 749+ Elizabeth (Betsey[333]).

748 Hannah Pierson married Richard Dey of Preakness, N.J., the father of Anthony Dey from whom Dey Street, New York City, is named.

749 Elizabeth (Betsey[334]) Pierson married Col. William Boyd of New York City.

55 Martha Pierson was born 1728[335] at Bridgehampton, Suffolk Co., N.Y. colony. She mar. [336] Stephen Jagger of Westhampton, Long Island, and had Jagger chd. [337]: Jonathan; Susanna, wife of William Halsey, Westhampton; David; Hannah, wife of Rev. Nathan Woodhull; Abigail, wife of Timothy Halsey, Gorham, N. J.; Hiram; and Josephus.

56 Joseph Pierson was born 1736 at Bridgehampton, Suffolk Co., N.Y. colony. His twin brother, probably the 59 John[338] mentioned by Lizzie Pierson, died in infancy. Joseph moved from Bridgehampton, Long Island to New York City, N.Y., where he married Anne Vielee of the family of General Egbert Vielee of New York City. They had no children. Joseph died about age 66 in 1802 at New York City, New York.[339]

---

[328]*DAR Patriot Index*, Centennial Edition, National Society of the Daughters of the American Revolution, 1994, part 3, p. 2258.

[329]Orange County Genealogical Society, New York, *The History of Orange County, New York*, records from the family of Silas Pierson, son of Josiah Pierson.

[330]Joseph R. Klett, *Genealogies of New Jersey Families*, Genealogical Publishing Co., Inc., Baltimore, Md., 1996, pp. 354 & 659.

[331]*DAR Patriot Index*, Centennial Edition, National Society of the Daughters of the American Revolution, 1994, part 3, p. 2258.

[332]Thomas B. Wilson, *Notices From New Jersey Newspapers 1781-1790*, Hunterdon House, Lambertville, N.J., 1988, p. 150.

[333]*Long Island Source Records From The New York Genealogical and Biographical Record*, Selected and Introduced by Henry B. Hoff, Genealogical Publishing Co., Baltimore, MD, 1987.

[334]*Long Island Source Records From The New York Genealogical and Biographical Record*, Selected and Introduced by Henry B. Hoff, Genealogical Publishing Co., Baltimore, MD, 1987.

[335]Orange County Genealogical Society, New York, *The History of Orange County, New York*, records from the family of Silas Pierson, son of Josiah Pierson.

[336]*Long Island Source Records From The New York Genealogical and Biographical Record*, Selected and Introduced by Henry B. Hoff, Genealogical Publishing Co., Baltimore, MD, 1987.

[337]*Long Island Source Records From The New York Genealogical and Biographical Record*, Selected and Introduced by Henry B. Hoff, Genealogical Publishing Co., Baltimore, MD, 1987.

[338]Lizzie B. Pierson, *Pierson Genealogical Records*, Joel Munsell, Printer, Albany, N.Y., 1878, p. 32.

[339]Orange County Genealogical Society, New York, *The History of Orange County, New York*, records from the family of Silas Pierson, son of Josiah Pierson.

57 Benjamin Pierson was born in 1741[340] at Bridgehampton, Suffolk Co., N.Y. colony. He mar. Sarah Gilbert of Newark, N. J., and moved to Richmond, Mass., in 1772 where his brother Paul was living. Benjamin also lived in N.Y. City, N.Y., and died ca. 1796[341] at Ballston, Saratoga Co., N. Y. (close to Malta, N.Y.). More specifically, Revolutionary War records[342] provide that Benjamin Peirson was a New Jersey man (mar. a woman from N.J.) that participated in the Revolutionary War and died 21 Mar 1797, age 57 years, and is buried in Briggs Cemetery, Malta, N.Y. (22 miles north of Albany, N.Y.). Benjamin's wife, Sarah Gilbert, died at Homer, Cortland Co., N. Y. in 1834 in her 95th year. They had chd. 116+ Jeremiah b. 1766; 117 Gilbert; 118 Caleb; 119 Isaac (of N. Y.); 120 Lydia (w. 1st of Mr. Dean and 2d of Mr. Ballard); 121 John; 122 Mary (w. of Mr. Ballard); 123 Joseph; 124 Sarah (Sally) (w. of Mr. Watrous of Boston, Mass.).

116 Jeremiah Pierson was born in 1766 in N.J., and resided at Ramapo, N.Y. He had children, most of whom were residing in Ramapo, N. Y. in 1878. The sons were in the iron business.

58 Susannah Pierson was born in 1737[343] at Bridgehampton, Suffolk Co., N.Y. colony. In 1776, Susannah's father, Josiah Peirson, died and left via will to Susannah after dividing up his land and buildings to three of his sons: "All the rest of my Estate (live stock, personal belongings, and cash) after paying my debts to be divided equally between Mathew, Sylvanus, Timothy and Susannah Pierson." Susannah is still single in 1776 at age 39 when her father wrote his will. She married ca. 1777 Daniel$_5$ Hedges (b.11 May 1734) (Daniel$_4$, Daniel$_3$ of Sagg, Stephen$_2$, William$_1$) of East Hampton, Long Island.[344] She was Daniel Hedges 2nd wife. Daniel Hedges[345] mar. 1st Sarah Baker by whom he had Hedges chd. Sarah, Nathan, Daniel, Abigail, Phebe, Caleb, Abraham, Hannah (wife of John$_5$ Pierson [Daniel$_4$, John$_3$, Theodore$_2$, Henry$_1$]), and Nathaniel. Daniel and Susanna had Hedges chd. Susanna b. 22 Mar 1778; and Martha b. 24 Apr 1780, mar. Abraham Osborn.

60 Jeremiah Peirson was born about 1752 at Southampton, Suffolk Co., N.Y. Colony[346]. He signed the Association of those Americans against the British in May 1775 at Southampton, County Hall, Suffolk Co., N.Y. (see Chapter 16). That is the last record found of him in Southampton. His activity in the Revolutionary War is unknown, but he eventually settled in up-state New York. He died[347] 16 Mar 1839 at age 86 years, and is buried at Briggs Cemetery, Malta, Saratoga Co., N.Y. He mar. 1st Hannah ____ (b. ca. 1756, d. 15 Jun 1796 at

---

[340]Orange County Genealogical Society, New York, *The History of Orange County, New York*, records from the family of Silas Pierson, son of Josiah Pierson.
[341]Orange County Genealogical Society, New York, *The History of Orange County, New York*, records from the family of Silas Pierson, son of Josiah Pierson.
[342]*Jerseymen in the Revolution*, p. 405, LDS microfilm 1294816, item 10, p. 106.
[343]Orange County Genealogical Society, New York, *The History of Orange County, New York*, records from the family of Silas Pierson, son of Josiah Pierson.
[344]Henry B. Hoff, *Long Island Source Records From The New York Genealogical and Biographical Record*, "Genealogy of Pierson - The Family of Margaret Pierson, Wife of John Jermain," Genealogical Publishing Co., Baltimore, MD, 1987.
[345]George Rogers Howell, *The Early History of Southampton, L.I., New York with Genealogies*, 2nd Edition, Weed, Parsons and Company, Albany, NY, 1887, p. 288.
[346]Family records in Orange County, N.Y., report that this Jeremiah was b. 1743 and d. 1747. The authors of Pierson Millennium think otherwise based on the Association being signed in 1775.
[347]Calendar N.Y. His manuscripts Vol. 1-58. LDS microfilm 1294816, item 10, p. 106.

age 40 yrs.), and 2d Ruth ___ (b. ca. 1755, d. 14 May 1836 at age 81 yrs.). His wives are buried in the same plot with him. He may have lived near his two brothers Benjamin (Ballston) and Paul (West Milton), both near Malta where Jeremiah is buried in Saratoga Co., N.Y. Jeremiah's children are unknown.

20a Sarah Peirson was born at Bridgehampton, Suffolk Co., N.Y. colony, about 1697 (based on being the youngest dau. in the 1698 Southampton township census, child spacing, and order of children in census and father's will). Her father died the year he wrote his will 28 Aug 1701[348], leaving her: "I give unto my three daughters Hannah Peirson, Sarah Peirson & Mary Peirson, each of them, one hundred pounds current money of this Province, or what may be equivalent thereto, when they shall come to ye age of twenty years, or at ye day of their marriage, as it shall be demanded." She was not yet age 20 nor was she married on that date in 1701.

20b Mary Peirson was born at Bridgehampton, Suffolk Co., N.Y. colony, about 1700 (based on not being in the 1698 Southampton township census, and her father's death in 1701). Her father died the year he wrote his will 28 Aug 1701[349], leaving her: "I give unto my three daughters Hannah Peirson, Sarah Peirson & Mary Peirson, each of them, one hundred pounds current money of this Province, or what may be equivalent thereto, when they shall come to ye age of twenty years, or at ye day of their marriage, as it shall be demanded." She was not yet age 20 nor was she married on that date in 1701.

---

[348]William S. Pelletreau, *Early Long Island Wills of Suffolk County, 1691-1703, With Genealogical and Historical Notes*, Francis P. Harper, New York, NY, 1897, pp. 239-41.
[349]William S. Pelletreau, *Early Long Island Wills of Suffolk County, 1691-1703, With Genealogical and Historical Notes*, Francis P. Harper, New York, NY, 1897, pp. 239-41.

Chapter 11
Descendants of Benjamin Peirson
Son of Henry

Benjamin Peirson is the son of Henry and Mary Peirson of Southampton, Suffolk Co., New York Colony. The following descendants of Benjamin Peirson (1655-1731) are based upon the footnoted research by the authors of *Pierson Millennium*. Lizzie Pierson's, *Pierson Genealogical Records*, lists his line as not traced, and George Rogers Howell's, *The Early History of Southampton*, lists him only as going to Elizabeth Town, New Jersey, and having descendants there. An every-name index is provided at the back of *Pierson Millennium*. The + symbol after an identifying number indicates more information is provided in a later paragraph of this chapter beginning with the same number. The numbering system used is designed to match Lizzie Pierson's book as many other chapters herein have done.

1 Henry Pierson[1] had chd. 2 John; 3 Daniel; 4 Joseph; 5 Henry, b. 1652, d. 1701; **6+ Benjamin**, b. 1655, d. 1731; 7 Theodore; 8 Sarah, b. Jan. 20, 1660/61. See chapter 8 for more children and information on 1 Henry Pierson's family.

6 Benjamin Peirson was born in 1655 at Southampton, Suffolk Co., N.Y. colony, and died in 1731 at Elizabeth Town, Essex Co., New Jersey. Tombstone in First Presbyterian Church Burying Ground, Elizabeth, New Jersey[2]: "Here lyeth ye body of Benjamin Pierson, decesed A° 1731 in the 77 year of his age." According to Arthur Newton Pierson in his 1945 book[3], no record of Benjamin's marriage or of his children have been found in the records of the Elizabeth Church, as the early records were destroyed with the burning of the church by the British in 1780. At a town meeting at Southampton on April 1, 1681[4], it was granted to Benjamin Pierson to have an acre and half of orchard land on the west end of his land at Little Worth, and what more can be spared after the highway is regulated at the discretion of the layers out. In 1681[5], Benjamin had cattle at Southampton as verified by ear mark registration that year. On September 1, 1683[6], the Estimate of the Town of Southampton for the year 1683 revealed Benjamin Peirson £51, and his older brothers Joseph Pierson £127, and Henry £136. Mary Peirson, the widow of Henry Pierson, married 2nd in May 1682 Rev. Seth Fletcher, with whom she went to Elizabethtown, N. J. According to Lizzie Pierson, her son Benjamin accompanied her to Elizabethtown.[7] But Benjamin is not

---

[1]Lizzie B. Pierson, *Pierson Genealogical Records*, Joel Munsell Printer, Albany, NY, 1878, p. 22.

[2]Wm. Ogden Wheeler and Edmund D. Halsey (of Morristown, NJ), Inscriptions on Tombstones and Monuments in the Burying Ground of the First Presbyterian Church and St. Johns Church at Elizabeth, New Jersey 1664- 1892, Morehouse & Taylor, New Haven, Conn., 1892, p. 29, No. 186.

[3]Arthur Newton Pierson, *Genealogy, the Pierson Family, the Marsh Family, the Clark Family, the Baker Family*, published by author, 1945, pp. 3-4, a copy is in Library of Congress, Washington, DC.

[4]*Town Records of Southampton*, NY, Liber A, No. 2, 1st Part, p. 147.

[5]*Town Records of Southampton*, NY, Liber A, No. 2, 2nd Part, p. 96.

[6]George Rogers Howell, *The Early History of Southampton, L.I., New York with Genealogies*, Second Edition, Weed, Parsons and Company, Albany, NY, 1887, pp. 44-5, and his reference is given as Doc. Hist. of N.Y., Vol. 2, page 536.

[7]Lizzie B. Pierson, *Pierson Genealogical Records*, Joel Munsell Printer, Albany, NY, 1878, p. 22.

corroborated as being at Elizabeth Town until October 11, 1687[8] when "Benjamen Pierson of Elisabeth towne in Jarsey" sells to Mathew Howell, Southampton property, described as one quarter of a lot of meadow in Quaquanantuck neck, and one quarter of a Lot in Assopstauke neck, and one quarter of a 390 Lot in Catchaponack, price 11 pounds 15 shillings.   To this document he signs his name "Benj Pierson" and his wife "Hannah Pierson" makes her mark. Witnessed by Job Sayre and Sam Whitehead. The bill of sale was entered in Southampton records in May 1694. On March 21, 1691[9], the land sold above officially passed from Benjamin's father, Henry Peirson, to Mathew Howell along with lots and 5 acres from Benjamin's brothers Joseph, Henry, and Theodore. In 1691[10], Benjamin's brother Theodore was using Benjamin's cattle earmarks at Southampton indicating that Benjamin no longer had cattle at Southampton. On 26 Oct 1695[11] in Southampton records, "Benj. Pierson of Elisabethtown" sells to Samuel Jagger a lot of meadow at North sea lying with his brother Joseph Pierson, and 1/2 lot of meadow at west neck bounded W by Geo. Harris and a small creek, S by common land, and 1/3 lot in Birch neck accabouge, surrounded by water except on S.E. side next to James White, and 1/3 of an amendment to said lot lying between two points of land. Benjamin sold his half fifty in commonage throughout the bounds of Southampton to Peter Noris prior to April 7, 1712[12].

Benjamin married Hannah ____, before 11 Oct 1687, and they had at least three children: 750+ Daniel, b. ca. 1688, d. 1743; 751+ Henry, b. 1 May 1690, d. 1750; and 752+ Sarah[13]. For the source of the children, see the will of 750 Daniel Peirson below and Ogden family records of Elizabeth, New Jersey, below under son 751 Henry Peirson.

750 Daniel Peirson was born ca. 1688, probably at Elizabethtown, and died before his will was proved on 16 Apr 1743 (Lib. D, p. 34). Daniel's will was written 17 Nov 1741[14] at Elizabeth Town, Essex Co., N.J. where he listed his brothers Henry Pierson and Jonathan Crane (brother-in-law). His Inventory was taken 30 Apr 1743 and was £71,16 shillings. He mar.[15] Sarah ____ and had chd. [16]: 753+ Daniel; 754 Phebe; 755 Sarah, probably mar. James Craige (see the paragraph on 753 Daniel Pierson below); 756 Stephen; 757 Hannah; 758 Abigail; 759+ David, b. ca. 1736; and 760 ____, an expected child (17 Nov 1741).

753 Daniel Pierson was the executor[17] of the James Craige estate in 1763. James Craige (b. 17 Sep 1726, d. 1763) of Elizabeth, N.J. (will NJ Archives 33:96), mar. 8 Feb 1744 Sarah ____ (b. 19 Feb 1728/9), and had Craige chd. Sarah b. 16 Mar 1745; James b. 8 Feb 1747; Lydah b.

[8] *Town Records of Southampton*, NY, Liber A, No. 2, 2nd Part, p. 171.

[9] *Town Records of Southampton*, NY, Liber A, No. 2, 1st Part, p. 194.

[10] *Town Records of Southampton*, NY, Liber A, No. 2, 2nd Part, p. 145.

[11] *Town Records of Southampton*, NY, Liber A, No. 2, 2nd Part, p. 219. Abstract.

[12] *Town Records of Southampton*, NY, Liber A, No. 2, 1st Part, pp. 240-241.

[13] Will of Jonathan Crane, dated 2 Apr 1744, of Newark, Essex Co., N.J., wife Sarah, chd. Samuel, Caleb, Elijah, Nehemiah, John, and Mary Johnson. Proved 1 Oct 1744. Lib. D, p. 181.

[14] Edited by A. Van Doren Honeyman, *Documents Relating to the Colonial History of the State of New Jersey*, First Series, Vol. XXX, "Calendar of New Jersey Wills, Administrations, etc., Vol. II 1730-1750, p. 379.

[15] Edited by A. Van Doren Honeyman, *Documents Relating to the Colonial History of the State of New Jersey*, First Series, Vol. XXX, "Calendar of New Jersey Wills, Administrations, etc., Vol. II 1730-1750, p. 379.

[16] Edited by A. Van Doren Honeyman, *Documents Relating to the Colonial History of the State of New Jersey*, First Series, Vol. XXX, "Calendar of New Jersey Wills, Administrations, etc., Vol. II 1730-1750, p. 379.

[17] Papers of Daniel Pierson, Rutgers University Library (part of Ms. accession 1810); Joseph R. Klett, *Genealogies of New Jersey Families*, Genealogical Publishing Co., Inc., Baltimore, Md., 1996, p. 728.

12 Dec 1748; Andrew b. 8 Jun 1751; Danyel b. 12 Dec 1753; and Sarah (2d) b. 31 Aug 1755. It is likely that James Craige's wife, Sarah, is 755 Sarah, dau. of 750 Daniel Pierson, based on 753 Daniel Pierson being James' executor and James & Sarah Craige having child Danyel.

759 David Pierson was born about 1736, and died 2 Apr 1788. He is buried in the burying ground of the First Presbyterian Church, Elizabeth, N.J., and his tombstone reads[18], "In memory of David Pierson who departed this life Aprl the 2d 1788 in the 52d year of his age." He mar. Elizabeth ____. She was born about 1735, and died 8 Jan 1793. She is buried in the same grave yard with her husband, and her tombstone reads[19], "In memory of Elizabeth, widow of David Pierson, who died January ye 8th 1793 in ye 58th year of her age."

751 Henry Peirson, son of Benjamin Peirson[20], was born 1 May 1690[21] at Elizabethtown, N.J., and died in 1750 (3 Jan 1748 will[22] at Elizabeth, N.J.). He married 1st[23] Jemima Ogden (b. 1692), dau. of John and Elizabeth (Plum) Ogden. He married 2nd Sarah ____.

"Jan. 3, 1748/9[24]. Will of Henry Person (Peirson) of the Borough of Elizabeth, Essex Co., New Jersey, Yeoman. Wife, Sarah. Children - Henry, John, Benjamin and Jemima, wife of James Arnet. Grandchildren - Henry, Jemima, and Elizabeth Skillman, children and James, deceased. Lands bought of Benjamin Meeker, John Clark, David Morehouse, deceased, Benjamin Lyon; land joining land of Benjamin Bond, bought of Joseph Meeker, deceased; land bought of John Blanchard, May 20, 1736; land bought of Benjamin Williams, deceased; land joining lands of Stephen Brown, Abraham Baker, Isaac Crane and Joseph Crane, deceased. Executors - sons Joseph and Benjamin. Witnesses - John Hinds, Michael Meeker, Jno. Oborn (John Osborn). Proved Sept. 22, 1750 (Lib. F, p. 341)."

Henry and Jemima had chd.[25], probably all at Elizabethtown, N.J.: 761+ Henry Peirson Jr., b. 1714, d.1757, mar. Unis (b. 1717, d. 1762); 762 Elizabeth, b. 1715; 763+ Jemima, b. 22 Dec 1717; 764+ John, b. ca. 1719; 765 Sarah, b. 1722; 766 Benjamin, b. 1724; 767 Hannah, b. 1726; 768 David, b. 1728; 769 Samuel, b. 1730; 770 Joseph, b. 1733; and 771 Mary, b. 1734.

761 Henry Peirson Jr. was born 20 Jan 1714, probably at Elizabethtown, N.J., and died 1757. The will[26] of "Henry Peirson", dated 26 Aug 1754, Borough of Elizabethtown, Essex Co., N.J., proved 29 Sep 1757, names his "wife Unis and his children David, Samuel (Daniel in

[18]Wm. Ogden Wheeler and Edmund D. Halsey, *Inscriptions on Tombstones and Monuments in the Burying Ground at the First Presbyterian Church ... at Elizabeth, New Jersey 1664-1892*, Morehouse & Taylor, New Haven, Conn., 1892, p. 57, No. 389.
[19]Wm. Ogden Wheeler and Edmund D. Halsey, *Inscriptions on Tombstones and Monuments in the Burying Ground at the First Presbyterian Church ... at Elizabeth, New Jersey 1664-1892*, Morehouse & Taylor, New Haven, Conn., 1892, p. 56, No. 387.
[20]*The Ogden Family (Elizabeth Town Branch)*, p. 51, found in the Elizabeth, NJ, library.
[21]*The Ogden Family (Elizabeth Town Branch)*, p. 51, found in the Elizabeth, NJ, library.
[22]Edited by A. Van Doren Honeyman, *Documents Relating to the Colonial History of the State of New Jersey*, First Series, Vol. XXX, "Calendar of New Jersey Wills, Administrations, etc., Vol. II 1730-1750, p. 376.
[23]*The Ogden Family (Elizabeth Town Branch)*, p. 51, found in the Elizabeth, NJ, library.
[24]Edited by A. Van Doren Honeyman, *Documents Relating to the Colonial History of the State of New Jersey*, First Series, Vol. XXX, "Calendar of New Jersey Wills, Administrations, etc., Vol. II 1730-1750, p. 376.
[25]*The Ogden Family (Elizabeth Town Branch)*, p. 51, found in the Elizabeth, NJ, library.
[26]Will of Henry Peirson, Borough of Elizabethtown, Essex Co., Secretary of State office, New Jersey, Liber 494, dated 26 Aug 1754, proved 29 Sep 1757.

other records), William, Abraham, Suruiah, Frances, and Sarah, all under age." He mar.[27]
Unis _____, and they had chd. [28]: 772+ William, b. 1734; 773 Sarah; 774+ David, b. 1737, d.
1790; 775 Abraham; 776+ Daniel, b. 1740; 777 Suruiah; and 778 Frances.

772 William Pierson was born 1734, and died 1819. He mar. Sara Wills. William settled[29]
in Westfield, N.J. David, Daniel, and William Pierson, brothers, migrated from Elizabeth,
N.J., to Westfield, N.J., and settled there sometime in the 1760's.[30] William Pierson[31], the
brother of David, was the ancestor of 779+ John Davis Pierson. In the July 1781 tax list[32] at
Westfield, Essex Co., N.J., William Pierson and his two brothers, Daniel and David Pierson,
are listed. Also listed[33] at Westfield that same date are Person (Abraham & Theophilus),
and Pierson (David Jr., David 3rd, Sylvanus, & William Jr.). Some of these last six may be
children of 772 William, especially William Jr.

779 John Davis Pierson had chd[34]. 780 John D.; 781 Blanchard; 782 Ralph; and others, in
New Jersey.

774 David Pierson was born 10 Feb 1737/8 at Elizabeth Town, Essex Co., New Jersey, and
died 26 Jun 1790 at Westfield, N.J.[35] He mar. 1760 Esther Bailey (b. 1744, d. 25 Mar 1788),
and came to Westfield, N.J., about 1760 where he erected a home on the lower Springfield
Road. David and his wife Esther joined the Presbyterian Church of Westfield, N.J., in 1763,
but in 1765 they joined the Baptist Church of Scotch Plains, N.J. "David Pierson served as a
Private, Essex County Militia," New Jersey, during the Revolutionary War. He "received
Certificate No. 1683, dated 15 Oct 1784, signed by Thomas Clark, for £4:13:9, for the
depreciation of his Continental pay in the Essex County Militia."[36] In the July 1781 tax
list[37] at Westfield, Essex Co., N.J., David Pierson and his two brothers, Daniel and William
Pierson, are listed. On 2 Oct 1782, he advertised[38] in the New Jersey Journal newspaper,
"David Pierson, Westfield, advertises a mare broke into his pasture." David and Esther
(Bailey) Pierson are both buried in the old burying ground of the Baptist Church in Scotch
Plains, N.J.[39] David and Esther had chd. 783 Stephen, b. 1762, moved to Ohio in 1816, mar.
Esther Robinson; 784 Hannah, b. 1765, d. 1830, moved to Ohio in 1816, mar. Jacob Beedle

[27] *The Ogden Family (Elizabeth Town Branch)*, p. 51, found in the Elizabeth, NJ, library.
[28] Arthur Newton Pierson, *Genealogy, Our Pierson Family, Marsh Family, Clark Family, Baker Family*, published by the author, 1945, Pierson Chart; his source presumed to be *The Ogden Family (Elizabeth Town Branch)*, p. 51, found in the Elizabeth, NJ, library.
[29] Lizzie B. Pierson, *Pierson Genealogical Records*, Joel Munsell, Printer, Albany, NY, 1878, pp. 64-65.
[30] Arthur Newton Pierson, *Genealogy, the Pierson Family, the Marsh Family, the Clark Family, the Baker Family*, published by author, 1945, p. 5A, a copy is in Library of Congress, Washington, DC.
[31] Lizzie B. Pierson, *Pierson Genealogical Records*, Joel Munsell, Printer, Albany, NY, 1878, pp. 64-65.
[32] MicroQuix, *Colonial America - Pre- 1790 Census Indexes, Tax Lists*, No. CD136, Automated Archives, Inc., 1992.
[33] MicroQuix, *Colonial America - Pre- 1790 Census Indexes, Tax Lists*, No. CD136, Automated Archives, Inc., 1992.
[34] Lizzie B. Pierson, *Pierson Genealogical Records*, Joel Munsell, Printer, Albany, NY, 1878, pp. 64-65.
[35] Arthur Newton Pierson, *Genealogy, the Pierson Family, the Marsh Family, the Clark Family, the Baker Family*, published by author, 1945, p. Pierson 6, and his reference is: Records of baptisms, marriages, and burials in the history of the Presbyterian Church, Westfield, New Jersey.
[36] Certification letter from the State of New Jersey, Office of the Adjutant General, Trenton, NJ, dated 15 Nov 1944.
[37] MicroQuix, *Colonial America - Pre- 1790 Census Indexes, Tax Lists*, No. CD136, Automated Archives, Inc., 1992.
[38] Thomas B. Wilson, *Notices From New Jersey Newspapers 1781-1790*, Hunterdon House, Lambertville, N.J., 1988, p. 146.
[39] Records of old burying ground of Scotch Plains, N.J.

1785; 785+ Squire (1st), b. 1767, d. 1849; 786 Daniel, b. 1770, mar.[40] Neijie Ockerman (Ackerman) 23 Sep 1798 at New Brunswick Dutch Church, New Brunswick, N.J.; 787 Moses (1st), b. 1774, died in infancy; 788+ Moses (2nd), b. 1776, d. 1857; 789 Samuel, b. 1778, unmarried; 790 David, b. 1783, moved to Ohio in 1816, mar. Sarah ____. Conflicts in the birth year of 786 Daniel (b. 1770) and 790 David (b. 1783) occur between that reported by Lizzie Pierson[41] and Arthur Pierson[42] (reversed from one another), but based upon the 1798 marriage date of 786 Daniel, the birth dates are listed correctly by Lizzie Pierson and are used here.

785 Squire Pierson 1st was born 20 Apr 1767 at Westfield, N.J., and died 4 Oct 1849. He mar. 4 Aug 1791 Nancy DeCamp (b. 1775, d. 1854), dau. of Moses and Sarah DeCamp. Squire 1st, his wife Nancy, and probably some of his children, excepting Squire 2nd, moved to Butler Co., Ohio about 1816. Both Squire 1st and his wife Nancy were buried in the old Bethel burying ground in Riley, Butler Co., Ohio. Squire 1st and Nancy had chd.[43] 791 Rebecca, b. 1792, mar. Abraham Jones; 792 Moses, b. 1794, mar. Eliza Martin; 793+ Squire 2nd, b. 1796, d. 1878; 794 Sarah, b. 1799, d. 1869, mar. Joseph D. Horton; 795 David, b. 1802, d. 1884, mar. Rebecca Trimbly; 796 Daniel, b. 1809, d. 1895, mar. 1st Mary Loftland, mar. 2nd Mary Byers; 797 Mary E., b. 1812, d. 1900, mar. Elija Rose; 798 Stephen, b. 1815, mar. Mary Ann ____; 799 Hiram, b. 1819, d. 1895, mar. Mary Moon.

793 Squire Pierson 2nd was born 1 Oct 1796 at Westfield, N.J., and died 23 Dec 1878. He mar. 1st 10 Mar 1817 Abigail (Abby) (b. 25 Jan 1799, d. 28 Apr 1862), dau. of Charles and Abigail (Denman) Marsh. He mar. 2nd, after Apr 1862, Harriet Kingsland. Squire 2nd lived on Gallows Hill Road in Westfield. All are buried in Fairview Cemetery, Westfield, N.J. All his children are by his 1st wife. Squire 2nd and Abby had chd. [44] 809 Irene, b. 1818, d. in infancy; 810 Orren, b. 1819, d. 1893, mar. Gertrude Kingsland and had 1 son & 2 daus.; 811 Sara Ann, b. 1822, d. 1900, mar. W. Baxter Muchmore and had 1 son & 1 dau.; 812 Mary Elizabeth, b. 1824, d. 1901, mar. John A. Smith and had 1 son & 1 dau.; 813 Evaline, b. 1827, d. 1905, mar. Ezra Miller and had 1 son & 2 daus.; 814 Everet M., b. 1830, d. 1902, mar. Elizabeth Williams and had 1 son & 3 daus.; 815 Harriet, b. 1833, d. 1868, unmarried; 816+ James Topping, b. 1835, d. 1909; 817 Lyman H., b. 1838, d. 1892, mar. 1st Arabella Hunt, mar. 2nd Nellie Topping, had 1 son; 818 George W., b. 1840, d. in infancy.

816 James Topping Pierson was born 7 Jun 1835 at Westfield, N.J., and died 13 Dec 1909. He mar. 23 Nov 1864 Catherine Crane Clark (b. 1 Aug 1837, d. 24 May 1926), dau. of Ephraim and Hannah (Baker) Clark. James Topping Pierson told his son, Arthur Newton,

---

[40]*New Brunswick Dutch Church Marriage Records 3*, New Brunswick, N.J.: "Daniel Pierson married Neijie Ockerman (Ackerman) 23 Sep 1798." (New Brunswick is 12 miles south of Westfield, N.J.)

[41]Lizzie B. Pierson, *Pierson Genealogical Records*, Joel Munsell, Printer, Albany, NY, 1878, pp. 64-65.

[42]Arthur Newton Pierson, *Genealogy, the Pierson Family, the Marsh Family, the Clark Family, the Baker Family*, published by author, 1945, p. Pierson 6, and his reference is: Records of baptisms, marriages, and burials in the history of the Presbyterian Church, Westfield, New Jersey.

[43]Arthur Newton Pierson, *Genealogy, the Pierson Family, the Marsh Family, the Clark Family, the Baker Family*, published by author, 1945, p. Pierson 6, and his reference is: Records of baptisms, marriages, and burials in the history of the Presbyterian Church, Westfield, New Jersey.

[44]Arthur Newton Pierson, *Genealogy, the Pierson Family, the Marsh Family, the Clark Family, the Baker Family*, published by author, 1945, p. Pierson 6, and his reference is: Records of baptisms, marriages, and burials in the history of the Presbyterian Church, Westfield, New Jersey.

the following family legend: "My father, Squire Pierson 2nd, told me that his father, Squire Pierson 1st, told him, before leaving for Ohio in 1816, that his father was a Revolutionary soldier, born in Elizabeth Town, and that his ancestors came to Elizabeth Town from Southampton, Long Island, about 1680." Research by Arthur Newton Pierson has shown this to be a true legend as recorded above. James Topping and Catherine Pierson were buried in the family plot at Fairview Cemetery, Westfield, N.J. They had chd[45]. 819+ Arthur Newton, b. 1867, d. aft. 1945, mar. 1899 Sadie M. Fowler; 820+ James Willis, b. 1872, d. 1920.

819 Arthur Newton Pierson was born 23 Jun 1867 at Westfield, N.J., and died after 1945 when he published his book[46]. He mar. 14 Mar 1899 at New York city, N.Y., Sadie M. Fowler, dau. of Robert A. and Mary Elizabeth (Drake) Fowler. Arthur Newton Pierson was elected to represent Union County in the New Jersey House of Assembly, and served from 1915 to 1922 inclusively. In the session of 1918, he was the Republican Majority leader, and in 1919 was Speaker of the House of Assembly. In 1923, he was elected to represent Union County in the Senate of New Jersey, and served in that body through 1932. In 1929, he was the Republican Majority leader in the Senate, and in 1930 was President of the Senate. During this term, he was Acting Governor of the State of New Jersey for two weeks during the absence of Governor Larsen. In 1934, he was elected by the Board of Chosen Freeholders as Treasurer of Union County, New Jersey, and was still holding that office in 1945. Arthur Newton and Sadie (Fowler) Pierson had chd. 821 Arthur Newton Jr., b. 16 Aug 1901, mar. 1st 23 Dec 1925 Eltse Van Saun, mar. 2nd 1 Jun 1935 Marcia P. Townley, mar. 3rd 20 Jun 1944 Meriam Coward Rice; 822 Elizabeth Fowler, b. 16 Oct 1903, mar. 1 Feb 1923 Lewis A. Kniffin and had 1 son & 1 dau.; 823 Katherine Clark, b. 23 Aug 1910, mar. 11 Jun 1929 H. Haines Turner and had 3 sons; 824 Margaret Fowler, b. 13 Feb 1913, mar. 1st 19 Jan 1935 Raymond Beck, mar. 2nd 12 Apr 1940 Lewis A. Kniffin.

820 James Willis Pierson was born in 1872, and died 1920. He mar. 1896 Cornelia F. Dodge. They had chd. 825 Helen Dodge, b. 1898, mar. 1924 Elliot M. Marfield; 826 James Topping, b. 1900, mar. 1923 Ruth Abinzin; 827 Phoebe Clark, b. 1914, mar. 1939 Tristram C. Dunn.

788 Moses Pierson (2nd) was born in 1776, and died in 1857, He mar. 1807 Elizabeth M. Brown (b. 1784, d. 1862). They had chd. [47] 800 William M., b. 1808, a minister in 1878 residing in Brooklyn, N.Y.; 801 Daniel M., b. 1810; 802 Charlotte, b. 1811; 803 George W., b. 1813; 804 David M., b. 1815; 805 John, b. 1816; 806 Charles, b. 1818; 807 Avaline, b. 1820; 808 Lydia, b. 1822.

776 Daniel Pierson was born in 1740, and died in 1822. He mar.[48] Elizabeth Allen, dau. of Joseph Allen of Washington Valley area of Somerset Co., N.J., not far from Scotch Plains (NJW:894R). Joseph Allen in his will (NJW:550R) named his son Joseph and son-in-law

---

[45] Arthur Newton Pierson, *Genealogy, the Pierson Family, the Marsh Family, the Clark Family, the Baker Family*, published by author, 1945, p. Pierson 6, and his reference is: Records of baptisms, marriages, and burials in the history of the Presbyterian Church, Westfield, New Jersey.

[46] Arthur Newton Pierson, *Genealogy, the Pierson Family, the Marsh Family, the Clark Family, the Baker Family*, published by author, 1945.

[47] Lizzie B. Pierson, *Pierson Genealogical Records*, Joel Munsell, Printer, Albany, NY, 1878, pp. 64-65.

[48] Joseph R. Klett, *Genealogies of New Jersey Families*, Genealogical Publishing Co., Inc., Baltimore, Md., 1996, p. 231.

Daniel "Person" as executors. Daniel was listed as Samuel in his father's will, probably because it was miscopied from the original handwritten will where it read Daniel. Daniel[49], and his brothers, William and David, migrated from Elizabeth Town, N.J. to Westfield, N.J. and settled there sometime in the 1760's. Daniel Pierson who was always known as a brother of David, purchased the farm west of his brother David and erected his home on the north side of East Broad Street near Springfield Avenue, Westfield. In 1765, Daniel and his wife Elizabeth joined the Baptist Church of Scotch Plains, N.J., as did his brother, David. In the July 1781 tax list[50] at Westfield, Essex Co., N.J., Daniel Pierson and his two brothers, William and David Pierson, are listed. Also listed[51] at Westfield that same date are Person (Abraham & Theophilus), and Pierson (David Jr., David 3rd, Sylvanus, & William Jr.). Some of these last six may be children of 776 Daniel.

763 Jemima Pierson was born 22 Dec 1717, and died 21 Nov 1804. She mar. 1742, James Arnett (b. ca. 1714, d. Oct 1778)[52], son of James Arnett Sr.

764 John Pierson was born about 1719, and died 10 Feb 1774. He was buried in the burying ground at the First Presbyterian Church, Elizabeth, N.J., and his tombstone reads[53], "Here lies ye body of John Peirson who departed this life Febry 10th 1774 in ye 55 year of his age." He mar. Abigail ____ (b. ca. 1728, d. 18 Mar 1782). She is buried in the same graveyard with her husband, and her tombstone reads[54], "Here lies what was mortal of Abigail Pierson the wife of John Pierson who departed this life March 18th A. D. 1782 in the 54 year of her age." They may have had these chd. at Elizabeth, N.J.: 888+ John, b. ca. 1746; and 889+ Jonathan, b. ca. 1750.

888 John Pierson[55] was born about 1746, and "died 11 Aug 1811 in the 66th year of his age." He was buried in the burying ground of the First Presbyterian Church, Elizabeth, N.J. He mar. 1st Rhoda ____ (b. ca. 1747, d. 20 Oct 1791 in the 44th year of her age), and 2d Phebe ____ (b. ca. 1760, d. 7 Apr 1834 aged 74 years). His two wives were buried in the same place as their husband. John and Rhoda may have had these chd. at Elizabeth, N.J.: 890+ Lewis; 891+ Oliver, b. ca. 1769; 892+ Elihu; 893+ William, b. 11 Mar 1777; and 894+ John.

---

[49]Arthur Newton Pierson, *Genealogy, the Pierson Family, the Marsh Family, the Clark Family, the Baker Family*, published by author, 1945, p. 5A, a copy is in Library of Congress, Washington, DC.

[50]MicroQuix, *Colonial America - Pre- 1790 Census Indexes, Tax Lists*, No. CD136, Automated Archives, Inc., 1992.

[51]MicroQuix, *Colonial America - Pre- 1790 Census Indexes, Tax Lists*, No. CD136, Automated Archives, Inc., 1992.

[52]Joseph R. Klett, *Genealogies of New Jersey Families*, Genealogical Publishing Co., Inc., Baltimore, Md., 1996, p. 112.

[53]Wm. Ogden Wheeler and Edmund D. Halsey, *Inscriptions on Tombstones and Monuments in the Burying Ground at the First Presbyterian Church ... at Elizabeth, New Jersey 1664-1892*, Morehouse & Taylor, New Haven, Conn., 1892, p. 11, No. 45.

[54]Wm. Ogden Wheeler and Edmund D. Halsey, *Inscriptions on Tombstones and Monuments in the Burying Ground at the First Presbyterian Church ... at Elizabeth, New Jersey 1664-1892*, Morehouse & Taylor, New Haven, Conn., 1892, p. 11, No. 46.

[55]Wm. Ogden Wheeler and Edmund D. Halsey, *Inscriptions on Tombstones and Monuments in the Burying Ground at the First Presbyterian Church ... at Elizabeth, New Jersey 1664-1892*, Morehouse & Taylor, New Haven, Conn., 1892, pp. 17-18, No. 90, 91, & 92.

890 Lewis Pierson[56] mar. Abigail ____, and had dau.: 895 Mary, b. 27 May 1791, d. 27 Aug 1793.

891 Oliver Pierson[57] was born about 1769, and died 17 Sep 1800 in his 31st year. He mar. Prudence ____, and they had chd.: 896 Charlotte, b. ca. 1794, d. 19 Aug 1814 in the 20th year of her age; and perhaps 897 Oliver, mar. Eliza (Chandler?), and had dau. 901 Mary Chandler (b. 8 Sep 1823, d. 8 Mar 1826).

892 Elihu Pierson[58] mar. Rebekah ____ and they had chd. 898 Prudence, b. 26 Jan 1795, d. 26 Apr 1797.

893 William Pierson[59] was born 11 Mar 1777, and died 22 May 1871. He mar. Catherine A. ____ (b. ca. 1779, d. 6 Apr 1866 in the 88th year of her age). They may have had chd.: 899 Daniel, mar. Joanna Sayre (b. 22 Mar 1793, d. 6 Apr 1819, bur. First Presbyterian Church, Elizabeth, N.J.), dau. of Samuel and Mary Sayre.

894 John Pierson[60] mar. Phebe ____, and they had chd. 900 Elihu, b. ca. 1805, d. 23 Feb 1832 in the 27th year of his age, bur. First Presbyterian Church, Elizabeth, N.J.

889 Jonathan Pierson[61] was born about 1750, and died 11 Jan 1790 in the 39th year of his age. He is buried in the burying yard of the First Presbyterian Church, Elizabeth, N.J. He may have had chd. 902 Jonathan[62], b. ca. 1791, d. 13 Mar 1864 in the 73rd year of his age (bur. First Presbyterian Church, Elizabeth, N.J.).

752 Sarah[63] Peirson mar. Jonathan Crane (d. 1744) of Newark, Essex Co., N.J. They had Crane chd. Samuel; Caleb; Elijah; Nehemiah; John; and Mary (who mar. John Johnson).

---

[56]Wm. Ogden Wheeler and Edmund D. Halsey, *Inscriptions on Tombstones and Monuments in the Burying Ground at the First Presbyterian Church ... at Elizabeth, New Jersey 1664-1892*, Morehouse & Taylor, New Haven, Conn., 1892, p. 56, No. 388.

[57]Wm. Ogden Wheeler and Edmund D. Halsey, *Inscriptions on Tombstones and Monuments in the Burying Ground at the First Presbyterian Church ... at Elizabeth, New Jersey 1664-1892*, Morehouse & Taylor, New Haven, Conn., 1892, p. 19, No. 98; p. 18, No. 93 & 96.

[58]Wm. Ogden Wheeler and Edmund D. Halsey, *Inscriptions on Tombstones and Monuments in the Burying Ground at the First Presbyterian Church ... at Elizabeth, New Jersey 1664-1892*, Morehouse & Taylor, New Haven, Conn., 1892, p. 11, No. 44.

[59]Wm. Ogden Wheeler and Edmund D. Halsey, *Inscriptions on Tombstones and Monuments in the Burying Ground at the First Presbyterian Church ... at Elizabeth, New Jersey 1664-1892*, Morehouse & Taylor, New Haven, Conn., 1892, p. 134, No. 917 & 918; p. 274, No. 1934.

[60]Wm. Ogden Wheeler and Edmund D. Halsey, *Inscriptions on Tombstones and Monuments in the Burying Ground at the First Presbyterian Church ... at Elizabeth, New Jersey 1664-1892*, Morehouse & Taylor, New Haven, Conn., 1892, p. 17, No. 88.

[61]Wm. Ogden Wheeler and Edmund D. Halsey, *Inscriptions on Tombstones and Monuments in the Burying Ground at the First Presbyterian Church ... at Elizabeth, New Jersey 1664-1892*, Morehouse & Taylor, New Haven, Conn., 1892, p. 18, No. 95.

[62]Wm. Ogden Wheeler and Edmund D. Halsey, *Inscriptions on Tombstones and Monuments in the Burying Ground at the First Presbyterian Church ... at Elizabeth, New Jersey 1664-1892*, Morehouse & Taylor, New Haven, Conn., 1892, p. 18, No. 94.

[63]Will of Jonathan Crane, dated 2 Apr 1744, of Newark, Essex Co., N.J., wife Sarah, chd. Samuel, Caleb, Elijah, Nehemiah, John, and Mary Johnson. Proved 1 Oct 1744. Lib. D, p. 181.

Chapter 12
Descendants of Theodore Peirson
Son of Henry

Theodore Peirson is the son of Henry and Mary Peirson of Southampton, Suffolk Co., New York Colony. The following descendants of Theodore Peirson (1669-1726) are copied from Lizzie B. Pierson, *Pierson Genealogical Records*, Joel Munsell, Printer, Albany, N.Y., 1878, pp. 33-34, as a framework to present new data upon. Lizzie Pierson's footnotes, errata, and related appendices are incorporated within the text which is modified by footnoted additional research by the authors of *Pierson Millennium*. An every-name index is provided at the back of *Pierson Millennium* whereas only heads of families were indexed in *Pierson Genealogical Records*. The + symbol after an identifying number indicates more information is provided in a later paragraph of this chapter beginning with the same number.

1 Henry Pierson had chd. 2 John; 3 Daniel; 4 Joseph; 5 Henry, b. 1652, d. 1701; 6 Benjamin, d. 1731; **7+ Theodore**; 8 Sarah, b. Jan. 20, 1660/61. See chapter 8 for more children and information on 1 Henry Peirson's family.

7 Theodore Pierson, was born 1669[1] at Southampton, Suffolk Co., New York colony, and he died[2] at Sagg (Sagaponack), Suffolk Co., N. Y. colony, May 7, 1726. On March 21, 1691/2[3] (Abstracted[4]), 4 lots and 5 acres of meadow allotted to Henry Pierson deceased, which now by agreement belong to Joseph, Henry, and Theodore Pierson, and Mathew Howell assignee to Benjamen Pierson, was sold by Theodore and his two brothers to Mathew Howell. After Theodore's father died in 1680, his mother Mary remarried to the Rev. Seth Fletcher in 1682, and pursuant to a prenuptial agreement, Mary took her three under-age children (Theodore at age 13 and his two youngest sisters), with her to Elizabethtown, New Jersey.

When Theodore reached age 21, he returned to Southampton on Long Island, where the town records begin about him in 1691. In 1691[5], "Theodore Pierson" had cattle in the Southampton township as confirmed by earmarks registered there "that was his brother Benjamin's." In 1693[6], he again recorded cattle earmarks in Southampton township. Theodore mar. ca. 1694 Frances[7] _____, and they lived at Sagg (Sagaponack), 1 mile east of

---

[1] George Rogers Howell, *The Early History of Southampton, L. I., New York, with Genealogies*, 2nd Edition, Weed, Parsons and Company, Albany, New York, 1887, p. 352.
[2] George Rogers Howell, *The Early History of Southampton, L. I., New York, with Genealogies*, 2nd Edition, Weed, Parsons and Company, Albany, New York, 1887, p. 352.
[3] *Town Records of Southampton*, NY, Liber A, No. 2, 1st Part, p. 194.
[4] Henry Hedges, Wm. Pelletreau, Edward Foster, *The Second Book of Records of the Town of Southampton, Long Island, N.Y. with other Ancient Documents of Historic Value*, John H. Hunt, Printer, Sag Harbor, NY, 1877, pp. 126-127.
[5] *Town Records of Southampton*, NY, Liber A, No. 2, 2nd Part, p. 145.
[6] *Town Records of Southampton*, NY, Liber A, No. 2, 2nd Part, p. 162.
[7] Based upon the greater Southampton, N.Y., area 1698 census including Sagg.

Bridgehampton. In 1696[8], the Estimate of the Township of Southampton listed three Piersons: Theodore £38; Joseph £75; and Col. Henry £130, the latter two being Theodore's brothers. In 1698, a census was taken in the Southampton township, and under the title "Mecox, Sagg, and Bridgehampton" was listed "Theoder Peirson," with "Frances Peirson," and children "Theoder Peirson" and "Ann Peirson." Frances was believed to be Theodore's wife because they had son John after the census. The child "Theoder" is believed to be Theodore's son Job who was born a year before the census and referred to in later town records as "Job." Thus this son is dubbed Theodore Job Peirson, believing him to have a middle name that his father does not have as indicated by him never being referred to as Jr. In 1711[9], Daniel Sayre of Bridgehampton wrote a letter to the "Chief Secretary at New York" advising that eleven men of Bridgehampton were engaged in offshore whaling, which list included "Capt. Theodore Pierson." On April 7, 1712[10], Theodore is confirmed by the town of Southampton as owning three quarters fifty in commonage throughout Southampton and is later in 1712[11] granted land accordingly at the Westward Division Speeunk Neck and Tanners Neck and Apocuck Neck. In 1720[12] and 1726[13], Theodore Pierson was elected trustee for the town of Southampton. The last town record mentioning Theodore was dated April 25, 1726[14], where it was mentioned in a Southampton Highways report that the northwest corner of Theodor Peirson's home lot was on Sagg Street in Sagg and that Abraham Peirson's lot and Theophilus Peirson's garden were nearby. Here, it was reported[15] that Theodore Pierson owned a blacksmith shop.

Theodore and Frances had chd. 21a Ann[16]; 21+ Job (Theoder in 1698 census), b. 1697, d. 1788; 22+ John; and 22a+ Gordon[17].

21 Theodore Job Pierson, Captain and Justice, was born 1697 at Sagaponack, Suffolk Co., New York colony, and died[18] there Feb. 28, (1768?) (this death date, provided by Howell, is wrong since Job signed the Association at Southampton in May 1775 along with 130 Job Pierson Jr., and as land was granted by Southampton to "Job Pierson Esq." in 1782). Job appeared in the July 4, 1776 Southampton census as 1 male & 1 female, while 130 Job Pierson Jr. was still living with his father Daniel. Thus, Job died Feb. 28, perhaps in 1786,

---

[8]Henry Hedges, Wm. Pelletreau, Edward Foster, *The Second Book of Records of the Town of Southampton, Long Island, N.Y. with other Ancient Documents of Historic Value*, John H. Hunt, Printer, Sag Harbor, NY, 1877, pp. 361-4.

[9]Co-Chairmen Mrs. Albert W. Topping & Everett C. Foster, Editor Paul H. Curts, *Bridgehampton's Three Hundred Years*, The Hampton Press, Bridgehampton, N.Y., 1956, p. 67.

[10]*Town Records of Southampton*, NY, Liber A, No. 2, 1st Part, pp. 240-41.

[11]*Town Records of Southampton*, NY, Liber A, No. 2, 1st Part, p. 246.

[12]*Town Records of Southampton*, NY, Liber B (Vol. 3), p. 133. Abstract.

[13]*Town Records of Southampton*, NY, Liber B (Vol. 3), p. 135.

[14]*Town Records of Southampton*, NY, Liber A, No. 2, 1st Part, pp. 289-90.

[15]Co-Chairmen Mrs. Albert W. Topping & Everett C. Foster, Editor Paul H. Curts, *Bridgehampton's Three Hundred Years*, The Hampton Press, Bridgehampton, N.Y., 1956, p. 10.

[16]From the greater Southampton, N.Y., area 1698 census including Sagg.

[17]This Gordon was provided by Lizzie Pierson as the son of 66 Jedidiah Pierson. But as the dates of the descendants were 100 years off and as George Rogers Howell provided a different Gordon as the son of 66 Jedidiah, these descendants are attached here as the only possible connection based on the children's names and dates. 22a Gordon is listed as 138 Gordon in Lizzie B. Pierson, *Pierson Genealogical Records*, Joel Munsell Printer, Albany, NY, 1878, p. 34.

[18]George Rogers Howell, *The Early History of Southampton, L. I., New York, with Genealogies*, 2nd Edition, Weed, Parsons and Company, Albany, New York, 1887, p. 352.

but definitely after the 1782 land grant. In the Southampton 1698 census 21 Job was listed as "Theoder," but other records have referred to him as Job. Job was granted land by the town of Southampton: in 1727[19] at Seder Swamps westward of the Little River; in 1738[20] at the Lower Division in Quaquanantuck Purchase; in 1738[21] at North Division in Quaquanantuck Purchase; in 1738[22] at timber land between the Indian line and East Hampton bounds; in 1745[23] at Sagg Harbor; in 1763[24] at Aucaubogue Division in Toppings purchase; in 1763[25] in the Little South Division as Capt. Job Pierson; and in 1782[26] at the Last Division in Toppings Purchase as Job Pierson Esq. (Justice status). In 1747[27], Job was one of the purchasers of 50 acres of land at Sagg, called Smiths Corner. Job held public offices at Southampton: in 1734[28] as trustee; in 1736[29] and 1737[30] as a Supervisor of intestate estates; in 1738[31] as trustee; in 1739[32] as assessor; in 1740[33] as trustee; in 1743[34] as trustee; in 1745[35], "Capt. Job Pierson" trustee; in 1746[36] Capt. Job Pierson chosen supervisor; in 1747[37], 1748[38], 1750[39], 1751[40], 1752[41], 1753[42], 1754[43], and 1755[44] "Justice Job Pierson" present for the town meeting; in 1751[45], 1752[46], and 1754[47] Justice Job Pierson chosen trustee; in 1756[48] Justice at meeting and signed his name "Job Peirson;" in 1757[49] Justice and trustee; in 1758[50] as Justice; in 1760[51] as Justice,

[19] *Town Records of Southampton*, NY, Liber A, No. 2, 1st Part, pp. 296-9.
[20] *Town Records of Southampton*, NY, Liber B (Vol. 3), pp. 166-73.
[21] *Town Records of Southampton*, NY, Liber B (Vol. 3), pp. 184-88.
[22] *Town Records of Southampton*, NY, Liber B (Vol. 3), p. 157.
[23] *Town Records of Southampton*, NY, Liber B (Vol. 3), pp. 143-6.
[24] *Town Records of Southampton*, NY, Liber B (Vol. 3), pp. 302-06.
[25] *Town Records of Southampton*, NY, Liber B (Vol. 3), pp. 320-24.
[26] *Town Records of Southampton*, NY, Liber B (Vol. 3), pp. 405-410.
[27] *Town Records of Southampton*, NY, Liber B (Vol. 3), p. 197. Abstract.
[28] *Town Records of Southampton*, NY, Liber B (Vol. 3), p. 137.
[29] *Town Records of Southampton*, NY, Liber B (Vol. 3), p. 138.
[30] *Town Records of Southampton*, NY, Liber B (Vol. 3), p. 138.
[31] *Town Records of Southampton*, NY, Liber B (Vol. 3), p. 138.
[32] *Town Records of Southampton*, NY, Liber B (Vol. 3), pp. 138-9.
[33] *Town Records of Southampton*, NY, Liber B (Vol. 3), p. 139.
[34] *Town Records of Southampton*, NY, Liber B (Vol. 3), p. 140.
[35] *Town Records of Southampton*, NY, Liber B (Vol. 3), p. 140.
[36] *Town Records of Southampton*, NY, Liber B (Vol. 3), p. 147.
[37] *Town Records of Southampton*, NY, Liber B (Vol. 3), p. 176.
[38] *Town Records of Southampton*, NY, Liber B (Vol. 3), p.201.
[39] *Town Records of Southampton*, NY, Liber B (Vol. 3), p.216.
[40] *Town Records of Southampton*, NY, Liber B (Vol. 3), p.218.
[41] *Town Records of Southampton*, NY, Liber B (Vol. 3), p.220.
[42] *Town Records of Southampton*, NY, Liber B (Vol. 3), p.8.
[43] *Town Records of Southampton*, NY, Liber B (Vol. 3), p.241.
[44] *Town Records of Southampton*, NY, Liber B (Vol. 3), p.247.
[45] *Town Records of Southampton*, NY, Liber B (Vol. 3), p.218.
[46] *Town Records of Southampton*, NY, Liber B (Vol. 3), p.220,
[47] *Town Records of Southampton*, NY, Liber B (Vol. 3), p.241.
[48] *Town Records of Southampton*, NY, Liber B (Vol. 3), p.261.
[49] *Town Records of Southampton*, NY, Liber B (Vol. 3), p.261.
[50] *Town Records of Southampton*, NY, Liber B (Vol. 3), p.262.
[51] *Town Records of Southampton*, NY, Liber B (Vol. 3), p. 273.

Supervisor, and trustee; in 1762[52] as Justice and Supervisor; and in 1764[53] as assessor where he was called Capt. Job Pierson. He mar. Hannah[54] _____ and they had chd. 62+ Lemuel, b. 1723; and 63+ Col. David.

62 Lemuel Peirson 3d was born in 1723 in Suffolk Co., New York Colony. He was referred to as Lemuel Peirson 3d when he registered his cattle firebrand "L. P." at Southampton in 1768[55]. The 3d designation was because Lemuel Sr., son of David Peirson, and Lemuel Jr., son of Lemuel Sr., distant cousins, were present in town. In May 1775, he signed the Association of Americans against British tyranny (see Chapter 16). In Sep and 18 Oct 1776, after the occupation of Long Island by the British during the Revolutionary War, Lemuel Peirson 3rd was moved from Bridgehampton to East Haddam, Conn., with three passengers by Capt. Hubbard Latham, Capt. Joshua Griffeth, and Capt. Elnathan Fellows. After the war ended in 1783, Lemuel returned to Bridgehampton on Long Island. On July 25, 1789[56], Lemuel and his son William witnessed a land transaction in Southampton township. On December 11, 1795[57], Lemuel Peirson sold a land lot in Topping's Purchase to John Horton which was witnessed by his wife Elizabeth and son William (this was the last town record for Lemuel, thus he died after 11 Dec 1795). Lemuel married[58] Elizabeth (his 2nd cousin), dau. of Abraham Peirson of Southampton, and they had chd. 127+ Samuel, b. 1 Jan 1753; 128+ William, b. 1762; and perhaps others.

127 Samuel Peirson[59] was born 1 Jan 1753 at Bridgehampton, Suffolk Co. N.Y. He mar. 17 Dec 1778 Jerusha Conklin, and died 13 Oct 1838. In May 1775, at age 22, he signed the Association of Americans against British tyranny at Southampton (Suffolk County Hall), N.Y. (see Chapter 16). On July 4, 1776, he was living with his father Lemuel 3d during the Southampton census (quantity of males shows all male children there). In 1776[60], "Samuel Peirson, son of Lemuel Peirson the 3d" registered his cattle brand S. P. at Southampton. In 1783[61], "Samuel Pierson of Sagg" registered his cattle earmark at Southampton. On 2 July 1787, he was among the signers of an agreement between the residents of Bridgehampton and Rev. Aaron Woolworth. In 1792[62], "Samuel Peirson, Bridge Hampton," registered a cattle earmark at Southampton that he bought of Col. David Peirson, his uncle. Samuel held Southampton town offices: in 1800[63] as Overseer of Highways 6th district; and in 1802[64] and 1805[65] as Fence Viewer. On January 3, 1803[66], Samuel and his brother

---

[52] *Town Records of Southampton*, NY, Liber B (Vol. 3), p. 328.

[53] *Town Records of Southampton*, NY, Liber B (Vol. 3), p.269.

[54] George Rogers Howell, *The Early History of Southampton, L. I., New York, with Genealogies*, 2nd Edition, Weed, Parsons and Company, Albany, New York, 1887, p. 352.

[55] *Town Records of Southampton*, NY, Liber B (Vol. 3), p. 341, Abstract.

[56] *Town Records of Southampton*, NY, Liber B (Vol. 3), p. 456, Abstract.

[57] *Town Records of Southampton*, NY, Liber B (Vol. 3), p. 473, Abstract.

[58] George Rogers Howell, *The Early History of Southampton, L. I., New York, with Genealogies*, 2nd Edition, Weed, Parsons and Company, Albany, New York, 1887, p. 352.

[59] Lizzie B. Pierson, *Pierson Genealogical Records*, Joel Munsell Printer, Albany, NY, 1878, p. 33.

[60] *Town Records of Southampton*, NY, Liber B (Vol. 3), p. 382, Abstract.

[61] *Town Records of Southampton*, NY, Liber B (Vol. 3), p. 419, Abstract.

[62] *Town Records of Southampton*, NY, Liber B (Vol. 3), p. 428, Abstract.

[63] *Town Records of Southampton*, NY, Liber B (Vol. 3), p. 491.

[64] *Town Records of Southampton*, NY, Liber B (Vol. 3), p. 497.

[65] *Town Records of Southampton*, NY, Liber B (Vol. 3), p. 519.

William Peirson manumitted a female slave named Peggy. Samuel and Jerusha had chd. 271 Joanna, b. Mar. 1, 1780 at Bridgehampton, L. I., mar. Ebenezer White; 272 Samuel Dayton, b. Oct. 4, 1786 at Bridgehampton, L. I., and d. there without issue; 273 Esther, b. Aug. 24, 1789 at Bridgehampton, d. before 1878, mar. D. H. Haines; 274+ Job b. 23 Sep 1791; 275 Mary, b. at Bridgehampton, Nov. 10, 1794, mar. 1815 Samuel Huntting Pierson.

274 Job Pierson[67], was born at Bridgehampton, L. I., 23 Sep 1791, and died 9 Apr 1860; mar. 24 Sep 1815 Clarissa T. Bulkeley, of Williamstown, Mass.; Mrs. Pierson died 1865. They had chd. 451 Sarah Jerusha b. 12 Dec 1816 Schaghticoke, N.Y. (w. of Philip T. Heartt, of Troy, N. Y., in 1839, and had 8 chd.), died 21 Jan 1866 Bloomfield, N. J.; 452 Samuel Dayton, b. 1819, d. 1850; 453+ Job, b. 1824; 454 Mary Bulkeley, b. 18 Aug 1825 Schaghticoke, N. Y. (w. of Oscar F. Winship, U. S. A., and had one son); 455+ John Bulkeley, b. 1828.

453 Job Pierson, Rev.[68], born 3 Feb 1824 Schaghticoke, N. Y.; graduated from Williams College 1842, and from Auburn Theological Seminary in 1847; ordained to the ministry in 1851. He mar. Rachel W. Smith, Feb. 7, 1849, at Geneva, N. Y. He now (1878) resides in Ionia, Mich., and is pastor of a church there. He had chd. 504 Clarissa Taintor b. 15 Sep 1850 Troy, N. Y. (w. of B. Chew of N. Y. city); 505 Samuel Dayton, b. Oct 1852 Pittsford, N. Y.; 506 John W. Smith, b. 1854 Pittsford; 507 Bowen Whiting b. 1858 Victor, N. Y.; 508 Philip T. Heartt, b. 1859 Victor, N. Y.

455 John Bulkeley Pierson[69], b. 7 Jan 1828 Schaghticoke, N. Y. (m. Mary Lockwood), now (1878) resides in Troy, N. Y.; had chd. 509 Mary L., b. 25 Oct 1863, and d. 13 Apr 1867.

128 Capt. William Pierson[70] was born 1762. He married[71] Ruth Hedges (b. 31 Dec 1766), the youngest dau. of Col. Jonathan and Phebe Hedges. In 1784[72], "William Peirson" registered a cattle ear mark at Southampton that he bought of Daniel Pierson (probably the nephew of William's grandfather Job). On 25 Jul 1789[73], William and his father Lemuel witnessed a land transaction at Southampton. On 11 Dec 1795[74], William and his mother Elizabeth Peirson witnessed a land transaction at Southampton for his father Lemuel Peirson. William held public office at Southampton: in 1796[75] as "Lieut. William Peirson" 6th district Overseer of Highways; in 1798[76] as "Capt. William Peirson" Trustee and Fence Viewer; in 1799[77] as "Wm. Peirson" Overseer of Poor and Trustee; in 1801[78] as Trustee; in 1803[79] as "Capt. Wm. Pierson" Assessor and Trustee; in 1804[80] as Trustee; in 1805[81] as

[66]Town Records of Southampton, NY, Liber B (Vol. 3), p. 504, Abstract.
[67]Lizzie B. Pierson, Pierson Genealogical Records, Joel Munsell Printer, Albany, NY, 1878, p. 33.
[68]Lizzie B. Pierson, Pierson Genealogical Records, Joel Munsell Printer, Albany, NY, 1878, p. 33.
[69]Lizzie B. Pierson, Pierson Genealogical Records, Joel Munsell Printer, Albany, NY, 1878, p. 33.
[70]Lizzie B. Pierson, Pierson Genealogical Records, Joel Munsell Printer, Albany, NY, 1878, p. 33.
[71]George Rogers Howell, The Early History of Southampton, L. I., New York, with Genealogies, 2nd Edition, Weed, Parsons and Company, Albany, New York, 1887, p. 290.
[72]Town Records of Southampton, NY, Liber B (Vol. 3), p. 421, Abstract.
[73]Town Records of Southampton, NY, Liber B (Vol. 3), p. 456, Abstract.
[74]Town Records of Southampton, NY, Liber B (Vol. 3), p. 473, Abstract.
[75]Town Records of Southampton, NY, Liber B (Vol. 3), pp. 477-8.
[76]Town Records of Southampton, NY, Liber B (Vol. 3), pp. 485-6.
[77]Town Records of Southampton, NY, Liber B (Vol. 3), p. 489.
[78]Town Records of Southampton, NY, Liber B (Vol. 3), p. 492.
[79]Town Records of Southampton, NY, Liber B (Vol. 3), p. 507.

Assessor; and in 1807[82] as Trustee. On 3 Jan 1803[83], William and his brother Samuel manumitted a female slave named Peggy. On 3 Apr 1804[84], the Commissioners of Highways of Southampton township described "The line by us established in front of Capt. Wm. Peirsons home lot which line runs straight from the NE corner of Deacon Hedges home lot to the SE corner of the shoemakers shop of Capt. Wm. Peirson." William and Ruth had chd. 276 Terril; 277 Alfred, b. 1793; 278 Thos. Jefferson; 279 Hiram.

63 Col. David Pierson[85] was the son of Job and Hannah Peirson. Col. David Peirson held public office in Southampton: in 1787[86] as Trustee; in 1789[87] and 1790[88] as Commissioner of Highways; and in 1791[89] as Trustee (that year also was elected Capt. David Peirson Trustee and David Peirson Jr. Fence Viewer, showing that these other Davids are different people). In 1792[90], Col. David Peirson sold cattle to his nephew Samuel Peirson. Col. David Peirson had chd. 129 David.

22 John Pierson was born about 1700 (based on his elder brother Job's birth of 1697), and died after 1763 (last Southampton town record). John was granted land at Southampton township: in 1727[91] at "Seder Swamps westward of ye Little River"; in 1738[92] at the lower (south) Division in Quaquanantuck Purchase; in 1738[93] in the north Division of Quaquanantuck Purchase; in 1738[94] at timber land between the Indian line and East Hampton bounds; in 1739[95] at Canoe place Division in Quaquanantuck Purchase; and in 1763[96] at the Little South Division in Southampton. "John Peirson" registered cattle earmarks at Southampton in 1729[97]. In 1738/39[98], "John Peirson of Bridge Hampton" and Elnathan White purchased 50 acres in Southampton from Thomas Chatfield of East Hampton and divided it between them. In 1740[99], John and his brother Job witnessed a land transaction at Southampton township. In 1742[100], "John Pierson, blacksmith," purchased 14 acres in Southampton township from Nathaniel Rusco, weaver. In 1746[101], John Pierson purchased three acres adjacent to his property at Sagg from Hezakiah

---

[80] *Town Records of Southampton*, NY, Liber B (Vol. 3), p. 511.

[81] *Town Records of Southampton*, NY, Liber B (Vol. 3), p. 519.

[82] *Town Records of Southampton*, NY, Liber B (Vol. 3), p. 530.

[83] *Town Records of Southampton*, NY, Liber B (Vol. 3), p. 504, Abstract.

[84] *Town Records of Southampton*, NY, Liber B (Vol. 3), pp. 525-6, Abstract.

[85] Lizzie B. Pierson, *Pierson Genealogical Records*, Joel Munsell Printer, Albany, NY, 1878, p. 33.

[86] *Town Records of Southampton*, NY, Liber B (Vol. 3), p. 434.

[87] *Town Records of Southampton*, NY, Liber B (Vol. 3), p. 448.

[88] *Town Records of Southampton*, NY, Liber B (Vol. 3), p. 455.

[89] *Town Records of Southampton*, NY, Liber B (Vol. 3), p. 457.

[90] *Town Records of Southampton*, NY, Liber B (Vol. 3), p. 428, Abstract.

[91] *Town Records of Southampton*, NY, Liber A, No. 2, 1st Part, pp. 296-299.

[92] *Town Records of Southampton*, NY, Liber B (Vol. 3), pp. 166-73.

[93] *Town Records of Southampton*, NY, Liber B (Vol. 3), pp. 184-88.

[94] *Town Records of Southampton*, NY, Liber B (Vol. 3), p. 157.

[95] *Town Records of Southampton*, NY, Liber B (Vol. 3), pp. 189-94.

[96] *Town Records of Southampton*, NY, Liber B (Vol. 3), pp. 320-24.

[97] *Town Records of Southampton*, NY, Liber A, No. 2, 1st Part, p. 299.

[98] *Town Records of Southampton*, NY, Liber B (Vol. 3), pp. 248-9. Abstract.

[99] *Town Records of Southampton*, NY, Liber B (Vol. 3), p. 115. Abstract.

[100] *Town Records of Southampton*, NY, Liber B (Vol. 3), p. 182, Abstract.

[101] *Town Records of Southampton*, NY, Liber B (Vol. 3), p. 182, Abstract.

Topping. In 1750[102], John sold land and an orchard at Great Orchard to Henry Howell which he originally purchased from Edward Howell. In 1761[103], John registered cattle fire brand "P" with Southampton. John Peirson had chd.[104] 64+ Daniel W.; 65+ Stephen; 66+ Jedidiah.

64 Daniel W. Pierson was born about 1736 (based on his eldest son's birth in 1758), and died after 1804 (last town record of him). In 1769[105], "Daniel Pierson" registered cattle ear marks at Southampton. In May 1775, Daniel signed the Association at Southampton of the Americans against British tyranny (see Chapter 16). He appeared in the July 4, 1776, census of Southampton, Suffolk Co., N.Y., east of the Watermill, with 3 males and 5 females. In 1784[106], Daniel sold cattle to William Peirson. In 1804[107], "Daniel Peirson" was one of three men who bonded 300 pounds to obtain 150 pounds from the town of Southampton to support the gospel at Sag Harbor. The last Southampton town record for Daniel on April 3, 1804[108] mentions a Commissioners of Highways report which describes a highway going "straight to the NE corner of Daniel W. Peirson's house." Daniel Pierson[109] had chd. 130+ Job, b. 1758; 131+ John, b. 1772; and 130a, b, c, & d, four daughters (1776 census).

130 Job Pierson[110] was born 1758 in Southampton township, Long Island, N.Y. He signed the Association of Americans against British tyranny at Southampton (County Hall, Suffolk Co., N.Y.) in May 1775 at age 16. During the Southampton census on July 4, 1776, he was still living at home with his father, 64 Daniel, who had all his children at home in 1776. He was in Capt. Ezekiel Mulford's 12th Company, Minutemen Regiment, during the Revolutionary War. On 26 July 1776, his military records provided[111]: Job Pierson (a Private), residence Southampton, age 17, born Southampton, 5 ft. 8 in. tall, dark complexion, brown hair, occupation blacksmith. Perhaps he married ____ Halsey (see children's names). In 1792[112], "Job Peirson" registered cattle ear marks at Southampton. He had chd. 280 James; 281 Halsey; 282 Alanson.

131 John Pierson[113] was born in 1772, and died in 1853. He married[114] Hannah (b. 12 Aug 1772), dau. of Daniel and Sarah (Baker) Hedges. They had chd. 283 Nathaniel; 284 John; 285 Daniel H. (Daniel Hedges?).

65 Stephen Peirson was the son of John Peirson. He[115] had chd. 132 James; 133 John.

---

[102]*Town Records of Southampton*, NY, Liber B (Vol. 3), p. 238, Abstract.
[103]*Town Records of Southampton*, NY, Liber B (Vol. 3), p. 271, Abstract.
[104]Lizzie B. Pierson, *Pierson Genealogical Records*, Joel Munsell Printer, Albany, NY, 1878, p. 34.
[105]*Town Records of Southampton*, NY, Liber B (Vol. 3), p. 344, Abstract.
[106]*Town Records of Southampton*, NY, Liber B (Vol. 3), p. 421, Abstract.
[107]*Town Records of Southampton*, NY, Liber B (Vol. 3), p. 513, Abstract.
[108]*Town Records of Southampton*, NY, Liber B (Vol. 3), pp. 525-6, Abstract.
[109]Lizzie B. Pierson, *Pierson Genealogical Records*, Joel Munsell Printer, Albany, NY, 1878, p. 34.
[110]Lizzie B. Pierson, *Pierson Genealogical Records*, Joel Munsell Printer, Albany, NY, 1878, p. 34.
[111]Frederic Mather, *The Refugees of 1776 from Long Island to Connecticut*, Genealogical Publishing Company, Baltimore, MD, 1972, p. 1005.
[112]*Town Records of Southampton*, NY, Liber B (Vol. 3), p. 429, Abstract.
[113]Lizzie B. Pierson, *Pierson Genealogical Records*, Joel Munsell Printer, Albany, NY, 1878, p. 34.
[114]George Rogers Howell, *The Early History of Southampton, L.I., New York with Genealogies*, 2nd Edition, Weed, Parsons and Company, Albany, NY, 1887, p. 288.
[115]Lizzie B. Pierson, *Pierson Genealogical Records*, Joel Munsell Printer, Albany, NY, 1878, p. 34.

66 Jedidiah Peirson was the son of John Peirson. In 1764[116] and 1770[117], "Jedediah Peirson" registered cattle ear marks with the Southampton township. In May 1775, he signed the Association of Americans against British tyranny at County Hall, Suffolk County, N.Y. In the July 4, 1776, Southampton census, east of the Watermill, he and is family were listed with 5 males (2 over age 16 and 3 under age 16) and 4 females (1 over age 16 and 3 under age 16). After the British invasion of Long Island, "Jedidiah Peirson from Southampton, E. Dist." (probably Bridgehampton) was moved to Stonington, Conn., in Sep 1776, with four in the family and his goods, by Capt. Ephraim Pendleton. On 2 July 1787, Jedidiah was among the signers of an agreement between the residents of Bridgehampton and Rev. Aaron Woolworth. He[118] had chd. 134+ Caleb, b. 1764, d. 1834; 135 Daniel; 136 Peleg; 137 Andrew; 138+ Gordon, b. 1787.

134 Caleb Pierson[119] was born in 1764, and died in 1834. On 2 July 1787, Caleb was among the signers of an agreement between the residents of Bridgehampton and Rev. Aaron Woolworth. In 1805[120], he was chosen town officer as Fence Viewer at Southampton. He may have held other Southampton offices, but the town records were not reviewed after 1807 by this author. He had son 286 Theodore.

138 Gordon Pierson[121] was born in 1787, and had wife Matsey (b. 1789). Gordon and Matsey had chd. 840 Theodore b. 1820, mar.[122] Phebe (b. ca. 1828), dau. of Benjamin Halsey Foster and Fanny Sayre; 841 David b. 1825, mar.[123] Helen, dau. of Rogers Cook; 842+ Elihu M. b. 1832; and 843 Jerusha b. 1834.

842 Elihu[124] M. Pierson was born in 1832. In the Arctic Ocean in 1865[125], Elihu M. Pierson was a crew member aboard one of the nine ships that were fired by the Confederate steamer *Shenandoah*. Capt. Jeremiah Ludlow of Bridgehampton lost his ship, the *Isaac Howland*. The affair was a ghastly tragedy, for Capt. Ludlow when taken aboard the *Shenandoah* begged Capt. Wardell to spare the fleet as the war was over, and showed him papers telling of the surrender of Lee. But Capt. Wardell called them "Yankee lies" and ordered the destruction. Capt. Jeremiah Ludlow's description of the scene chills the blood. Nine great whaling ships, full of oil, the very wooden framework soaked with oil, became "great forks of flame, blood red, tipped with pitchy smoke ... around the doomed craft the very sea burned." Others in Bridgehampton involved in the nine-ship fleet were Capt.

[116]*Town Records of Southampton*, NY, Liber B (Vol. 3), p. 282, Abstract.

[117]*Town Records of Southampton*, NY, Liber B (Vol. 3), p. 347, Abstract.

[118]Lizzie B. Pierson, *Pierson Genealogical Records*, Joel Munsell Printer, Albany, NY, 1878, p. 34.

[119]Lizzie B. Pierson, *Pierson Genealogical Records*, Joel Munsell Printer, Albany, NY, 1878, p. 34.

[120]*Town Records of Southampton*, NY, Liber B (Vol. 3), p. 519.

[121]George Rogers Howell, *The Early History of Southampton, L. I., New York, with Genealogies*, Weed, Parsons and Company, Albany, NY, 1887, p. 353.

[122]George Rogers Howell, *The Early History of Southampton, L. I., New York, with Genealogies*, Weed, Parsons and Company, Albany, NY, 1887, p. 251. Phebe also married Elihu Pierson according to p. 353 of Howell's book.

[123]George Rogers Howell, *The Early History of Southampton, L. I., New York, with Genealogies*, Weed, Parsons and Company, Albany, NY, 1887, p. 213.

[124]George Rogers Howell, *The Early History of Southampton, L. I., New York, with Genealogies*, Weed, Parsons and Company, Albany, NY, 1887, p. 353.

[125]Co-Chairmen Mrs. Albert W. Topping & Everett C. Foster, Editor Paul H. Curts, *Bridgehampton's Three Hundred Years*, The Hampton Press, Bridgehampton, N.Y., 1956, pp. 69-70.

Benjamin Halsey and Gurden Pierson Ludlow. Elihu M. Pierson mar.[126] Phebe, dau. of B. Halsey Foster, and they had a dau. 844 Clara F. b. Dec. 1862 (or Jan 1863).

22a Gordon Pierson[127] had chd. 287+ Elihu b. 1734; 288 Theodore; 289 Peleg; 290 Mary (of N. J.); 291 Esther (lived with Elihu at the time of his marriage); 292 Joseph, d. 1755.

287 Elihu Pierson was born[128] 1 Aug 1734 at Southampton, Suffolk Co., N.Y. colony, and died[129] 12 Jul 1812 in New Jersey. He moved to Orange, N.J., about 1776, and taught school there. During the Revolutionary War, Elihu was a Private in the New Jersey militia.[130] "Elihu Peirson" was on tax lists[131] in Newark Twp., Essex Co., N.J., in Feb. 1780, Jul. 1781, Feb. 1782, Jul. 1782, and Jul. 1783. "Elihu Pierson" appeared in a census record[132] in July-August 1789 at Newark Twp., Essex Co., N.J. He married Catharine Baldwin of Orange, N.J., and they had chd., all born at Southampton, Suffolk Co., N.Y., before they moved to New Jersey: 456 Hannah, b. Jan. 13, 1762; 457 Stephen, b. Jan. 5, 1764; 458 Silas, b. Apr. 16, 1766, d. 1787; 459+ David b. Mar. 7, 1769; 460 Daniel, b. Sept. 22, 1772; 461 Phebe, b. Aug. 25, 1776, d. 1815, mar. Stephen Dodd.

459 David Pierson was born Mar. 7, 1769 at Southampton, Suffolk Co., N.Y. He married 90 Joanna Pierson, dau. of 45 Caleb Pierson of New Jersey (the 90 and 45 reference numbers are from the Descendants of Thomas Pierson Sr. of Chapter 13). They had chd. 510 Elizabeth, b. 1795; 511 Phebe, b. 1797; 512+ Aaron, b. Mar. 22, 1802; 513 David Austin, b. 1808; and 514 Geo. Ambrose, b. 1812.

512 Aaron Pierson was born Mar. 22, 1802. He married Mary Cook of Caldwell, N.J., and they had chd. 515 Phebe J., b. 1830; 516 David Munroe, b. 1832; and 517+ Theodore Francis, b. 1834.

517 Theodore Francis Pierson was born 1834 in New Jersey. He mar. M. C. Dodd of Bloomfield, N.J., and they lived in Orange, N.J. By 1878, they had five children.

[126]George Rogers Howell, *The Early History of Southampton, L. I., New York, with Genealogies*, Weed, Parsons and Company, Albany, NY, 1887, p. 353. Phebe also married Theodore Pierson according to p. 251 of Howell's book.
[127]Lizzie B. Pierson, *Pierson Genealogical Records*, Joel Munsell, Printer, Albany, NY, 1878, p. 34.
[128]*DAR Patriot Index*, Centennial Edition, National Society of the Daughters of the American Revolution, 1994, part 3, p. 2257.
[129]*DAR Patriot Index*, Centennial Edition, National Society of the Daughters of the American Revolution, 1994, part 3, p. 2257.
[130]*DAR Patriot Index*, Centennial Edition, National Society of the Daughters of the American Revolution, 1994, part 3, p. 2257.
[131]MicroQuix, *Colonial America - Pre-1790 Census Indexes, Tax Lists*, No. CD136, Automated Archives, Inc., 1992.
[132]MicroQuix, *Colonial America - Pre-1790 Census Indexes, Tax Lists*, No. CD136, Automated Archives, Inc., 1992.

Chapter 13
Descendants of Thomas Pierson Sr.
American Immigrant

The following descendants of Thomas Pierson Sr. (1634-1701) are copied from Lizzie B. Pierson, *Pierson Genealogical Records*, Joel Munsell, Printer, Albany, N.Y., 1878, pp. 34-47 and pp. 78-87, as a framework to present new data upon. Lizzie Pierson's footnotes, errata, and related appendices are incorporated within the text which is modified by footnoted additional research by the authors of *Pierson Millennium*. An every-name index is provided at the back of *Pierson Millennium*. The + symbol after an identifying number indicates more information is provided in a later paragraph beginning with the same number in this chapter.

1 Thomas Pierson Sr. was christened[1] 6 Aug 1634 at Dewsbury, Yorkshire, England, son of Rev. Samuel Pierson of Dewsbury (brother of Rev. Abraham Pierson of Branford, Ct.). See Chapter 4 for parents, siblings, and ancestors of Thomas. After completing his apprenticeship as a weaver in England, Thomas emigrated to Branford, Connecticut, about 1661, where he joined his uncle, Rev. Abraham Pierson. Thomas Pierson was called Thomas Sr.[2] to distinguish him from Rev. Abraham Pierson's son Thomas (d. before 1684). Both Thomas's had home-lots set off to them in Newark, N.J., and both are mentioned in various official positions, up to 1684; therefore some confusion concerning them has arisen.

Thomas Pierson Sr.[3] is first recorded in America at Branford, Connecticut. The Town Records of Branford say Thos. Pierson mar. Nov. 27, 1662, Maria Harrison (dau. of Richard Harrison, b. ca. 1596 of West Kirby, Cheshire, England, d. 25 Oct 1653 Branford, Conn.)[4], both of Branford. Thomas was one of the signers of Heads of Families at Branford Oct. 30, 1666, that agreed to move to Newark, New Jersey. Accordingly that fall, with Rev. Abraham Pierson at their head, they went to Newark. At Newark, Thomas took his six-acre home-lot, to which each settler was entitled, on what is now (1878) the center of Newark, New Jersey. He was made townsman in 1677, constable in 1679, and grand juryman in 1680. He appraised the property of Rev. Abraham Pierson in 1678, whose will he witnessed in 1668.

Excerpts from the will[5] of Thomas Pierson: "Jan. 12, 1697-8. The will of Thomas Pierson Sr. of Newark, New Jersey. Children -- Samuel, Thomas (youngest son), Hannah, Abigail, Mary, Elizabeth. Real and personal estate. Son(-in-law), Samuel Lyon, executor. Witnesses

---

[1] Samuel Joseph Chadwick, *The Registers of Dewsbury, Yorkshire, Vol. 1, 1538-1653*, Joseph Ward & Co., Dewsbury, Record Series of the Yorkshire Archaeological Society, no publication date given (near 1900), pp. 123, 125, 130, 136, 141, 147, 160, 165.

[2] Lizzie B. Pierson, *Pierson Genealogical Records*, Joel Munsell, Printer, Albany, NY, 1878, Note E, p. 75.

[3] Lizzie B. Pierson, *Pierson Genealogical Records*, Joel Munsell, Printer, Albany, NY, 1878, pp. 34-35.

[4] Joseph R. Klett, *Genealogies of New Jersey Families*, Genealogical Publishing Co., Inc., Baltimore, Md., 1996, pp. 250-252.

[5] Edited by A. Van Doren Honeyman, *Documents Relating to the Colonial History of the State of New Jersey*, Volume II -- 1730-1750, The Unionist-Gazette Association, Printers, Somerville, N.J., p. 563.

-- Zophar Beech, Jonathan Tichnar, Benjamin Lyon. Proved March 3, 1700/1. May 1, 1701 letters of administration issued to Samuel Lyon of Newark (E. J. D., Lib. G, pp. 278-279)."

Thomas and Maria had chd. 2+ Samuel b. 1663, d. 1730; 3 Hannah; 4 Elizabeth; 5 Abigail; 6 Mary (mar. Samuel Lyon); and 7+ Thomas b. 1678, d. 1758.

2 Samuel Pierson was born at Branford, Connecticut, in 1663, and moved to Newark, New Jersey, with his parents at age 3. He married Mary Harrison (b. 1664, d. 15 Nov 1732), dau. of his uncle Sgt. Richard Harrison (b. ca. 1622). He moved to Orange, N.J., and was a carpenter. He was a deacon in the old 1st Presbyterian church of Orange. He died 19 Mar 1730, and was buried in the "old graveyard, with an honorable memorial" (written Samuel Pairson on tombstone) at Orange. They had chd.: 8+ Joseph, b. 1693, d. 1759; 9+ Samuel, b. 1698, d. 1781; 10+ James[6] (who moved to Lake Champlain [borders New York and Vermont], and died there leaving son Moses); 11+ Daniel (Judge), b. 1703, d. 1777; 12+ Caleb; 13 Jemima; 14 Mary, m. Samuel Dodd (1695-1773); 15 Hannah, b. 1729, d. 1794.

8 Joseph Pierson was born in 1693, and died in 1759. He lived and died in Orange, N.J. Joseph mar. Hepzibah Camp (b. 1696, d. 1769), and they had chd. 18 Sarah, b. 1718, d. 1737, m. Tim. Meeker, mother of Jos. Meeker & Mrs. Isaac Smith; 19 Jemima, b. 28 Aug 1734, d. 17 Sep 1819, m. Benj. Munn (1730-1818); 20+ Patience; 21+ Bethuel, b. 1721, d. 1791; 22 Joseph; 23 Eliz., d. young; 24 Mary, d. 1763; 25 Eliz. 2d, b. 1735, d. 1763, m. ____ Taylor.

20 Patience Pierson married 31 Joseph Pierson, son of 13 Joseph Pierson Jr. (see numbers 13 and 31 of Chapter 9). 31 Joseph Pierson bought land 2 miles west of Morristown, N.J., 1741, and settled there. See the descendants of Joseph and Patience Pierson in Chapter 9.

21 Bethuel Pierson (Dea.), b. 1721, d. 1791, mar. 1st Eliz. Riggs (b. 1725, d. 1776), dau.[7] of James Riggs, and 2d widow Taylor. He was ruling elder of the old 1st church of Orange, N.J., the last 23 years of his life. He was buried in the old graveyard at Orange, N.J. He contributed toward the 1st church parsonage, 1748. He was listed Sep.1, 1755, as a Newark Twp., Essex Co., N.J., freeholder. On 7 May 1783, he advertised[8] in the New Jersey Gazette newspaper, "Bethuel Pierson, Orange, Essex Co., advertises for a runaway Negro man, Pompey, about 37 years old." In 1786, the Orange academy (Orange, N.J.) was established, of which Deacon Bethuel was one of the trustees. He had chd. 53+ Joseph, b. 1754, d. 1835; 54+ Cyrus, b. 1756, d. 1804; 55 Rhoda; 56 Mary.

53 Joseph Pierson, b. 1754, d. 1835, mar. 1st Hannah (1763-1802), dau. of Aaron Baldwin, and 2d Rebecca Campbell. They lived in So. Orange, N.J. Joseph was ruling elder in the old 1st church of Orange, after his father's death, 1791. He had chd. 104 Betsey, b. 1776, d. 1825, mar. Ezra Gildersleeve (1771-1846); 105 Nancy, mar. J. Davie of Ky.; 106+ Bethuel; 107+ Calvin; 108 Sarah; 109 Rachel; 110 Joseph.

---

[6] 10 James Pierson may not be the son of 2 Samuel Pierson. Instead he is believed to be the orphaned James Peirson who came to New Jersey from Wales and England about 1715 to apprentice, then went to Lake Champlain, died there, and left a son Moses. He had to serve his indebtedness until reaching adulthood to pay for his passage, which was probably paid by 2 Samuel Pierson, a carpenter. 10 James may be a distant relative of 2 Samuel Pierson in England.

[7] Joseph R. Klett, *Genealogies of New Jersey Families*, Genealogical Publishing Company, Inc., Baltimore, Md., 1996, p. 624.

[8] Thomas B. Wilson, *Notices From New Jersey Newspapers 1781-1790*, Hunterdon House, Lambertville, N.J., 1988, p. 47.

106 Bethuel Pierson, mar. Elizabeth Crowell, and had chd. 238 Hannah, mar. ____ Henderson; 239+ John; and 240 Emily, mar. ____ Pye.

239 John Pierson, of Illinois, had chd. 630 Bethuel; 631 Major Lucius; 632 Elizabeth; 633 Harriet; 634 William; 635 John.   239 John had grand-child C. Davie, by which of his children is unknown.

107 Calvin Pierson, mar. Sally Stockman, and had chd. 241 William; and 242 Matilda.

54 Cyrus Pierson, M.D., b. 1756 at So. Orange, N.J., d. 1804, mar. 69 Nancy Pierson (dau. of 30 Dr. Matthias Pierson of this chapter).   Cyrus graduated from Princeton college 1776; and studied medicine under Dr. Darcy.   Dr. Cyrus Pierson was licensed[9] to practice physic and surgery in N.J. on 28 May 1788, and practiced in So. Orange, N.J.   He moved to Caldwell, N.J., and practiced there 4 years; then to Woodbridge, N.J., where he had an extensive practice until his health failed.   He then moved to Newark, N.J., where he associated himself with Dr. S. Hays, with whom he continued to practice until his death in 1804.   He was buried in the old cemetery in Orange, N.J., but when the Rosedale Cem. opened there, his remains, with others of his family, were moved to it.   Cyrus and Nancy Pierson had chd. 111 Horace, b. 1791, d. 1814; 112 Harriet, b. 1793, unmar.; 113 Sarah D., b. 1796, d. 1852, unmar.; 114 Charlotte, b. 1798, d. 1839, mar. Uzal Crane; 115 Caroline R., b. 1800, d. 1851; 116 Charles, b. 1802, d. 1829; 117+ Cyrus, b. 1804, d. 1862, mar. Angeline Holmes.

117 Cyrus Pierson, b. 1804, d. 1862, had chd. 243 Charles; 244 Adolphus; 245 Wm. Holmes; 246 Caroline R.; 247 Harriet; 248 Eliza H.; 249 Angeline C.; 250 Anna A.; 251 Cyrus F.

9 Samuel Pierson, b. 1698, d. 1781, mar. Mary Sargeant (b. 1700, d. 1779).   He was born at Orange, N.J., and lived all his life between the mountains, tilling the soil.   He had chd. 26 Eunice, b. 1722, m. Isaac Williams; 27 Rebecca, m. Jotham Condit; 28+ Samuel; 29+ John; 30+ Matthias, b. 1734, d. 1809; 31 Mary, b. 1736, d. 1816, m. Nathaniel Williams (1733-1782); 32+ Joseph, b. 1736; 33 Joanna, m. Joseph Taylor; 34+ Zenas.

28 Samuel Pierson died 1781[10].   He mar. Phoebe, dau. of Joseph Harrison.   He was a farmer at Orange, N.J. and died 1699.   Samuel and Phoebe had chd. 57+ Erastus, b. 1753, d. 1837; 58+ Jabez; 59 Sarah, b. 1761, d. 1788, m. Isaac Conner; 60+ Bethuel, b. 1767; 61+ Enos; 62 Lydia, d. 1817; 63 Jotham, b. 1772, d. 1794, m. Lillis Condit; 64 Rebecca, b. 1 Oct 1769, d. 28 Aug 1849, mar. 79 Linus Pierson, son of 32 Joseph of this chapter (see 79 Linus Pierson).

57 Erastus Pierson, b. Nov. 6, 1753, d. Nov 1837 Orange, N.J., mar. Eunice, dau. of Abel Freeman, lived in Orange, N.J.   He was an officer in the Rev. War; was wounded & taken prisoner by the British.   He had chd. born in Orange, N.J.: 118 Rhoda, b. 1781, d. 1861; 119+ Moses; 120 Lydia, b. 1787, d. 1876; 121+ Aaron; 122+ Caleb; 123+ Jotham, b. 1794.

119 Moses Pierson was born in Orange, N.J. where he lived.   He had chd. 252 Ira, b. 1809; 253 Rhoda H., b. 1811; 254 Mary S., b. 1814; 255 Wm. J., b. 1817.

---

[9]Thomas B. Wilson, *Notices From New Jersey Newspapers 1781-1790*, Hunterdon House, Lambertville, N.J., 1988, p. 257.
[10]In Lizzie Pierson's *Pierson Genealogical Records*, she provides a death year of 1751 for 28 Samuel Pierson. However, since he had children born in 1753 and 1772, among others, the death date cannot be correct. Perhaps it was meant to be 1781, but no proof of that guess has been found.

121 Aaron Pierson mar. Elizabeth Bedford and had chd. 256 Albert, b. January 14, 1816; 257 Erastus H., b. May 9, 1817 (lived in Paterson, N.J.); 258 Edwin A., b. Nov. 12, 1818 (lived in St. Louis); 259 Eunice T., b. Dec. 19, 1820; 260 Henrietta, b. Nov. 23, 1822; 261 Martha E., b. Dec. 6, 1824; 262 Mary Ann, b. Feb. 27, 1827; 263 Aaron W., b. Feb. 9, 1829; 264 Jane, b. May 11, 1831; 265 James M., b. July 27, 1833; 266 Hannah, b. Sept. 3, 1835.

122 Caleb Pierson, soldier in War of 1812, mar. 1st 170 Electa and 2d 172 Melinda, daus. of 80 Joseph Pierson of this chapter, lived in Orange, N.J., and had chd. 267 Joseph Austin, b. 1824, d. 1862; 268+ Moses Freeman, b. 1826; 269 Chas. Wilbur, b. 1827; 270 Mary L., b. 1830, d. 1851; 271 Alfred Leander, b. 1833; 272 Ira M., b. 1837, now (1878) lives in Newark, N.J.

268 Moses Freeman Pierson, b. Jan. 19, 1826, was a soldier in the Civil War; and had chd. 471 Helen A.; 472 Emma F.; 473 Charles; 473 Robert G.; 475 Maggie; 476 Anne; 477 Julia; 478 Clara; and 479 Alfred.

123 Jotham Pierson, in War of 1812, b. 1794 Orange, N.J., d. 1868, m. Hannah (d. 1845, dau. of Samuel Williams), had chd.: 273 Eunice, b. 1824, m. ___ Stagg; 274 Harriet E., b. 1827, m. ___ Condit; 275+ Samuel W., b. June 1829; 276 George H., b. January 1835, d. Feb. 1852; 277+ Linus E., b. Nov. 1837; 278 Bethuel W., b. Nov. 1839; 279+ Jotham S., b. June 1842.

275 Samuel W. Pierson was born June 16, 1829 in Orange, N.J., and had chd. 480 Alice G.

277 Linus E. Pierson was born Nov.3, 1837, in Orange, N.J., and now (1878) lives in Newark, N.J. He had chd. 481 Lilian M.

279 Jotham S. Pierson, was born in Orange, N.J., June 2, 1842, and had chd. 482 Eleanor; 483 Eliz.; and 484 William B.

58 Maj. Jabez Pierson, b. vic. of Orange, N.J., lived So. Orange, N.J., mar. Martha, dau. of Stephen Harrison, had chd.: 124+ Israel; 125+ Amzi; 126 Louisa, b. 1800, d. 1867, m. Aaron M. Condit; 127 Lydia, b. 1810, d. 1851, m. Bethuel D. Harrison (b. 1810, son of Stephen).

124 Israel Pierson, born at So. Orange, N.J., mar. Mary A. Willis, and had chd. 280 Elias; 281 Amzi, who lives in Newark, N.J. (1878), and is a printer (mar. A. M. Terhune); 282 Willis; 283 Charles L. (who mar. A. L. Mains).

125 Amzi Pierson, born at So. Orange, N.J., mar. Mary Riker and M. Cockefair, and had chd. 284 Chas.; 285 Lydia.

60 Bethuel Pierson, was born between the mountains (Orange, N.J. area), 1767, d. 1814, bur. in old graveyard at Orange, N.J.; mar. Mary, dau. of Matthew Condit, and had chd. 128 Jabez P. (who mar. H. Robinson, lived in Orange, N.J., and left no chd.); 129 Elijah (of Orange, N.J., and never married); 130 Henry (of Orange, N.J., mar. 1st Sarah Williams, 2d Harriet Jones, and left no chd.); 131+ Hiram; 132 Miranda (w. of Capt. Aaron Peck of Orange, N.J.); 133 Sarah (w. of Caleb Baldwin of Orange, N.J.); 134 Charles H., d. young; 135+ Charles H.; all born in Orange, N.J.

131 Hiram Pierson, was born at Orange, N.J., mar. Mary ____, and had chd. 286 William, and 287 Charles H., both of N.Y.

135 Charles H. Pierson, was born at Orange, N.J., mar. Emily King, now (1878) lives in Newark, N.J., and had chd. 288 Hiram; 289 Maria; 290 George; 291 Sarah; 292 Augusta.

61 Enos Pierson was born in 1762[11] between the mountains in N.J. (his father was a farmer at Orange, N.J.), and died about 1837.   Enos lived in Orange, N.J.   During the Revolutionary War, he was a Private in the New Jersey militia.[12]   He mar. Abigail[13] Cockefair, and they had chd. 136+ Ira, b. 1788; 137+ Lewis, b.1790, d. 1875; 138+ Daniel, b. 1796, d. 1872; 139 Enos, b. 1805 (who left home in Orange, N.J., when young and none of his descendants are known); 140 Sarah, m. Bethuel Williams (son of Samuel); 141 Phebe, b. 1798, m. Silas Dodd Condit (son of Japhia); 142 Mary, m. Lewis Williams (son of Samuel).

136 Ira Pierson, born 1788 in Orange, N.J., mar. Jemima, dau. of Simon Condit, moved to Delaware Co., Ohio, where he died 1873, and had chd. (born in Ohio): 292 Munson; 293 Thompson; 294 Hannah; 295 Pyrena; 296 Catherine; 297 Arzea; 298 Simon; 299 Phebe; 300 Francis, perhaps the one that mar.[14] Mary F. Ross; 301 Albertus.

137 Lewis Pierson b. in Orange, N.J., 1790, served as volunteer in the War of 1812, and died Jan. 17, 1875.   He mar. L. Crane, and had chd. 302 Caleb C., b. July 20, 1822, in Orange, N.J. (he now [1878] resides at Perth Amboy, N.J.).

138 Daniel Pierson born 1796 in Orange, N.J., but moved to Akron, Ohio, where the last years of his life were spent.   He died in 1872.   In Orange, N.J., he married Margaret, dau. of Uzal Harrison, by whom he had chd. 303+ Philander S., b. Dec. 19, 1821; 304+ Ashbel H., b. Sept. 10, 1824; 305 Sarah E., b. Feb. 17, 1828; 306 Albert, b. Feb. 17, 1832, d. 1832; 307 Enos, b. June 16, 1836 (lives in Ohio); 308 Lydia, b. Sept. 16, 1838.

303 Philander S. Pierson, born in Orange, N.J., Dec. 19, 1821, moved with his parents to Ohio in childhood, afterwards returned to N.J., and now (1878) lives at Caldwell, N.J., and is county collector of Essex county, N.J.

304 Ashbel H. Pierson, born in Orange, N.J., Sept. 10, 1824, moved with his parents to Ohio in childhood, afterwards returned to the east, now (1878) resides in Philadelphia, Pennsylvania.   He had chd. 485 Daniel H., b. Nov. 24, 1847; 486 Mary Edith, b. Apr. 12, 1856, d. 1857; 487 Harry N., b. Jan. 18, 1865.

29 John Pierson, born between the mountains (Orange, N.J., area), mar. Phebe Allen, and had chd. 65 Mary (w. of S. Crowell); 66 Caleb (who mar. A. Ball); 67 Joanna (w. of Ebenezer Matthews); 68 Phebe (w. of John Pool).

30 Matthias Pierson, M.D., was born June 20, 1734 between the mountains (Orange, N.J., area), lived in Orange, N.J, all his days, died there May 9, 1809, and was buried in the old graveyard beside his kindred; his remains with those of his wife were afterwards moved to Rosedale Cemetery.   He mar. Phebe Nutman (b. 1742, d. 1826), dau. of Isaac Nutman, of Elizabeth, N.J.   His district of practice embraced the region now (1878) occupied by So. Orange, Orange, Bloomfield and Caldwell, N.J., and to the border of Morris Co., which

---

[11]*DAR Patriot Index*, Centennial Edition, National Society of the Daughters of the American Revolution, 1994, part 3, p. 2257.

[12]*DAR Patriot Index*, Centennial Edition, National Society of the Daughters of the American Revolution, 1994, part 3, p. 2257.

[13]*DAR Patriot Index*, Centennial Edition, National Society of the Daughters of the American Revolution, 1994, part 3, p. 2257.

[14]Viola E. Shaw and Barbara S. Parker, *Madison, New Jersey Presbyterian Church Vital Records 1747-1900*, The Presbyterian Church of Madison, Madison, N.J., 1982, p. 250.

during most of his life he traversed on horseback. During the Revolutionary War, the family fled to the mountains for safety, and the British occupied his house in Orange, N.J. He was one of the corporators of the Orange Academy founded 1785. The Central Presbyterian church of Orange now (1878) stands nearly on the site of the Dr.'s old house. He had chd. 69 Nancy, b. Sept. 8, 1765, d. Aug. 1851, mar. 1790, 54 Cyrus Pierson, M.D. (54 of this chapter), of Orange, N.J.; 70 Sarah (Sally), b. May 21, 1768, m. 1st Rev. Bethuel Dodd and 2d J. Ballard, and lived in Orange, N.J.; 71+ Isaac, b. Aug. 15, 1770; 72 Fanny, b. Mar. 20, 1773, d. Aug. 1828, mar. 1796 Israel Crane of Bloomfield, N.J., and had Crane chd. Mary (b. 1798, d. 1805), Eliz. (b. 1800, mar. E. Beach), Matthias (b. 1802, mar. S. Baldwin), Abigail (b. 1804, mar. Dr. I. Dodd), Mary (b. 1807), James (b. 1809, mar. P. Crane), Phebe (b. 1811, d. 1814); 73+ Matthias, b. June 13, 1775, d. Jan. 4, 1812; 74+ William, b. July 24, 1778, d. Jan. 1844; 75 Mary (Polly), b. Oct. 14, 1781, d. Apr. 4, 1804, never mar.; 76 Harriett, b. Dec. 29, 1786, d. 1840, mar. 1806 Daniel Stryker of Orange, N.J., had Stryker chd. Mary, John, Phebe, Daniel, and Isaac.

71 Isaac Pierson, M.D., b. Aug. 15, 1770 at Orange, N.J., d. Sept. 22, 1833. He graduated at Princeton College, 1789. He succeeded to his father's practice, with whom he pursued his medical studies and continued in practice until his death. He was a fellow of the Medical Society of New Jersey, having been its president in 1827. He was sheriff of Essex County, N.J., and afterwards represented his district in the 20th and 21st congress of the U.S. He mar. 1795 Nancy Crane (b. 1775, d. 1841), dau. of Aaron Crane of Bloomfield, N.J. They lived in Orange, N.J., where the Central Presbyterian Church now (1878) stands. They had chd. 143+ William, b. 1796; 144+ Albert, b. 1798; 145 Phebe S., b. Feb. 26, 1801, d. May, 1877, mar. Stephen Condit (son of Joseph) of Orange, N.J., and had Condit chd. Sarah, Frances, Charles, Albert, Harriet, & Stephen; 146 Fanny, b. July 22, 1803, d. June, 1874, mar. Daniel Jessup (b. 1795, d. 1876) of Florida, N.Y.; 147+ George, b. Oct. 16, 1805; 148+ Edward, b. Apr. 27, 1808, d. Mar. 18, 1866; 149+ Aaron, b. Feb. 28, 1811, d. Aug. 10, 1863; 150 Isaac, b. July 20, 1813, d. May 1, 1841; 151 Harriet, b. Mar. 12, 1816, d. Jan. 15, 1871, mar. Wm. L. Collins of Hartford, Conn., a merchant, and they had Collins chd. Edward, Mary L., Ellen, Frances, William, & Alice; 152 Sarah Ann, b. Mar. 21, 1820, mar. Roderick Terry of Hartford, Conn., and had Terry chd. Henry T. (a professor in a government college in Japan in 1878), Anna, Jennie, Harriet, & Edith.

143 William Pierson, M.D., born Dec. 4, 1796, in Orange, N.J., and died 1882. He graduated at Princeton College 1816. He married Margaret (d. 1853), dau. of Rev. Asa Hillyer. He was a sheriff of Essex Co., N.J., and later the Mayor of Orange, N.J. William and Margaret had chd. 309 Jane Riker; 310 Anne; 311 a babe d. young; 312+ William, b. 1830; 313+ Edward Dixon, b. 1833; 314 Margaret Riker, d. young.

312 William Pierson, M.D., born in 1830 in Orange, N.J., studied medicine with his father, to whose practice he succeeded, and is the 4th Dr. Pierson, of Orange, in direct descent, all of whom have resided within a few rods of the same spot. He mar. 14 May 1856 Belle Adams, and had chd. 488 Margaret; 489 Louisa; 490 Isabella D., b. 1872, d. 1874.

313 Edward Dixon Pierson, born in 1833 in Orange, N.J., died 30 Mar 1882 Orange, N.J., was graduated at Princeton College 1854, studied law, and began the practice of it in Orange, N.J. At the breaking out of the rebellion (Civil War), he enlisted as a volunteer in the U.S. service, and served as Captain in Sherman's division, until the war closed. He then

resumed his law practice in Orange where he now (1878) resides. He mar. Lelia James, and had chd. 491 Edith; 492 William; 493 Annie R., b. 1875, d. 1876.

144 Albert Pierson, Rev., was born Dec. 17, 1798 at Orange, N.J., and died[15] at the same place, June 10, 1864. He graduated at Princeton 1816 (with his bro. Wm.). Though by profession a minister, he became a teacher. He was principal of the Bloomfield Academy, and afterwards principal of the classical school at Orange, N.J., for many years. He mar.[16] April 7, 1827, in Bloomfield, N.J., Jane Armstrong, dau. of Rev. Amzi Armstrong. Albert and Jane had chd. 315+ William Hugh; 316 Edward (d. young); 317 Frances J. and 318 Sarah R., twins (Sarah mar. Jacob L. Halsey); 319 George, a clergyman; 320+ Albert F.

315 William Hugh Pierson, M.D., born in Orange, N.J., where he practiced medicine for a while. He was a surgeon of the U.S. Navy, during the Civil War, and now (1878) lives in Bloomfield, N.J. He married Annie Van Liew, and had son 528 John.

320 Albert F. Pierson[17] was born Dec. 19, 1838 in Orange, N.J. At age 17, he went to Kendall Co., Illinois, engaging in agriculture there. At the outbreak of the Civil War, he enlisted in Company K, 20th Illinois Infantry. He was discharged in New York Nov. 1862, and returned to Orange, N.J. In June 1863, he re-enlisted in Captain Robert's independent company of Newark, N.J., with which he served a short time, and returned to Orange, N.J. In 1868, he organized the firm of A. F. Pierson & Company, engaged in the coal and wood business. Albert mar. Oct. 19, 1876, Adelaide Decker (d. May 11, 1897), dau. of John W. and Maria Louise (Hawes) Decker. They had chd. 636 Albert H., attending Princeton College in 1898; and 637 Alfred, d. age 5.

147 George Pierson, Rev., was born Oct. 16, 1805 at Orange, N.J., and died[18] in 1880. He graduated at Princeton College 1823, and studied for the ministry. He was colleague with Dr. Hillyer in the 1st church of Orange, a short time. Then the brick church (2nd Presbyterian Church of Orange, N.J.) was built, and he was installed the pastor. He remained there a few years, and a short time in Wantage, N.J. But his life's work has been done in Florida, Orange Co., N.Y., where he preached the gospel for 40 years. He mar. 1st Eliza L. Day (b. 1805, d. 1856, dau. of Stephen D. Day), of Orange, N.J., and after Eliza's death, mar. 2d Caroline Stall of Port Jervis, N.Y. He had chd. 321 Sarah Ann, who mar. David McNair of Dansville, N.Y.; 322+ Wilson G.; 323 Isaac, d. young; 324 Caroline Elliott, mar. Rev. Samuel Jessup of Oneida, N.Y.; 325+ Stephen Day; 326 Fanny, d. young; 327 Mary, d. young; 328 Ellen C.

322 Wilson G. Pierson, born in N.J., moved with his parents to Florida, N.Y., when young, where he now (1878) lives and owns a dairy farm. He married Sarah C. Wheeler, and had chd. 494 Charles W.; 495 Eliza D.

---

[15]*Biographical and Genealogical History of the City of Newark and Essex County, New Jersey*, The Lewis Publishing Company, New York and Chicago, 1898, p. 157.

[16]*Biographical and Genealogical History of the City of Newark and Essex County, New Jersey*, The Lewis Publishing Company, New York and Chicago, 1898, p. 157.

[17]*Biographical and Genealogical History of the City of Newark and Essex County, New Jersey*, The Lewis Publishing Company, New York and Chicago, 1898, p. 157-158.

[18]*Biographical and Genealogical History of the City of Newark and Essex County, New Jersey*, The Lewis Publishing Company, New York and Chicago, 1898, p. 157.

325 Stephen Day Pierson, resides in Florida, N.Y., where he owns a dairy farm. He married Phebe Duzenberre, and had chd. 496 Fanny; 497 Harriet W.

148 Edward Pierson, was born Apr. 27, 1808, in Orange, N.J., and died in Newark, N.J., Mar. 18, 1866. All the early part of his life was spent in Orange, and the latter part in Newark. He was for some years the sheriff of Essex Co., N.J., and afterwards engaged in the insurance business. He died suddenly at Newark. He married Phebe Baldwin (d. 1883) of Orange, N.J., and had chd. 329 Matilda; 330 Harriet C.; 331 Aaron D., d. young; 332 Edward, b. 1843, d. 1869 (a young man of promise).

149 Aaron Pierson, was born Feb. 28, 1811, in Orange, N.J., and died Aug. 19, 1863 in Hartford, Conn., and was buried beside his kindred in Rosedale Cemetery in Orange, N.J. His early days were spent in Orange, and the last 13 years in Hartford, engaged in the wholesale drygoods business. He married Mary C. Ogden (b. 1813, d. 1876) of Parsippany, N.J., and had chd. 333+ John Ogden; 334+ Stephen Condit; 335+ Isaac; 336+ Lizzie Benedict.

333 John Ogden Pierson, was born in Orange, N.J., in childhood (1850) moved to Hartford, Conn., where for a time he engaged in business with his father. Later he worked for insurance companies in Hartford, Conn., and Chicago, Ill. He mar. 1st Miss Lewis, 2d Emily Chickering of Boston, Mass., and had chd. 498 Kate Lee; 499 Fred. Hudson; 500 Alice F., d. young.

334 Stephen Condit Pierson, was born in Orange, N.J., moved in childhood (1850) to Hartford, Conn. He graduated at Yale College 1864, and Scientific school 1865. He was a city surveyor in Meriden, Conn., where he still (1878) resides. He mar. Hannah P. Latimer of Simsbury, Conn., and had chd. 501 Guy Rowland P. (d. young); 502 Decius Latimer; 503 Mary Caroline O.; 504 Antoinette P.

335 Isaac Pierson, Rev., was born in Orange, N.J., and moved in childhood (1850) to Hartford, Conn. He graduated at Yale College 1866, and Andover Theological Seminary 1869. In 1870, he went to Northern China as a missionary of the A. B. C. F. M. He mar. Sarah E. Dyer of Cambridgeport, Mass.

336 Lizzie Benedict Pierson, was probably born in Orange, N.J., before 1850. She moved with her parents in 1850 (if she was born in Orange), to Hartford, Conn. Sometime after her father died in 1863 at Hartford, she moved to Andover, Mass., where she was the author of *Pierson Genealogical Records*, published in 1878. After writing the book, she went to China in 1878 to be a missionary with her brother, Rev. Isaac Pierson who had earlier gone to China in 1870 as a missionary. She entrusted her book to Rev. George Rogers Howell (author of *The Early History of Southampton, L.I., New York*) as editor and to ensure its publication, which occurred March 1878. It is unknown to the authors of *Pierson Millennium* if she married, if she returned from China, or when she died. However, Lizzie Pierson has our lasting respect as an author of Pierson records. In her book, Lizzie attempted to connect all Pierson family lines to the family of Rev. Abraham Pierson, last of Newark, N.J., but was unable to make the connections. *Pierson Millennium* fulfills Lizzie Pierson's goal by making those family connections in England for most Pierson lines of the 1600's immigrants.

73 Matthias Pierson, born June 13, 1775, at Orange, N.J., and died Jan. 4, 1812. He was a tobacconist in Orange. He mar. 1801, Polly Baldwin, and had chd. 153 David S., b. June

1802, d. young; 154 Laetitia, d. young; 155+ James, b. June 1807; 156+ Laetitia 2d, b. Feb. 1810, d. Mar. 1866; 157 Matthias, b. Aug. 1817, d. 1832.

155 James Pierson was born June 1807, and died in 1881. He was a carpenter and lived in Newark, N.J. He had chd. 337 Mary J.; 338 Orville.

156 Laetitia B. Pierson, born Feb. 1810, married H. Price of New Jersey.

74 William Pierson, was born July 24, 1778, and died Jan., 1844. He was a hatter, and owned and lived on property adjoining the place of his brother, Dr. Isaac Pierson, in Orange, N.J. William married 1806 Sally Day (d. 1843), and had chd. 158 Sarah, b. June 1807, d. Oct 1843, mar. Wm. Frame and had Frame chd. Jane & Harriet; 159+ Matthias, b. May 1809; 160 Sidney, b. Sep. 1810, d. 1843, never mar.; 161+ Horace, b. June 1814; 162 Mary, b. July 1818.

159 Matthias Pierson was born May 1809 in Orange, N.J. He was a hatter. He mar. Maria (b. 1810, dau. of Charles King). They had chd. 339 Emily, mar. G. Baldwin; and 340 Alice.

161 Horace Pierson, was born June 1814 in Orange, N.J. He lived in Bloomfield, N.J. in 1878. He mar. 1st Rhoda A. Smith (dau. of Daniel) of Orange, N.J., and 2d M. Oakes of Bloomfield, N.J. He had, by his 1st wife, a son 341+ William S., b. Apr. 9, 1841, d. 1861. He had , by his 2d wife, chd. 342 Fred O., b. Nov. 1847; 343 Ella K., mar. G. H. Seymour, and had Seymour chd. Alice & Maude.

341 William S. Pierson, was born Apr. 9, 1841, at Bloomfield, N.J. In the year of the rebellion (Civil War), he enlisted in the 1st Minnesota Regiment of artillery. At the first battle of Bull Run, he was wounded and taken prisoner. After the battle was over, he was taken to Richmond, Virginia, where he died.

32 Joseph Pierson was born 1736[19] at Orange, N.J., and continued to live there. He mar. Rebecca, dau.[20] of Joseph and Hannah Smith, and had chd. 77a Hannah[21], b. 18 Jan 1763 Orange, N.J., d. 15 Mar 1816, mar. Simon Condit (b. 1761, d. 1839)[22], and had Condit chd. Electa (b. 1783), Mary (b. 1785), Joseph (b. 1787), Naomi (b. 1790), Jemima (b. 1792), Jotham (b. 1794), Alvin P. (b. 11 Jun 1801, d. 1 Feb 1883, m. Maria Jacobus), & Hannah (b. 1805); 77 Eunice, b. 1760, d. 1842, mar. Samuel Williams (b. 1754, d. 1824, son of Samuel Williams)[23]; 78 Electa, mar. Zenas Tichenor (son of David); 79+ Linus, b. 7 Feb 1768; 80+ Joseph.

[19]Jotham H. & Eben. Condit, *Genealogical Record of the Condit Family, Descendants of John Cunditt a Native of Great Britain Who Settled in Newark, N.J., 1678 to 1885*, Ward and Tichenor, Newark, N.J., 1885, Appendix, "The Pierson Family," pp. 376-380.
[20]Jotham H. & Eben. Condit, *Genealogical Record of the Condit Family, Descendants of John Cunditt a Native of Great Britain Who Settled in Newark, N.J., 1678 to 1885*, Ward and Tichenor, Newark, N.J., 1885, Appendix, "The Pierson Family," pp. 376-380.
[21]Jotham H. & Eben. Condit, *Genealogical Record of the Condit Family, Descendants of John Cunditt a Native of Great Britain Who Settled in Newark, N.J., 1678 to 1885*, Ward and Tichenor, Newark, N.J., 1885, Appendix, "The Pierson Family," pp. 376-380.
[22]Jotham H. & Eben. Condit, *Genealogical Record of the Condit Family, Descendants of John Cunditt a Native of Great Britain Who Settled in Newark, N.J., 1678 to 1885*, Ward and Tichenor, Newark, N.J., 1885, Appendix, "The Pierson Family," pp. 376-380.
[23]Jotham H. & Eben. Condit, *Genealogical Record of the Condit Family, Descendants of John Cunditt a Native of Great Britain Who Settled in Newark, N.J., 1678 to 1885*, Ward and Tichenor, Newark, N.J., 1885, Appendix, "The Pierson Family," pp. 376-380.

79 Linus Pierson[24] was born 7 Feb 1768 in Orange, N.J., and died 16 Mar 1817. He mar. ca.1795, 64 Rebecca Pierson (b. 1 Oct 1769, d. 28 Aug 1849), his 1st cousin, dau. of 28 Samuel Pierson of this chapter. They had chd. 163+ Jotham, b. 1796; 164 John S., b. 26 Sep 1797, d. 11 Jul 1822, never mar.; 164a Phebe H., b. 18 Jul 1799, d. 1 Nov 1799; 165 Lydia, b. 10 Jul 1800, d. 1865, mar. Benjamin Clark (b. 1803); 166+ Samuel L., b. 30 Jan 1803; 167+ Erastus, b. 12 Apr 1805; 168+ Joseph Morris, b. 8 Aug 1807.

163 Jotham Pierson was born 1796, and died 4 Apr 1828. He lived in Orange, N.J. He mar. Mary Edwards, and had chd. 344 Edward; 345 Samuel; 346 John.

166 Samuel L. Pierson was born 30 Jan 1803, lived in Newark, N.J. in 1878, and died 1879. He mar. Eliza, dau. of John Perry, and had chd. 347 Phebe, mar. ____ Barrister; 348 John; 349 Linus; 350 Anna, mar. ____ Pierson.

167 Erastus Pierson was born 12 Apr 1805 in Orange, N.J. He drove a stage between Orange and Newark, N.J., and lived in E. Orange, N.J. He mar. Abby S. Baldwin (b. 1807, d. 1875), dau. of Ebenezer, and had chd. 351 Jotham; 352 Mary Ann, m. ___ Harrison.

168 Joseph Morris Pierson, Rev., was born 8 Aug 1807 in Orange, N.J., and died in 1873. He was a minister of the Methodist church. He mar. Abby Edwards, and had chd. 353 Mary Riggins; 354 Henry; 355 Albert; 356 Morris; 357 Charles Wesley (who mar. M. Hunter).

80 Joseph Pierson was born in Orange, N.J., and lived there. He mar. Rachel Vincent, and had chd. 169 Sally, d. about 1873, mar. ____ Jones; 170 Electa, b. 1799, d. 1842, mar. 122 Caleb Pierson; 171 Charlotte, mar. ____ Thompson, joined the Shakers; 172 Melinda, b. 1804, d. 1843, was the 2d wife of 122 Caleb Pierson; 173 Mary, mar. 1st Ira Pierson, and 2d Jno. Riggs; 174 Rachel, never mar.; 175 Eliza, never mar.; 176 Linus, mar. R. Peck and went to Ohio to live, his wife died and he mar. again in Ohio.

34 Zenas Pierson was born and lived between the mountains in Orange, N.J., and was a farmer. He mar. Betsey Nixon, and had chd. 81 Samuel, mar. 1st L. Ward, 2d M. Young; 82 Phebe, mar. D. Ross; 83 Zenas, mar. C. Townley; 84 Moses.

10 James Pierson was said to be the son of 2 Samuel Pierson in Lizzie Pierson's book[25] and said James was said by Lizzie to have moved to Lake Champlain and died there leaving son Moses. However, in information provided to Lizzie Pierson by John S. Pierson[26] of New York, she presents a James Peirson, who was sent out to the colonies, about 1715, when he was 16 years old. On his arrival in America, this James Peirson was either sold or apprenticed in New Jersey, till he should become of age, to pay for his passage over. He had a son Moses who settled on property inherited from his father at Lake Champlain. This must be the same James! Thus, it is concluded that 10 James Pierson is not the son of 2 Samuel Pierson, but rather a carpenter apprentice purchased by 2 Samuel Pierson by paying James' passage on his arrival in New Jersey. It is possible that James is a distant English cousin of 2 Samuel Pierson with prior arrangements by letter, though such connections have yet to be found. A possible christening record for James is: "Jacobus

---

[24]Linus Pierson Family Record. The records (GSNJ number 2467) were copied by Charles Carroll Gardner from an 1828 Bible printed by H. & E. Phinney. It's present whereabouts are unknown. The records are published in Joseph R. Klett, *Genealogies of New Jersey Families*, Genealogical Publishing Co., Inc., Baltimore, Md., 1996, p. 594.

[25]Lizzie B. Pierson, *Pierson Genealogical Records*, Joel Munsell, Printer, Albany, NY, 1878, p. 35.

[26]Lizzie B. Pierson, *Pierson Genealogical Records*, Joel Munsell, Printer, Albany, NY, 1878, p. 78.

Person c. 24 Apr 1698, Elland, Yorkshire, England, father Jos. Person" with no brothers or sisters listed in the 1994 IGI[27] for Elland. Elland is located 9 miles west of Dewsbury, Yorkshire, England, where 2 Samuel's grandfather (Rev. Samuel Pierson) resided (see Chapter 4 under Thomas Pierson Sr. of Yorkshire). Other Piersons exist at Elland whose given names (i. e. Abraham, & James) match the family of Thomas Pierson Sr., but the connections have not been investigated via Parish records due to insufficient time prior to publication.

James Peirson's first memories were of living in a fine house, in luxury, with his father an old man, and his mother much younger, there being one or two sisters, much older than himself, but no brothers. He remembers the death of both his father and mother, and his being placed by his friends in a farm house in Wales for his health. Thence, after some time, he was taken by an uncle or brother-in-law, and put on board a ship bound to America, in order to inherit the property belonging to the lad. After arriving in New Jersey, James worked, having before him the purpose of returning to England and Wales, to claim his rights, as soon as able. But he married Esther Williams, and settled down, first in or near Newark, N.J., and afterwards at Hanover, N.J., and then decided to wait until his son Moses was old enough to go for him, which he never did. His will is dated Sept. 3, 1761, at Hanover, N.J., and provided for his wife and four daughters, and gives the rest of his property to his son Moses. In that document, James and his wife's names are spelled Peirson, though the signature seems to be Pirson. James and Esther had chd. 529+ Moses, b. Oct. 17, 1733; 530 Ruth, mar. Nathaniel Tichenor, and had Tichenor chd. Hannah, Esther, & Aaron; 531 Hannah, mar. ____ Baldwin; 532 Martha, mar. ____ Bowers; and 533 Esther, married.

529 Moses Peirson was born Oct. 17, 1733 in Newark, N.J. He always spelled his name Peirson. He lived at Parsippany, N.J., from 1754 to 1770. He mar. March 27, 1754, Rachel Smith (b. Oct. 13, 1735, d. Mar. 22, 1813). Being obliged to sell his property in New Jersey in order to pay off the indebtedness of his father incurred for the benefit of a son-in-law, he bought (or inherited from his father) 1,000 acres, or more, of wilderness land in Vermont, bordering Lake Champlain, and moved upon it with his family in 1770. He built a block house of hewn logs and a log barn. The name of Shelburn was given to the place where he lived. At one time, four sons, and three daughters were settled upon portions of this tract at Shelburn.

Condensed from an article[28] by Moses' youngest daughter, Rhoda: When the 13 colonies declared their independence in 1776, Canada was under British rule and became a nearby enemy to Shelburn. Raiding parties were sent out from Canada to the suburbs of the new United States with Shelburn being the nearest settled place to Canada. In the fall of 1777, they had fears of being disturbed by the British, and a small company of men were sent to Mr. Peirson's relief under the charge of Lt. Barnum. There being no trouble, a part of the company left in Feb. 1778, leaving 15 remaining with Mr. Peirson including Lt. Barnum. On March 12, 1778, the "Battle of Shelburn" took place. The attacking party numbered 57, some being Indians, and some supposed to be Tories or British soldiers disguised as

[27]The Church of Jesus Christ of Latter-Day Saints International Genealogy Index on CD ROM program FamilySearch.
[28]Newspaper article, "A Bit of Local Centennial History," by Mrs. Rhoda (Peirson) Foot, written in 1860, and published Sept. 5, 1877, in the Free Press, Burlington, Vt.

Indians. It was later confirmed that British soldiers had participated. It was an hour before dawn when the guard heard the enemy coming, forgot to fire his gun, and ran into Moses Peirson's log cabin shouting, "They are coming, they are coming!" The men sprang to their feet and caught their guns, but at that instant the house was fired upon. Moses Peirson got out of bed, reached up to the beam for his rifle, and a bullet went through his shirt leaving two holes in it. His body was untouched by the bullet. The men had to get their chance at firing from the small windows. Lt. Barnum gave orders until a bullet struck him in the breast. He fell across a kettle and his blood ran into it. He died there. The Tories set the house on fire with port-fire, which was discovered and put out with beer. During the battle, Mrs. Rachel Peirson was in the bed with her youngest daughter Rhoda, 10 months old, and her other three daughters were in another bed next to her. Capt. Sawyer took command, and the firing was too hard for the Tories. They skulked behind the house, and when one peeped out, he was shot at from the house. The battle lasted until the sun was an hour high. The Tories then crept off as they could on the ice of Lake Champlain. The Tories crossing the ice were seen to cut a hole in the ice and put in some that died. Some Tories behind the barn cried for quarter, and were told to come forward if they wanted quarter. Six Tories were taken prisoner. Six more Tories were found dead around the cabin and one was a great stout Indian. Three of the Whigs were killed, including Lt. Barnum, and some others wounded. None of Moses Peirson's family were injured. The Whigs were put in coffins, but one big hole was dug for the enemy where they were all piled in together. The Indian was thrown in first with his face downward, an old Dutchman calling out "dig your way down to hell."

The British authorities, exasperated by the repulse of their party, offered a large reward for the body of "the notorious rebel Moses Peirson, " dead or alive. An order of the Vermont Council of Safety, directed to Captains Ebenezer Allen and Isaac Clark, alludes to the affair as "Capt. Sawyer's late signal victory over the enemy at Shelburn," orders them to go to his relief, to secure the wheat at Shelburn, and to remove all inhabitants they could not protect, within their lines on Otter Creek. Shortly, Moses Peirson with his family started on the ice for Shoreham, Vermont, 32 miles to the south, with their horse-teams. The cattle were driven by land through the woods. There the family made a stop, found a place on Mr. More's farm, and stayed until next fall.

About this time, some scouts from Canada came out and burned Moses Peirson's house and barn and all the other buildings at Shelburn. From Shelburn, the scouts next went 13 miles south to Vergennes, Vt., where they burned all the log houses and took some prisoners. Among the prisoners was Moses Peirson's eldest daughter, Mrs. Sarah Van Arnum, her husband Isaac, and year old son Miles. They were all kept in a prison at Quebec until the war was over, when they were exchanged.

When Moses Peirson's family left Shoreham in the fall of 1778, they went to Rutland, Vt., 25 miles to the southeast of Shoreham, and remained there and in Clarendon, 7 miles south of Rutland, till peace was declared. But Moses had left his cattle and hogs and two oldest sons, Ziba (age 17) and Uzal (age 15), to kill their meat and try their lard before following. They had completed their work at Shoreham and were ready to start their journey on the following morning. But before dawn a British squad came, fired on the house, which frightened the cattle and they all fled to the woods. The two boys, Ziba and Uzal, and Mr. More, on whose farm they had lived, were made prisoners with others they had found in the town and taken to the British fort at St. John, New Brunswick. The British set fire to the house and burned the meat and lard. When they arrived at St. John, Ziba was handcuffed and locked up while his younger brother Uzal was allowed the run of the fort. The captain took Ziba's pocket compass from him. Later, Ziba's handcuffs were moved and he was also given his freedom within the fort. In March 1779, the captain was leaving on another scouting expedition and came to Ziba and shook his hand leaving the pocket compass in Ziba's hand. A day or two later, Ziba and Uzal made good their escape while the sentinel slept, holing up at a house used as a church until the next night and reached the woods. Then they started on their journey back through woods and clearing, sometimes finding barns to sleep in. They became so faint and hungry that they hit an ox on the head with a hatchet that they found, then cut his throat and skinned the thighs, and took the skin to wrap up their feet, and ate some of the meat. They stole food whenever they could. By April, the snow began to melt and they had to walk through muddy water and snow. They came to Lake Champlain and made a raft to cross. When they reached land they let the raft go and then discovered they were on an island, probably the Isle of Mott. They made another raft, and left the island. Making landfall, they could walk but slowly now due to sore feet and worn moccasins. It was May before they arrived at their father's farm at Shelburn, but they found no friends there and nothing to eat but birds which they killed and ate. They stayed there several days, resting, and then proceeded to Rutland. They arrived in Rutland 40 days after they had escaped. The news of their arrival spread rapidly. One man took his horse and rode from house to house to proclaim the news. Men, women and children flocked to see them and many were the tears of joy shed by their friends at seeing them again, for they had imagined that they were killed by Indians.

When the war was over in 1783, Moses Peirson returned with his family to the place in Shelburn, Vt., that he had left. He died there Feb. 28, 1805. Moses and Rachel had chd., the first eight born at Parsippany, N.J., and the last two at Shelburn, Vt.: 534 James, b. Oct. 3, 1755 at Parsippany, N.J., d. Dec. 14, 1775 of consumption at Shelburn, Vt.; 535 Sarah, b. Oct. 12, 1757, d. ca. 1823 in Richland Co., Ohio, m. Isaac Van Arnum and had Van Arnum chd. (all b. in Shelburn except Geo.) Miles, George F. (b. in Quebec 1779), Rachel, Ethan Allen, & Heman; 536 Zillah, b. July 5, 1759, d. at Hector, N.Y., she mar. Jared Post and had Post chd., all b. at Shelburn, James, Hiram (both drowned, aged 10 and 12, with their father in Lake Champlain about 1796), Henry (moved to Ohio), Polly (mar. ____ Dee, and lived and d. in Georgia, Vt.), Sally (mar. ____ Tyler), Laura (b. 1792, d. Apr. 15, 1814), and Sophia (d. Mar. 7, 1814, aged 19); 537+ Ziba, b. May 9, 1761; 538+ Uzal, b. May 4, 1763; 539+ William, b. Jan. 15, 1765; 540 Hannah, b. Mar. 13, 1767, mar. ____ Rich of Richland, N.Y.; 541+ Samuel, b. Jan. 7, 1770; 542 Martha, b. Apr. 9, 1772, d. Sep. 4, 1832, mar. 1st Nehemiah Prey of Shelburn and had Prey chd. Tubal & Susan, mar. 2d Isaac Newton Russell of Shelburn and had Russell chd. Ellis McArby & William Pierson (Dr., surgeon 5th Vt. Regiment); 543 Rhoda, b. May 27, 1777 Shelburn, Vt., mar. Uric Foot of Shelburn, Vt., and they had Foot chd. Horace (married) and Henrietta (both living at Auburn, N.Y.), and William (who resides [1878] at Buffalo, N.Y.).

537 Ziba Pierson was born May 9, 1761, at Parsippany, N.J., and died Nov. 7, 1820 in Shelburn, Vt. He moved in 1770 with his father to Shelburn, Vt., was taken prisoner (1778-9) by the British during the Rev. War (see description under his father Moses), and inherited his father's homestead at Shelburn in 1805. He mar. May 24, 1787, Hannah

Campbell (b. Jan. 24, 1766, d. Aug. 7, 1847 in Shelburn) of Voluntown, Windham Co., Conn., and they had chd., all born in Shelburn, Vt., 544 James, b. Jan. 11, 1789, d. July 24, 1793 at Shelburn; 545 David, b. June 30, 1790, d. Dec. 7, 1794; 546 Esther, b. Nov. 28, 1791, d. Dec. 17, 1794; 547 Hannah, b. July 1, 1793, d. July 11, 1793; 548 Betsey, b. Nov. 5, 1794, d. Oct. 6, 1795; 549 Nancy, b. Apr. 25, 1797, d. June 29, 1867 at Bedford, Canada, mar. July 3, 1822, George Clayes (b. Jan. 22, 1796, d. Nov. 30, 1866 Bedford) and had Clayes chd. George, and Sophia; 550 Lucy, b. Sep. 29, 1799, d. Mar. 28, 1866 at Shelburn, mar. there May 3, 1826 Henry S. Morse (b. April 1800, d. 1875 at Massena, N.Y.), and had Morse chd. Henry Pierson, Caroline, Emily, and Henry P.; 551 Moses Campbell, b. Oct. 29, 1801, d. Oct. 21, 1814, at Shelburn, Vt.; 552 Clara, b. July 21, 1804, m. 1st Nov. 14, 1822, William Read (d. Nov. 7, 1823 without chd.) of Burlington, Vt., 2d Feb. 19, 1827, Luther Martin Hagar (b. Sep. 24, 1804), and had Hagar chd. Sarah Clara, Maria Ellen, Julius Martin, Katherine Almira and Caroline Frances (twins), and George Ingersoll.

538 Uzal Pierson was born May 4, 1763, at Parsippany, N.J., and died Jan. 11, 1836. He moved in 1770 with his father to Shelburn, Vt., was taken prisoner (1778-9) by the British during the Rev. War (see description under his father Moses). He lived on a portion of his father's 1,000 acres at Shelburn, Vt. He mar. Dorcas Frisbie (b. June 10, 1767, d. May 22, 1848), and had chd. 553+ John, b. Feb. 17, 1790; 554+ Uzal, b. Nov. 7, 1791; 555 Edward, b. Dec. 2, 1793, mar. 1829 Abiel Bacon and had chd. 562 Smith (living in Chicago 1878) and 563 Isaac; 556 Betsey, b. Jan. 9, 1796, unmarried; 557 Mary, b. Apr. 28, 1798, at Shelburn, Vt., d. Aug. 13, 1842, at Willoughby, Ohio, mar. Nov. 6, 1836, Earl Smith (b. Apr. 6, 1795, at Waitsfield, Vt.) and had a Smith chd. Emma Frisbie; 558 Marcia, b. Feb. 28, 1800, d. June 30, 1847, mar. twice, last to Albert Rowleson, no chd.; 559+ Smith Frisbie, b. Aug. 29, 1802; 560+ Hiram, b. Aug. 11, 1804; 561 Lucina, b. Jan. 19, 1808, d. Mar. 4, 1870, mar. Sep. 17, 1828, Isaac Smith (b. Sep. 16, 1812), no chd.

539 William Pierson was born Jan. 15, 1765, at Parsippany, N.J., and moved with his father to Shelburn, Vt. He mar. 1st _____ Wolcott, 2d Sally Rouse. About 1810, the family moved to near Vevay, Indiana. He had chd., all born at Shelburn, by which mar. is not known: 564 Harry; 565 James; 566 William; 567 Maurice; 568 Ovid; 569 Luna; 570 Rowena (d. in New York).

541 Samuel Pierson was born Jan. 7, 1770, at Parsippany, N.J. He mar. Ruth Hastings and went to Cayuga Co., N.Y., about 1811. They had chd. 571 Fanny, d. in Chautauqua, N.Y.; 572 Lewis; 573 Rhoda; 574 Samuel; 575 Rachel; 576 James; 577 Allen; and others.

553 John Pierson was born Feb. 17, 1790, and died in 1859 at Honolulu, Sandwich Islands. He mar. 1812, Abigail Saxton (d. 1868). He went to the Sandwich Islands (Hawaii), where he accumulated a large property. John and Abigail had chd. 578 Adeline, b. 1814, mar. John Craig and had Craig chd. John & George; 579 Betsey, b. 1815; 580 Alexander Edw., b. 1816; 581 Rosamund; 582 Louisa; 583 John Saxton; 584 Moses Fred.; 585 Helen; 586 Araminta, mar. George Saxton, resides (1878) at Hammanton, N.J., and had 6 children.

554 Uzal Pierson was born Nov. 7, 1791, and died Aug. 2, 1872. He mar. Nov. 10, 1813, Polly Smith (b. Sep. 14, 1793, d. June 1, 1848), and had chd. 587 Hanson C., b. Oct. 8, 1814, d. June 12, 1848, at Tyler, Ill., mar. Sep. 12, 1844, Elizabeth Comstock (d. Sep. 2, 1845) and had son 597 George (b. June 4, 1845, d. Aug. 18, 1845); 588 Addie A., b. Dec. 4, 1816, at Shelburn, Vt., where she d. Oct. 16, 1863, mar. Feb. 18, 1838, Oscar L. Holabird (d. May

1870) of same place, and had Holabird chd.(all at Shelburn) Eugene F., Alice, Oliver, William, Polly, Ellen, and James H.; 589 Helen M., b. Mar. 30, 1819, mar. Dec. 11, 1844, Curtis J. Pattridge, and had Pattridge chd., all residing (1878) in Burlington, Vt., Mary E., Hanson C., Frank S., George P., Fanny C., and Clara H.; 590+ Edward, b. Aug. 15, 1821; 591 Jane, b. July 3, 1823, mar. Dec. 28, 1846, George J. Pattridge, reside at Shelburn, and had Pattridge chd. Lucy J., Frederic W., William P., Henry N., Emma C., Helen M., Adelia, and Anna F.; 592 Mary R., b. Oct. 26, 1825, d. July 3, 1864, mar. Dec. 10, 1849, Enos Peterson of Burlington, Vt., and had Peterson chd., born at Burlington, Mary, Enos Jr., Edward P., Cornelia, Catherine E., and Walter; 593 Cornelia, b. June 27, 1828, d. Mar. 27, 1832, at Shelburn; 594 Allen Smith, b. Dec. 18, 1830, d. Mar. 17, 1832; 595 Cornelia, b. Aug. 8, 1833, d. Sep. 20, 1871, mar. Jan. 16, 1866, Horace R. Nash of Burlington, Vt., no children; 596 John Henry, b. Oct. 6, 1838, mar. Apr. 18, 1864, Eleanor L. Lawton, and had chd. 598 Charles (b. Dec. 17, 1866).

559 Smith Frisbie Pierson was born Aug. 29, 1802, at Shelburn, Vt. He mar. Apr. 29, 1829, Lydia Tabor, and had chd, all born at Shelburn, Vt., except Richard: 599+ Richard Irving, b. Aug. 7, 1830, at Charlotte, Vt.; 600 Betsey E., b. May 3, 1832, d. Apr. 21, 1873, at Brooklyn, N.Y., where her chd. now (1878) reside, mar. Dec. 26, 1855, Fred. S. Blinn, and had Blinn chd. Addie L., Carrie J., and Walter F.; 601 Emma L., b. Sep. 20, 1834, mar. Oct. 22, 1862, Oliphant P. Hartley at Janesville, Wis., live in Brooklyn, N.Y., and have Hartley chd. Irving P., and Emma L.; 602 John Tabor, b. Oct. 10, 1836, d. Jan. 29, 1841; 603+ Henry Morse, b. Aug. 3, 1838; 604 James Smith, b. Dec. 8, 1840, mar. Dec. 5, 1871, Lucille Blake, and living (1878) at Mt. Vernon, N.Y.; 605 Mary Jemima, b. Oct. 21, 1842, and now (1878) living at Shelburn, Vt.

560 Hiram Pierson was born Aug. 11, 1804, and died Aug. 29, 1860, near Pike's Peak, Colorado, killed by a band of cattle thieves. He mar. May 1826 Maria Holabird (b. 1804 Shelburn, d. May 1869 at New Milford, Ill.). He left Vermont in 1842, and went to Milwaukee, then Winnebago Co., Ill., California, and other points west. He had chd. 606 Irvin H., b. Feb. 11, 1825, at Shelburn, Vt., d. Jan., 1828; 607 Harriet M., b. Oct. 4, 1828, at Shelburn, Vt., mar. Mar. 29, 1848, Frederick H. Maxwell, and had 9 Maxwell children; 608 Lucy, b. May 17, 1830, at Shelburn, Vt., resides (1978) at Milwaukee, Wis., mar. Oct. 24, 1848, at Beloit, Wis., George H. Mitchell, had Mitchell chd. Stanley, and Alice Maud (wife of Ceylon Lyman); 609 Lucina, b. Apr. 14, 1833, at Shelburn, Vt., d. May 1849; 610 Charles, b. Oct. 10, 1837, at Shelburn, Vt., mar. at Denver, Colo., Maria Ulin, and had 6 children; 611 Ellen T., b. Apr. 23, 1839, at Shelburn, Vt., d. Apr. 1877, at Denver, Colo., mar. 1869 Albert Kneeland, and had one child; 612 Alice M., b. Aug. 6, 1843, at Winnebago, Ill., mar. Nov. 1867 to W. A. Judd of Dubuque, and had one daughter; 613 Clara J., b. Apr. 22, 1845, mar. Dec. 25, 1871, Philip Ireland, at Denver, Colo., and has (1878) one daughter; 614 Marion A., b. Nov. 28, 1848, at Winnebago, Ill., mar. Nov. 10, 1868, Alfred Graham, at New Milford, Ill., and has (1878) one daughter.

590 Edward Pierson was born Aug. 15, 1821. He mar. 1st Sep. 12, 1844, Sarah Comstock (d. Oct. 21, 1848), 2d Feb. 4, 1850, Maria A. Smith, and now (1878) lives at Spring Valley, Rockland Co., N.Y. He had, by his 1st wife, chd. 615+ William George, b. Dec. 27, 1845; 616 Jason E., b. Jan. 31, 1848, at St. George, Vt., and lives (1878) in Geneva, Nebraska. Edward had, by his 2d wife, chd. 617 Sarah, b. Aug. 1853, mar. June 22, 1872, Peter E. Kelly; 618 Susan, mar. Nov. 9, 1874, John A. Cook; 619 Enos.

615 William George Pierson was born Dec. 27, 1845, and was living (1878) in Brooklyn, N.Y. He mar. Nov. 12, 1866, Mattie W. Fifield, and had chd. 628 William, b. Jan. 23, 1867; and 629 Edward E., b. Feb. 8, 1869.

599 Richard Irving Pierson was born Aug. 7, 1830. He mar. July 14, 1853, at Massena, N.Y., Abbie M. Douglas, and had chd. 620 Richard I., b. June 17, 1855, at Shelburn, Vt., d. July 16, 1859; 621 Clarissa L., b. Nov. 24, 1859, at Janesville, Wis.; 622 Emma L., b. Feb. 12, 1862, at Janesville, Wis.; 623 Walter C., b. Jan. 11, 1865, at Burlington, Vt., d. July 28, 1865; 624 Fanny P., b. Sep. 7, 1868, at Burlington, Vt., d. Sep. 8, 1868.

603 Henry Morse Pierson was born Aug. 3, 1838. He mar. 1st July 6, 1866, at Wheeling, W. Va., Annie E. Shaw (d. Dec. 28, 1871, at Brooklyn, N.Y.), and 2d Aug. 25, 1875, Mrs. Frances A. Creevey. He was living (1878) at Brooklyn, N.Y. He had chd., all by his 1st wife: 625 Frank J., b. Aug. 4, 1867, at Steubenville, Ohio, d. July 19, 1868; 626 Frederick H., b. Oct. 2, 1868, d. May 13, 1874, at Jessup, Iowa; 627 George S., b. Dec. 27, 1871, at Brooklyn, N.Y., d. Dec. 30, 1871.

11 Daniel Pierson (judge) was born 1703 in Orange, N.J., where he continued to live until his death in 1777. He was known as Judge, and mar. Jemima Ogden (b. 1709, d. 1776), dau. of John Ogden of Orange, N.J. They had chd. 36+ Nathaniel; 37 Jonas; 38 Daniel, went to Pompton, N.J.; 39 Aaron, went off with the British; 40 James, went off with the British; 41 Jemima; 42 Abigail.

36 Nathaniel Pierson[29] mar. Mehetable Herrick and had chd. 640+ Joanna, b. 16 Oct 1749; and perhaps others.

640 Joanna Pierson[30] was born 16 Oct 1749 and died 7 Jan 1825 at age 75[31]. She mar. 20 Mar 1769 Daniel Beach (b. 16 Nov 1743, d. 31 Dec 1824)[32], son of Josiah and Annas (Day) Beach of Newark, N.J. Daniel Beach's home was at North Caldwell, Essex Co., N.J. Daniel and Joanna had Beach chd.: Mehetable, b. 26 Aug 1771, d. 10 Nov 1837, mar. ____ Crowell; Jonathan, b. 7 Oct 1773, d. 12 Apr 1842[33]; Nathaniel, b. 16 May 1776, d. 21 Jun 1808; Mary, b. 20 Nov 1778, d. 31 Mar 1844, mar. 1st ____ Monroe, 2d 13 Apr 1811 Samuel Tenneswood; Charles, b. 7 Aug 1781, d. 7 Sep 1817; Sarah, b. 30 Dec 1784, d. 3 Nov 1827, mar. ____ Munn; Daniel D., b. 2 Nov 1787, d. 25 May 1841.

12 Caleb Pierson was born in Orange, N.J., and lived there. He mar. 1st Ruth Ogden and 2d Sarah ____. Caleb died intestate and the records of administration[34] were dated Sep. 22, 1743; "Caleb Peirson" of Newark, Essex Co., N.J.; administratrix Sarah Peirson, the widow; Samuel Baldwin and John Tomkins, fellow bondsmen (Lib. D, p. 90). Caleb and Ruth had

[29] Joseph R. Klett, *Genealogies of New Jersey Families*, Genealogical Publishing Co., Inc., Baltimore, Md., 1996, p. 669.

[30] Joseph R. Klett, *Genealogies of New Jersey Families*, Genealogical Publishing Co., Inc., Baltimore, Md., 1996, p. 669.

[31] Gravestone records at Caldwell Presbyterian Church Yard, GMNJ 2:14, et seq.

[32] Gravestone records at Caldwell Presbyterian Church Yard, GMNJ 2:14, et seq.

[33] Gravestone records at Caldwell Presbyterian Church Yard, GMNJ 2:14, et seq.

[34] A. Van Doren Honeyman, *Documents Relating to the Colonial History of the State of New Jersey*, First Series, Vol. 30, "Calendar of New Jersey Wills, Administrations, Etc.," Vol. II, 1730-1750, The Unionist-Gazette Association, Printers, Somerville, N.J., 1918, p. 374.

chd. 44 Thomas, mar. Ruth Harrison, and lived and d. in Bloomfield, N.J.; 45+ Caleb, b. 1738; 46 Elizabeth, mar. J. Martin; 47 Jemima, mar. Jedia Lindsley.

45 Caleb Pierson was born 1738 in Orange, N.J., and died[35] in 1801 in N.J. He lived in Bloomfield and Caldwell, N.J. During the Revolutionary War he was a Private in the New Jersey militia.[36] He mar. Joanna Baldwin (b. 1745), and had chd. 85 Sarah, mar. David Ogden; 86+ John; 87 Elizabeth, b. 1767, d. 1793, mar. Linus Dodd (1765-1825); 88+ Jeptha, b. 1775; 89+ Israel; 90+ Joanna; 91+ Abraham; 92 Jane, d. young; 93+ Elijah, b. 1779; 94 Lydia, mar. James Crockett and had Crockett chd. David, John, & Caleb; 95 Naomi, mar. Simeon Baldwin; 96 Rhoda, mar. ____ James, and had James chd. Joseph & Uriah.

86 John Pierson was born in New Jersey, mar. Susanna Russell, and moved to Seneca Falls, N.Y. He had chd., all born in N.Y. state: 177+ Reuben D.; 178+ Calvin; 179+ Ogden; 180 Moses, d. young; 181 Smith, d. young; 182 Jeptha, went off in early life and was never heard from; 183 Phebe; 184 Polly G.; 185 Rhoda; 186 Lucy; 187 Peggy Maria; 188 Betsey.

177 Reuben D. Pierson was born in Seneca Falls, N.Y. He had chd. 358 John E.; 359 Elias; 360 Susan; 361 Cyrus; 362 Cynthia.

178 Calvin Pierson was born in Seneca Falls, N.Y. He had chd. 363 George; 364 Chas.; 365 Frank; 366 Reuben; 367 Eugene.

179 Ogden Pierson was born in Seneca Falls, N.Y. He had chd. 368 Forest; 369 Addison; 370 Phebe; 371 Maria.

88 Jeptha Pierson was born in 1775 in N.J., d. 1857, mar. Sally ____, and lived in Caldwell, N.J., where some of his descendants now (1878) reside. He had chd. 189 Nancy; 190+ Caleb; 191 Joanna; 192+ John; 193+ Cyrus; 194+ Stephen S.; 195+ Bethuel H.; 196+ Abiather H. (twin of 195 Bethuel); 197 David H., d. young; 198 Sally Maria, mar. J. Schuyler.

190 Caleb Pierson, of New Jersey, had chd. 372 Harvey (who went to Iowa to live); 373 Nancy; 374 Daniel, of N.J.; 375 Joseph.

192 John Pierson had chd. 376 William; 377 Caroline; 378 Marcus; 379 Catherine; 380 Mary; 381 Charles (lives in Georgia); 382 George (of New Haven, Conn.); 383 John; 384 Willis; 385 Albert (of Mass.).

193 Cyrus Pierson was born in New Jersey, and moved to Michigan. He had chd. 386 Hiram (Mich.); 387 John (Mich.); 388 Timothy (Indiana); 389 Rebecca.

194 Stephen S. Pierson was born was born in New Jersey, and had chd. 390 James (Ohio); 391 Sarah; 392 Chas., d. young; 393 Frederick (N.J.).

195 Bethuel H. Pierson, of Arkansas, joined the U.S. Army and died in Missouri in 1836. He had chd. 394 Elizabeth; 395 Samantha.

---

[35]*DAR Patriot Index*, Centennial Edition, National Society of the Daughters of the American Revolution, 1994, part 3, p. 2257.

[36]*DAR Patriot Index*, Centennial Edition, National Society of the Daughters of the American Revolution, 1994, part 3, p. 2257.

196 Abiather H. Pierson, lived in Iowa, and had chd. 396 William (Iowa); 397 Marcus (Iowa); 399 Cyrus (Ky.); 400 Jeptha (Iowa); 401 Thos. (Iowa); 402 Georgiana (Iowa); 403 John (Iowa).

89 Israel Pierson, born in New Jersey, moved to Paris, Ky., and lived there. His descendants still (1878) live there. He had chd. 199 John; 200 Eliza; 201 Priscilla; 202 George C.; 203+ Thornton P.; 204 Sally M.; 205+ Thos. W.; 206+ James Trotter.

203 Thornton P. Pierson, of Kentucky, had chd. 404 Mary L., mar. P. N. Norton; 405 Virginia; 406 James M.; 407 Chas. E.; 408 Sarah E.; 409 Georgiana; 410 Emma J., mar. J. Temperly; 411 Carrie; 412 Anna E., mar. A. Smith; 413 Alice; 414 Uzal; 415 Irene; 416 Joseph.

205 Thomas W. Pierson, of Kentucky, had chd. 417 Mary E., mar. J. J. Jones; 418 John J.

206 James Trotter Pierson, of Kentucky, had chd. 419 Anna E.; 420 George I.; 421 Beatty; 422 Willie and 422a Jane; 423 Sallie; 424 Kittie; 425 Mary; 426 Frank.

90 Joanna Pierson, mar. 459 David Pierson of Long Island, son of 287 Elihu Pierson (numbers 459 and 287 are from Chapter 12.) She had chd. 1795 to 1812: Elizabeth, Phebe, Aaron, David Austin, and George Ambrose. Their record is given under 459 David Pierson in the "Descendants of Theodore Peirson", Chapter 12, near the end of the chapter.

91 Abraham Pierson, was in Bloomfield or Caldwell, N.J. He mar. Jemima Miller, and had chd.207 Israel; 208 Albert M. (now [1878] residing in Newark, N.J.); 209 Jacob; 210 Eliza; 211 Joseph; 212 Sarah Ogden; 213 Caleb Ward; 214 Lydia; 215 Mary W.; 216 Abraham; 217 Jane and 217a Joanna (twins); 218 Julia Ann; 219 Phebe H. The children live (1878) in N.J. and N.Y.

93 Elijah Pierson, b. 1779 Caldwell, N.J., d. 1862 Orange, N.J., m. 1st Martha Williams (b. 1784, d. 1851), 2d Mary Williams, a sister. He had chd., all born at Caldwell: 220 James C., d. young; 221 Louisa, b. 1807, mar. Aaron Dodd (b. 1805, d. 1860) of Orange, N.J.; 222+ Elijah B., b. 1809/10; 223+ Calvin D., b. 1811; 224 Maria, b. 1813, m. Sam. Crane (b. 1810); 225+ Caleb Nelson, b. 1815; 226+ David Harrison, b. 1818; 227+ Nathan Williams, b. 1821.

222 Elijah B. Pierson, born in 1809 or 1810 in Caldwell, N.J., went to Ohio to live. He mar. Sally, dau. of John Mingus. He died in 1876 in Ohio aged 66 years. They had chd. 427 Martha; 428 Mary; 429 Grant W. (of Ohio).

223 Calvin D. Pierson was born in 1811 in Caldwell, N.J., and lived in Orange, N.J. He mar. 1st Lavinia Dodd, and 2d Margaretta Dodd. He was a painter in Orange, N.J. He had chd., by which wife is unknown: 430 Samuel D.; 431 David (died); 432 David A.; 433 Lavinia C.; 434 Martha; 435 Elijah; 436 Morris D.; 437 Charles; 438 Frank; 439 William. The children live (1878) mostly in Orange, N.J.

225 Caleb Nelson Pierson was born in 1815 in Caldwell, N.J., and moved to Ohio. He mar. Jane E. Crane, and had chd. 440 Joseph W.; 441 Walter C.; 442 Caleb C.; 443 Maria C.; 444 Janet F.; 445 Orville A.; 446 John D.; 447 Julia C. This family was in Ohio in 1878.

226 David Harrison Pierson (Rev. and Ph.D.), was born in 1818 in Caldwell, N.J., and moved to Elizabeth, N.J., where for many years he has been a successful teacher of a classical school for boys, and where he now (1878) resides. He mar. Caroline Peck (dau. of

Capt. Aaron Peck, of Orange, N.J., and grand-daughter of Bethuel Pierson of Orange, N.J.). He had chd. 448 Henry M.; 449 James A.; 450+ David H., b. 1806; 451 George P.; 452 Mary H.; 453 Caroline P.

450 David H. Pierson was born 10 Sep 1806, and died[37] 27 Mar 1891 at age 84 years 6 months 17 days. He was a farmer[38] at Madison, N.J. He mar. [39] Sally Ann Scofield (b. 13 Oct 1806, d. 14 Oct 1872 at age 66 years 1 day), sister of Albert Scofield. She transferred[40] May 8, 1857 to Presbyterian Church, Madison, N.J., from 1st Presbyterian Church, Morristown, N.J. They had dau. [41] 638 Susan Bishop, mar. [42] 16 Feb 1859, Edwin P. Burroughs, son of C. C. Burroughs, cabinet maker of Madison, N.J.

227 Nathan Williams Pierson, born in 1821 in Caldwell, N.J., resides (1878) in Virginia, mar. Susan, dau. of Abiathar Harrison, and had chd. 454 Emma L.; 455 Fred H., mar. Miss Matthews; 456 Edward; 457 Harriet; 458 Robert; 459 Harry; 460 Susan H.

7 Thomas Pierson, was born in Newark, N.J., in 1678, and died Mar. 5, 1758, in Orange, N.J. He was buried in the old graveyard at Orange. He went from Newark to Whatnong Plain (now Morris Plain) where he bought a tract of land and settled on it, about 1685. He commenced running a saw mill at that place, which, with the original land, has remained in the family ever since. In 1878, this place was occupied by 228 John Henry Pierson, who was Lizzie Pierson's informant for his family as reported in her 1878 book, *Pierson Genealogical Records*. He had chd. 16+ Timothy, b. 1710, d. 1777; 17 Silas.

16 Timothy Pierson was born in 1710, probably at Whatnong Plain, N.J., and died in 1777. He mar. Mary ____ (d. 1788). They were both buried at Morristown, N.J. In 1752, Timothy sold land at Newark, N.J., formerly owned by Thomas Pierson (his father). Timothy posted[43] for strays at Hanover, N.J., on 2 Nov 1753, 8 Nov 1759, and 8 Dec 1772. In May 1776, he was on the poll list[44] as "Timo Pierson" with place of abode at Hanover. His will names his chd. 48 Thomas; 49+ Samuel, b. 1748, d. 1789-90; 50 Phebe; 51 Keziah; 52 Experience, d. 1793.

49 Samuel Pierson was born 1748 (probably at Whatnong Plain), and lived on the old place owned by his father and grand-father. Samuel died 1789 or 90, and was buried at

[37] Viola E. Shaw and Barbara S. Parker, *Madison, New Jersey Presbyterian Church Vital Records 1747-1900*, The Presbyterian Church of Madison, Madison, N.J., 1982, p. 249.

[38] Viola E. Shaw and Barbara S. Parker, *Madison, New Jersey Presbyterian Church Vital Records 1747-1900*, The Presbyterian Church of Madison, Madison, N.J., 1982, p. 252.

[39] Viola E. Shaw and Barbara S. Parker, *Madison, New Jersey Presbyterian Church Vital Records 1747-1900*, The Presbyterian Church of Madison, Madison, N.J., 1982, p. 249.

[40] Viola E. Shaw and Barbara S. Parker, *Madison, New Jersey Presbyterian Church Vital Records 1747-1900*, The Presbyterian Church of Madison, Madison, N.J., 1982, p. 249.

[41] Viola E. Shaw and Barbara S. Parker, *Madison, New Jersey Presbyterian Church Vital Records 1747-1900*, The Presbyterian Church of Madison, Madison, N.J., 1982, p. 249.

[42] Viola E. Shaw and Barbara S. Parker, *Madison, New Jersey Presbyterian Church Vital Records 1747-1900*, The Presbyterian Church of Madison, Madison, N.J., 1982, p. 252.

[43] Harriet Stryker-Rodda, *Some Early Records of Morris County, New Jersey 1740-1799*, published under the patronage of Morris County Archives Publications Committee, Polyanthos, Inc., New Orleans, La., 1975, pp. 33, 36, & 43.

[44] Harriet Stryker-Rodda, *Some Early Records of Morris County, New Jersey 1740-1799*, published under the patronage of Morris County Archives Publications Committee, Polyanthos, Inc., New Orleans, La., 1975, p. 98.

Morristown. In 1798, the Hanover Twp., Morris Co., N.J., Ratables[45] showed that Samuel's wife (her name not given, listed as mother of Timothy and Stephen) was living with her sons Timothy and Stephen on 130 acres worth 20£. He had chd. 97+ Timothy, b. 1772, d. 1851; 98+ Stephen, b. 1777; 99 Joseph; 100 Ebenezer; 101+ Samuel, b. 1785; 102+ Isaac; 103+ Silas.

97 Timothy Pierson was born in 1772, and died in 1851. His home was on the old place at Whatnong Plain, N.J. In 1798, the Hanover Twp., Morris Co., N.J., Ratables[46] showed that Timothy was living with his mother and brother Stephen on 130 acres worth 20£. He had chd. 228+ John Henry, b. 1822; perhaps 228a+ Henry W.; and nine others.

228 John Henry Pierson was born in 1822 at Morris Plain, where he spent his life, and still (1878) keeps the saw mill running. He had chd. 461 James H.; 462 Henry W.; 463 Edward H.; 464 John H.

228a Henry W. Pierson[47] was connected to this family because 228 John Henry had a son 462 also named Henry W. 228a Henry W. was of Mendham, N.J., and is probably the eldest son of 97 Timothy Pierson's 11 children. He mar. Nov. 29, 1821, Joan (Joanna) Crowell (d. Dec. 13, 1858, bur. Hillside Cem., Madison, N.J.) of Green Village, N.J. They had dau. 639 Caroline C., mar. Charles W. Burch.

98 Stephen Pierson was born 1777. In 1798, the Hanover Twp., Morris Co., N.J., Ratables[48] showed that Stephen was living with his mother and brother Timothy on 130 acres worth 20£. He had chd. 229+ Edward; 230 Stephen, had no children; 231 Charles, had no children; 232 Samuel, had no children; 233 Anna; 234 Eliza.

229 Edward Pierson, was born 1813, and had chd. 465+ Stephen; 466 Charles; 467 Phillip B.; 468 Samuel; and 469 Laura.

465 Stephen Pierson was a physician who, in 1878, was living and practicing medicine in Morristown, N.J. He was a graduate of Yale College, and served his country during the Civil War.

101 Samuel Pierson was born in 1785. He had chd. 235+ Lewis Jr., b. 1822.

235 Lewis Pierson Jr. was born in 1822. It is not clear why he was called Jr., but another Lewis, senior to him in age, must have been present in town. He was a manufacturer of carriages in Morristown, N.J. Lewis had son 470 Lemuel E.

102 Isaac Pierson, had chd. 236 Abiram of Ohio.

103 Silas Pierson, had chd. 237 Charles.

---

[45]Harriet Stryker-Rodda, *Some Early Records of Morris County, New Jersey 1740-1799*, published under the patronage of Morris County Archives Publications Committee, Polyanthos, Inc., New Orleans, La., 1975, p. 170.
[46]Harriet Stryker-Rodda, *Some Early Records of Morris County, New Jersey 1740-1799*, published under the patronage of Morris County Archives Publications Committee, Polyanthos, Inc., New Orleans, La., 1975, p. 170.
[47]Viola E. Shaw and Barbara S. Parker, *Madison, New Jersey Presbyterian Church Vital Records 1747-1900*, The Presbyterian Church of Madison, Madison, N.J., 1982, p. 250.
[48]Harriet Stryker-Rodda, *Some Early Records of Morris County, New Jersey 1740-1799*, published under the patronage of Morris County Archives Publications Committee, Polyanthos, Inc., New Orleans, La., 1975, p. 170.

Chapter 14
Descendants of Stephen Pierson
American Immigrant

The following descendants of Stephen Pierson (1642/3-1739) are copied from Frederick Lockwood Pierson[1], *The Descendants of Stephen Pierson of Suffolk County, England and New Haven and Derby, Conn.*, Walsh & Griffen, Printers, Amenia, N.Y., 1895, as a framework to present new data upon. Most of the information in Lizzie Pierson's book[2] on this family was provided to her by Frederick Lockwood Pierson in 1877. Since that time, Frederick Lockwood Pierson has published his 1895 book, which significantly modifies and corrects Lizzie's published information. The numbering system used in this chapter is matched to Frederick Lockwood Pierson's 1895 book, thus added numbers are either by adding a letter to an existing number to identify a different person, or by new numbers beginning at 500. Some additional research by the authors of *Pierson Millennium* is included and footnoted. An every-name index is provided at the back of *Pierson Millennium*. The + symbol after an identifying number indicates more information is provided in a later paragraph beginning with the same number in this chapter.

1 Stephen Pierson, the immigrant ancestor, of Branford and Derby, Connecticut, was christened[3] 13 Feb 1642/3 at Ubbeston, Suffolk County, England. His parents were Edward Peirson and Anne Clough (see Stephen Pierson of Suffolk County, England, in chapter 4 for more detail). The widow Anne (Clough) Peirson sent Stephen to Branford, Connecticut, for a carpenter apprenticeship at age 11. Stephen's father, Edward Peirson Jr., was christened 10 Jul 1600 at Ubbeston, Suffolk County, England (father Edward Sr.), and died while a king's soldier about 1645, probably a casualty of the English civil war.

Stephen Pierson was apprenticed to Thomas Mulliner of Branford, Conn., to learn the carpenter trade, and landed at New Haven in 1654. Mulliner first appeared in New Haven in 1640. June 30, 1657, Stephen Pierson testified in court in New Haven in a case of slander brought by Meeker against Mulliner for saying that Meeker's pigs were bewitched. In Oct., 1658, Stephen Pierson appeared in the Probate Court at New Haven in a complaint made against Thomas Mulliner for not fulfilling an agreement to teach him the carpenter trade. On March 15, 1667, Stephen Pierson was one of eight recorded residences of Derby, then called Paugassett, and in all probability was there in 1666. His first wife, and mother of all his children, was Mary Tomlinson, daughter of Henry Tomlinson and his wife Alice _____ of Stratford, Connecticut.

---

[1]Frederick Lockwood Pierson, *The Descendants of Stephen Pierson of Suffolk County, England and New Haven and Derby, Conn., 1645-1739*, Walsh & Griffen, Printers, Amenia, N.Y., 1895.

[2]Lizzie B. Pierson, *Pierson Genealogical Records*, Joel Munsell, Printer, Albany, N.Y., 1878.

[3]LDS microfilm No. 0919634, Church of England, Parish Church of Ubbeston (Suffolk Co.), original Parish Registers, 1555-1837.

Henry Tomlinson was in Watertown, Mass., in 1644; went to Milford, Conn., in 1652; and then to Stratford, Conn., in 1665, where he died in 1681. His widow, Alice, married John Birdsey Sr. under a contract of Oct. 8, 1688.

Henry Tomlinson[4] (c. 22 Nov 1606 St. Peters, Derby, Derbyshire, England)[5] was son of George Tomlinson and Maria Hyde of Yorkshire, England (mar. 19 Jan 1600/1 at St. Peters, Derby, Derbyshire, England)[6]. They moved from Yorkshire to Derby, Derbyshire. Henry was a weaver by trade. Georgius (George) Tomlinson (c. 16 Aug 1567, Howden, Yorkshire, England, father Johannis (John) Tomlinson)[7] had mother Barbara. The location of George Tomlinson's christening at Howden is interesting in that the ancestors of Henry Peirson of Southampton, Long Island, New York Colony (1640), the Rev. Abraham Pierson of the same place and time, John Pierson of Lynn, Massachusetts (1637), Thomas Pierson of Branford, Connecticut (1662) and probably Bartholomew Pierson of Watertown, Massachusetts (1639) all descend from Howden, Yorkshire, England.

Stephen Pierson had a home lot of 3 1/2 acres on the original town street on meeting-house hill, called also New Haven Sentinel hill. Stephen's 1st wife, Mary Tomlinson, died at Derby, Conn., Sept. 25, 1715, and he mar. 2d Esther ____. His will, dated Sept. 2, 1733, provides for his wife, Esther; eldest son Stephen, junior, 20 shillings; daughter Sarah Twitchell, 80 pounds; daughter Mary Baldwin, 80 pounds; son Abraham and daughter Bathsheba Blackman, of Stratford, heretofore provided for. His son, Abraham, was appointed executor. Stephen died at Derby, Conn., May 14, 1739, aged 96. His Inventory, dated Dec. 4, 1739, is as follows, viz.: Welchman's lot, 100 pounds; barn and homestead, 360 pounds; 80 acres of land in Quaker Farms purchase, 44 pounds; another piece of land in Bear Hill district, 85 pounds; one old Bible, 5 shillings; one other Bible, 6 shillings; and other small articles; amounting in all to 631 pounds, 9 shillings, three pence.

Stephen Pierson had children, all by his 1st wife, Mary Tomlinson, and all born in Derby, Conn., except Sarah: 1a Sarah[8] (b. ca. 1664[9], if age 16 at marriage, possibly at Milford or Stratford), mar. 21 Jan 1679/80 John Twitchell; 2+ Stephen Jr.; 3 Mary, b. ca. 1673, mar. 19 Sep 1700 Josiah Baldwin; 3a Joseph[10], b. ca. 1675, who drew lots in Derby March 12, 1702, (probably a son of Stephen); 4 John, b. ca. 1678, probably a bachelor, d. ca. 1704; 5 Bathsheba[11], b. ca. 1684, mar. Adam Blackman of Stratford, Conn.; 6+ Abraham (Sgt.), b. 1681; 7 Daniel, b. ca. 1687, who drew lots in Oxford 1713 (probably a son of Stephen).

[4]Frederick Lockwood Pierson, *The Descendants of Stephen Pierson of Suffolk County, England and New Haven and Derby, Conn., 1645-1739*, Walsh & Griffen, Printers, Amenia, N.Y., 1895, p.32, notes & errata.
[5]Parish records of Derby, Derbyshire, England.
[6]Parish records of Derby, Derbyshire, England.
[7]*The Registers of the Parish of Howden, Co. York*, Vols. I (published 1904, marriages 1542-1644 and baptisms 1542-1659), & II (published 1905, burials 1543-1659), edited by G. E. Weddall, privately printed for the Yorkshire Parish Register Society, Beck & Inchbold Ltd., Printers, Oriel Press, Leeds, Yorkshire, England.
[8]Renumbered from 1 in Frederick Lockwood Pierson's book to 1a, to allow 1 to be used for her father, Stephen, who was not numbered there.
[9]From the old history of Derby it appears that Stephen Pierson had two children born before 1670, their names were not given, but this fits Sarah and Stephen Jr.
[10]Frederick Lockwood Pierson, *The Descendants of Stephen Pierson of Suffolk County, England and New Haven and Derby, Conn., 1645-1739*, Walsh & Griffen, Printers, Amenia, N.Y., 1895, p.32, notes & errata.
[11]Out of birth order, based upon her estimated birth of 1684.

2 Stephen Pierson Jr. was born ca. 1668[12] at Derby, Conn., was the eldest son of Stephen Sr., and died intestate 1744 at Derby, Conn. He mar. 12 Oct 1697 Mehetabel Canfield (b. 2 Jul 1671 Milford, Conn.), dau. of Thomas Canfield. In 1717, a town assessor appraised his property at £51. They had chd. 8 Elizabeth, b. Jan. 12, 1699, in Derby, Conn., mar. ____ Bennett; 9+ Thomas; 10 John, b. 1705 Derby, Conn., d. Jan. 25, 1789 Huntington, Conn., mar. a dau. of Benj. Scrivener of Norwalk, Conn., had son 500 William (wife Hannah); 11 Job, b. Oct. 5, 1707, Derby, Conn., d. 1 746-7 Derby, mar. Sarah ____, and had sons 501 Stephen & 502 Samuel; 12 Phebe, b. in Derby, mar. William Fanton; 13 Abigail, b. in Derby, mar. Mar. 30, 1738, was 1st wife of James₄ St. John[13] (b. Mar. 30, 1708, d. 1756, ancestors James₃, Matthias₂, Matthias₁); 14+ Jonathan, b. May 6, 1716.

9 Thomas Pierson was born in Derby, Conn., and died 1772 at Derby. He mar. 1st Feb. 22, 1727/8 at Norwalk, Conn., Ruth Holbrook (d. Oct. 14, 1737), dau. of Abil Holbrook of Derby, and mar. 2d Mar. 7, 1738, widow Elizabeth Thomas of Norwalk, Conn. He was known as Thomas Jr. in Derby town records because of the presence of an unrelated Thomas Pierson Sr., who was one of the first settlers of Derby (Thomas Pierson Sr. held a commission from King George and purchased lands from O'Kennuch, the chief of the Sagamore Indians, a portion of which is still [1878 comment] held by that Pierson family)[14]. On Dec. 8, 1728, Thomas and his 1st wife Ruth were among the list[15] of persons who owned the half-way covenant during Rev. Stoddard's ministry in Woodbury, Conn. He lived in Norwalk, Conn., and purchased land in Derby in 1758. In 1773, after his death, his two sons, Timothy and Nathan, divided his property. He had chd., all by his 1st wife Ruth, all at Norwalk, Conn.: 21 Mehetabel, b. Jan. 13, 1729/30 at Norwalk, Conn., mar. Theophilus Hanton of Norwalk, Conn.; 22+ Timothy, b. Nov. 7, 1732; 23+ Nathan, b. Nov. 27,1734; 24 Hannah, b. in Norwalk, Conn., mar. Nov. 7, 1751, Enos Bradley of Derby, Conn.

22 Timothy Pierson (Parsons) was born Nov. 7, 1732 at Norwalk, Conn., and died at Reading, Conn. He mar. Mar. 9, 1756, at Fairfield, Conn., Elizabeth Couch (b. June 13, 1735), dau. of Samuel Couch. Timothy's family opposed his marrying Elizabeth Couch because she was poor, but he married her anyway. He spelled his surname Parsons. He resided for a time at Saugatuck, Fairfield Co., Conn. Timothy and Elizabeth Parsons had chd. 43 Sabary, b. Feb. 26, 1758, mar. Frances Andrews, moved to Newark, N.J., and had sons and daughters; 44+ Abigail, b. Apr. 20, 1760; 45+ Daniel, b. Mar. 30, 1762; 46+ Abraham, b. Feb. 20, 1764; 47 Samuel, b. Dec. 15, 1765, d. when son George was very young, was a doctor and resided in Columbus, Ohio, had son 504 George M. (a lawyer and member of congress), one of George's daughters married Prince Von Liner of Prussia[16]; 48 Elijah, b. Feb. 6, 1768, had sons, 505 Jared and 506 Timothy (d. in Georgetown, Conn.), and dau. 507 Betsey (mar. Lemuel Adams of Reading, Conn. and had Adams chd. Lemuel & Stephen); 49 Betty, b. Nov. 7, 1770; 50 Hannah, b. Aug. 12, 1773; 51 Eleanor, b. July 22, 1775; and 52 Aaron, b. Jan. 12, 1779.

---

[12]From the old history of Derby it appears that Stephen Pierson had two children born before 1670, their names were not given, but this fits Sarah and Stephen Jr.
[13]Orline St. John Alexander, *St. John Genealogy*, The Grafton Press, New York, N.Y., 1907, p. 35.
[14]Lizzie B. Pierson, *Pierson Genealogical Records*, Joel Munsell, Printer, Albany, N.Y., 1878, p. 75, note K.
[15]Cothren's *History of Ancient Woodbury*.
[16]Frederick Lockwood Pierson, *The Descendants of Stephen Pierson of Suffolk County, England and New Haven and Derby, Conn., 1645-1739*, Walsh & Griffen, Printers, Amenia, N.Y., 1895, p.32, notes.

44 Abigail Pierson (Parsons) was born Apr. 20, 1760 in Fairfield Co., Conn. She may have came to Newark, N.J., with her brother Sabary about 1780. She may be the Abigail Pierson[17] that mar. 20 Nov 1783 Samuel Leonard (b. ca. 1757, d. 24 Mar 1822 in Morristown, N.J., a Rev. soldier) and had Leonard chd.: Samuel (mar. Sarah Haines); Nancy (mar. Phillip Condict); Mary A. (mar. Peter Dickerson, later div.); Joanna (mar. Ira Moore); and at least 3 other Leonard children.

45 Daniel Pierson (Parsons) was born Mar. 30, 1762. He settled in Tioga Co., N.Y. He had chd. 114 Samuel, M.D., settled in Columbus, Ohio; 115 Uriah; 116 Betty; 117 Clara; 118 Hannah; 119 Eunice; 120 Lydia; 121 Mary; 122 Daniel; 123 Burr.

46 Abraham Pierson (Parsons) was born Feb. 20, 1764. He mar. Urana Starr. They had chd. 124+ Starr, b. Feb. 15, 1793; 125 Betsey, mar. Rufus H. Pickett of Ridgefield, Conn.; 126 Laura, was the 1st wife of Moses G. Betts of Fairfield, Conn., his 2d wife was Laura's niece, 250 Caroline Pierson.

124 Starr Pierson (Parsons) was born Feb. 15, 1793, and died Jan. 25, 1867 in Newark, N.J. He mar. Oct. 15, 1814, Elizabeth Spear (b. Apr. 6, 1792, d. Apr. 1, 1869) of Bloomfield, N.J. They had chd. 250 Caroline, b. Mar. 12, 1816, 2d wife of Moses G. Betts, his 1st wife was her aunt 126 Laura Pierson (Parsons); 251 William, b. Dec. 20, 1817; 252 Charles, b. Mar. 6, 1820, resided in Newark, N.J.; 253 Walter, b. Dec. 25, 1822, resided in Newark, N.J.; 254 Laura, b. Apr. 13, 1824, resided in Bloomfield, N.J.; 255 Rev. Benjamin, b. Jan. 6, 1826, went to Michigan; 256 Cyrus, b. Mar. 18, 1828, lived in Bloomfield, N.J.; 257 Abraham, b. Aug. 3, 1830, resided in Newark, N.J.; 258 Henry Clay, b. May 12, 1833, resided in Newark, N.J.

23 Nathan Pierson was born Nov. 27, 1734, at Norwalk, Conn. He mar. Nov. 17, 1756, Amy Smith. They had chd. 53 David; 54 Thomas; 55+ Abel; 56 Nathan Jr., mar. Sarah Fairchild, had son 508 William (d. Sep. 10, 1811, aged 9 months); 57 Ruth; 58 Rebecca; 59 Sarah; 60 Hannah.

55 Abel Pierson mar. Hannah Fairchild. They had chd. 127+ Nathan; 128 Hannah; 129+ Abial; 130 Abel, mar. Merib Lyman, settled in Newark, N.J., and had children & grandchildren; 131+ Sheldon, b. 1791; 132 Sophia, mar. Bennet Hine of Naugatuck, Conn., Sophia d. leaving one son who died before 1895.

127 Nathan Pierson died Oct. 17, 1822, age 40, in Derby, Conn. He mar. Sally Swift. They had chd. 259 John Swift, d. June 21, 1874 in Brooklyn, N.Y., mar. Eliza Jennings (d. young) of Fairfield, Conn., and had son 517 John Augustus; 260 Abel, d. unmarried; 261 Edward, mar. Sarah Bennett and had dau. 518 Sarah Medora (d. July , 1879, unmarried); 262 Abigail, d. unmarried; 263 Martha B., mar. Augustus Studwell.

129 Abial Pierson mar. Dec. 25, 1806, Irene Holbrook, and moved to Burton, Ohio, after having all his children in Derby, Conn. They had chd. 338 Julius Egbert, bap. May 1, 1814, Derby, Conn.; 339 David Holbrook, bap. May 12, 1816, Derby, Conn.; 340 Melissa Holbrook, bap. Aug. 23, 1818, Derby, Conn.; 341 Irene, bap. Oct. 27, ____; 342 Nathan Josiah, bap. Sep. 5, 1826, Derby, Conn.

---

[17]From a June 1988 query from Sharon Holley of Budd Lake, N.J., in the Morris NJ Genealogy Club newsletter.

131 Sheldon Pierson was born 1791 in Derby, Conn. He mar. Hepsey Peet, and lived in Trumbull, Conn. They had chd. 264+ William R.; 265 Sheldon P. Jr., mar. Oct. 11, 1855, Lydia J. Hawley, no children.

264 William R. Pierson was born Nov. 8, 1818. He mar. Oct. 4, 1846, Augusta Wheeler (b. Nov. 2, 1822). They resided at Nichols Farms, Conn. They had chd. 400 Mary Augusta, b. Sep. 26, 1847, mar. Sep. 26, 1866, Lorenzo B. Nichols (d. Oct. 5, 1876); 401 America, b. Feb. 25, 1850, unmarried; and 402 Sarah Medora, b. Mar. 28, 1852, d. Aug. 20, 1854.

14 Jonathan Pierson was born May 6, 1716, at Derby, Conn., and died at Ridgefield, Sullivan Co., N.Y. He mar. Mar. 5, 1739, Mary Bates (d. Feb. 16, 1755, at Derby, Conn.). They had chd. 25 Martha, b. Jan. 12, 1740, d. young; 26 Elias, b. June 23, 1743; 27 Osborn, d. in Ohio (tradition); 28+ Bartholomew; 29 David, d. in Sharon, Conn. (tradition); 30+ Jonathan Jr., b. 1751; 31 Martha 2d, b. Mar. 4, 1753.

28 Bartholomew Pierson was born[18] about 1750 in Connecticut, and died[19] after 1803 when he was in New York. Family tradition says he died in Pennsylvania. He mar.[20] Hannah Balch. During the Revolutionary War he was a Private in the Connecticut militia.[21]

30 Jonathan Pierson Jr. was born 1751, and died Sep. 7, 1818, at Reading, Conn. He mar. Elizabeth Thomas of Norwalk, Conn. They had chd. 61+ Elias O. 2d, b. 1780; 62+ Samuel, b. 1785; 63+ Noah, b. Jan. 30, 1795; 64 Sarah, mar. Turney Osborn of Norwalk, Conn., and had Osborn sons, John (a teacher in Norwalk) and Gregory (of Weston, Conn.); 65 Phebe, mar. Alfred Rockwell of Marcellus, Onondaga Co., N.Y.

61 Elias O. Pierson 2d (Parsons) was born 1780 and died Sep. 29, 1851, at Weston, Conn. Elias adopted the spelling of his surname as Parsons. He mar. Abigail Fanton, and they had son 133 Charles Meeker, b. June 1, 1815, in Reading, Conn., d. Aug. 2, 1888, bur. Easton, Conn., mar. Huldah M. Somers and had one child 514 David Somers (b. Oct. 18, 1842).

62 Samuel G. Pierson was born 1785, and died Jan. 8, 1851, in Reading, Conn. He mar. Hannah Hoyt. They had chd. 134 Daniel, d. 1875 Norwalk, Conn.; 135 Andrew, who resides (1895) in Norwalk, Conn.

63 Noah Pierson (Parsons) was born Jan. 30, 1795, and died Jan. 23, 1885, in Liberty, Sullivan Co., N.Y. Noah adopted the spelling of his surname as Parsons. He mar. Jan. 27, 1822, Harriet Sanford (b. Mar. 26, 1798, d. May 16, 1849 Liberty, N.Y., had bros. George and Samuel [of Reading, Conn.]). Noah and Harriet had chd. 136 Ebenezer S., b. Sep. 20, 1822, mar. May 23, 1849, Harriet Griswold and had chd. 515 Thomas (lived at Walton, Delaware Co., N.Y.), and 516 F. L. (engineer at a steam saw mill in same area [Delaware Co., N.Y.]); 137 Mary E., b. Apr. 21, 1824, mar. Nov. 23, 1848, Eri Chamberlain; 138 John T., b. Oct. 23,

---

[18]*DAR Patriot Index*, Centennial Edition, National Society of the Daughters of the American Revolution, 1994, part 3, p. 2256.

[19]*DAR Patriot Index*, Centennial Edition, National Society of the Daughters of the American Revolution, 1994, part 3, p. 2256.

[20]*DAR Patriot Index*, Centennial Edition, National Society of the Daughters of the American Revolution, 1994, part 3, p. 2256.

[21]*DAR Patriot Index*, Centennial Edition, National Society of the Daughters of the American Revolution, 1994, part 3, p. 2256.

1825, mar. Nov. 26, 1850, Martha Young; 139 Samuel G., b. May 17, 1827, drowned Oct. 12, 1846; 140 Sarah C., b. Apr. 4, 1829, d. Mar. 3, 1830; 141 Sarah C. 2d, b. Dec. 11, 1830, mar. May 14, 1860, James W. Smith (they resided in Iowa in 1895); 142 Noah B., b. Jan. 14, 1833, killed at the Civil War battle of Cedar Mountain Sep. 19, 1862; 143 Esther C., b. Sep. 22, 1835, d. Sep. 6, 1869, mar. Nov. 23, 1854, John Brundage; 144 Alfred R., b. Aug. 31, 1837, killed in the Civil War battle of Cedar Mountain Aug. 9, 1862; 145 Le Grand, b. Jan. 17, 1840, d. May 11, 1840; 146 Hannah E., b. Apr. 8, 1841, d. Feb. 12, 1865, mar. Mar. 5, 1859, John F. Burch; 147 Harriet A., b. Mar. 9, 1843, mar. Dec. 3, 1873, Arthur McKinney.

6 Abraham Pierson Sr., Sgt., was born 1681 Derby, Conn., and died May 12, 1758. He was a selectman in 1711 and frequently afterwards until 1741[22]. On the assessors list in 1717, he was listed with £48, 10s. His will, dated Apr. 26, 1750, was recorded at New Haven, Conn. He mar. Sarah ____, and had chd. 15 Sarah, b. Aug. 19, 1705, mar. Aug. 24, 1727 at Derby, Thomas Bassett; 16+ Abraham Jr., b. July 26, 1707; 17 Mary, b. Oct. 26, 1712, d. 1791 in Newtown, Conn., mar. May 1732 John Sheppard (b. Oct. 26, 1708, son of John Sheppard and Abigail Allen) of Milford, Conn.; 18 Hannah, b. Aug. 4, 1715, mar. June 12, 1734, in Derby, Conn., Solomon Chatfield; 19+ Stephen 3d, b. Mar. 4, 1720; 20 Bathsheba, b. Dec. 1, 1726, mar. Ephraim Parker.

16 Abraham Pierson Jr. was born July 26, 1707, and died 1781. He mar. Apr. 10, 1731, Susannah Wooster (b. July 25, 1713), dau. of Sylvester and Susannah Wooster of Milford, Conn. Abraham Jr. and Susannah had chd. 32+ Oliver, b. Mar. 25, 1732; 33 Stephen 4th, b. 1738, d. May 7, 1763, leaving a widow (Mary Camp?) and dau. 503 Sarah; 34 Elizabeth, mar. Samuel Wooster; 35+ Capt. David, b. Jan. 17, 1748; 36+ Abraham 3d, b. Feb. 11, 1746; 37 Avis, b. Oct. 11, 1751.

32 Oliver Pierson was born Mar. 25, 1732. He mar. Hannah Peet. They had chd. 66 Sarah, bap. Sep. 20, 1750, mar. ____ Baldwin; 67+ Joseph, eldest son; 68 Anna, bap. July 25, 1756, mar. ____ Hotchkiss; 69 Amos 2d, bap. Nov. 20, 1757, mar. 1790 Sarah Johnson; 70 Huldah, bap. June 3, 1759; 71 Susannah, bap. May 9, 1762; 72 Hannah, bap. May 26, 1765; 73 Isaac 3d, bap. Apr. 12, 1767; 74 Lucy, bap. Aug. 21, 1768; 75 David, bap. Nov. 25, 1770, mar. Mar. 6, 1791, Anna Botsford.

67 Capt. Joseph Pierson (eldest son) died in Cazenovia, N.Y. He mar. Sarah Sizer of Middletown, Conn. They had chd. 148 Oliver, settled in Monticello, N.Y.; 149 Abel, lived with his father in Cazenovia, N.Y.; 150+ William, b. May 18, 1775; 151 Sarah, bap. Apr. 28, 1782; 152 Martin; 153 Reuben; 154 Josiah; 155 Isaac; 156 David; 157 Polly; 158 Ichabod Spencer, a lawyer of Utica, N.Y.; 159 Ruby; 160 Lucy.

150 William Pierson was born May 18, 1775, lived to be over 80 years old, and died in Illyria, Ohio. He mar. Betsey Sawyer (d. Cornwall) of Cornwall, Conn. A story is told that William bit a rattlesnake with his teeth to preserve his teeth, which it is said never decayed. They had chd. 266 Polly, b. Feb. 28, 1801, mar. John Slade and had Slade chd. Merritt (mar. Sarah Wedge) and Michael; 267 Paulina, b. Nov. 19, 1803, d. Winsted, Conn., mar. Roswell Perry; 268 Maria, b. Feb. 16, 1807; 269 Cornelia, b. Sep. 29, 1809, d. in Michigan, mar. Joseph Driggs; 270 Ruby, b. Mar. 5, 1813; 271 Clark, b. Mar. 12, 1817, married; 272 Oliver, b. Oct.

---

[22]Frederick Lockwood Pierson, *The Descendants of Stephen Pierson of Suffolk County, England and New Haven and Derby, Conn., 1645-1739*, Walsh & Griffen, Printers, Amenia, N.Y., 1895, p.32, notes.

29, 1821, resided in Ohio, had chd. 518 William H. and 519 Adelia (mar. Mr. Gardiner & resided in Kansas).

35 Capt. David Pierson (Parsons) was born Jan. 17, 1748, and died Mar. 12, 1812, at Amenia, N.Y., in his 64th year. He mar. Oct. 29, 1766, Lois Thompson (d. Mar. 7, 1812, in her 62nd year), dau. of Capt. Jabez Thompson (a sea captain) and his wife Sarah of Derby, Conn. They settled in Amenia, N.Y. They spelled their name Parsons. They had chd. 76 Sarah, b. Oct. 28, 1767, mar. Samuel Falkner; 77+ Joel; 78 Thompson, mar. Sally Welch, settled at Chenango Co., N.Y.; 79 David, d. at the Forks, N.Y., 12 miles from Binghamton; 80+ Truman; 81+ Joseph, b. about 1778; 82 Henrietta, mar. John Bayles of Catskill, N.Y.; 83 Lois, mar. Samuel Hood of Amenia, N.Y.; 84 Betsey, mar. Leman Bosworth and moved to Ohio; 85 Apame, mar. John Palmer of Poughkeepsie, N.Y.

77 Joel Pierson (Parsons) mar. Phebe Bayles. They had chd. 161+ Orrin; 162 Austin; 163 Jabez; 164 Milton; 165 Eli; 166 Laura; 167 Phebe; 168 Anna; 169 Paulina, d. at the manor unmarried; 170 George, resided in Wayne Co., Pennsylvania.

161 Orrin Pierson (Parsons) mar. Betsey Prosier. They had chd. 273 Austin, mar. Betsey Weaver; 274 Jabez, mar. Catharine Prosier; 275 Milton, mar. Eliza ____; 276 Eli, d. in Hudson, N.Y., unmarried; 277 Laura, mar. 1st Joel Westfall and had 2 sons, mar. 2d Abiah Palmer and had Palmer son Abiah Jr.; 278 Phebe, resided in Hudson, N.Y., unmarried in 1895; 279 Anna, mar. and soon died, left no heirs.

80 Truman Pierson (Parsons) died in Cairo, Greene Co., N.Y. He mar. Sally Barlow. They had chd. 171 Electa, mar. ____ Richmond of Cairo, Greene Co., N.Y.; 172 Barlow, mar. ____ Barker of Catskill, Greene Co., N.Y.; 173 Sanford; 174 Sarah, mar. ____ Bevins; 175 Eunice Boyd, mar. William H. Hayes; 176 Joel, moved to Ohio; 177 Philo, moved to Ohio; 178 Clark, moved to Ohio; 179 Harriet, mar. ____ Lockwood of New York city, N.Y.

81 Joseph Pierson (Parsons) was born about 1778, and died Mar. 12, 1812, aged 34, at Amenia, N.Y. He mar. Polly Darling (d. May 27, 1851, aged 67). They had chd. 180 Parnel, b. Feb. 13, 1802, mar. Henry Bird and had Bird son Milo; 181 Julia, b. Feb. 20, 1804, mar. Augustus Jarvis; 182+ Warren, b. 1805; 183 Almira, b. Nov. 11, 1809, d. Apr. 16, ____, mar. Milton Andrews; 184 Mary Ann, b. Nov. 11, 1812, d. Oct. 7, 1876, mar. George Delevan.

182 Warren Pierson (Parsons) was born in 1805, and d. Aug. 1, 1872, at Amenia, N.Y. (killed by a two-year-old bull). He mar. Caroline Rowe (d. June 5, 1885, age 71, of cancer). They had chd. 280 Theron W., b. Apr. 9, 1838, mar. Feb. 28, 1861, Mary C. Burton (b. June 27, 1840), resides (1887) in Washington, D. C., and had chd. 520 Warren (b. Jan. 2, 1862) and 521 Harry (b. Feb. 16, 1871); 281 Charles A., b. Dec. 27, 1842, mar. Oct. 6, 1874, Julia Smith, resided in 1884 in Amenia, N.Y., had chd. 522 Carrie (b. Mar. 26, 1877) and 523 George (b. Sep. 5, 1880); 282 Frank, twin with Frances, b. May 28, 1851, d. May 17, 1881 in Amenia, N.Y., unmarried; 283 Frances, twin with Frank, b. May 28, 1851, mar. prior to 1895.

36 Abraham Pierson 3d was born Feb. 11, 1746, and died in 1779/80. He mar. July 2, 1767, Keziah Lines (d. May 16, 1803, at Woodbridge, Conn.) of New Haven, Conn. At Abraham 3d's death, his living chd. were Levi, Lines, Mary, Patty, Hannah, and Amos (probate court record). Abraham and Keziah had chd. 86 Susannah, b. Mar. 10, 1768, mar. May 17, 1790, Lewis Loveland; 87 Abraham, b. and d. the same day; 88 Abraham 4th, bap. July 29, 1781; 89 Lines, bap. May 23, 1773, d. in 1832 Woodbridge, Conn., had chd. 509 Abraham 5th, 510

Jeremiah, 511 Merritt, 512 Lois, and 513 Harriet (mar. a Baldwin of Woodbridge); 90 Levi, b. Mar. 25, 1771, mar. Emily ____ and lived in Orange, Conn.; 91 Harriet, mar. 2d E. Russell, resided in Orange, Conn., and had a large family; 92 Mary; 93 Patty; 94 Hannah; 95 Amos.

19 Stephen Pierson 3d was born Mar. 4, 1720, in Derby, Conn., and died there in 1754. He mar. June 15, 1738, Hannah Munson (b. Mar. 7, 1721, d. in Alford, Berkshire Co., Mass.), dau. of John and Elizabeth Munson of Derby, Conn. Stephen Pierson 3d's will is dated Feb. 2, 1753. After Stephen 3d died, his widow Hannah Pierson mar. Elijah Davis and had Davis chd. Jabez (lived in Alford, Mass.), Hannah (mar. 3 times), and others. Stephen 3d and Hannah had chd. 38+ Enoch, b. June 18, 1739; 39 Elijah, b. Dec. 26, 1740, in Derby, Conn., d. young and unmarried; 40+ Rachel, b. Sep. 16, 1742; 41 Daniel, b. Apr. 29, 1744, married, was a soldier in the Revolutionary War, left his wife for misconduct in his absence and took his two children and went west to parts unknown; 42+ Eli, b. 1750.

38 Capt. Enoch Pierson was born June 18, 1739, in Derby, Conn., and died Oct. 1, 1827. He mar. 1st Feb. 11, 1761, in Newtown, Conn., Abigail Clogstone (b. Mar. 22, 1738, Reading, Conn., d. June 6, 1807) of Reading, Conn. He mar. 2d Oct. 8, 1809, Abigail Royce (maiden name) (d. Nov. 12, 1823), widow of Dea. Silas St. John. Enoch, at age 16, went as a servant of an officer to Canada during the French war of 1755. He returned and learned the carpenter trade, worked in Newtown, Conn., till he moved to Ellsworth, Conn., April 9, 1764. The homestead he first purchased of John Jackson of 14 acres contained a house, barn, and orchard. He was a selectman and constable and represented Sharon, Conn., in the General Assembly in October 1795. Capt. Enoch was five feet ten inches high, weighed 180 pounds, and had gray eyes and brown hair. His 1st wife, Abigail Clogstone, was tall and bony, with black eyes and hair. Enoch had chd., all by his 1st wife, Abigail: 96+ Betsey, b. Mar. 17, 1762; 97+ Mary Wakeman, b. Nov. 5, 1763; 98+ Abigail, b. Jan. 5, 1766; 99+ Amirillis, b. Sep. 2, 1768; 100+ Stephen, b. Aug. 11, 1771; 101+ Enoch Jr., b. May 9, 1773; 102+ Freeman Washington, b. Mar. 16, 1776; 103+ Amideus, b. Apr. 29, 1780.

96 Betsey Pierson was born Mar. 17, 1762, in Newtown, Conn., and died May 14, 1829. She mar. Dea. Calvin Peck (d. Sep. 1, 1847) of Greenwich, Conn. They had Peck chd. Polly, Enoch Pierson, George Whitfield, Sarah, Amirillis, Betsey, Laura, John Calvin, and Samuel Ferris.

97 Mary Wakeman Pierson was born Nov. 5, 1763, in Newtown, Conn. She mar. David Tryon of Nine Partners, N.Y., and moved to Middleberg, Schoharie Co., N.Y. They moved again to New Connecticut, Ohio. Mary Wakeman Pierson was named after the Wakeman's of Fairfield, Conn.; her mother being Abigail Clogstone, and Nicholas Clogstone married Mary Wakeman of Fairfield, a near relative of Rev. Wakeman of Fairfield. Mary and David had Tryon chd. Betsey, Amelia, Aurelia, Oliver, Alma, Phebe, Freeman, Eunice, Harriet, David, Stephen, and Enoch.

98 Abigail Pierson was born Jan. 5, 1766, in Ellsworth, Conn., and died Aug. 1, 1848, in her 84th year, at Stanwich, Conn. She mar. Joel Hoyt of Stanwich, Conn. Joel Hoyt was drowned in the river June 6, 1805, aged 49 years 2 months and 20 days. This Hoyt family was buried in their family burying ground on their farm in Stanwich, Conn. Abigail and Joel had Hoyt chd.: Mehetabel, b. June 16, 1791, d. Jan. 29, 1810, unmarried; Freeman, b.

Jan. 16, 1795, d. Mar. 16, 1869, aged 74, mar. Lorina Finch (d. Mar. 21, 1861, aged 81, in Stanwich), no children.

99 Amirillis Pierson was born Sep. 2, 1768, in Ellsworth, Conn. She mar. John Wells of Amenia, N.Y., and settled in Nobletown, N.Y., where all of their children were born. Later they moved Amsterdam, N.Y., at which place both Amirillis and John Wells died. They had Wells chd.: Abigail, Anna, Julia, John Jr., Almena, and Pierson (d. at age 15 in Amsterdam, N.Y.).

100 Stephen Pierson was born Aug. 21, 1771, in Ellsworth, Conn., and died Dec. 9, 1839 (suicide with opium). He mar. Nov. 14, 1790, Hannah Curtis (d. Feb. 3, 1844) of Danbury, Conn. Stephen and Hannah had chd. 215 Ada, b. June 16, 1792, d. Jan. 9, 1813, unmarried; 216 Abigail, b. Apr. 28, 1794, d. without issue, was the 2d wife of Lewis Burr Sturges; 217+ Zillah, b. Apr. 5, 1796; 218 Miritta, b. Jan. 5, 1798, d. Jan. 14, 1813, age 15, unmarried; 219+ Stephen Curtis, b. Nov. 19, 1799; 220 Betsey Maria, b. Oct. 9, 1801, mar. 1st Joseph Heath, 2d Alexander Conn, had Heath chd. Abigail (b. 1823) and Lewis; 221 Lucy, b. Mar. 26, 1805, d. July 2, 1805; 222 Lucy Lovina, b. Mar. 31, 1807, d. Nov. 16, 1809; 223+ Heman King, b. Dec. 22, 1808; 224+ Noah Seth, b. Feb. 26, 1811.

217 Zillah Pierson was born Apr. 5, 1796, and died Sep. 2, 1843, at age 47. She mar. Clark Sherwood (d. Feb. 19, 1854, age 65). They had Sherwood chd.: Stephen Pierson, b. Jan. 28, 1814, mar. 1st July 13, 1834, Mary Hitchcock (d. Feb. 6, 1855), mar. 2d Oct. 10, 1855, Jerusha Stark (d. Sep. 16, 1872, age 54); Mary, b. July 26, 1817, d. Apr. 5, 1823; Henry, b. Mar. 24, 1819, d. May 27, 1820; Seth Curtis, b. Sep. 10, 1821, d. Dec. 24, 1857; Lois Ann, b. July 19, 1827.

219 Stephen Curtis Pierson was born Nov. 19, 1799, and died Feb. 13, 1869. He mar. 1st Nov. 19, 1822, at Sharon, Conn., Sabra Heath (b. Apr. 6, 1798, d. Sep. 4, 1838, in Eugene, Vermillion Co., Indiana), dau. of Obadiah and Diana (Waller) Heath. Stephen mar. 2d Sarah Cooper (b. Ellsworth, Conn., d. there Aug. 14, 1888, age 82). Stephen had chd., all by his 1st wife Sabra: 289+ Henry Clark, b. June 6, 1823; 290 Miritta(?) Cecilia, b. July 13, 1826, Ellsworth, Conn., mar. May 18, 1847, Alonzo Kingsley (b. Oct. 3, 1828) of New Preston, Conn.; 292[23] Milo Curtis, b. July 13, 1828, d. June 24, 1890, at age 61, heart disease, mar. Feb. 20, 1866, Mary Maria Elmore (an Irish girl of Albany, N.Y.), no children; 293 Amelia Jane, b. Aug. 6, 1833, Ellsworth, Conn., d. Jan. 8, 1885, in New Preston, Conn., of pneumonia, mar. Aug. 1, 1856, at Patterson, N.Y., James Harvey Moore (b. Jan. 30, 1833, Sharon, Conn.), had Moore chd. Robert, John, & Estelle; 294 Charles Elmore, b. Apr. 15, 1835, d. young in Eugene, Ind.; 295 Stephen Curtis, b. Aug. 26, 1838, d. young in Eugene, Indiana.

289 Henry Clark Pierson was born June 6, 1823 in Ellsworth, Conn., and died Oct. 27, 1864, in Tonawanda, Erie Co., N.Y. He mar. Nov. 4, 1851, at Pawling, N.Y., Charity Slocum (b. May 13, 1823, Pawling, N.Y.). They had chd. 403 Emma, b. Dec. 25, 1852, Millville, Orleans Co., N.Y., mar. Sep. 14, 1873, R. J. Dean; 404 Mary Elizabeth, b. Apr. 10, 1858, d. May 17, 1859; 405 Henry Clark, b. Nov. 7, 1864, Tonawanda, Erie Co., N.Y.

---

[23]Number 291 has been skipped by Frederick Lockwood Pierson in his 1895 book, thus it is skipped here.

223 Heman King Pierson was born Dec. 22, 1808, died Oct. 31, 1890, in Ashtabula, Ohio, of softening of the brain, and was buried in Tallmadge, Ohio. He mar. Janette Upson (d. Jan. 27, 1884, Tallmadge, Ohio) of Watertown, Conn. They had chd. 296 Fredrick, d. young, unmarried; 297 Almira, d. young, unmarried; 298+ Elizabeth, b. Sep. 11, 1837.

298 Elizabeth Pierson was born Sep. 11, 1837, and died in North Easton, Mass. She mar. Sep. 6, 1857, James H. Bailey (b. Oct. 9, 1835). They had Bailey chd.: Nettie B., b. Mar. 14, 1860; Minnie A., b. July 23, 1862; Lillie A., b. Apr. 18, 1865; and Francis E., b. July 24, 1868.

224 Noah Seth Pierson was born Feb. 26, 1811, and died May 1, 1875, Unadilla, Otsego Co., N.Y.. He mar. 1st Susan Lattison, and mar. 2d Feb. 21, 1864, Mary E. Fuller (b. Aug. 9, 1845, Unadilla, Otsego Co., N.Y.). After her husband's death, Mary Fuller mar. again. Noah had chd. by his 1st wife Susan: 299 Charlotte, mar. ____ Fox; 300 Edwin, d. young, unmarried; 301 James, mar. Miss ____ Howe of Cornwall, Conn.; and 302 Adelbert. Noah had chd. by his 2d wife Mary: 303 Nettie Jane, b. Feb. 24, 1865, mar. Wm. Ostrander; 304 Evaline, b. July 6, 1869, mar. Edward Nichols; and 305 Stephen Curtis, b. Aug. 27, 1872, unmarried.

101 Enoch Pierson Jr. was born May 9, 1773, in Ellsworth, Conn., and died Sep. 10, 1835. He mar. Feb. 8, 1795, Amy Studley (d. Feb. 9, 1846) of Ellsworth, Conn. Enoch Jr. had blue eyes, dark hair, was six feet tall, and weighed over 200 pounds. He had no sons. Enoch Jr. and Amy had chd. 225 Polly, d. without issue, mar. Philander Hatch of New Preston, Conn.; 226 Ruth, twin with Amy, d. unmarried; 227 Amy, twin with Ruth, mar. Burr Camp of New Preston, Conn.; 228 Mary Ann, d. Mar. 6, 1846, unmarried; 229 Caroline, d. Apr. 13, 1852, mar. Dr. Russell Everett and had Everett chd.: Enoch Pierson (mar. 1st Helen Sophronia Everett, 2d Emily Goodenough); and Richard Floyd (mar. Catherine St. John).

102 Freeman Washington Pierson was born Mar. 16, 1776, in Ellsworth, Conn., at the homestead, and died July 21, 1861, age 85, of a shock of palsy (couldn't speak after the palsy attack until he died). He mar. 1st Oct. 1797, Mary Skiff (b. Sep. 23, 1774, at Ellsworth, d. Nov. 18, 1846) of Ellsworth, Conn. He mar. 2d Miss Maria Boardman, who survived him and died in Bridgewater, Conn. He was a well read, intellectual man and often selectman and constable. Freeman was five feet ten tall, weighed 196 pounds, eyes black, hair dark which he lost by fever and became bald. Mary Skiff, mother of all his children, was about five feet four tall, weighed 200, blue eyes, and dark brown hair. Freeman and Mary Skiff had chd. 230+ John, b. Nov. 6, 1799; 231 Betsey, b. Jan. 17, 1802, d. Mar. 26, 1885, in Sharon, Conn., bur. Ellsworth, Conn., mar. 1st Oct. 4, 1818, Edmund Miles Bennett (b. Nov. 22, 1796, Sharon, d. Sep. 10, 1830, while blasting a well in Ellsworth) of Sharon, Conn., mar. 2d Apr. 3, 1842, Charles Lockwood (b. Apr. 13, 1797, d. Sep. 28, 1852, Greenwich) of Greenwich, Conn., Betsey had no children; 232+ Daniel, b. Sep. 14, 1804; 233+ Paulina, b. Mar. 15, 1806; 234 Mary Louisa, b. Dec. 11, 1812, d. Sep. 6, 1888, bur. in Ellsworth, Conn., mar. Jan. 6, 1841, Augustus L. Peck (d. Jan. 22, 1883, of dropsy) of Ellsworth, Conn. They had no children.

230 John Pierson was born Nov. 6, 1799, in Ellsworth, Conn., at the old homestead, died Dec. 14, 1888 at Stanwich, Conn., and is buried there. He mar. Nov. 30, 1821, Sarah Lockwood (b. Sep. 19, 1799, Greenwich, d. May 21, 1883, Stanwich, of typhoid pneumonia, bur. Stanwich) of Greenwich, Conn., dau. of Frederick and Deborah (Reynolds) Lockwood. John Pierson was 5 feet 8 inches tall, weight 150 lbs., dark brown hair, and gray eyes. John

and Sarah had chd. 306+ Frederick Lockwood, b. Sep. 23, 1822; 307 Mary Elizabeth, b. Nov. 19, 1823, d. May 25, 1844 in Kent, Conn., bur. in Sharon, Conn., mar. Apr. 27, 1843, Charles B. Bates of Sharon mountain, Conn.; 308 Harriet Louisa, b. Feb. 17, 1826, mar. Nov. 26, 1851, Henry Kirke White of White Hollow, resided at Winchester, Conn., and had White chd. Josephine, Elizabeth, Albert Pierson, & Frances Louisa, all born in Sharon Great Hollow; 309 John Albert, b. Apr. 6, 1828, mar. widow Jane (Briggs) Groesbeck of Saratoga, N.Y., had son 524 Albert Briggs (b. Torrington, Conn., & drowned there); 310 Caroline, b. Aug. 7, 1830, d. Dec. 18, 1867, in Bridgeport, Conn., bur. in Sharon, Conn., mar. Mar. 27, 1850, Frederick A. Hotchkiss of Sharon Valley, Conn., had Hotchkiss chd. Mary, Carrie Louisa, Franklin Augustus, and Hattie; 311 Sarah Augusta, b. Feb. 13, 1833, d. Aug. 27, 1866, Bridgeport, Conn., bur. in Sharon, Conn., mar. Oct. 26, 1853, Marcus Coon, no heirs; 312 Frances Aphelia, b. Dec. 5, 1834, mar. Nov. 27, 1856, Josiah Hawley Mills of Northeast Center, N.Y., had Mills chd.: a son (d. young) and Emma Cordelia; 313 Cordelia, b. Nov. 5, 1837, unmarried; 314 Augustus, b. Oct. 31, 1840, d. Aug. 8, 1842.

306 Frederick Lockwood Pierson was born Sep. 23, 1822, in Ellsworth, Conn., at the old homestead. He mar. Feb. 2, 1851, at Ellsworth, Conn., Susan Skiff (b. Mar. 2, 1832). Frederick is five feet 8 inches tall, 160 lbs., gray eyes, and light brown hair. Susan is five feet 4 inches tall, 136 lbs., black eyes, and black hair. Frederick was the author of *The Descendants of Stephen Pierson*[24], published in 1895, from which most of the material on the descendants of Stephen Pierson in this chapter was obtained. Frederick and Susan had chd. 411 Mary, b. July 10, 1852, d. May 13, 1888, mar. Oct. 26, 1875, Joseph White (d. Apr. 14, 1889), had White chd. Clara Louisa (b. May 28, 1883); 412 Edward, b. Mar. 3, 1856, mar. Jennie Landon (d. May 22, 1891, without issue); 413 Eliza, b. Apr. 19, 1860, mar. Jan. 2, 1895, Marshall B. Hopkins; 414 George, b. Oct. 26, 1867, d. Mar. 1, 1894, unmarried.

232 Daniel Pierson was born Sep. 14, 1804, in Ellsworth, Conn., and died Apr. 13, 1854, of typhoid fever, in Ellsworth, Conn., at the old homestead. He mar. Sep. 14, 1828, Electa Ann Reed (b. Feb. 18, 1808, d. Sep. 20, 1885, Independence, Iowa, was insane in her last days) of Sharon, Conn., dau. of Benjamin and Prudence (Smith) Reed (formerly of Darien, Conn.). Daniel studied law and was admitted to the bar at Litchfield, Conn., after he was 40 years old. He was a good scholar and had an uncommon good memory. Daniel was five feet 8 inches tall, weighed 184 lbs., and had dark brown hair and black eyes. Daniel and Electa had chd. 315+ George Benjamin, b. Mar. 27, 1830; 316 Julia Ann, b. Nov. 27, 1833, d. Sep. 13, 1835, Ohio.

315 Dr. George Benjamin Pierson was born Mar. 27, 1830, in Sharon, Conn. He mar. 1st Elizabeth Hatch (d. 6 months after her marriage) of Kent, Conn. He mar. 2d May 26, 1859, at Independence, Iowa, Sophia W. Edgecomb (b. Dec. 29, 1841). George studied medicine with Dr. Hatch of Kent, Conn., practiced awhile in Middlebury, Conn., and moved to Independence, Iowa, after the death of his father. He practiced at Independence for a time, keeping a drug store, enlisted in a Cavalry Regiment during the Civil War, and afterwards moved to Hooper, Nebraska. George and Sophia had chd. 415 Charles Herbert, b. Oct. 16, 1860, Independence, Iowa; 416 Laura Winslow, b. Dec. 11, 1864, Independence, Iowa, mar.

---

[24]Frederick Lockwood Pierson, *The Descendants of Stephen Pierson of Suffolk County, England and New Haven and Derby, Conn., 1645-1739*, Walsh & Griffen, Printers, Amenia, N.Y., 1895.

Oct. 5, 18(84?), in Colorado, Mr. _____ Layner; 417 Henry E., b. Sep. 23, 1866, Independence, Iowa.

233 Paulina Pierson was born Mar. 15, 1806, and died Jan. 3, 1892, in Gorham, Ontario Co., N.Y. She mar. Nov. 20, 1827, Ethan Lord (d. Feb. 23, 1871, in Gorham, hurt by being thrown from a wagon and died soon after) of Ellsworth, Conn. They had Lord chd.: a son, d. young; Marietta, b. Ellsworth, Conn., resided in Gorham, unmarried; Flora Louisa, b. Ellsworth, Conn., mar. Feb. 25, 1879, Frank Foster, resided in Gorham, Ontario Co., N.Y.

103 Amideus Pierson was born Apr. 29, 1780, in Ellsworth, Conn., died July 31, 1866, and buried at Ellsworth, Conn. He mar. Feb. 7, 1808, Aurelia Miles (b. July 10, 1784, d. Jan. 13, 1871, age 86, bur. Ellsworth) at Watertown, Conn., dau. of Richard and Margaret (Scott) Miles. They had chd. 235 Laura Ann, b. July 29, 1810, d. Dec. 25, 1880, mar. Samuel F. Peck (her cousin), had Peck dau. Charlotte; 236 Charles Miles, b. Mar. 13, 1812, d. Aug. 2, 1872, in Norfolk, Conn., bur. at Ellsworth, Conn., unmarried; 237+ Almira, b. Mar. 6, 1815.

237 Almira Pierson was born Mar. 6, 1815. She was the 2d wife of Henry St. John, son of Silas and Olive (Barstow) St. John. They had St. John chd.: Charles Pierson, b. Aug. 20, 1839; Aurelia Miles, b. June 5, 1844; Cordelia M., b. Apr. 8, 1846; Pluma Barstow, b. Dec. 30, 1848; and Isabel, b. Nov. 17, 1859.

40 Rachel Pierson was born Sep. 16, 1742, in Derby, Conn., and died June 26, 1815, at North Colebrook, Conn. She mar. Henry Clinton (d. Apr. 15, 1814, at North Colebrook, Conn., in his 87th year). He was a farmer and resided a while in New Milford, Conn. They had a large family. Some of them emigrated to Newark Valley, Tioga Co., N.Y. They had Clinton chd. Henry, d. in Wisconsin; Sheldon, d. in Wisconsin; Samuel, d. in Pennsylvania; Lyman 1st, d. in Newark Valley, Tioga Co., N.Y.; Clara or Clarana, mar. Ira Andrus of Colebrook, Conn., d. there, and left a large family; Elijah Pierson, bapt. Apr. 18, 1762.

42 Eli Pierson Sr. was born 1750 in Derby, Conn., and died May 22, 1822, aged 72 years, at Egremont, Mass. He mar. Sarah Hinman (d. Mar. 9, 1815, in her 68th year, at South Egremont, Mass.) of Derby, and was a farmer. Eli and Sarah had chd. 110 Betsey, b. Derby, Conn., never married; 111+ Lewis, b. 1772; 112 Sarah, b. Derby, Conn., never married; 113 Lucy, b. Derby, Conn., a fine looking intelligent young lady, was thrown from a wagon and crippled for life, had no use of her lower limbs, and occupied a swing bed the remainder of her days, which were not few, never married.

111 Lewis Pierson (Parsons) was born 1772 in Derby, Conn., and died May 10, 1859, in Egremont, Mass. He mar. Esther Smith (d. Oct. 4, 1829, age 54) of Derby, Conn., dau. of Elijah Smith of Oxford, Conn. They spelled their surname Parsons. Lewis and Esther had chd. 242 Elijah, b. 1798, d. Apr. 5, 1861, South Egremont, Mass. (suicide), wagon maker, unmarried; 243+ Eli Jr., b. 1799; 244 Maria, unmarried, d. of palsy in Egremont, Mass.; 245 Esther, mar. Charles Beers and had Beers chd.: Eliza Ann, Maria, Frank, and Fanny, resided in Marcellus, Onondaga Co., N.Y.; 246 Anna, b. 1806, d. Aug. 30, 1833, unmarried; 247+ Lewis Smith; 248 Sarah, d. Nov. 29, 1877, Sheffield, Mass. (she and her husband were murdered by a man that hung for it), 2d wife of David Stillman (d. Nov. 29, 1877, Sheffield) of Sheffield, Mass., had a Stillman dau. (d. young), and a Stillman son Charles.

243 Eli Pierson Jr. was born in 1799, and died May 4, 1860, in Egremont, Mass. He mar. Clarissa Tuller (d. Egremont, Mass.). He learned the blacksmith trade from his uncle, Isaac

Smith of Oxford. Eli Jr. had chd., all born in Egremont, Mass., and those living in 1895 were in California: 325 Emmeline, mar. Levi Baldwin, resides (1895) in California; 326 Margaret, mar. ____ Hawley; 327 William Eli, d. Aug. 29, 1857, in his 21st year; 328 George C.; 329 John L.; 330 Foster E.; 331 Sanford W.; 332 Charles; 333 Albert.

247 Lewis Smith Pierson was born in Egremont, Mass. He mar. Elizabeth Boardman of Sheffield, Mass. They had chd. 334+ George L.; 335 Sarah, mar. Hopkins Candee of Sheffield, Mass.; 336 Levi, mar. Mary E. Andrews of Northfield, Conn.; 337 Arthur, married and resided at Ashley Falls, Massachusetts.

334 George L. Pierson mar. Mary Huggins of Sheffield, Mass., and resided at Canaan, Conn. They had chd. 418 George Willis, b. Nov. 5, 1865; 419 Joseph Lewis, b. Feb. 8, 1867, mar. Clara E. Baldwin; 420 Mary Louisa, b. May 6, 1869; 421 Frederick Smith, b. Feb. 26, 1871, mar. Eva K. Corbit, had son 525 Julius C. (b. June 30, 1894).

Chapter 15
Descendants of John Pearson of Lynn
American Immigrant

The following descendants of John Pearson (1608-1679) are copied[1] from Lizzie B. Pierson, *Pierson Genealogical Records*, Joel Munsell, Printer, Albany, N.Y., 1878, pp. 57-58, as a framework to present new data upon. Lizzie Pierson's footnotes, errata, and related appendices are incorporated within the text which is modified by footnoted additional research by the authors of *Pierson Millennium*. An every-name index is provided at the back of *Pierson Millennium*. The + symbol after an identifying number indicates more information is provided in a later paragraph beginning with the same number in this chapter.

John Pearson of Lynn (1608-1679) is likely the first cousin of Rev. Abraham Pierson (1611-1678) of Branford, Conn., and Newark, N.J., and John is likely the second cousin of Henry Peirson (1615-1680) of Lynn, Mass., and Southampton, Long Island. See Chapter 4 for details. John Pearson of Lynn, Massachusetts, was christened[2] 8 Dec 1608 at Howden, Yorkshire, England, parents John and Jane Pearson who married 19 Feb 1603/4 at Howden, Yorkshire, England. John's father died in 1636 and John came to Lynn, Massachusetts, the following year in 1637. He had wife Maudlin and children at Lynn and Reading, Massachusetts, and died at Reading in 1679 at age 71. See Chapters 3 & 4 for ancestors, and below for descendants. This chapter is not intended to be an authoritative list of descendants of John Pearson, but rather a limited list by which new and experienced family genealogical researchers may tie into the English data presented in this book.

1 John Pearson was christened[3] 8 Dec 1608 in Howden, Yorkshire, England. He married Maudlin ____, they arrived at Lynn (then Saugus), Mass., in 1637, and moved to Reading, Mass. in 1639. John Pearson is said to have been one of seven men who founded the church and town of Reading in that year. John Pearson died at Reading, Mass. in 1679. John and Maudlin had chd. 2 Mary, b. Lynn, Mass., mar.[4] 3 Dec 1663 Thomas Burnett; 3 Bertha, b. Lynn, Mass.; 4 Sarah, b. Lynn, Mass.; 5+ John, b. 1650/53 Reading, Mass.; and 6 James, b. Reading, Mass.

5 Capt. John Pearson was born 1650/53 at Reading, Mass., and died in 1720. He mar. T. (probably Tabitha) Kendall, was representative of the town of Lynn 1702 till 1710, and was known as "Capt." They had chd. 7 James, b. 1678, mar. H. Swaine; 8 Tabitha, mar. J.

---

[1]Lizzie B. Pierson, *Pierson Genealogical Records*, Joel Munsell, Printer, Albany, New York, 1878, page 57.

[2]*The Registers of the Parish of Howden, Co. York*, Vols. I (published 1904, marriages 1542-1644 and baptisms 1542-1659), & II (published 1905, burials 1543-1659), edited by G. E. Weddall, privately printed for the Yorkshire Parish Register Society, Beck & Inchbold Ltd., Printers, Oriel Press, Leeds, Yorkshire, England.

[3]*The Registers of the Parish of Howden, Co. York*, Vols. I (published 1904, marriages 1542-1644 and baptisms 1542-1659), & II (published 1905, burials 1543-1659), edited by G. E. Weddall, privately printed for the Yorkshire Parish Register Society, Beck & Inchbold Ltd., Printers, Oriel Press, Leeds, Yorkshire, England.

[4]George Rogers Howell, *The Early History of Southampton, L.I., New York*, 2nd Edition, Weed, Parsons and Company, Albany, NY, 1887, p. 206.

Goodwin; 9 John, b. 1684 Lynn, Mass., mar. É. Batcheller; 10 Rebecca, b. 1686; 11+ Kendall, b. 1688; 12 Susanna, b. 1690 Lynn, Mass., mar. D. Gould; 13 Mary b. 1692, mar. G. Eaton; 14 Thomas, b. 1694 Lynn, Mass.; 15 Ebenezer, b. 1696 Lynn, Mass.; 16 Sarah; 17 Abigail; 18 Elizabeth b. Lynn, Mass.

11 Kendall Pearson was born 1688 at Reading, Mass., and died in 1763. He mar. L. Boardman, and had chd. 19+ Thomas, b. 1709.

19 Thomas Pearson was born 1709, and died 1773. He mar. A. Lewis, and they had chd. 20+ William, b. 1732; 21+ Ebenezer, b. 14 May 1736; 22 Thomas, b. 1736?, and d. young; 23+ Samuel, b. 1739; 24 Hannah, b. 1741; and 25 Susanna, b. 1743.

20 William Pearson was born in 1732, probably in Mass., and died in 1804 at Windsor, Vt. He mar. M. Jaquith, and had chd. 26+ William, b. 1756; 27 Nabby, b. 1758; 28 Thomas, b. 1759; 29 Sallie, b. 1761, d. 1795, mar. Capt. Burnham; 30 Hannah, b. 1762, d. 1839, mar. 41 Samuel Pearson, son of 23 Samuel Pearson of this chapter; 31 Lydia, b. 1764, d. 1846, mar. S. Hubbard; 32 Thomas, b. 1766, d. 1794 Windsor, Vt., mar. ____ Sherwin; 33 John, b. 1768, d. young; 34 John, b. 1770, d. 1862 Windsor, Vt., mar. L. Moore; 35 Benjamin, b. 1773, d. 1843 Woodstock, Vt., mar. P. More, had son 58 Benjamin of Reading, Vt.; 36 Polly, b. 1775, d. young.

26 William Pearson was born 1756, and died in 1836. He lived at Windsor, Vt. William mar. 40 Hannah Pearson, dau. of 23 Samuel Pearson (see 23 and 40 near end of this chapter), and had chd. 49 Hannah, b. 1782, d. 1840, mar. E. Holden; 50+ William, b. 1785, d. 1864, mar. A. Brockway; 51 Lois, b. 1786, d. 1866, mar. J. Holden; 52+ Abiel, b. 1789, d. 1875 Poultney, Vt., mar. O. Bliss; 53+ Ira, b. 1791; 54+ Dennis, b. 1794, d. 1838, mar. B. Parker; 55+ Leonard, b. 1796, d. 1873, mar. M. Buck; 56 Lynda, d. young; 57+ Calvin, b. 1802, d. 1854, mar. S. Pearson.

50 William Pearson was born in 1785, and died in 1864. He married A. Brockway, and had chd. 70 Philander, b. 1804, mar. U. Allard of Reading, Vt.; 71 Azula, b. 1807, d. 1852, mar. A. D. Allard of Reading, Vt.; 72 Alvin, b. 1810, d. 1838, mar. L. Allard of Reading, Vt.; 73 Sarah, b. 1812, mar. G. Weeding; 74 Roxana, b. 1817, mar. A. Holt of Sherburne, Vt.

52 Abiel Pearson was born in 1789, and died in 1875 at Poultney, Vt., where he lived at death. He mar. O. Bliss, made his home at Clarendon Springs, Vt., and had chd. 75 Lucy; 76 Caroline, mar. J. Bailey; 77 Calvin, b. 1814, of Windsor, Vt.; 78 Olive (d. young?); 79 Olive, b. 1818, mar. J. Flowers; 80 Alice, mar. G. W. Field; 81 Angeline, d. 1868, mar. J. Bramble; 82 Martha, d. 1868, mar. W. Jenney; 83 Diana, mar. H. Lincoln; 84 Vesta; 85 Susan.

53 Ira Pearson was born in 1791. He mar. S. J. Pollard of Ludlow, Vt. He was a minister of the gospel for 19 years, and was still living in 1878 at age 87 at Newport, N.H. He had chd. 86 Ira, b. 1817, d. 1858, of N.Y. city; 87 John William, b. 1819, of Lowell, Mass.; 88 Sophia J., b. 1821, mar. J. M. Emerson; 89 James, d. young; 90 Charles Edmunds, b. 1830, d. 1863, was a physician, mar. 1st A. Piper, and 2d M. Morill.

54 Dennis Pearson was born in 1794, and died in 1838. He mar. B. Parker, and had chd. 91 Cynthia, b. 1817, mar. D. Smith; 92 Leonard, b. 1819, mar. S. Rice of Northfield, Mass.; 93 Casandana (Cassandra?), mar. R. Bowman; 94 Amasa, b. 1824, mar. M. Amdon of Rutland,

Vt.; 95 Larnard, b. 1827, mar. A. E. Pearson; 96 Charles H., b. 1829, mar. D. A. Cutting of Rutland, Vt.; 97 Philetta, mar. D. Campbell; 98 Anna, mar. S. Wright.

55 Leonard Pearson was born in 1796, and died in 1873. He lived at Windsor, Vt., mar. M. Buck, and had chd. 99 Henry S., b. 1824, of Chelsea, Mass., mar. E. Fifield; 100 Celestia, of Windsor, Vt., mar. J. B. Maynard.

57 Calvin Pearson was born in 1802, and died in 1854. He mar. S. Pearson, and lived in Windsor, Vt. He had chd. 101 Polly, of Hartland, Vt., mar. S. Rogers; 102 John S., of Rutland, Vt., mar. ____ Kendall.

21 Ebenezer Pearson was born[5] May 14, 1736 in Mass., and died[6] June 6, 1779 in New Hampshire. During the Revolutionary War, he was a Private in the New Hampshire militia.[7] It is not clear if his death was caused by the war. He mar.[8] Mary Thompson, and they had chd. 37+ Ebenezer, lived in Milford, N.H.; 38 Ezekiel, lived in Woodstock, Vt.

37 Ebenezer Pearson lived in Milford, N.H., and had chd. 59 James, lived in Milford, N.H.

23 Samuel Pearson was born in 1739, and died in 1823. He lived at Windsor, Vt., mar. B. Gray, and had chd. 39 Bridget, b. 1759, d. 1825, mar. A. Boutwell; 40 Hannah, mar. 26 William Pearson, son of 20 William Pearson of Windsor, Vt. (see 26 and 20 of this chapter); 41 Samuel, b. 1763, d. 1847, of Reading, Vt., mar. 30 Hannah Pearson, dau. of 20 William Pearson of this chapter; 42 Olive, mar. S. Whitcomb; 43 Chloe, of Reading, Vt., mar. ____ Peabody; 44+ Cornelius G., b. 1768; 45 John, b. 1770, d. 1822; 46 Lydia, mar. ____ Spencer; 47 Rhoda, mar. O. Davis; 48 Lucy, mar. J. Holden.

44 Cornelius G. Pearson was born in 1768, and died in 1849. He mar. P. Benjamin, settled in New York city, N.Y., and had chd. 60 Samuel; 61 Lewis; 62 Polly; 63 Sally; 64 Daniel; 65 Hosea; 66 Asa.

---

[5]*DAR Patriot Index*, Centennial Edition, National Society of the Daughters of the American Revolution, 1994, part 3, p. 2257.

[6]*DAR Patriot Index*, Centennial Edition, National Society of the Daughters of the American Revolution, 1994, part 3, p. 2257.

[7]*DAR Patriot Index*, Centennial Edition, National Society of the Daughters of the American Revolution, 1994, part 3, p. 2257.

[8]*DAR Patriot Index*, Centennial Edition, National Society of the Daughters of the American Revolution, 1994, part 3, p. 2257.

Chapter 16
Some Pearson/Peirson/Pierson Men
In the Revolutionary War (1776-1783)

In 1775, Associations were formed throughout the thirteen British colonies in America composed of male inhabitants from 16 to 50 years of age capable of bearing arms. The signers of these Associations took the following oath:

"Persuaded, that the salvation of the rights and liberties of America, depends, under God, on the firm union of its inhabitants, in a vigorous prosecution of the measures necessary for its safety; and convinced of the necessity of preventing the anarchy and confusion, which attend a dissolution of the powers of government; We, the freeholders, and inhabitants, of _____, being greatly alarmed at the avowed design of the ministry, to raise a revenue in America; and, shocked, by the bloody scene, now acting in the Massachusetts Bay, do, in the most solemn manner, resolve never to become slaves; and do associate under all the ties of religion, honour, and love to our country, to adopt and endeavour to execution, whatever measures may be recommended by the Continental Congress; or resolved upon our Provincial Convention, for the purpose of preserving our Constitution, and opposing the execution of the several arbitrary, and oppressive acts of the British Parliament; until a reconciliation between Great-Britain and America, on constitutional principles, (which we most ardently desire) can be obtained; and that we will in all things follow the advice of our General Committee, respecting the purposes aforesaid, the preservation of peace and good order, and safety of individuals, and private property. Dated in ___ May, 1775."

County Hall, Suffolk County, N.Y., May 1775 (Associations 30.154, 30.158, 30.162, & 30.197).

Abraham Peirson (No. 19, Chap. 10)	Lemuel Peirson Jr. (No. 78, Chap. 10)
Daniel Peirson (No. 64, Chap. 12)	Lemuel Peirson 3d (No. 62, Chap. 12)
David Peirson (No. 79, Chap. 10)	Mathew Peirson (No. 50, Chap. 10)
David Peirson Jr. (No. 39, Chap. 10)	Mathew Peirson 2d (No. 44, Chap. 10)
Henry Peirson (No. 101, Chap. 10)	Nathan Peirson (No. 85, Chap. 10)
Isaac Peirson (No. 80, Chap. 10)	Samuel Peirson (No. 127, Chap. 12)
Jedediah Peirson (No. 66, Chap. 12)	Silvanus Peirson (No. 51, Chap. 10)
Jeremiah Peirson (No. 60, Chap. 10)	Stephen Peirson (No. 43, Chap. 10)
Job Peirson (No. 21, Chap. 12)	Theophilus Peirson (No. 89, Chap. 10)
Job Peirson Jr. (No. 130, Chap. 12)	Timothy Peirson (No. 53, Chap. 10)
John Peirson (No. 93, Chap. 10)	Zebulon Peirson (No. 45, Chap. 10)
Lemuel Peirson (No. 38, Chap. 10)	Zecheriah Peirson (No. 86, Chap. 10)

Josiah Peirson refused to sign the Association (probably No. 20, age 80, Chap. 10).

County Hall, Suffolk County, N.Y., May 1775 (Associations 30.166, & 30.175)

Samuel Peirson (No. 69, Chap. 9)	Timothy Pierson (No. 68, Chap. 9)

Cornwall Precinct, Orange Co., N.Y., Signers of the Association, 1775

Silas Pierson (No. 48, Chap. 10)	Silas Pierson Jr. (No. 96, Chap. 10)

Col. David Mulford, commander of the 2nd Regiment of Suffolk County, reported a statement of his Regiment on 10 Feb 1776. The nine companies totaled 760 officers and privates, of which three companies were furnished by Southampton, three by Bridgehampton, and two from East Hampton. The staff officers were Lt. Col. Jonathan Hedges, 1st Maj. Uriah Rogers, 2d Maj. George Herrick, Captain David Howell, Captain John Dayton, Captain David Pierson[1] (No. 79, Chap. 10), Captain David Fithian, Captain Stephen Howell, Captain William Rogers, Captain Josiah Howell, Captain Samuel L'hommedieu, Captain John Sanford, Adjutant John Gelston, Quarter Master Phineas Howell, Sergeant Major Lemuel Pierson[2] (No. 78, Chap. 10), and Drum Major Elias Matthews. In addition to those named, Colonel Mulford's Regiment included 18 Lieutenants, 9 Ensigns, 36 Sergeants, 9 Drummers, 9 Fifers, and 670 Rank and File.

Capt. David Pierson (No. 79, Chap. 10), commander of the 2nd Southampton Company of the Minutemen Regiment, had under his command 2 Lieutenants, 1 Ensign, 4 Sergeants, 1 Drummer, 1 Fifer, and 60 Rank and File. The enlisted men included[3] on 10 Feb 1776:

Abraham Pierson (No. 94, Chap. 10)	John Pierson (No. 93, Chap. 10)
Elias Pierson (No. 90, Chap. 10)	Lemuel Pierson (No. 78, Chap. 10)
Isaac Pierson (No. 80, Chap. 10)	Zachariah Pierson (No. 86, Chap. 10)
Job Pierson (No. 130, Chap. 12).	

Capt. Zephaniah Rogers was commander of the 1st Company (raised for protection to the inhabitants and stock of Long Island). His men included[4] on said reporting dates:

26 July 1776: Elias Peirson, Corp., residence Southampton, age 28, born Southampton, 6 ft. 6 in. tall, dark complexion, dark hair, occupation weaver. See 90 Elias Pierson in Chapter 10.

10 Aug. 1776: John Peirson, Sergt. See 93 John Pierson in Chapter 10.

Capt. Ezekiel Mulford was commander of the 12th Company. His men included[5] on said reporting date:

26 July 1776: Lemuel Pierson, Sergt., residence Southampton, age 32, born Southampton, 5 ft. 8 in. tall, dark complexion, dark brown hair, occupation weaver. See 78 Lemuel Pierson Jr. in Chapter 10.

26 July 1776: Job Pierson, residence Southampton, age 17, born Southampton, 5 ft. 8 in. tall, dark complexion, brown hair, occupation blacksmith. See 130 Job Pierson in Chapter 12.

---

[1] Capt. David$_5$, Lemuel$_4$, David$_3$, Col. Henry$_2$, Henry$_1$
[2] Sgt. Lemuel$_5$, Lemuel$_4$, David$_3$, Col. Henry$_2$, Henry$_1$
[3] Frederic Mather, *The Refugees of 1776 from Long Island to Connecticut*, Genealogical Publishing Company, Baltimore, MD, 1972, pp. 995-996.
[4] Frederic Mather, *The Refugees of 1776 from Long Island to Connecticut*, Genealogical Publishing Company, Baltimore, MD, 1972, pp. 1003-1004.
[5] Frederic Mather, *The Refugees of 1776 from Long Island to Connecticut*, Genealogical Publishing Company, Baltimore, MD, 1972, p. 1005.

Census of the Town of Southampton, 1776[6] (Piersons only)

July 4, 1776, East of Watermill:　　　Males (>50,>16,<16). Females (>16,<16).　　　Total 21 families.

Heads of Families	Males	Females	Author's Remarks
Abraham Pierson[7]	1 (1,0,0)	1 (1,0)	see No. 19, Chapter 10.
Daniel Pierson[8]	3	5	see No. 64, Chapter 12.
David Pierson Jr.[9]	1	3	see No. 39, Chapter 10.
David Pierson[10], Capt.	1 (0,1,0)	4 (1,3)	see No. 79, Chapter 10.
Jedidiah Pierson[11]	5 (0,2,3)	4 (1,3)	see No. 66, Chapter 12.
Job Pierson[12]	1	1	see No. 21, Chapter 12.
Josiah Pierson[13]	2	3	see No. 20, Chapter 10.
Lemuel Pierson[14]	3 (1,1,1)	4 (2,2)	see No. 38, Chapter 10.
Lemuel Pierson Jr.[15], Sgt.	1 (0,1,0)	2 (1,1)	see No. 78, Chapter 10.
Lemuel Pierson 3d[16]	3 (0,3,0)	3 (1,2)	see No. 62, Chapter 12.
Matthew Pierson[17]	2 (1,1,0)	1 (1,0)	see No. 50, Chapter 10.
Mathew Pierson Jr.[18]	2	1	see No. 44, Chapter 10.
Nathan Peirson[19]	2	2	see No. 85, Chapter 10.
Silvanus Pierson[20]	1 (1,0,0)	2 (1,1)	see No. 51, Chapter 10.
Stephen Pierson[21]	1	1	see No. 43, Chapter 10.
Theophilus Pierson[22] (Ens.)	4 (0,1,3)	3 (1,2)	see No. 89, Chapter 10.
Timothy Pierson[23]	1	4	see No. 53, Chapter 10.
Zachariah Peirson[24]	2 (0,1,1)	2 (1,1)	see No. 86, Chapter 10.
Zebulon Pierson[25]	4 (1,2,1)	4 (1,3)	see No. 45, Chapter 10.

July 22, 1776, West of the Watermill:

Elias Pierson[26]	3 (1,2,0)	4 (3,1)	see No. 90, Chapter 10.
Timothy Peirson[27]	4	6	see No. 68, Chapter 9.

---

[6]Henry Hedges, Wm. Pelletreau, Edward Foster, *The Third Book of Records of the Town of Southampton, Long Island, N.Y. with other Ancient Documents of Historic Value*, John H. Hunt, Printer, Sag Harbor, NY, 1878, Appendix, pp. 391-399.

[7]Abraham$_3$, Col. Henry$_2$, Henry$_1$

[8]Daniel$_4$, John$_3$, Theodore$_2$, Henry$_1$

[9]David Jr.$_4$, David$_3$, Col. Henry$_2$, Henry$_1$

[10]Capt. David$_5$, Lemuel$_4$, David$_3$, Col. Henry$_2$, Henry$_1$

[11]Jedidiah$_4$, John$_3$, Theodore$_2$, Henry$_1$

[12]Job$_3$, Theodore$_2$, Henry$_1$

[13]Josiah$_3$, Col. Henry$_2$, Henry$_1$

[14]Lemuel$_4$, David$_3$, Col. Henry$_2$, Henry$_1$

[15]Sgt. Lemuel Jr.$_5$, Lemuel$_4$, David$_3$, Col. Henry$_2$, Henry$_1$

[16]Lemuel 3d$_4$, Job$_3$, Theodore$_2$, Henry$_1$

[17]Matthew$_4$, Josiah$_3$, Col. Henry$_2$, Henry$_1$

[18]Mathew Jr.$_4$, Abraham$_3$, Col. Henry$_2$, Henry$_1$

[19]Nathan$_5$, Capt. Nathan$_4$, Theophilus$_3$, Col. Henry$_2$, Henry$_1$

[20]Silvanus$_4$, Josiah$_3$, Col. Henry$_2$, Henry$_1$

[21]Stephen$_4$, Theophilus$_3$, Col. Henry$_2$, Henry$_1$

[22]Ens. Theophilus$_5$, Stephen$_4$, Theophilus$_3$, Col. Henry$_2$, Henry$_1$

[23]Timothy$_4$, Josiah$_3$, Col. Henry$_2$, Henry$_1$

[24]Zachariah$_5$, Capt. Nathan$_4$, Theophilus$_3$, Col. Henry$_2$, Henry$_1$

[25]Zebulon$_4$, Abraham$_3$, Col. Henry$_2$, Henry$_1$

[26]Elias$_5$, Stephen$_4$, Theophilus$_3$, Col. Henry$_2$, Henry$_1$

[27]Timothy$_5$, Samuel$_4$, Henry$_3$, Lt. Joseph$_2$, Henry$_1$

Henry, Job Jr., John, and Samuel Peirson, who signed the Association in 1775 (being at least age 16), do not appear as separate families in the 1776 census because they are still living with their fathers, Matthew, Daniel, Zebulun, and Lemuel Peirson 3d, respectively. In each case, all known male children for Matthew, Daniel, Zebulun, and Lemuel Peirson 3d are accounted for in the number of males present in the census.

From *Documents Relating to the Colonial History of the State of New York*[28], the following New York participants in the Revolutionary War are listed:

David Peirson, Capt., officers of Col. David Mulford's 2d Battalion, 3d Company, commissions issued 13 Sep 1775.
David Pierson, Capt., report of Col. David Mulford's 2d Regiment of Militia in Suffolk Co. 10 Feb 1776.
David Pierson, Capt., officers of the Regiment of Minute Men under Col. Josiah Smith, 2d Southampton Company, commissions issued 23 Feb 1776. See 79 Capt. David Pierson in Chapter 10.

Johannes Persen, Ensign, Col. Abraham Hasbrouck's Northern Regiment of Ulster Co., N.Y., 1st Company, commissioned 25 Oct 1775.
Joh's Persin, 2d Lieut., Col. Abraham Hasbrouck's Northern Regiment of Ulster Co., N.Y., Bogardus' Company (1st Company), changes in the Regiment 19 Feb 1778.

John Pierson, Private, New York Line, 3rd Regiment, 7th Company, entered the Company 24 May 1777, in the war, and died 17 Apr 1778 (Military Register).

John Pierson, Private, New York Line, Hazen's 2d Canadian, Assembly Papers 15-236 (containing petition for bounty land).

John Persen, Ensign, New York Levies and Militia, 11th Regiment (Coxsackie and Groote Imbocht), Changes in the Regiment, 20 June 1778.
John Person, 2d Lieutenant, New York Levies and Militia, 11th Regiment (Coxsackie and Groote Imbocht), Changes in the Regiment, 3 May 1779, Dubois' Co. (2d Lt. Benjamin J. Dubois resigned).

Lemuel Pierson, Sergeant Major, report of the Col. David Mulford's 2d Regiment of Militia in Suffolk Co. 10 Feb 1776. See 78 Lemuel Pierson Jr. in Chapter 10.

Silas Pierson, Capt., Col. Jesse Woodhull's East Orange or Cornwall Regiment (Orange Co., N.Y.), officers commissioned 15 Sep 1775 for a 7th Goshen Company.
Silas Pierson, Capt., report of Col. Jesse Woodhull to Albany Congress, 1 March 1776, "that through the unhappy dissatisfaction in the Company of his Regiment, whereof Silas Pierson has been appointed Captain, the said company will be useless in their present state and he therefore requested the Congress to provide some relief in the premises."
Silas Pierson, Capt., Col. Jesse Woodhull's East Orange or Cornwall Regiment (Orange Co., N.Y.), officers re-appointed with no change 21 Feb 1778, 7th Goshen Company. See 48 Capt. Silas Pierson in Chapter 10.

[28]Berthold Fernow, Editor, Documents Relating to the Colonial History of the State of New York, Vol. 15, State Archives Vol. 1, Weed, Parsons and Company, Printer, 1887.

Theophilus Peirson, Ensign, officers of the 2d Battalion, 3d Company, commissions issued 13 Sep 1775. See 89 Theophilus Pierson in Chapter 10.

At the beginning of the Revolutionary War, 1776, many Piersons had settled in New Jersey including descendants of the Rev. Abraham Pierson of the Newark area, Benjamin Peirson of Long Island who had settled in the Elizabeth Town, New Jersey, area and other Pierson migrations such as Piersonville in Morris County.

The Friends of the Joint Free Public Library of Morristown and Morris Township, N.J., published the following Pierson participation in the war from Morris County, New Jersey[29]:

Aaron Pierson, b. 1746, d. 2 Jan 1803, Private in Morris Co., N.J. militia (S-719). He lived in Hanover Township; married Mary Howell 25 Nov 1766; is buried in First Presbyterian Church Yard, Morristown, N.J. See 67 Aaron Pierson in Chapter 7.

Benjamin Pierson Sr., b. 1736, d. 1 Jan 1792, Lieut. & Capt. in Morris Co., N.J. militia, Eastern Battalion (S-405). He was born near the present Convent Station; son of Benjamin, brother of Elijah; married Phebe Raynor 3 Nov 1756; buried in First Presbyterian Church Yard, Morristown, N.J. (D.A.R. 43052, 46354, 95049, 106722, 115262). See 64 Capt. Benjamin Pierson in Chapter 7.

Benjamin Pierson Jr., b. 25 Nov 1757, d. 10 Feb 1832? Served as Private in Capt. Daniel Pierson's Co., Morris Co., N.J. militia (S-719). Son of Elijah; he lived on the homestead near the Convent Station; married Abigail Condict 22 Dec 1779; is buried in First Presbyterian Church Yard, Morristown, N.J. (D.A.R. 109262, 46354, 126151, 12567). See 93 Benjamin Pierson in Chapter 7.

Daniel Pierson, b. 1750, d. 15 Dec 1831. Served as 2d Lieut., Capt. Imlay's Co., 3rd Regiment, Continental Army. He was discharged with his battalion (S-21; 161). He was born in Morristown, N.J., son of Benjamin; married Prudence King 19 Feb 1784. They "built and dwelt in the Wood house," southeast corner of Pine and South Streets, Morristown, now site of the Community Theater. He died in Dayton, Ohio. (GMNJ) Pension: S4-272. See 70 Lt. Daniel Pierson in Chapter 7.

David Pierson, b. 29 Aug 1763, d. 22 Mar 1824. Served as Private in Morris Co., N.J. militia (S-719). He was the son of Benjamin and Phebe Raynor; married Abigail Thompson; buried in First Presbyterian Church Yard, Morristown, N.J. (D.A.R.) See 100 David Pierson in Chapter 7.

Isaac Pierson, b. 1755, d. 19 Aug 1825. Enlisted in April 1775 at Southampton, New York, in Capt. John Hulbut's Co., 2nd N.Y. Regiment, and in 1776 in Capt. David Pierson's Co., N.Y. Regiment. He came to Morristown in 1788 and settled at "Piersonville," northeast of Morristown. He was called "Long Island Pierson." He was a shoemaker by trade; married 1st Hannah ____, 2nd Mary ____. Lived with his son Maltby G. Pierson at the time he applied for a pension in 1823. (GMNJ) Pension: R8246. See 80 Isaac Pierson in Chapter 10.

---

[29]Barbara Hoskins, *Men From Morris County New Jersey Who Served in the American Revolution*, Friends of the Joint Free Public Library of Morristown, Morristown, New Jersey, 1979, pp. 144-146.

John Pierson, b. 24 May 1758, d. 11 Feb 1827. Served as Private from Morristown, N.J., in Capt. Richard Cox's Co., and was wounded at Germantown (S-720). He was born in Essex Co., N.J.; married Sarah Van Dyke; died in Martinsburg, Ohio. Pension: BLWt. 8646. (D.A.R. 43887, 48897).

Joseph Pierson, served as Private in Capt. Austin Bayley's Company, Morristown, and in State Troops (S-720). He lived in Morris Township, N.J. Pension: S3693. See 866 Joseph Pierson in Chapter 9.

Matthias Pierson, served with brother Samuel in Col. Spencer's Regiment, Continental Army (S-21). He owned land in Cincinnati, Ohio, and is buried in Hamilton Co., Ohio.

Robert Pierson, b. 5 Nov 1759, d. 8 Sep 1843. Served as Private, Corp., & Sgt. in Morris Co., N.J. militia, also Continental Army (S-266; 720). He enlisted in Parsippany, N.J.; later lived in Randolph Township, N.J.; married 1st Mary Dalrymple, 2nd Elizabeth Price, 3rd Mrs. Margaret (Clark) Youngs. Pension: Margaret W5561. (D.A.R.)

Samuel Pierson, b. 10 Apr 1748, d. 4 May 1790. Served as Private in Morris Co., N.J. militia and in Col. Spencer's Regiment, Continental Army, Capt. Jonathan Holmes Co. (S-266; 720). He married Rebecca Garrigus in 1769; is buried in First Presbyterian Church Yard, Morristown, N.J. (D.A.R.)

Samuel Pierson, b. 1753, d. 1839. Served in Morristown, N.J. militia 1778; reputed to be one of Washington's Life Guards (Munsell: 193). He lived in Madison, N.J.

Shadrack Pierson, served as Private in Morris Co., N.J. militia (S-720). He was born on Long Island, N.Y., and moved to New Jersey in 1770. He lived in Morris Township and Mendham Township, Morris Co., N.J., then moved again to upper New York state in 1785. See 83 Shadrach Pierson in Chapter 10.

Stephen Pierson, b. 1732, d. 13 Sep 1793. Served as Private in Morris Co., N.J. militia (S-720). He was born in Bridgehampton, Long Island; died in New Vernon, N.J.; married Elishabe Wood; is buried First Presbyterian Church Yard, Morristown, N.J. (D.A.R. 101331, 76898, 138169, 188132, 134802) (S.A.R. 40763).

Uriah Pierson, b. ca. 1723, d. 24 May 1811 at age 88. Served as Private in Morris Co., N.J. militia (S-720). During the Revolutionary War, he lived in Morris Township, Morris Co., N.J.; was a freeholder in Mendham Township, Morris Co., N.J., in 1793; and died in Randolph Township, N.J. in 1811.

William Pierson, served in Morris Co., N.J. militia (S-720). He lived in Morris Township, N.J.

Other Pierson participants during the Revolutionary War in New Jersey include:

Caleb Pierson was born 1738 in Orange, N.J., and died[30] in 1801 in N.J. He lived in Bloomfield and Caldwell, N.J. During the Revolutionary War he was a Private in the New Jersey militia.[31] He mar. Joanna Baldwin. See 45 Caleb Pierson in Chapter 13.

---

[30] *DAR Patriot Index*, Centennial Edition, National Society of the Daughters of the American Revolution, 1994, part 3, p. 2257.

David Pierson, b. 10 Feb 1737/8, of Westfield, N.J., served as Private in the N.J. militia. See 774 David Pierson in Chapter 11.

Enos Pierson was born in 1762[32] in N.J. (his father was a farmer at Orange, N.J.), and died about 1837. Enos lived in Orange, N.J. During the Revolutionary War, he was a Private in the New Jersey militia.[33] He mar. Abigail[34] Cockefair. See 61 Enos Pierson in Chapter 13.

Erastus Pierson, b. Nov. 6, 1753, d. Nov 1837, mar. Eunice ____, lived in Orange, N.J., and died there, on his farm. He was an officer in the Revolutionary War; was wounded and taken prisoner by the British. See 57 Erastus Pierson in Chapter 13.

Pierson participants during the Revolutionary War in Connecticut include:

Abraham Peirson[35], from Bridge Hampton, Suffolk Co., N.Y., served in Col. Smith's N.Y. Minutemen Regiment and in the Connecticut militia. See 94 Abraham Pierson, Chapter 10.

Bartholomew Pierson was born[36] about 1750 in Connecticut, and died[37] after 1803 when he was in New York. Family tradition says he died in Pennsylvania. He mar.[38] Hannah Balch. During the Revolutionary War he was a Private in the Connecticut militia.[39] See 28 Bartholomew Pierson in Chapter 14.

Daniel Pierson was born Apr. 29, 1744, probably at Derby, Conn., where his father Stephen was born and died. He married, was a soldier in the Revolutionary War, and left his wife for misconduct in his absence and took his two children and went west to parts unknown. See 41 Daniel under children of 19 Stephen Pierson 3d in Chapter 14.

Pierson participants during the Revolutionary War in Vermont include[40]:

Moses Peirson was born Oct. 17, 1733 in Newark, N.J. He married March 27, 1754, Rachel Smith. He lived at Parsippany, N.J., from 1754 to 1770. In 1770, he moved with his family to a 1,000-acre tract of wilderness land in Vermont, bordering Lake Champlain, and called

---

[31]*DAR Patriot Index*, Centennial Edition, National Society of the Daughters of the American Revolution, 1994, part 3, p. 2257.
[32]*DAR Patriot Index*, Centennial Edition, National Society of the Daughters of the American Revolution, 1994, part 3, p. 2257.
[33]*DAR Patriot Index*, Centennial Edition, National Society of the Daughters of the American Revolution, 1994, part 3, p. 2257.
[34]*DAR Patriot Index*, Centennial Edition, National Society of the Daughters of the American Revolution, 1994, part 3, p. 2257.
[35]Abraham$_5$, Zebulun$_4$, Abraham$_3$, Col. Henry$_2$, Henry$_1$
[36]*DAR Patriot Index*, Centennial Edition, National Society of the Daughters of the American Revolution, 1994, part 3, p. 2256.
[37]*DAR Patriot Index*, Centennial Edition, National Society of the Daughters of the American Revolution, 1994, part 3, p. 2256.
[38]*DAR Patriot Index*, Centennial Edition, National Society of the Daughters of the American Revolution, 1994, part 3, p. 2256.
[39]*DAR Patriot Index*, Centennial Edition, National Society of the Daughters of the American Revolution, 1994, part 3, p. 2256.
[40]Lizzie B. Pierson, *Pierson Genealogical Records*, Joel Munsell, Printer, Albany, N.Y., 1878, footnotes pp. 79-84.

it Shelburn. During the Revolutionary War in late 1777, Capt. Sawyer and part of his company were on hand in Shelburn at Moses Peirson's to protect the settlers from possible British attack. On March 12, 1778, the "Battle of Shelburn" took place. The attacking party numbered 57, some being Indians, and some supposed to be Tories or British soldiers disguised as Indians. It was later confirmed that British soldiers had participated. With the help of Moses, the British were repelled and some of them captured. The British authorities, exasperated by the repulse of their party, offered a large reward for the body of "the notorious rebel Moses Peirson, " dead or alive. An order of the Vermont Council of Safety, directed to Captains Ebenezer Allen and Isaac Clark, alludes to the affair as "Capt. Sawyer's late signal victory over the enemy at Shelburn," orders them to go to his relief, to secure the wheat at Shelburn, and to remove all inhabitants they could not protect, within their lines on Otter Creek. See 529 Moses Peirson in Chapter 13 for more details of the battle and family.

Uzal Pierson, son of Moses, was born May 4, 1763, at Parsippany, N.J., and died Jan. 11, 1836. He moved in 1770 with his father to Shelburn, Vt., was taken prisoner (1778-9) by the British during the Revolutionary War (see the description under Ziba Pierson below). He lived on a portion of his father's 1,000 acres at Shelburn, Vt. He mar. Dorcas Frisbie. See 538 Uzal Pierson in Chapter 13.

Ziba Pierson, son of Moses, was born May 9, 1761, at Parsippany, N.J., and died Nov. 7, 1820 in Shelburn, Vt. He moved in 1770 with his father to Shelburn, Vt. During the Revolutionary War, he lived at Shelburn, Vt., but after the Battle of Shelburn, moved temporarily to Shoreham, Vt. When Moses Peirson's family left Shoreham in the fall of 1778, they went to Rutland, Vt., 25 miles to the southeast of Shoreham. But Moses had left his cattle and hogs and two oldest sons, Ziba (age 17) and Uzal (age 15), to kill their meat and try their lard before following. They had completed their work at Shoreham and were ready to start their journey on the following morning. But before dawn a British squad came, fired on the house, and captured the two boys, Ziba and Uzal, and Mr. More, on whose farm they had lived. They, with others they had found in the town, were taken as prisoners of war to the British fort at St. John, New Brunswick, Canada. The British set fire to the house and burned the meat and lard. In March 1779, Ziba and Uzal made good their escape from the fort at St. John while the sentinel slept, holing up at a house used as a church until the next night and reached the woods. They arrived in Rutland, Vt., 40 days after they had escaped. Ziba inherited his father's homestead at Shelburn in 1805. He mar. May 24, 1787, Hannah Campbell. See 537 Ziba Pierson in Chapter 13 for a more complete story and family.

Pierson participants during the Revolutionary War in New Hampshire include:

Ebenezer Pearson was born[41] May 14, 1736 in Mass., and died[42] June 6, 1779 in New Hampshire. During the Revolutionary War, he was a Private in the New Hampshire

---

[41]*DAR Patriot Index*, Centennial Edition, National Society of the Daughters of the American Revolution, 1994, part 3, p. 2257.

[42]*DAR Patriot Index*, Centennial Edition, National Society of the Daughters of the American Revolution, 1994, part 3, p. 2257.

militia.[43] It is not clear if his death was caused by the war. He mar.[44] Mary Thompson. See 21 Ebenezer Pearson in Chapter 15.

The British Occupation of Long Island 1776-1783

After the British abandoned Boston in March 1776, British General Sir William Howe prepared an expedition against New York City. Anticipating the enemy's move, General George Washington moved his American army, including the two Suffolk County Regiments and Minutemen, southward to defend the strategic port. Between August 22nd and 25th, 1776, Howe, with the aid of a British fleet under his brother, Admiral Lord Richard Howe, landed 20,000 troops on the southwestern end of Long Island. Here, the American General Israel Putnam commanded a force of about 7,000 men. On the British left (west) General James Grant faced the American right wing under General William Alexander, known as Lord Sterling. To the east, German General Philip von Heister, commanding a force of Hessian mercenaries, opposed General John Sullivan. On the night of August 26th, Howe unleashed his main effort, a wide circling movement to the east led by General Sir Henry Clinton. On the following morning, Clinton struck the left rear of the American position, caving it in. Only desperate rear-guard fighting enabled the American army to fall back behind the defenses on Brooklyn Heights. The Americans suffered 1,500 casualties including 200 killed. The British suffered 400 casualties and managed to capture American Generals John Sullivan and William Alexander.

Howe's army pressed forward all along the line, but did not assault the Brooklyn breastworks. Instead, the British commander began a siege operation. However, on the night of August 29th, Washington skillfully withdrew Putnam's army to Manhattan Island. Two weeks later, Washington made a second retreat to Harlem Heights at the northern end of the island. This move prevented his army from being outflanked when the British crossed the East River to land at Kip's Bay on September 15th. The battle had taken place on Long Island 75 miles west of Southampton, but all of Long Island was captured by the British.

After the battle of Long Island, the remnants of the 2nd Regiment and Minutemen were reconstructed and commissioned 13 Sep 1776 at a mainland site into the 2nd Battalion of Suffolk County with nine companies. The 3rd Company was commanded by Capt. David Pierson[45], and his staff included 1st Lt. Daniel Hedges[46], 2nd Lt. David Sayre, and Ensign Theophilus Pierson[47]. This reorganization took place, as reported by the orders of Washington, "in order that such as was needed to protect their homes should return, and others as preferred could enlist under a new organization."

---

[43]*DAR Patriot Index*, Centennial Edition, National Society of the Daughters of the American Revolution, 1994, part 3, p. 2257.
[44]*DAR Patriot Index*, Centennial Edition, National Society of the Daughters of the American Revolution, 1994, part 3, p. 2257.
[45]Capt. David$_5$, Lemuel$_4$, David$_3$, Col. Henry$_2$, Henry$_1$
[46]Husband of Susanna Peirson and son-in-law of Josiah Peirson.
[47]Ens. Theophilus$_5$, Stephen$_4$, Theophilus$_3$, Col. Henry$_2$, Henry$_1$

To escape British occupation and a demand for an oath of allegiance to England, many Long Island families took refuge on the mainland during the Revolutionary War, traveling first to the American-held state of Connecticut. The Peirsons among those families were[48]:

Capt. David Peirson[49], from Bridge Hampton to East Haddam, Connecticut on 2 Sep 1776, with five persons and goods, he was brought from Sag Harbor by Capt. Elijah Mason. He served in Col. Mulford's Regiment, Col. Smith's Regiment, and in Col. Drake's Provisional Regiment. See 79 Capt. David Pierson in Chapter 10. Frederic Mather[50] attributes the title of Colonel to Capt. David Peirson after the war, but this is in error. Col. David Peirson was the son of Job and Hannah Peirson.

Corp. Elias Peirson[51], from Sagaponack in Bridge Hampton to East Haddam, Connecticut, in Sep 1776, brought to Connecticut by Capt. John Harris. He served in Col. Smith's Regiment. See 90 Elias Pierson in Chapter 10.

Jedidiah Peirson[52], from Southampton, E. Dist. (probably Sag Harbor or Bridge Hampton) to Stonington, Connecticut, in Sep 1776. He was brought over, with four in the family and his goods, by Capt. Ephraim Pendleton. See 66 Jedidiah Pierson in Chapter 12.

Lemuel Peirson[53], his effects were moved from Sagaponack to Stonington, Connecticut, in Sep 1776 by Capt. David Sayre. On 16 Sep 1776, with ten of his family, he was moved from Sagaponack to East Haddam, Connecticut, by Capt. Joshua Griffeth. See 38 Lemuel Pierson in Chapter 10.

Sgt. Lemuel Peirson Jr.[54], from Sagaponack to East Haddam, Connecticut, in Nov 1776, moved over by Capt. Joshua Griffeth. He served in Col. Mulford's and Col. Smith's Regiments. See 78 Lemuel Pierson Jr. in Chapter 10.

Lemuel Peirson 3rd[55], from Bridge Hampton to East Haddam in Sep and 18 Oct 1776, with three passengers. He was moved by Capt. Hubbard Latham, Capt. Joshua Griffeth, and Capt. Elnathan Fellows. See 62 Lemuel Pierson 3d in Chapter 12.

Matthew Peirson[56], from Bridge Hampton to Stonington and East Haddam, Connecticut. In Sep 1776, with one passenger and goods, he was moved by Capt. Isaac Sheffield and on 27 Sep 1776, with six passengers and goods, he was moved by Capt. Ephraim Pendleton. He is the twin of Silvanus Peirson. See 50 Matthew Pierson in Chapter 10.

---

[48] Frederic Mather, *The Refugees of 1776 from Long Island to Connecticut*, Genealogical Publishing Company, Baltimore, MD, 1972, pp. 504-8.

[49] Capt. David$_5$, Lemuel$_4$, David$_3$, Col. Henry$_2$, Henry$_1$

[50] Frederic Mather, *The Refugees of 1776 from Long Island to Connecticut*, Genealogical Publishing Company, Baltimore, MD, 1972, pp. 505.

[51] Corp. Elias$_5$, Stephen$_4$, Theophilus$_3$, Col. Henry$_2$, Henry$_1$

[52] Jedidiah$_4$, John$_3$, Theodore$_2$, Henry$_1$

[53] Lemuel$_4$, David$_3$, Col. Henry$_2$, Henry$_1$

[54] Sgt. Lemuel Jr.$_5$, Lemuel$_4$, David$_3$, Col. Henry$_2$, Henry$_1$

[55] Lemuel 3rd$_4$, Job$_3$, Theodore$_2$, Henry$_1$

[56] Matthew$_4$ (twin of Silvanus), Josiah$_3$, Col. Henry$_2$, Henry$_1$

Mathew Peirson Jr.[57], from Sagaponack to Stonington, Connecticut, with one passenger and goods, in Sep 1776 by Capt. Hubbard Latham. He was the son of Abraham Pierson. See 44 Matthew Pierson in Chapter 10.

Silvanus Peirson[58], from Sagaponack to Stonington, Connecticut, Sep to Dec 1776, with four passengers and goods, by Capt. Josephus Fitch, Capt. Isaac Sheffield, Capt. John Miner 2d, and Capt. Hubbard Latham. He is the twin of Matthew Peirson. See 51 Silvanus Pierson in Chapter 10.

Stephen Peirson[59], from Bridge Hampton to Stonington, Connecticut, in Sep 1776 by Capt. Eliphalet Budington. See 43 Stephen Pierson in Chapter 10.

Ens. Theophilus Peirson[60], from Bridge Hampton to Stonington, Connecticut, in Sep 1776, with five passengers and goods, by Capt. Amos Pendleton; and in Oct 1776, with five passengers and goods, by Capt. David Sayre. See 89 Theophilus Pierson in Chapter 10.

Zebulun Peirson[61], from Bridge Hampton to Saybrook, Connecticut, in Sep 1776, his effects were moved by Capt. Zebulon Stow; to East Haddam, Connecticut, on 16 Sep 1776, five in the family and goods were moved by Capt. Joshua Griffeth. See 45 Zebulon Pierson in Chapter 10.

Zechariah Peirson[62], from Sagaponack to East Haddam, Connecticut, on 2 Sep 1776, one person and goods by Capt. Elijah Mason; and also in Sep 1776, five persons and goods to Chester, Connecticut, by the same Captain. See 86 Zechariah Pierson in Chapter 10.

On Long Island, the British troops were quartered in the villages. Sir William Erskine, the British General, had his headquarters in Southampton. Houses left vacant by the refugees were immediately appropriated to the use of the British soldiers. During the remainder of the war, the inhabitants were cut off from affording any open aid to the cause of freedom. Yet, a clandestine communication was kept with the people and places on the main land. Swift whale boats from the Connecticut main land were used by the island's refugee soldiers for lightning attacks on British outposts.

During all seven years and three months (26 Aug 1776 to 25 Nov 1783), the island groaned under the oppressive occupation of their soil by the British. They were exposed to suffering and outrages from both sides. The continental Whigs (Americans against the British) carried off the Island's livestock and produce, and the British punished the islander's for letting it go. There was much lawless action by the British soldiers including the taking of anything and vandalism such as demolishing furniture. Many stories were told of events during the occupation - some about Peirsons.

In one story told, the soldiers came to the house of Lemuel Peirson and turned him out. Against their orders, Lemuel was determined to carry off some of his furniture and,

[57] Mathew Jr.$_4$, Abraham$_3$, Col. Henry$_2$, Henry$_1$
[58] Silvanus$_4$ (twin of Matthew), Josiah$_3$, Col. Henry$_2$, Henry$_1$
[59] Stephen$_4$, Theophilus$_3$, Col. Henry$_2$, Henry$_1$
[60] Ens. Theophilus$_5$, Stephen$_4$, Theophilus$_3$, Col. Henry$_2$, Henry$_1$
[61] Zebulun$_4$, Abraham$_3$, Col. Henry$_2$, Henry$_1$
[62] Zechariah$_5$, Capt. Nathan$_4$, Theophilus$_3$, Col. Henry$_2$, Henry$_1$

although the soldiers stood over him with drawn sword, he persisted and got his way. This is probably Lemuel4 (David3, Col. Henry2, Henry1).

In another story, the soldiers came to Lemuel Peirson's house to secure any plunder that might offer itself. Mrs. Peirson was alone in the house with young children, but bravely met them at the door with a kettle of hot water and threatened to scald the first man who attempted to enter her doors. The British soldiers quietly retreated. From this description (with young children), it could only have been Sgt. Lemuel Peirson Jr.'s second wife, Mary, who had young children Henry and Franklin at home.

In 1778, the Americans made a Treaty of Alliance with France. The British under Sir Henry Clinton, fearing that the French fleet would enter the Delaware river cutting off their position at Philadelphia from New York, marched his army to New York. Later in 1778, the British took Savannah, Georgia. In 1780, the British took Charleston, South Carolina. A band of frontiersmen under Isaac Shelby and John Sevier routed a British raiding party of 1,000 regulars from a ridge of Kings Mountain, South Carolina. The British survivors fled in disorder. Swift American raids by such leaders as Andrew Pickens, Francis Marion (the "Swamp Fox") and Thomas Sumter constantly harried the British forces. In 1781, Gen. Daniel Morgan with about 950 men, under orders from Gen. Nathaniel Greene, won an overwhelming victory against the British at Cowpens, South Carolina. This was followed by a battle with the main British force under Lord Cornwallis (2,200 men) and Generals Greene and Morgan's American forces (4,500 men) at Guilford Courthouse, North Carolina, on March 15, 1781. The Americans won this battle and Cornwallis retreated with a fourth of his army dead or wounded to Wilmington, North Carolina, where he was reinforced to over 6,000 men.

Cornwallis planned to attack Lafayette who led 3,000 American troops at Richmond, Virginia. But Lafayette stayed just out of reach of Cornwallis's troops and was reinforced by Wayne with about a 1,000 men. Cornwallis became fearful of being trapped himself and turned eastward toward the sea to be near the British fleet. Lafayette followed, and at Williamsburg, Cornwallis turned to attack the reinforced Lafayette, but Lafayette again stayed out of reach. Lord Cornwallis then went on to Yorktown, Virginia, where he was reinforced by another 1,000 men and prepared his defense. Lafayette called on General George Washington for help. Gen. Washington, Gen. Jean Rochambeau (Commander of French land forces in America), and Admiral Francois de Grasse (Commander of the French fleet) seized this opportunity to trap Cornwallis with the main British army. On August 30, 1781, Adm. De Grasse's fleet of 24 ships arrived off Yorktown. Cornwallis was now trapped between enemy land and sea forces. An English fleet of 19 ships attempted to rescue Cornwallis but failed. In September, 1781, Gen. Washington's and Gen. Rochambeau's men joined those of Lafayette to bring their strength to 16,000 men. Gen. Washington was put in charge of closing the trap. But as the trap began to close, Lord Cornwallis surrendered his 7,247 British soldiers to the American. This surrender on October 19, 1781, ended the Revolutionary War. However, Long Island remained occupied by the British because official peace treaties were not yet signed.

Twice during the war, England made offers of peace to win back the Americans. Lord North and Parliament in 1778 promised to yield on all points in the dispute. But it was too late. The American Congress had already declared America's freedom and the American spokesmen stated the United States would remain a separate nation. After the surrender of Cornwallis in October, 1781, the American Congress named five commissioners - John Adams, John Jay, Benjamin Franklin, Thomas Jefferson, and Henry Laurens - to make a treaty of peace with England. The commissioners were instructed not to make peace without the knowledge and consent of France. Only Adams, Jay, and Franklin were present for the negotiations. Fearing that Spain and France were ready to betray the United States, Adams and Jay outvoted Franklin, decided to ignore the French Alliance, and negotiated a preliminary peace treaty with England, which was signed at Paris, France, November 30, 1782. The Americans secured their independence and the land west to the Mississippi river. The Americans were permitted to fish in the waters off Newfoundland but could not dry or cure their catches on the island. Under the treaty, Congress was to recommend that the states compensate the British Loyalists for property taken from them during the war. No laws were to be passed to prevent the payment of debts owed by Americans to British merchants. The northern boundary of the United States was to include the line of the Great Lakes, and citizens of both the United States and Britain were to have use of the Mississippi river. France accepted this treaty, made final on September 3, 1783, by the Treaty of Paris. On the same day a peace was concluded between England and her European foes.

For another two months and 22 days after the Treaty of Paris was signed, the British occupied Long Island. This was not an intentional act of obstinacy by the British. There was no means of instant communication at that time. Thus, orders for the British troops had to be hand written on paper and dispatched by sailing ship (a seven to ten week voyage across the Atlantic Ocean, depending on the winds). Further, the sailing ships to transport the British troops home to England also had to be dispatched. Given these conditions, the British had acted expeditiously to remove their troops from Long Island after the treaty became official. And on November 25, 1783, the residents of Long Island were again free to return to their homes and lead peaceful lives.

The five (or less) Peirson families that had remained on Long Island during the British occupation and the 16 Peirson families that had evacuated to Connecticut (all descendants of Henry Peirson) now breathed their first breaths of the new freedom and began to repair the damage to home and property. The losses had been great, including much furniture, farm animals, crops, farm tools, and structure damage or destruction. A few Peirson deaths were recorded during this period but it is unknown if they were caused by the British. Some Peirson families sold their Long Island property making their new homes in New Jersey (i.e. Piersonville 1788 of "Long Island Pierson"), and other places of opportunity. With the United States now extending westward to the Mississippi river, a slow westward emigration of Peirson families began - to fill opportunities for land and wealth.

Now that the Revolutionary War was over, a question remained. Who was to return and who was to leave the Suffolk County area of Long Island out of the 21 Peirson families that existed there before the war in 1776? The following two records reveal which Peirsons were residents of Southampton in 1784 and of Bridgehampton in 1787, now totaling 24 families.

The following Piersons were among the signers of an agreement between the residents of Southampton and the Rev. Joshua Williams dated 30 Dec 1784[63]:

Elias Pierson (No. 90, Chap. 10)   Samuel Pierson (No. 69, Chap. 9)
Elias Pierson Jr. (No. 248, Chap. 10)   Timothy Pierson (No. 68, Chap. 9)

The following Peirsons were among the signers of an agreement between the residents of Bridgehampton and Rev. Aaron Woolworth dated 2 July 1787:

Abraham Peirson (No. 94, Chap. 10)   Matthew Peirson (No. 50, Chap. 10)
Caleb Peirson (No. 134, Chap. 12)   Mathew Peirson Jr. (No. 44, Chap. 10)
Charles Peirson (No. 249, Chap. 10)   Samuel Peirson (No. 127, Chap. 12)
David Peirson (No. 79, Chap. 10)   Silvanus Peirson (No. 51, Chap. 10)
Henry Peirson (No. 101, Chap. 10)   Stephen Peirson (No. 43, Chap. 10)
Jedidiah Peirson (No. 66, Chap. 12)   Theophilus Peirson (No. 89, Chap. 10)
Job Peirson (No. 130, Chap. 12)   Timothy Peirson (No. 53, Chap. 10)
John Peirson (No. 93, Chap. 10)   William Peirson (No. 47, Chap. 10)
Lemuel Peirson (No. 38, Chap. 10)   Williams Peirson (No. 95, Chap. 10)
Lemuel Peirson Jr. (No. 78, Chap. 10)   Zebulon Peirson (No. 45, Chap. 10)

---

[63] George Rogers Howell, *The Early History of Southampton, L. I., New York, with Genealogies*, Albany, New York, 2nd Edition, 1887, pp. 112-113.

Chapter 17
The Pierson Island Legend
and Piersonville, New Jersey

The Pierson Island Legend

In a 1991 letter from the New Zealand Piersons to the American Piersons[1], Jenny Pierson reported this New Zealand Pierson family legend: "Having arrived in America (from England), the Pierson family was supposed to have owned an island in New York harbour. They (the New Zealand Piersons who descended from William Pierson of Cairo, Greene Co., N.Y.) believe this was sold long before the first Pierson came to New Zealand (1860)."

Henry Peirson came to Southampton, Long Island (currently in the state of New York), in 1640. He was a step-son of John Cooper who was a member of the company that purchased eight square miles for the town on Long Island in 1640. Before 1643, Henry obtained a 1 acre home lot as his share of the town and later he participated in 1648 when home lots were expanded to 3 acres. He purchased an additional lot from John White to increase his share in the town property and in portions of later town additions. When he died, after 40 years in Southampton, his property was worth 1256 pounds, 1 shilling, two pence[2]. Long Island's westward end is in New York harbor and this long narrow island extends 120 miles eastward along the Connecticut coast lying about 16 miles from the mainland. Surely, this is the island in the New Zealand Pierson Island legend. Henry Peirson held many town and county offices at Southampton between 1640 and 1680, not the least of which were Southampton town and Suffolk County clerk, register, and recorder. In these duties, he had most of the ownership papers of the town intermittently in his possession for about 20 years from 1650 to 1669. The following receipt[3] was recorded in the town records when he turned over the documents to John Howell Junior in 1669:

"Southampton, May the 10th, 1669. Whereas I, Joseph Rainer Cunstable, and I, Isaack Halsey Overseer, having determined with the rest of o' copartners, the overseers of this towne, to take the books of records out of the hands of **Henry Peirson**, wee having chosen another, namely John Howell Jun, to that office of Recorder, doe hereby acknowledge to have received this day of him the said **Henry Peirson** for the Town's use as follows: one bundle of papers wherein amongst the rest is the Original of ye Indian's deed for the town's lands witnessed by **Mr. Abraham Pierson**, with ye copy of the said deed signed as Recorded, and the Original deed from Mr. James Farret on which is the award of Mr. Winthrop with Mr. Farret's memorandum, and another deed of Mr. Farret's with a copy of the first of them, and the Articles of agreement with the Indians in ye year 1649. Governor

---

[1] Letter from Mrs. Jenny Pierson, Wellington, New Zealand, to Richard Pierson, California, U.S.A., dated 18 September 1991, p. 2.

[2] George Rogers Howell, *The Early History of Southampton, L.I., New York with Genealogies*, Second Edition, Weed, Parsons and Company, Albany, NY, 1887, p. 348.

[3] Henry Hedges, Wm. Pelletreau, Edward Foster, *The Second Book of Records of the Town of Southampton, Long Island, N.Y. with other Ancient Documents of Historic Value*, John H. Hunt, Printer, Sag Harbor, NY, 1877, p. 353-354.

Niccolls his determination concerning the Towne. Mr. Topping and **John Cooper**, a copy of it recorded. Capt. Toppings deed with his Assignment on ye back of it to the towne. The original of the Indians deed assuring ye lands to the Towne which they bought of Capt. Topping, a copy of it recorded. Mr. Scott's deed to the Towne for ye meadows & land to Peaconnet, the deed for the hearbidg of the beach, with **John Cooper's** Assignment. The final conclusion with Southold Committees concerning the Accabauk meadows, ye order for payment of ye countries rate in 67, ye copy of the letter intended to bee sent to ye Governor in 69, more ye great book of records with a parchment cover, more the old book of records, with a large bundle continued part of the blue book & many other writings, more 3 great roles of papers, and the two books of records of cattle & some time in ye hands of Mr. Laughton, Memoranda, with ye copy of ye said deed signed as recorded and is delivered in amongst ye papers, with a copy of ye Articles of Agreement with ye Indians recorded, wee say received ye above mentioned writings and books, &c by us with our copartners, witness our hands the day & year above written.

Joseph Raynor, Jonas Bower, Isaac Halsey (his mark), and Thomas Cooper
In presence of: John Jessup (his mark) and John Laughton"

Patent of Gov. Edmund Andros, 1676

Henry Peirson also represented the town on many occasions with others. In 1676, the town obtained a patent from Governor Andros which names 15 townsmen including **Henry Pierson** that represent Southampton. This patent[4] describes the large portion of Long Island attributed to Southampton:

"Edmund Andros, Esq., Lieut. and Governor General under his Royal Highness James Duke of York and Albany &c. of all his Territories in America to all to whom these presents shall come sendeth Greeting. Whereas there is a certain Towne in the East Riding of Yorkshire upon Long Island commonly known by the name of South Hampton, situate, lying and being on the South side of the said Island, toward the Maine Sea, having a certain Tract of Land, thereunto belonging. The Eastward bounds whereof extend to a certain place or plaine, called Wainscott, where the bounds are settled betwixt their neighbours of the Towne of East Hampton, and them. Their Southern bounds being the Sea and so runs westward to a place called Seatuck, where a Stake was sett as their farthest extent that way. Then Crossing over the Island to the Northward to Peaconock great River and so to run Eastwards alongst the north bounds to the Eastermost point of Hogg-Neck, over against Shelter Island, Including all the Necks of Land and Islands, within the afore described Bounds and Limits. Now for a Confirmation unto the present Free holder, Inhabitants of the said Towne and precincts, know yee, that by vertue of his Majesty's Letters, Patents, and the Commission and Authority, unto mee given by his Royall Highness, I have Ratifyed Confirmed and granted; And by these presents, do hereby Ratifie Confirme and grant, unto John Topping, Justice of the Peace, Capt. John Howell, Thomas Halsey Senior, Joseph Raynor, Constable, Edward Howell, John Jagger, John Foster and Francis Sayers, Overseers; Lieut. Joseph Fordham, **Henry Pierson**, **John Cooper**, Ellis Cooke, Samuel Clarke, Richard Post and John Jennings, **as Patentees**, for and on the behalfe of themselves

---

[4] Henry Hedges, Wm. Pelletreau, Edward Foster, *The Second Book of Records of the Town of Southampton, Long Island, N.Y. with other Ancient Documents of Historic Value*, John H. Hunt, Printer, Sag Harbor, NY, 1877, p. 347-349.

and their Associates, the Freeholders and Inhabitants of the said Towne, their Heires, Successors and Assignes, All the afore mentioned Tract of Land, with the Necks and Islands within the said bounds sett forth and described as aforesaid, Together with all Rivers, Lakes, Waters, Quarrys, Wood, Land, Plaines, Meadows, pastures, marshes, fishing, hawking, hunting and fowling, And all other Proffits, Commodities, Emoluments and hereditaments, to the Said Towne, Tract of Land and premises, within the limits and bounds aforementioned described, ... And that the place of their present Habitacon and abode shall continue and retaine the name of South Hampton, by which name and Stile, it shall be distinguished and knowne, in all Bargaines and Sales Deeds, Records and writings. They the said Patentees and their Associates their Heires Successors and Assignes making Improvement on the said Lands, and Conforming themselves according to Law, And yeilding and paying therefore yearly and every year, as an Acknowledgment, or Quit Rent, one fatt Lamb, unto such officer, or officers, there in Authority as shall bee Empowered to receive the same. Given under my hand and sealed with the Seale of the Province in New Yorke, the first day of November, in the Eight and twentieth yeare of hid Ma'ties Reigne Anno. Domini, one thousand, six hundred Seventy Six.

(Signed) E. Andros
Examined by mee and Recorded: Mathias Nicolls, Secr."

Patent of Gov. Thomas Dongan, 1686

November 23, 1686[5]. At a Southampton town meeting, it was agreed that Major John Howell should go to New York about the present affair of making good their title to Southampton lands called into question at Shinnecock. There were chosen six men to be a committee to give Major Howell his instructions: "Mr. Edward Howell, **Henry Pierson**, Mathew Howell, Thomas Cooper, Obadiah Rogers, and **Joseph Pierson**." Henry and Joseph were sons of Henry Peirson Sr. This visit to Fort James resulted in the "Patent of Gov. Dongan" abstracted below:

December 6, 1686[6]. "PATENT OF GOV. DONGAN. Thomas Dongan Capt. General Governor in Chief and Vice Admiral in and over the Province of Newyorke and Territorys depending thereon in America &c. under his Majesty James the second By the grace of God King of England Scotland France & Ireland Defender of the faith &c. To all whom this shall come sendeth Greeting. ... Whereas of late some difference hath happened betweene the Inhabitants of said towne of Southampton and the Indyans adjacent to said towne concerning the bounds above specifyed ... Now Know Yee that I the said Thomas Dongan ... do finde that the Freeholders of the Towne of Southampton have lawfully purchased the lands ... do grant Ratifye Release and Confirme unto Major John Howell, Thomas Hallsey Senior, Edward Howell, John Jagger, John Foster, Francis Sayres, Joseph Fordham, **Henry Pearson**, Samuell Clarke, Job Sayers, William Barker, Isaac Halsey Freeholders & Inhabitants of Southampton herein after erected and made one body Corporate and Politique ... I do ... command ... that they shall forever have hold use and enjoy all the libertyes ... according to the tenure .. In Testimony Whereof I have caused the seale of the

---

[5] *Town Records of Southampton*, NY, Liber A, No. 2, 2nd Part, p. 116.
[6] George Rogers Howell, *The Early History of Southampton, L.I., New York with Genealogies*, Second Edition, Weed, Parsons and Company, Albany, NY, 1887, p. 460-4.

said Province to be hereunto affixed and these presents to be entered in the Secretaryes Office. Witness my hand at Fort James the sixth day of December - One thousand six hundred eighty six & in the second yeare of his said Majestyes Reigne.

(signed) Thomas Dongan."

The original eight square miles of Southampton was less than one percent of Long Island which would allot about 100 acres apiece to the original share holders of the town. However, as the town purchased more and more land to distribute to its citizens with property owning "rights," some of the original shareholders were now the owners of as much as several hundred acres. But the land was not evenly distributed as some settlers bought land and future "rights" from those leaving. Some family surnames held as much as 3,000 acres (Howell).

Will of Col. Henry Peirson, 1701

The Peirsons, including 21 land-owning Peirson families, together owned about 1,000 acres of Long Island in 1776. The will of Col. Henry Peirson, below, is an example of individual Peirson family land ownership:

August 28, 1701[7]. Colonel Henry Peirson wrote his will this date, confirming his eight children, given unabridged:

"In ye name of God, Amen. I, Henry Peirson, belonging to S'hampton in ye County of Suffolk on Island of Nassau (Long Island) in ye Province of New York, being thro God's goodness in perfect strength of memory, though weak in body & not knowing ye day of my appointed change, do make this my last Will & testamt as followeth -

First - bequeath my soul to God who gave it & my body to ye earth decently to be buried & for yt estate which it hath pleased God to bless me with, I dispose of it as followeth -

I give unto my eldest son, John Peirson, his heirs & assigns forever, my home lot with all ye housing & fencing thereupon & also all my beach close & also two lots of land in Hog Neck No. 39 & No. 47 & also my land & swamp at ye head of Sag swamp & also all my meadow at ye North side at ye great meadow & at Smith's meadow & also a quarter of a share at Meantake, one horse, two oxen, two cows & ten sheep -

I give unto my son, David Peirson, to him, his heirs & assigns forever, all that piece of land lying in Bridgehampton on ye West side of ye street bounded with ye land of Robt. Norris, Stephen Hedges & Josiah Hand on ye South; with Sag pond on ye West; with ye land of ye sd Norris on ye North, & with ye street on ye East thereof & also all my meadows at Noyack & also one half quarter of a share at Meantake & one horse, two steers of 3 year old & two cows & ten sheep & twenty five pound in money or what shall be equivalent when he shall come to ye age of twenty one years -

I give unto my son, Theophilus Peirson, all yt piece of land yt I bought of Mr. Peregrine Stanburgh, called ye Swamp Close & also two fifty pound allotments of land in Hog Neck, one of which was my father's No. 41, ye other I bought of Benjamin Foster No. 26, all which

---

[7]William S. Pelletreau, *Early Long Island Wills of Suffolk County, 1691-1703, With Genealogical and Historical Notes*, Francis P. Harper, New York, NY, 1897, pp. 239-41.

said land I give unto him, ye sd Theophilus Peirson, his heirs & assigns for ever - Also one horse, two steers, two cows, ten sheep & twenty five pounds in money, or what may be equivalent thereto, when he shall come to ye age of twenty one years & also one Eighth part of a share at Meantake -

I give unto my two younger sons, Abraham Peirson & Josiah Peirson, to them, their heirs & assigns forever, equally to be divided, all yt piece of land which I bought of ye town of S'hampton & of Christopher Leaming, called ye Wood Close, bounded with a highway on ye South, with ye land of Theophilus Howell & ye parsonage land on ye East, with ye land of Capt. Topping, Benoni Flint and common land on North, with ye land of Robt. Norris & a highway on ye West thereof & also a fifty pound commonage throughout ye bounds of S'hampton & also four acres of land lying in S'hampton, join to ye east end of ye lot of Joseph Peirson & I do give unto each of them, my sd two sons, Abraham & Josiah Peirson, twenty five pounds in money, one horse, two steers, two cows & ten sheep as they shall come to ye age of twenty one years -

But if it shall please God to take away any of my sons by death before they come to ye age of twenty one years, then his or their part so taken away shall be equally divided amongst those of my sons surviving -

I give unto my three daughters Hannah Peirson, Sarah Peirson & Mary Peirson, each of them, one hundred pounds current money of this Province, or what may be equivalent thereto, when they shall come to ye age of twenty years, or at ye day of their marriage, as it shall be demanded, but if any of my sd daughters shall be taken away by death before they shall come to ye age of twenty years or marriage, then her or their part so taken away shall be equally divided among ye rest of my children then surviving -

I do make my well beloved wife, Susannah Peirson, whole & sole Executrix of this my last will & testamt & my will is that my sons, as they come to fitting age, shall be teached to reade & write well & bound out to trades -

In witness whereof, I hereunto set my hand & seal the 28 day of August 1701 - And I desire Mr. Ebenezer White & brother (in-law) Abraham Howell to be overseers to my children & see that this, my will, be duly executed -

Henry Peirson [Seal]

In presence of us: Benoni Flint, Theo. Peirson (brother of Col. Peirson), Jno Morehos."

Pierson Island Legend Conclusions

Peirson ownership of land on Long Island beginning in 1640 and lasting for more than 200 years, along with Henry Peirson and his son, Col. Henry Peirson, being named in the Southampton Gov. Andros and Gov. Dongan Patents in 1676 and 1686, respectively, explains the development of the Pierson Island Legend and the extent of its validity.

Piersonville, New Jersey

Piersonville[8] was established about 1730 by Benjamin$_4$ Pierson (Abraham$_3$, Thomas$_2$ Jr., Rev. Abraham$_1$). It was a large and beautiful tract of land located three miles east of Morristown, New Jersey, on the road from Whippany to E. Hanover (now Madison), a portion of which land was occupied by the Roman Catholic convent and school in 1878.

41 Benjamin Pierson[9] was born at Newark (New Jersey) in 1701 and died in 1783. He moved from Newark to a tract of land called Piersonville, which he afterwards divided among his children, the most of whom settled thereon. He mar. Patience Coe, who d. in 1785; and had chd. 61+ Elijah, b. 1728 or 1730 in Newark or Piersonville, d. 1795; 62+ John, b. 1731 near Morristown (Piersonville); 63 Sarah, b. 1733 (w. of ____ Cook, and mother of Benj. Cook of Bottle Hill); 64+ Benjamin, b. 1736 near Morristown (Piersonville), N.J., settled near the old homestead, d. 1794; 65+ Moses, b. 1738 near Morristown (Piersonville), d. 1768; 66+ Isaac, b. ca. 1742 near Morristown at Piersonville; 67+ Aaron, b. 1746 at Piersonville, d. 1803 (?); 68 Keziah (w. of Dea. Munson); 69 Abraham; 70+ Daniel, b. 1750 in Morristown, d. 1831.

61 Elijah Pierson, was born 1728 or 30 in Newark or Piersonville, and settled on a farm near Green village, N. J., and died in 1795, and was buried at Morristown. He had chd. 91 George; 92 Moses (who never married); 93 Benjamin; 94 Sarah (w. of ____ Crane); 95 Jane (w. of ____ Durham); 96 Phebe (w. of ____ Furnam).

62 John Pierson, was born near Morristown at Piersonville, in 1731, and had chd. 97 Catherine (w. of ____ Cook, and mother of Dr. Silas Cook); 98 Mary (w. of I. Spaulding); 99 Ruth (w. of I. Spining).

64 Benjamin Pierson, was born near Morristown, at Piersonville, N. J., in 1736, settled near the old homestead, and died in 1794. His wife Phebe, died in 1799. He had chd. 100 David, b. 1763; 101 Hannah, b. 1794; 102 Gabriel; 103 Patience.

65 Moses Pierson, born 1738, near Morristown, at Piersonville, and died 1768, had chd. 104 Keziah.

66 Isaac Pierson, born near Morristown, at Piersonville, about 1742, perhaps had chd. 105 Darius; 106 Penira.

67 Aaron Pierson, was born at Piersonville, near Morristown, N. J., 1746; he lived on his father's homestead, and died about 1803. He had chd. 107 Ebenezer D.; 108 Charlotte, d. 1846, (w. of Wm. Jones, and had 9 chd., of whom Charlotte mar. A. Canfield and Louisa mar. O. L. Kirkland).

70 Daniel Pierson was born near Morristown, at Piersonville, N. J., in 1750, and died in Dayton, Ohio, in 1831. "He served in the Jersey line of the Continental Army, and was present at the battle of Monmouth. Early in the century, in order to educate his family, he moved to the village of Morristown and built the substantial house on the corner of South and Pine streets, now (1878) known as the Wood house, and not long after emigrated with his whole family, except Charles, to Dayton, Ohio." He mar. Prudence King, who survived

---

[8]There is also a Pierson, Michigan, but its origin has not been investigated.
[9]Lizzie B. Pierson, *Pierson Genealogical Records*, Joel Munsell, Printer, Albany, NY, 1878, pp. 17-19.

him 6 yrs. He had chd. 109 Clarissa, b. 1785 Morristown, N.J., d. 1863 Cincinnati, Ohio, mar. ____ Davies; 110 Charles Edwin, b. 1787, d. 1865; 111 John A., b. 1789, d. 1811; 112 William H., b. 1791, .d. 1820; 113 Eliz. Ann, d. 1794; 114 Henry A., b. 1795.

42 Abraham Pierson, was born in Newark, 1707 and died 1777 in Morristown, N. J. He lived on a farm in Morristown opposite his brother 41 Benjamin (who called his tract of land Piersonville). Perhaps Abraham's farm was included in the area called Piersonville. He mar. Mary ____ (who died in 1782), and had chd. 71 Abraham; 72+ Darius; 73+ Isaac, b. 1737; and some others.

In 1771, a census was taken at Morris Township, Morris Co., N.J., which includes Piersonville, about half of which Peirsons are identified:

Head of Family	Probable Identity (ref. Numbers in Chapter 7)
Benjamin Peirson	41 Benjamin, son of Abraham
Elijah Peirson	61 Elijah, son of 41 Benjamin
John Peirson	62 John, son of 41 Benjamin
John Peirson Jr.	(not identified)
Isaac Peirson	66 Isaac, son of 41 Benjamin
Abraham Peirson	42 Abraham, brother of 41 Benjamin
Joseph Peirson	(not identified)
Joseph Peirson Jr.	(not identified)
William Peirson	(not identified)
Willis Peirson	(not identified)
Ruth Peirson	99 Ruth, dau. of 62 John, wife of I. Spining

In 1788, Isaac$_6$ Peirson, son of Lemuel$_5$ Peirson (David$_4$, Col. Henry$_3$, Henry$_2$, William$_1$) of Sagg, part of Bridgehampton, Suffolk Co., Long Island, N.Y., moved to Piersonville, N.J.

80 Isaac Pierson, was born 1755, on L. I. In 1788[10], he moved to New Jersey, and settled on a tract of land near Morristown, known as Piersonville. He was commonly called "Long Island Pierson" to distinguish him from the other Pierson families of New Jersey (that also resided at Piersonville, see above). He had chd. 206+ Elisha, b. 1781; 207 Eleazar, b. 1785; 208+ Maltby G., b. 1795; 209+ George; 210+ Henry; 211 Miller; 212+ Isaac.

206 Elisha Pierson[11], born on L. I. in 1781, moved with his father to New Jersey when he was a child (1788), and resided in Morristown (or Piersonville), and had chd. 386 John; 387 Sidney; 388 Eliza; 389 Harriet; 390 Hannah.

208 Maltby G. Pierson[12], was born 1795 in New Jersey at Piersonville, mar. S. Voorhees, and lived in New Jersey. He had chd. 391 Isaac N. (mar. R. Post); 392 Aaron (mar. S. Birch, and has a daughter Mrs. Dr. Cooper of Westfield, N. J.); 393 Charles J. (mar. M. Cobert); 394 Henry W. (mar. M. Budd); 395 David L. (mar. E. Berry); 396 Maltby G. (mar. C. Muchmore); 397 Allen H. (never married); 398 Wm. (never mar.); 399 Mary Ann; 400 Hannah N.; 401 Harriet; 402 Ellen C.; 403 Sarah L.; and one other daughter.

---

[10]Lizzie B. Pierson, *Pierson Genealogical Records*, Joel Munsell, Printer, Albany, NY, 1878, p. 30.

[11]Lizzie B. Pierson, *Pierson Genealogical Records*, Joel Munsell, Printer, Albany, NY, 1878, p. 30.

[12]Lizzie B. Pierson, *Pierson Genealogical Records*, Joel Munsell, Printer, Albany, NY, 1878, p. 30.

209 George Pierson[13], born in N. J. (Piersonville?), had chd. 404 Oliver; 405 Miller; 406 Eliz.; 407 Temperance. This family said to be of California.

210 Henry Pierson[14], born in N. J. (Piersonville?), had chd. 408 Charles; 409 Caroline.

212 Isaac Pierson[15], born in N. J. (Piersonville?), had chd. 410 Edward; 411 Henry; 412 Cecilia; 413 Eliza; 414 Mary.

---

[13]Lizzie B. Pierson, *Pierson Genealogical Records*, Joel Munsell, Printer, Albany, NY, 1878, p. 30.
[14]Lizzie B. Pierson, *Pierson Genealogical Records*, Joel Munsell, Printer, Albany, NY, 1878, p. 30.
[15]Lizzie B. Pierson, *Pierson Genealogical Records*, Joel Munsell, Printer, Albany, NY, 1878, p. 30.

Appendix A
Parish Records 1542-1660
Howden, Yorkshire, England

Among the English counties, the largest number of Pearson family records of all spellings appear in Yorkshire. Within Yorkshire, the largest number of Pearson families appear in Sheffield and the second largest group in Howden located 18 miles southwest of Beverley in the East Riding of Yorkshire. There are two Howden's in Yorkshire, but all the Pierson records are at the one in East Riding. Howden also has the largest group of Pearson families near the now lost vill of Pericne located 18 miles to the northeast of Howden.

In the 16th century, the Parish of Howden included the Townships of Asselby, Balkholme, Barmby, Belby, Cotness, Howden, Kilpin, Knedlington, Laxton, Linton, Newland, Metham, Saltmarshe, Skelton, Thorpe, and Yokefleet - an area of twenty square miles of flat alluvial land, forming part of the Baronial Liberty of the Bishops of Durham. Chapels were built at Barmby and Laxton - about four miles from Howden - and resident Curates appointed. Additionally, several records occur for the locations Barnell, Boothe, Duncotts, Howden Dike, and Swinefleet.

Vicinity of Howden Parish in Yorkshire

The following Howden Parish records are taken from *The Registers of the Parish of Howden, Co. York*, Vols. I (published 1904, marriages 1542-1644 and baptisms 1542-1659), & II (published 1905, burials 1543-1659), edited by G. E. Weddall, privately printed for the Yorkshire Parish Register Society, Beck & Inchbold Ltd., Printers, Oriel Press, Leeds, Yorkshire, England:

"Julie 1546. George Pearson & Agnes ux. xxvij." This is the form provided. Dates will be provided together below instead of the day in Roman numerals at the end. Occasionally, the day in Roman numerals is replaced with "ult." which is an abbreviation for the Latin "ultimo die" meaning "final day" (last day of the month). Also "primo" is occasionally used in lieu of the Roman numerals to represent the first day of the month. "Ux." is an abbreviation for "uxor" which is Latin for "wife." Dates are provided in the Julian calendar by the Parish registers. Thus, the Julian calendar sees March 25 as the first day of the new year, and March as the first month of the new year. To avoid confusion, the year for dates from January 1 through March 24 will be shown as Julian/Gregorian (i.e. 14 Jan 1610 is 14 Jan 1610/11) prior to 1752.

> "The Register of All the Weddings of Howden, Knedlington & Boothe
> Beginning the 14th Day of September in the Year of our Lord 1543."

27 Jul 1546, George Pearson & Agnes (no surname given).

> "Here Begineth the Register of All the Wedding within the Whole Parish of Howden
> Beginning the Eighth of June Anno Dom. 1550."

22 Apr 1553, Richard Bartlemew, Alice wife of Bernbie (Barmby).
11 Jun 1553, Willm. Pearson, Isabell, of Booth (Botheby in 1550, place name Booth near Howden, called Booth's Ferry in 1651).
16 Sep 1560, Robert Pearson, Hellen, of Howden.
23 Jan 1562/3, William Peerson of Asselby, Julian Collin.
20 May 1565, Robert Peerson of Howden, Margaret Freman.
25 Jan 1567/8, Richard Cowper of Belby, Jennett.
26 Nov 1569, John Cowper of Howden, Isabell.
18 Jun 1570, Robert Fawne of Howden, Elizabeth Trounce.
2 Dec 1570, William Bowes of Howden, Isabell Peerson.
8 May 1571, William Dun Junr of Howden, Jennet Pearson.
23 Oct 1571, John Cowper of Howden, Elizabeth Binds.
15 Jun 1572, John Pearson of Saltmarshe, Dorothie Wells.
10 Aug 1572, Thomas Richardson of Howden, Alice Pearson.
23 Nov 1572, Thomas Pearson of Howden, Elizabeth Fawne.
17 Aug 1573, Robert Pearson of Howden, Margaret Aske.
27 Apr 1574, Henrie Pearson, Margaret Williamson of Howden.
20 May 1574, Henrie Potter of Barlby, Margaret Cowp(er).
15 Sep 1577, Thomas Middleton of Hamelton (Hambleton?), Marion Peerson.
5 Jul 1579, Richard Pearson of Howden, Alice Hartfirth.
15 Nov 1579, John Pearson of Saltmarshe, Elizabeth Webster. (Second wife)
19 Oct 1581, William Pearson of Kilpin, Alison Bushbie.

18 Jun 1582, Thomas Raner of Howden, Margaret Peerson.

5 Aug 1583, Richard Leaven of Gowle (Goole?), Joan Peerson.

15 Nov 1584, John Peerson of Skelton, Elizabeth Stamp.

31 Jul 1591, Thomas Pearson of Saltmarshe, Agnes.

23 Jun 1594, John Cowper of Howden, Alice.

2 Oct 1597, Christopher Pearson of Howden, Jane.

19 Feb 1603/4, John Pearson of Howden, Jane.

27 Nov 1608, Edward Cowper of Skelton, Elizabeth Bamtor.

28 Nov 1608, Robert Rainforth of Saltmarshe, Ann Pearson.

27 Aug 1610, George Pearson of Howden, Elizabeth.

9 Nov 1611, Richard Cowper of Saltmarshe, Margaret Dawson.

9 May 1613, Ralfe Cowper of Kilpin, Mary Martin.

11 Jul 1613, Richard Cowp(er) of Saltmarshe, Agnes Storye.

30 Jan 1615/16, William Smythson of Cotness, Barbara Pearson.

15 Nov 1621, Phillip Pearson of Yokefleet, Jane Cowper.

5 Feb 1624/5, Thomas Richman of Osgodby, Elizabeth Pearson.

11 Nov 1628, Richard Pearson of Saltmarshe, Elizabeth Wilson.

2 May 1629, Thomas Jewett of Saltmarshe, Grace Pearson.

15 Nov 1633, Thomas Garton of Yokefleet, Ann Cowper.

15 Oct 1635, Leonard Branton of Knedlington, Elizabeth Pearson.

20 May 1638, Thomas Pearson of Barmby, Marie Underwood.

7 Sep 1641, John Pearson of Howden, Marie Robinson.

"Thomas Richinson of Howden and Joane Pearson of the same married by Phillipp Saltmarsh Esq. (according to an Act of Parliament in the case provided) in the presence of Richard Watterhouse of Asselby & Lowrence Thompson of the same, 16 May 1654."

"Savage Pearson of Laxton in the Parish of Howden, grasman, and Anne Lyon of Balkholme in the said parish, Widdow, was married at Saltmarshe by Phillip Saltmarsh Esq. (witnesses unreadable), 17 Jan 1655/6."

"Lawrence Graburne of Saltmarshe in the parish of Howden, husbandman, and Margaret Pearson of Skelton in the said parish, spinster, was married at Saltmarshe by Phillip Saltmarsh Esq. in presence of Phillip Pearson her father and Arthur Kirby both of Skelton, 28 Jan 1655/6."

"Robert Pearson of Howden, glover, and Ailse Wrey of the same, spinster, was married at Howden by Phillip Saltmarsh Esq. in presence of Robert Sawer and William Durham, 21 Oct 1656."

Parish of Howden Baptism Records

"November 1542. Agnes filia Georgii Sandes de Belby die xv." This is the form of the record provided. "filia" is Latin for "daughter, female offspring," "gemelli" is Latin for "twin or twin-born" and "filius" is Latin for "son, male offspring." "de" means "of." "die" means "day" (day of the month). "xv" for example is small Roman numerals for "15." The day will be grouped with the month and year below and the Julian year stated as before (10 Jan 1610 is 10 Jan 1610/11).

12 Mar 1543/4, Johanna, dau. of Robert Colling of Skelton.

18 Mar 1543/4, Alicia, dau. of Thomas Freeman of Skelton.

24 Jul 1545, Robert Pearson, no parent given.

9 Dec 1545, Alicia, dau. of Robert Colline of Skelton.

16 Jul 1546, Alicia Pearson, no parent given.

12 Oct 1546, Alicia Pearsonne, no parent given.

28 Nov 1546, Alicia Pearsonne, no parent given.

26 Apr 1547, Margareta Freeman, no parent given (see father of Alicia Freeman c. 18 Mar 1543/4). (Wife of Robert Peerson)

20 Jul 1548, Katherina, dau. of Thomas Pearson.

17 Feb 1548/9, Juliana, dau. of Stephan Colling. (Wife of William Peerson?)

5 Oct 1549, Agnes, dau. of Johannis (John) Wheelewrighte.

18 Nov 1549, Thomas, son of Johannis (John) Pearsonne.

3 Apr 1550, Georgius (George), son of Guilieli (William) Pearsonne.

25 Nov 1550, Georgius (George), son of Georgii (George) Pearson of Howden.

17 Feb 1551/2, Alicia, dau. of Georgii (George) Pearsonne of Howden.

17 Apr 1552, Cuthbertus, son of Guilieli (William) Pearson of Howden.

16 Sep 1552, Robert, son of Johannis (John) Wheelewright of Howden.

5 Feb 1553/4, Margareta, dau. of Richardi (Richard) Bartholomew of Barmby.

26 Feb 1555/6, Anna, dau. of Richard Pearson.

7 Jul 1555, Francis, dau. of Richardi Bartholomewe of Barmby.

1 Aug 1557, Thomas, son of Richardi Bartlemewe of Barmby.

28 Sep 1561, Agnes, dau. of Thomas Ellerton alls. Cowp(er) of Knedlington.

7 Dec 1561, Janeta, dau of Robert Pearson of Howden.

25 Oct 1562, Thomas, son of Thomas Ellerton als. Cowp(er) of Knedlington.

24 Jan 1562/3, Elsabetha, dau of Johannis (John) Stamp of Kilpin. (Wife of John Peerson)

7 Feb 1562/3, Francis, son of Robert Pearson of Howden.

24 Oct 1563, Dorothea, dau of Guillmi (William) Pearson of Asselby.

13 Aug 1564, Elizabetha, dau of Robert Pearson of Howden.

2 Jun 1565, Elizabetha, dau of Johannis (John) Webster of Barnby. (Wife of John Pearson?)

22 Oct 1565, Nicholaus, son of Robert Pearson of Howden.

30 Dec 1565, Margareta, dau of Guillmi (William) Peerson of Asselby.

23 Mar 1565/6, Emma, dau of Robert Pearson of Duncotts.

28 Feb 1567/8, Johannes (John), son of Robert Pearson of Duncotts.

16 May 1568, Katherina, dau of Robert Pearson of Howden.

27 Oct 1569, Agnes, dau of Richard Cowper of Belby.

27 Dec 1570, Thomas, son of Guillmi (William) Pearson of Asselby.

20 Jan 1570/1, Reginoldus, son of Johannis (John) Cowper of Howden.

24 Mar 1570/1, Isabella, dau of Robert Fawne of Howden.

22 Mar 1571/2, Margareta, dau of Johannis (John) Williamson of Skelton.

26 Sep 1572, Dorothea, dau of Johannis (John) Cowper of Howden.

23 Jan 1572/3, Alicia, dau of Robert Pearson of Howden.

2 Feb 1572/3, Nicholaus, son of Guillmi (William) Pearson of Asselby.

25 Mar 1574, Johannes (John), son of Johannis (John) Pearson of Saltmarshe.

18 Apr 1574, Elizabetha, dau of Thomas Pearson of Howden.

17 Jul 1574, Thomas, son of Guilmi (William) Pearson of Asselby.

17 Apr 1575, Elizabetha, dau of Johannis (John) Cowper of Howden.

13 Jul 1575, Johanna, dau of Thomas Pearson of Howden.

21 Oct 1575, Juliana, dau of Robert Pearson of Howden.

6 Dec 1576, Catherina, dau of Robert Pearson of Howden.

19 Sep 1577, Guilmus (William), son of Thomas Pearson of Howden.

1 Mar 1577/8, Elenora, dau of Johannis (John) Cowper of Howden.

24 Feb 1579/80, Elena, dau of Thomas Pearson of Howden.

29 May 1580, Elizabetha, dau of Richard Pearson of Howden.

15 Sep 1580, Robertus, son of Johannis (John) Pearson of Saltmarshe.

15 Jan 1581/2, Cicilia, dau of Johannis (John) Pearson of Saltmarshe.

8 Apr 1582, Georgius, son of Richard Pearson of Howden.

12 Jan 1582/3, Johes. (John), son of Johes. (John) Pearson of Saltmarshe.

10 Feb 1582/3, Dorothea, dau of Thomas Pearson of Howden.

26 Sep 1584, George, son to Richard Pearson of Howden.

8 Apr 1585, Isabell, dau to John Pearson of Saltmarshe.

13 Oct 1585, Elizabeth, dau to Edward Pearson of Howden.

22 Oct 1585, Edward, son to John Pearson of Howden.

25 Dec 1586, Robart, son to John Peareson of Howden.

6 Apr 1587, Edward, son to Richard Pearson of Howden.

13 Nov 1587, Joane, dau to John Pearson of Saltmarshe.

13 Jan 1587/8, Elizabeth, dau to Edward Pearson of Howden.

20 Feb 1588/9, Ellinor, dau to John Pearson of Howden.

20 Mar 1589/90, Marie, dau to Edward Pearson of Howden.

8 Oct 1590, John, son to Nicholas Pearson of Howden.

7 Dec 1591, Thomas, son to Nicholas Pearson of Howden.

17 Sep 1592, Jane, dau to John Pearson of Howden.

23 Sep 1592, John, son to Edward Pearson of Howden.

6 Apr 1593, Tomasine, dau to Thomas Pearson of Saltmarshe.

30 Sep 1593, Henrie, son to Nicholas Pearson of Howden.

22 Oct 1594, Barbara, dau to Edward Pearson of Howden.

1 Dec 1594, William, son to Thomas Ellerton als. Cowp(er) of Belby.

31 Jan 1595/6, Philip, son to Thomas Pearson of Saltmarshe.

20 Mar 1595/6, Henrie, son to Edward Pearson of Howden.

22 May 1597, Richard, son to Edward Pearson of Howden.

6 Jan 1597/8, Robart, son to Nicholas Pearson of Howden.

31 Jul 1598, An, dau to Edward Pearson of Howden.

16 Dec 1598, Thomas, son to Thomas Pearson of Saltmarshe.

21 Jun 1599, Milisant, dau to Christopher Pearson of Howden.

14 Aug 1599, Tomisine, dau to Edward Pearson of Howden.

30 Aug 1600, John, son to Christopher Pearson of Howden.

25 Feb 1600/1, Ralfe, son to Elizabeth Cowper of Howden.

11 Jan 1601/2, Margaret, dau to Thomas Pearson of Saltmarshe.

2 Jun 1602, Thomas, son to Ralfe Cowper of Cotness.

20 Dec 1602, William, son to Christopher Pearson of Howden.

2 Jul 1603, Elizabeth, dau to John Pearson of Barmby.

3 May 1604, Elizabeth, dau to John Pearson of Howden.

20 Apr 1605, An, dau to Ralfe Cowper of Cotness.

27 Apr 1605, Grace, dau to Thomas Pearson of Saltmarshe.

9 Oct 1605, Elizabeth, dau to John Pearson of Howden.

25 Oct 1605, William & An, children to John Pearson of Barmby.

25 Dec 1605, Margaret, dau to Jane Cowper of Barnell.

3 May 1606, Marie, dau to Robart Underwoode of Barmby.   (Wife of Thomas Pearson)

5 Nov 1607, William, son to John Pearson of Howden.

3 Sep 1608, Grace, dau to John Pearson of Barmby.

8 Dec 1608, John, son to John Pearson of Howden.

28 Oct 1610, Thomas, son to John Pearson of Barmby.

9 Feb 1610/11, Frances, dau to John Pearson of Howden.

6 Mar 1610/11, Brigett, dau to George Pearson of Barmby.

16 Jan 1612/3, Thomas, son to John Pearson of Howden.

6 Feb 1612/3, Savage, son to John Pearson of Barmby (on the Marsh).

6 Feb 1612/3, Elizabeth, dau to George Pearson of Howden.

17 Dec 1614, William, son to John Pearson of Howden.

23 Jul 1615, John, son to George Pearson of Howden.

2 Mar 1615/6, Dorothie, dau to John Pearson of Barmby (on the Marsh).

11 Feb 1616/7, An, dau to John Pearson of Howden.

1 Feb 1617/8, Jane, dau to George Pearson of Howden.

27 Mar 1619, Mary, dau to John Pearson of Howden.

27 Nov 1619, Robert, son to John Pearson of Barmby.

9 Apr 1620, Nicholas, son to George Pearson of Howden.

11 Nov 1620, Edward, son to John Pearson of Howden.

23 Oct 1622, George, son to George Pearson of Howden.

15 Dec 1622, Jane, dau to John Pearson of Howden.

25 Jan 1622/3, Thomas, son to Phillipp Pearson of Skelton.

8 Jan 1624/5, Elizabeth, dau to John Pearson of Howden.

15 Mar 1625/6, Margaret, dau to Phillip Pearson of Skelton.

3 Jun 1626, Robart, son to George Pearson of Howden.

19 Jul 1626, Joseph, son to Margaret Pearson of Skelton.

29 Mar 1629, An, dau to Phillip Pearson of Skelton.

26 Sep 1629, Alice, dau to George Pearson of Howden.

28 Jan 1630/1, Frances son & Jane dau to John Fuller of Howden.

20 Jan 1631/2, John, son to Phillip Pearson of Skelton.

19 Nov 1634, Robert, son to Phillipp Pearson of Skelton.

24 Jun 1636, John, son of John Pearson of Kilpin.

25 Nov 1637, Phillip, son to Phillip Pearson of Skelton.

5 Aug 1638, An, dau to John Pearson of Kilpin.

22 Jan 1638/9, John, son to Thomas Pearson of Asselby.

12 Feb 1640/1, John, son to John Pearson of Howden.

27 Apr 1641, Bartholomew, son to Thomas Pearson of Asselby.

24 Jan 1641/2, An, dau to John Pearson of Howden.

23 Jan 1643/4, Sara(?), dau to John Pearson of Barnell (Barnhill).

2 Nov 1644, An, dau to John Pearson of Asselby.

8 Jul 1649, Joseph, son to Robert Pearson of Asselby.

27 Apr 1651, George, son to Robert Pearson of Howden.

Christened 16 Jan 1652/3, Robert, son to Robert Pearson of Asselby.

Borne 16 Jan 1653/4, Stephen, sonn to John Pearson of Asselby, Husbandman.

Borne 24 Apr 1654, George, son to Thomas Peeres (Peereson?) of Barnill (Barnhill).

Borne 10 Mar 1654/5, Francis, son to Ann Pearson of Skelton.

Borne 14 Feb 1655/6, Anne, dau to Richard Fuller of Howden, soldier.

Borne 24 Feb 1655/6, Robert, sonn to Robert Pearson of Asselby, taylor.

Borne 4 Jul 1656, Sarah, dau to John Pearson of Asselby, bruster (brewer?).

Christened 9 Dec 1657, Jane, dau to Savage Pierson of Laxton.

"A Register of All the Burials of Howden, Knedlington, & Boothe,
Beginning in September 1543."

Thomas Peerson buried 6 Jun 1545.

Agnes Peerson buried 10 Jul 1546.

Catherine Pearson buried 7 Oct 1546.

John Pearson buried 18 Mar 1546/7.

Thomas Peerson buried 1 Jan 1547/8.

Margaret, dau to William Pearson buried 10 Mar 1549/50.

"The Register of All the Burialls of Saltmarsh, Cotnes, Metham, Yockflet (Yokefleet), & Feild
Houses Beginning July 1545 through April 1549."

John, son to Thomas Peerson, buried 30 Sep 1545. (Thomas Pearson of <u>Saltmarshe</u> was
buried 27 Mar 1569)

"Here Begineth the Register of All the Burialls within the Whole Parish of Howden 19 May
1550, According as the Curats Were Commanded After the Dissolving of the Churche."

John, son to George Peerson of Howden, buried 12 Dec 1550.

Jennet, dau. to John Whelewright of Howden, buried 28 Feb 1550/1.

George, son to William Peerson of Howden, buried 16 Nov 1551.

Agnes Peerson of Boothe buried 16 Sep 1552.

Robart, son to John Whelewright of Howden, buried 1 Dec 1552.

Agnes Peerson of Asselby, widow, buried 19 Jan 1552/3.

Margaret, dau. to Richard Bartlemew of Barmby, buried 10 Feb 1553/4.

Frances, dau. to Richard Bartlemew of Barmby, buried 25 Sep 1555.

Alice, wife to Richard Bartlemew of Barmby, buried 25 Nov 1557.

Henrie Cowper of Thorp buried 2 Dec 1557.

Dorothie, dau. to George Peerson of Howden, buried 19 Dec 1559.

Elizabeth, dau. to Robert Pearson of Howden, buried 13 Aug 1564.

Elizabeth Pearson, died at Howden, buried 6 Jan 1564/5.

Alice, dau. to William Pearson of Asselby, buried 14 Aug 1565.

Isabell, wife to William Pearson of Boothe, buried 20 Dec 1567.

Catherine, dau. to Robert Pearson of Howden, buried 6 Nov 1568.

Thomas Pearson of Saltmarshe, buried 27 Mar 1569.

Joan, dau. to Robart Pearson of Howden, buried 17 May 1569.

George Pearson of Howden buried 8 Feb 1569/70.

Old John Pearson of Howden buried 21 Oct 1570.

Thomas, son to William Pearson of Asselby, buried 22 Dec 1570. (Probably should have been entered as 27 Dec 1570, copying or initial error, he was c. 27 Dec 1570)

Isabell, wife to John Cowper of Howden, buried 23 Jan 1570/1.

Agnes Pearson of Howden, wid., bur. 28 May 1571. (w. of George Pearson late of Howden)

Ranold, son to John Cowper of Howden, buried 2 Aug 1571.

Robart Fawne of Howden, buried 16 May1572.

Margaret wife to Robert Pearson of Howden, bur. 30 Nov 1572. (1st w. Margaret Freeman)

Nicholas son to William Pearson of Asselby, buried 19 Feb 1572/3.

John Wells of Cotness, buried 27 Mar 1573.

John son to John Pearson of Saltmarshe, buried 29 Apr 1574.

Alice dau. to Robart Pearson of Howden sho'k., buried 11 May 1574.

Elizabeth dau. to Thomas Pearson of Howden, buried 19 Aug 1574.

John son to John Pearson of Boothe, buried 4 Nov 1574.

Em. Fenton mother to the said child (John above), buried 8 Nov 1574.

Julian dau. to Robert Pearson of Howden cordwainer, buried 28 Oct 1575.

Joane dau. to Thomas Pearson of Howden butcher, buried 13 Mar 1577/8.

Dorothie wife of John Pearson of Saltmarshe, buried 12 Jul 1578. (Dorothie Wells).

John Collin died at Skelton 15 May 1579.

Elizabeth dau. to Richard Pearson of Howden, buried 27 Jan 1580/1.

Ellinor wife to Robert Pearson of Howden, buried 19 Sep 1581.

Robart Pearson of Howden butcher, buried 18 Nov 1581.

Eleanor dau. to Thomas Pearson of Howden, buried 3 Nov 1582.

John son to John Pearson of Saltmarshe, buried 24 Jan 1582/3.

Frances dau. to Robert Pearson of Howden, buried 1 Dec 1583.

William Pearson of Boothe, buried 9 Jan 1583/4.

George son to Richard Pearson of Howden, buried 26 Jan 1583/4.

Thomas Pearson of Howden, buried 15 Feb 1583/4. (Father of William)

Edward son to John Pearson of Howden, buried 24 Nov 1585.

John son to John Pearson of Saltmarshe, buried 18 Jul 1586.

Alice wife to William Pearson of Kilpin, buried 3 Mar 1586/7. (Alison Bushbie)

Alice dau. to Edward Pearson of Howden, buried 3 Apr 1587.

Isabell dau. to John Pearson of Saltmarshe, buried 4 Jul 1587.

Jane dau. to John Pearson of Saltmarshe, buried 15 Nov 1587. (Chr. Joane 13 Nov 1587)

Alice dau. to John Cowper of Howden, buried 26 Feb 1587/8.

William Pearson of Kilpin, buried 16 Mar 1587/8.

Robart son to John Pearson of Howden, buried 8 May 1588.

John Pearson of Saltmarshe, buried 3 Jun 1588.

John son to Nicolas Pearson of Howden, buried 9 May 1589.

Robart Pearson of Swinefleet, buried 13 Sep 1589.

Agnes Wheelewright of Howden, buried 1 Sep 1590.

Isabell Pearson of Saltmarshe, widow, buried 19 Dec 1590.

John Pearson of Howden, buried 1 Oct 1592.

Jone dau. to John Pearson of Howden, buried 11 Oct 1592. (Christened Jane 17 Sep 1592)

Elizabeth Pearson of Howden widow, buried 15 Oct 1592. (Wife of John Pearson?)

Elizabeth wife to John Cowper, buried 14 Nov 1592.

Isabell wife to Edward Pearson of Howden, buried 9 Dec 1592.

John son to Edward Pearson of Howden, buried 23 Apr 1593.

Jone wife to Richard Pearson of Howden, buried 21 Oct 1593.

Alice wife to Richard Pearson of Howden, buried 26 Nov 1593. (Alice Hartfirth)

Richard Pearson of Howden, buried 17 Dec 1593.

Henrie son to Nicolas Pearson of Howden, buried 3 Jan 1593/4.

Richard son to Richard Pearson of Howden, buried 25 May 1595.

John Wells of Saltmarshe, buried 1 Oct 1595. (Father of Dorothie Wells?)

Henrie son to Edward Pearson of Howden, buried 7 Jun 1597.

Robert son to Nicolas Pearson of Howden, buried 10 Jan 1597/8.

John Cowper, a stranger, buried 9 Apr 1598.

Nicolas Pearson of Cotness, buried 11 Dec 1600.

Elizabeth dau. to John Pearson of Howden, buried 19 Nov 1604.

Jone dau. to Henry Pearson of Howden, buried 29 Jan 1604/5.

Alice Pearson, a servant of Howden, buried 2 Apr 1605.

Thomas Pearson of Saltmarshe, buried 29 Dec 1605.

Richard Pearson of Saltmarshe, buried 10 Mar 1605/6.

Elizabeth dau. to John Pearson of Howden, buried 17 Sep 1607.

William son to John Pearson of Howden, buried 16 Nov 1607.

Frances dau. to John Pearson of Howden, buried 14 Sep 1612.

Margaret wife to Richard Cowper of Saltmarshe, buried 16 Sep 1612.

Brigett dau. to George Pearson of Howden, buried 12 Mar 1612/3.

John Pearson of Cotness, young man, buried 25 Jan 1614/5.

John Cowper of Howden, buried 2 Oct 1616.

Edward Pearson of Howden, buried 22 Aug 1619.

An Pearson of Howden, excommunicated 23 May 1620.

Jane dau. to George Pearson of Howden, buried 19 Jul 1621.

Nicholas son to George Pearson of Howden, buried 16 Nov 1621.

Marie dau. to John Pearson of Howden, buried 22 Nov 1621.

A son to Phillip Pearson of Skelton, buried 30 Dec 1621.

Jane dau. to John Pearson of Howden, buried 1 Sep 1624.

Dorcas Pearson of Howden, buried 17 Oct 1624.

Joseph son to Margarett Pearson of Skelton, buried 31 Jul 1626.

John Pearson of Barmby, buried 6 Apr 1627.

Richard Cowper of Saltmarshe, buried 16 Oct 1628.

Elizabeth wife to William Pearson of Howden, buried 20 Sep 1629.

John Pearson of Howden, buried 7 Feb 1635/6.

John son to John Pearson of Kilpin, buried 19 Sep 1636.

An Pearson of Barmby, widow, buried 22 Jun 1638.

Elizabeth wife to Richard Pearson of Laxton, buried 3 Oct 1639.

John son to Thomas Pearson of Asselby, buried 26 Dec 1639.

Bartholomew son to Thomas Pearson of Asselby, buried 1 May 1641.

Thomas son to Phillip Pearson of Skelton, buried 26 May 1643.

An dau. to John Pearson of Howden, buried 31 Jul 1643.

Marie dau. to Robert Pearson of Asselby, buried 30 Sep 1643.

A son to John Pearson of Asselby, buried 28 Oct 1643.

Richard Pearson of Howden, buried 13 Sep 1644.

Katheran dau. to Richard Pearson late of Howden, buried 21 Sep 1644.

George son to George Pearson of Howden, buried 20 Feb 1645/6.

Elizabeth wife to George Pearson of Howden, buried 24 Dec 1647.

William son to Robert Pearson of Howden, buried 25 Mar 1650.

Stephen son to John Pearson of Asselby, buried 27 Feb 1650/1.

Issabel wife of Christopher Person of Booth, buried 9 Feb 1652/3.

Wife to Alexander Pearson of Laxton, buried 3 Mar 1652/3.

George Pearson of Howden buried 6 Dec 1653.

Jane, wife to Phillip Pearson of Skelton buried 11 Dec 1653. (Jane Cowper)

Joseph sonn to Thomas Pearson of Asselby buried 29 Dec 1653.

Anne dau to Robert Pearson of Asselby buried 4 May 1654.

Francis son to Anne Pearson of Skelton, spinster, buried 17 Jul 1655.

John Pearson son to Phillipp Pearson of Skelton, young man, buried 27 Oct 1655. (c. 1631/2)

A son to Robert Pearson of Asselby, tailor, buried 3 Nov 1655.

Ann wife to Robert Pearson of Howden, glover, buried 10 Jul 1656.

Mary Pearson of Asselby, widdow, buried 16 Oct 1656.

Mary Pearson of Barmby, spinster, buried 30 Nov 1656.

Robert son to Robert Pearson, buried 7 Dec 1657. (of Asselby?)

Phillip son to Phillip Pearson of Skelton, buried 19 Feb 1657/8.

Anne wife to John Pearson of Howden, buried 22 Jun 1658.

John son to Savage Pearson of Laxton, buried 17 Dec 1658.

Phillip Pearson of Skelton, buried 2 Apr 1663.

William Pearson of Barmby, buried 3 May 1665.

Anne dau. to John Pierson of Skelton, buried 17 Dec 1666.

Savage Peirson of Balkholme, buried 4 Feb 1666/7.

Mary wife to Thomas Peirson of Asselby, buried 21 Jan 1670/1.

Thomas Pierson of Asselby, buried 26 May 1672.

Anne dau. to Robert Pierson of Asselby, buried 19 Aug 1678.

Barbara wife of John Pierson of Skelton, buried 30 Jan 1678/9.

Ann wife to Robert Pearson of Asselby, buried 12 Apr 1681.

Robert son to John Pearson of Asselby, buried 7 Jun 1686.

Robert Pearson of Asselby, buried 29 Nov 1687.

Analysis of Family Groups in Howden

In the following analysis, the seven Pearsons labeled A through G are believed to be siblings of the oldest Pearson generation at Howden. Their children are indented under them and grandchildren indented further, etc.:

A. John Pearson, called "Old John Pearson" in his burial record, was born about 1517, and buried 21 Oct 1570 at Howden. He married 1st about 1538 Catherine _____ (bur. 7 Oct 1546 at Howden, Knedlington, or Booth - all within Howden parish), and married 2nd about 1548 Elizabeth _____ (bur. 6 Jan 1564/5 at Howden).

Probable children by John Pearson's 1st wife Catherine:

1. Robert Pearson, born ca. 1539, butcher, bur. 18 Nov 1581 Howden, of Howden at marriage, m. 16 Sep 1560 Hellen (Ellinor) _____ (bur. Ellinor 19 Sep 1581 Howden), children christened or buried at Howden;

   (1) Janeta c. 7 Dec 1561;

   (2) Francis (M) c. 7 Feb 1562/3;

   (3) Elizabeth c. 13 Aug 1564, bur. 13 Aug 1564;

   (4) Nicholas c. 22 Oct 1565, of Howden at children's christenings and burials;

      (a) John bur. 9 May 1589;

      (b) John c. 8 Oct 1590;

      (c) Thomas c. 7 Dec 1591 (Inherited Moscraft near Beverley), see chapter 3 for more details;

      (d) Henrie c. 30 Sep 1593, bur. 3 Jan 1593/4;

      (e) Robert c. 6 Jan 1597/8, bur. 10 Jan 1597/8.

   (5) Katherina c. 16 May 1568, bur. 6 Nov 1568;

   (6) Joan bur. 17 May 1569;

   (7) Alicia c. 23 Jan 1572/3, bur. 11 May 1574;

   (8) Catherine c. 6 Dec 1576;

   (9) Frances (F) bur. 1 Dec 1583.

2. William Peerson, born ca. 1541, bur. 16 Mar 1587/8, of Kilpin at burial, of Asselby (2 miles west of Howden within Howden parish) at 1st marriage, m. 1st 23 Jan 1562/3 Julian Collin (d. ca. 1581), m. 2nd 19 Oct 1581 Alison Bushbie (bur. 3 Mar 1586/7), William of Kilpin at 2nd marriage, William of Asselby at children's christenings, all by first wife Julian;

   (1) Dorothea c. 24 Oct 1563;

   (2) Alice bur. 14 Aug 1565;

   (3) Margareta c. 30 Dec 1565;

(4) Thomas c. 27 Dec 1570, bur. 27 Dec 1570;

(5) Nicholas c. 2 Feb 1572/3, bur. 19 Feb 1572/3;

(6) Thomas c. 17 Jul 1574 (m. 14 Aug 1593 Grace Marshall at Guiseley, Yorkshire, lived at Bradford, Yorkshire, and later Guiseley, and had a son (among others) Rev. Abraham Pierson c. 22 Sep 1611 at Guiseley, Yorkshire, who went to America 1639), see chapter 4 for more details.

(7) Christopher b. ca. 1576, of Howden at marriage, m. 2 Oct 1597 Jane ____ at Howden, Christopher of Howden at children's christenings, all children christened at Howden;

    (a) Milisant c. 21 Jun 1599;

    (b) John c. 30 Aug 1600;

    (c) William c. 20 Dec 1602.

(8) John b. ca. 1580, bur. 7 Feb 1635/6 (will at Beverley 1636), of Howden at marriage, m. 1st 19 Feb 1603/4 Jane ____ at Howden (she d. ca. 1617), m. 2nd ca. 1618 Mary ____ (mentioned in John's will, bur. 16 Oct 1656 Howden, of Asselby ,widow at burial), "John of Howden" at all children's births which are at Howden;

John had children by his first wife Jane:

    (a) Elizabeth c. 3 May 1604, bur. 19 Nov 1604;

    (b) Elizabeth c. 9 Oct 1605, bur. 17 Sep 1607;

    (c) William c. 5 Nov 1607, bur. 16 Nov 1607;

    (d) John c. 8 Dec 1608, (mentioned in his father's will 1636, eldest living son, went to America 1637), see chapter 4 for more details;

    (e) Frances (F) c. 9 Feb 1610/11, bur. 14 Sep 1612;

    (f) Thomas c. 16 Jan 1612/13, mentioned in his father's will 1636, see chapter 4 for more details;

    (g) William c. 17 Dec 1614, not mentioned in his father's 1636 will (died before 1636?);

    (h) An c. 11 Feb 1616/7, not mentioned in her father's 1636 will (mentioned as sister Hannah of Edward in 1650 at Beverley);

John had children by his second wife Mary:

    (i) Mary c. 27 Mar 1619, bur. Marie 22 Nov 1621;

    (j) Edward c. 11 Nov 1620, mentioned in his father's will 1636, for more detail see chapter 4;

    (k) Jane c. 15 Dec 1622, bur. 1 Sep 1624;

(l) Elizabeth c. 8 Jan 1624/5, mentioned in her father's will 1636, for more detail see chapter 4.

3. John Pearson, born ca. 1543, bur. 18 Mar 1546/7 (no parent given) at Howden, Knedlington, or Booth;

4. Agnes Pearson, born ca. 1545, bur. 10 Jul 1546 (no parent given) at Howden, Knedlington, or Booth.

Probable children by John Pearson's 2nd wife Elizabeth (Thomas is a proven son):

5. Thomas Pearson, butcher, c. 18 Nov 1549 Howden, father John, bur. 15 Feb 1583/4 Howden, of Howden at marriage, m. 23 Nov 1572 Elizabeth Fawne at Howden, of Howden at children's christenings and burials at Howden;

    (1) Elizabetha c. 18 Apr 1574, bur. 19 Aug 1574;

    (2) Johanna c. 13 Jul 1575, bur. Joane 13 Mar 1577/8;

    (3) Guilmus (William) c. 19 Sep 1577 (William probably went to Olney, Buckinghamshire, m. Wyborro Griggs 1609 and had son Harry (Henry) Peirson 1615 who went to America 1639, William bur. 1616 Lavendon, Buckinghamshire), see chapter 3 for more details;

    (4) Elena c. 24 Feb 1579/80, bur. Eleanor 3 Nov 1582;

    (5) Dorothea c. 10 Feb 1582/3.

6. Henrie Pearson, born ca. 1551, of Howden, m. 27 Apr 1574 at Howden, Margaret Williamson of Howden;

    (1) Jone bur. 29 Jan 1604/5;

7. Jennet Pearson, b. ca. 1553, m. 8 May 1571 William Dun Jr at Howden;

8. Marion Pearson, born ca. 1559, m. at Howden 15 Sep 1577 Thomas Middleton of Hambleton (12 miles west of Howden);

9. John Peerson, born ca. 1561, of Skelton at his marriage, bur. 1 Oct 1592 Howden, m. 15 Nov 1584 Elizabeth Stamp of Kilpin at Howden (bur. 15 Oct 1592), John was of Howden at the christenings of all his children, all children were christened or buried at Howden;

    (1) Edward c. 22 Oct 1585, bur. 24 Nov 1585;

    (2) Robart c. 25 Dec 1586, bur. 8 May 1588;

    (3) Ellinor c. 20 Feb 1588/9;

    (4) Jane c. 17 Sep 1592, bur. Jone 11 Oct 1592.

10. Edward Pearson, born ca. 1563, of Howden at burial, bur. 22 Aug 1619, m. 1st ca. 1584 Isabell _____ (bur. 9 Dec 1592), m. 2nd ca. 1593 Anne (reference 1615 Howden land transaction[1] for Edward Pearson and Anne his wife), "Edward of Howden" at all of his children's christenings and burials, all children's christenings and burials at Howden:

Edward had children by his first wife Isabell:

(1) Elizabeth c. 13 Oct 1585 (based on a younger sister Elizabeth below perhaps this Elizabeth died young);

(2) Alice bur. 3 Apr 1587;

(3) Elizabeth c. 13 Jan 1587/8;

(4) Marie c. 20 Mar 1589/90;

(5) John c. 23 Sep 1592, bur 23 Apr 1593;

Edward had children by his second wife Anne:

(6) Barbara c. 22 Oct 1594, m. 30 Jan 1615/6 William Smythson of Cotness at Howden;

(7) Henrie c. 20 Mar 1595/6, bur. 7 Jun 1597;

(8) Richard c. 22 May 1597;

(9) An c. 31 Aug 1598, "An Pierson excommunicated 23 May 1620" (either this An, or her mother Anne, or C. 1. (1) John Pearson's wife An);

(10) Tomisine c. 14 Aug 1599.

11. Joan Peerson, born ca. Jan 1564/5, m. 5 Aug 1583 Richard Leaven of Goole at Howden.

B. Thomas Pearson, of Saltmarshe at burial, bur. 27 Mar 1569, had children, some probable:

1. Thomas, bur. 6 Jun 1545 at Howden, Knedlington, or Booth;

2. John, son to Thomas Peerson, bur. 30 Sep 1545 Saltmarshe;

3. Alicia Pearson, c. 12 Oct 1546 Howden (no parent given);

4. Thomas Pearson, bur. 1 Jan 1547/8 at Howden, Knedlington, or Booth;

5. Katherina, dau. of Thomas Pearson, c. 20 Jul 1548;

6. John, b. ca. 1550, of Saltmarshe at burial, bur. 3 Jun 1588, m. 1st 15 Jun 1572 Dorothie Wells (bur. 12 Jul 1578), m. 2nd 15 Nov 1579 Elizabeth (Isabell?) Webster (Isabell Pearson of Saltmarshe, widow, bur. 19 Dec 1590, and Isabella Webster c. 27 Oct 1560, father Milanis (Miles) Webster of Barmby), John of Saltmarshe at all children's christenings and burials:

[1]The Yorkshire Archaeological Society, *Record Series Vol. 53, Yorkshire Fines for the Stuart Period Vol. I*, Edited by William Brigg, Printed for the Society, 1915, p. 49.

Child of John by his first wife Dorothie Wells:

(1) John c. 25 Mar 1574, bur. 29 Apr 1574;

Children of John by his second wife Isabella Webster:

(2) Robert c. 15 Sep 1580;

(3) Cicilia c. 15 Jan 1581/2;

(4) John c. 12 Jan 1582/3, bur. 24 Jan 1582/3;

(5) Isabell c. 8 Apr 1585, bur. 4 Jul 1587;

(6) John bur. 18 Jul 1586;

(7) Joane c. 13 Nov 1587, bur. Jane 15 Nov 1587.

7. Thomas, b. ca. 1568, of Saltmarshe at burial, bur. 29 Dec 1605, of Saltmarshe at marriage, m. 31 Jul 1591 Agnes _____, Thomas of Saltmarshe at all children's christenings;

(1) Tomasine c. 6 Apr 1593;

(2) Philip c. 31 Jan 1595/6, of Skelton at burial, bur. 2 Apr 1663, of Yokefleet at marriage, m. 15 Nov 1621 Jane Cowper (bur. 11 Dec 1653, wife of Phillip Pearson of Skelton), Philip of Skelton at all children's christenings and burials;

(a) A son bur. 30 Dec 1621;

(b) Thomas c. 25 Jan 1622/3, bur. 26 May 1643;

(c) Margaret c. 15 Mar 1625/6, of Skelton at marriage, m. 28 Jan 1655/6 at Saltmarshe, Lawrence Graburne of Saltmarshe, husbandman, witnesses Phillip Pearson, her father, and Arthur Kirby, both of Skelton;

(d) An c. 29 Mar 1629;

(e) John c. 20 Jan 1631/2, bur. 27 Oct 1655 (a young man);

(f) Robert c. 19 Nov 1634;

(g) Phillip c. 25 Nov 1637, bur. 19 Feb 1657/8.

(3) Thomas c. 16 Dec 1598;

(4) Margaret c. 11 Jan 1601/2;

(5) Grace c. 27 Apr 1605, m. 2 May 1629 Thomas Jewett of Saltmarshe.

C. William Pearson, born ca. 1523, of Howden, had children at Howden;

1. Robert c. 24 Jul 1545 (no parent given);

(1) John , b. ca. 1581 (no christening, no parent of record), bur. 6 Apr 1627 of Barmby (4 miles west of Howden within the Howden parish), m. ca. 1602 An (Bartholomew?) (bur. 22 Jun 1638, widow of Barmby). They had children at Barmby:

(a) Elizabeth c. 2 Jul 1603, m. 5 Feb 1624/5 Thomas Richman of Osgodby;

(b) William c. 25 Oct 1605, bur. 3 May 1665 of Barmby;

(c) An c. 25 Oct 1605 (twin of William?);

(d) Grace c. 3 Sep 1608;

(e) Thomas c. 28 Oct 1610, bur. 26 May 1672 of Asselby (2 miles west of Howden within the Howden parish), m. 20 May 1638 Marie Underwood (Mary bur. 21 Jan 1670/1). They had children at Asselby:

> i. John c. 22 Jan 1638/9, bur. 26 Dec 1639;
>
> ii. Bartholomew c. 27 Apr 1641, bur. 1 May 1641;
>
> iii. Joseph bur. 29 Dec 1653.

(f) Savage c. 6 Feb 1612/3, bur. 4 Feb 1666/7 of Balkholme, m. 17 Jan 1655/6 Anne Lyon of Laxton, had child;

> i. John bur. 17 Dec 1658 of Laxton.

(g) Dorothie c. 2 Mar 1615/6;

(h) Bartholomew b. ca. 1618 (not recorded at Howden), went to America 1639;

(i) Robert, tailor, c. 27 Nov 1619, bur. 29 Nov 1687, m. ca. 1642 Ann _____ (bur. 12 Apr 1681), had children at Asselby;

> i. Marie bur. 30 Sep 1643;
>
> ii. Joseph c. 8 Jul 1649;
>
> iii. Robert c. 16 Jan 1652/3, bur. a son 3 Nov 1655;
>
> iv. Ann bur. 4 May 1654;
>
> v. Robert b. 24 Feb 1655/6, bur. 7 Dec 1657;
>
> vi. Anne bur. 19 Aug 1678.

(j) Dorcas bur. 17 Oct 1624 (no parent given).

2. Margaret bur. 10 Mar 1549/50;

3. George c. 3 Apr 1550 (bur. 16 Nov 1551);

4. Cuthbert c. 17 Apr 1552.

D. George Pearson, born ca. 1525, bur. 8 Feb 1569/70 at Howden, m. 27 Jul 1546 Agnes _____ (bur. 28 May 1571 Howden), had children, all at Howden;

1. John bur. 12 Dec 1550;

2. George c. 25 Nov 1550;

3. Alicia c. 17 Feb 1551/2, m. 10 Aug 1572 Thomas Richardson of Howden;

4. Richard Pearson, b. ca. 1556, bur. 17 Dec 1593 at Howden, of Howden at marriage, m. 5 Jul 1579 Alice Hartfirth (bur. 26 Nov 1593) at Howden, Richard of Howden at all children's christenings, children christened at Howden;

> (1) Elizabeth c. 29 May 1580, bur. 27 Jan 1580/1;

> (2) George c. 8 Apr 1582, bur. 26 Jan 1583/4;

> (3) George c. 26 Sep 1584, bur. 6 Dec 1653, m. 27 Aug 1610 at Howden, Elizabeth _____ (bur. 24 Dec 1647 Howden), George of Howden at marriage and christening of children after Brigett, was of Barmby when Brigett christened, all children christened at Howden;

>> (a) Brigett c. 6 Mar 1610/11, bur. 12 Mar 1612/3;

>> (b) Elizabeth c. 6 Feb 1612/3, m. 15 Oct 1635 Leonard Branton of Knedlington;

>> (c) John c. 23 Jul 1615, husbandman, of Asselby at children's christenings, all children christened at Howden;

>>> (i) A son bur. 28 Oct 1643;

>>> (ii) An c. 2 Nov 1644;

>>> (iii) Stephan bur. 27 Feb 1650/1;

>>> (iv) Stephan b. 16 Jan 1653/4;

>>> (v) Sarah b. 4 Jul 1659, bur. 25 Sep 1659;

>>> (vi) Robert bur. 7 Jun 1686.

>> (d) Jane c. 1 Feb 1617/8, bur. 19 Jul 1621;

>> (e) Nicholas c. 9 Apr 1620, bur. 16 Nov 1621;

>> (f) George c. 23 Oct 1622, bur. 20 Feb 1645/6;

>> (g) Robert c. 3 Jun 1626, glover of Howden when wife Ann died in 1656, m. 1st Ann _____ (bur. 10 Jul 1656), m. 2nd 21 Oct 1656 Ailse Wrey at Howden, Robert of Howden at children's christening and burial;

>> Children by Robert's first wife Ann:

>>> (i) William bur. 25 Mar 1650;

>>> (ii) George c. 27 Apr 1651.

>> (h) Alice c. 26 Sep 1629.

> (4) Edward c. 6 Apr 1587.

5. Dorothie bur. 19 Dec 1559.

E. Richard Pearson, born ca. 1533, m. about 1554;

> 1. Anna c. 26 Feb 1555/6 Howden.

F. Robert Pearson, born ca. 1540, bur. 13 Sep 1589 Swinefleet (located 4 miles south of Howden on the south side of the River Ouse within Howden Parish);

G. Alicia Pearson c. 16 Jul 1546 at Howden (no parents given).

There are remaining a few Pearson records in the Howden parish records which could not be placed in a family. However, these Pearson records still appear in the front of this appendix in date order with the other Pearson christenings, marriages, and burials.

Appendix B
Problem Research for 1600s Immigrants

Deacon John Pearson of Rowley, Massachusetts, 1643

Deacon John Pearson's origins before Rowley have been given differently by the following three authors:

"1 John Pearson[1] (Deacon), came from Essex county, England, in pursuit of religious freedom, and settled in Rowley, Mass., in 1643. He mar. Dorcas _____; and died in Rowley, Dec. 22, 1693. In 1643, he set up the earliest saw-mill in America (the running of which has been continued by some of his descendants ever since). He was made freeman of Rowley, probably in 1647; was representative from 1678, for several years. Was the first Deacon of the old Rowley church, and was an earnest advocate of the gospel truths. In the Colonial Records his name often appears, and was written Peirson; but his descendants write it Pearson. He had chd. 2 Mary; 3 John, b. 1644; 4 Eliz.; 5 Samuel, b. 1648; 6 Dorcas; 7 Mary; 8 Jeremiah, b. 1653; 9 Sarah; 10 Joseph, b. 1656; 11 Benjamin, b. 1658; 12 Phebe; 13 Stephen, b. 1663; and 14 Sarah."

Deacon John Pearson[2] was "born about 1616 in England and came to Ipswich, Massachusetts, at the age of 30. Remained in Ipswich a short time before moving to Rowley, Massachusetts."

"Deacon John Pearson[3] was not of the first company but a very early settler, probably 1643. It is tradition in the family that he was a native of Yorkshire, England. The date of his birth is not known, though probably before 1610. His name is first mentioned on the Rowley records in the birth records of his children, 1643. He was made freeman, 26 May 1647, and ordained Deacon of the Rowley Church 24 Oct 1686."

In the data provided by the first source, *Pierson Genealogical Records*, John Pearson was born in Essex county, England. Search of English records via the International Genealogical Index provided no possible christening record. However his death date of 22 Dec 1693 is considered a very good clue in determining the range of his birth year. If we assume that he lived to about age 83, he would have been born about 1610 or later.

In the data provided by the second source, *Four Generations of the Descendants of John and Dorcus Pearson of Rowley Massachusetts in 1643*, John Pearson was born about 1616 and came to Ipswich, Massachusetts, at age 30. That would mean that he came to Ipswich about 1646, yet he was at Rowley by 1643. Thus it is concluded that this source is inaccurate, at least about the age.

In the data provided by the third source, *The Early Settlers of Rowley, Massachusetts*, John Pearson arrived at Rowley in 1643, was probably born before 1610, and was ordained as Deacon to the Rowley Church in 1686. If his birth and Deaconship dates are correct as

---

[1]Lizzie B. Pierson, *Pierson Genealogical Records*, Joel Munsell, Printer, Albany, New York, 1878, p. 54.
[2]The book, *Four Generations of the Descendants of John and Dorcus Pearson of Rowley Massachusetts in 1643*, reference 17 Aug 1996 E-mail from Katharine Ulatt of Wisconsin to Roberta Pierson of California.
[3]Blodgette and Jewett, *The Early Settlers of Rowley, Massachusetts*.

given, then he became a Deacon at age 76 or older. This seems a little old to take on this job, though possible. Thus, it is suspected that the birth year before 1610 is inaccurate. This source also mentioned that it was family tradition that John Pearson was a native of Yorkshire, England. This is in direct difference to Essex county, England mentioned by *Pierson Genealogical Records*. Since Essex county data struck out and family tradition is mentioned, the origin of Yorkshire, England is believed to be more accurate.

If we assume that John was at least age 21 when he married and age 22 when his first child Mary was born in 1643 at Rowley, then Deacon John Pearson was born in 1621 or earlier. Based on all of the above, a computer search in English IGIs was conducted in Yorkshire for the christening of John Pearson between 1600 and 1621. Twenty three records met a criteria which looked for a father John (based on Deacon John Pearson's children's names which included John as the first male child). Within these 23 records, one stood out because the mother's name was Elizabeth which is also one of Deacon John's children's names. That record read:

> "John Pearson christened 16 Dec 1619, father John Pearson, mother Elizabeth Denton, Sheffield, Yorkshire, England."

The normal way to see if this theory holds water, is to obtain the Parish records for Sheffield and try to determine if this John, c. 16 Dec 1619, died young or married and stayed and had children. If none of these things occur, that is some support for the choice that he left town without dying though not a proof of him being the right John. No record of a John Pearson marrying a Dorcus was found in English IGI records. Unfortunately, Sheffield is the town which contained the largest number of Pearsons (all spellings) in Yorkshire in the 1600s. There are numerous John Pearsons in Sheffield, and separating them is sometimes difficult. But parish recorders usually tried to identify which of them was which some way. Occasionally, one can even find a church record reference to a person going to America, if you're lucky! No relation of the John Pearson/Elizabeth Denton family of Sheffield to other New England Pearson immigrant families of Yorkshire is known, though a connection is possible. Obviously, more work can be done here, but that is left to the descendants of Deacon John Pearson to conduct as it will not be timely for this book. Remember, surname spelling in England of that era was established by the recorder and not the family. So look at all the Pearson spellings.

Samuel Peirson of Philadelphia, Pennsylvania, 1699

"Samuel Peirson[4], emigrated from Yorkshire, England; and settled in Philadelphia about 1699. He belonged to the Society of Friends; was twice married. He and family removed to the back settlements in North Carolina; and in the war which ended in 1763 (French and Indian wars) is said to have been murdered, with all his family (except two children) by the Indians. By his first wife he had chd. 2 Samuel; 3 Thomas; 4 George; 5 Mary; and 6 Elizabeth."

In making a computer search for a Samuel Peirson, christened between 1678 and 1698 in Yorkshire, in the English IGIs, none were found. However, it is known that an earlier

---

[4]Lizzie B. Pierson, *Pierson Genealogical Records*, Joel Munsell, Printer, Albany, New York, 1878, p. 59.

family at Dewsbury, Yorkshire, exists: a Rev. Samuel Pierson (c. 27 Feb 1603/4 Guiseley, Yorkshire) with father Thomas (c. 17 Jul 1574 Howden, Yorkshire) and son Samuel (c. 11 Apr 1632 Dewsbury, Yorkshire). This matches the children's names of Samuel Peirson of Philadelphia by his first wife. Therefore, a search of the son Samuel's (c. 1632), or his brothers', families should be made, starting with the parish records of Dewsbury, Yorkshire, England, looking for a grandson Samuel (born about 1670?) who could be our Samuel of Philadelphia in 1699. See Thomas Pierson Sr. in Chapter 4 of this book for more details on this family. Obviously, more work can be done here, but that is left to the descendants of Samuel Peirson of Philadelphia to conduct as it will not be timely for this book.

Unidentified Passengers to America

"The Endeavor," George Thorp, master, arrived (location unknown) 29 July 1683[5].

> John Pierson of Poormell
> Thomas Pierson, mason, of Poormell
> Mary Pierson, wife of Thomas

Comments on Using LDS IGIs

A large number of parish records of the 1500s and 1600s in England have been entered into the Church of Jesus Christ of Latter-Day Saints (LDS) International Genealogical Index (IGI), available on CD ROM (compact-disk read-only-memory) through the FamilySearch computer program at LDS local Family History Centers throughout the world. Those records are identified by the categories "christened" and "marriage" with exact dates. Available parish death or burial records have not been entered into the IGI. And when identifiers of a person are given in parish records, such as "of Barmby" or "butcher," these identifiers are not entered into the IGI.

Comments on Completeness of Available Parish Records

Keeping parish records began wide-spread compliance in England about 1600. But tensions leading to the English Civil War began about 1620 and records were sparse from 1620 to 1640 when they became almost non-existent until 1660, when the Civil War was over and the Puritans no longer in charge of government. In addition to sparse and non-existent records, some existing parish records were destroyed in the 1640s during the English Civil War. Thus, the record that you are looking for may not exist today. Let us hope that this situation does not dampen your research efforts too much. The authors of *Pierson Millennium* wish you luck!

Comments on Searching for Parents in England

Remember, in the 1500s and 1600s, it was against the law to have more than one given name in England. Thus, identities for common names like John are a nightmare. However, it was common for the husband's father's name to be given to his first son, and that followed by the wife's father's name, and then (as with the immigrant Rev. Abraham

---

[5]H. Stanley Craig, Salem County New Jersey Genealogical Data Prior to 1800, Vol. I, published by H. Stanley Craig, Merchantville, N.J., no publication date (microfilmed by the LDS church 15 Nov 1977), p. 297.

Pierson) children were named after the husband's or wife's siblings. This is <u>very consistent</u> in England, <u>except</u> when a father dies while his son is too young to remember him - then no family given names are carried down by the son (as with the immigrant Henry Peirson).

Place Index

Name Index

Hannah E., 180
Jonathan, 161
Jonathan Col., 205
Jonathan Lt. Col., 250
Martha, 190
Nathan, 190
Nathaniel, 190
Phebe, 190, 205
Ruth, 205
Samuel O., 180
Sarah, 190
Sarah (Baker), 190,
    207
Stephen, 157, 190, 266
Susanna, 190(2)
Susannah, 190
Tristrum, 108
William, 190
Heim
    Antoinette Louise, 146
    Raymond G., 146
Hendee
    A. L., 149
    Hannah, 148
    R., 148
Henden
    Edward, 76
    Elizabeth (Chrich), 76
    John, 76(2)
    Simon, 75(2)
    Susan (Brickenden), 76
    Symon, 76
    Thomasin, 75(2), 76
Henderson, 213
    Hannah, 213
Hendirson
    Katherine, 79
Herrick
    Abigail, 135
    Austin, 135
    Edward, 135(2)
    George, 134
    George 2d Maj., 250
    Herman, 134
    James, 107, 113
    Mary, 134
    Mehetable, 226
    Nathan, 177
    Phoebe, 134
    Stephen, 134
    William, 134(5)
    William Pierson, 134
Hildreth
    Ephraim, 175
    James, 155

Joshua, 186
Peter, 182, 184
Sarah, 186
Thomas, 107, 108, 111
Hillyer
    Asa Rev., 216
    Dr., 217
    Margaret, 216
Hinds
    John, 195
Hine
    Bennet, 234
    Sophia, 234(2)
Hineman
    Mary, 140
Hinkel
    Elizabeth, 172, 187
Hinman
    Sarah, 242
Hitchcock
    Mary, 239
Hitchens
    Rosemarie Joan, 139
Hitt
    Angela Blair, 171
    Jeffery Scott, 171
    Joni Marlene, 171
    Samantha Christine,
        171
Hoeltzel
    Rosa, 146
Holabird
    Addie A., 224
    Alice, 225
    Ellen, 225
    Eugene F., 225
    James H., 225
    Maria, 225
    Oliver, 225
    Oscar L., 224
    Polly, 225
    William, 225
Holbrook
    Abil, 233
    Irene, 234
    Ruth, 233
Holden
    E., 246
    Hannah, 246
    J., 246, 247
    Lois, 246
    Lucy, 247
Holley
    Jane, 138
    Jenny, 138

Mary (Lewis), 139
Sara, 138, 139
William, 139
Holmes
    Angeline, 213
    Jonathan Capt., 254
Holt
    A., 246
    Roxana, 246
Hood
    Lois, 237
    Samuel, 237
Hopkins
    Eliza, 241
    Marshall B., 241
    Oceanus, 84
Horton
    John, 204
    Joseph D., 197
    Piersa, 173, 187
    Sarah, 197
Hosmer
    A., 150
    Amanda, 150
    Mary Ann, 150
    Sophia M., 150
    T. B., 150
    W. T., 150
Hotchkiss, 236
    Anna, 236
    Caroline, 241
    Carrie Louisa, 241
    Franklin Augustus, 241
    Frederick A., 241
    Hattie, 241
    Mary, 241
    S. C., 91
Howard
    Thomas, 43
Howe, 257(3)
    (also see Howes)
    Daniel, 106
    Diadama, 144
    F. S., 100
    Miss, 240
    Mr., 108
    Richard Lord Adm.,
        257
    William Sir Gen., 257
Howell, 266
    Abraham, 154, 267
    Ann, 173, 187
    Arthur, 164
    Capt., 117
    Col., 155(2)

Daniel, 130
David Capt., 250
Edward, 106(2), 109,
    111, 113(3),
    120, 123, 207,
    264, 265
Edward Mr., 265
Elizabeth, 130, 140
Eva M., 146
Frank, 146
George Rogers, 1, 125
George Rogers Rev.,
    218
Gilbert, 143
Henry, 207
John, 108, 111(2), 113,
    120, 123, 124,
    147, 155
John Capt., 264
John Capt., 117(2)
John Jr., 127, 263(2)
John Maj., 153, 154,
    155, 265(2)
Josiah Capt., 250
Maj., 265
Martha, 188
Mary, 99, 253
Mathew, 119, 124(2),
    194(2), 201(2),
    265
Matthew Col., 155
Mr., 108
Mrs., 113(3)
Nathan Lt., 156
Nathaniel, 181
Phineas Quarter
    Master, 250
Prudence, 155, 178(2)
Richard, 105, 111, 113
Stephen Capt., 250
Susanna, 164
Susannah, 153(2)
Theophilus, 155, 177,
    181, 267
Howes
    Daniel, 35(2), 115
    Jane (Brymley), 115
Hoyt, 238
    Abigail, 238(2)
    Freeman, 238
    Hannah, 235
    Joel, 238(3)
    Lorina (Finch), 239
    Mehetabel, 238
Hubbard

Gilbert, 184, 190
Gordon, 202, 208(3), 209
Grace, 52, 53(2), 56, 90, 273, 276(2), 285, 286
Grace (Marshall), 51, 53, 282
Grace (Plumb), 150
Grant W., 228
Grizel, 79(2)
Guillmus, 39
Gustavus C., 151
Guy Rowland P., 218
H. P. (Brown), 151
H. (Irish), 151
H. (Slusser), 152
H. (Robinson), 214
H. (Swaine), 245
Halsey, 207
Hamden, 150
Hamilton W., 91
Hamilton Wilcox D. D., 91
Hanah, 155
Hannah, 49, 59(2), 60(2), 91, 93, 94, 97, 101, 102(2), 133, 137, 144(2), 147, 148, 149, 151, 155, 156, 157(2), 160, 161, 162, 182, 189(2), 190(2), 191(2), 194(3), 195, 196, 204, 206, 209, 211, 212(2), 213, 214(2), 215, 219, 221, 223, 224, 233(2), 234(2), 236(2), 237, 238(2), 239, 246(4), 247(2), 253, 258, 267, 268, 269, 282
Hannah (Balch), 235, 255
Hannah (Baldwin), 212
Hannah (Barrett), 148
Hannah (Campbell), 223, 256

Hannah (Church), 137(2)
Hannah (Coe), 98
Hannah (Curtis), 239
Hannah (DeLong), 144
Hannah (Fairchild), 234
Hannah (Green), 160(3)
Hannah (Hedges), 207
Hannah (Hoyt), 235
Hannah (Munson), 238
Hannah (Peet), 236
Hannah Amarillis, 149
Hannah Ann, 144, 145
Hannah C., 152
Hannah N., 162, 269
Hannah P. (Latimer), 218
Hannah widow, 238
Hanson C., 224
Harlow W., 92
Harriet, 140, 162(2), 197, 213(3), 216, 229, 238(2), 269(2)
Harriet (Jones), 214
Harriet (Kingsland), 197
Harriet C., 218
Harriet E., 139, 150, 214
Harriet Louisa, 241
Harriet M., 151, 225
Harriet P., 151
Harriet W., 218
Harriette, 185
Harry, 33(2), 35(2), 79(3), 103, 104, 224, 229, 283
Harry N., 215
Harvey, 176, 227
Hattie B., 142
Hattie E., 185
Helen, 224
Helen (Cook), 208
Helen A., 214
Helen Dodge, 198
Helen M., 98, 225
Hellen, 37, 38, 272, 281
Heman King, 239, 240
Henrie, 38, 40, 74, 272, 275(2), 279(2), 281, 283, 284

Henrietta, 214
Henry, 5, 8(2), 27, 28, 30, 32(4), 33(4), 34(16), 35(3), 40, 42, 45(2), 47(2), 48(5), 49(6), 50(4), 51(2), 55(4), 57(2), 58(7), 59(2), 63, 74, 75(8), 76(5), 79(3), 83(2), 84, 87(4), 88(2), 101(2), 102(2), 103(10), 104(8), 105(12), 106(4), 107(2), 108(3), 109(10), 111(4), 112(5), 113(4), 114(11), 115(4), 116(4), 117(3), 118(9), 119(3), 120(15), 121(13), 122(4), 123(6), 124(9), 125(5), 126(2), 127(6), 128(4), 129(8), 130(4), 132, 135, 140, 144, 145, 150, 153(8), 154(10), 155(5), 156(3), 158, 159(2), 162(3), 164(6), 165, 166(2), 172, 174, 175, 176, 183, 184(3), 185(2), 187, 190, 193(7), 194(5), 195(6), 201(7), 214, 220, 232, 245, 249, 252, 260(2), 261, 262, 263(5), 264(3), 265(3), 266, 267(2), 269(2), 270(2), 279, 283, 292
Henry A., 100(2), 269
Henry Adelman, 145
Henry C., 150
Henry Clark, 239(3)
Henry Col., 110, 114, 124(2), 128,

153(5), 154(4), 155(4), 156, 163, 164, 177, 181, 187(2), 202, 260, 266(3), 267, 269
Henry E., 242
Henry Esq., 185(3)
Henry J., 145(2)
Henry Jr., 119, 153(2), 195(2)
Henry Lt., 117, 154(2)
Henry Lt. Col., 155(2)
Henry M., 229
Henry Martyn, 132
Henry Morse, 225, 226
Henry Mulford, 185(2)
Henry R., 172(2)
Henry R. Esq., 172
Henry R., 185
Henry Rayner, 144, 145
Henry S., 247
Henry Sr., 265
Henry W., 162, 230(5), 269
Hepsey (Peet), 235
Hepzibah (Camp), 212
Herbert, 145
Herbert Prescott, 145
Herman L., 150
Herrick Roosevelt Philetous, 5, 139
Hiel, 166(5), 167(3)
Hiel Jr., 167(2), 168(7), 169
Hiel Sr., 167(3)
Hillary, 29, 32
Hiram, 149(2), 179, 197, 206, 214(3), 224, 225, 227
Horace, 213, 219(2)
Horace L., 100
Horatio, 150(2)
Hosea, 247
Hugh, 29, 32(2), 36(2), 37, 49(2), 72(2)
Huldah, 236
Huldah (Churchill), 149
Huntting, 180
Ian Nathanial, 171
Ichabod Spencer, 236
Ida, 172
Inez, 137

Sarah Medora, 234,
235
Sarah Ogden, 228
Sarah R., 217
Sarah widow, 226
Savage, 56, 273, 276,
277, 280(2), 286
Saye, 30, 69, 70
Scott Wayne, 171
Selma (Van Cise), 146
Seth W., 152
Shadrach, 164(4),
165(12), 187(2),
254
Shadrach Private, 164
Shadrack Private, 254
Shane Johnson Gullery,
139
Sheldon, 234, 235
Sheldon P. Jr., 235
Sidney, 162, 219, 269
Sila, 174
Silas, 95, 96, 143(4),
144(7), 145,
148, 174, 175,
177, 178(5),
179(2), 180(6),
182(2), 183(2),
184, 209, 229,
230(2), 249
Silas Capt., 144(2),
183(2), 252(5)
Silas Jr., 183(3), 249
Silas Rayner, 145
Silas Spencer, 145(2)
Silas Sr. Capt., 183
Silvanus, 142, 143(3),
144(6), 172(2),
178, 186(14),
187, 188, 249,
251, 258,
259(2), 262
Simon, 91(2), 215
Smith, 224, 227
Smith Frisbie, 224, 225
Solon, 176
Sophia, 140, 166, 185,
234, 241
Sophia J., 97, 246
Sophia M., 150
Sophia W. (Edgecomb),
241
Squire 1st, 197(5), 198
Squire 2nd, 197(5), 198
Squire Henry, 185

Stanley King, 150
Starr, 234
Stephen, 8, 28, 47,
62(5), 63(11),
64(10), 164,
175(12), 176,
180, 194, 196,
197, 207(2),
209, 230(9),
231(9), 232(7),
233, 238,
239(4), 241,
249, 251,
255(2), 259(2),
262, 277, 280,
287(2), 289
Stephen 3d, 236,
238(4)
Stephen 4th, 236
Stephen Condit, 218(2)
Stephen Curtis, 239(3),
240
Stephen Day, 217, 218
Stephen H., 97(3)
Stephen Jr., 63, 232,
233
Stephen Private, 254
Stephen S., 227(2)
Stephen Sr., 233
Steven, 63, 64
Submit, 91
Suruiah, 196(2)
Susan, 35, 74, 225,
227, 240,
241(2), 246
Susan (Cone), 161
Susan (Harrison), 229
Susan (Lattison), 240
Susan (Skiff), 241
Susan Bishop, 229
Susan E., 150
Susan H., 229
Susan Lynn
(Robinson), 171
Susanah Mrs., 155
Susanna, 44, 53, 90,
91, 102, 164,
246(2)
Susanna (Russell), 227
Susannah, 102, 151,
152, 154(4),
155, 156(4),
182, 183, 184,
186, 188(4),

190(5), 236(2),
237, 267
Susannah (Howell),
153
Susannah (Wooster),
236
Susannah Mrs., 156
Sylvanus, 164, 174,
176, 182(3),
184(2), 186(3),
188, 190, 196,
199
Sylvester Condit, 95
Symon, 73(2)
Syrena S. (Prescott),
145
T. (Kendall), 245
Tabitha, 245
Taphena, 101
Temperance, 149, 162,
270
Terril, 206
Thankful, 91
Theodore, 114, 119,
124(5), 125,
126(3), 127,
128, 153,
154(2), 190,
193, 194(2),
201(12),
202(14), 203,
208(2), 209,
228, 267
Theodore Capt., 202
Theodore Francis,
209(2)
Theodore Job, 202
Theodore Job Capt.,
202
Theodore Job Justice,
202
Theodore Roosevelt,
142
Theodosia, 94(2)
Theophilus, 53, 90(2),
102(3), 155(2),
156(2), 163(8),
164(3), 175(4),
176(6), 196,
199, 202, 249,
251, 253, 259,
262, 266, 267
Theophilus Ens.,
175(5), 176,
253, 257, 259

Thomas, 8, 26(4), 28,
29, 30(11),
31(6), 32(9), 35,
36(4), 37, 38(5),
39(8), 40(2), 47,
49(11), 50(2),
51(7), 52(12),
53(2), 55(14),
56, 57(2), 59(7),
60(15), 61(2),
62(3), 63, 64(2),
69(12), 70(7),
72(6), 74(8),
75(2), 76(7),
77(3), 79, 81(2),
90(3), 173,
211(11), 212(2),
226, 228,
229(3), 232,
233(3), 234,
246(6), 272,
273(2), 274(5),
275(10), 276(7),
277(6), 278(5),
279(4), 280(3),
281, 282(3),
283(2), 284(5),
285(4), 286,
290, 291(3)
Thomas C., 150
Thomas Henry Anson,
138
Thomas Jefferson, 206
Thomas Jr., 90, 94(2),
233, 268
Thomas Mrs. (Brooke),
69(3)
Thomas Mrs. (Barnes),
70
Thomas Mrs. (Brooke),
70
Thomas Sr., 8, 62(3),
77, 209, 211(6),
221(2), 233(2),
291
Thomas W., 228(2)
Thompson, 215
Thornton P., 228(2)
Timothy, 73(2),
133(10), 134(4),
140, 141,
142(2), 143(2),
148, 182(3),
184, 186,
188(8), 190,

227, 229(5),
230(7), 233(3),
249(2), 251(2),
262(2)
Tomasine, 275(2), 284,
285
Truman, 237
U. (Allard), 246
Unis, 195(2), 196
Uriah Private, 254
Ursula, 48(2), 56(3), 57
Uzal, 101, 222(2),
223(3), 224(3),
228, 256(5)
Van Renslaelaer, 150
Vashti Maria, 150
Vesta, 246
Virginia, 228
Walter C., 226, 228
Warren, 237
Watson, 188
Wautier, 8, 25, 30(3),
78(2)
Welthy, 151
Willelmi, 44
Willelmus, 44
William, 5, 8, 26(2),
28(2), 30(4),
32(8), 33(7),
34(3), 35(7),
36(7), 39(6),
40(3), 41, 42(2),
44(6), 45(2),
48(2), 51(2),
52(2), 55(10),
56, 58, 59(4),
72(4), 73, 74(2),
79(2), 92,
103(6), 104(3),
130(5), 132,
134, 135(9),
136(6), 140(3),
141, 162, 172,
174(2), 176,
178(2), 180(2),
183(2), 196(9),
199(3), 200,
204(3), 205(7),
206(2), 207,
213(2), 214,
216(3), 217(2),
219(2), 223,
224(2), 226,
227, 228(2),
233, 234,

236(3), 246(7),
247(3), 254,
262, 263,
269(3), 272(3),
274(8), 275(2),
276(3), 277(4),
278(5), 279(2),
280(2), 281(3),
282(3), 283(3),
285, 286(2), 287
William A., 148
William B., 166, 214
William C., 144
William Capt., 205(3),
206(2)
William Clark, 144,
146
William Corp., 135
William D., 137
William Dr., 216(2)
William Eli, 243
William Ens., 135
William George, 225,
226
William H., 100(2),
136(2)
William H. Capt.,
136(2)
William H., 166, 237,
269
William Henry, 97, 141
William Holmes, 213
William Hugh, 217
William Hugh Dr., 217
William J., 213
William Jr., 196(2),
199
William Lt., 205
William M., 198
William Nelson,
166(2), 172
William R., 185,
235(2)
William S., 149,
150(2), 219(2)
William Seward, 93(3)
William Seward Dr.,
93
William T., 146
William Tracy, 146
Williams, 262
Willie, 132, 228
Willis, 214, 227, 269
Wilson G., 217(2)
Winfield, 142

Winfield S., 150
Winfield Scott, 142(2)
Winifred, 145
Winifred May, 169
Wyborro, 33, 35, 103,
104
Wyborro (Griggs),
33(2), 36, 44(2),
45, 48, 103(2),
283
Wyllis, 93
Zachariah, 174(2), 250,
251
Zebulon, 130, 178(3),
179(6), 249,
251, 252(2),
259(2), 262
Zechariah, 173, 174(8),
259(2)
Zecheriah, 249
Zenas, 213, 220(2)
Ziba, 222(2), 223(8),
256(7)
Zillah, 223, 239(2)
Zipporah, 158
Peck
Aaron Capt., 214, 229
Amirillis, 238
Augustus L., 240
Betsey, 238(2)
Calvin Dea., 238
Caroline, 228
Charlotte, 242
Enoch Pierson, 238
George Whitfield, 238
John Calvin, 238
Laura, 238
Laura Ann, 242
Mary Louisa, 240
Miranda, 214
Polly, 238
R., 220
Samuel F., 242
Samuel Ferris, 238
Sarah, 238
Peet
Hannah, 236
Hepsey, 235
Peirce
William Master, 85
Pelton
George, 168(2)
George Mrs., 168
M., 151
Pendleton

Amos Capt., 176, 259
Bryan, 124
Ephraim Capt., 184,
208, 258(2)
Mary, 124
Penney
Jennifer, 139(3)
Jenny, 83
John James, 139
Thelma Elizabeth
(Collins), 139
Pequot Indians, 110
Percy
Alan, 4, 7
Henry, 1(2)
Piers, 1
Serlo, 4
William, 1, 3(2), 4(7),
5(2), 6(8), 7(3),
19, 20, 23(2), 30
Perkins, 185
Sarah A. Rossiter, 185
Perry
Eliza, 220
John, 220
Orra, 149
Paulina, 236
R., 149
Roswell, 236
Perse
John, 56
Persen
Johannes 2d Lt., 252
Johannes Ens., 252
Person
John 2d Lt., 252
John Ens., 252
Peters
Hugh, Rev., 48
Peterson
Catherine E., 225
Cornelia, 225
Edward P., 225
Enos, 225
Enos Jr., 225
Mary, 225
Mary R., 225
Sally, 136
Walter, 225
Petty
Edward, 182
Martha, 182(2)
Philipot
John Esq., 76
Phillen

Polly, 224
Prudence, 241
Rachel, 221, 255
Rachel W., 205
Rebecca, 219
Rhoda A., 219
Richard, 107, 108, 111
Sarah C., 236
William Col., 156
Smythson
Barbara, 273, 284
William, 273, 284
Somers
Huldah M., 235
Soverhill
E. P., 145
Spaulding
I., 96, 268
Mary, 268
R. P., 93
Spear
Elizabeth, 234
Speece
Abigail Joanna, 169
Bowen Wesley, 169
Nancy Jane (Dull), 169
Spencer, 188, 247
Alanson, 188
Col., 254(2)
Evelina, 150
Harvey, 188
J. C. Dr., 150
Lydia, 247
Polly, 188
Spining
I., 96, 268, 269
Ruth, 268, 269
Stagg, 214
Eunice, 214
Stall
Caroline, 217
Stamp
Elizabeth, 40, 59, 273, 283
Elsabetha, 274
John, 274
Stanborough
Josiah, 106, 111(2)
Mr., 108, 112(2)
Peregrine, 163, 266
Peregrine Mr., 266
Stanhope
Richard, 51
Stanley
M. B., 150

Stapleton
James Hornsby, 138
Olla Mary Frances, 138
Stark
Jerusha, 239
Starr
Urana, 234
Steenwyck
Mr., 117(3)
Stephens
Nicholas, 116
Thomas, 154, 181
Stevens
Annetta, 149
B. E., 149
Lydia, 149
Stewart
Sally, 173, 187
Sarah, 173, 187
Stillman
Charles, 242
David, 242
Sarah, 242
Stirk
Christian, 79
Stockman
Sallie, 213
Stoddard
Rev., 233
Storre
Marie, 54(3), 55
Mary, 54
Thomas, 54(3)
Storrs
Charles B., 150
Henry M., 150
Vashti Maria, 150
Storye
Agnes, 273
Stow, 188
Mary, 188
Mr., 188
Polly, 188
Zebulon Capt., 179, 259
Strathclyde Welsh
Eugenius, 15
Stratton
Martha, 158
Richard, 107, 108
Stryker
Daniel, 216(2)
Harriett, 216
Isaac, 216
John, 216

Mary, 216
Phebe, 216
Stuart
Mary, 145
Studley
Amy, 240
Studwell
Augustus, 234
Martha B., 234
Sturges
Abigail, 239
Lewis Burr, 239
Styles
J., 102
Sullivan
John Gen., 257(2)
Sumter
Thomas, 260
Sutliff, 142
Amanda W., 142
Sutton
Ann (Howell), 173, 187
Anne, 173, 187
Elizabeth Ann, 173, 187
Fanny (Seward), 173, 187
James, 173, 187
Jeremiah, 173, 187
Jonathan, 173(2), 187(2)
Joseph, 173(4), 187(4)
Joseph Pierson, 173, 187
Julia Ann (Beach), 173, 187
Martha, 173(2), 187(2)
Martha (Upson), 173, 187
Martha Lupton, 173, 187
Mary, 173(2), 187(2)
Patience, 173, 187
Piersa (Horton), 173, 187
Rebecca, 173, 187
Sally (Stewart), 173, 187
Sarah (Stewart), 173, 187
Shadrach, 173, 187
Uriah, 173(2), 187(2)
Zebulon, 173, 187
Swain
H., 245

Lieut., 90
Thomas, 52
Swift
Sally, 234

- - T - -
Tabor
Lydia, 225
Tailcoat
Mr., 113
Talmage
Robert, 108
Thomas, 107, 111
Thomas Jr., 108
Thomas Sr., 108
Taverner
Henry, 86, 87
Taylor, 212
Elizabeth, 212
Joanna, 213
Joseph, 213
widow, 212
Temperly
Emma J., 228
J., 228
Tenneswood
Mary, 226
Samuel, 226
Terhune
A. M., 214
Terry
Anna, 216
Edith, 216
Harriet, 216
Henry T., 216
Jennie, 216
Roderick, 216
Sarah Ann, 216
Thomas, 106
Thomas
Elizabeth, 235
Elizabeth widow, 233
Thompson, 220
Abigail, 97, 253
Abigail (Haines), 101
Charlotte, 220
Jabez Capt., 237
Jonathan Dea., 101(3)
Lisa Marie, 171
Lois, 237
Lowrence, 273
Mary, 247, 257
Sarah, 237
Thomson
John, Rev., 44
Thomas, 108(3)

Thorp
   George master, 291
   Ida Mae, 170
Tichenor
   Aaron, 221
   David, 219
   Electa, 219
   Esther, 221
   Hannah, 221
   Jonathan, 60, 212
   Nathaniel, 221
   Ruth, 221
   Zenas, 219
Tiffany
   C., 151
Tillesworth
   Elizabeth, 76
   William, 76
Tomkins, 90
   John, 226
   Michel, 90
Tomlinson
   George, 232
   Alice, 62(2), 231
   Alice widow, 232
   Barbara, 63, 232
   George, 62(2), 63(3),
        232(2)
   Henry, 62(5), 231,
        232(3)
   John, 63, 232
   Maria (Hyde), 62,
        63(2), 232
   Mary, 62, 63(2), 231,
        232(2)
Tomson
   Grizel, 79
Topping, 125
   Abigale, 155
   Capt., 177, 181,
        264(2), 267
   Elnathan, 113
   Hezakiah, 206
   John, 113, 118, 123,
        125, 264
   Josiah, 130, 177
   Mr., 264
   Nellie, 197
   Sarah, 164
   Silvanus, 178
   Sylvanus, 182, 184
   Thomas, 107, 113(2)
Townley
   C., 220
   Marcia P., 198

Treat
   Robert, 90
Trenchard
   George, 102
Trevore
   William, 84
Trimbly
   Rebecca, 197
Trounce
   Elizabeth, 272
Tryon
   Alma, 238
   Amelia, 238
   Aurelia, 238
   Betsey, 238
   David, 238(3)
   Enoch, 238
   Eunice, 238
   Freeman, 238
   Harriet, 238
   Mary, 238
   Mary Wakeman, 238
   Oliver, 238
   Phebe, 238
   Stephen, 238
Tuller
   Aurilla, 91
   Clarissa, 242
Turner
   H. Haines, 198
   Katherine Clark, 198
   S., 150(2)
Tusten
   Benjamin Sr. Col., 183
Tuthill
   C. L., 100
   Nancy, 140
   Silas, 140
Twitchell
   John, 63, 232
   Sarah, 232(2)
Tyler, 223
   Sally, 223

- - U - -
Ulin
   Maria, 225
Underwood
   Marie, 57, 273, 276,
        286
   Robert, 276
Upson
   Janette, 240
   Martha, 173, 187

- - V - -
Vale
   Thomas, 109, 111(2)
Valentine
   Miss, 98
Van Arnum
   Ethan Allen, 223
   George, 223
   George F., 223
   Heman, 223
   Isaac, 223
   Miles, 222, 223
   Rachel, 223
   Sarah, 223
   Sarah Mrs., 222
Van Cise
   Selma, 146
Van Dyke
   Sarah, 254
Van Liew
   Annie, 217
Van Orden
   Peter, 135
   Peter S. Brig. General,
        135
Van Rensselaer
   Kiliaen, 155
Van Saun
   Eltse, 198
Van Vechten
   John Capt., 135(2)
Van Wagenen
   Eliza (Burnett), 145
   Sarah Armeda, 145
   Simon, 145
Vassall, 86(4)
   Samuel, 86(3), 87
Vedder
   E., 150
   S. J., 150
Veghte
   Mary, 141
Vielee
   Anne, 183, 189
   Egbert General, 189
Vincent
   Rachel, 220
Vivion
   Christopher, 34, 87
von Heister
   Philip Gen., 257
Von Liner
   Prince of Prussia, 233
Voorhees
   S., 162, 269

- - W - -
Wade
   M. J., 151
Wadsworth
   William, 113
Wakeman, 238
   Mary, 146, 238
   Rev., 238
Walker
   John, 41
Wall
   John, 102
Wallace
   William, 78(2)
Waller
   Diana, 239
Walsworth
   E. B. Rev., 151
   Sarah, 151
Walton
   Henry, 106
Ward
   A., 97
   Clarissa, 149
   J., 102
   Jeh'd, 92
   John, 90
   L., 220
   Mr., 92
   Sgt., 90
   T., 149
Wardell
   Capt., 208(2)
Warner
   Daniel, 174
   Olive, 174
Washington, 257(3)
   Gen., 260(3)
   General, 176, 254
   George Gen., 257, 260
   Martha, 142
Waters
   Mary P., 166
   Mr., 166
Watrous, 188
   Mr., 190
   Rebecca W., 150
   Samuel Capt., 150
   Sarah, 151, 190
   Susannah, 188
Watson
   Margaret, 79
Watterhouse
   Richard, 273
Weaver

Betsey, 237
Webb
  Alexander, 132
  Maria, 132
Webster
  Elizabeth, 272, 284
  Elizabetha, 274
  Isabell, 284
  Isabella, 284, 285
  John, 274
  John Esq., 113
  Miles, 284
Wedge
  Sarah, 236
Weeding
  G., 246
  Sarah, 246
Welbe
  George, 106
Welch
  Sally, 237
Welchman, 232
Wells
  Abigail, 239
  Almena, 239
  Amirillis, 239(2)
  Anna, 239
  Dorothie, 272, 278,
      279, 284, 285
  John, 239(2), 278, 279
  John Jr., 239
  Julia, 239
  Mr., 113
  Pierson, 239
  William, 107
Wemple
  Julia B., 142
  Stephen, 142
Westfall
  Joel, 237
  Laura, 237
Wetherby
  Charles, 167(2), 171,
      172
  Edmund, 101
  Eliza, 167, 171, 172
Wheat
  Frances Irene, 146
  Leonard, 146
Wheeler
  Augusta, 235
  S. A., 97
  Sarah C., 217
Wheelock
  P., 151

Wheelwright, 89
  Abigail, 48, 53(5), 54,
      55(4), 89
  Agnes, 274, 278
  Alice, 54
  Elizabeth, 54
  Elizabeth (Smyth), 53,
      54(2)
  Elsabeth, 54
  Isabel, 54(3)
  Jennet, 277
  John, 48, 53(4), 54(21),
      55(3), 274(2),
      277(2)
  John Rev., 89
  Katherine, 54
  Marie, 54
  Marie (Storre), 54(2),
      55
  Mary, 53, 54(3), 55(2)
  Mary (Storre), 54
  Robert, 54, 274, 277
  Susan, 53, 54(2), 55(2)
  William, 54
Whitbeck
  C. M., 151(2)
Whitcomb
  Olive, 247
  S., 247
White
  Albert Pierson, 241
  Clara Louisa, 241
  Ebenezer, 205, 267
  Edmund, 56
  Elizabeth, 140, 241
  Elnathan, 130, 177(2),
      206
  Frances Louisa, 241
  George G., 140
  Harriet Louisa, 241
  Henry Kirke, 241
  James, 194
  Joanna, 205
  John, 104, 107, 108,
      111, 112, 113,
      118, 263
  Joseph, 241
  Josephine, 241
  Mary, 241
  Peregriene, 84
Whitehead
  Sam, 194
Wick
  William, 135
Wickham

Joseph, 124
Wilkinsen
  Joan, 73
Williams
  Benjamin, 195
  Bethuel, 215
  Elizabeth, 197
  Esther, 221
  Eunice, 213, 219
  Hannah, 214
  I., 213
  Joshua Rev., 133, 143,
      176, 177, 262
  Lewis, 215
  Martha, 228
  Mary, 213, 215, 228
  Nat., 213
  Samuel, 214, 215(2),
      219(2)
  Sarah, 214, 215
Williamson
  John, 274
  Margaret, 40, 272, 283
  Margareta, 274
Willis
  M. A., 214
Willman
  Isaac, 107, 111, 113(2)
Wills
  Sara, 196
Wilson
  Elizabeth, 273
  M. V. Rev., 145
  Mary Calista Adelaide,
      145
Wingate
  Mr., 86
  Mrs., 86
Winship
  Mary Bulkeley, 205
  Oscar F., 205
Winthrop
  Governor, 58
  John, 87
  John Esq., 106
  John Governor, 87
  John Maj., 117
  Maj., 117(4)
  Mr., 263
Wolcott, 224
Wood
  Elishabe, 254
  George, 108, 111
  John, 34, 87
  Jonas, 111(3), 112

Woodbridge
  Ruth, 93
  Timothy Rev., 93
Woodhull
  Hannah, 189
  Jerusa, 143
  Jerusha, 143
  Jesse Col., 183, 252(3)
  Nathan Rev., 189
Woodruff
  John, 107
  John Jr., 113
  John Sr., 113
Woolley
  Kylie, 139
Woolworth
  Aaron Rev., 174, 175,
      176(2), 179(2),
      180(2), 185,
      186, 188, 204,
      208(2), 262
  Rev., 158, 184
Wooster
  Elizabeth, 236
  Samuel, 236
  Susannah, 236(2)
  Sylvester, 236
Wrey
  Ailse, 273, 287
Wright
  Anna, 247
  Hannah, 180
  Hannah E., 180
  Malsey, 180(2)
  Morgan P., 180
  Nymphas, 180(3)
  S., 247
  Sarah, 174
  Sophia (Halsey), 180

- - Y - -
Yost
  Daniel, 141
  Emily Amanda, 141
Young
  M., 220
  Margaret Mrs., 254
  Martha, 236

www.ingramcontent.com/pod-product-compliance
Lightning Source LLC
Chambersburg PA
CBHW080227270326
41926CB00020B/4178